Zoltán Székely

Béla Bartók

Zoltán Székely in 1921 at the time of his Hungarian debut.

Székely and Bartók

·

The Story of a Friendship

CLAUDE KENNESON

AMADEUS PRESS
Reinhard G. Pauly, General Editor
Portland, Oregon

Jacket front illustration: Zoltán Székely and Béla Bartók in the garden in Nijmegen, Holland, 1925. Photography Igminia Everts. The Székely Collection. Handcolored by Jenny Poon, Photogra-fix Restorations, Edmonton.

Jacket back illustration: Photography Kurt Julius. The Koromzay Collection.

Endpiece illustration (following Chapter Twenty-eight): Photography Monte Greenshields. Courtesy of the Banff Centre Archives.

Letter A-39 is reprinted by permission of Faber and Faber Ltd.

ISBN 0-931340-70-5

Printed in Singapore

AMADEUS PRESS
The Haseltine Building
133 S.W. Second Ave., Suite 450
Portland, Oregon 97204-3527, U.S.A.

Library of Congress Cataloging-in-Publication Data

Kenneson, Claude.
    Székely and Bartók : the story of a friendship / Claude Kenneson.
      p.   cm.
    Discography: p.
    Includes bibliographical references (p.   ) and index.
    ISBN 0-931340-70-5
    1. Székely, Zóltan, 1903-   . 2. Violinists—Hungary—Biography. 3. Bartók, Béla, 1881-1945. 4. Composers—Hungary—Biography.
    I. Title.
    ML385.K45   1994
    780'.92'2439—dc20
    (B)   93-33524
                                                        CIP
                                                        MN

To "Mientje"

Igminia Székely-Everts (1898–1990)

"I have seen with my own eyes
Stravinsky and Schoenberg standing
on their chairs in the Gran Teatro La
Fenice in Venice to applaud Zoltán's
performance of his Solo Sonata!"

Contents

Foreword   ix
Preface   xi
Acknowledgments   xiv

1903–1923

Chapter One Village Life in Hungary   1
Chapter Two The Franz Liszt Academy of Music   8
Chapter Three Jenő Hubay and Zoltán Kodály   17
Chapter Four Alliance with Béla Bartók   28
Chapter Five A Stellar Season, 1921–22   36
Chapter Six Off to Holland   47
Chapter Seven With Bartók in Holland   59
Chapter Eight A Tour to Spain   69

1924–1937

Chapter Nine The Festival at Venice   79
Chapter Ten The "Michelangelo" Stradivarius   95
Chapter Eleven The Year of the Rhapsodies   108
Chapter Twelve In Hungary with Bartók   121
Chapter Thirteen From London to Warsaw   133
Chapter Fourteen The Bartóks in Santpoort   146

1938–1945

Chapter Fifteen   The New Hungarian String Quartet   167
Chapter Sixteen   Paris and North Africa   177
Chapter Seventeen   Bartók's New Masterpiece   194
Chapter Eighteen   Occupied Holland   208

1946–1972

Chapter Nineteen   The Beethoven Cycle   231
Chapter Twenty   New York Debut   239
Chapter Twenty-one   Southern California   252
Chapter Twenty-two   Aspen   264
Chapter Twenty-three   Australia   280
Chapter Twenty-four   Alberta   295
Chapter Twenty-five   "Exit without Tears"   308

1973–1993

Chapter Twenty-six   The Banff Years   321
Chapter Twenty-seven   Farewell to Budapest   336
Chapter Twenty-eight   The Academy of String Quartets   350

Appendix A   Béla Bartók Letters   369
Appendix B   Performance Practice   403
Appendix C   Members of the Hungarian String Quartet
        (1935–1972)   420
Appendix D   Compositions and First Performances by Zoltán
        Székely   426
Appendix E   Discography   432

Notes   445
Selected Bibliography   475
Index   479

Illustrations follow pages 46, 94, 190, 238, and 318.

Foreword

For almost four decades, Zoltán Székely and the Hungarian String Quartet provided music lovers the world over with performances of the greatest works in the classical canon—the quartets of Haydn, Mozart, Beethoven, Schubert, and Brahms. This magnificent repertoire was further enriched by premieres or early performances of string quartets by Paul Hindemith, Igor Stravinsky, Darius Milhaud, Arthur Honegger, William Schuman, Heitor Villa-Lobos, Aaron Copland, Walter Piston, and Elizabeth Maconchy. But the jewel in the crown of Zoltán Székely and the Hungarian String Quartet was the monumental cycle of six quartets by Székely's lifelong friend, compatriot, and musical collaborator, Béla Bartók.

In addition to the quartets, Székely was intimately involved with Bartók's two Rhapsodies for Violin and Orchestra, the second of which was dedicated to him and which he played in its world premiere with the Budapest Philharmonic under the direction of Ernst von Dohnányi. Székely also played the first performance of the Second Rhapsody outside Hungary—with the Amsterdam Concertgebouw led by Pierre Monteux. In 1939, he played the world premiere of Bartók's Violin Concerto with the Concertgebouw conducted by Willem Mengelberg. "To my dear friend Zoltán Székely," Bartók wrote on the front of the score.

In Székely, Bartók did indeed find a sympathetic and responsive interpreter of his music. Bartók was greatly interested in the rich and

variegated folk-music traditions of eastern Europe, and the tempes-
tuous music of peasant violinists contributed much to the distinc-
tive character of his works. Among Székely's many gifts was the ability to assimilate and understand the peasant idiom in all its sensuality
and fiery temperament, as anyone who ever heard his performance of
Maurice Ravel's gypsy piece, *Tzigane*, will be able to attest.

Bartók's music presented a daunting challenge to early twentieth-century listeners. The groundbreaking performances of Székely
and the Hungarian String Quartet changed this. The dissonances,
unfamiliar scales, and driving rhythmic patterns soon came to be
understood as integral parts of a larger musical soundscape that Bartók conceived—one that included intense romantic and sensual
elements, combined with brilliant use of formal structure. Today the
six quartets of Bartók, along with other major works in his large
oeuvre, are treasured landmarks in the development of twentieth-
century musical styles.

Székely and Bartók: The Story of a Friendship is peopled by many of
the most accomplished composers, conductors, soloists, and chamber musicians of the middle fifty years of the twentieth century. The
story involves various heads of state of the interwar years, of World
War Two, and of the postwar and Cold War eras. We also meet (in
sometimes charming and previously unknown anecdotes) major
writers, poets, painters, filmmakers, and actors of the years from 1920
to 1970. Székely's emigration from Hungary to the Netherlands, his
marriage to the love of his life, Mientje Everts, his efforts to assist
Bartók during the late 1930s, and his determination to establish himself and his quartet in a stable environment in America are all part of
the fabric of *Székely and Bartók*. This volume also contains correspondence from Bartók to the Székelys that spans the duration of the
friendship. And, for the specialist seeking insight into problems of
musical performance, the appendixes offer detailed technical guidance derived from Székely's eighty years of musical experience. It is a
rich feast indeed.

Brian Lorne Harris
4 October 1993

Preface

I met Zoltán Székely in 1957 when I first heard a concert by the Hungarian String Quartet. When I went backstage to greet him I shook his hand, but dared not say his name because I had no idea how to pronounce it properly. Later I learned that he was quite accustomed to being called Sze-ke-ly in Holland (where he had lived for twenty-seven years) and in the United States. I also learned to approximate the Hungarian pronunciation by saying the name in two syllables, accenting the first, with the vowel *e* in the second as in the word keg: Say-ke. I begin with this suggestion for readers who may also find the name difficult to pronounce.

Zoltán Székely and I became colleagues and friends during the many visits of the Hungarian String Quartet to western Canada during the 1960s. In 1967 I had the privilege of meeting his wife, Mientje, who often traveled with him on concert tours. Our first conversation ran the gamut from music criticism in the Japanese press to the protocol for quartet wives on tour. An avid amateur photographer, Mientje soon produced a small, red wallet containing photographs. "This was Bartók's favorite!" she said, pointing to a well-worn snapshot of the composer taken in Nijmegen in 1925. Thirty-five of the illustrations that appear in this book are photographs taken by her between 1925 and 1960.

It was immediately apparent that this charming, gregarious Dutch woman was not only devoted to Zoltán Székely, her adoring husband, but to the violinist Zoltán Székely, *primarius* of the Hungarian String Quartet and dedicatee of Bartók's Violin Concerto. Throughout their seventy years together, she constantly stoked the flame of Zoltán's career. During the early years of their marriage she traveled with him to all his concert engagements, kept account of his professional affairs, and was his personal representative to various concert managers. Until the end of her life she was his best friend. Their story is an enchanting and poignant one for all who enjoy music and musicians.

After the Hungarian Quartet was disbanded in 1972, the Székelys spent three consecutive summers in the Canadian Rockies where Zoltán taught chamber music at the Banff Centre before accepting the position of violinist-in-residence there in 1975, an engagement that brought them permanently to Canada. In the summer of 1973, David Leighton (then president of the Banff Centre) had the visionary idea of documenting the artistic collaboration between Zoltán Székely and Béla Bartók. He began this task by taping a series of personal interviews with Zoltán and Mientje. Although Mientje's health had begun to fail, the taped interviews reveal her remarkable spirit. Her sense of personal history was truly a gift and her devoted chronicling of Zoltán's life story is a phenomenon in itself.

When the Banff Centre decided at the end of 1990 to create an archive to celebrate the life and career of Zoltán Székely, I was invited to direct a project which involved assessing his music library, personal papers, press clippings, photographs, lecture notes, and the memorabilia of the Hungarian String Quartet. After Zoltán and I had spent several months together that winter discussing music and musical ideas, I proposed writing his biography. When he finally agreed to my proposal, I told David Leighton of my plan to write *Székely and Bartók: The Story of a Friendship* and he immediately entrusted me with his 1973 collection of taped interviews which became the genesis of this book.

Important information appears in the Appendix which may be of considerable interest to the lay reader as well as to musicians and scholars: articles on performance practice, membership of the Hungarian String Quartet, Székely's compositions and first performances, and a discography. Of particular significance is Appendix A which contains the collection of extant correspondence from Béla Bartók to the Székelys from the period 1923 to 1940. Carefully preserved for seventy years, this collection survived the troubled years of World War Two and was brought to the United States by Mientje Székely in

1950 where it now remains with their son, Frank Székely-Everts. The sons of Béla Bartók—Béla Bartók, Jr., (Budapest) and Péter Bartók (Florida)—have made possible the publication of their father's un-published letters to the Székelys. The brief musical examples in items 6, 21, 38, 41, 43, and 44 are published by permission of Boosey and Hawkes, Inc. The letter A-39 originally published as number 213 in *Béla Bartók Letters* by János Demény is republished by permission of Faber and Faber Ltd.

Bartók's correspondence written in Hungarian or German is pre-sented in an English translation by János Csaba and Almut Chateau that preserves the composer's unique style of personal expression, his idiosyncratic punctuation, and several brief musical examples in his own script. The content of thirty-five of these items appears in various forms in the text to illuminate the narrative. Along with eleven additional ones, they can be read in their entirety and in chronological order in Appendix A.

For musicians and scholars this book provides a record of Szé-kely's and Bartók's unique insights into the music revealed through their shared history, letters, and discussions of performance practice. The story of the Hungarian String Quartet from its formation in Buda-pest in 1935 until its final concert at Dartmouth College in 1972 is based on the vivid recollections of the three living members of the en-semble—Zoltán Székely, Dénes Koromzay, and Gabriel Magyar—and on the well-preserved memorabilia from the Koromzay Collection.

For our generation and those following, *Székely and Bartók: The Story of a Friendship* is an account of a cultural history, a "golden moment" for the musical art in the twentieth century.

Claude Kenneson
4 May 1993

Acknowledgments

I thank my friend Zoltán Székely for his generosity and trust in permitting me such an intimate view of his life. His charm, good humor, and hospitality, like his practical assistance, never faltered during the unforgettable three years we spent together at Banff talking about his life and his art.

Without the assistance of Dénes Koromzay and Gabriel Magyar, the other two living members of the Hungarian String Quartet, it would have been impossible to establish the many facts necessary to chronicle the ensemble's distinguished career.

Dr. David S. R. Leighton, past president of the Banff Centre, whose idea it was in 1973 to write about the remarkable friendship between Béla Bartók and Zoltán and Mientje Székely, has shared his valuable, early research with me. I am grateful to him for the genesis of this book.

Among the artists, builders, and dreamers of the Banff Centre, I gratefully acknowledge Isobel Moore Rolston, Székely's chosen pianist and faithful friend; Thomas Rolston, whose intention it is to preserve the legacy of Székely's artistic life for posterity; and Jorie Adams, manager of the Music Division, without whose practical assistance this book could not have progressed from day to day.

The Banff Centre greatly assisted me throughout the writing of this book, giving access to its archival resources and technical expertise to utilize those resources. Particular thanks are due Ben West, Technical Services; Robert Foley and Debbie Rosen, librarians; Monte Greenshields, photographer, and his assistant, Cheryl Bellows; Kenneth Murphy, executive director of the Banff International String Quartet Competition; Katherine Loram and Tod Spence-Perkins, my research assistants; and the office staff of the Music Division.

Acknowledgment with appreciation is also made to Jaap Schröder, Lorand Fenyves, János Starker, and László Funtek for their personal contributions; to Professor László Somfai, head of the Bartók Archívum and the Institute for Musicology of the Hungarian Academy of Sciences; and the sons of Béla Bartók—Béla Bartók, Jr., and Péter Bartók—who have made possible the publication of their father's unpublished letters to the Székelys.

I express my gratitude to János Csaba for his enormous contribution as Hungarian translator. To Anita de Vey Mestdagh for her insightful translation of all Dutch materials and to Almut Chateau, H. M. Fracchia, Erwin Warkentin, and Gérard Guénette for expert translation of additional German, Italian, and French language materials, I am deeply indebted.

Others whose efforts have assisted the creation of this book and to whom I owe thanks are Frank Székely-Everts, Ubbo Scheffer, the Board of Directors of the Amsterdam Concertgebouw, the late Paul D. Fleck, Adám Friedrich, Kató Havas, Bonnie Hampton, Gwen Hoebig Moroz, Marina Hoover, and David Gollon, librarian of the Pitkin County Library in Aspen, Colorado.

Acknowledgment of permission to republish documentary materials is made to the following among many contributors: Faber and Faber, Ltd., for letter 213 from Béla Bartók Letters edited by János Demény (see A-39 in Appendix A); European American Music Distributors Corporation, agent for Universal-Edition (Vienna), for an illustration from Székely's Sonata, Op. 1; and Boosey and Hawkes, Inc., for excerpts from Béla Bartók's Violin Concerto which appear in his letters to Zoltán Székely.

The Canadian musicologist Brian Harris offered invaluable advice throughout the writing of this book. For his intellectual and moral support I owe my deepest personal gratitude.

1903–1923

The parish church at Kocs where László Székely registered Zoltán's birth in 1903. PHOTOGRAPHY ADÁM FRIEDRICH.

Chapter One

Village Life in Hungary

I remember a certain moment when I stood at the door and
listened as my father played the violin at home for friends. I
would have liked a violin when I was six, and perhaps I
would have started earlier than I did, but I simply didn't get
a violin.

With these words, Zoltán Székely began to recount the story of
his life one winter's day in 1990. Through the frosted windows of
Lloyd Hall at the Banff Centre loomed the magnificent snowbound
panorama of the Canadian Rockies, an awesome confirmation of Alberta's harsh winter, but the warmth of Székely's apartment held that
scene at bay. Inside it was cozy, *gezellig* as his Dutch wife, Mientje,
would have said.

Apparently not eager to comment further on the fleeting memory
of his turn-of-the-century childhood in Hungary, Székely revealed
nothing more at that moment. Instead he sat quietly studying a large
map that he had unfolded on his lap. He had begun his odyssey, a
journey of recollection during which he would try to recapture the
essence of his own past that had begun ninety years earlier.

In the silence that ensued, one wondered what could be learned
about this rather shy, white-haired gentleman who sat musing in his
favorite chair, surrounded by bookcases overflowing with well-worn

1

string quartet scores, his Stradivarius violin, the "Michelangelo," nearby in its open case. What could be learned about him before he became what he is today—one of the great living violinists of the twentieth century

"I was born here at Kocs," he said at last, tapping the map with his fingertip. "And here is Süttö near the Danube," he continued, having traced the familiar route to the northeast. "We lived there when I was yet a small boy." After a moment, he asked himself, "But where is Körmöczbánya? No longer in Hungary," he concluded, his fingertip moving to the north in search of Körmöczbánya, the small town now claimed by modern Slovakia and called Kremnica.

As he located these villages where he had lived as a child, he began to speak of almost-forgotten images: a glimpse of the Danube flowing past the village of Süttö, lying between Komárom and Esztergom; peasant children at play in the dusty road, their fathers hard at work at the nearby quarry, extracting high-quality limestone called "red marble" from the surrounding terrain; and finally the country doctor's house where the sick came to be healed by his father, Dr. László Székely. This house at Süttö was the first childhood home Zoltán remembered clearly.

> At Süttö we had a nice house with sufficient room for my father to conduct his medical practice at home. I remember that in this small village he also practiced dentistry, and for this he used a mechanical chair such as one sees in a barber shop. It was raised or lowered with a foot pedal as we had no electricity. I remember that once he pulled one of my teeth as I sat in this chair, having approached me with a smile, his dental apparatus concealed in his sleeve.
>
> My sister Piroska and I often played with the peasant children in that little village. In fact, we liked best playing in our barn where horses had once been stabled. She and I were fond of gymnastics at that age—she was seven, I was five—so we conceived a kind of gymnastic show which we frequently performed in our barn before an audience made up of these village children. We even charged an admission. Probably a penny.
>
> And there was always music-making at Süttö. My mother had taken singing lessons in Budapest. She sang and Piroska played the piano, but it was my father's violin playing that interested me most. However, as a very small boy I practically did not hear classical music because my parents did not

play that sort of music. Let us not forget that we lived in such very small villages that the musicians I heard there were often the real Hungarian type.

He remembers little about Kocs, his birthplace. He was still an infant when his family left Kocs (pronounced "coach"), moving from one country village to another. Although he never returned to Kocs, he later learned the significance of its name from Zoltán Kodály, who was interested in etymology.

In the Middle Ages many important continental routes passed through Hungary. One of these, known as the Butcher's Road, became an important commercial route leading from Budapest to Vienna. The village of Kocs is situated on this route about twenty-five kilometers southeast of the town of Komárom near the Danube and not far from Budapest. It was at Kocs that the first light horse-drawn carriage for fast, long-distance travel was constructed. The coach, as the vehicle was called, quickly changed the nature of travel in Europe, and the name of the village was introduced as a common noun into the Hungarian language and into several foreign languages as well.

Kézdi Vársárhely, a Transylvanian village far from Kocs and the ancient Butcher's Road, was the birthplace of Zoltán's father in 1875. As a young man László Székely moved from the Haromszek district in Transylvania, where he had spent his youth, to Szeged, the traditional economic and cultural center of the southern part of Hungary's Great Plain. When he arrived there in 1895, Szeged had been almost completely rebuilt after its great flood of 1879 and was admired not only for its ancient university but also for the many imposing buildings of its inner city and for its famous paprika, an important ingredient of Hungarian cuisine.

After completing his medical studies at the University of Szeged by writing a thesis that investigated tuberculosis, László Székely moved to Budapest to begin his medical career. Since childhood he had been fascinated by the music of the gypsies; although not trained as a classical musician, the young doctor played the violin "by heart" in the Hungarian style. In Budapest he eventually knew many gypsy violinists personally, including Laczi Rácz who enjoyed enormous popularity in the cafe life of the city.

Rácz could be heard in the evenings at the Nemzeti Cafe at 15 Ráday Street, where he played the violin as he strolled among the

tables speaking to his ardent followers, one of whom was László Székely. This extraordinary violinist, the son of Páli Rácz, was said to
represent the thirty-sixth generation of violinists in the Rácz family.
Whether such a succession of gypsy violinists could have been a reality is not certain; however, Laczi Rácz's fame was legendary, and
his calling card grandly announced him as "The thirty-sixth Rácz
Laczi, King of the Gypsies, principal memory musician of the five
continents."[1]

Laszló Székely met Erzsébet Strausz in Budapest and married her
there in 1900. Soon after their wedding, the young couple moved to
the village of Kocs where at the age of twenty-five Dr. Székely began
his medical career as a district physician. As the official doctor of the
Komazo district, he served the medical needs of the small, rural community, yet still found time to enjoy country life and to indulge his
favorite pastime—playing the violin.

Their first child was born in 1901 at their village home, 2 Kocs,
when Erzsébet Székely was only eighteen. They named her Piroska,
the Hungarian name for Little Red Riding Hood of the nursery tale.
Two years later at three o'clock in the afternoon on 8 December 1903,
their son was born in the same house. When the boy was three days
old, Dr. Székely registered his birth with Ödön Kedrish, the acting
registrar of the Komazo district, and then had his name entered into
the records of the parish church, in accordance with Catholic tradition. He was named Zoltán.

Zoltán began attending public school in the autumn of 1908 before he turned six years old. When he reached the third grade, his violin lessons began modestly in a violin class given at his public school.
Although his introduction to the violin came comparatively late (he
was nearly nine), his remarkable natural talent showed itself almost
immediately. Within a few years his youthful career rivaled that of
the precocious *Wunderkinder* who, in part, represented the Hungarian
school of violin playing during the early twentieth century.

It seems I had a good soprano voice as a child. Before
playing the violin at the public school I sang in the school
choir. When I did begin my violin lessons they progressed so
quickly and so easily that the result was beyond the expectation of my parents. To get us to work more diligently, the
teacher of my first violin class at school had the habit of rewarding us with a *krajcár*, a coin now worth about one cent.
I always won those.

Because my parents were concerned about the quality of my education in these small places, after I began studying the violin I was sent to live in Budapest for one year with my maternal grandparents. My mother's generation of the Strausz family had abandoned their Germanic family name in favor of the more patriotic surname, Zoltán. (This was a somewhat unusual choice since in Hungary Zoltán is a familiar given name for men.) Although my aunt had married and moved away, there in my grandparents' home at 40 Gróf Zichy Jenő Street I had three uncles. One of my uncles, the young writer Siegmund Zoltán, was musically gifted and played the violin nicely.

At the end of the school year when I had completed the fourth grade of public school, I left my grandparents' home in Budapest and returned to the provinces once more to live with my parents in Körmöczbánya, where my father by then had become the town's doctor.

In 1913 the Székelys moved from their familiar house in Süttö near the Danube to a house in Körmöczbánya, a northern mountain village nestled on hills where sheep grazed outside the medieval gate. Located in the central Carpathian Mountains, Körmöczbánya was connected to the rest of the country by a railway line that passed through the valley of Bartos, then climbed into a higher valley, entered a tunnel, and finally emerged at the Körmöczbánya Station. From the station a winding road flanked by trees led across a meadow to the town itself. Much of the town's medieval character had been preserved, and for that reason it was a favorite gathering place for those interested in the ancient Franciscan monastery and the Town Hall with its wealth of archives. However, in the early twentieth century when the Székely family lived there, Körmöczbánya was most important because it contained the Mint, the only one in Hungary.

On his return from Budapest in the fall of 1913, Zoltán was admitted to the Reáliskola or Modern School in Körmöczbánya, an institution that provided an alternative curriculum to that of the traditional *gymnasium* (secondary school) that Piroska attended. From the fifth year of his education, Zoltán began learning French and German at the Reáliskola rather than the classical languages, Latin and Greek, studied by the students at the secondary school.

Village life in Körmöczbánya offered its own unique social aspects. As a member of an amateur orchestra, Dr. Székely enjoyed taking part in the village music-making. When the orchestra played light music by Offenbach or Rossini, he "played by ear" even when the others played with their music because he had difficulties reading music well. However, he was a very good musician in his way and loved to play his violin in the orchestra.

On weekends Dr. Székely and his gentlemen friends often spent a cordial afternoon together. At these times when the men enjoyed themselves drinking a few glasses of beer and bowling, the young women and the ball boys went outside to the courts and played tennis. At that time in Hungary, tennis was not necessarily accepted as a reputable game for women, but Erzsébet Székely enjoyed the sport and played well. She became a strong player who met the athletic challenge of playing against men and sometimes played in competitive matches on a provincial basis. Zoltán became a ball boy and soon learned to play tennis when he joined his mother on the courts for her weekend games. In his own estimation he became "a good player, but no, not an international player," although he later competed in many tennis matches in Holland and eventually in 1928 played at the Queen's Court, Wimbledon.

Once Zoltán began studying the violin he became engrossed in music; from the outset violin playing absorbed his interest. Because his parents sensed the magnitude of his talent, they became convinced that they must plan a musical career for him and seriously began to consider a move from Körmöczbánya to Budapest where Zoltán would have the best opportunity to study.

> In Körmöczbánya I studied the violin with a teacher who was the organist at the church. A sort of general musician, this man also played both the violin and the piano. In fact, he did everything. Of course his teaching was probably not of a very high standard. It could not have been for there was not a high level of teaching in the provinces in Hungary at that time.
>
> When I was about to leave Körmöczbánya to live in Budapest at age eleven, he said to me, "If later I ever read your name in the newspaper when you have become famous, then I will have the feeling that I had something good to do with all this!"

The Székely family moved to Budapest during the summer of 1914. Dr. Székely himself taught Zoltán for a brief period since his son was not yet sufficiently trained to enter the Franz Liszt Academy of Music. Dr. Székely knew an excellent violin teacher in Budapest he hoped would accept his son as a private pupil. When this was arranged, he told Zoltán, "Now you will study the violin with my good friend Kőszegi." Dr. Székely felt certain that Zoltán's lessons with Sándor Kőszegi would assure his admission to the academy, and in this he was correct.

As for Piroska's artistic future, a musical career was not a serious consideration although her parents recognized that she had made progress as a piano student; however, they knew that she, too, would prosper in Budapest where she could continue her academic education in a fine secondary school. Piroska did continue to study the piano in Budapest, as a pupil of Madame Jámbor, a colleague of Sándor Kőszegi and the mother of the prodigy pianist, Agi Jámbor. An excellent student, Piroska graduated from the *gymnasium*, had additional music lessons from the composer Leó Weiner, and performed frequently as piano accompanist in her brother's early recitals.

In the wake of a natural disaster—a devastating tornado struck Budapest on 23 July 1914—the Austro-Hungarian Empire broke off relations with Serbia as a result of the assassination of Archduke Franz Ferdinand in Sarajevo. In the chaotic aftermath of these events, the specter of war descended on Budapest as it would on Vienna, Paris, London, and distant St. Petersburg.

In the autumn Dr. Székely was called away to war. During those troubled years at the beginning of the war, the children would have to face the challenge of a new life in an enormous city of almost a million people, a metropolis from which their father was absent. Erzsébet Székely, now thirty-one and secure living in Budapest, the city of her birth and the home of her parents and brothers, moved into the center of the city so that Piroska and Zoltán might live near their schools and the Franz Liszt Academy.

Their new home was a modest apartment on the fourth floor of a large apartment building in Pest. There was a lift, but this elevator was seldom used in those frugal war days since this required tipping a porter. When Piroska practiced the piano, which was in the parlor, Zoltán often fled with his violin to the privacy of the bathroom to continue his own practicing. Although the sounds of music came from the Székelys' apartment for many hours each day, the neighbors never complained. Perhaps it was heartening to hear the talented youngsters playing music in such uncertain times.

Chapter Two

The Franz Liszt Academy of Music

Sándor Kőszegi, Zoltán's new violin teacher in Budapest beginning in 1914, had a good reputation as a violinist. A former pupil of Joseph Bloch, with whom Zoltán would later study, Kőszegi was the leader of the second violins of the Royal Opera Orchestra. With his three colleagues, Schuster, Hollós, and Kárpáthy, he took part in many chamber music concerts in Budapest as first violinist of his own string quartet.

According to Halsey Stevens, Sándor Kőszegi appeared with Béla Bartók as pianist on 8 June 1903 to give the first performance of one movement of Bartók's Sonata for Violin and Piano (1903).[1]

This performance was Bartók's last appearance as a student at the academy, and it occurred when the young composers in Hans Koessler's composition class presented a concert of their works. The program comprised the works of eight young composers: Albert Heidlberg, Elek Radó, Imre Kálmán, László Toldy, Pál Redl, Albert Szirmai, Ozmán Kasics, and Béla Bartók. The evening concluded with Bartók's and Kőszegi's performance of the Finale (Allegro vivace) of Bartók's youthful work.[2] This early sonata was apparently incomplete at the time of this recital since Bartók mentions in a letter to his mother written ten weeks later, dated 23 August 1903, that he was kept rather busy composing the slow movement (Andante con variazioni) of the work.[3]

The completed sonata was performed in Budapest by Jenő Hubay and Béla Bartók on 25 January 1904. The next month Bartók gave his first chamber music performance outside of Hungary, at the Bösendorfer Saal in Vienna on 3 February 1904; he shared a recital with the Fitzner Quartet, his contribution being a performance of his Sonata for Violin and Piano (1903) with Rudolf Fitzner.[4] Later in 1905 Bartók performed the sonata in Paris during an extended trip to France, where he competed unsuccessfully for the Prix Rubinstein. In a letter to his mother, Bartók explained that since the jury insisted his Quintet for Piano and Strings (1904) was too difficult to be learned in the assigned time, he performed the Sonata for Violin and Piano (1903) instead, although he had difficulty finding a violinist until Lev Zeitlin, a pupil of Leopold Auer, agreed to take part in the performance.[5]

Székely recalls a conversation with the composer in 1930 concerning Bartók's participation in the Rubinstein Competition:

> Bartók wanted to introduce himself to the public in Paris in his dual role as piano virtuoso and composer, and his Rhapsody, Op. 1, composed the previous year, was one of the works he chose to accomplish this.
>
> Bartók always kept a warm place in his heart for this work. Once when we happened to talk about his failure in the Rubinstein Competition, which had taken place at least twenty-five years earlier, he still expressed his displeasure about the event. Though he was not vain at all, in this case he felt hurt. He never understood why the prize was not awarded to him for his Rhapsody which later he still considered a work of quality and certainly ranking far above everything presented by the other competitors.
>
> With his typical sarcastic humor he remarked to me, "Nevertheless, there were some people who liked my Rhapsody, for instance, my landlady who always came to listen to the performances of the competition. She got so angry when I did not win, that in her rage at the jury she reduced the price of my room from nine to seven francs!"

The early Sonata for Violin and Piano (1903), Bartók's first venture in this genre, is important in that with the Quintet for Piano and Strings (1904), it delineates the end of his preparatory period. With these two compositions, Bartók begins the catalogue of his works in the 1921 autobiographical sketch entitled *Selbstbiographie.*[6]

Bartók's early performances with violinists Sándor Kőszegi, Jenő Hubay, and Rudolf Fitzner indicate a predilection for performing the chamber music works for violin and piano that was already evident during his boyhood in Transylvania. Among his later sonata partners at various periods were the violinists Jelly d'Arányi, André Gertler, Joseph Szigeti, Ferenc Vecsey, Imre Waldbauer, Ede Zathureczky, and, of course, Zoltán Székely with whom Bartók appeared frequently in violin sonata performances during the period 1921 to 1938.

During the year-and-a-half of his boyhood in 1914–15 when Zoltán studied with Sándor Kőszegi, he reached the stage of violinistic advancement required to study the forty-two études of Rodolphe Kreutzer. From that fact one might surmise that an unusual acceleration had begun in his acquisition of instrumental prowess.

Remarkable talent, highly intelligent self-guidance, and an unswerving inclination to sacrifice nothing of the music he performed in order to favor the merely sensational aspects of violin playing characterized Zoltán's youthful virtuosity. Of his playing at age seventeen an early critic remarked, "He does not add anything to the music that does not come from it; his struggle is logical, great, and now we can also say victorious."[7]

In addition to his violin lessons with Kőszegi, he continued his academic education at the Reáliskola in Budapest. The students at this school who chose music as their main subject usually went to the Franz Liszt Academy as private students, took lessons from an official teacher there, and were examined by the academy at the end of the year.

I remember that when I was in the third year at the Reáliskola my violin examination at the academy conflicted with the academic examinations, but fortunately I was excused from the school examinations. Dr. Horváth, our director at the Reáliskola, had a certain respect for the academy and an understanding of such things. He knew that the emphasis in my life was entirely on music.

I entered the Franz Liszt Academy when I was eleven years old and remained a violin student there for a period of six years. On 13 June 1921 I received the Master's diploma.

There were four levels of violin instruction at the academy which were intended to comprise twelve years of study.

I began my study at the third-year level, then completed each of three courses in only six years. The preparatory violin class with Joseph Bloch, which usually took four years, I did in two; again, I completed Hubay's academy violin class in two years instead of the usual four; and his master class I completed in two years, the normal period for that course.

Joseph Bloch, who taught the preparatory violin class, had studied at the academy with Karl Huber, the father of Jenő Hubay, and at the Paris Conservatory with Charles Dancla. For six years Bloch had been the second violinist of the Hubay-Popper String Quartet. During an earlier period this famous string quartet was much admired by Johannes Brahms, whose complete chamber music repertoire the ensemble introduced to the Budapest audience, including several world premieres.

Joseph Bloch began a long teaching career in Budapest in 1889, first as violin teacher at the Hungarian National Academy of Music, then from 1890 to 1900 as violin teacher at the Nemzeti Zenede, the National Conservatory, which was founded in 1840 and renamed the Béla Bartók Musical Training College in 1949. From 1908 Bloch became the director of violin pedagogy at the Franz Liszt Academy and taught the preparatory violin class. He was also a composer, producing a number of pedagogical violin pieces, chamber music, orchestral pieces, and a violin concerto which was performed by Joseph Szigeti.[8]

Székely recalls his early years at the Franz Liszt Academy:

When we came exactly at two o'clock for the preparatory violin class, Joseph Bloch had the habit of sitting in his private room reading the newspaper. As good a reputation as the Hungarian school of violin playing had, its operations were sometimes not very specific. Fifteen minutes after the scheduled class time, Bloch would arrive in our classroom, and we would finally all settle down to work. He had a straight chair where he always sat with his violin in his hand. Without fail he played pizzicato accompaniments to all that went on. If something was wrong in the playing, he tapped his foot for attention. Apparently that was all he thought to do until the next time an error occurred when he would again tap his foot, say, "Once more," then return to his pizzicato.

Bloch required some of his former pupils to prepare us

for his violin classes. This was a tradition at the academy and Hubay did the same. Once each week there was a violin lesson from a deputy teacher. In my case, it was Sándor Kőszegi, the former pupil of Joseph Bloch with whom I had studied previously, who gave me these lessons. I remember that Kőszegi no longer knew how Bloch required certain works to be studied, for instance Kreutzer's trilling study, but despite this fact we continued to have these lessons since that was the system at the academy.

During those early years at the academy it was required that the violin students study a second instrument. We had to learn to play the piano, and it was Alajos Tarnay who taught us. At best Tarnay's teaching was superficial. He often read the newspaper *during* the lessons. He didn't even consider giving real classes.

I know only that although one was a "Bloch student," there was a required examination for the pupils in the preparatory violin class. The nature of my final examination in that class was seemingly exceptional. Because Joseph Bloch found me the best of his students, there was a kind of exemption. He had just written a new cadenza for Viotti's Concerto No. 22. The jury didn't ask much of me, just that I play that cadenza.

Later I prepared the Violin Concerto, Op. 45, by Christian Sinding for the admission examination to the academy violin class. Already I was not the ordinary student, and this was evident to them. In the 1917–18 season, two years earlier than expected, I was sent forward to the next level of instruction, the academy violin class. It was then that I became a pupil of Jenő Hubay.

In 1916 during my second year at the academy, I had harmony classes with the composer Leó Weiner.[9] Weiner gave these classes entirely from memory, as he paced about the room never having to refer to the text of the figured basses he discussed in great detail. For Weiner this was a year of transition when he continued to teach harmony but also began teaching his new chamber music class.

The next season he concentrated on teaching chamber music and gave up his normal appointment as a theorist. As a chamber music teacher he had a certain artistic reputation, and all the talented students appreciated him. I don't know how the average ones reacted, but we found his class very interesting. Leó Weiner was an exceptional teacher. There were real things to be learned in the way he taught us.

Because I had completed the preparatory violin class in only two years, there were certain theoretical studies that had yet to be learned since one could not overlap attendance in the harmony classes. Knowing the situation of my theoretical studies, my father invited one of Leó Weiner's young assistants, Maria Weiss, to join us on an unusual summer vacation in 1917 in order to tutor me in harmony. She played both the violin and the piano and had accompanied me at the piano in a performance of Vieuxtemps' *Ballade et Polonaise* in a student recital at the academy.

My father served as a regimental surgeon on a Red Cross train that transported Yugoslavian prisoners of war. Somehow he made it possible for our family and my tutor to spend the summer holiday together near the army camp. Because there was a military band made up of these Yugoslavians, I decided to try my hand at composition, and I wrote a military march for their band. I was about fourteen at that time.

A year later I was again able to visit my father who was serving as doctor for the military forces in Galicia, not on the front lines but somewhere sufficiently safe that I could join him for a few days. I remember that one of the unusual events of that visit was that he allowed me to ride a certain small, white pony if I wished. I had never ridden horseback before but I was eager to try. All went well until I reached the railroad tracks just as a train was approaching. The engineer blew the whistle. This startled the horse, and I was thrown but fortunately not hurt.

I immediately mounted the horse again and continued to ride. My father appeared about that time in a horse-drawn wagon and suggested we ride along together. When we reached a bridge my horse became nervous again, probably still "spooked" by the incident with the train. Once on the bridge he bolted. I was thrown again for the second time in the same morning and so ended my equestrian adventure in Galicia!

When classes resumed at the academy, I became one of Leó Weiner's favorite students in his new chamber music class. Whether it was right or wrong I don't know, but he would always say, "Székely. Show it!" and I would demonstrate the passage in question. Weiner had coached the Léner

String Quartet,[10] and everyone who understood his role in their success appreciated his abilities. I was encouraged when once he said to me, "I would like to see you in a quartet."

It happened that while I always played quartets, I took part in all the other ensembles as well. I was one of the violinists at the academy who played the viola with pleasure, and I remember that we played Mozart's Trio, K. 498 ("Kegelstatt"), a work for clarinet, viola, and piano. Weiner listened as we played. He stopped us and said, "Play it once more." We played again. "That is good. Interesting." He was pleased that each time in a certain episode we had played the same nuance, a sort of ritenuto, and this showed him that we were gaining a certain understanding of this Mozart work.

My first chamber music performance at the academy was in a piano trio during the time I was in Weiner's class. I joined Pál Hermann, cellist, and pianist George Herzog[11] for a performance of Beethoven's Trio, Op. 70, No. 2 ("Ghost").

With Leó Weiner I played his First Sonata for Violin and Piano, Op. 9, but not the second. The earlier work is dedicated to Hubay with whom he had a better relationship than did Kodály or Bartók. When Weiner and I rehearsed his sonata, one remark he made about a certain passage in the last movement was "Telmányi played it so—at the frog—and he found it possible." Although I couldn't do that bowing very well at that time in such a fast tempo, I attempted it since Weiner knew it was possible due to his knowledge of Emil Telmányi's great technical ability.

Other Weiner works we played often at that time either at the academy or in private concerts were the First String Quartet (1908) and the String Trio (1909). In 1922 Weiner's Second String Quartet, Op. 13, won the Elizabeth Sprague Coolidge Prize and was performed in Washington, D.C., bringing him a certain reputation in American musical circles.

I heard the Budapest premiere of Weiner's Second Violin Sonata, Op. 11. This was played by Eugene Ormandy and Lily Keleti. I remember that on this occasion Kodály said to me, "This is a masterpiece." At that time I accepted his remark as satirical, but later I realized it was a masterpiece in every respect.

Ormandy's violin recital did not draw a full house so we students were able to slip in. We simply gave a tip to the usher and sneaked into an empty seat. That was the usual way for academy students. "Sneaking" it was called, and we did it almost every time. There were so many concerts to be heard that buying tickets became too expensive for a student. I remember that once we sneaked in and sat *under* the platform to hear the orchestra. That was not the best place, of course.

I didn't visit Leó Weiner in later years. When I was in his chamber music class we had a certain relationship of student and professor, but somehow we were not connected later since we had moved in somewhat different musical directions. However, in 1925 when he proposed a new work for violin and orchestra which he planned to call Violin Fantasy, he wrote to me saying that as soon as he finished it, he would have it copied and sent to me, and then we should play it either with the Philharmonic Society or on a composer's evening, or it could be a world premiere in one of the festival concerts of the International Society of Contemporary Music. He concluded by saying that we had plenty of time to talk about this matter, for first the work had to be written, and unfortunately he could not even predict when that would happen.[12] Since those days of his proposed Violin Fantasy, the international status of Leó Weiner has grown.

In an interview in 1981, Dénes Koromzay, the original violist of the Hungarian String Quartet, commented on the growth of Weiner's status and the continued interest in his work:

> If you talk to any successful Hungarian musicians who came out of the academy between 1917 and 1965, during which time Weiner had an incredibly long tenure of almost fifty years, they will say that the only person from whom they learned how to make music was Leó Weiner.
>
> At our time, in the early 1930s, the teaching at the academy was absolutely concentrated on technique and virtuosity, and we got very little if any advice on how to make music. Certainly if Weiner hadn't been at the academy there wouldn't have been chamber music.
>
> This man loved chamber music so much—loved music so much—that he taught a master class every single afternoon. Sándor Végh and I were always at his classes and listened even if we didn't play. He was fascinating because he brought us to understand what music-making really is, totally divorced from virtuosity or the solving of technical problems. And he was the only one who took this approach at that time.

If you ask Georg Solti, who graduated at the same time as I did, he will say exactly the same thing—that Leó Weiner taught us how to make music. The whole succeeding generation was under Weiner's influence. In 1980 at Indiana University, János Starker organized a Leó Weiner Festival to which he invited everybody who was connected with Weiner, and there was even a competition for performances of Weiner's works, the Weiner *Concours*.[13]

Chapter Three

Jenő Hubay and Zoltán Kodály

By 1917 when Székely was studying the violin with Jenő Hubay[1] in the academy violin class, Hubay was already clearly at odds with Kodály and Bartók. Recalling his student years, Székely spoke candidly about Hubay's teaching and his attitude toward the modernist movement in music and its Hungarian protagonists.

> When one reads in print what Hubay had to say about Bartók, it is usually a recognition of Bartók's great talent, but in his heart I think Hubay was seriously against the modernist movement because he did not understand it. His musical taste really didn't go further than the music of Wagner.
>
> During the second year that I studied with Hubay we experienced an erratic time. That was the time of the first Communist Revolution in Hungary during which Hubay escaped to Switzerland. In his absence János Koncz, his former pupil who had graduated in 1913, was his teaching substitute. During a lesson with Koncz, I played a work by Max Reger for solo violin, and he didn't say a word about this music. He didn't know it, and perhaps he was not interested in it.
>
> I wanted to distance myself from the standard repertoire, and I remember, for instance, that I never studied Bruch's Concerto in G Minor nor Lalo's *Symphonie espagnole* with Hubay. I didn't ask Hubay what I should play since he was

quite free in that matter, but I had conflicts with him regarding repertoire from time to time during the war years. In the case of certain works Hubay had feelings beyond the music itself. When I played the Dvořák Violin Concerto for him, he was very upset. For him this was not a musical matter, but a very personal one. Because he had experienced political difficulties in Czechoslovakia, he would allow no Czech music.

When I was still in Hubay's academy violin class, I was a member of the Academy Orchestra for one year and was then released from that commitment. I remember that I played a solo with orchestra for the first time when Hubay conducted a performance at the academy of Franz Liszt's *Hungarian Coronation Mass,* which was composed in Budapest in 1867. I stood up from my place in the violin section and walked to the podium to perform the violin solo in the Benedictus. Ede Zathureczky also appeared as a soloist in that concert.

At that period when I was not practicing the violin or attending a class, I enjoyed visiting Mor Zala's music store near the academy or the bookstore owned by István Léderer on Erzsébet Street. It was possible to browse through great stacks of music on the upper floor at Zala's store. There I constantly found one interesting work or another, and each time I added it to my collection of music since Zala allowed me a form of credit. Of course when a certain time arrived he presented me with a bill. Since I could not pay this bill from my own pocket I had to explain the situation to my father who was quite surprised at the extent of my purchases; however, he understood my urge to acquaint myself with the violin repertoire and gave me the money to set things right with Zala.

As a fourteen-year-old student I started to go to many concerts. I heard Emil Telmányi play. He had a reputation as a serious musician and was the favorite violinist of Ernst von Dohnányi. They frequently played sonatas together. Once I heard Telmányi play a solo recital which included Wieniawski's *Valse Caprice,* and I was amazed that he played with such virtuosity. In 1917 I heard Telmányi play the world premiere of Dohnányi's Violin Concerto in Budapest with the Philharmonic.

In 1918 Telmányi married the painter Anne Marie Nielsen, the daughter of composer Carl Nielsen, and settled in Copenhagen. I never met him again, but I know he married again in later years. He formed an ensemble for early music, a family quintet, of which he, the violist Annette Schiøler, who was his wife, and their three daughters, all professional violinists, were the members. He died in 1988 and was buried on what would have been his ninety-sixth birthday.

In 1918 came the moment when I first got into the modernist movement. In March I heard the first performance of Bartók's Second Quartet played by the Waldbauer Quartet. At that time in my youth I went so far as to think that Imre Waldbauer was the best violinist. Such a virtuoso! While we were still young students, the Waldbauer Quartet was very active. They lived for playing certain things for the first time. They were in the whole modernist movement. That was their time!

Imre Waldbauer had formed a string quartet eight years earlier, in 1910, expressly to perform the new quartets of Kodály and Bartók. The members of the quartet were all young men who had just finished their studies at the Franz Liszt Academy. János Temesváry played second violin; Antal Molnár was the violist. All were former pupils of Hubay. The cellist, Jenő Kerpely, was a protégé of Dávid Popper. When Popper died in 1913, Kerpely succeeded him as professor at the academy. From the outset the ensemble was known as the Waldbauer-Kerpely Quartet, but on their many concert tours in Europe they were sometimes called the Hungarian String Quartet.

In Ferenc Bónis' book, *Béla Bartók: His Life in Pictures and Documents*, Bartók and Kodály appear in a photograph taken in 1910 with the Waldbauer-Kerpely Quartet at the time of its debut.[2] On 17 and 19 March of that year, the first programs devoted exclusively to the works of Kodály and Bartók took place in Budapest. After nearly one hundred rehearsals the new Waldbauer-Kerpely String Quartet gave the world premieres of the two composers' first string quartets.

The Bartók concert on 19 March included not only his String Quartet No. 1, Op. 7, which had been finished on 29 January 1907, but also a number of piano pieces and the early Quintet for Piano and Strings (1904), in which Bartók joined the ensemble as pianist. In a letter written shortly thereafter to Sándor Kovács in Paris, Bartók commented on these two important concerts. He enthusiastically praised the results of the Kodály evening, mentioning that the Budapest music publisher, Rózsavölgyi, had asked to publish Kodály's String Quartet and piano pieces. He extolled the Waldbauer-Kerpely Quartet—apparently the young performers had played exceedingly well.[3]

When the Viennese publisher, Universal-Edition, wished to publish Bartók's Quintet for Piano and Strings (1904) twelve years later, the composer found that part of the manuscript was missing and beyond his recall. When this fact was mentioned to Ernst von Dohnányi, well known for his memory feats, he went to the piano and recreated the missing passages which he had seen sixteen to eighteen years earlier, thus enabling the composer to recapture what was lost.[4]

The Waldbauer-Kerpely Quartet undertook its first European concert tour in 1911 and performed Bartók's new quartet in Amsterdam, The Hague, Paris, Berlin, and Vienna. Four years later, Bartók began composing his Second Quartet. It was completed in October 1917; Bartók dedicated it to the Waldbauer-Kerpely Quartet, who presented its premiere on 3 March 1918. By the time of this first performance, there had been a change of personnel in the quartet, with another Hubay pupil, violist Egon Kornstein (later known as Egon Kenton in North America), replacing Antal Molnár.

After leaving the quartet, Antal Molnár became a professor at the Franz Liszt Academy in 1919, remaining there until his retirement in 1959. Molnár is a founder of modern Hungarian musicology and was a prolific composer. His written work included the first analysis of Bartók's music and the first monograph on Kodály.[5] Among his compositions is the Suite for Violin and Piano written in 1929 and dedicated to Zoltán Székely.

Imre Waldbauer attributed the formation of his original quartet in 1910 to an awakening interest in the avant-garde at a time when Schoenberg's *Transfigured Night* and the chamber music of Debussy and Ravel were the only music of the period considered new.[6] On the occasion of their twenty-fifth anniversary, the Waldbauer Quartet gave a gala celebration performance at the academy on 29 March 1935, recreating, in part, the Kodály-Bartók concerts of 1910. On that evening not only were the two composers' first quartets performed, but Kerpely and Bartók played Kodály's Sonata for Cello and Piano as well.[7]

The Waldbauer Quartet played for the last time in 1946 after thirty-six years of concertizing. The occasion was the Hungarian premiere of Bartók's Sixth Quartet in Budapest. Soon after their famous ensemble was disbanded, both Kerpely and Waldbauer emigrated to the United States. Kerpely began teaching at Redlands University in California. Waldbauer assumed a position at the State University of

Iowa where he continued to perform the quartet repertoire, leading the University of Iowa String Quartet until his death in 1953.

In the aftermath of the First World War, Hubay's master class consisted of only five violinists: György Beimel, Endre Braun, Ilona Fehér, Lilla Kálmán, and Zoltán Székely. By June of 1920, three of these—Beimel, Fehér, and Kálmán—had completed their studies. The following season, 1920-21, eight new violinists joined the master class. They were Irma Bárány, Marianna Breuer, Miklós Fehér, László Hajós, Anna Herrnfeld, Pál Kernács, László Sándor, and Ede Zathureczky.[8]

Only two of Zoltán Székely's classmates had outstanding careers. Ede Zathureczky, a favorite of Hubay, later became the director of the academy (1943–56). He emigrated to the United States and taught at Indiana University from 1957 until his death. Ilona Fehér, after 1949, became a very successful violin teacher in Israel, where she was the first teacher of Shmuel Ashkenasi, Shlomo Mintz, and Pinchas Zukerman.

The master class in 1920 in itself did not represent Székely's idea of what teaching should be, although Hubay's pedogogical approach at other periods is described somewhat differently by others.[9]

> In my opinion Hubay's master class was not a real teaching class. One was supposed to "do it well," and Hubay did not go into very specific details. Somehow the work was supposed "to go by itself," and while Hubay sometimes said such things as "light bowing," which was one of his favorite bowing techniques, nobody specifically instructed us. The principle seemed to be "prepare the next piece for next time," and the result was supposed to be good in itself. I don't know, maybe this way in which he behaved with his students was accepted. It seemed that the prevailing attitude was that whatever one did, one was good, perhaps the best, and one could not do better, or maybe it was the case that some students communicated better with him than I did. Perhaps Hubay simply had good luck in that he had a lot of fine students, or perhaps he taught differently at another time when he was younger. At any rate, I am not very enthusiastic about what he did.
>
> That he sat at the piano and accompanied as each one came up, rarely disrupting anyone, was a little bit similar to Joseph Bloch with his pizzicato accompaniment. A class that lasts for only two hours from three to five o'clock in the

afternoon is a fairly short class for a dozen students. He would choose somebody to play. They would probably play a concerto which he would accompany at the piano. He would say some instructive things—in fact, he occasionally stopped to say, "you are not loose enough."

Of course we learned something. Certainly. We learned just by listening to the others. Probably it would have saved me a lot of time simply to find out for myself what was necessary for my own development.

Hubay kept a copy of his Stradivarius, a violin made by Zimmer in Budapest, at the academy, but he did not even unpack it. I don't know if he felt he had completely abandoned the violin at that time; anyway, he didn't play the violin to the class. As well, he no longer appeared in public at that time since the Hubay-Popper Quartet was by then disbanded.

We studied the unaccompanied Bach works. I eventually played in public three of the six works which were the least often heard at that time: the two sonatas—those in A minor and C major—and the Partita in B minor. Hubay had his own printed edition of these works and taught the articulations as they appeared in his publication. For instance in the movement called *Double* of the B minor Partita he chose to play *spiccato* in certain passages, and so we also approached it in that manner.

The articulations in these works present difficult questions, of course, but at the time I studied them with Hubay as a young boy, I simply followed his solutions. Later when I thought seriously about these matters I attempted to arrive at a logical and consistent treatment of the articulations and tried to unify the notated rhythms in the fugues of the Bach sonatas, for instance.

In the case of Hubay's own compositions, I remember pieces which I played for him much to his surprise. For instance, when I played for him the *Ballade and Humoreske*, Op. 104, which he dedicated to Joan Manén, the work was fresh in print. His satirical remark was "This is something for you." Perhaps he thought I was so sour that this *Humoreske* was a kind of satire in my case. I also played the *Walzer Paraphrase*, Op. 105, which is dedicated to Joseph Szigeti. One of Hubay's pupils, Emilia Hermann, played this work with the Academy Orchestra for the first time in 1918.

For my first concert in Budapest with orchestra I played

three concertos: Brahms, Sibelius, and Hubay's *Concerto all'antica*. Hubay conducted. I was the only one in the master class who studied the Sibelius Violin Concerto, the work dedicated to Hubay's pupil, Ferenc Vecsey. Even though we pursued this together, his true opinion about the Sibelius concerto I never knew.

While Hubay had played Bartók's early sonata with him in a Budapest concert in 1904, by my time at the academy, Hubay was definitely opposed to the modernist movement and personally antagonistic toward Bartók and Kodály. He did not change his view as their compositions became more widely accepted by the public.

I have many personal recollections of memorable performances of Bartók's works, dating from 1918, when I first heard his Second Quartet. At such occasions I began to sense a definite reversal of the public opinion that arose when neither the public nor the musicians could understand him sufficiently, the time when instead of encouragement, the opposition to his music became vivid, sometimes violent, and Budapest, the place which represented the center of Hungary's cultural activities, rejected him.

This reversal started with the production of his ballet, *The Wooden Prince*, in May 1917. Bartók was accustomed to unsatisfactory, badly prepared performances of his orchestral works in Hungary. But this time the conductor, an Italian by the name of Egisto Tango, devoted the unheard-of number of thirty rehearsals to this difficult score. This extraordinary preparation promptly bore fruit. The work became an immediate success and was accepted by the public and critics alike.

Székely's closest friend at the academy was the seventeen-year-old cellist, Pál Hermann. One of the most promising cello talents of his generation, Hermann studied in Budapest with Adolf Schiffer, the pupil of Dávid Popper, who was the professor in charge of the undergraduate cello classes at the Franz Liszt Academy. In addition, Hermann was a composition student of Kodály and in 1918 already had a number of compositions to his credit.

The Hermann family lived in Buda very near the Margithid, or Margaret Bridge, that unusual structure that forms an obtuse angle in midstream from which a short leg leads to the Margaret Island in the Danube. The Hermann home was a favorite refuge for Hermann and

Székely. There they worked on their compositions and practiced chamber music together.

Hermann happened to be on the same trolley as Kodály[10] when they both were returning to their homes in Buda one afternoon in the spring of 1918. The cellist had in his possession the score of Székely's String Trio since these young friends frequently studied and compared each other's newest works. Hanging on the outside of the tram as he traveled homeward, Hermann spoke through the open window to Kodály who was seated inside. When Hermann approached his stop, he began to whistle a passage from Székely's composition, the score of which he suddenly put into Kodály's hand as they parted. Kodály took home the manuscript of Székely's String Trio and studied it.

> Why Pál showed Kodály that score, I don't quite know, but he took it and was interested. At that period Kodály was already teaching composition at the academy. When he spoke to me later he said something really extremely nice. "Just come and see me," he said. From that moment on, I had private composition lessons from Kodály. Pál and I never paid a cent for our lessons. It was a matter of pure interest and friendship. Through that event of Pál's having given him my score, we became close to Kodály. Pál and I went together very regularly during the summer of 1918 to have our lessons at Kodály's villa in Buda, a house built on the Rózsadomb, the Hill of Roses.
>
> I was industrious. When I had a spare moment and had a compositional idea, I immediately set to work on it. This was important because every week we needed to have some new material to present to Kodály. At Kodály's home Pál and I often went into the garden and sat with him under the cherry tree, or we went on long walks with him. He was not talkative. In fact, he did not talk except for a few words from time to time. During our composition lessons we began to have a sort of intimate musical relationship with Kodály. Now, of course, when I say "intimate" you have to understand that seventy years ago the relationship between professor and student was not as it is nowadays. We always had a sort of distance, yet I would say he treated us like his own children. Mrs. Kodály was very charming as well. The friendship we had with them was lovely. What we learned from Kodály was real. It was a beautiful time!

Kodály was very reserved about offering opinions on our work, but sometimes he dropped a hint. His opinion regarding my early Duo for Violin and Cello composed in Budapest when I was seventeen was that he was amazed by the Scherzo and found the unison at the end especially interesting. Whether the character of the piece interested him I don't know. He once said that I had a gift for musical invention that was different from Pál's. Maybe Kodály was right about this.

On another occasion when Pál and I performed Brahms' Double Concerto at the academy, I was told that we had different styles. Pál's style was enthusiastic and outgoing while mine was more reserved. However, in my day as a young composer I tried everything, but Pál did not—and we were of the same school and the same time period. Temperaments are so different!

I remember that the unpublished manuscripts of both Bartók's Second Quartet and Kodály's Second Quartet were once lying on Kodály's piano when Pál and I were at his home for a composition lesson. Kodály handed the scores to us. We took them home to study and spent day and night doing so. We were deeply impressed, and soon we seemed to know them by heart.

I imagine there was a certain point during this period when Kodály was not so interested in Bartók's works. After the Second String Quartet, Bartók's harmonic method became severe, unlike that of his *Allegro barbaro*, one of the sensations of the day. In his oeuvres, the *Allegro barbaro* seems only a small piece, but it is an important one, and it was also easily accessible to the public.

Kodály's musical language was more conservative than Bartók's, but very much his own. I think he never accepted the new atonality, and it remained strange to him. Kodály never said modernism was wrong, but he just didn't really accept it as a composer although he accepted the direction which Bartók took for himself.

One can even see that in various works Bartók was influenced to some degree, let us say, by Kodály's music, particularly with respect to the use of Hungarian folk music—the use of certain folk idioms. As an example, take the slow movement of Bartók's Fourth Quartet. Kodály's influence is certainly evident there. But, of course, if you compare it to the second movement of Kodály's Second Quartet, which is essentially in the same spirit, then you are bound to hear an immense difference in how the two composers worked out the same idea. There is no doubt, however, that this Bartók movement, Non troppo lento, does reveal Kodály's influence. I don't know what Kodály really thought of these later works of Bartók. That is a question, since they followed such different paths.

Kodály himself had produced masterpieces during this period: the First String Quartet (1908), the Duo for Violin and Cello (1914), and the Sonata for Solo Cello (1915), among others. In fact, Kodály gave us a new musical language, and the early masterpieces I note are very important in expressing this. Perhaps in the end Kodály simply was not prolific enough. Of course there are very specific things, interesting things about his compositions. The cellists I knew like Pál Hermann were very excited by the Solo Sonata.

I was very interested in the new music. At the academy, which for me was the center of music at that time, the students knew little about the modernist movement, and they did not care for it. During my second year in the academy violin class, we tried to form a musical club in 1918–19 to educate ourselves more completely about these matters. We asked Leó Weiner to preside over the meetings, but after only two gatherings the whole thing was abandoned.

Political disturbances began in Hungary with the end of the war when the Hapsburg Empire collapsed. On 16 November 1918, Hungary was proclaimed a republic and Count Mihály Károlyi came to power. Within a month Czechoslovakian, Rumanian, and Yugoslavian armies invaded Hungary's border provinces and met little resistance from the new government. Károlyi resigned and turned the government over to the journalist, Béla Kun, the founder of the Hungarian Communist Party.

The months that followed brought chaos to Hungary. The national currency became worthless. Hunger was widespread in Budapest. When a Rumanian army marched toward Budapest in July of 1919, Béla Kun and his followers fled to Vienna. Soon a counter-revolution took place, and by 4 June 1920, Budapest was in mourning with the realization that the Kingdom of Hungary was now reduced to one-third its previous size.

During the brief reign of the Hungarian Republic of Councils, Kodály, Dohnányi, and Bartók were members of the Directory of Music Council led by Béla Reinitz. Dohnányi served as director of the Franz Liszt Academy. With the resurgence of a new conservative regime, an effort was made to dismiss several musicians from their posts, including Imre Waldbauer and Zoltán Kodály. In the case of Kodály, the inquiries failed to produce his dismissal, but Hubay, now director of the academy, originated the idea of sending him on leave to a humbler position, hoping that during his absence a plan would arise to prevent his return.[11] Bartók drafted a letter to Hubay in January of 1920, stating that he would resign from his position as a professor out of solidarity with his persecuted colleague, but Kodály refused this sacrifice and bore his burden alone.[12]

Székely at sixteen was spared an awareness of the difficulties.

Kodály had spare time for our lessons because he had been re-lieved for a year from his duties, as one can read in every book. I was absorbed in music entirely, and I must say I was not interested in these political things at that age. I didn't feel all the misery that happened around me. Children don't always feel these things, and at that time we were still young boys. In fact, as young people we were perhaps younger than students of today. This is an important difference.

Chapter Four

Alliance with Béla Bartók

Emil Herrmann, the Berlin violin dealer (who later worked in New York), had some connection with Jenő Hubay and came to Budapest every year with a small collection of instruments for sale. When Zoltán was first a student of Hubay, Erzsébet Székely, who was astute in business matters, acquired from Herrmann a French violin made by François Pique. However, sometime in 1919 the family decided to commission a contemporary violin from János Tóth, who was then regarded as the best living Hungarian violin maker. The new violin was finished in 1920 in Tóth's shop at 10 Lajos Kossuth Street in Budapest. Zoltán recalled that his mother traded the François Pique violin toward its price, which was at that time probably three hundred florins.

The Tóth violin made for me was in the style of Guada-gnini, and in fact some parts of it may have been authentic and from an earlier period. Until 1927 when I acquired the "Michelangelo" Stradivarius, all my performances were given on this Tóth violin, which was a fine violin with a great tone. Years later I purchased yet another Tóth violin for my father who by then lived in Dunavarsány, a village about a half-hour's journey from Budapest.

During my time in Hubay's master class an exceptional thing happened to me. I appeared twice as soloist with the

Academy Orchestra. On the first occasion, in 1920, I played the Brahms Violin Concerto with Hubay conducting. That was the first time I played on the new Tóth violin. Later in 1921 at the end of the season, Pál Hermann and I performed the Double Concerto by Brahms with the Academy Orchestra; in Hubay's absence this performance was conducted by Nándor Zsolt.[1]

The Great Hall of the Franz Liszt Academy was the scene of two concerts on the last weekend of April in 1920. On Saturday evening, 24 April, the first performance of Kodály's new string trio, the Serenade for Two Violins and Viola, took place in a chamber music concert by the Waldbauer-Kerpely Quartet, a musical event thought by Bartók to be the sole sensation of a Budapest season especially poor in novelties.[2] Székely had heard this new work a few days earlier in a private concert at Imre Waldbauer's home, a Kodály afternoon attended by many composers, including Dohnányi and Bartók.

On the morning of 25 April three young violinists from Hubay's master class appeared in a concert devoted to concerto performances. Hubay conducted the Academy Orchestra that Sunday morning as Lilla Kálmán, György Beimel, and Zoltán Székely faced the supreme challenge of the soloist's role. Kálmán began the concert with a performance of Beethoven's Violin Concerto. The Eighth Concerto by Louis Spohr followed with Beimel as soloist. Finally Zoltán Székely appeared on the platform and played Brahms' Violin Concerto with resounding success.

Székely's Brahms performance was greeted enthusiastically by the press who extolled his excellent technique and understanding and assured the public that he could now be considered a finished artist.[3] This was extravagant praise for the sixteen-year-old boy from Kocs who in only seven years of study had progressed from modest lessons in a rural public school violin class to the stage of the Great Hall at the Franz Liszt Academy in Budapest.

Following Székely's first performance of Brahms' Violin Concerto at the academy, there was a performance of chamber music restricted to the works of Beethoven. Székely appeared on this program with Béla Szigety,[4] violist, and Pál Hermann, cellist, playing Beethoven's String Trio in G Major, Op. 9, No. 1. A brief critical review proclaimed that "The most promising hope for Hungarian chamber music was Székely with his purest classical style."[5]

By the spring of 1920, Székely had won the critics' admiration so often reserved for the *Wunderkind* violinists such as Vecsey and Kerékjártó who had emerged on the scene before him. Supported by this critical recognition of his outstanding abilities both as soloist and chamber musician, Székely soon claimed an unassailable position in the musical life of the capital, appearing often in Budapest during the next two years. He garnered an enviable reputation from the press, including many accolades from Aladár Tóth, the most important Hungarian music critic during the years between the wars.[6]

During his youth Székely heard the famous child wonder, violinist György Kerékjártó, as well as pianist Erwin Nyiregyházi, the Hungarian prodigy who was the subject of an investigation into the nature of infant musical talent carried out by Dr. Géza Révész, director of the Psychological Institute at the University of Amsterdam.[7]

Székely has this to say about the sometimes unresolved musical fate of precocious children:

> Happily I cannot include myself among the genuine *Wunderkinder* because I played for the public for the first time at the age of fourteen, far too respectable an age for a genuine child wonder.
>
> During my first year at the academy I heard the violinist György Kerékjártó. He had studied first with Gusztáv Szerémi, then with Hubay. In 1914 he was in Hubay's master class and later played a recital in Budapest where I saw him come on the stage carrying *two* violins. He put one of them on the piano seemingly *just in case*.
>
> Although it is said that at his violin recitals he engendered great enthusiasm—the audience would sometimes carry him on their shoulders to his hotel—apparently his destiny was the variety stage, where he gained a certain reputation. I heard that he ended his days in California, having appeared in at least one movie. He lived a comparatively long life and died in 1962.
>
> Another famous prodigy was the Budapest pianist Erwin Nyiregyházi. He studied with István Thomán, then went to Dohnányi in Berlin but later returned to Budapest when Dohnányi came to teach at the academy in 1916. Nyiregyházi made his debut in America in 1920 but ten years later became a recluse and didn't play again in public for forty years until he was rediscovered in San Francisco in 1973. At that time he played several recitals hoping to raise the money nec-

essary to cover the medical bills of his ninth wife, Elsie Swan. I met Professor Révész in Amsterdam in 1937 in Bartók's company. He seemed eager to discuss his psychological studies about precocious children with Bartók. I cannot say how interested Bartók was in such matters, but the psychologist was certainly interested in Bartók's views.

I am very glad that I did not have to exhibit my own artistry at too early an age. I believe that this can be very bad for one's development. A child may be very talented by nature and may even have great virtuosity, but when not given sufficient time for the true development of musical knowledge, the risk is run that such a child may be stopped when still only at the beginning point.

If the general musical culture has not developed properly by the time such a child grows up, the fate of the *Wunderkind* may be a very bad one. Perhaps this is the reason that so many precocious violinists and pianists who were a phenomenon in their early youth and even very well known to the public are later never heard of again.

When at seventeen I appeared as soloist in a performance of Brahms' Violin Concerto at the Vigadó, the principal concert hall in Budapest, I think people could not yet call me a grownup, but already a certain maturity was evident, and inside myself I was "grown up." However, I knew that I should keep studying and never think that I had already arrived.

Székely appeared with his sister, Piroska, in several recitals outside of Budapest in the fall of 1920. They performed at Győr, Esztergom, then Nagymegyer. In Győr and Esztergom Székely's program included works by Christian Sinding, Enrico Bossi, César Cui, and Leone Sinigaglia, already indicating his search for a unique repertoire. "This pale, blond-haired boy who appeared on the stage, totally calm and self-contained," wrote the critic in Esztergom, "moved the hearts and souls of the audience."[8]

At Nagymegyer the recital was organized as a benefit to help victims of a recent fire. Piroska Székely recited a poem written by Gyula Strausz, art songs followed the reading, then Székely played Charles de Bériot's *Scène de ballet* and Franz Drdla's Serenade. The critic at Nagymegyer concluded by saying, "According to the signs we saw, he will soon be able to stand up before all the great cities of the world and win them over."[9]

Ernst von Dohnányi dominated the Budapest concert season of

1920–21. Like only Hans von Bülow before him, Dohnányi performed all the piano works of Beethoven. In celebration of the 150th anniversary of Beethoven's birth, he appeared sixty-two times as conductor, solo pianist, or chamber musician during a four-month period which began in October, then left Hungary on 25 January 1921 to tour the United States.

Székely turned seventeen on 8 December 1920, midway in this busy concert season when Dohnányi captured the almost undivided attention of the Budapest audience with his Beethoven performances. A few months later on 16 February 1921, Székely and his sister took part in a concert at the Vigadó in Buda sponsored by the Christian National Party, which supported a high standard of culture in the capital. The evening began with a lecture and the singing of old Hungarian songs with the accompaniment of the *tárogatón*, an ancient Hungarian woodwind instrument similar to the Islamic shawm. A group of art songs followed, then Székely played the Larghetto and Capriccio from Hubay's *Concerto all'antica*.

Because Hubay had gone to Switzerland, Székely and Hermann prepared their performance of Brahms' Double Concerto with Hermann's teacher, Adolf Schiffer. Nándor Zsolt conducted the Academy Orchestra on 25 February in a concert that presented not only Székely and Hermann but also two violinists—Pál Kernács[10] who played Bruch's Concerto in G Minor and Ede Zathureczky who played Glazounov's Violin Concerto.

"Székely's best success this year has been the Double Concerto by Brahms which he played with the most promising of the young cellists, Pál Hermann," wrote Aladár Tóth in *Nyugat*, one of the most forward looking and valued literary journals.[11] Tóth had not heard Hermann's solo playing before, but Hermann's superior ability won the critic's praise.

Sometime in March of 1921 there was a conversation between Kodály and Bartók during which it was first proposed that Bartók and Székely play together in public. Székely recalls the events resulting from that proposal:

> It is safe to say that they were the best of friends, these two, and had such conversations. In this case, perhaps they felt that in me there was a talent and their actions could make my progress easier.

When I first knew them, their youth had passed and they had already had a long friendship, and, in my opinion, no rivalry whatsoever existed between them. On the contrary, Kodály always wrote wonderful articles about the new Bartók works, and when times were difficult politically, for example, Bartók would stand up for Kodály in turn. They got along very well with each other, both artistically and personally.

In March of 1921 Kodály arranged my first important meeting with Bartók. This was the first opportunity for him to hear me privately. Kodály said, "Take your work with you!" Since I was fairly well advanced in composition, I had a certain work for solo violin. I decided that I would play my composition, the Sonata for Solo Violin, for Bartók at our first meeting.[12]

This meeting took place in Bartók's home at 2 Gyopár Street. It marked the beginning of a long friendship between us. It became a happy day for me and also a significant one. I think it must have made its imprint on my whole future career, because as an outcome of this encounter not only did I win Bartok's friendship but as an immediate practical result he chose me as a partner for many concerts.

At the time when I first met Bartók he was nearly forty years old. I imagine that meeting him for the first time would have been a somewhat bewildering experience for anybody, not only for me, insofar as it was hard to believe that this man of such dignified modesty and simple appearance, this small, frail person who spoke with such a pleasant, quiet voice, clear and disciplined, could be the creator of such powerful, sometimes almost savage music like *Allegro barbaro* or *The Miraculous Mandarin*.

The Bartóks were extremely nice to me during that first visit. He asked me to play for him, and afterwards we had a conversation during afternoon tea. His wife, Márta Bartok,[13] joined us as we talked. Shortly after this first meeting I received a message from him that he would like to play with me.

We rehearsed two sonatas. For a Budapest concert at the academy on 23 April he planned for us a performance of Debussy's Sonata for Violin and Piano (1916–17), and on 25 April he wished to perform Beethoven's Sonata, Op. 47 ("Kreutzer") at a smaller concert in Ujpest, a suburb of Budapest which had its own auditorium in the City Hall.

During the weeks ahead, Bartók took part in two concerts at the academy that were of great interest to the new music movement. On 16 March he joined Waldbauer and Kerpely in a performance of Ravel's Piano Trio in a program that included Kodály's Duo for Violin and Cello and Schumann's String Quartet, Op. 41, No. 1. Five weeks later on 23 April with Zoltán Székely and Madame Erzsi Gervay, he presented a program of works by Debussy, Schoenberg, and Stravinsky: Debussy was represented by ten selections from his *Préludes* for piano and by the Sonata for Violin and Piano (1916–17), Schoenberg by *Drei Klavierstücke*, Op. 11 (1909), and Stravinsky by the four art songs, *Quatre Chants Russes*, and *Piano Rag Music* Nos. 1 and 2 (1920). (Plate 2)

Bartók submitted a brief article entitled "Lettera di Budapest" to the Turin-based journal, *Il Pianoforte*, in which he described the organization of this April concert with its rather daring program. At the conclusion of his article, he acknowledged Székely: "The Debussy Sonata's violin part was played by the young but already outstanding Zoltán Székely with a musicality that bears great promise."[14]

The Budapest critics caught the spirit and purpose of the 23 April concert. In the opening lines of his review in *Pesti Hirlip*, Izor Béldi wrote, "Béla Bartók introduced to his faithful followers some works by composers of other countries who seem to believe in an artistic credo similar to his own."[15] In the German-language newspaper, *Pester Lloyd*, Géza Molnár found the academy filled with the modern spirit, and commented on Bartók's performance of the Debussy *Préludes*, "The sounds that Bartók brought forth are familiar to him, totally natural and human."[16]

Aladár Tóth wrote in *Nyugat* that he found the performance of the Debussy sonata remarkable because of "Bartók's rigorous, hardspined approach so ably complemented by Székely's violin playing," then continued with an astute summation of Székely's notable performances of the season, recognizing his unique musicianship and unusual approach to the violin in which, it seemed to Tóth, he was not at all tempted by sentimentalism.[17]

Bartók's own compositions figured prominently in a concert presented at the auditorium of the City Hall in Ujpest two days later on 25 April. He played many of his piano works, and soprano Izabella Nagy, accompanied by pianist Adolf Szikla, performed his songs. The concert ended with a performance of Beethoven's Sonata, Op. 47 ("Kreutzer") with Székely as violinist. (Plate 3)

Székely recalls Bartók's satisfaction with their early performances, during which a successful alliance was formed that led to many joint recitals during the subsequent seventeen years:

> These concerts in which I joined Bartók for the first time in performances of sonatas by Debussy and Beethoven must have proved satisfactory to him. But of course the remarkable thing is the fact that somebody of the stature of Bartók played with a student and found his work worthwhile.
>
> What was so extraordinary was that he did not care that I should have a big name, for of course in this period he played from time to time with various well-established artists including Imre Waldbauer, Jelly d'Arányi, and Emanuel Feuermann.

Not pleased with Székely's exuberant artistic collaboration with Bartók, Jenő Hubay admonished his young pupil. He suggested that any further public performances with Bartók might endanger the conclusion of his studies at the academy. However, nothing came of this warning; Székely's final month at the academy followed its normal course, and he completed his preparations for the graduation examination for the Master's diploma scheduled for 8 June.

Székely's short program for the examination was accompanied by Oszkár Dienzl, a well-known Budapest accompanist who was so familiar with the violin repertoire that he often played the encore pieces for violin recitals from memory. Székely began with the Andante and Presto movements from Bach's Partita No. 3. Joined by Dienzl, he then played both Hubay's *Concerto all'antica* and Joseph Joachim's Variations for Violin and Orchestra. He received his Master's diploma from the Franz Liszt Academy five days later, on 13 June 1921, officially concluding his years as a student in Budapest at the age of seventeen.

Chapter Five

A Stellar Season, 1921–22

Bartók and Székely again appeared in a concert at the Vigadó in the autumn of 1921. The big hall was full on 12 November, and the printed programs ran short by several hundreds. Somewhat outside the framework of a composer's evening, they began with a performance of the Sonata in E Major by J. S. Bach, then Bartók performed Zoltán Kodály's exceptional piano work, *Zongoramuszika* (Seven Pieces for Piano) Op. 11. After the intermission, Bartók returned to play a large group of his own piano works. The program concluded with the first Budapest performance of Szymanovsky's impressionistic work, *Mythes*, Op. 11, for violin and piano, a new composition in which Bartók took considerable interest. (Plate 4)

An important musical figure in Poland, Karol Szymanovsky had lived on his estate at Timoshovka in Ukraine throughout the First World War and during that period composed *Mythes*, Op. 11, for the violinist Paul Kóchanski and later performed it with him in Moscow and St. Petersburg. The third piece of the group, *La Fontaine d'Aréthuse* (The Fountain of Arethusa), eventually became one of Szymanovsky's best-known compositions. At the time of the Budapest performance of the work, Szymanovsky had returned from Ukraine to Warsaw where eventually he was recognized as the most important force in the new music of Poland.

Bartók had ordered copies of all Szymanovsky's published piano and violin works and piano compositions from Universal-Edition in 1921. He was studying them precisely at the time of composing his Violin Sonata No. 1, Op. 21. While Szymanovsky's influence is not evident in Bartók's musical style, János Kárpáti, the Hungarian scholar, acknowledges that Bartók's treatment of the instruments, especially the violin, recalls the texture of Szymanovsky's violin pieces.[1]

During the month that followed this November concert, Bartók continued work on his important Violin Sonata No. 1, Op. 21, completing it on 12 December. At last he had provided himself with a formidable new chamber music work for forthcoming recitals with his violin partners. The world premiere was given by Mary Dickenson-Auner, violinist, and Eduard Steuermann, pianist, on 8 February 1922 in Vienna at the Mittlerer Konzerthaus-Saal. Bartók did not play the sonata himself until March and April of 1922, when he performed it in both London and Paris with the Hungarian violinist, Jelly d'Arányi, to whom it is dedicated.

Jenő Hubay now seemed to take less notice of Székely's artistic association with Bartók, a collaboration that had caused him considerable displeasure. An event was fast approaching that Hubay hoped would eclipse all that had gone before and create a sensation in Budapest—Székely's gala debut performance with the Royal Opera House Orchestra. Hubay would conduct the concert, in which three large works would be presented—the Brahms Violin Concerto, Hubay's *Concerto all'antica*, and the relatively new Violin Concerto in D Major, Op. 47, by Jean Sibelius.

In an interview preceding the concert, the young violinist expressed his love for the classical repertoire, for composing, and for playing with Bartók:

> I love equally violin playing and composing. I would like to be successful in both as Liszt and Mozart were. I love most the works of Brahms, Beethoven, and Bach. I do not like Paganini at all and hardly ever play his music. On my debut concert there will be works by Brahms, Hubay, and Sibelius with orchestral accompaniment. My professor will conduct the orchestra.
>
> Not too long ago I appeared in a concert with Béla Bartók, and during this year I will appear in all of Bartók's concerts in Budapest. The master has said that I will be his only violin partner. I would like to have several more concerts this winter, then I would like to travel abroad.

At home I practice five or six hours each day, but this is
very little. I should really practice more, but unfortunately I
have little time since I am still going to the Sixth *Réal* [the
tenth grade]. Abroad I would like to receive the Doctor of
Music degree which is impossible at home.[2]

Hubay's plan for the concerto evening was well-conceived. The
three works were chosen for Székely's abilities; for his own part, the
performance of his *Concerto all'antica* would again confirm Hubay's
eminence as a composer. And, of course, the Sibelius concerto had
been associated from the beginning with the Hungarian school of
violin playing and Hubay's remarkable pupil, Ferenc Vecsey, to
whom it is dedicated.

"For a moment we were taken aback as the first notes sounded on
his violin," wrote one critic about Székely's performance of the
Brahms concerto at the Vigadó, "because a seventeen-year-old blond
child was standing on the podium, but a fully developed artist was
making this music."[3] Another critic observed, "Missing from this
searching and slowly unfolding talent is the immediacy of childish
charm, simplicity, and trust since he is already full of deep delving
and understanding of the rhythm and structuring of the works."[4]

Székely's concert plans continued to unfold as his confidence
grew. Before the New Year he performed Beethoven's Violin Concerto in Budapest and made his debut in Vienna at the Kleiner Konzerthaus-Saal.

In the all-Beethoven concert at the Vigadó on 25 December 1921,
Emil Abrányi, who had returned to his native Hungary from Germany in 1911 to become conductor at the Royal Opera House,
directed the Symphony Orchestra of the Városi Theatre. The program
included the *Egmont* Overture, the Sixth Symphony, and the Violin
Concerto with Székely "playing with the beauty of classic sunshine."[5]

Three days later Székely was in Vienna. He traveled there from
Budapest on the Red Cross train on which his father was the doctor.
With pianist Erich Meller he rehearsed his recital, which included
Joachim's Variations, the Beethoven Violin Concerto with Hubay's
cadenzas, Bach's Solo Sonata in A Minor, and a group of short pieces
he had chosen to close the recital: Tor Aulin's *Nordic Dance,* Cyril
Scott's *Mélodie et danse nègre,* and Philipp Scharwenka's *Alla Polacca.*

"Anyone with a good ear will notice that this lad sings a song of
a higher order," wrote the critic of the *Neues Wiener Journal,* "and he

will become a man to watch for in the future."[6] In the crowd of new artists making debuts in Vienna, Székely was no interloper but a welcome violinist with a magnificent technique and a musical intellect that easily probed the depths of the works he played. Yet while he was called "the new Kreisler" in Vienna, no impresario came forward to claim him as his own. He returned to Budapest immediately.

Székely spent New Year's Day of 1922 rehearsing with Pál Hermann for their duo recital scheduled for 2 January at the academy. This was the first of many duo recitals presented by the two young artists between 1922 and 1939 in Hungary, Holland, England, Germany, and Switzerland. In the course of these performances, they brought the great duo repertoire, including their own compositions for violin and cello, to the attention of a public especially interested in new music.

The first half of the program contained works by Haydn, Enrico Bossi, and Friedrich Hermann, the talented Leipzig composer who had been violist of the Joachim Quartet. The centerpiece of the concert was Zoltán Kodály's 1908 masterpiece, the Duo for Violin and Cello.

The Budapest critics especially liked the Six Bagatelles by Bossi and Kodály's very energetic and original Hungarian work which was the high point of this rare artistic event, a violin and cello duo recital with the very young but already well-known players. As one critic noted, "They were totally in unity, with high artistic goals, and a large audience rewarded them very deservedly."[7]

Bartók had plans for yet another recital on 18 January. Székely would join him on the platform—on this occasion not as a violinist but as a violist. Hubay would draw on Székely's talent as a violist as well. Székely comments:

> As a violist I played the pieces that none of the viola pupils at the academy played because they were not yet sufficiently advanced. I remember that the viola professor at that time was Gusztáv Szerémi, the first violist of the Opera Orchestra. Not only did Bartók invite me to perform as a violist, but on at least two different occasions, Hubay invited me to appear with him as a violist in chamber music afternoons at his home.

In 1894 Hubay had married the Countess Rosa Cebrain. They lived in Buda in a palace on the Danube. By 1922 the Hubay-Popper

Quartet had disbanded, and Hubay no longer appeared in public. Instead he gave musical *soirées* on Sundays at his home for an invited audience of aristocrats.

Occasionally Hubay gave a master class at his home, inviting the parents of his students to accompany their children to the Hubay palace. Székely recalls his several visits to the Hubay home:

> I remember going with my mother to Hubay's palace near the Danube. Our parents were always excited over these visits to Hubay's home, because otherwise they were not often invited there.
>
> Somewhat later Hubay invited me to take part in one of his Sunday *soirées*. I played the viola in a performance of the Brahms Sextet, Op. 18. Hubay took the leading part of course.
>
> I am still amazed at the circumstances of that performance. I cannot remember that we rehearsed at all. I didn't know the work, and although the second viola part I played is not complicated, granted, it is sufficiently complicated for someone to play with no rehearsal. Hubay must have trusted my experience since I had played before as violist in chamber music. My parents were not invited on that occasion, or probably they would have remembered something about the event and we would have spoken of it.
>
> Several weeks after that I appeared with Bartók in the first Budapest performance of Ernest Bloch's new Suite for Viola and Piano, then Hubay again invited me to take part in one of his Sunday *soirées*. This time it was to be a performance of the Quartet in G Minor by Robert Volkmann. Hubay led the quartet, László Sándor played second violin, I played viola, and Miklós Zsámboky was the cellist. To begin the concert Hubay was joined by the pianist Wilhelmus Henrik for a Mozart sonata, then Mrs. Imré Peto sang songs by Brahms, Tchaikovsky, and Hubay accompanied by her husband.
>
> Lorand Fenyves,[8] my friend who studied at the academy with Hubay in the 1930s, also remembers taking part in Hubay's private concerts during his childhood. He recalls that it was a tradition on New Year's Eve and the high point of the evening's concert that Hubay would perform the Bach Chaconne for his guests.

The Hubay palace was destroyed during the Second World War. However, photographs of its interior appear in Maria Zipernovsky's book on Hubay. The music room appears sparsely furnished: a grand piano, a few works of art, a bronze statue of Hubay. During Hubay's Sunday gatherings, the room was nearly filled with beautiful, artistically created chairs for the guests, who often included aristocrats and statesmen. After the music, Countess Cebrain held the attention of the guests at tea served upstairs in a studio where there was an enormous stove tiled with biblical scenes. From that setting the guests finally took their leave with farewells to the countess and her husband.

In a setting quite different from that of the Hubay palace, the Bartók concert at the Vigadó on 18 January was once again devoted to modern music. It began with six selections from the *Préludes* by Claude Debussy, and Bartók then played his own *Eight Improvisations on Hungarian Peasant Songs*, Op. 20. Bloch's Suite for Viola and Piano followed the intermission with Székely playing the viola. (Plate 5)

The suite was written for the 1919 Elizabeth Sprague Coolidge Competition, which it won on Mrs. Coolidge's casting the deciding vote. Louis Bailly, violist of the Flonzaley Quartet, and pianist Harold Bauer gave the world premiere that year at the Berkshire Festival in Pittsfield, Massachusetts. The performance by Székely and Bartók was the Budapest premiere, as noted in the March 1922 issue of the Parisian journal, *La Revue Musicale*, in an article written by Zoltán Kodály.[9]

A review in *Magyarság* by Aurél Kern showed that not everyone easily followed the progressive ideas in Bartók's *Eight Improvisations*. Shocked by Bartók's relentless modernity, Kern admitted that he did not quite understand the *Improvisations* and did not trust the sincerity of the evening's public who so faithfully applauded the new music. He found Bartók's advance into the realm of modernism too quick and wrote, "Did Wagner ever stand so far from his own age during *Tristan*, certainly daring for the time—was he as far away from his own age as Bartók is today?"[10]

The tunes on which the Op. 20 *Improvisations* are based are genuine peasant songs, some of them from Bartók's *Hungarian Folk Song Collection*, a theoretical work of examples of folk song which was completed in October 1921 and published in 1924. The seventh improvisation, dedicated to the memory of Claude Debussy, was published in the *Tombeau de Claude Debussy* as Bartók's contribution.

In 1904 the singing of Lidi Dósa, an eighteen-year-old peasant girl, had drawn Bartók's attention to some real Hungarian peasant tunes. For Bartók it was a revelation that would influence all his subsequent creations. After hearing the *Improvisations* in 1921, Székely began to realize the significance of Bartók's abstraction of authentic folk song and to appreciate his rigorous pursuit of ethnomusicological research.

Until his encounter with Lidi Dósa, Bartók shared with others the belief that Hungarian music was synonymous with gypsy music. Suddenly he came to realize that something else did exist in the songs of the peasants, something genuinely Hungarian, of immense artistic value and great significance to musical and general ethnology.

The impact of his realization was such that Bartók decided to investigate further, and together with his like-minded confrère, Zoltán Kodály, they started to collect these folk tunes.

Equipped with such primitive devices as the original Edison phonograph with wax cylinders, they undertook many tiresome and exhausting expeditions to meet the peasants. They lived among them and tried to record as many folk songs as possible.

After long years of their persevering effort, the collection increased to a stupendous number of songs which provided the spark for a momentous artistic and scientific movement.

One month after Bartók completed his First Violin Sonata, Márta Bartók wrote on 3 March 1922 on behalf of her husband (then on a tour in Transylvania) to Professor Géza Révész in Amsterdam. This letter, which launched a month-long correspondence between the Bartóks and Révész, was in answer to Révész' inquiry about Bartók's availability for a lecture, and possibly a recital, in Amsterdam. While none of their proposals came to fruition, the correspondence seems to have given impetus to the idea of Bartók's appearing in Holland.[11]

After his tour in Transylvania, Bartók went to England where the d'Arányi sisters arranged a private concert for him at the Hyde Park residence of the Hungarian *chargé d'affaires* on 14 March. After returning from a concert at Aberystwyth in Wales, Bartók was guest of honor at a reception given by Dorothy Moulton Mayer. There he met, among many others, Edward Dent, who would later play an important role in the success of the International Society for Contemporary Music.

Bartók appeared in a much-publicized recital at the Aeolian Hall on 24 March 1922. It was attended by more than twenty critics who reviewed the program of Mozart, Kodály, and Bartók. Before the intermission, singer Grace Crawford joined the composer in selections from his *Eight Hungarian Folk Songs*. Bartók and d'Arányi launched the second half with the long-awaited public performance in London of his First Violin Sonata.[12] Arthur Bliss, who was in the audience, later wrote the composer speaking of the sincere and remarkable expression of compositional technique involved in the work.[13]

Bartók and Jelly d'Arányi performed the First Violin Sonata in a Paris recital on 8 April that had been arranged by *La Revue Musicale*. Darius Milhaud and Francis Poulenc both attended this concert at the Théâtre du Vieux Colombier and later sent Bartók their congratulations.[14] A week later Bartók wrote to his mother telling her the news of Paris, particularly of the success of the concert and of the First Violin Sonata, and about a dinner party at the home of Henri Prunières during which he met Ravel, Szymanowsky, Stravinsky, and others, probably members of Les Six.[15]

The next day Bartók left Paris for Frankfurt, where his two important stage works, *Duke Bluebeard's Castle* and *The Wooden Prince*, were produced. This was the first time any of his stage works had been performed outside Hungary.

Four months later in Salzburg, two important Hungarian chamber music works were presented during August at the Internationale Kammermusikaufführungen. Bartók's First Violin Sonata brought the opening concert on 7 August to a close in a performance by violinist Mary Dickenson-Auner and pianist Eduard Steuermann who had given the world premiere in Vienna. A few days later in a program dominated by the works of English composers, Kodály's Serenade for Two Violins and Viola, Op. 12, was performed with great success.

These new-music concerts were organized by a group of young Viennese composers including Rudolf Réti, Egon Wellesz, and Paul Stefan, and took place during the Salzburg Festival of 1922. After the success of these concerts, some of the twenty composers present in Salzburg decided that this first international music festival after the First World War should become a regular event. Bartók and Kodály, along with Anton Webern, Paul Hindemith, Arthur Honegger, and Darius Milhaud were the principal protagonists in the formation of a new organization that would become known as the International Society for Contemporary Music.

The ISCM's headquarters were set up in London, where the first constitution was worked out at a conference in January 1923. This constitution stated that the aim of the society was the promotion of contemporary music without regard for aesthetic trends or the nationality, race, religion, or political views of the composer. This policy would be put to the test in the years ahead when conflicts occurred between those countries whose committees disagreed on the question of the promotion of only the avant-garde as opposed to any other contemporary music thought to be worthy of the interest of the society. However, in the early years, interest was entirely focused on staging the first festivals in Salzburg under the new auspices of the ISCM.[16]

The chamber music of Bartók and Kodály was heard again in Salzburg the following summer. Bartók's Second Violin Sonata appeared in the opening concert and Kodály's Sonata for Solo Cello, Op. 8, in the final concert of the first ISCM Festival in August of 1923. Pál Hermann had previously played Kodály's Solo Sonata at one of Schoenberg's private performances in Vienna in 1920. With the success of his Salzburg performance of Kodály's masterpiece in 1923, he and Imre Waldbauer were invited to perform Kodály's Duo for Violin and Cello at the ISCM Festival in Salzburg the following year. These early festival performances in Salzburg established an international reputation for the chamber music works of Bartók and Kodály and for the outstanding instrumentalists who performed them.

Because there was a twenty-year difference between their ages, during this period Székely and Bartók developed a friendship based primarily on the artistic ventures they undertook together, although their relationship was to evolve more completely in later years. During the 1920s, however, Bartók was touring abroad and meeting international colleagues, enjoying the success appropriate to his age and accomplishment, while Székely was still establishing himself as a performer in Budapest.

The next step in Székely's career was to give a debut recital at the Vigadó. The pianist György Kósa, a former pupil of Dohnányi, was chosen to accompany the recital. A Budapest composer of some reputation, Kósa had studied composition with Albert Siklós and Victor Herzfeld as well as having had some instruction from Bartók. He had also traveled as piano accompanist with violinists and other artists in Germany, Austria, and Italy. Székely and Kósa appeared together for the first time in an evening of poetry and music at the academy on 22 January 1921. A new sonata by the Englishman Cyril Scott, whose

modernistic music was much admired by Debussy, formed the centerpiece of an evening of poetry readings from the works of Walt
Whitman, Franz Werfel, Kurt Heynicke, and Lajos Kassák.

Székely's recent debut recital in Vienna was the basic model for
the Budapest concert on 2 February. Joseph Joachim's Variations
opened the program, but instead of the Beethoven work, the Concerto in B Minor, Op. 11, by Hermann Zilcher followed. An exact
contemporary of Bartók, Zilcher was the Frankfurt composer who,
like Bartók, had toured as pianist for Ferenc Vecsey. After the intermission Székely played the demanding Solo Sonata in A Minor by
Bach, then closed the concert with a group of pieces: Hubay's *Elegia
and Lepke*, Scott's *Mélodie et danse nègre*, and Scharwenka's virtuosic
Alla Polacca.

The *Pesti Napló* critic, Keleti, wrote enthusiastically about the
well-chosen program, noting Székely's lack of mannerism, his outstanding rhythm, and the depth of expression he brought to his virtuosity. Keleti concluded, "Despite his youth, he is already a fully
grown artist who will bring glory to himself."[17]

Many of Jenő Hubay's most successful pupils had established international careers after their debuts in Budapest by going abroad,
where foreign concert managers presented them in recitals in Berlin,
Vienna, or London. Before the First World War there was a steady
exodus of young Hungarian violinists from Budapest: Ferenc Vecsey
left in 1903, Joseph Szigeti in 1905, and Emil Telmányi in 1911. The
d'Arányi sisters had established themselves in London by 1914. Two
important violinists of a later generation, Erna Rubinstein and István
Pártos, had gone to Holland.

Eighteen-year-old Székely now seemed destined for an international career, but until his Hungarian concert commitments were fulfilled, he remained at home with his family in Budapest, a city where
the aftermath of war still brought chaos to everyday life. His desire
to go abroad intensified as he searched for a way to accomplish his
departure during a time when Hungary was recovering from war and
revolution.

After the Easter holiday in 1922, Dr. László Székely proposed a
plan for his son's trip abroad. Jenő Hubay wrote a statement on behalf
of his brilliant former pupil which would serve as an introduction:

> Székely, who is now only eighteen years old, is in command
> of the entire violin repertoire. He plays the familiar classical

pieces with complete mastery of technique, with a maturity and sensitivity well beyond his years. He plays the brilliant virtuoso pieces with great technical expertise. He is thoroughly musical, and is also very experienced in the area of chamber music. I have no doubt that when Székely steps onto the world scene he will receive acclaim everywhere and will rise to the upper echelons of modern virtuosi.[18]

Plate 1. The Franz Liszt Academy of Music in Budapest. PHOTOGRAPHY ADÁM FRIEDRICH.

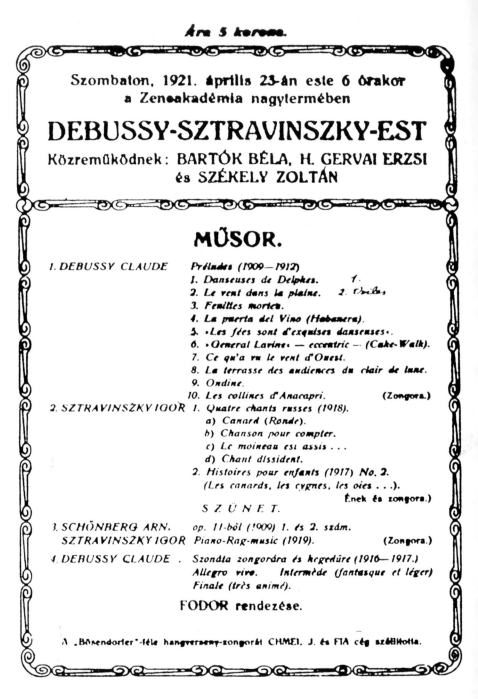

Plate 2. On 23 April 1921 Bartók and Székely played an early Budapest performance of Debussy's Sonata for Violin and Piano at the academy. THE SZÉKELY COLLECTION.

UJPESTI ZENEMŰVELŐ EGYESÜLET
(CONSERVATORIUM)

Az 1921. évi április hó 25-én, hétfőn az ujpesti városháza dísztermében Bartók Béla m. kir. zeneakadémiai tanár, zeneszerző, Nagy Izabella énekművésznő, Székely Zoltán hegedűművész szereplésével és Szikla Adolf conservatoriumi igazgató, m. kir. operaházi karmester vezetésével rendezett

MŰVÉSZHANGVERSENY

MŰSORA:

1. *a)* Bartók: 15 magyar parasztdalból a 7—15. szám. (Régi táncdalok).
   b) Este a székelyeknél. *c)* Medvetánc. *d)* Allegro barbaro.
   Zongorán előadja a szerző.
2. *a)* Gluck: Ária az „Orfeusz" c. operából.
   b) Grieg: Die Sennerin.
   c) Brahms: Von ewiger Liebe.
   Énekli: Nagy Izabella.
   Zongorán kiséri: Szikla Adolf.
3. *a)* Bartók: Szonatina. *b)* III. burleszk. *c)* 1. és 2 sirató ének. *d)* 1. román tánc.
   Zongorán előadja a szerző.

SZÜNET.

4. Bartók: Három székely parasztdal:
   a) Istenem, istenem áraszd meg a vizet...
   b) Töltik a nagyerdő utját..
   c) Asszonyok, asszonyok, hadd legyek társatok...
   Énekli: Nagy Izabella. Zongorán kiséri a szerző.
5. Beethoven: Kreutzer szonáta, op 47. — Adagio sostenuto. Presto. — Andante con Variazioni. — Finale. Presto.
   Hegedűn és zongorán előadják: Székely Zoltán és Bartók Béla.

Kezdete pont 6 órakor.

Az egyes számok alatt az ajtókat zárva tartjuk.

Az Egyesület IV. HÁZI hangversenyét az ujpesti városháza dísztermében május 9-én, hétfőn este 6 órai kezdettel rendezi.

E műsor ára 3 korona.

Terminus nyomda Budapest

Plate 3. On 25 April 1921 Bartók and Székely played Beethoven's Sonata Op. 47 ("Kreutzer") at the City Hall in Ujpest. THE SZÉKELY COLLECTION.

FODOR HANGVERSENYIRODA IV. VÁCZI-UTCA 1.
(könyvkereskedés) Telefon: 88—61.

Szombaton, 1921. november 12-én este 8 órakor
a fővárosi Vigadóban

BARTÓK BÉLA

zongora- és szerzői estje

Közreműködik: SZÉKELY ZOLTÁN hegedűművész.

MŰSOR

1. BACH J. S. . . . . . . 3. szonáta zongorára és hegedűre
(E-dur.)
Adagio. — Allegro. — Adagio ma non tanto
Allegro.

2. KODÁLY ZOLTÁN . Zongoramuzsika, op. 11.
(Első előadás.)
1. Lento. 2. Székelykeserves. 3. Il pleut dans la
ville. 4. Sírfelirat. 5. Tranquillo. 6. Székely nóta.

S Z Ü N E T.

3. BARTÓK BÉLA . . . a) 14 zongoradarabból, op. 6.
2. Allegro giocoso. 3. Andante. 4. Grave
(régi magyar népdal). 5. Vivo (tót népdal).
6. Lento. 7. Allegretto molto capriccio.
8. Andante sostenuto. 9. Allegretto grazioso·
10. Allegro. 12. Rubato.

b) 3 burleszk, op. 8.
1. Perpatvar. 2. Kicsit ázottan. 3. molto vivo,
capriccio.

c) 1. román tánc.

4. SZIMANOVSZKY KAROL . . . Mythes, op. 11, zongorára és hegedűre (Budapesten először).
1. La Fontaine d'Arethuse.
2. Narcisse.
3. Dryades et San.

A „Bösendorfer"-féle hangversenyzongorát CHMELL J. és FIA cég szállítja.

Plate 4. On 12 November 1921 Bartók and Székely played the first Budapest performance of Karol Szymanowsky's *Mythes*, Op. 11, at the Vigadó. THE SZÉKELY COLLECTION.

Szerdán, 1922. január 18-án este fél 6 órakor
a fővárosi Vigadó nagytermében

BARTÓK BÉLA

zongora- és szerzői estje

SZÉKELY ZOLTÁN közreműködésével.

MÜSOR

1. DEBUSSY . . . . Préludes.
   1. Danseuses de Delphes.
   2. La puerta del Vino. (Habanera.)
   3. „Les fées sont d'exquises dan-
      seuses".
   4. „General Lavine" eccentric.
      (Cake-Walk).
   5. Des pas sur la neige.
   6. La sérénade interrompue.
   7. Les collines d'Anacapri.

2. BARTÓK . . . . . 8 zongoradarab magyar népdalok
   fölött, op. 21. (Első előadás.)
   Andante (attacca). — Allegro capriccioso. — Lento (attacca). — Allegretto scherzando (attacca). — Vivace.
   Allegretto rubato. — Lento (attacca).
   Allegro vivace.

S Z Ü N E T.

3. BLOCH-ERNEST . Suite zongorára és violára.
   (Budapesten először.)
   1. Lento, Allegro. 2. Allegro ironico.
   3. Lento. 4. Molto vivo.

Plate 5. On 18 January 1922 Bartók and Székely played the first Budapest performance of Ernest Bloch's Suite for Viola and Piano at the Vigadó. THE SZÉKELY COLLECTION.

Plate 6. The façade of the Vigadó. PHOTOGRAPHY ADÁM FRIEDRICH.

Plate 7. Bartók's home at 4 Desző Szilágyi Square in Budapest where he composed his Second Violin Sonata in 1922. PHOTOGRAPHY ADÁM FRIEDRICH.

Plate 8. The home of Igminia Everts at 127 Berg en Dalscheweg in Nijmegen. THE SZÉKELY COLLECTION.

Plate 9. Igminia Everts as a young violin student in Nijmegen in 1915. THE SZÉKELY COLLECTION.

Plate 10. An audience gathers at the entrance to the Kleine Zaal of the Amsterdam Concertgebouw in 1917. COURTESY OF HET CONCERTGEBOUW NV.

Plate 11. The concert platform in the Kleine Zaal of the Amsterdam Concertgebouw. COURTESY OF HET CONCERTGEBOUW NV.

Chapter Six

Off to Holland

Dr. László Székely had many friends among the doctors who served on the Red Cross trains. One of those friends was in charge of a very special train called the Children's Train. It traveled back and forth between Budapest and Holland, which had been neutral during the war. In Holland there were committees devoted to relief work which brought children from Hungary to spend some time with foster families in Holland.

Shortly after Zoltán had traveled on his father's train to Vienna to play his debut recital there, Dr. Székely had a conversation with the doctor of the Children's Train and asked him, "Don't you know anybody in Holland that my son could stay with?" Fortunately for Zoltán's future, Dr. Székely's friend kept this question in mind during the Easter holiday of 1922 when the Children's Train brought a large group of Hungarian youngsters around the ages of fifteen or sixteen to Holland to be temporarily domiciled at Nijmegen[1] with Dutch foster families.

The children were met at the station in Nijmegen by the local Red Cross Committee which included a remarkable young woman named Igminia Everts. During a conversation with Dr. Székely's friend about the welfare of the children, she asked him in her friendly way, "What are you going to do for Easter?" He replied, "I am going to stay on the train. I have no money and can't go elsewhere." Miss

47

Everts immediately offered an invitation on behalf of her family, and the doctor gladly accepted. Later at the Everts' home when the conversation turned to musicians and artists, he told the family about his friends, Dr. Székely and his son, Zoltán, the brilliant young Hungarian violinist.

Zoltán Székely was eager to find the way to establish his international career and felt a Hungarian artist had to go abroad to do this. He knew that Bartók's fame had started only when he was abroad, that his career had gained momentum as a result of his successful international performances as pianist and composer. When suddenly Székely had his opportunity to go to Holland with an invitation to stay with the Everts family in Nijmegen, he traveled on the Children's Train.

There seemed to me to be promise in Holland for a Hungarian violinist such as myself. Two young Hungarian violinists who were pupils of Hubay, Erna Rubinstein and István Pártos, one of Hubay's favorites who was four years ahead of me at the academy, had established themselves very successfully in the musical life in Holland.

Hubay suggested I play for Karl Muck, a conductor he knew well. Muck was then guest conductor of the Amsterdam Concertgebouw Orchestra. Hubay's statement written on my behalf would serve as an introduction to him once I reached Holland and could arrange an appointment to meet him.

I traveled alone on my first trip to Holland. It was not a difficult trip for me since I had already had the experience of going to Vienna. My first impression of Holland was that it was a very quiet, peaceful country. It offered another orientation to life and reminded me of Hungary as it had been earlier during my childhood.

The train trip took two days, and when I finally arrived at the station in Arnhem near Nijmegen I was met by the Everts family. I did not yet know Dutch and Igminia Everts knew only a little Hungarian which she had learned from the children, so at our first meeting we spoke entirely in German. At first it was a little bit strange since we couldn't talk very much, but in the months ahead in Nijmegen I studied hard and soon learned Dutch.

Igminia, who was to become my wife in 1926, came from Helmond, a small town near Eindhoven. Her father, Jacobus

Everts, owned a factory in this industrial region. During his childhood, Mr. Everts had learned a certain respect for musicians who frequently visited his family at their garden house. When he grew up he became a very good amateur musician. He both played the cello and sang in choirs. Apparently he had a beautiful voice and enjoyed singing as a baritone soloist in oratorios, which were very much *en vogue* in Holland. At the time when I first knew him he was still a choir member. Igminia's mother, Anna Everts Balbian-Verster, was a fairly good pianist and I think she had once studied for the profession, but at that time this kind of pursuit was not the fashion for such a person in Holland.

When Igminia was a child of ten her father decided he did not wish to spend the rest of his life as a businessman. Having made this decision, he moved his family from Helmond to a large, stately home at 127 Berg en Dalscheweg in Nijmegen. Igminia's parents belonged to the choral society, Toonkunst, and eventually really devoted their lives to music and musicians.

Igminia, who was called Mientje by her family and close friends, studied the violin as a child with a pupil of Carl Flesch who lived in Nijmegen. As she grew up, Mientje met many distinguished musicians who visited her family, including the violinists Aldo Antonietti, Bronislav Hubermann, and Jacques Thibaud, pianists Myra Hess and Marcel van Gool, singers Birgit Engbell and Ilona Durigó, and cellist Gerard Hekking.

In May 1919 she even met the young Hungarian violinist, István Pártos, when he first appeared in Holland and caused great excitement with his concerts. She asked that István Pártos be invited to their home. During his visit she happily taught him to ride a bicycle although the boy's parents thought the idea far too dangerous, fearing he might fall and injure himself. A year later, Mientje lost her young Hungarian friend when at the peak of his youthful career, seventeen-year-old Pártos died tragically from influenza in Amsterdam.

Mientje Everts became deeply involved in the Red Cross relief movement. In 1920, when she was twenty-two, she visited Hungary for the first time, traveling as a volunteer with other relief workers on the Children's Train to Budapest to return four hundred Hungarian children to their families in Hungary after their visit to Holland. She wrote about this adventure in her travel diary:

On Wednesday we left from the station at Arnhem. We went first to Zavenaar and then into Germany, passing through Würzburg, Nuremberg, and Passau, where I saw the Danube for the first time. When we entered Austria, I saw Linz, Vienna, and Bruck. I saw the Danube again at Komárom when we finally arrived in Hungary. There the crops were still in the fields. I saw country women with their heads covered in colorful kerchiefs and wearing embroidered shawls on their shoulders. At noon on the 28th of August we arrived at the East Train Station in Budapest with the four hundred children and there I began my vacation.[2]

When she returned to Holland, she began to learn Hungarian from the children with whom she dealt in her relief work. She had a strong commitment to these young Hungarians visiting Holland. Some of the children she knew were in Holland for years before returning to Hungary. Some even remained permanently in her country.

During Székely's first visit to Holland, Mientje Everts was thrilled by the young violinist's presence in her family's home, and soon she was completely prepared to devote herself to his artistic needs. In later years she liked to joke, "He came for three weeks and stayed for three years!" For Székely this first visit proved to be a significant opportunity in the creation of his new career. On the basis of the recommendation from Hubay, he was able to play for Karl Muck and several other conductors.

One of these was the Finn, Georg Schnéevoight.[3] Originally a cellist, Schnéevoight was a very popular conductor in Holland. He led the Residentie Orchestra of The Hague in its summer concerts at the Kurzaal in Scheveningen, a suburb of the capital. Székely played Sibelius' Violin Concerto, Op. 47, for Schnéevoight and was immediately engaged to perform that work. Unfortunately, Dr. Géza de Koos, an important impresario in Amsterdam, intervened, perhaps on behalf of one of the artists under his management. Schnéevoight was convinced to abandon the performance of the Sibelius concerto only a few days before the concert date. Székely's appearance was rescheduled for a Sunday matinée concert of the Residentie Orchestra on 23 July with Ignaz Neumark conducting.

A new problem arose when the repertoire was changed. Neumark suggested Székely select several brief genre pieces in place of the Sibelius concerto which he felt would not suit the matinee audience.

There were no orchestrations available for the works Székely wished to present. Not to be defeated, he disappeared into his room for a day and night with the piano scores of Paul Juon's *Berceuse* and Henri Vieuxtemps' *Ballade et Polonaise*. He orchestrated the accompaniments and copied the orchestral parts. Such industry and commitment were characteristic of the young violinist who knew perfectly well how to achieve results. The concert was a great success, and Székely had won the respect of Mientje Everts and her family.

After his debut at the Kurzaal in Scheveningen, Székely began searching for a concert manager in Amsterdam.

With the assistance of the Everts family, I approached various managers and soon learned that the Dutch impresarios required a tremendous amount of money to arrange concerts. The response of Mr. Everts to the situation was, "Don't you listen to them. They should pay *you* to play!"

It was Mientje who found the solution to the financial problem of my hiring a manager. She made a personal sacrifice to raise the necessary funds, selling her own violin to finance my early recitals.

Eventually I went not to Géza de Koos, but to an old-fashioned impresario, Hans Augustine, who arranged an introductory recital. That took place a little later, in the province of Zeeland, and it was well received.

Thus having begun to establish myself in Holland, I decided to return to Hungary for a short visit in the late summer of 1922 to see my family and to renew my friendship with Bartók.

On 21 August 1922, Bartók wrote to his wife, Márta, who was away, to tell her that recently Zoltán's mother, Erzsébet Székely, had rung his doorbell early one morning. He had run to the door in his dressing robe to greet her, and they had made the plan that later in the morning the entire Székely family would come for a visit to discuss the possibility of a concert in Holland.[4] A week after the meeting with the Székely family, Bartók wrote his wife again to describe a first reading with Zoltán of the unfinished Second Violin Sonata.[5] A third letter was posted to her a few days later describing a certain point he had reached in the composition and again mentioning a rehearsal of the unfinished work with the young violinist.[6]

When Székely visited Bartók in his home at 4 Dezső Szilágyi

Square during the last week of August 1922, they spent their time together in a large room that contained his old grand piano and antique furniture including a very old Hungarian cupboard.

> When I arrived, Bartók was working on the Second Violin Sonata, and he showed me the manuscript. Since I had my violin with me, he proposed we play through the sonata although it was not yet completed.
>
> We played this difficult work as far as the recapitulation in the second movement, where the tremolo begins—the point he had reached in composing it. After we had played, Bartók remarked that certain things would come next in the work although these things were not yet written down. Evidently I was the first violinist to see a part of this work and to play it with him since that was the very first time he had showed it to anyone.
>
> During those visits I asked him about the Violin Concerto which it was rumored he had written for Stefi Geyer. I told him that I had heard that such a work existed and asked if it would be possible to see it. As he had no other violin works yet, except the First Violin Sonata and perhaps something from his youth, I was interested in the possibility that an unplayed concerto existed.

During 1907–08, Bartók intended to compose a three-movement violin concerto, each movement of which would portray a different aspect of the young violinist Stefi Geyer. He only completed two movements, then separated from her. He dedicated the work to her and gave her one copy of the manuscript as a token of his love.

Probably around 1914, Bartók incorporated the first movement (Allegro giocoso) of this two-movement concerto as the first movement of *Two Portraits*, Op. 5 (the opus number he intended for the unpublished concerto). Earlier he had called the theme of the concerto the "Stefi Geyer *leitmotif*," and this motif appears in several of his piano compositions of that period, notably the presto waltz, *Ma Mie qui danse*, the last piece from Fourteen Bagatelles, Op. 6. An orchestrated version of this bagatelle, but without solo violin, serves as the second movement of *Two Portraits*, Op. 5.

Bartók did not allow the early violin concerto to be published during his lifetime; however, Stefi Geyer kept her copy of the manuscript, and after her death in 1958 and fifty years after its composition, the work was given its first performance in Basel with Hans-Heinz Schneeberger, violinist, and the Basel Chamber Orchestra conducted by Paul Sacher. It was published posthumously in 1959 by Boosey and Hawkes.

No doubt Bartók could have shown his copy of the manuscript to Székely when he requested to see it had he intended it to be performed in its original form, but that, of course, was not his wish. In 1990 Székely recalled:

> When I inquired about this concerto, he made no answer whatsoever. He simply turned away and went out of the room as though he hadn't heard my question. At the moment I thought he was going to get the music, but when he returned he never mentioned it at all. These early works he never showed to anybody.
>
> As everyone now knows, Stefi Geyer had been his classmate at the academy and they were romantically involved. Even if his romantic involvement with Stefi Geyer was one reason for withholding this work he wrote for her, I think that is not enough reason for him not to have made the early Violin Concerto public. Maybe he never intended to bring this music out as a concerto.
>
> During this summer in Budapest when I visited my family and the Bartóks, I had sufficient time to think over my recent stay in Holland. Since an invitation had been made to return to Nijmegen for another visit with the Everts family, I decided to go back to Holland for the 1922–23 season.

After his return to Nijmegen, Székely learned the Violin Concerto by Sir Charles Stanford, an Irish composer whose works seemed to remain virtually unknown outside Great Britain. At the end of his first month back in Holland, Székely appeared as guest soloist in a choir concert at St. Steven's Church in Nijmegen. He played the Adagio from Stanford's concerto accompanied by the organist, Willem De Vries.

The Nijmegen critic found his tone "delicious" and thought his Tóth violin was a very beautiful instrument; the Stanford work was considered not very special, although the critic did think it was wonderfully played by this very young Hungarian whose future seemed so promising.

Székely's study of new works that were somewhat outside the

mainstream of the repertoire was a rewarding experience for him and for his audiences.

> At that time I was interested in playing compositions which were not known, in order to create something new. In the real world of concert giving we are somewhat cruel and forget these works eventually. I played certain works, but abandoned them later since one cannot keep on with all things. For instance, in my time a very popular work was the Violin Concerto by Karl Goldmark, but now it is ignored. Of course, for us it was important because Goldmark had certain connections to Hungary and in Budapest we played his works often.
>
> Even with the well-known composers there are series of works which it would be worthwhile to play, but one cannot do so for lack of time. We make selective choices even with the works of the great masters, even with Mozart and Haydn, since no one can keep up with all the repertoire.

During this period the design of Székely's early recitals was still based on tradition, containing works from various style periods, but most significantly, presenting a repertoire unlike the traditional one preferred by most of his contemporaries. The programs usually opened with a pre-classical work. After that followed a sonata or sometimes even a concerto performed with piano reduction, such a practice being common in the earlier part of the century. After the intermission came a series of smaller pieces, and the program concluded with a virtuosic showpiece.

Rarely heard genre pieces appeared in Székely's recitals much to the delight of audiences somewhat jaded by the typical fare frequently heard in violin recitals during the years between the wars.

> For that part of my violin recitals devoted to smaller pieces I found some very nice gems, for instance the pieces of Lili Boulanger, the sister of Nadia Boulanger, who didn't write more than one or two works since she died at the young age of twenty-four. I frequently performed Leone Sinigaglia's work called *Rapsodia piemontese*. Sinigaglia had a certain reputation then. Later in Italy I met this very talented man who composed in a style similar to Dvořák's. Pieces by Christian Sinding, Alfredo d'Ambrosio, and the Russian-born composer, Paul Juon, all appeared in my early recitals in Holland.

One day a certain Dutch pianist who accompanied me in those early years complained to Mientje that "Székely makes me work in those rehearsals as though I have been hired for life!" Of course such accompanists were often easily satisfied, but while I hated the idea that every time there was a recital more rehearsals were necessary, I nevertheless loved to be quite precise when working.

Until later when I played such recitals almost exclusively with Géza Frid, the Hungarian pianist who settled in Amsterdam as my accompanist, I had several pianists in Holland. Among them were Willem Kerper, Marcel van Gool, Bernard Tabbernal, and the Austrian, Paul Schramm. When the international touring began I appeared with other pianists: Ferran Ember, Ernst Wolff, Ivor Newton, Rae Robertson, Max Deutsch, Felix Petyrek, and Dante Alderighi. In my late career, when I was no longer leading the Hungarian String Quartet and had returned to playing recitals, I performed and recorded exclusively with the Scottish-Canadian pianist, Isobel Moore.

And there were the recitals with Bartók. These had a different repertoire than the usual violin recitals of the period. His taste was for Bach, Mozart, Beethoven, and Schubert, and on occasion the works of Brahms, Debussy, and Ravel. And of course his own compositions, the sonatas and the rhapsodies, appeared in these recitals.

An important opportunity came to the young violinist in November of 1922 when Martin Spanjaard, the conductor of the Arnhem Symphony Orchestra, invited him to appear as soloist in five concerts. Born in Holland, Spanjaard trained in Germany, later accepting guest engagements in Berlin and Vienna. He was an able piano accompanist to various singers, and he composed several large orchestral works that remained unplayed. In Holland he was long associated with the Arnhem Symphony Orchestra. He invested heavily in the financial affairs of the organization but in 1933 withdrew from his prominent position, and shortly after that, while suffering from a depression, commited suicide.

Following the 1922 performances, Székely became a frequent soloist with the Arnhem Orchestra, appearing in both Arnhem and Nijmegen at the invitation of Spanjaard. During the decade that followed, he was heard with the Arnhem Orchestra in the works of Dvořák, Hubay, Juon, Sinigaglia, d'Ambrosio, Brahms, Beethoven, and Glazounov, and in a final performance at Arnhem on 25 November 1933, he played Viotti's Concerto No. 22 and Ravel's *Tzigane*.

For his debut with the Arnhem Symphony Orchestra, Székely chose two programs linking together either the Violin Concerto by Dvořák and Hubay's *Variations on a Hungarian Theme* or a different combination for matinee concerts that used the Hubay *Variations* and the two short works, *Berceuse* by Paul Juon and Leone Sinigaglia's *Rapsodia piemontese*.

Eight different critics seized upon certain undeniable aspects of Székely's violin playing and musicianship that were evident during these performances. They found his tone very beautiful because of its timbre and volume, and especially so on the lower strings. They noted that he projected this tone equally with tenderness or with power and always with perfect intonation. In addition, the unusual ease with which he played the most difficult passages showed the bowing to be as developed as the left-hand technique, where the harmonics, trills, and double stops were "incredibly perfect," the technique "masterful."

Perhaps more telling than this amazing unanimity of opinion concerning Székely's technical prowess were the more personal observations: "From the first moment, the artist won the audience, and they were more enthusiastic than I have seen them before."[7] And "A harmonious wonder of youth and maturity, Székely is a boy and I hope he will stay a boy for all his life."[8]

In December of 1922 Székely's playing came to the attention of the conductor Evert Cornelis, a Debussy specialist and a leading new-music advocate in Holland. An Amsterdamer, Cornelis conducted both the Amsterdam Opera and the Amsterdam Concertgebouw Orchestra for a decade, then assumed the conductorship of the Utrecht Symphony Orchestra in 1920. Szekely's performance of the Dvořák Violin Concerto on 13 December was a resounding success, and the press forecast that his path to the big concert halls would soon be assured.

While Hubay's recommendation to Karl Muck had enabled Székely to introduce himself, nothing further had developed in Amsterdam because Muck had gone to Germany to conduct the Hamburg Philharmonic. It therefore became important for Székely to play for Willem Mengelberg, the permanent conductor of the Amsterdam Concertgebouw Orchestra. Mengelberg, the most celebrated Dutch conductor, was a champion of the music of Gustav Mahler and

Richard Strauss and a conductor whose Beethoven performances were greatly admired.

Trained in his native Utrecht and at the Cologne Conservatory, Mengelberg obtained his first important conducting post in Lucerne when he was only twenty-one. Three years later he returned to Holland to lead the fledgling Amsterdam Concertgebouw Orchestra that had been established in its new concert hall for less than a decade. For the next half century, Willem Mengelberg was responsible for leading the Amsterdam Concertgebouw Orchestra to international fame as one of Europe's supreme virtuosic orchestral ensembles. During his tenure he made his influence felt in other countries—England, Germany, Italy, Russia—but it was in New York that he enjoyed the greatest success outside Holland.

Mengelberg consolidated his international career beginning in 1921, when he was appointed music director of the New York Philharmonic, a position he held while still engaged by the Amsterdam Concertgebouw and until Arturo Toscanini succeeded him in 1928.

The artistic association that began with Székely's playing for Mengelberg in December of 1922 lasted for more than two decades, culminating in the first performance of Bartók's new Violin Concerto in 1939 and, shortly thereafter, his brief appointment as second First Concertmaster during the troubled, early years of the Second World War.

Székely arrived at his audition for Mengelberg prepared to play from a large repertoire of concertos; however, Mengelberg unexpectedly requested to hear a quite different repertoire.

> I prepared five concertos—Brahms, Beethoven, Sibelius, Mendelssohn, and Mozart—but this audition was a strange thing. Mengelberg called me into his studio at the end of an orchestra rehearsal, but then excused himself while he changed and went for a shower. He asked me to play in the meantime. I had expected someone would probably accompany me at the piano, but no, there was no one.
>
> At that time I had a fairly good repertoire of solo works, and so I played him everything including my transcription of Friedrich Hermann's Scherzo for the viola.[9] After this I paused, thinking I was finished with the audition, but I heard him call from the shower, "Now, play some Bach!"
>
> Evidently pleased by my performance, he wrote this statement: "Mr. Székely has played for me, and I am de-

lighted to recognize in him a young artist who is musically
highly gifted, in whom currently a high level of technical
and musical development has been reached. Mr. Székely
without a doubt belongs to the group of the best young violin artists, and I highly recommend him to every concert
director as a soloist."[10]

Chapter Seven

With Bartók in Holland

In Budapest Bartók had completed his Second Sonata for Violin and Piano on 22 November 1922, one month before Székely played for Mengelberg. This was the sonata that Székely had played with him at his home in Dezső Szilágyi Square in August of 1922, when composition of the work was still in progress. Bartók's international reputation as a chamber music composer was greatly enhanced by the emergence of his two sonatas for violin and piano. His eventual performances of the works with Székely as a favorite sonata partner would bring a daring, new artistic impact to the many recitals in which they collaborated until 1938.

The Waldbauer-Kerpely Quartet and Béla Bartók performed an all-Bartók evening entitled *Melos-Kammermusik Abend*, for the subscribers of the musical periodical *Melos* on 7 February 1923. This important concert engagement in Berlin provided the opportunity for the first performance of the Second Violin Sonata. The program included two works: the String Quartet No. 1, Op. 7, which the Waldbauer-Kerpely Quartet had played first on 19 March 1910, twelve years earlier; and the Second Violin Sonata in its world premiere, performed by Imre Waldbauer with Bartók as the pianist.

Bartók soon proposed a concert with Székely in Paris. However, Henri Prunières[1] could not make arrangements similar to the successful ones of the previous season, so the idea of the Paris recital was abandoned. Bartók also proposed a Budapest recital with Székely in which they would present the first performance in Hungary of the new Second Violin Sonata and would include Stravinsky's five-movement Petite Suite for Violin, Clarinet, and Piano arranged from *L'Histoire du Soldat* in 1919. In a letter dated 19 January 1923 he wrote, "Around the 25th I will send the piano and violin parts of the Sonata as well as the violin part of the Stravinsky."[2] Knowing that Székely was planning a trip to England to introduce himself there to several prominent musicians, Bartók had prepared a letter of introduction for the young violinist to the writer and critic, Michel Calvocoressi, which he included.[3]

Unfortunately, as these concert negotiations unfolded, Székely was not able to accept this particular engagement in Budapest because of previous professional commitments in London. Bartók wrote again on 25 February 1923:

> Dear Székely!
>
> I am sorry that you cannot come to the concert. It was impossible to postpone the thing, so the concert will take place and the Stravinsky cannot be played, of course. [Ede] Zathureczky will play the Sonata; it will go quite well, I believe.
>
> I ask you to send back the Sonata and the Stravinsky part as soon as possible.
>
> With greetings and best wishes,
> Bartók[4]

Székely then suggested to Bartók a series of recitals in Holland in Amsterdam, Rotterdam, and Utrecht. The concerts in Amsterdam and Rotterdam took place the following April, producing the third and fourth performances of the Second Violin Sonata, but the scheduling of the Utrecht recital caused a good deal of difficulty, and that engagement was ultimately canceled.

Székely went to England for the first time in February of 1923, where in London he was the guest of the singer Dorothy Moulton Mayer, the wife of industrialist Robert Mayer and a patron of young performing artists. While in London, the nineteen-year-old violinist played privately for two leading English conductors, Eugene Goosens and Sir Henry Wood. Székely hoped that these auditions would lead to his future engagements in England.

Bartók had contacted Edwin Evans who, in turn, introduced Székely to Goosens, who had been associated with Thomas Beecham's operatic enterprises and had conducted a season of concerts with his own orchestra in London. Goosens heard Székely's audition on 23 February 1923 shortly before leaving England for America, where he had been engaged as conductor of the Rochester Philharmonic Orchestra. Later in 1931, having established himself in the United States, Goosens succeeded Fritz Reiner as conductor of the Cincinnati Symphony Orchestra when the celebrated Hungarian conductor left his post to teach at the Curtis Institute of Music in Philadelphia.

After Székely had played through Goosens' Violin Sonata, No. 1 (1918) with him, he continued with the Brahms Violin Concerto. Goosens described his impressions:

> I have listened several times to the marvelous playing of Zoltán Székely and am full of admiration for him—as violinist and musician alike. His playing of the Brahms concerto alone stamps him as a great artist, and his sympathetic rendering of every kind of music from classic to ultra-modern is wholly admirable.[5]

A few days after having played for Goosens, Székely again played the Brahms concerto, this time at the Queen's Hall in London for Sir Henry Wood, the most eminent English conductor of his day and the innovator of the famous Promenade Concerts in Queen's Hall in 1895. At the time he listened to Székely in London, Sir Henry had recently been appointed professor of conducting at the Royal Academy of Music while continuing to direct the Promenade Concerts, having declined the conductorship of the Boston Symphony Orchestra as successor to Karl Muck. After hearing Székely he invited him to appear in the "Proms" and immediately wrote from the Queen's Hall, "I have heard Mr. Zoltán Székely play the first movement of the Brahms Violin Concerto and I consider he has a great talent and should take a fine position as a soloist."[6]

In London Székely soon met Arnold Bax and Ralph Vaughan Williams. He also visited Joachim's grandniece, the Hungarian violinist Adila Fachiri-d'Arányi, and at her home was introduced to the young English conductor, Adrian Boult.

In late March of 1923 Székely traveled to Germany to give his first recital. In Berlin he stayed with Pál Hermann, who was now studying the cello with Hugo Becker at the Staatliche Hochschule. Together they searched Berlin's libraries and museums for violin and cello duos to present in their forthcoming chamber music recitals.

Székely's Berlin recital took place at the Bechstein-Saal on 29 March 1923. Dr. Ernst Wolff, a well-known scholar and an expert on the lieder of Robert Schumann, was the pianist. Two short works, *Romanze* by Victor von Herzfeld and *Capriccio* by Niels Gade, opened the program. Well known at one time, the composers of these genre pieces are virtually forgotten in the late twentieth century, although Herzfeld had been a professor of music theory in Budapest and second violinist of the Hubay-Popper String Quartet, and the prolific Danish composer Niels Gade, friend of Felix Mendelssohn, was the founder of the Copenhagen Conservatory.

The recital continued with Dvořák's Violin Concerto played with the piano reduction. After the intermission Székely played the Largo and Allegro from Bach's Third Solo Sonata, and concluded the evening's program with Joachim's Variations, a work he had played with success in Vienna and Budapest.

The Berlin critics were enthusiastic about Székely's performance and found him an outstanding violinist. The recital clearly had awakened high expectations; in fact they were already considering him an artist to be reckoned with. They admired his large, broad tone and spirited, clean technique and were captivated by the warmth of his style, especially when he allowed it free rein in passionate cantilena passages. The success of this Berlin concert seems to have rested on his being able to combine his great bravura abilities and his demonstrative Hungarian temperament to convey his musical insight.

The critic of the *Berliner Börsen-Zeitung* wrote, "Everything about him is completely natural, he becomes one with his instrument, he does not merely play upon it—and when he plays one pleasantly forgets that one is in a concert hall."[7]

Béla Bartók's arrival in Amsterdam was eagerly anticipated by late April of 1923. On tour in France, he played at the Théâtre des Champs Elysées, returned to Budapest, then arrived in Amsterdam on 28 April, the day of the first concert.

Mientje Everts especially looked forward to his arrival since it would be their first meeting. Fifty years later in conversation with David Leighton she vividly recalled that encounter:

> I wanted very much to meet Bartók and assist the artists
> at the concert, so Zoltán and I traveled to Amsterdam from

Nijmegen the day before the concert. My first encounter with Bartók was to be a rather unusual one.

Since I had been invited to stay with my aunt, Miss Rie de Balbian-Verster, the very well-known Dutch painter, I did so. Zoltán stayed in a hotel. The next morning we got a message from the hotel that Zoltán was not feeling at all well and was running a high fever. I rushed to the hotel and when I arrived he insisted that he would play despite his illness and wanted me to go to the railway station and meet Bartók who would arrive in the afternoon.

In those years the international trains were very irregular, and I remember running from one platform to another whenever an international arrival was announced. All I had to help find Bartók was a small photo. At last, about half-past six, an international train from Budapest arrived. The heavy stream of passengers pushed its way to the exit, and with the help of that little photo I suddenly recognized Bartók. How I did this in such a crowd, I don't know.

He was rather surprised not to find Zoltán at the station, but when I explained the situation he wanted to go as quickly as possible to the hotel. He was very tired from the long trip but wanted to talk to Zoltán immediately. Although still not well, Zoltán seemed to revive somewhat when he saw Bartók. He promised him firmly that he would play that evening no matter what happened. In the meantime it had gotten rather late. After having a hasty snack and dressing for the concert, both artists were finally ready to go. We drove to the Concertgebouw and found the audience already waiting in the hall.

As they had not rehearsed the Second Violin Sonata together, Bartók wanted very much to have at least some kind of rehearsal. There was no piano in the soloist's room of the Kleine Zaal, the small hall of the Concertgebouw used for chamber music recitals, but with all their powers of persuasion they succeeded in having a guard open the soloist's room of the Groote Zaal where the orchestra concerts were held. The guard even agreed to light a gas stove, as it was very cold that evening and Zoltán was shivering all over. They did manage to rehearse a few passages of that very difficult sonata.

There was a marvelous review in the paper the next morning. How they could play this sonata for an audience when they never played it together—and nearly without rehearsal—is amazing!

During the concert I was too nervous to go into the hall, so I listened from backstage. When suddenly there was a pause during the very first page and no music sounded I was afraid that Zoltán had given up or fainted, but then they continued. Later I realized that there was a general pause in the sonata at that point!

Because Mientje was backstage during the performance, she could not see, but heard Székely loudly demand, "Zurück! zurück!" ("Back! back!") much to the surprise of Bartók—and the audience—when two of his pages were turned simultaneously, a further complication caused by the inept page turners of which there were two, one at the piano turning for Bartók, the other standing beside Székely. However, despite the unusual circumstances that beleaguered the performance, Bartók was pleased with the concert and soon reported its unusual events to his wife, Márta.[8]

After their first encounter, Béla Bartók and Mientje Székely remained close friends until the desperate world conditions of 1939 finally separated them when Bartók left Europe for the United States.

"Bartók was always very friendly and open hearted toward me," Mientje recalled.

I think that he knew from that unexpected start that I not only admired him, but that he could count on me whatever happened. This first encounter was so emotional that even though he was a very "closed" person, I saw that he gave me his friendship right away.[9]

Székely played only Bartók's Second Sonata in this Amsterdam concert, but Bartók played his own piano works and those of Scarlatti and Debussy. The next day the whole recital was repeated in Rotterdam, but still without rehearsal because Székely had not yet recovered.

After these performances in Amsterdam and Rotterdam, Bartók went to London where he stayed at the South Kensington home of Duncan and Freda Wilson. Later His Majesty's Chief Inspector of Factories, Wilson was a keen amateur pianist and enthusiast for Bartók's music. During Bartók's subsequent London visits when he was frequently the Wilsons' house guest, he gave Duncan Wilson piano lessons.[10]

Bartók wrote to Székely from London on 1 May 1923:

Dear Székely!

The concert in Utrecht will be on May 11. I will arrive there that morning, thus we can have a thorough and <u>calm</u> rehearsal in the afternoon. I hope you have completely recovered and won't get sick before Utrecht.

Many greetings,

Bartók[11]

Bartók wrote again from London on 4 May 1923:

Dear Székely!

They found more engagements here for me than I expected, therefore I cannot return before the 13th.[12] I sent a telegram and a letter to Suikerman[13] that he should move the concert in Utrecht to the 14th or 15th. I hope he will be able to do it; I asked him to notify you of the new date. I seem to remember that you are free on these days. If the Utrecht concert will take place, I will arrive there on the morning of the concert and plan to stay at the Hotel des Pays-Bas.

Many greetings,

Bartók[14]

Bartók and Jelly d'Arányi[15] performed the Second Sonata in London on 7 May 1923. This London premiere was the fifth time the work had been played in public and the first time that Jelly d'Arányi, the violinist to whom the work is dedicated, performed it.

On the following day, 8 May, another postcard from Bartók arrived in Nijmegen from London:

Dear Székely!

Suikerman has not responded to date concerning the concert in Utrecht, thus no doubt it will be canceled; I have to make a decision about when I leave here regardless of Utrecht. I depart on the evening of the 14th because even on that afternoon I have some business here which, of course, I would not have accepted if I had received news from Suikerman; but now I cannot wait any longer.[16] I am sorry that the concerts in Holland had this many hurdles. Would you please send the Sonata to my address in Budapest. I haven't yet spoken with Taylor or Goosens.

Many greetings,

Bartók[17]

For decades Székely made astute observations of Bartók's work habits as a composer. They discussed matters of composition both in rehearsal and in conversation. Székely occasionally saw manuscripts of Bartók's works in progress and frequently performed from annotated manuscripts before his new works were released by the publisher. Székely recalls:

> For the two early performances of the Second Sonata in Holland, I played from a manuscript which I later sent back to Bartók. I got the manuscript beforehand, of course, and studied it, otherwise one couldn't play such a work. The work only came out in print a year or two later.
>
> It is interesting that it was often his way to completely finish a section of a new work while the rest was just in sketches, but when he finished a movement, that was done. Regarding the Second Sonata, I couldn't say whether or not when he completely finished it he returned to change any of the parts he had completed earlier. In order to make that judgment, one would have to see the original manuscript and to have the later ones and compare them, which all the musicologists do nowadays.
>
> During a later period in the case of the orchestration of his Violin Concerto, Bartók said to me, "I had such great difficulties in scoring this because usually when I compose a work, I have exactly in mind what I want to do. I put it down in a sketch, not exactly a piano sketch, that is not necessary, often I already have the piano version ready. It would be much faster, would save time, if I would have exactly fresh in my memory what I want to do in the scoring. When I orchestrate I should write it down right away, as though composing, rather than later as instrumentation."
>
> This is, of course, a very bold, a very daring statement to say—"I should put these ideas down right away in my score." That proves again that Bartók had a very detailed imagination about what he notated although probably from time to time he allowed small differences.
>
> He did sometimes return to a work and improve it, but I think that was not the usual thing. Whether hearing a performance would have helped him in some way, that could be, but he never talked about that sort of thing. Such matters he considered so much a part of his intimate, inner life that he did not like to speak about them and rarely did, and then he only just gave hints.

As far as I know, he worked on only one composition at a time, but he told me, "Once I start, I work fast." He could compose a string quartet in a few weeks. All his biographies emphasize that once he started composing, he worked long hours through the day and into the night. He worked this way when he composed even with the strain of years and years of nonstop, heavy schedules that combined concerts, composing, his scientific work, and teaching (that is to say, he did all of these things at the same time). These things kept him away from his composing, of course, and he may have had a much greater output if he had been in more favorable circumstances. That is why he didn't like to teach. He didn't like to teach, and he didn't like to concertize. It is a paradox: one likes it and one dislikes it.

At the Amsterdam and Rotterdam concerts in April of 1923 the difficulties and the seriousness of Bartók's new Second Violin Sonata did not escape the notice of the Dutch critics, who were eager to hear Bartók's music. However, it seemed to them that the new work demanded a very special technique that did not show very much about the violinistic side of Székely's playing. They noted that a program limited to one new work could hardly do justice to this very special, musical violinist. However, the critic of Amsterdam's *Het Handelsblad* wrote, "There is something strongly individual in his very special and suggestive rhythm and in the particular timbre of his playing, and all this fascinates and captivates the audience very strongly."[18]

The critic of the *Nieuwe Rotterdamsche Courant* was simply confounded by the work itself, as perhaps were others in the audience unaccustomed to Bartók's expressionist style in the Second Sonata. "They played a composition of Bartók and we didn't understand one note of it. . . . Maybe this music is written for other ears than ours."[19] An opposite view was expressed by the critic of the *Dagblad van Rotterdam*. "There burns in this Sonata a mighty passion which in the following moment drops into an irresistible tenderness."[20]

In the late twentieth century Bartók scholars have given new perspective to the compositional significance of the two sonatas for violin and piano which are experimental works in Bartók's oeuvre. János Kárpáti has remarked that the proximity of the writing of the two works, as though composed in a single burst of creative energy, and their Schoenbergian structures took Bartók to the threshold of dodecaphonic composition.[21] However, Ferenc Bónis has observed that while Bartók had thought it possible to synthesize tonal folk music with the principles of atonal development, he later rejected this idea and moved away from the expressionism of the second Viennese school.[22]

After Bartók's departure, Székely finished the season on 4 May 1923 with a violin recital accompanied by Marcel van Gool in the Kleine Zaal of the Amsterdam Concertgebouw. Although Erna Rubenstein had moved on to an international career and the young István Pártos was dead, the memory of their performances had not faded. Two years after Székely's arrival on the scene, Theo van der Bijl acknowledged the Dutch reign of a triumvirate of Hungarian violinists in his review in *De Tijd*: "Next to Erna Rubenstein and István Partós we now have the third Hungarian wonder, Zoltán Székely, who is only nineteen."[23]

Comparisons were drawn. The musical intensity of Partós' playing and the unique style of Rubinstein's performances were remembered as the most admirable traits of those two artists. On the other hand, Székely was thought to be unsentimental and to possess a bigger sense of style. If Partós had moved his audiences to tears, Székely inspired his audiences to admiration, for his playing was not of the intimate sort but triumphed rather by etching the great musical lines with his expansive tone, projecting to the audience the subtle inner processes of his musicianship.

Chapter Eight

A Tour to Spain

My very rapidly developing friendship with Bartók had suffered somewhat when I left Hungary as a boy to live in Holland, since we no longer had the opportunity to see each other regularly. However, Bartók's visit to Holland in the spring of 1923 renewed our friendship, and this friendship deepened during my subsequent trips to Hungary and our ensuing recitals together.

My impression was that as a man, Bartók was honest to the extreme and straightforward even if he had to be harsh. I learned to appreciate his open and firm yet kind and friendly manner, and his fine sense of humor. The impression might have been different for a stranger, on account of the shyness and reserve which he could not entirely overcome even in his later years. Besides, he was uncompromising in his everyday life, as well as in his profession.

He wouldn't hesitate, for instance, to express his disapproval to an artist or conductor if a performance of his work did not satisfy him. Thus it is easily understandable that such characteristics did not advance his career much, nor did they make him win many friends among his colleagues or people in the world of music. Notwithstanding, Bartók earned more and more recognition. One success followed another, and it would take quite a time to enumerate all of them.

In the summer of 1923 in Nijmegen, Székely knew nothing of several pivotal events rocking Bartók's personal life. After he returned to Budapest from his tour in Holland and England, Bartók was occupied throughout the summer of 1923 with the composition of the Dance Suite for Orchestra. During these months of intense creativity, Bartók was suddenly distressed to learn that he had to appeal for the recognition of his mother's new Czech citizenship. She experienced great difficulties in Poszony: her citizenship was in question and her pension was imperiled as a result of the new geographical borders resulting from the Treaty of Trianon.

Having dealt with this difficulty concerning his mother, Bartók experienced a personal crisis later in July when his marriage of fourteen years to Márta Ziegler Bartók ended abruptly in divorce. However, by late August he had married again, this time to another of his students, Ditta Pásztory, who had studied in his piano class the previous year.[1]

Three months after his marriage to Ditta Pásztory, Bartók's new Dance Suite was performed for the first time in Budapest. The world premiere took place on 10 November 1923 at a concert celebrating the fiftieth anniversary of the federation of Budapest from the three cities of Pest, Buda, and Obuda. At that concert Dohnányi conducted the Budapest Philharmonic in three important commissioned works: his own Festival Overture, Op. 31, based on patriotic music; Kodály's *Psalmus Hungaricus*, a choral setting of Mihály Vég's paraphrase of Psalm 55; and Bartók's Dance Suite for Orchestra which incorporated Rumanian and Arabic influences as well as Hungarian. The Dance Suite was such a success that there were more than fifty performances within the year in Germany alone.

Székely had gone to Knokke–Le Zoute on the seacoast in West Flanders during early September of 1923 to hear the great violinist Eugène Ysaÿe in recital. Ysaÿe's contract as conductor of the Cincinnati Symphony Orchestra had allowed him only the summer months at home in Belgium. However, in 1922 Fritz Reiner succeeded him in Cincinnati, and Ysaÿe was once more in residence at La Chanterelle, his villa at Knokke–Le Zoute. Here his friends and colleagues, among them the Thibaud-Casals-Cortot Trio, gathered to play chamber music and on occasion to hear Ysaÿe play. Székely recalls his first meeting with Ysaÿe:

> When I had heard Ysaÿe's recital at Knokke, his playing was no longer as it had been. He had just passed his sixty-fifth

birthday and was not well. Somewhat later he suffered the amputation of his right foot due to diabetes. Whether that health crisis was the reason he turned so strongly to composing at the end I don't know.

Many of his compositions that nobody had heard before suddenly came to our attention. He seemed to print them all. Many of them were orchestral, composed in his symphonic poem style a little bit *à la* César Franck. I was interested in these works.

When I visited Ysaÿe at the beginning of my career, I had the opportunity to play for him. On that occasion I played the Mendelssohn concerto and one of his own pieces which I often played in recitals, the *Berceuse de l'enfant pauvre*, Op. 20, for violin and piano. When I had finished playing his piece, he said to me, "*Je n'ai jamais pensé c'était . . . si triste*" (I never thought that it was . . . so sad).

I appreciated this compliment from Ysaÿe. Before we parted he wrote a page for me which said, "After having heard the young artist, Mr. Zoltán Székely, I am happy to be able to say that, among the violinists of the new generation, he is certainly one of the most remarkable. Zoltán Székely possesses great ability and has beautiful technical qualities also. Feelings." He signed his name and the place: Eugène Ysaÿe, Le Zoute, 12 September 1923.[2]

On his return from visiting Ysaÿe, Székely gave two concerto performances in Holland, one in Gouda on 7 October, where he performed the Mendelssohn concerto with the Residentie Orchestra of The Hague conducted by Johann Jäger, and the other in Nijmegen on 11 October with the Arnhem Symphony Orchestra, Martin Spanjaard conducting. Jeanne Landré, critic of the *Nijmeegsche Courant*, wrote, "When Székely entered the hall there was a feeling of 'welcome' from the audience."[3] They had come to hear Székely play an unfamiliar work, Violin Concerto No. 2 by Alfredo d'Ambrosio.[4] The Nijmegen presentation of the d'Ambrosio concerto, a work dedicated to Jacques Thibaud, was Székely's only performance of this composition simply because no conductor other than Martin Spanjaard asked for it.

Very often the concertos Székely championed met with no sustained interest from conductors who were usually eager to present more orthodox music to the public. Undaunted, Székely continued his quest for a unique repertoire, searching for unfamiliar works of significant artistic merit and promoting the composition of new music. (Fifteen years later this would result in his persuading Béla

Bartók to compose his Violin Concerto, one of the great masterpieces of the twentieth century.)

Following these concerto performances, Székely undertook a concert tour in Holland with pianist Marcel van Gool. They began in Friesland. After a recital at Leeuwarden, a Friesian town completely enclosed by waterways, they gradually made their way to southern Holland where they played at Delft, the birthplace of Vermeer, then ended the tour with a performance at Rotterdam, Holland's second largest city and then the largest seaport in the world, built astride the most important waterways in Europe, the Rhine and the Maas.

Székely's new edition of an anonymous Italian sonata from the mid-eighteenth century began these recitals. He had realized its figured bass from the manuscript no. 1266 that he had discovered in Munich in the collection of the Baierische Staatsbibliothek. In addition, Székely performed the suite of four pieces, *Quasi Ballata, Appassionata, Un poco triste*, and *Burleska* by the Czech composer-violinist, Josef Suk, the son-in-law of Dvořák. After the Mendelssohn concerto, Philipp Scharwenka's Polonaise in D Minor ended the programs.

Having set out to establish himself in Holland, Székely was rapidly building his reputation as a concert violinist in a country where violin performance was held in the highest esteem. He confidently searched for new works to include in his unusual repertoire, considering music from every style period, but particularly the works of twentieth century composers. By the mid-1920s, Dutch impresarios would publicize the fact that the young Hungarian had performed concerts in every music center in the country, and frequently in many of the small villages as well.

There had been ample evidence during his composition lessons with Kodály that he had a remarkable aptitude for creating violin music. Despite his interest in the new-music movement, as a composer Székely moved with a certain caution controlled by an unerring sense of timing. Even though he had played his Sonata for Solo Violin for Bartók at their first meeting, by 1923 he had not performed his own compositions in public. While he may have had some doubt about the promise of his work for cello and orchestra begun in Budapest during 1920, he eventually recast it for violin and orchestra, then made a version of it for violin and piano, and by 1923 recognized its merit as a violin piece. In the autumn when he felt it was time for Székely, the composer, to emerge, his interest turned not to his Sonata for Solo Violin, the bold work he had presented to Bartók at their first meeting, but to this quite different composition. In 1923 for the first time Székely included one of his own compositions in his recital programs. He presented his short work, Allegro for Violin and Piano, within a group of pieces that included compositions by Enrique Granados, Cyril Scott, and Alfredo d'Ambrosio.

Székely made his first international tour to Spain in December of 1923. In Madrid and Barcelona he appeared in a series of recitals with the Hungarian pianist, Ferran Ember. While Ember may be forgotten today, in the musical life of Madrid in the 1920s he was admired for his virtuosity and his cultivated musicianship. Contrasting the ages of the performers, the critic of *ABC Madrid* wrote, "Zoltán Székely is by far a child in age, but with youthful ardor and remarkable dominion over his noble instrument, he brought happy results to all he played."[5]

The programs Székely presented for Madrid's Sociedad Filharmónica were considered extraordinarily novel and included many composers whose names were unknown in Madrid. On 10 December he performed works by Veracini, Dvořák, Ravel, Poldowsky,[6] Manén, Hubay, and Scharwenka. The next evening he played a somewhat different program: the Italian sonata discovered in Munich, as well as works by Sinding, Granados-Kreisler, Ravel, Cyril Scott, Manén, d'Ambrosio, and his own composition, Allegro for Violin and Piano. The critic of *El Sol* reported the performance of Székely's composition: "The Allegro by Székely has a curious melodic line entrusted to the violin with many beautiful harmonic moments in the piano."[7] In Madrid for the first time in his career, Székely was acknowledged and applauded in his double role as composer and interpreter.

Székely and Ember ended their tour in Barcelona where in 1923 a particularly rich musical life had evolved around the Orquestra Pau Casals, then celebrating its fifth season. Violinists such as Kreisler, Thibaud, Ysaÿe, Adila and Jelly d'Arányi, and Mathieu Crickboom appeared frequently as soloists with Casals' orchestra, whose repertoire, although predominantly classical and romantic, did include works by the twentieth-century Spanish composers and others such as Kodály, Malipiero, Milhaud, Schoenberg, and Stravinsky. A few months after Székely's first visit to Spain, the thirty-three-year-old English conductor, Adrian Boult, made a pilgrimage to Barcelona in order to attend Casals' rehearsals and to conduct two British works during May at the Palau de Musica Catalana, where Székely and Ember had played so successfully on 18 December 1923.[8]

Señor Walter, the Barcelona critic of *La Vanguardia*, found Székely a surprisingly natural violinist in whose hands the labor of the performance was disguised and the sentiment restrained, the better to interpret each page. "His technique is agile and clear, the tone of his violin is beautiful, and the expression is attractive."[9] The applause lasted long after each work, including Székely's Allegro.

"His tone is large and robust, and there is a truly exceptional, grand artistic temperament that dominates all his faculties," wrote the reviewer for the *Diario Del Comercio*, "and in his Allegro demonstrates the serious temperament of the composer."[10] *La Publicitat* reported that "Mr. Székely appeared as composer on the second half with his Allegro, a compact work of great interest which establishes the personality of the composer as the fine product of the young national school of Hungarians that counts Bartók and Dohnányi as prestigious figures."[11]

After the concert, the entire audience went with the violinist through the streets of Barcelona to his hotel and wanted to be invited inside, but naturally the management of the hotel objected to this exuberant display. Normally, concerts in Spain start very late, so this unusual event happened after midnight when the entire street was filled with enthusiastic concert-goers wanting to be near Székely, the sounds of the last encore, Rimsky-Korsakov's *Song of India*, lingering still in their memories.

In Holland, the impresario Ernst Krauss took an interest in managing Székely's concert tours after the success of the Spanish engagements. A German poet and idealist, Krauss was a well-known international concert director in Amsterdam. He offered Székely a January tour with the Viennese pianist Paul Schramm, who had an established reputation in Holland.

The tour began in North Brabant in the industrial town of Tilburg, then took the artists to s'Hertogenbosch (the birthplace of the painter Hieronymous Bosch), Gorinchem, Helder, Baarn, Eemland, and Vlissingen.

Their programs were based on a variant of the model Székely had used since his Budapest debut three years earlier, with Schramm performing a group of solos before the intermission.[12] The audiences were delighted. One critic observed that in Székely's case where still waters ran deep, "the tone was miraculous, as it was with Erna Rubenstein, and if one weren't looking at the solitary figure on the platform, when he plays double stops one would think it was an entire ensemble!"[13]

Krauss planned a major recital midway in the tour. It was scheduled for 26 January in the Kleine Zaal of the Amsterdam Concertgebouw with a different pianist, Marcel van Gool, a favorite in Amsterdam. The following day in Vlissingen when the tour with Paul
Schramm resumed, an entirely new program was improvised much
to the surprise of the audience and the artists. When Székely and
Schramm arrived at the concert hall, they discovered that the music
of the tour repertoire had been accidentally left behind at the Concertgebouw the night before. The duo offered a spontaneous performance of the Mendelssohn concerto when a piano reduction of that
work was found at the last moment.

For his Amsterdam recital with Marcel van Gool, Székely turned
to the French composers, presenting a program somewhat different
from that played on the tour with Paul Schramm. Székely played his
own composition, Allegro for Violin and Piano, which he had recently introduced in Spain. After the intermission, the group of genre
pieces took on a new aspect with Ysaÿe's *Berceuse*, Op. 20, Ravel's
Pièce en forme de Habanera, Roger-Ducasses' *Allegro Appasionato*, and
Darius Milhaud's *Le Printemps*. The closing group comprised the ever-
popular *Serenate* by d'Ambrosio and Leone Sinigaglia's *Rapsodia
piemontese*.

With the exception of d'Ambrosio's *Serenate*, all these short works
were new to the Amsterdam audience. Székely's playing of his own
composition intensified the public's interest in modernity; the critic
remarked that this work made him eager to hear other pieces Székely
had written and boldly heralded him as "the most interesting violinist of our time."[14]

The Dutch critics had come to realize by now that Székely was an
unusual virtuoso for his era in that he inevitably placed his virtuosity in the service of his well-considered musical ideas. Solving the
serious musical problems was probably more important to him than
dazzling performances of the traditional virtuoso pieces. He seemed
not to want to bewitch the audience, even though he possessed the
means to do so, and at twenty-one his intellect inevitably showed
him another way to accomplish his aspirations. Perhaps when he
was least conscious of pursuing the virtuosity of violin playing, he
succeeded best in becoming profoundly conscious of pursuing music
itself.

1924–1937

Mientje carried this snapshot taken in Nijmegen in 1925 ("Bartók's favorite!") in her small, red wallet for sixty-five years. PHOTOGRAPHY IGMINIA
EVERTS. THE SZÉKELY COLLECTION.

Chapter Nine

The Festival at Venice

"A first London recital is always an event of great import for a foreign artist," remarked the critic of the *Daily Telegraph* on the morning of 11 April 1924 following Székely's debut at the Aeolian Hall:

> That this should be so is so gracious a compliment to English musicians that they must needs incline towards friendliness on these occasions. Mr. Zoltán Székely, the young Hungarian violinist who gave his first London recital at the Aeolian Hall yesterday, can not only claim friendship, but admiration, too.[1]

Friendship and admiration—these sentiments must have been very welcome to the young man of twenty, offered as they were from the bounty of the great musical culture of London. For Székely, whose career embraced a pattern of artistic associations with living composers and their new music, friendship and admiration would play a great role in his innumerable concerts in England.

For his first Aeolian Hall recital he had chosen Rae Robertson to join him. The Scottish pianist and his wife, Ethel Bartlett, later performed widely in Europe and America as Bartlett and Robertson, duo pianists.[2] Székely's program was drawn from the group of works that had recently occupied his attention: music by Veracini, Dvořák,

Scott, Milhaud, Aulin, Ysaÿe, Inghelbrecht, d'Ambrosio, and Sini-gaglia represented unusual recital fare for London. Whereas in Vienna he had been dubbed "the new Kreisler," the critic of the *Morning Post* felt that "In its finish, his style reminds one of Heifetz."[3]

The series of small modern works that concluded the program led to the opinion that Székely's playing was peculiarly suited to the uncompromising demands of contemporary composers, but appraisals held his violinistic abilities to the mirror of an international standard:

> Though little more than a lad, and not over robust at that, Székely produces a powerful tone which is beautifully rounded. . . .[4]

> He is a fine violinist with just the bite to his playing that denotes the genuine article and furthermore, he plays delightfully in the middle of every note. . . .[5]

> It was abundantly clear from the very outset that his accomplishment was unusually secure when with his right arm he can at will obtain a tone of poignant sweetness, or a warmth and virility impossible to resist. . . .[6]

Two weeks later Székely again appeared at the Aeolian Hall with Rae Robertson; however, the second recital on 25 April had a new dimension. Arnold Bax, the outstanding British composer, joined Székely as pianist for the opening work, that composer's Sonata No. 2 for Violin and Piano. The critic of the *Daily Telegraph* wrote:

> There was some uncommonly brilliant playing at Aeolian Hall on Friday when Zoltán Székely amply confirmed the favourable impression he had already created as a violinist who is not only highly endowed in a technical sense, but who is possessed also of genuine interpretative ability. So much was evident enough in the performance of Arnold Bax's Second Sonata with the composer at the piano. Only an artist with a singularly alert musical sense could have grasped the complex idiom of that exacting work so fully as had this youthful player. No doubt the authority possessed by the composer's assistance had a great deal to do with the feeling of unity conveyed by a reading that left no point of beauty undiscovered. But there was no mistaking the fact that Mr.

Székely had thought the work out for himself, and had made it so much his own that he was never at a loss in finding what one felt to be precisely the right shade of tone or turn of phrase to give the whole something of the inevitableness that belongs of right to a true piece of interpretation. His playing here rose with the utmost ease to the height of the subject.[7]

The *Daily Mail* concurred: "One of the best performances Arnold Bax's Second Sonata has ever had was that given at the Aeolian Hall,"[8] while the *Daily Graphic* went one step further in suggesting that "Zoltán Székely, the violinist, did Mr. Bax a favour last night. . . ."[9]

At the time Székely appeared at the Aeolian Hall in 1924, Lionel Powell was one of the best established impresarios in London. With his business partner, Henry Holt, he had created an important agency for concert management on New Bond Street and served as director of the Royal Albert Hall Sunday Concerts, the London Symphony Orchestra Concerts at Queen's Hall, and perhaps of most importance, the popular International Celebrity Subscription Concerts. The roster of violinists who appeared in England under the Powell and Holt management included Cecilia Hansen, Alma Moodie, Erica Morini, and the giants: Kreisler, Kubelik, Prihoda, Ysaÿe, and Zimbalist. To this list Lionel Powell would soon add Zoltán Székely's name. Székely recalls:

> After the success of my Aeolian Hall recitals, Powell became interested in me for his International Celebrity Concert Series. He arranged my first appearance in the Royal Albert Hall in a joint recital with John McCormack, then engaged me for his series. Over the years he presented me often in joint recitals with outstanding singers of the day—John McCormack, Evelyn Scotney, the Kedroff Vocal Quartet, and Feodor Chaliapin.
>
> Powell had a motto: "Never leave the platform cool! Never!" These concerts were exciting events.

In the joint recital with the Irish tenor, John McCormack, on 4 May 1924, Székely relied once more on Hubay's *Variations on a Hungarian Theme*, a work well suited to his ardent temperament and his strong, uncompromising tone. He also played d'Ambrosio's *Serenate* which had gained such favor on his Dutch tours and the brilliant Polonaise in D Minor of Scharwenka.

McCormack had made his debut at the Manhattan Opera House in New York in *La traviata* in 1909, and from that period onward, his repertoire of serious music grew as he presented the works of Handel and Mozart and the monuments of German lieder. For the London audience of 1924, the legendary tenor and the young Hungarian violinist proved an incomparable combination on the concert platform.

The *Daily Telegraph*, which had become Székely's journalistic champion during the Aeolian Hall recitals, now made certain that the public understood that a unique musician had arrived in their midst. "This was a performance brimful of genuine musical impulse; one felt that this young player had an almost infallible instinct for values and contrasts."[10]

Among the throng of well-wishers gathered backstage at the Royal Albert Hall were Mr. and Mrs. Jaap de Graaff-Bachiene, waiting to offer Székely their congratulations. Jaap de Graaff, a connoisseur and collector of the paintings of the modern Belgian school, had come to the concert with his wife, Loes, an ardent music lover, and found himself overwhelmed by the young violinist's playing.

De Graaff, a Dutch businessman whose profession had nothing to do with art, had lived in England for a number of years. In the sophisticated ambience of his London home on Millfield Lane, de Graaff greatly enjoyed his enormous collection of more than two hundred paintings and equally enjoyed knowing that his protégés were at the forefront of their artistic movement.

Székely recalls that backstage with his wife, Jaap de Graaff said:

> You played so beautifully that I feel you deserve one of the fine violins. You must search around, and when you find the violin that you really like—I don't care what it is—then I will make it possible for you to play on that violin.

True to his word, Jaap de Graaff acquired a fine violin on Székely's behalf later in 1927. Székely recounts his offer:

> He didn't say right away, "I give it to you," but rather, "You will play on that violin," and after I had played on it for two decades, it was given to me as a gift after the end of the Second World War. I have had the "Michelangelo" Stradivarius for almost sixty years now due to the generosity of Jaap de Graaff who heard my concert in the Royal Albert Hall and believed in my promise.

Following these successful appearances in London, Székely and his father began to discuss the prospect of going to America together during the summer of 1924. László Székely was then almost fifty years old. He had spent the ten years since the outbreak of the war as a regimental surgeon in Hungary, serving the needs of prisoners of war being transported on Red Cross trains or somewhat later as a doctor employed by the railroad system to tend to the medical needs of railroad workers. He yearned to travel abroad with his son, to see what life was like in the United States, and to consider trying to begin a new medical practice in America.

In the company of his father, Székely sailed from Europe in the fall of 1924, bound for New York City, unaware that their adventure in America might not be successful.

I was still a very young man, of course. Only twenty-one. From the time of my debut in Budapest in November 1921, not yet three years of my career had passed, but Lionel Powell was willing to give me excellent recommendations following my appearance with John McCormack in the Royal Albert Hall. As we made those plans during the summer of 1924, we had no idea what might await us in America.

In the autumn my father and I crossed the Atlantic from Rotterdam to New York City on the Holland-America Line. After our arrival in America we soon began to meet interested persons who tried to help make contacts with various managers.

I saw again my first teacher from Budapest, my father's friend, Sándor Kőszegi, who was by then a member of the New York Philharmonic.[11] The composer Edgar Varèse, chairman of the International Composers' Guild in New York City, wrote a letter of introduction on my behalf stating that I was very highly recommended to him by Bartók who was anxious to have me as a collaborator for his piano and violin works. Several Hungarian friends in New York tried to better my position, among them a pianist who was willing to make an introduction to the Hungarian conductor, Fritz Reiner, who was in New York to audition musicians for his orchestra, the Cincinnati Symphony.

I played for Reiner, who offered me a position in the first violin section. I had no idea then how a violinist in America could proceed in a soloist's career from an orchestral position, not even from a concertmaster's position, although some violinists, such as Joseph Gingold, were able to accomplish this. After some careful consideration, I did not accept Reiner's offer since it did not fully satisfy my expectations. At twenty-one I was very much under the influence of certain career expectations which resulted from my training as a soloist at the Franz Liszt Academy.

We spent time not only in New York City but in Philadelphia as well. I did have some engagements, the first one in Albany, New York, but they were not significant. By now my father began to realize that, in his own case, it would be impractical for him to attempt to establish a new medical practice in America. Meanwhile, my mother and sister, who had stayed in Budapest, and the Everts in Nijmegen waited for good news.

My father's sister had lived in America for some years, but unfortunately he was quite out of touch with her. She was an actress who lived in Los Angeles and had toured in America performing roles in the Hungarian language for the expatriate Hungarians living in the larger cities.

Although he tried in 1924, my father was unable to make contact with our family members in America, so I didn't meet them then. I could not have imagined in 1924 that twenty-five years later I myself would live in Los Angeles and there meet my cousin, Bella Poganyi, the daughter of the actress who had since passed away, and Bella's daughter, Márta Holt.

The turning point in our dilemma came when I received a telegram from Kodály that my Sonata for Solo Violin had been chosen for a performance in Venice at the forthcoming Festival of the International Society for Contemporary Music. With this good news we decided to leave America.

In March we sailed from New York City on a Greek liner bound for Hamburg. When the ship reached France, we disembarked at Le Havre, then traveled by train to Holland. During that Atlantic crossing, I began to realize that our return to Europe was not a bad decision.

While this unsuccessful American venture resulting from insufficient management had taken valuable time, I had learned many necessary things about building my career and sensed that the experience that lay ahead in Venice would be very important to me. There I would meet famous musicians, composers such as Malipiero, Schoenberg, and Stravinsky, and renew acquaintances with my old musician friends. This would be a welcome relief for me after our abortive attempt in America. I don't know of a better thing than to move in the atmosphere of real artists, and the Festival at Venice gave me this opportunity once more.

And I would soon see Mientje again.

Székely returned to Holland to live again in the Everts' home in Nijmegen. He resumed his Dutch concerts in April of 1925, appearing in both Rotterdam and The Hague with the pianist Bernard Tabbernal. Székely's return was welcomed by the press. "Before he was good," wrote the critic of *De Telegraaf*, "but now he is even better, a violinist of the first rank with warmth, life, and happiness in the playing and a real artist's soul."[12] The *Avond Post* reviewer wrote, "He stands without moving, but at the same time his inner life goes out from him like the rays of the sun, and he creates an atmosphere that takes the public out of this world into a dream."[13]

In April Székely played for the first time in Paris. At the Salle Gaveau he and Swiss pianist Edwin Fischer were featured in two joint appearances. At the first concert they performed with the Orchestre Colonne conducted by Gabriel Pierné. After Mozart's Overture to *Le nozze di Figaro*, Edwin Fischer played Beethoven's Piano Concerto No. 3, then Székely performed Brahms' Violin Concerto. Székely's performance of the Brahms concerto was seen as an "honorable confrontation" by the critic Marc Pincherle. The work was often unjustly decried in Paris at the time—because by its symphonic nature it was thought to be out of proportion with the demands of the genre. In *Le Monde Musical*, Pincherle observed that "Sobriety is one of the master qualities of M. Zoltán Székely, a violinist of great talent and a very confident musician."[14]

A week later Székely and Fisher were heard again at the Salle Gaveau, the concert hall that was to become Székely's favorite. In this joint recital, pianist Max Deutsch accompanied the violinist until near the end of the evening, when Edwin Fisher joined him for Schubert's Rondo brillant, Op. 70. On that occasion they verified the impression of the earlier concert. Székely had won the confidence of the Parisian audience.

Upon his return to Holland following these two appearances in Paris, Székely was visited in Nijmegen by his old friend, the cellist Pál Hermann. Hermann was by then enjoying a successful career in Berlin, where he performed with an early music ensemble and continued to compose. With the eminent Dutch conductor, Eduard Van

Beinum, as pianist, Székely and Hermann performed several joint recitals at Canisius College, a large Catholic institution in Nijmegen. Van Beinum played Debussy's *Préludes*, and with Székely performed a new sonata by the Dutch composer Lou Lichtveld. Székely and Hermann played Ravel's new duo, the Sonata for Violin and Cello. With the acquisition of this new duo, they launched their preparations for even-more-ambitious programs of the highly specialized repertoire for violin and cello.

The summer of 1925 passed pleasantly: Székely continued his preparations for the concert in Venice, and Mientje began making plans to go with him to Italy. Székely would be the sole representative of Hungary's composers at the Venice Festival, and the excitement mounted in August as the time drew near for their train trip to Italy.

"When Zoltán's Sonata for Solo Violin was chosen for the 1925 chamber music concert of the International Society of Contemporary Music, it was Kodály who sent the telegram to tell him of the invitation," Mientje recalled.

> He advised Zoltán to go to Venice and perform his own work. My parents agreed that I should accompany my friend (we were not yet married, of course) and when we arrived a few days before the Festival began, there was Ravel's *Tzigane* scheduled for performance but with no one willing to play it because of its great difficulty. Zoltán agreed to play the *Tzigane* on the second chamber music concert, then began searching for the right pianist. Finally it was decided that Felix Petyrek would play Ravel's new work with him.[15]

The first chamber music concert took place on 4 September in the Gran Teatro La Fenice. A new Sonata for Cello and Piano by the Spanish cellist-composer, Gaspar Cassadó opened the program. Cassadó performed his own work with the pianist Giulietta Gordiagiani von Mendelssohn. Samuel Feinberg, a piano professor from the Moscow Conservatory, appeared next on the program playing his Sonata No. 6 for Piano, one of ten such works that he wrote in his lifetime.

Székely's Sonata for Solo Violin followed the Steinberg work. The twenty-two-year-old violinist performed his sonata that he had played for Bartók at his home in Budapest before their first public concerts together. Three more compositions came after Székely's sonata: works by Max Butting, Ladislav Vycpálek, and Leos Janácek.[16]

"I have seen with my own eyes Stravinsky and Schoenberg standing on their chairs in the Gran Teatro La Fenice to applaud Zoltán's performance of his Solo Sonata," Mientje recalled.

> Not only were the composers impressed with his work, but the critics as well. One of the great advantages for the composers whose works appeared in these festival concerts was the fact that the international press was always in attendance. Fifteen critics wrote brief notices about Zoltán's sonata.

On 1 October the *Musical Courier* announced to its American readership the success of his performance: "Zoltán Székely's Sonata for Solo Violin, played by the composer himself, shows a healthy preoccupation with the problems of the instrument and a structural ability which in one so young (he looks barely twenty) must be considered highly promising."[17]

Székely's captivating Sonata for Solo Violin was a palpable success reported widely in the press. In Wiesbaden: "The finale revealed that there was as much daring in his composing as there was bravura virtuosity in his playing."[18] In Leipzig: "In it a strong vitality is at work that uses as its creative source the technique of that instrument so masterfully played by the composer himself."[19] In Prague: "Music and nerve, intellect and rhythm of the finest sophistication, of the most filigree-like interweaving of psyche and sound, substance and creative unity—these are represented by the name Zoltán Székely."[20]

Professor Hans Hermann, writing for *Signale* in Berlin, found Székely to be a violinist of the highest order. Of his composition he wrote, "Passion, energy, technical ability, grandiose sound are all present, just the understanding of most listeners was missing, a fact that troubles me, because this sonata stands head and shoulders above similar products."[21]

The next night the large audience gathered once more at the Gran Teatro La Fenice to hear new works by another group of composers that comprised the Austrian, Erich Korngold; the Italian, Vittorio Rieti; and a large contingent of French composers, including Jacques Ibert, Arthur Honegger, Albert Roussel, and Maurice Ravel.[22]

At the climax of the evening Zoltán Székely and Felix Petyrek played Ravel's Tzigane; the night made a deep and lasting impression on the Italian audience and on the representatives of the international press.

"The International Music Festivals fulfill a very useful role when they allow the young composer to be heard," Székely said to Aladár Tóth during an interview in Budapest a few months after his success in Venice:

As Kodály wrote in one of his outstanding essays, "a musical creation is really finished only on the concert platform." Truly, a composer only knows then, when he hears his music from the podium, whether he has expressed everything he wanted in a work. That is why I was happy when my Sonata for Solo Violin was accepted by the committee for the Venice Festival.

My sonata was very well received by the critics and all the other composers there. To me this meant more than the explosive Italian audience's applause. It is true that with a few exceptions the critics don't always stand out with their individual opinions, but during the concert one of my acquaintances heard two well-known critics discussing my sonata. One said, "It is not so modern. There is a lot of Debussian effect." The other said, "But it must be good. Look, Schoenberg is applauding it enthusiastically." For one of my good reviews I can thank not the sonata itself, but Schoenberg's applauding it!

Actually the biggest success in Venice was Schoenberg's. A lot of people found Stravinsky's turn toward conservatism a kind of betrayal and, what is more, they thought he was bluffing. The ultra-modern musicians have been angered at their leader Stravinsky just as the cubists suffered when Picasso became conservative. The biggest sensation of Stravinsky's appearance was when he announced that one of his fingers was injured and therefore he would play his composition "with only nine fingers." He played well even in this way and according to some he played so well that his tenth finger did take part although it didn't show!

Among the Germans I find Paul Hindemith the most talented. He is the most sincere and he makes sense, but naturally the truly great artistry is not entirely evident yet. Recently he won the American Coolidge Prize, the same that our own Leó Weiner has won, and from that nice prize he bought an old tower and on top of it he made an apartment. I must say that Hindemith's tower has nothing to do with the "ivory tower."

Modern Hungarian music doesn't have to be pushed any

more in foreign lands. Audiences love to hear Bartók and
Kodály. The new generation is lucky that it follows such
giants.[23]

As an immediate result of the success in Venice, Emil Hertzka,
director of Universal-Edition, offered the young composer a contract
with the famous music publishing firm in Vienna. The Sonata, Op. 1,
Violino Solo and Székely's celebrated transcription for violin and
piano of Bartók's *Rumanian Folk Dances* were published in 1926.
These were followed in 1927 by the publication of Székely's *Polyphon
et Homophon*, Op. 2, a duo for violin and cello.

Meanwhile, the Everts' home in Holland was to receive another
visit from Béla Bartók during October of 1925. He arrived in Nijmegen a few days before playing two recitals with Székely which were
planned for 5 October in Arnhem and 6 October in Utrecht. Mientje's
mother, Anna Everts, understood perfectly the singular needs of her
guest and provided the serene atmosphere that would make his visit
pleasurable.

"My mother was wonderful," Mientje recalled. "She understood
Bartók's wish to have privacy and avoided having any other guests
during his stay in our home."

> He could take his meals when he wanted and be out of doors
> when he wished—he enjoyed the privacy of the garden
> where he spent many hours each day—and often he would
> go to his room perhaps to work or think. And of course he
> and Zoltán rehearsed. He seemed very happy indeed.

One of Székely's musical accomplishments which eventually
brought him universal recognition from violinists was his 1925 transcription of Bartók's *Rumanian Folk Dances*. The transcription was
first performed in recitals in Arnhem and Utrecht. Székely recalls:

> Bartók and I planned three sonatas for these concerts:
> Bach, Mozart, and Brahms. He would play a group of his own
> compositions for piano ending with *Allegro barbaro*, then just
> before the intermission we played two works together, the
> *Improvisation* of Ernest Bloch and my new transcription of
> his *Rumanian Folk Dances*.
> Bartók had written the *Rumanian Folk Dances* in 1915 and
> dedicated this piano work to his friend Professor Ion Buşiţia,

the art master in the Belényes school in Rumania who had helped him in preparing his trips for the collection of Rumanian folk songs.

In Nijmegen we rehearsed my transcription, and our performance in Arnhem was the first time it was played. We did not work together at all on this transcription. I made it completely before he arrived. Technically speaking there are just a few compositional changes which are not in the original. I used other tonalities, for instance.

Bartók was very pleased. Of course, at that time this transcription was something new. Later in 1926 when my transcription was published by Universal-Edition in Vienna, he wrote a letter to his friend Buşiţia telling him that during the summer my transcription for violin and piano had been printed and that my work was "very ably done."[24]

The audience particularly liked Bartók's performance of the *Allegro barbaro* with its sonorous bass and its sharp rhythms in the melody, a contradiction which he showed masterfully. The critic in Arnhem realized that Bartók's compositions were surprising because he had reclaimed the power of folk song which was too often forgotten. In the *Rumanian Folk Dances* his use of the folk music sources was "unlike that of the composers of the romantic school who went too far making things nice which were meant to be naked and honest."[25] Their playing of the classical repertoire was praised lavishly: "The crowning moment of the evening was Brahms' Sonata in D Minor when the artists were at their best, completely worthy of Brahms," wrote the critic of *Het Daagblad van Arnhem*.[26]

The next day, the recital was performed in Utrecht. The critics found Bartók's strong personality and incredible originality impressive, and equally so his piano virtuosity and the unity of his ensemble playing with Székely. The clarity of the Bach performance and the fleet tempos in Mozart's sonata arrested the attention of the critic of the *Utrechtisch Nieuwsblad*, who wrote about their performance of Székely's new transcription: "A very unusual alternation of directness and restraint gave a very lively character to their playing in the *Rumanian Folk Dances*."[27]

Bartók remained in Nijmegen for another week before departing from the Everts' home. Before he returned to Hungary, he appeared on 15 October as soloist with the Amsterdam Concertgebouw

Orchestra under the direction of Pierre Monteux. His Rhapsody, Op.1, for Piano and Orchestra and the Dance Suite for Orchestra formed the program with Berlioz' *Symphonie fantastique*.

Székely returned to the stage in late October to perform Brahms' Violin Concerto and Ravel's *Tzigane* in Arnhem and Nijmegen with the Arnhem Orchestra, Martin Spanjaard, conducting. When he came on stage in Nijmegen people immediately began to yell; suddenly the audience had begun a spontaneous celebration. He brought the full maturity of his talent to their stage and they realized it, but more than that, Székely had become one of their own. He performed the Brahms concerto masterfully, and the orchestra played with him with such unity that it was a pleasure to hear. The cadenza was his own.[28]

After the performance of Ravel's *Tzigane*, the Dutch public could no longer be called restrained. "The audience cried and laughed in turn and brought him back to play an encore," wrote Jeanne Landré.[29] The critic of *De Gelderlander* summed it up: "People do not have to love it—it just happens, it is in the air. We will have to call Székely one of the greatest of our time."[30]

In early November Székely and pianist Géza Frid returned to Hungary to play a series of recitals in Budapest, Györ, and Szeged. These three Hungarian performances established a professional liaison that would last throughout the following decade of Székely's solo career. Géza Frid was a pianist whose abilities suited Székely's needs. Frid's natural musicianship and his musical training shared aspects of Székely's—both were students of Kodály—and made him a logical choice as Székely's accompanist.[31]

"Székely left us for foreign lands as a child and came back as a world famous violinist," wrote Aladár Tóth in *Pesti Napló* upon Székely's return to Hungary. This review of the Székely-Frid recital served as a prelude to Székely's appearance with Bartók two weeks later:

> Besides Vecsey and Szigeti, he is the greatest Hungarian violinist. An incredibly sure technician, he is also an incredibly sure musician. Even amongst these few musician-virtuosos Székely deserves a very special place since he is practically a reformer of violin playing.
>
> It became truth again that nothing enriches the instrument more than the solving of problems which are seemingly far from its nature. . . . Székely has declared war on those aspects of violin playing that are merely virtuosic,

and, in his hands, the violin has been reborn in the spirit of music, and thus it has remained, in fact, a shining, sparkling, gorgeously sounding instrument.

Székely is a virtuoso, but he is a virtuoso of a puritan musical spirit. One needs a tyrannical, stubborn, and strict temperament to solve such problems and reach the goals. The force and unique direction of his intense fantasy is certainly the basic characteristic of our artist's poetic spirit.

The most popular piece of the concert was naturally Ravel's *Tzigane*. Székely handled the virtuoso effects on which this work is based with the greatest ease, seeming to make fun of the difficulties. It is no wonder he conquered the Venice Festival with this work. We must give the greatest respect to the pianist, Géza Frid, who is not only an excellent accompanist, but is a total master.[32]

A few days later the two young artists appeared in Györ, the large Hungarian city midway between Vienna and Budapest. In medieval times the Benedictine Abbey of Pannonhalma at Györ was the center of ecclesiastical culture and remains the only early Gothic church in Hungary. The local Song and Music Club organized the recital at the Lloyd Concert Hall, filling the house with an expectant audience. At the end of the evening, a performance of Hubay's *Csárdás scène* brought storms of relentless applause that summoned encores, and the audience's enthusiasm was shared by Székely with Géza Frid, his masterful pianist.

From Györ, Székely and Frid traveled south to Szeged where the program was repeated. "In the club of Hungarian violinists—Vecsey, Telmányi, János Koncz, Stefi Geyer, and Erna Rubenstein," wrote critic Péntek in the *Szegedi Napló*, "Székely is a real pearl in the history of the violin to the glory of Hungarian art and the pleasure of two continents."[33]

Having reestablished his eminence in his own country, Székely appeared once more at the Vigadó with Béla Bartók on 24 November. The audience was eager to hear Székely and Bartók together again, playing sonatas of Bach and Beethoven, and Bartók's own First Violin Sonata, in a recital that had been previously postponed because of Bartók's illness.

After this important concert, Sándor Jemnitz, the gifted Budapest composer and the critic for *Népszava*, expressed his idea that Bartók's music was itself creating performers more able to play the works by their talent and perception, and consequently Bartók's compositions were now being heard as they should be and the public was benefiting. At the heart of this matter was Székely, the truly modern violinist of Hungarian musical life. In his review, Jemnitz described Székely's mission and concluded that, "After Václav Talich[34] pulled the shroud off the true face of the Dance Suite, now Székely forms a perfect understanding of the First Violin Sonata."[35]

In *Pesti Napló* Aládar Tóth wrote one of his most searching reviews:

> In the Vigadó Tuesday evening there was a sonata concert by Béla Bartók and Zoltán Székely, both the pride of Hungary, one of Hungarian composition, the other of Hungarian violin playing. Bartók is the greatest performing individual that we have seen at the piano up to now. When such an exceptional artist finds a worthy violin partner, the audience can prepare for the highest level of enjoyment. Székely is not only a worthy partner, but a congenial partner. The absolutely, totally unmistakable musicality which is characteristic of Bartók's piano playing is not missed in Székely's violin playing either.
>
> They are both strict musical thinkers. Whatever they have discovered as the most meaningful thought, those things they performed without any restraint or artificial coloring and in the straightest way and in its naked truth. The only function of those shining tone colors is to make the outline of the work more understandable and its poetic substance clearer and self evident. They are elementary colors, those from the Bösendorfer and those from the terrific Tóth violin.
>
> We don't have to repeat that Bartók's piano playing is the most gigantic, the purest poetry. We do not find in any other performing artist such deep, creative intensity and crystal clear, sweet lyricism. In Beethoven's violin and piano sonata not even d'Albert nor Dohnányi can sing with such concentrated rich fantasy, with such high-flying yet truly deep human idealism. One wonders where can be found a more worthy interpreter of Bach than Bartók. Fischer or d'Albert in their soul no doubt live closer to the great German classics, yet it is still no less gripping an event when a totally Hungarian temperament with such wonderful intelligence can so completely identify with the German genius.

And this difference between the temperaments totally disappears when Bartók plays his own work. In its shaking, volcanic outbursts, in its pagan, mystic shiverings, in its ancient melancholy, painful melodies, and finally blood-boiling, wild outbursts, this miraculous vision of the world has never been painted more distinctly than by these artists. Székely's unbelievable playing had a lot to do with this. Székely is also a poet and after his Beethoven and Bach, we can really see how truly great a poet he is. However, in this Bartók work it is not enough to have a poetic understanding. Here one needs unbelievable musicality and technical knowledge. Székely presented us this very complicated musical structure so clearly that it was as if he had been playing a Schubert rondo, and the most demanding technical problems were solved magically. Only a great master can do this.

The audience was totally under the influence of the artists. The Vigadó's lights were turned down twice, and they had to be turned up again twice because the audience would not go. Bartók's *Rumanian Dances* were given as the encore. Now Bartók's art is no longer for a select few, but belongs to the whole audience and now not only for the foreign audience, but the Hungarian audience as well.[36]

Plate 12. Zoltán Székely appears in London in 1924 at the Aeolian Hall. THE
SZÉKELY COLLECTION.

Herrn und Frau J. de Graaff-Bachiene herzlichst gewidmet

SONATE

I

Zoltán Székely, Op. 1

Appassionato, ma in tempo molto moderato (♩= 72-74)

Universal-Edition Nr. 8466

Plate 13. Zoltán Székely's first published work, Sonata, Op. 1, for Violin Solo.
PHOTOGRAPHY MONTE GREENSHIELDS. THE SZÉKELY COLLECTION. COPYRIGHT RE-
NEWED. ALL RIGHTS RESERVED. USED BY PERMISSION OF EUROPEAN AMERICAN MUSIC
DISTRIBUTORS CORPORATION, SOLE U.S. AND CANADIAN AGENTS FOR UNIVERSAL-
EDITION.

Plate 14. Igor Stravinsky on St. Mark's Square in Venice, 8 September 1925.
PHOTOGRAPHY IGMINIA EVERTS. THE SZÉKELY COLLECTION.

Plate 15. Philip Lazar, Gian-Francesco Malipiero, Mario Castlenuovo-Tedesco, and Zoltán Székely in Venice, 1925. PHOTOGRAPHY IGMINIA EVERTS. THE SZÉKELY COLLECTION.

Plate 16. Paul Hindemith in his "Tower House" in Frankfurt, 1925. PHOTOGRAPHY IGMINIA EVERTS. THE SZÉKELY COLLECTION.

Plate 17. An early autograph manuscript of Székely's celebrated transcription of Bartók's *Rumanian Folk Dances*. PHOTOGRAPHY MONTE GREENSHIELDS. THE SZÉKELY COLLECTION.

Plate 18. Béla Bartók and Zoltán Székely in the Everts' music room in Nijmegen, 1925. PHOTOGRAPHY IGMINIA EVERTS. THE SZÉKELY COLLECTION.

Plate 19. Zoltán Székely and Béla Bartók in the garden in Nijmegen, Holland, 1925. PHOTOGRAPHY IGMINIA EVERTS. THE SZÉKELY COLLECTION.

Plates 20 and 21. Béla Bartók. PHOTOGRAPHY IGMINIA EVERTS. THE SZÉKELY
COLLECTION.

Plate 22. Géza Frid and Zoltán Székely in Nijmegen before leaving for a concert tour in Hungary in 1925. PHOTOGRAPHY IGMINIA EVERTS. THE SZÉKELY COLLECTION.

Plate 23. Zoltán Székely appears in London at the Royal Albert Hall in 1926.
PHOTOGRAPHY BERSSENBRUGGE. THE SZÉKELY COLLECTION.

Plate 24. Igminia Everts at the time of her marriage to Zoltán Székely in 1926. THE SZÉKELY COLLECTION.

Plate 25. Zoltán Székely
and Arthur Honegger at
the Zurich Festival in
1926. PHOTOGRAPHY
IGMINIA SZÉKELY. THE
SZÉKELY COLLECTION.

Plate 26. Zoltán Székely
and Zoltán Kodály at
the Zurich Festival.
PHOTOGRAPHY IGMINIA
SZÉKELY. THE SZÉKELY
COLLECTION.

Plate 27. Zoltán Kodály, Willem Pijper, Zoltán Székely, and Emil Hertzka, director of Universal-Edition, at the Zurich Festival. PHOTOGRAPHY IGMINIA SZÉKELY. THE SZÉKELY COLLECTION.

Plate 28. Zoltán Székely, Zoltán Kodály, and Carlos Salzedo with their unidentified hostess in Zurich. PHOTOGRAPHY IGMINIA SZÉKELY. THE SZÉKELY COLLECTION.

Plate 29. Zoltán Székely
at Pontresina in 1926.
THE SZÉKELY COLLECTION.

Plate 30. Zoltán Székely
and Zoltán Kodály on
the tennis courts in
Nijmegen in 1927.
PHOTOGRAPHY IGMINIA
SZÉKELY. THE SZÉKELY
COLLECTION.

Plate 31. Zoltán and Emma Kodály in Nijmegen in 1927.
PHOTOGRAPHY IGMINIA SZÉKELY.
THE SZÉKELY COLLECTION.

Plate 32. Zoltán Kodály at the station in Nijmegen in 1927.
PHOTOGRAPHY IGMINIA SZÉKELY. THE SZÉKELY COLLECTION.

Plate 33. The "Michelangelo" Stradivarius of 1718. COURTESY OF MAX MÖLLER, AMSTERDAM.

Plate 34. Darius Milhaud, Heinrich Burkhard, and Béla Bartók at the Frankfurt Festival in 1927. PHOTOGRAPHY IGMINIA SZÉKELY. THE SZÉKELY COLLECTION.

Plate 35. Guus Everts, Zoltán Székely, and Géza Frid on tour in the Fiat in Switzerland in 1927. PHOTOGRAPHY IGMINIA SZÉKELY. THE SZÉKELY COLLECTION.

Plate 36. Géza Frid, Guus Everts, and Zoltán Székely in Florence in 1927. PHOTOGRAPHY IGMINIA SZÉKELY. THE SZÉKELY COLLECTION.

Plate 37. King Gustav of Sweden and Zoltán Székely playing tennis at the Monte Carlo Tennis Club in 1933. PHOTOGRAPHY IGMINIA SZÉKELY. THE SZÉKELY COLLECTION.

Plate 38. Zoltán Székely and Imre Waldbauer playing tennis in Budapest in the 1930s. PHOTOGRAPHY IGMINIA SZÉKELY. THE SZÉKELY COLLECTION.

Plate 39. Bartók's home at 10 Kavics Street in Budapest where his Second Rhapsody was dedicated to Székely in 1928. PHOTOGRAPHY ADÁM FRIEDRICH.

Plate 40. Maurice Ravel and Zoltán Székely with Michel Calvocoressi at the station in Monfort l'Amaury, France, in 1929. PHOTOGRAPHY IGMINIA SZÉKELY. THE SZÉKELY COLLECTION.

Plate 41. Zoltán Székely and James Ensor in Ostende, Belgium, in 1929. PHOTOGRAPHY IGMINIA SZÉKELY. THE SZÉKELY COLLECTION.

Plate 42. Carl Flesch in Florence in 1930. PHOTOGRAPHY IGMINIA SZÉKELY. THE SZÉKELY COLLECTION.

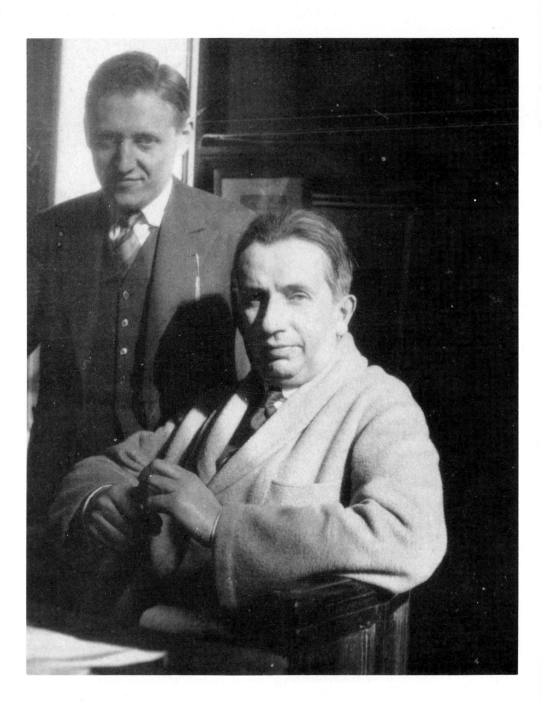

Plate 43. Zoltán Székely and Alfredo Casella in Rome in 1930. PHOTOGRAPHY
IGMINIA SZÉKELY. THE SZÉKELY COLLECTION.

Plate 44. Leone Sinigaglia and Zoltán Székely in Milan in 1930. PHOTOGRAPHY
IGMINIA SZÉKELY. THE SZÉKELY COLLECTION.

Plate 45. Feodor Chaliapin. A self-caricature, 1930. PHOTOGRAPHY MONTE
GREENSHIELDS. THE SZÉKELY COLLECTION.

Plate 46. Zoltán Székely and Feodor Chaliapin in London in 1930. PHOTOG-
RAPHY IGMINIA SZÉKELY. THE SZÉKELY COLLECTION.

Plate 47. Pál Hermann and Zoltán Székely in Nijmegen in 1930. PHOTOGRA-
PHY IGMINIA SZÉKELY. THE SZÉKELY COLLECTION.

Plate 48. Zoltán Székely and Karol Szymanovsky in Warsaw in 1931. PHO-
TOGRAPHY IGMINIA SZÉKELY. THE SZÉKELY COLLECTION.

Plate 49. Performing Ravel's *Tzigane* in the Groote Zaal of the Amsterdam Concertgebouw on 19 January 1932. COURTESY OF HET CONCERTGEBOUW NV.

Plate 50. The Carlo Tononi violin of 1730. COURTESY OF MAX MÖLLER, AMSTERDAM.

Plate 51. The Kolisch String Quartet and Zoltán Székely in Nijmegen in 1934. (Left to right: Eugene Lehner, Felix Kuhner, Rudolf Kolisch, Zoltán Székely, and Benar Heifetz.) PHOTOGRAPHY IGMINIA SZÉKELY. THE SZÉKELY COLLECTION.

Plate 52. The Rhapsody in Bloemendaal designed by Gerrit Reitveld in 1935. THE SZÉKELY COLLECTION.

Plate 53. Zoltán Székely in his studio at The Rhapsody in 1935. THE SZÉKELY COLLECTION.

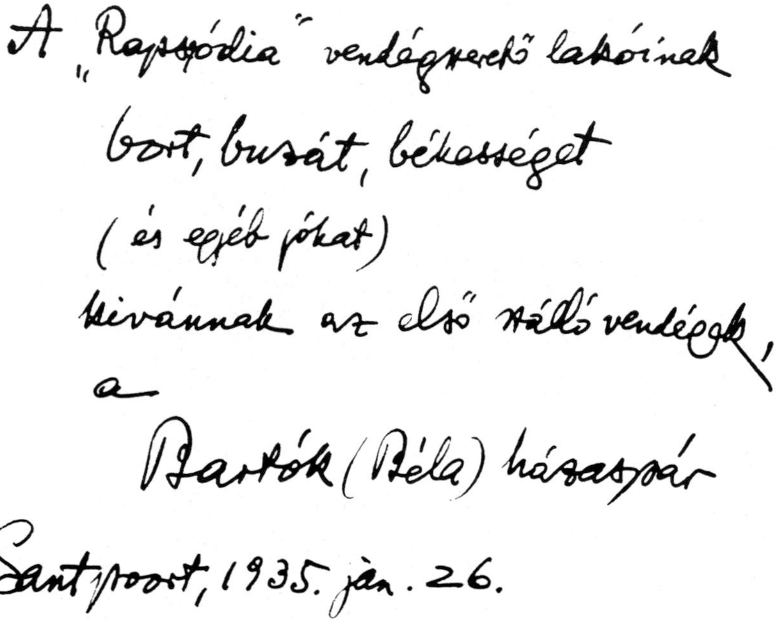

A „Rapszódia" vendégszerető lakóinak
bort, búzát, békességet
(és egyéb jókat)
kivánnak az első szálló vendégek,
a
Bartók (Béla) házaspár
Santpoort, 1935. jan. 26.

Plate 54. Bartók is the first to sign the guest book at The Rhapsody on 26 January 1935. PHOTOGRAPHY MONTE GREENSHIELDS. THE SZÉKELY COLLECTION.

Plate 55. Béla Bartók and Zoltán Székely rehearsing at The Rhapsody in 1936.
PHOTOGRAPHY IGMINIA SZÉKELY. THE SZÉKELY COLLECTION.

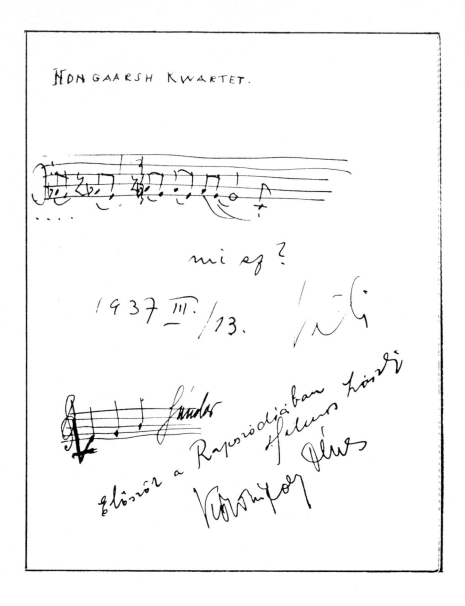

Plate 56. The New Hungarian String Quartet signs the guest book at The Rhapsody on 13 March 1937. PHOTOGRAPHY MONTE GREENSHIELDS. THE SZÉKELY COLLECTION.

Chapter Ten

The "Michelangelo" Stradivarius

A month later, a capacity audience filled the Teatro Paganini in Genoa, the scene of Székely's first Italian recital after the success of the ISCM festival concerts in Venice. His virtuosity and exquisite sensitivity affirmed themselves in every piece he played from Veracini to Hubay. The enthusiasm of the audience grew even more intense during the second half when Mario Castelnuovo-Tedesco's *Ritmi* was especialy savored as was the *Rapsodia piemontese* of Sinigaglia. "At the end, after being wildly applauded, he gave four encores," wrote the critic of *Il Cittadino*, "and sharing the triumph was the gifted pianist Géza Frid who accompanied him masterfully."[1]

Székely and Frid appeared at the Sala Scarlatti in Palermo a few days later at the invitation of the Concert Office of Sicily and its director, Traselli Varvara. To the Sicilian audience, Székely's playing, with its technical force and interpretive mastery, compared favorably with that of the most noted and world-famous violinists who had appeared before them. "We had heard him at Venice at the International Festival last September," wrote the critic of *l'Ora*, "and at that time we had carried back with us an unforgettable impression of a violinist with a pure bowing style and a correct touch."[2] Székely reconfirmed that impression and, in Veracini and Mozart, again revealed his elegant style. Castelnuovo-Tedesco's *Ritmi*, a new musical work for Palermo, was especially well received, and Scharwenka's

Polacca ended the program. The artists returned to the stage to play Chaminade's *Spanish Serenade* and Bartók's *Swing Song*.

In Venice Székely again performed Ravel's *Tzigane* which had brought him such success during the International Festival a few months earlier. At the Sala del Liceo Civico Musicale Benedetto Marcello, Székely and Frid were guest artists for the Società Veneziana del Quartetto and offered a program of Veracini, Dvořák, Ravel, Manén, Sinigaglia, and d'Ambrosio, ending the evening with Henri Vieuxtemps' *L'Orage*.

"With the liveliness of his interpretations and the great warmth that he knows how to lend to every composition," wrote the critic of the *Gazzetta di Venezia*, "he stirred the most vivid admiration of the public which applauded him with ever-increasing enthusiasm and called him repeatedly to the stage at the end of every piece."[3]

At the end of this first Italian tour, Székely went to Donaueschingen in Germany for a performance of Dvořák's Violin Concerto and Sinigaglia's *Rapsodia piemontese*. One of Germany's most important summer festivals was the one at Donaueschingen. Under the direction of Heinrich Burkard, the Donaueschinger Kammermusiktage finally became so large that the location was changed to Baden-Baden, and Burkard, Paul Hindemith, and Joseph Haas became the organizers. During the winter season, Burkard continued to guide the work of the Gesellschaft der Musikfreunde zu Donaueschingen, conducting the orchestral concerts.

Burkard invited Székely to Donaueschingen because he knew from having heard him in Venice in September that this violinist appealed directly and unforgettably to the emotions. With his wonderful, clean technique and opulent tone, Székely produced the artistic results at his Donaueschingen concert that Burkhard had promised. As always, he played with great sympathy, free of all affectation and exaggeration. His musicality never allowed the content of what he played to become obscured by his virtuosity. Both in technique and spirit, Székely's playing delighted the public and convinced the critics. The audience accorded him a well-deserved ovation, and the critic of the *Donaueschingen Tageblatt* wrote, "The sensation of the concert was the soloist, the young Zoltán Székely from Budapest, who is no Hungarian gypsy-type like the ones so often seen and heard in Budapest itself or often in Vienna, but a God-gifted artist with, unless I'm very much mistaken, a bright future ahead of him."[4]

In London Lionel Powell planned the 1926 tour for his International Celebrity Concerts to feature a vocal ensemble from Russia, the Kedroff Quartet, Zoltán Székely, and soprano Evelyn Scotney. Ivor Newton was the pianist. The tour began in London with a gala concert in the Royal Albert Hall on 17 January 1926. In this mixed recital, Székely's repertoire featured the Concertpiece in A Major by Saint-Saëns and short works by Pablo Sarasate, Fritz Kreisler, Mendelssohn, and Hubay.

During this winter tour of 1926 Székely played in nineteen cities: London, Hanley, Nottingham, Sheffield, Dublin, Belfast, Glasgow, Dundee, Edinburgh, Blackburn, Bradford, Newcastle, Hull, Birmingham, Halifax, Leicester, Liverpool, Cardiff, and Bristol. Midway during the tour, the artists appeared again in the Royal Albert Hall in London with new repertoire, and on that occasion Székely played Bloch's *Improvisation*, the *Rapsodia piemontese* of Sinigaglia, d'Ambrosio's *Serenate*, and Hubay's *Csárdas scène*.

Throughout this tour Székely's performances were praised. He was called "a violinist for whom difficulties do not appear to exist," "a virtuoso with a big future," and "a new star of the first magnitude in the fiddler's firmament." In the *Birmingham Gazette* the critic wrote humorously that "Zoltán Székely, a brilliant violinist possessing the advantage of a name that knocks out of competition such dull, drab cognomens as John Smith, George Brown, and Thomas Green, none of which could ever be associated with high-flying romantic art, was the third of the ravishing features of an evening that enchanted the audience and sent them home enraptured."[5]

During Székely's extended tour in Great Britain, Ernst von Dohnányi invited him to perform his Violin Concerto in the forthcoming Dohnányi Cycle in Berlin. He made this invitation as the result of a suggestion by Bartók, who had written to him in November proposing that Székely perform the concerto on this important occasion, reminding him of the Venetian success of Ravel's *Tzigane*.[6]

While touring life demanded the daily travel, disciplined practice, and brilliant virtuosic performances widely recognized as the normal lifestyle of the concert artist, Székely met an even-greater challenge during the final weeks of this tour of Great Britain: he completed his study of Dohnányi's Violin Concerto and prepared a demanding London recital for the London Contemporary Music Centre scheduled for 2 March.

Pál Hermann arrived from Berlin in late February to meet Székely

and pianist Arthur Alexander in London to rehearse the new Trio for
Violin, Cello, and Piano by Rebecca Clarke, an English composer-
violist who was then enjoying a successful international career. In
this March concert Hermann played Hindemith's Solo Sonata,
demonstrating once more that he was a remarkably good cellist with
an astonishing memory and comprehension of the modern idioms.
Kodály's Duo for Violin and Cello was prominent on the program,
and Székely and Alexander performed Ravel's *Tzigane* brilliantly to
end the recital.

Only ten days remained for Székely to complete the learning of
Dohnányi's Violin Concerto for the Berlin performance. He remained
in London for a week to practice, then traveled to Berlin to rehearse
with the orchestra on 12 March 1926, the day of the concert.

The Dohnányi cycle in Berlin was divided into three concerts featuring Dohnányi as composer, conductor, and pianist. Székely performed the Violin Concerto in the first concert, an evening devoted
to Dohnányi as composer and conductor.[7] The stellar performance
by Székely (the only other featured artist in the Dohnányi cycle
besides Dohnányi himself) and the attractiveness of Dohnányi's
Ruralia Hungarica brought the artists a prolonged ovation after the
concert in the Blüthnersaal. Dr. Schmidt, the critic for the *Berliner
Tageblatt*, praised the soloist: "Zoltán Székely's performance of the
Violin Concerto shows him at the top of his form, playing with shining tone and magnificent verve."[8]

Recalling his youthful performance of the Dohnányi work, Székely acknowledges that certain difficult achievements are readily possible for the young:

> In retrospect certain things amaze me. That I finished
> learning the Dohnányi concerto and memorized it in two
> weeks while on tour in England makes me wonder "Just how
> did I do that?" I know that in the previous summer I had
> started to learn this concerto but I never got further than two
> movements, then suddenly I had only a few weeks to pre-
> pare the work for the concert in Berlin. We made it with one
> rehearsal in the morning. The concert was that night.
>
> It is one of the longest concertos, probably forty-five min-
> utes, but I just had no problem at that time with the memory.
> There are many similar passages with the same entrance but
> with new endings so that you have to really memorize thor-
> oughly. While the music is naturally flowing, there are cer-

tain turns and modulations that must be securely learned.

I think that originally it was planned that Georg Ku-lenkampff[9] would play that engagement. When I was invited to play this work with the composer conducting the Berlin Symphony Orchestra, it was a unique performance for me.

Dohnányi is a good composer, on the verge of really good. Kodály, for example, considered him the master of the variation form. The last movement of the Violin Concerto is in that form.

I had hoped to play this concerto one last time at the end of my public career in a performance at the Banff Festival of the Arts in Canada, but after an illness, the plan was abandoned.

From Berlin Székely returned to Holland for the first of his many appearances with the Amsterdam Concertgebouw Orchestra, with Willem Mengelberg conducting. His performance of Dvořák's Violin Concerto began a long artistic collaboration with Mengelberg and the Concertgebouw Orchestra. On an evening concert that began with Weber's Overture to *Oberon* and ended with Tchaikovsky's Sixth Symphony, Theo van der Bijl found Székely's playing as beautiful as ever and wrote in *De Tijd*, "He is a violinist with character, and while he does not like sentimentality, he has a beautiful singing tone and a specialness in the balance between the musical and the technical possibilities."[10] Holland's major critic, L. M. G. Arntzenius, found Székely's playing strong and serious, musical, and very healthy; he wrote in *De Telegraaf*, " He reshapes the piece during the playing, makes the details clear, and it is as though he doesn't like to overdo specific violinistic things."[11] Székely's specialization in modern music and this very good *entrée* in 1926 prompted the Amsterdam Concertgebouw Orchestra to present him frequently, and this it did for more than a decade—until Székely curtailed his solo engagements in favor of quartet playing.

On tour again in Holland during April, Székely played with pianist Bernard Tabbernal in The Hague, Zwolle, Heerenveen, Amsterdam, s'Hertogenbosch, and Venlo. The recital at the Amsterdam Concertgebouw again elicited praise from Arntzenius, who wrote in *De Telegraaf*:

A very good musician, an important program, and a wonderful violin. The total impression was warmth. Before he played, he had already won the match. His reputation has been made, so there is no longer debut fever. Indeed, he is an incredible musician, someone whose love for art is deep and serious, who honors the beauty of the pieces. A very strong and often warm tone lives in his playing. He is many-sided. He has a fine harmony between his violinistic abilities and his general musicianship. He touched the audience in a deep way with both the Ravel *Tzigane* and the Brahms sonata. There was despair, there was tragic tension, the quiet melancholy of Boulanger, and the power of Bartók with its gypsy effects and new harmonies. It was a rich, interesting evening.[12]

The friendship between Zoltán and Mientje that had begun the day of Zoltán's arrival at the train station in Arnhem in 1921 was transformed by now into a bond of mutual and profound love. They decided to marry in the early summer.

Their wedding took place in a simple civil ceremony in s'Gravenhage on 12 June 1926. Among those in the small wedding party were Mientje's sister, Jeanne, and their mother, Anna Everts (Jacobus Everts had passed away after a long illness). Mientje's best friend, Tilla van der Grintken, was the maid of honor. After the wedding ceremony, Mientje was issued a Hungarian passport at the office of the Hungarian Consul, Hungarian citizenship now conferred because of her marriage to a Hungarian citizen.

Zoltán and Mientje departed from The Hague for their honeymoon in Switzerland. When their train passed through Venlo, their friends, the Van der Grinken family, waved their congratulations from the platform to the newly wed couple bound for Zurich.

A new adventure had begun. Born of such remarkable circumstances, their marriage would endure the passing of seven decades, the vicissitudes of war, the stress of Zoltán's demanding international career, and Mientje's final illness in Canada.

In Zurich they attended the fourth annual festival of the International Society for Contemporary Music. There they had a reunion with old friends and colleagues, among them Kodály and Arthur Honegger, whose great choral works, Kodaly's *Psalmus Hungaricus* and Honegger's *Le Roi David*, began the celebration. This was the first performance of Kodály's *Psalmus Hungaricus* outside Hungary and was conducted by Andreas Volkmar with Karl Erb as the tenor soloist.

After the Zurich Festival, the Székelys traveled to Pontresina, a resort town in the Swiss Alps, where unfortunately Mientje contracted chicken pox and had to miss the joy of mountain climbing with Zoltán.

When they returned to Holland after their honeymoon, they lived in a small villa at 275 Kwakkenbergweg in Nijmegen. This was the new home of Anna Everts where she had lived since the death of her husband, Jacobus. Until 1935, the Székelys continued to live there three months out of each year while they were in Holland.

During this time they lived away from Holland for extended periods—in Wiesbaden, Germany, and on the French Riviera near Cap Martin. On the Riviera they rented a comfortable villa near the sea below the castle in a small community named Roquebrune. There they enjoyed the marvelous climate and the village's solitary but excellent restaurant.

Zoltán enthusiastically played tennis in the best of conditions at the Monte Carlo Tennis Club, which was outside the city on the road to Menton. Among his tennis partners was King Gustav of Sweden. For a while, living at Roquebrune was so pleasant that the Székelys contemplated making the French Riviera their permanent home.

When the Székelys were first married, Piroska Székely came to Holland for a visit. Mientje and her mother were hopeful that Piroska would marry and stay in Holland, but that was not to happen. As Zoltán recalled:

> After her visit to Holland, my sister returned to Hungary and soon married Károly Mártonyi. Because the housing situation was very difficult, they lived with our parents in their big house in the little town of Dunavarsány near Budapest.
>
> They had two children, both sons. Piroska tried to continue her musical life in Dunavarsány although the opportunities were not very significant in that small village.
>
> Piroska died young in 1930. Since my father was a doctor he had a certain opinion about her sudden illness, but the Budapest doctors made a different judgment. She died of the complications of appendicitis. Her sons were still young and continued to live with my parents when their father married again to a local school teacher. Years later the younger son was shot down in the 1956 revolution in Hungary. The elder son and his family still live in that same house in Dunavarsány.
>
> At a certain time after the death of my parents, that house became mine since the later communist regime al-

lowed Hungarian composers to own such property. Of course I could make no use of it until recently when I was able to give it to my nephew during a time of political change.

In the late 1930s, another of my relatives came to visit us in Holland. This was my cousin Frigyes. We had known each other as children. Our mothers were sisters, the two daughters of the Strausz family. We had played together in his father's vineyard and gone swimming in the river nearby during my family's visits to his home in the country.

We encouraged Frigyes to remain in Holland, concerned that he might be conscripted into some kind of military service should he return to Hungary. He managed well in Holland and eventually found a position abroad as an electrical engineer with a mining company in Lima, Peru. He settled permanently in South America, never to return to Europe.

During his second concert tour of Italy in December of 1926, Székely was accompanied by the Roman pianist, Dante Alderighi.[13] The tour began in Naples on 12 December with a recital for the Società Amici della Musica Napoli. After Tartini's Sonata in B Minor and Mozart's Concerto No. 6, K. 219, the remainder of the program consisted of various works heard for the first time in Naples: Ravel's *Tzigane*, Bloch's *Improvisation*, Alfredo Casella's *Scherzo*, Malipiero's *Il canto della lontananza* (The song of the distance), and Suk's *Burleska*. The program concluded with Sarasate's *Introduction and Tarantella*.

As had been the case on his first Italian tour, Székely immediately won the positive response of audience and critics alike. In Naples, the reviewer of *Il Giorno* wrote, "In all these works not heard before in Naples the artist showed a great precision of technique, an energetic touch, and a strong and vibrant hand, so much so as to win himself much applause and also the request of repeated performances."[14]

In Rome Székely and Alderighi performed three recitals. The first was at the Reale Accademia Filarmonica Romana on 13 December. Aspiring violin soloists appeared in Rome from everywhere in Europe, notably from Germany, Hungary, and Bohemia, all playing some modern works as well as the venerable compositions of the past. After their recitals and perhaps a day or two of sightseeing, they left Rome with new press cuttings in which their efforts had been recorded: "Among the numerous foreign violinists who assault the City, it is appropriate to give the post of honor to Zoltán Székely, a pupil of the famous Hubay, who gave a concert yesterday, winning applause as a technician and interpreter of uncommon merit," wrote the critic of *La Tribuna*, following the recital at the Filarmonica.[15] *Il Messaggero*'s reviewer commented, "With a rich and varied program, consisting not of over-played compositions but rather of compositions which were new to us, Zoltán Székely proved himself to be an admirable artist, furnished with an excellent technique and an uncommon stylistic sense."[16]

Vittorio Rieti's new work based on a pentatonic scale, *Variazioni su una tema cinese* and Mario Castelnuovo-Tedesco's *Ritmi* captured the interest of the audience because these works were not yet well known in Rome. The critic of *Il Popolo di Roma* wrote, "Among the selections he offered us, and we are pleased to note that both older and modern Italian pieces were well represented, were two compositions by our own young composers that won the unanimous approval of the audience."[17]

The next day Székely appeared at the intimate Sala Capizucchi on the Piazza Campitelli in Rome, where from a small audience he received a reception no less enthusiastic than the one he obtained from the huge crowd at the Reale Accademia Filarmonica Romana. Again the critic of *Il Messaggero* responded, "Székely is a truly exceptional, able, and intelligent artist who has learned to win an audience handily with his technical ability and sure interpretive intuition."[18]

In 1926 there was probably no amateur violinist more enthusiastic about the presence of foreign violinists in Rome than Benito Mussolini. He frequently invited visiting artists, among them Fritz Kreisler, to give private concerts at his home on the Via Rasella. For a young concert violinist such as Székely, an invitation to play a private recital for the head of state, also a violinist, was one to be valued in 1926 when the question of Hitler's ultimate influence had not yet occurred to visitors in Italy. Many world politicians, including Winston Churchill, tried to meet Mussolini when they were in Italy, some with little success. At the request of the Hungarian Embassy, Székely gave three such private recitals at Mussolini's home. The first in 1926 was with Dante Alderighi, Géza Frid joined him for the second in 1929, and in 1930 he performed with the composer-pianist Alfredo Casella.

Mussolini cordially greeted Székely and Alderighi and enthusiastically congratulated them after hearing works by Veracini, Gluck, Schubert, Ravel, Chaminade, and Hubay during the private concert on 20 December 1926. A notice from Mussolini's office appeared the following day in Rome's *Il Piccolo*: "The violinist Székely is clearly a great artist as is evident in his careful and precise touch, ultra-virtuosic technique, and forceful interpretation."[19]

The Székelys spent the winter at home in Nijmegen. In the early spring, Zoltán, Emma Kodály, and the great Hungarian tenor, Ferenc Székelyhidy, came to the villa at 275 Kwakkenbergweg. Székely recalls the circumstances of their visit:

> Kodály made his debut as a conductor in April when he led a performance of his *Psalmus Hungaricus* in Amsterdam with the choir of the Oratorium Vereenigung and the Amsterdam Concertgebouw Orchestra. The choir sang in Hungarian from a specially prepared phonetic transcription of the text.
>
> In Nijmegen Kodály and I even found time to play a game of tennis, although he was not a very good player. His sport was figure skating. Later we saw them off at the train station when they returned to Hungary.

Although Jaap de Graaff had offered in 1923 to provide a fine violin for the young violinist's future concerts, Székely allowed several years to pass until Mientje insisted during the spring of 1927 that he take advantage of de Graaf's generous offer made backstage at the Royal Albert Hall in London.

> In London I visited William E. Hill's firm on Wardour Street. They had a beautiful Strad, and I wanted it. The next morning Mientje telephoned to see what they thought about an offer I had made and was told, "Sold by cable to America."
>
> I learned that the Berlin expert Keszler had two other Strads. I decided to go to Berlin immediately, but there was a railway strike in England and only one last train going to the coast. There seemed to be no place on this train, but finally two seats were found, one for Mr. Visser, the famous explorer and mountain climber of the Karakoram Expedition, and the other for me.
>
> When I reached Berlin, one of the Strads had already gone. Paul Godwin, who had married Keszler's daughter, had been given the violin as a wedding present. Godwin was later the violist of the Netherlands Quartet. The other Strad was not suitable for me and besides they asked an incredible amount for it.

Then I heard there was a luthier in Paris who might have a Stradivarius for sale. That was at the firm of Maucotel et Deschamp, near the old Vuillaume shop at 46 rue Croix-des-Petits-Champs. I had seen Emile Maucotel once, but he had since died. Deschamp ran the business. He was a former orchestra violinist, not a violin maker but a connoisseur who had become Maucotel's business partner in 1903.

He knew that on the Spanish border there was a very rich man who had a very well-preserved Stradivarius violin which he might be interested in selling. It was the "Michelangelo" Stradivarius of 1718.

As to the question of previous owners, no one seems to know about that with certainty. Even Deschamp was vague on this point. On his document of authenticity he mentions a certain aristocrat, the Count of Gabriac. At another time, he said the violin had come from Russia. I don't know which story to believe. Perhaps it did belong to an aristocratic amateur, and maybe somebody did bring it from Russia. Whatever the case, there is no doubt about the origin of this violin. On this everyone agrees, although Simone Sacconi had the opinion that it might have been made slightly later, in the year 1724.

Jaap de Graaff met me in Paris to carry out the plan he had first imagined backstage at the Royal Albert Hall years before. We went to the Salle Gaveau on rue la Boëtie, and there on the stage of that fine concert hall I played the violin hoping that I could make a decision about its potential as a concert instrument. I decided in favor of this violin, and de Graaff acquired it from Maucotel et Deschamp on my behalf.

Occasionally, especially when I was younger, I sometimes wondered if a Stradivarius of a larger model might not have had a more powerful tone than the "Michelangelo," but this violin was extremely well suited to quartet playing.

In 1927 when de Graaff purchased the violin in Paris, he gave me a present of a Voirin violin bow. Later when I realized that this bow did not entirely suit me, I went back to Deschamp and exchanged it for a Pecatte bow, then later for a completely unplayed violin bow by Vigneron. Somewhat later I acquired a Dodd bow that had been Ysaÿe's, and this became my favorite bow. I also have a fine Nürnberger bow that had belonged to Ferdinand Helmann and a Dominique Pecatte, as well as a Swiss Vidoudez bow made by Emile Ouchard.

For Székely it was again a time for composing music. In Pontresina on 5 July 1926 he had begun work on his Cello Concerto, a composition that Pál Hermann found very interesting. With renewed interest, discipline, and sufficient time to work carefully, he was determined to solve the compositional problems presented by the new work before committing anything to paper. The lives of such devoted musicians are lives of methodical absorption; for Székely, the composer, each day was spent adding note to note, phrase to phrase. He worked on the concerto until he completed the first movement in Baden-Baden on 12 August 1927. Unfortunately this promising work remains unfinished more than sixty years later. Although the remaining movements exist in the form of sketches, Székely has no plan to complete the work.

In June of 1927 the Skékelys visited with Bartók at the chamber music festival in Baden-Baden, where Bartók surprised the public with his new Sonata for Piano (1926). It was also at this festival that the Kolisch Quartet introduced Alban Berg's *Lyric Suite.*

There was much new evidence of change at the Baden-Baden Festival. Nikolai Lopatnikoff and Karl Haas generated special effects on a prepared piano one afternoon, followed in the evening by a presentation of a new photographic invention (*Lichtbild*) with examples of combinations of film and music, sound and visual art—music especially composed for film. Franz Schreker and Arnold Schoenberg each discussed the new invention, speaking to the audience from the screen on film. Hindemith made musical illustrations for *Felix the Cat* in an animated film. The public debated the new media on the terrace during intermission.

Attention was given to new stage works. There was a new *Singspiel* by Kurt Weill, *Aufstieg und Fall der Stadt Mahagonny* (Rise and Fall of the Town of Mahagonny), a satire on life in America to a libretto by Bertholt Brecht. Hindemith's opera *Hin und Zurück* (There and Back), achieved a marked success with its clever plot. Darius Milhaud took the mythological history of the kidnapping of Europa for his opera *L'Enlèvement d'Europa* (The Kidnapping of Europa) while Ernst Toch adopted the fairy tale, *Die Prinzessin auf der Erbse* (The Princess and the Pea).

The ISCM held its fifth International Festival at Frankfurt am Main immediately following the festival at Baden-Baden. The Székelys remained in Germany to attend this important musical event.

We saw Bartók again in Frankfurt during July, and this was a friendly continuation of our being together in Baden-Baden.

Furtwängler conducted when Bartók played his First Piano Concerto on 1 July with the Frankfurt Opera Orchestra. But he was probably not the man who should have conducted that performance, his preference being not for the contemporary.

To me this performance was not a great success. I think that one of the main reasons was the bad programming. The First Piano Concerto is somewhat under the influence of Stravinsky. The second movement is probably the finest part, extreme in its finesse and full of percussion with the strangest *pianissimo* effects. That extremely fine work was simply "killed" by all that came before it. I still remember that piece, *The Dance in Place Congo*, by the American Henry Gilbert. That was *loud* with all its drums and percussion.

At the end of the concert we heard the Fifth Symphony of Carl Nielsen, and that received an ovation.

At the second orchestra concert, after performances of works by Claude Delvincourt, Raymond Petit, and Emil Axman, the Swiss pianist Walter Frey made a deep impression on the public with his brilliant playing of Ernest Toch's Piano Concerto, Op. 38, the most spontaneous success of the evening.

For one concert of this festival, Alois Hába and Erwin Schulhoff gave an evening of quarter-tone music. Another concert, with the theme of humor in music, was directed by Herman Scherchen and included works by Hindemith, Strauss, Honegger, and Stravinsky.

Rudolf Kolisch played the difficult violin part in Alban Berg's *Kammerkonzert* for piano, violin, and thirteen wind instruments at a final chamber music concert, and the festival closed with a performance of Aaron Copland's work for chamber orchestra, *Music for the Theater*.

Chapter Eleven

The Year of the Rhapsodies

I met Norbert Salter in Berlin early in 1927. He was a German concert agent interested in arranging concert engagements for me in several European cities in which I was not yet well known—Prague, Stockholm, Warsaw, and Oldenburg, among others.

After the festivals in Germany in 1927 I played the Glazounov concerto and Ravel's *Tzigane* with the Oldenburg Landesorchester, then a recital with Géza Frid in Prague. These were the first performances in which I played on my Stradivarius.

With concerts in Budapest, Vienna, Amsterdam, Madrid, London, Paris, Berlin, and Rome, Székely had garnered an international reputation in a very short time. After Székely played for the first time in Czechoslovakia, the Prague audience knew from its own experience that he was a violinist of sensitive temperament and genuine accomplishment. The critic of the *Prager Tagblatt* wrote, "Székely played Ravel's *Tzigane* and made an incredible impression because his rhythm is electrifying, and in his tone there is something that carries you away."[1]

Back in Holland, Székely appeared again in Arnhem and Nijmegen in October performing Glazounov's Violin Concerto with Martin Spanjaard conducting the Arnhem Orchestra. After recitals in Apeldoorn, Koog aan de Zaan, and Soest, Székely and Frid gave a recital in Nijmegen on 15 November 1927 during which they performed Ravel's new Sonata for Violin and Piano for the first time in Holland. Concerts followed in Winterswijk, Hilversum, and Enschede. On 28 November 1927 Ravel's Sonata for Violin and Piano appeared again, this time on a major recital in the Kleine Zaal of the Amsterdam Concertgebouw. This was the first performance of Ravel's new sonata in Amsterdam.

"Some weeks ago we had to postpone this concert due to the illness of the violinist," wrote Paul Sanden in *Het Volk*, "but happily this opportunity came again since we would have missed one of the best evenings of the season."[2]

In his usual cogent style, L. M. G. Arntzenius reviewed the recital in *De Telegraaf*:

A brilliant violinist, a fine instrument, a good accompanist, and a beautiful program make us thankful to the organizers that this evening went on after Székely's illness. It was one of the most interesting evenings of the season. Székely chose a program of which he could be proud. The Bach Solo Sonata in C Major was incredible with its fugue, perhaps the biggest piece written for the violin. Then came the premiere of the Ravel sonata with its new sound. With radiant tone and severe, deep concentration, Székely mastered these works. The Bach fugue and the Ravel with its "Blues" and all its shine were miraculous.[3]

Before leaving again on tour, Székely joined conductor Eduard van Beinum and the Haarlem Symphony Orchestra for a performance of the Glazounov Violin Concerto, then spent a quiet holiday in Nijmegen with Mientje, his seventh Christmas season in Holland. Soon after the holiday, Mientje's cousin, Guus Everts, joined the Székelys and Frid on their first automobile tour to Italy and did much of the driving from Nijmegen to Livorno. The ease of their journey convinced Székely that traveling by automobile instead of train when touring in Europe was both practical and enjoyable.

Indeed it is tiring and difficult to be on tour, but I made it easier by doing everything by car when possible. In this way I went from Venice to Stockholm in my Fiat in 1927 and was one of the first musicians in Europe to have toured by automobile.

Once we arrived in Livorno for our third Italian tour, we were greeted by the sponsors of the concert. As introductions were being made, Frid, who was in a jolly mood, announced Guus Everts as "the celebrated Dutch tenor," and this little joke made everyone rather uneasy since the poor man could neither read a note of music nor sing at all.

When one of the organizers asked what was his repertoire, he said the first name that came into his head. "Wagner!" The organizer responded politely saying, "I hope we will hear you next year. You, Guus Everts, the first tenor of Holland."

That evening we played our recital at the Teatro Goldoni in Livorno, and the tour was launched. The next day we had to play in Florence, and since we thought the concert would be in the evening, Mientje kept my tails separate. When we arrived in the early afternoon we found, much to our surprise, that the concert was scheduled as a matinée. Normally one doesn't play in tails at a matinée, just a jacket, so quickly, all the suitcases had to be taken out to find the proper clothes.

I had to be really fast since we had only just arrived and it was already nearly time to begin the recital. In the midst of very precious paintings in the Palazzo Pitti, we improvised a changing room near the Sala Bianca where the concert was to take place. As I buttoned my jacket, the audience was already waiting for our recital to begin, a recital that would include the first performance of Ravel's sonata in Florence.

I remember that on another occasion in yet another country, I forgot my tails on a journey, but there was a tenor appearing in the concert with nearly the same build, and happily we did not have to appear at the same time, so we changed back and forth and overcame the problem.

After a recital in Lecce, we traveled to Rome, where we appeared at the Reale Accademia Filarmonica Romana on 30 January and again presented Ravel's sonata, in its first performance in Rome. The evening began with Veracini, Bach, and Glazounov's concerto. After Ravel's sonata, we played Italian works: Pizzetti's *Tre canti*, Castelnuovo-Tedesco's *Capitan Fracassa*, and the Paganini Caprices Nos. 20 and 24 in the arrangement for violin and piano by Szymanovsky.

After a few pleasant days in Rome, Guus Everts ended his vacation with us and took the train back to Holland, while Mientje, Frid, and I drove on to Sicily for a recital in Palermo.

For that concert we played the same program we had given in Rome with the exception of substituting for Ravel's sonata the Rondo brillant, Op. 70, by Schubert, a work I played often during my career.

With some time left to enjoy ourselves in Italy, we traveled to Venice before leaving for Stockholm for a recital at the Royal Academy of Music on 6 March. For the final segment of the journey we shared the driving and enjoyed ourselves thoroughly until we reached northern Germany near the Baltic Sea. Frid was at the wheel when suddenly a tire blew out. We hit a tree. No one was injured, but it was necessary to leave the Fiat in Germany and take the boat to Sweden. Despite this accident, we arrived safely and on time in Stockholm.

We ended the concert in Stockholm with *Midsummer's Dance* by Tor Aulin, the Stockholm violinist considered the greatest Scandinavian violinist since Ole Bull. As a composer and conductor Tor Aulin was a great champion of the modern Swedish composers, and many of his own violin compositions had a certain popularity in those days.

We returned to Germany by sea, claimed the repaired automobile, and continued the tour. In Frankfurt I met Pál Hermann to rehearse for one of our duo recitals which took place a few days later for the concert series of the Frankfurt Kammermusikgemeinde.

The Hungarian pianist Agi Jámbor, daughter of Piroska Székely's teacher in Budapest, had already performed that season in the Frankfurt series, as had Artur Schnabel, Emanuel Feuermann, and the Roth Quartet, of which Pál Hermann was the cellist. For their duo recital, Székely and Hermann presented works by Haydn and Mozart, the Divertimento by Ernst Toch, and *Sonata da camera* (1925) written for them by their compatriot, Mátyás Seiber, a Kodály pupil who had a successful career in London. They ended the evening with the transcription for violin and cello of Bartók's *Rumanian Folk Dances*.

"Zoltán played tennis everywhere he went," Mientje recalled in her journal in 1968.

He always traveled with tennis racquets in his suitcase. In 1928 he played four matches on the Queen's Court at Wimbledon. In those years the Frenchman Jean Borotra and Bill Tilden from America were the great names in tennis. I prayed

Zoltán would not strain his arm at the end of that competition since he was playing a concert the last night in London. Just to assuage his musical fans he entered the English competition under the pseudonym Spielman, which in Dutch means "a man who plays." An amusing thing about that event was that Zoltán tensioned his racquet by tuning it to the piano. For that competition his racquet had a nice sound!

During the 1930s Zoltán often played doubles in Monte Carlo with King Gustav of Sweden and two English girls who played regularly at the club. King Gustav, an extremely tall man, no longer young, would always position himself at the net. At other times Zoltán played tennis with his colleagues, the Koromzays, the Moskowskys, and even Imre Waldbauer. Of course in Holland, he had many good tennis partners, young people who played well.

My husband believed that sports were necessary for an artist to bring change to his point of view. Once in Holland, he was playing at the championship in Nijmegen just at the time that he had a radio broadcast. In the middle of the games he left in the car, rushed to Hilversum, played his pieces, and rushed back, having changed, and arrived just in time to play again and win second prize. Once in Arnhem he got a first prize at a tennis game, and in Roermond that night he had a big success as a violinist. Of course Zoltán is not the only one who combined art and sport. Once in England we saw Heifetz at a golf game in the afternoon then later that evening in the Albert Hall giving a concert.

Bartók crossed the Atlantic for the first time in December of 1927 to undertake a two-month concert tour in the United States. He began his recitals with a brief lecture in English, then played programs made up mainly of his own piano works. He returned to Europe on the SS *George Washington* in the company of Pablo Casals and Mario Corti, the Italian violinist.

In Budapest during the spring, the Bartóks moved to a villa at 10 Kavics Street in which they occupied the ground floor. When the Székelys were in Budapest in late summer, they were invited to dinner at the Bartóks' home in Buda. Székely recalls this exciting evening:

> The dinner party at the Bartóks' home was in one of those rooms with all the Hungarian embroidery and the furniture painted in the Hungarian peasant style, even the chairs.

Bartók was in a jovial mood. You could see there was something in the making. We talked, then a little bit later he came up with two manuscripts. He said, "I have a surprise for you. I have written two rhapsodies. One is for you; one is for Szigeti." It was clear that he had not yet shown these manuscripts to anybody else. He said, "You may choose which one you like for the dedication."

That was 1928—for me, the year of the rhapsodies! There must be almost a year's difference between the composition of the two rhapsodies, but I am not sure. I happened to choose the Second Rhapsody because I preferred it, but that doesn't mean that the First Rhapsody was already dedicated to Szigeti. On the contrary, these works were not written specifically for a specific person. If I had chosen the First rather than the Second Rhapsody, then the situation of the dedications would be reversed. Later that evening after the excitement of seeing the new rhapsodies, Bartók invited me to listen with him to the early recordings of his folk music collection.

While Bartók was away in September, Székely visited Ditta Bartók to get the manuscript parts of the new violin works so that he and Bartók could rehearse them when the composer returned home. Because Bartók had not written the metronomic indications in the scores, Ditta showed them to Székely since she knew them well. She and her husband had played through these new works several times on two pianos. On 14 September Székely and Bartók rehearsed the new violin pieces for the first time.[4] A month or so later, Bartók wrote to Szigeti and mentioned the new Rhapsody to him suggesting that they meet to discuss it.[5]

During his long career Székely devoted himself to the study and performance of the First and Second Rhapsodies. His interpretations are authentic in the true sense of the word—he witnessed Bartók's intentions firsthand and continued to investigate these masterworks through his own lifetime of research. That Székely knew to play *not* what appeared to be written in Bartók's notation in every instance is an important aspect of his mastery of performance practice in these works.

There are certain instructions that one *cannot know* from the notation of the rhapsodies, and that is always a hard problem. In the fifth measure of the *Friss* (fresh) movement of the Second Rhapsody with the entrance of the violin solo, Bartók expected a definite style of bowing. Now anybody who plays it, plays it at the frog with lifted bow strokes, because something about it inspires one to do that. But that is not correct. The bow should not be lifted, but instead the passage played on the string in the peasant style. If Bartók had been a violinist, he would have given it another marking and indicated "on the string." Usually violinists play it wrong in this respect. In both the Violin Concerto and in the finale of the Fourth Quartet, we often have the problem of whether or not to lift the bow in such passages.

I remember that later when I played the premiere of the Second Rhapsody in the orchestral version with Dohnányi conducting, Bartók was very satisfied and said, "You played it very well. You played it like a peasant." In this remark he was referring to this style of on-the-string bowing that I have mentioned. The gypsies do not play with lifted bowings, but rather "on the string," and this was what Bartók had in mind, so that justifies playing these passages in the way he preferred. I play it that way, and I recommend it be played that way.

There are certain cimbalom effects that can be made in the piano part of the First Rhapsody. [The cimbalom is a dulcimer-like Hungarian instrument used for centuries exclusively by gypsies.] In the Tempo della prima parte at measure 30, this effect appears in the orchestration. In the 1940 recording with Szigeti, made at the Library of Congress,[6] Bartók seems to play such an effect on the piano, and later Isobel Moore tried something similar in our recording and performances. Both pianists have made some "sound effects," in this instance creating that cimbalom effect.

I remember that I visited Szigeti once at his home in Switzerland. At that time he must have been eighty-two or eighty-three. I posed a question regarding the passage at measure 16 in the First Rhapsody. I was interested in this passage in double stops with the bass on the G string. "How did you play that?" I asked. "As it is written, of course," was his answer. Later I listened again to his performance recorded at the Library of Congress. There is no question, Szigeti did not play it as written. As written it is not playable. Theoretically it may seem so, but it is not. What is evident here is the question, how trustworthy is one's memory?

I never played this passage as Bartók wrote it, at least to play it so that anything comes of it. That is not possible.

These chords one can never play as a solid chord, only broken, and since the same finger is necessarily repeated, the original passage is far-fetched. Of course certain chords one can play if harmonics are introduced into it, but practically speaking the original passage is not possible. Fortunately the *ossia* (alternative) passage is comfortable and sufficient.

On 15 November 1938, when Bartók and Székely played together for the last time in an all-Bartók concert in Amsterdam, the program ended with a performance of the First Rhapsody. On that occasion Bartók chose to play the second ending of the work. Bartók's preoccupation with the endings of the two rhapsodies is in itself an interesting study. Until the late 1930s Székely was the periodic recipient of Bartók's various changes to these works and has this to say about the endings:

> Endings! There are so many composed for the two rhapsodies. Somehow Bartók was not entirely satisfied and continued to make these changes. When we played the First Rhapsody on the Bartók Evening in Amsterdam in 1938, we played the second ending. In that work there was an original first ending, then came a second ending, and there is an option mark and one may choose between them. In the 1940 recording with Szigeti, Bartók plays the second ending. He preferred the second ending for some reason, and I didn't ask him why. Very remarkable. Did his preference for that second ending mean that playing it so is the correct version? In my recording of the First Rhapsody with Isobel Moore, we played the first ending instead, with its recapitulation of the first theme and the cadenza.
>
> The endings he composed for the Second Rhapsody offer a unique problem. There are many—four or five. I have discussed these with the Hungarian scholar, László Somfai, who is interested in this matter. At first Bartók tried just a few notes, then he made a longer ending. My colleague, Lorand Fenyves, plays the original edition since he likes it better, but that ending is not really inspired somehow. Perhaps Bartók made that original ending because the First Violin Sonata has a similar ending, and that is the character of it. The later version has a somewhat sweet character and is not really a fiery ending as it was originally. There are a few good ideas there, but not as would befit such a work, so while maybe the orig-

inal ending had some similarities with the First Sonata, it was better. It was in character.

When I had played the Second Rhapsody for the first time in Budapest, I used the first printed version of the ending. Later it was changed and I played it for years—and with Bartók, too—in the second version, and then he made a new ending which he incorporated into both the orchestral and piano versions. As late as 1936 I inquired of him if the most recent changes had been put into the orchestral materials of the Second Rhapsody by Universal-Edition, because he had changed it suddenly and made a new ending and sent it to me before we were to play it in Amsterdam. Since I planned to play it in Brussels and elsewhere with orchestra during this period, I was anxious to know if the endings were already the same for both versions. If I were to learn this new ending and then arrive at an orchestra concert and have to play the old formula again, that would have been very annoying.

One of the endings in manuscript I never played. I cannot now remember the exact date when I put it into my score as a revision. I have an unrevised early edition where I have the various changes inserted in *Lichtpaus* (photocopied) slips of manuscript in Bartók's own writing, and since that is what I used in performance, I must have got them directly from him.

Some things are mysterious. At the time when such revisions are made, one may remember the sequence of the changes, but later it is sometimes difficult to reconstruct the order of such events.

By 1938, ten years after the Second Rhapsody was composed, I must have had all the improvements. Since I have the original manuscript, I often played from it in the early years. I also have *Lichtpaus* copies of all the revisions and must have had them before the war, because during the war there was no communication with Bartók. That is something I don't quite understand: I have a *Lichtpaus* copy of Bartók's final revision of the ending of the Second Rhapsody which is inserted in my old, pre-war Universal-Edition performance copy, yet Bartók is said to have made this revision later in America in 1945. In fact, the inserted changes in my performance copy and the changes that appear in the revised 1947 edition published by Boosey and Hawkes are identical. This makes me conclude that Bartók must have already made these changes before the war and sent them to me since I have these annotations in his hand with his final solutions.

Both Bartók and Székely were under the concert management of the Fodor Agency in Budapest in 1928. Their impresario arranged for Székely to play two performances in Budapest during October: a recital on 23 October at the Franz Liszt Academy with Géza Frid and a performance of the Dvořák Violin Concerto with the Budapest Philharmonic, Dohnányi conducting, on 28 October. On 30 October before Székely and Frid left Budapest on tour, they took part in a house concert in Budapest that was sponsored by the Budapesti Orvosok Kamarazeneegyesületéne, a doctors' chamber music club, to which Székely's father belonged.

They traveled to Prague where they played Ravel's Sonata for Violin and Piano which was still new to Czechoslovakia. Later Pál Hermann joined them in Germany for an evening of chamber music in Bremen where they played a private concert. After music of Handel, Veracini, and Beethoven, Frid played his composition, *Podium Suite*, which he had introduced in Budapest. The evening ended with the Trio in F Major by Saint-Saëns.

In Holland in the Groote Zaal of the Amsterdam Concertgebouw on 19 November, Székely appeared with Frid in a recital that brought something absolutely new to the Dutch public, the world premiere of Bartók's Second Rhapsody. To those who judged the violinists of his generation in Holland in 1928, Székely seemed to have something of a prophet's power to excite and stimulate the audience with Bartók's new music. The work in manuscript that Székely had recently brought back from Budapest ended the first part of the recital which began with Tartini's Sonata in G Minor ("Devil's Trill"), followed by Schubert's Sonatina in D Major. After the first performance of Bartók's new Rhapsody, the memorable evening continued with Pizetti's *Canto* and *Capitan Fracassa* by Castelnuovo-Tedesco and concluded with the virtuosity and fireworks of Ravel's *Tzigane*.

Before going to Germany to appear in a performance of Glazounov's Violin Concerto in Weimar with the Deutsches Nationaltheater Orchester conducted by Ernst Praetorius, Székely paid a tribute to Lucien Capet, the great French violinist who had died in Paris the previous December. The Capet String Quartet, an ensemble specializing in the performance of the Beethoven cycle, had appeared at the Amsterdam Concertgebouw in 1926 and 1927 and was much admired in Holland. At the end of their February recital in Haarlem, Székely and Frid played, in memoriam, Lucien Capet's *Poème* for violin and piano.

Not only did the International Society for Contemporary Music

arrange international festivals, but the various national sections of
the society gave series of concerts as well. The London Contemporary
Music Centre represented the British national section of the ISCM.
Székely returned to London with Pál Hermann to join Géza Frid in a
concert on 19 February which presented four works in their first London performances for the British Music Society at the Court House,
Marylebone Lane. During this extended visit to London, the musicians were the house guests of Mr. and Mrs. Jaap de Graaff. There
Bartók visited as well.

At the concert on Marylebone Lane, Székely and Frid began the
evening with the Sonata for Violin and Piano by the Swiss composer
Robert Bernard. Hermann and Székely continued with Mátyás
Seiber's *Sonata da camera*, a work written for them which they had recently played in Frankfurt. From Kodály's Seven Pieces for Piano (Op.
11), Frid played three pieces: *Méditation*, *Il pleure dans mon coeur
comme il pleut sur la ville*, and *Székely keserves* (lament). Székely and
Hermann ended the evening's concert with the new Duo for Violin
and Cello by Erwin Schulhoff, the Czechoslovakian composer who
with Alois Hába had worked on the problems of quarter-tone music.

Bartók and Székely played in London in 1929. Before their arrival
an article appeared in the *Radio Times* encouraging listeners to accord
greater respect to Bartók's music and not to switch off their sets un-
thinkingly.[7] For those who remained tuned to the BBC on 4 March
1929, there was a broadcast of the first performance in England of
Bartók's two rhapsodies. Székely recalls:

> In London we gave a performance of Bartók's works for
> the BBC's third season of concerts of contemporary music at
> the Arts Theatre Club in Great Newport Street.
> Bartók performed his Piano Sonata and three pieces from
> *Out of Doors*, both composed in 1926. Together we played my
> transcription of the *Rumanian Folk Dances* and the first Eng-
> lish performances of the two rhapsodies for violin and piano.
> Bartók was pleased with this performance of the rhapsodies
> and wrote Ditta to say that I had played the rhapsodies beau-
> tifully, especially the second one.[8]
> Later at Oxford we gave a sonata evening. It was a very
> cold night, I remember. After the concert, which was well
> attended, there was a big supper party and, of course, many
> Oxford professors were invited, and all sat at a big table in
> the shape of a horseshoe.

In the best English tradition, there was one toast after the other, then silence when everyone stood. Bartók did not stand up. He just sat down and said, "I think Mr. Székely will be glad to answer all your toasts." I was twenty-five at that time and never in my life had made a toast. How I brought it off in that illustrious company, I don't remember, but I did it. Making my first toast was for me one of those cruel social pleasantries.

About this tour in England in 1929, Mientje recalled:

After a brief visit in the home of the de Graaffs, Zoltán and I stayed in an apartment at the Mount Royal Hotel near Marble Arch. These were the first English flats I had known about and since Zoltán disliked always eating in restaurants, living at the Mount Royal was a good solution since there was a small kitchen and I could prepare meals there. For a while Bartók came to dinner every day until I suddenly became ill with influenza. He continued his daily visits during my illness, always bringing me an exotic flower or maybe an unusual compote of some kind—something special. He was so close to us, Bartók was.

Later when we all went walking in London, the streets were icy. When I crossed the road to take some correspondence to Zoltán's managers, Ibbs and Tillet, I ran too quickly and fell in the middle of the road. A car came along and Bartók dashed into the icy street and took me away. Later I said to Zoltan, "He risked his life for me," and I tell this to show that there was a kind of wonderful friendship with Bartók, and we were always very proud of that.

Székely and Hermann had each composed significant works for violin and cello duo. Now came an opportunity to play a duo recital again at the Wigmore Hall in London, where the artists had a large following. Székely's duo, *Polyphon et Homophon*, Op. 2, which had been published by Universal-Edition in 1927, was featured in a program that included the duos by Ravel and Kodály. "Their rhythm, tone, phrasing, and technique are all of the same perfection and we were directly convinced of their absolute superiority," wrote the critic of the *Morning Post*.[9] Székely and Hermann were praised in the *Times* and the *Observer*. The critic of the *Daily Telegraph* wrote, "The concert only with duos for violin and cello without accompaniment seemed to us quite something, but if the musicians are of the level of Székely and Hermann and the composers are of the level of Ravel, Bartók, Kodály, and Székely himself, then it is a pleasure of the first order to listen."[10]

Before the Székelys returned to Holland in mid-March, there was a house concert at the de Graaff's home in London. The concert honored the tenth year of the Society of Dutch Women in London, an organization in which Loes de Graaff was active. At her splendid house concerts, all the performers were Hungarians, Zoltán, Pál, and Géza, except the singer, Miss McDonald. After 1937, when the de Graaffs moved to France, their home on Millfield Lane was owned by the pianist, Sir Clifford Curzon.

Chapter Twelve

In Hungary with Bartók

Mientje and I traveled with Géza Frid to France in April of 1929 to meet Maurice Ravel. Since I had decided that I would like to play *Tzigane* and the Sonata for Violin and Piano for him, Bartók wrote a letter of introduction for me to Ravel from Rome on 15 March 1929 telling him of my interest in his works.[1]

I often included *Tzigane* on my recitals and with Frid had already presented the Violin Sonata extensively in Holland, Italy, and Czechoslovakia, with first performances in Amsterdam, Genoa, Florence, Rome, and Prague.

We met Calvocoressi in Paris, and he joined us in our visit to Ravel. From Paris we traveled to nearby Montfort l'Amaury, where Ravel lived in his home called Le Belvédère—now the Ravel Museum. When Ravel went to Paris he stayed in hotels. He was very warm and talkative, and he wanted to hear his violin sonata first. As we played he turned Frid's pages. During *Tzigane* he sat down and took his Siamese cat on his lap. When we had finished playing he gave a few comments and seemed to be happy about our performance.

He characterized the interpretation of those two works in this way: "In *Tzigane* one can be free—that is in the form of a *fantasia*—but in the sonata one should be very strict."

He went to his bar and showed us a lot of flasks upon which he commented. We spent a very sociable hour with him while he chatted about many things, including a new revue at the Moulin Rouge, all the time stroking his cat who he said was king of the house. Later he took us to the station, where he said goodbye very cordially and gave a bouquet to Mientje. That visit was a once-in-a-lifetime event, the only time I met with Ravel.

A letter to Mientje from Universal-Edition in Vienna had arrived in Holland during their absence. Because she had sent the recent English reviews to the publisher, they had written to express their interest in the success of the several Hungarian works that had been played in London, including the transcription of Bartók's *Rumanian Folk Dances*. In addition, the letter contained a new proposal from an editor at Universal-Edition who wanted Székely to make a violin transcription of Kodály's *Hary János Suite*, either of the whole suite or of its parts.

The editor also offered to send a special letter in which he would ask Székely to record Bartók's *Rumanian Dances* because these dances were played incredibly often, and people had asked for a recording. He felt that the recording companies were not as conservative as before, and it was now more necessary to bring out modern works because serious musicians and a part of the public were interested in modern music and bought many new records of such modern pieces.[2]

While Székely did not make the proposed Kodály transcription, he did later record his transcription of Bartók's *Rumanian Folk Dances* for Decca in London.

The Székelys and Frid set out for their fourth tour to Italy at the end of March. In Turin Székely played the Glazounov Violin Concerto with the Orchestra Stabile Municipale in the Teatro Regio. Giuseppe Antonicelli conducted the performance, which began with Schumann's Symphony No. 3 and ended with Respighi's suite for small orchestra, *The Birds* (1927). Frid joined Székely on the platform for a performance of Ravel's *Tzigane*, the first performance of the work in Turin.

The next day in Florence, they played at the British Institute at the Palazzo Antinori, then went on to Rome. On 4 April the Székelys joined Bartók and Szigeti at Gogol's favorite Roman cafe, the Cafe Greco, which the melancholy Russian novelist had frequented during his long stay in Rome. They spoke of a recent performance of the

Second Violin Sonata during which the audience was unusually noisy, something that was upsetting to Szigeti although Bártok claimed to be more used to such things.[3]

While in Rome, Székely received a message from the Hungarian Embassy that Benito Mussolini again wanted him to play a private concert at his home on the Via Rassela as he had done two years before. The Székelys and Frid were expected at Mussolini's residence at half past nine in the evening, Mientje in evening gown and the gentlemen in tails. The program would be their choice.

"Promptly at nine the car came for us at the little hotel where we were staying," Mientje recalled.

It took us through Rome to the Via Rassela where we went up on a lift to Mussolini's home. An elderly lady who looked after Mussolini received us and took our coats. We walked down a long hallway at the end of which waited Mussolini dressed in evening clothes and standing with his arms crossed. After a cordial greeting he led us into a very large room which was his library, showed us first an enormous, sculpted eagle received from his admirers, then a recent photo of Fritz Kreisler on his piano.

Since Zoltán had made a choice of works which Mussolini might want to hear—music by Tartini, Jongen, Manén, d'Ambrosio, Sinigaglia, Paganini, and Bartók—the playing began.

After Sinigaglia's *Rapsodia piemontese* they paused. Suddenly concerned, Mussolini asked the artists if they were not tired, or maybe the room was too hot for them, and if so, the doors should be opened; then deciding it was time for refreshments, he rang a bell, and the elderly woman reappeared.

Evidently she was the only person serving him. Now she poured champagne and presented bon-bons. Mussolini raised his glass. "I drink to your health and your future success," he said. Then he brought his glass to his lips but did not drink, since evidently it was not his habit.

Székely recalls that on the round table in front of Mussolini, there were piles of books and magazines including one thick, heavy work which was the first part of a new Italian lexicon on which, Mussolini told them, two thousand people were working.

Later when we talked about Holland, I told him that Nijmegen was my most beloved city, and again Mussolini surprised us with his remarks: "Nijmegen has a university, doesn't it? And Leiden and Delft, too. But the latter city is already famous because of its beautiful porcelain."

Mussolini asked me to write down the exact names of the pieces we had played. When I sat myself at his writing table to do so, he said, "I will write a piece myself about you for the Italian press."

For a few minutes he continued to chat. He spoke about his own musical training, telling us that he played the violin every day, having studied it in his youth. He said that when the people of Italy had learned about this, they had sent him hundreds of violins, and these were lying unused in two or three wagons. He intended to give these wagonsful of violins to the talented youth of Italy.

Having finished our refreshments, Frid and I concluded our concert with Paganini's Caprice No. 24 and my transcription of Bartók's *Rumanian Folk Dances*.

When the evening ended, Mussolini said, "Wait a minute, I will call my car to take you home." He walked with us to the end of the corridor, kissed Mientje's hand, then said goodbye to us in a very friendly way. A few minutes later we were riding in the official car through Rome's almost deserted streets. A few people stared after us, because everyone in the city knew Mussolini's Isotta Fraschini!

When we arrived at the hotel it was nearly midnight, so we all retired for the night, having spent more than two hours with Il Duce, indeed a strange evening in my busy artist's life.

In the morning, as he had promised, the newspapers carried a brief notice which ended, "His Excellency, the Head of State, was enthusiastically pleased with the excellent interpretations."[4]

Mientje remained in Rome to vacation while Frid and Székely drove south to play two more engagements in coastal towns. After their first concert an unusual adventure befell them. They were approached at their hotel by the police, who promptly put them under house arrest, much to their surprise. They begged to know what was happening and were finally told that the police had information that a spy was known to be traveling south in a Fiat with papers identifying him as Zoltán Székely.

Frid immediately brought to their attention that only the previous evening they had played a concert in the home of Mussolini and that the notice had appeared in every newspaper. Surely this must be a case of mistaken identity! Nevertheless, they were detained in their hotel rooms, but not before Székely telephoned Mientje in Rome, only to find that she was also being held.

Of course they missed the next engagement. In the afternoon they peered from their rooms into the hallway to find that the police were gone. They went to the police station to inquire about their status, and no one there was willing to speak of the matter. It was as though nothing at all had occurred since by then the police must have realized their error. They drove immediately back to Rome, got Mientje, and left Italy for home.

Pál Hermann came from Berlin to Holland to meet the Székelys on their return from Italy. On 15 May in Aerdenhout, an affluent suburb near Amsterdam, they presented a duo recital and on that occasion performed a new transcription of a Haydn work, Kodály's Duo for Violin and Cello, Johan Halvorsen's *Sarabande with Variations on a Theme by Handel*, and the *Grand Duo Brillant* by Friedrich Hermann, the violist-composer of the Joachim Quartet, a composition they had discovered years before in Berlin.

After Hermann's departure, the Székelys returned to London in June as house guests of the van den Berg family, friends of the de Graaffs, who lived in a palatial home near Buckingham Palace. In London their host was known as the Butter King since he owned the Blue Band Butter Company. On this trip they brought their automobile from Holland and enjoyed motoring in London.

Van den Berg had organized a concert at the Wigmore Hall on behalf of the Dutch Benevolent Society. Maartje Offers, a Dutch contralto, sang Strauss songs and Saint-Saëns' aria "Mon coeur s'ouvre à ta voix" from *Samson et Delilah*. The Dutch String Quartet—Herman Leydensdorff, Julius Röntgen, Bram Mendes, and Thomas Canivez—performed several short works including Hugo Wolf's *Italienische Serenade*. With Frid, Székely ended the concert with a performance of Ravel's *Tzigane*.

This was one of Székely's early collaborations with Maartje Offers, who was an outstanding singer. Fred Gaisberg, head of recording for His Master's Voice in London, was particularly interested in recording this fine contralto. While Maartje Offers remained a favorite artist in England, she did not have great success in Holland, where the

principal activity for singers was still the oratorio. At this period, Gaisberg decided to have Székely make a test recording of Hubay's *Csárdas scène*. Later, Antonia Kossar, Székely's Dutch manager, was able to
arrange his first two 78 rpm recordings for Decca.

The Székelys went to Ostende in Belgium later in the summer.
There Székely performed Brahms' Violin Concerto at the Ostende
Kursaal with François Rasse conducting. A pupil of Ysaÿe, Rasse was
then the director of the Conservatory at Liège. They remained near
Ostende for a vacation, living at the Littoral Palace in Middelkerke.

Jaap de Graaff's enthusiasm for the painters of the Belgian school
prompted him to suggest that Székely meet James Ensor, the great
Flemish painter, while in Ostende. To show his admiration for
Ensor's work, Székely decided to play a private concert for him and
his colleagues. Ensor's picturesque studio was not spacious enough
for the sonority of the Stradivarius, so the concert was given at another studio, at 36 rue Adolphe Buyl, where a few music lovers, in-
tellectuals, and artists gathered.

In such intimate circumstances, and accompanied by Frid, Székely entranced the audience. On 8 September 1929 in *Le Phare*,
Claude Berniers wrote a sweeping, more-poetic-than-usual account of
the evening during which the audience seemed transported elsewhere as soon as they heard the very first notes from the Michelangelo Strad. "Under the hands of this 'savant' a whirlwind of dreams
and images, a flow of laughter and sobs, suddenly comes forth from
the magical instrument, the very essence of life itself."[5]

They returned to Nijmegen in October so that Székely could prepare the Beethoven Violin Concerto. When Martin Spanjaard had
proposed an all-Beethoven concert—the *Coriolanus* Overture, the
Violin Concerto, and the Fifth Symphony—to launch the 1929–30
season of the Arnhem Orchestra, he had once more invited Székely to
appear as soloist in Nijmegen and Zutphen. In these performances of
the Beethoven concerto, Székely's virtuosity was again a source of
amazement, especially in the seldom-played cadenzas by Vieuxtemps.

Two recitals followed immediately, one in Haarlem at the Stadsschouwburg, a municipal theater west of the Grote Markt, and another at the Amsterdam Concertgebouw where on 13 November
1929 the program featured the Ravel sonata along with Joseph Jongen's *Poème Héroïque*, Filip Lazar's *Trois Danses*, and Beethoven's
Sonata, Op. 47, ("Kreutzer").

Székely began to plan the repertoire for his forthcoming Budapest concerts which were to take place during October. With Dohnányi conducting the Budapest Philharmonic he would play the premiere of Bartók's Second Rhapsody with orchestra.

I suggested to Dohnányi that we also play another, shorter work. I recommended Tartini's "Devil's Trill" in an arrangement with string orchestra by the German, Kalder, but Dohnányi didn't accept this proposal. While I was sorry that we didn't play the Kalder arrangement, this important program was finally decided: Rezsö Kókai's *Preludium and Scherzo*, the Second Rhapsody of Bartók, Respighi's Dance Suite, and the Symphony in D Minor by Franck.

I knew Dohnányi best in this early period, having played his Violin Concerto in Berlin, then later in 1928 the Dvořák Violin Concerto in Budapest where he conducted the Philharmonic. I didn't see him again after the war and had no contact with him at the end when he lived in America.

Joseph Szigeti played the first performance of the orchestral version of Bartók's First Rhapsody in Königsberg on 1 November 1929. Herman Scherchen conducted. During the period that followed, both Szigeti and Székely appeared in a marathon series of concerts in Budapest presenting the two rhapsodies in their alternate forms with piano or orchestra.

Szigeti and Bartók played the first Budapest performance of the First Rhapsody in the piano version on 22 November. Two days later, Székely played the world premiere of the orchestral version of the Second Rhapsody with the Budapest Philharmonic under the direction of Dohnányi. Finally, on 26 November, Bartók and Székely played a concert at the Franz Liszt Academy where they presented both rhapsodies in the piano versions.

Because Szigeti had played in Budapest just before me, presenting the First Rhapsody, the public had the unusual opportunity of hearing these two works in their various forms in quick succession.

On Sunday morning, 26 November, the Philharmonic Society staged an open dress rehearsal at the academy. This celebration was for the orchestra, Dohnányi, and especially for Bartók. This was the dress rehearsal of the evening concert, which offered the first chance for the Budapest public to hear Bartók's Second Rhapsody with orchestra.

It was inevitable that critics would compare both the artists and the new works. Géza Molnar wrote in *Pester Lloyd*, "How lucky we are to have two such violinists, the sublime Szigeti with his ideal tone and the refreshingly bittersweet Székely with his realistically tight approach."[6] Aladár Tóth went somewhat further in his *Pesti Napló* review:

> The new work's interpreter, the young generation's most outstanding violin talent, Zoltán Székely, made us feel the monumental musical tensions of the work beautifully. It was not in vain that Bartók dedicated this Rhapsody to him. For the young artist no technical passage is too difficult. He has an ideally balanced violin style devoid of any posturing, and a cool seriousness of interpretation that ensures the total success of the work.
>
> This Second Rhapsody creates a worthy pair with the First Rhapsody, which was introduced here by Szigeti only a couple of days ago. Somehow this one is on an even larger scale and is also more distilled. The instrumental folk music improvisation has a virtuosity, a swing, which in the First Rhapsody comes out in a very unabashed fashion, but here is shown in a deeper perspective.[7]

A controversy now arose between the critic Emil Haraszti and Bartók over Haraszti's review in *Budapest Hirlap* on 26 November. The press had wielded its power against Székely, perhaps to serve Haraszti's own purposes: in comparing both the artists and the works, he had ultimately termed Székely's performance "anemic . . . not made up for by the young artist's intellect."[8]

The next day a brief statement from Bartók appeared in the *Budapest Hirlap* in which he declared the "ideal perfection" with which Székely had played. "I could not have placed my work in better hands," he concluded.[9]

Nine years earlier in 1920, Székely had met Lily Berg, who later married Emil Haraszti. He recalls the circumstances of their meeting:

> Lily Berg was a composer whose string trio we once played at Pál Hermann's home. As I accompanied her back to Pest, where she and I both lived, we spoke of her string trio. I told her my opinion of that work which was probably not so flattering. She never forgave me. Perhaps that had some connection with Haraszti's review. One might wonder whether

Haraszti simply disliked Bartók, even though he later wrote books about him.[10]

Bartók's reaction to Haraszti's review is interesting. While he often would not react for himself, when it was other persons under fire he was immediately fighting for them—Kodály and others—but not for himself.

Two days after the appearance with the Philharmonic, Bartók and Székely played a recital at the academy. On that program they performed Ravel's sonata together for the first time and Beethoven's Sonata, Op. 47 ("Kreutzer"), a work with which they had begun their artistic collaboration in 1921. Perhaps most importantly, they played both the new rhapsodies in their piano versions.

The critics of *Pesti Hírlap* and *Pester Lloyd* agreed that hearing both rhapsodies in the same evening, and hearing them performed by Bartók and Székely, was a revelation. Palma Ottlik wrote in *Pesti Hírlap*, "Together they [the two rhapsodies] gave us an even more complete picture of the continuous evolution of Bartók's creativity and an even more perfect picture because next to the composer was the same artist playing both works."[11] The reviewer for *Pester Lloyd* commented, "And now that we have heard the two works on the same evening we can appreciate the intimate relation, the same musical spirit which beats in both works, the tension between the wide-arched, forceful melody and the heavy, occasionally elemental rhythm."[12]

In *Pesti Napló*, Aladár Tóth once again presented his assessment with great probity:

> Székely outdid himself. Not counting Huberman, Bartók probably could not have found a better partner for the "Kreutzer." In this piece, Heifetzian superiority, Kreislerian detailed work—these things are useless. Here the only thing that can save the violinist from a total fading out is that he can follow the great line of the formal conception. . . .
>
> Bartók played the "Kreutzer" sonata for us a few years ago with the world-famous Marteau.[13] That he could play it much better now than then is especially Székely's doing. Marteau's playing practically disappeared next to Bartók's piano playing, but Székely's violin playing reminded us constantly that the "Kreutzer" is a violin and piano sonata. The audience was practically intoxicated. The artists had to return to the podium many times, and finally, which is unusual for a sonata evening, they had to give an encore, the

Rumanian Folk Dances of Bartók in Székely's transcription.

The other big event of the concert was the introduction of Bartók's two new rhapsodies with piano instead of orchestra. The two compositions were played recently with orchestra accompaniment, but we must say that whatever the piano lacks of the orchestra's rich colors, it was more than made up for by the composer's inspired interpretation. Only now could we see what a sketchy idea we got from these two masterpieces with the orchestra. Bartók's piano playing gave wings to the violinist as well. Székely played his incredibly difficult part even more surely than he did a few days ago with the orchestra. The other piece on the program was Ravel's already known new sonata. It is a shapely piece without much content. But it has more shape than absence of content, and therefore it gives pleasure, and especially when it is performed as perfectly as it was by Bartók and Székely.[14]

An intense period of musical activity followed Székely's return from Budapest. He turned his attention to Darius Milhaud's Violin Sonata (1917), the prominent new work to appear in his forthcoming recitals in Utrecht, Heemsted, Heerlen, and Turnhout. In March he went again to Italy to play in Florence, Rome, and Milan. In Florence he was assisted at the piano by Mario Castelnuovo-Tedesco in a recital at the British Institute. A few days later while enjoying their stay in Florence, the Székelys visited Carl Flesch, who was there to perform Brahms' Violin Concerto.

After a recital with Géza Frid at the Conservatorio Verdi in Milan, Székely met Leone Sinigaglia, the Milanese composer whose *Rapsodia piemontese* he had so often performed. Székely played for him the Violin Concerto, Op. 20, dedicated to Arrigo Serato, with which Sinigaglia had introduced himself as a composer in 1901. After their meeting, Sinigaglia inscribed Székely's score, "To the illustrious artist, Zoltán Székely. 4 April 1929."

In Rome Székely acquired a new violin that he had commissioned from Simone Sacconi. He had first heard about Sacconi in Germany, when he visited the workshop of Emil Herrmann and was told that Sacconi had made a fine cello for Gaspar Cassadó. Later in Rome Sacconi agreed to make a violin for Székely, to be ready for delivery during this spring visit.

Székely appeared in Rome with the Orchestra of the Accademia di Santa Cecilia, under Mario Rossi's direction. He performed Dvořák's

Violin Concerto and the world premiere of a new work written for him by Mario Castelnuovo-Tedesco, *Variazioni sinfoniche*, a set of variations for violin and orchestra which ended with a fox-trot variation. When the audience demanded an encore, a grand piano was brought on stage and Géza Frid accompanied Székely in Ravel's *Tzigane*. Székely chose that moment to put aside his Stradivarius and play the new Sacconi violin for the first time in public. Almost thirty years later in New York, he sold this violin to Sacconi's private collection, since the violin maker had no such example of his own work from the 1930s.

During the following days, Székely and Frid appeared twice more in Rome, once before the guests of the Légation Royale de Hongrie, and then before the students of the Accademia di Santa Cecilia. As he had done twice before, Székely appeared in a private recital for Benito Mussolini at his home on the Via Rasella on 24 February.

On this occasion Székely was joined by composer-pianist Alfredo Casella, whom he had first met at the Venice Festival in 1925. An important leader of the new-music movement in Italy, Casella enjoyed an international reputation in 1930 that was enhanced by his recent sharing with Bartók of the first prize in the Musical Fund Society of Philadelphia competition.

Casella was a prolific writer on music. He was editor of the journal *Ars Nova* and founder of the Società italiana di musica moderna (later known as the Corporazione delle Musiche Nuove, the Italian national section of the ISCM), an educational venture devoted to Italian musical culture.

For Mussolini's private recital, the artists performed works of Veracini, Hubay, Manén, Kreisler, and Friedrich Hermann, and the featured work of the evening, the Sonata in D Minor by Brahms.

Ten days later in London, the plan to perform Pál Hermann's *Grand Duo* came to fulfillment with a first performance of the new work in the Wigmore Hall. To open the program Székely and Hermann played their arrangement of four two-part Inventions by J. S. Bach, followed by a duo by Fiorillo, and Pál Hermann's new work. Ravel's Sonata for Violin and Cello came after the intermission, and the concert ended with Halvorsen's *Sarabande with Variations on a Theme by Handel*.

When Székely returned to Holland there was a letter from Bartók written 24 March 1930 explaining that Mr. Schamschula, who was to organize concerts for them in Prague and Brno, had not responded. Székely recalls:

Our concerts in Czechoslovakia did not materialize, but perhaps this was for the best since Bartók had already been ill for three weeks with a skin inflammation and was uncertain whether he could go to Berlin where he was to play with Szigeti.

He also wrote about the performance rights of the orchestral versions of the two rhapsodies, sole performance rights he had given to both me and Szigeti out of friendship.

He ended the letter speaking of his concern about a performance in Liège where the organization seemed unable to pay a conductor's fee. He was adamant that he would not pay such a fee on principle.[15]

Albert Van Raalte, then in charge of the Utrecht Orchestra, had proposed an all-Sinigaglia concert to be broadcast from Hilversum where he frequently led the radio orchestra. During the spring Székely prepared himself for the first performance in Holland of Sinigaglia's Violin Concerto, Op. 20. The broadcast concert took place as summer drew to its end. It began with Sinigaglia's best known work, the Overture to *Le Baruffe Chiozote*, Op. 32; the Violin Concerto followed, and the orchestral work, *Danze Piemontese*, Op. 31, brought the unique broadcast to a close.

Chapter Thirteen

From London to Warsaw

Bartók composed two new quartets during 1927–28. He completed the Third Quartet in Budapest during September of 1927. This followed his participation at the festivals in Frankfurt and in Baden-Baden during which time he had visited with his friends, the Székelys.

During 1928 Bartók entered the Third Quartet in an international competition sponsored by the Musical Fund Society of Philadelphia. Almost a year later, Bartók received news that the first prize, in the amount of six thousand dollars, had been divided equally between himself and Alfredo Casella, whose winning work was the Serenata for Clarinet, Bassoon, Trumpet, Violin, and Cello, composed in 1927 as Op. 47. The second prize was also divided. The English composer Harry Waldo Warner, violist of the London Quartet, shared it with Carlo Jachino, professor of the Conservatorio in Parma. Warner received the third prize as well.[1]

Bartók dedicated the Third Quartet to the Musical Fund Society of Philadelphia, who held the exclusive performing rights for three months after the prize was awarded. Following that period, the BBC mounted the broadcast performance premiere of the work in London on 12 February 1929 with the Vienna (Kolisch) Quartet.[2] On 19 February 1929 it was given its first public performance by the Wald-bauer Quartet at the Wigmore Hall in London, preceding by a few

weeks the first English performances of the rhapsodies given by Bartók and Székely at the Arts Theater Club in Great Newport Street.
With this February performance, the Waldbauer Quartet gained the
distinction of having given the public premieres of Bartók's first three
quartets. Two days later on 21 February, the Vienna Quartet performed the Third Quartet in Frankfurt within the framework of the
ISCM concert series.

Bartók began composing his Fourth Quartet in July of 1928 and
finished it in September, one year after completion of the Third Quartet. Bartók later dedicated this monumental Fourth Quartet to the
Belgian Pro Arte String Quartet; however, the venerable Waldbauer
Quartet played the first performance in Budapest on 20 March 1929,
only one month after their Wigmore Hall premiere of the Third Quartet. The Waldbauer Quartet had now given four first performances of
Bartók's quartets.[3] The occasion of this concert was a Bartók evening
at the academy which, in addition to the premiere, included performances of the Third Quartet, *Out of Doors* suite, the vocal solo version
of *Village Scenes* sung by Mária Basilides, and the first performance of
the cello version of the First Rhapsody played by Jenő Kerpely.[4]

The Belgian impresario, Gaston Verhuyck-Coulon, asked on 22
February 1929 that Bartók send the parts for the Third and Fourth
Quartets to the Pro Arte Quartet. They performed the Fourth Quartet
in Berlin early in October of 1929 and again on 21 October in Vienna,
then requested that Bartók dedicate the work to them, which he did.
János Kárpáti suggests that the international reputation of the Belgian Pro Arte Quartet and possibly Bartók's wish to seek a wider audience for the new work prompted this decision.[5]

Székely went again to London at the request of Lionel Powell
after playing several concerto engagements at the beginning of the
1930–31 season in Wiesbaden, Haarlem, Groningen, and Antwerp.
There he joined another tour of the International Celebrity Subscription Concerts, this time with Feodor Chaliapin.

The Székelys arrived in London a few days before the first concert
which was to be a special Sunday event on 23 November at the Royal
Albert Hall.

On 26 November I telephoned Bartók at the Hotel
Rubens. He was in London to play his early work, the Rhapsody, Op. 1. I told him that I was in London to begin a tour
with Chaliapin, that Ivor Newton was the pianist, and we

would play a sonata by Porpora and Ravel's *Tzigane* on Sunday at the Royal Albert Hall.

After Bartók's concert Mientje and I met him and the conductor Jenő Szenkár who had directed the 1926 world premiere of *The Miraculous Mandarin* in Cologne. This was at a reception in South Kensington at the home of Bartók's friend, Duncan Wilson.

Székely's tour with Feodor Chaliapin began and ended in London. It took the artists to Manchester, Hull, Bournemouth, Edinburgh, Glasgow, Inverness, Bristol, and Brighton, concluding with a BBC broadcast on 14 December. At the time of his appearances with Székely for Powell's subscription concerts, the famous Russian *basso* was living in Paris. Considered one of the greatest singing actors, Chaliapin immortalized the role of Boris Godunov in Mussorgsky's opera. He had first appeared in London in 1913 in Thomas Beecham's seasons of Russian opera at Covent Garden and remained extremely popular with the English audiences throughout his career.

Canadian pianist Gerald Moore, who was Chaliapin's accompanist on one of Powell's earlier Celebrity tours, has related that instead of programs, concert booklets containing the numbered translations of many works which might or might not be sung at each appearance were sold at the Chaliapin concerts.[6] Chaliapin boldly announced from the stage the work to be sung next by calling out the appropriate number in the booklet. While it seemed to the audience that the *basso* improvised these choices from an enormous list, he most often selected the same works during each new concert!

During the tour in 1930 Chaliapin often stood backstage to listen to Székely's violin playing and seemed always to enjoy hearing him play Ravel's *Tzigane*.

After our concert in Hull, Mientje and I watched Chaliapin draw a remarkably good caricature of himself, a sort of self portrait which he then gave to me as a souvenir. [Plate 45] A week later in Glasgow when we returned to the Central Hotel after the concert, we were greeted by Chaliapin. He had arranged a birthday party that evening to celebrate my turning twenty-seven. During the party Ivor Newton sat with us while everyone came by and signed a postcard which we sent to Mientje's mother in Holland.

In late December Pál Hermann returned to Holland to join Székely in a recital at the Amsterdam Concertgebouw. During his visit a
new idea was born. Why not create a new ensemble to play piano
trios? With the decision made, they asked the Hungarian pianist
Louis Kentner, then living in London, to join them in the venture.
Together in Nijmegen, the trio prepared a concert of modern works,
including Ernest Bloch's Three Nocturnes and Ravel's Piano Trio. The
Székely Trio, as the new ensemble was called, appeared several times
in successful concerts in Amsterdam, Vlissingen, and Hilversum, and
in London on 19 February 1931.

Later that spring, after many concerts in Holland, Székely met
Hermann in Frankfurt for a radio broadcast of a duo recital, then
went to Wiesbaden, Frankfurt, and Warsaw to play Brahms' Violin
Concerto.

Mientje and I spent some time living in Wiesbaden during this period, and I often played tennis at a club there; one
of my occasional partners was the wife of the mayor. Eventually she insisted that she and her husband, who were
friends of the conductor Carl Schuricht, suggest to Schuricht
that I play with the Städtisches Kurorchester of which he was
the music director.

This I did on on 15 May 1931. Schuricht conducted a
performance of Hans Fleischer's Fourth Symphony, then I
performed Brahms' Violin Concerto, Ravel's *Tzigane*, and
Sinigaglia's *Rapsodia piemontese*. A few days later Schuricht
conducted the Brahms concerto for me in Frankfurt.

In Warsaw I played the Brahms concerto again, this time
with the Warsaw Philharmonic conducted by Gregor Fitelberg. He was the father of Jerzy Fitelberg, the talented composer. While in Warsaw I also played a recital with Géza Frid
and gave a radio broadcast on which I played Hindemith's
Solo Sonata. I saw Karol Szymanovsky in Warsaw, and we
had a good visit.

To finish the season in late May, Székely and Frid played a recital
in Aerdenhout near Haarlem. The program included a group of dance
works. After the music of Veracini, Bach, and Ravel, they performed
Székely's transcription of Bartók's *Rumanian Folk Dances*, Joachín
Nin's *Suite espagnole*, and Sinigaglia's *Rapsodia piemontese*.

Székely devoted the summer of 1931 to the concertos of Beethoven, Brahms, and Mendelssohn. On 7 July he joined Albert van

Raalte and the Amsterdam Concertgebouw Orchestra for a performance of the Beethoven Violin Concerto in an all-Beethoven concert. On 3 August he played the Brahms Violin Concerto at the
Kurhaus in Scheveningen with The Hague's Residentie Orchestra.
Again Van Raalte conducted. Commenting on Székely's performance, the critic of *De Avond Post* wrote, " He has a pure feeling for
style and a perfect technique, and this puts his music making above
the material world."[7] This concert was repeated one week later in a
radio broadcast of the Residentie Orchestra. By now, Van Raalte had
become a prominent figure at Algemeene Vereeniging Radio Om-
roep, or AVRO, an important Dutch broadcasting system. There he
would eventually build the radio orchestra, the Omroeporkest, into
a highly accomplished ensemble.

Meanwhile summer drew to a close, and Székely returned to London. It had been eight years since he first played for Sir Henry Wood;
now on 6 September 1931, matured by years of performances
throughout Europe, the violinist appeared in the Promenade Concerts at Queen's Hall. Sir Henry conducted the performance of Mendelssohn's Violin Concerto with the BBC Symphony. It was an
evening with many soloists including Evelyn Scotney, Székely's colleague from the Celebrity Concert tours, singing the "Bell Song" from
Delibes' *Lakmé*, organist Berkely Mason playing Boëllmann's *Fan-
taisie dialoguée*, and the French composer Francis Poulenc performing
as soloist in his *Aubade* for piano and eighteen instruments.

Following his success with the "Blues" from Ravel's Violin
Sonata, Székely's interest turned toward new genre pieces that uti-
lized the jazz element: Louis Gruenberg's *Jazzette*, George Gershwin's
Short Story, and Aaron Copland's *Ukelele Serenade*. On 8 November
1932 in the Kleine Zaal of the Amsterdam Concertgebouw, he and
Frid performed a program of considerable novelty, contrasting the
music of Veracini, Viotti, and Sinigaglia with the Milhaud sonata and
the jazz group.

In mid-December, Székely received a letter from Bartók in Vienna
with the good news that he would be coming for a visit in February,
since his management had not completely filled his itinerary with
engagements.

> Bartók told me that he had completed a new piano con-
> certo by disconnecting himself from all economic problems
> and working for a few weeks in enforced peace. Later he men-
> tioned that his Sonatina for Piano was just published in

a transcription for violin and piano. At the beginning of summer he had written forty-four little duos for two violins similar to *For Children*. He brought these duos with him to Nijmegen.

He was desperate to rent a different house in which to live in Budapest and wrote, "We are swamped by problems not the least of which is finding a new home (for May). . . . If we cannot find one I don't know what will happen for I vowed I'd rather be hanged than live in the same house with strangers. (My neighbors bought a radio last year, a piano this year! The latter was positioned so that it manages to pollute all of our rooms. There are days when one hears fifty times the charming melody of [a silly song]). . . ."[8]

It is now widely known that Bartók had financial difficulties throughout his career, although he was an extraordinarily thrifty person, at times even frugal perhaps. The salaries paid by the Hungarian Academy of Sciences were never really sufficient for the professors posted there. For that reason they were required to teach privately or else play concerts in order to make money on the side. Salaries were very poor in those days. Today better salaries are negotiated by staff associations and the like at all academic institutions, something unheard of at that time. One was caught up in a highly bureaucratic system and simply categorized. Even as an artist one was classified that way.

Besides being inadequately paid, he and his wife were periodically plagued with sickness which made it impossible for them to work. On top of all that, his scientific projects, that is, his investigations into folklore, were financed out of his own pocket. This work he always did completely on his own without support of any kind.

For these reasons, he was often forced to accept concert tours which really did not appeal to him. And he no longer enjoyed teaching. He would have preferred only to compose and continue his research. Later in America the situation was even worse. Had he been in a position to accept a staff position in Seattle and proceed with his research as he had hoped, his last years would probably have been very pleasant.

Bartók wrote on 29 December 1931 wishing us a happy new year and telling me that he would play his new concerto in Paris on 21 February 1932. He would thus be able to arrive in Nijmegen on the morning of 22 February to stay for five days, leaving by the Hook of Holland, the place from which the boats sail for Harwich, to London and on to Glasgow for a recital on 28 February.[9]

Bartók was our guest at Mientje's mother's villa at 275 Kwakkenbergweg on the outskirts of Nijmegen. A funny little episode which shows Bartók's thoroughness occurred during the first evening of this visit when he came into the living room with his *44 Duos for Two Violins*—primarily an educational work, but one full of artistic beauty. This work was not composed in one short period, but over a length of time. Now it was finished and he wanted to submit it to his editor. Helping him with the sorting, I was puzzled about the order in which to put the first five pieces intended for beginners because they had to be organized in the correct sequence from the easiest to the most difficult.

As I thought about this, Bartók interrupted me suddenly and with twinkling eyes made me the following proposition: "I have an idea," he said. "Let us pretend we are two beginners! Hand me a violin and I assure you that I will sound like a beginner. But you, a professional, have to take a handicap which should put your violin playing back to the stage of a child. Let us play the first five duos, but we will make a slight adjustment. Why don't you reverse your bow and violin. Hold your violin with your right hand and bow it with your left. That little trick may put us on even terms."

Now this is a remarkable feeling if you have never done it before, but somehow you still have the reflex and some feeling for playing. We played the duos in this way and succeeded in finding the correct sequence.

Before his visit Bartók had worked on some French translations on his way to Paris, Edgar Varèse had checked them over in Paris, and Mientje typed them for him in Nijmegen so he could send them off. He had a good rest with us and liked this house in its nice, quiet neighborhood. He went for long walks on the hilly, forested area nearby.[10]

After Bartók's visit and a recital in Venlo, I played two concerts at the Concertgebouw for the concert organization called Kunst Voor Allen (Art for All) and Pál Hermann joined me on the second one, which was a program devoted to the music of Debussy and Ravel. With Géza Frid I played the Debussy Sonata for Violin and Piano; then Pál and Géza played Debussy's Cello Sonata. Before the intermission Pál and I played Ravel's Sonata for Violin and Cello, and I ended the evening with *Tzigane*.

During this time I was preparing the Concerto for Violin and Chamber Orchestra (1928) by the Dutch composer Guillaume Landré who was the son of a another Dutch musician, Willem Landré. Guillaume Landré was a pupil of Willem Pijper and had also studied law in Utrecht.

This work is a bit unusual in some respects. The chamber orchestra accompaniment is without violins, and the first two movements are connected. The cadenza is accompanied by the double basses and percussion and the finale, Presto, is a kind of perpetual motion.

Pierre Monteux, a guest conductor in Amsterdam since 1925, conducted the Amsterdam Concertgebouw in that first performance of the Landré concerto on 24 January 1932. At the dress rehearsal he became anxious because he was afraid that I might miss an entrance in this quick movement. He said, "It will be all right if we just come out together in the finale." Fortunately, it was all right. This was the concert when I also played Bartók's Second Rhapsody with orchestra for the first time in Holland.

As one Amsterdam critic wrote, "We can say now that in our country it is possible to play modern, difficult pieces and still be appreciated, but Dutch instrumentalists will have to remember that they learned this lesson from a stranger, the Hungarian violinist Zoltán Székely, who didn't make it easy for himself nor for the audience or Monteux and the orchestra."[11]

That the Bartók Second Rhapsody was inspired to the last note was the perception of the critic of the *Maasbode*. The endlessly variable folk music that generated the work seemed to be just waiting for the genie's touch. In this case, Bartók was the genie who had shaped the new work in an authentic folkloric tradition, inspired by the ancient beginnings of a national consciousness.[12]

Willem Pijper, in 1931 the president of the Dutch National Section of the ISCM, had composed an unaccompanied violin work and he brought it to Székely in Nijmegen. Székely studied it, then played it for him, and the composer dedicated this Sonata for Violin Solo to him. Székely performed Pijper's new work at two ISCM concerts in Amsterdam in March of 1932.

Pál Hermann came for those ISCM concerts and on 22 March we played in Amsterdam for the organization Kunst

Voor Allen. The next day the recital was repeated in the Amsterdam Conservatory. We played Kodály's Duo for Violin and Cello and the first performance in Holland of Ernst Toch's Divertimento. Pál performed a new unaccompanied work by Bertus van Lier, a pupil of Pijper in Amsterdam and later a conductor, composer, and music critic in Utrecht. On those programs I performed Pijper's new Solo Sonata, and we ended the concerts with the duo version of Bartók's *Rumanian Folk Dances*.

In Rotterdam the conductor Eduard Flipse was a sort of pioneer for new works. Notwithstanding his weak orchestra, he did what he could to promote new literature. In December 1932 he asked me to perform again the new Violin Concerto by Landré that I had played in Amsterdam with Monteux. He also programmed a work by the father, Willem Landré, called *In Memoriam Matris*. In that concert I also played the Mendelssohn concerto.

Nine days later I played the Landré concerto for the third time, on that occasion with the Utrecht Orchestra directed by Henri van Goudoever. I also played Mozart's Concerto in A Major with my own cadenzas.

Pál Hermann and I met in Winterthur, Switzerland, in January to perform a duo recital for the Musikkollegium Winterthur. In addition to Kodály's duo and Bartók's *Rumanian Folk Dances*, we played two transcriptions: four two-part Inventions by Bach and Mozart's Duo, K. 423, originally composed for violin and viola.

Later that month, Géza Frid and I went to Paris to take part in a concert of contemporary music for the series, "Triton," at the École Normale de Musique on rue Cardinet. We played the first Paris performance of Bartók's Second Rhapsody that evening. In addition, I opened the concert with another first performance in Paris, Bohuslav Martinů's new Second Sonata, with Martinů at the piano.

In the 1930s a violin collector in Amsterdam died, and his collection came up for sale. Székely found a Petrus Guarnerius violin in that collection, a rather big model, played on it, and bought it. At the same time Max Möller, the famous Dutch dealer, purchased another Petrus Guarnerius from that collection which later proved to be a violin by Carlo Tononi. Since Székely was not entirely satisfied with the violin he had bought, Möller said he was willing to exchange violins with him, but that he must pay an additional amount. The exchange was made, and from 1933 Székely owned the wonderful Venetian violin by Carlo Tononi.

Even the greatest experts are a little bit hesitant to identify these instruments of the Venetian school by a group of makers who all worked in Venice at the same time: Petrus Guarnerius, Sanctus Seraphin, Gobetti, Montagnana, and Tononi. My Carlo Tononi violin was made in 1730 and in size and quality of tone is very similar to my Strad although its tone lacks the sweetness of that instrument and has a different character. During my career I did not play often on the Tononi violin, only during a period of a few months when my Strad was in the shop of Pierre Vidoudez in Switzerland; but it is one of the most beautiful Venetian violins I have ever seen.

About this time, Bartók had proposed that we play a concert in Glasgow; however, he wrote from Budapest on 20 October 1933 to say, "Unfortunately it seems that even £10 is too much for the Scots so Glasgow is out." He spoke of Eric Chisholm, the pianist in whose home he usually stayed in Glasgow. Chisholm had sent his regards to me. He was the president of Glasgow's Active Society for the Propagation of Contemporary Music. Now Bartók wondered if a concert Mientje and I were negotiating in Budapest would come about.[13]

I wrote to him in London, and he replied on 8 November to tell me that Eric Chisholm could do nothing about concert arrangements in either Glasgow or Edinburgh and to tell me that he was sorry our Budapest concert would not materialize.[14]

In the meantime I went to England to play in October. In London there was to be a meeting with the most important leaders in 1933 at the round-table talks of the Commonwealth Economic Conference. For this occasion the British government requested a concert from me. Sir Akbar Hydari, the prime minister of Hyderabad,[15] then a state in India, was so interested in the recital that he invited me to a personal meeting at the Hyde Park Hotel where he and his party were staying.

I received this message when I was playing a tennis game and didn't really understand it too clearly, so unfortunately I appeared before my hosts in my tennis clothes. After I offered my apology they made me feel very comfortable. What is more, when they saw that I liked tennis they gave us free tickets to Wimbeldon. On that occasion Mientje got no fewer than twenty-one arm bracelets as gifts from Sir Akbar's royal party.

While still in England on 25 October 1933, I gave a recital with pianist William Probert-Jones at the Kendrick School in Reading. The principal work on that program was Willem Pijper's new Solo Sonata that I had played recently in Amsterdam. The school was damp and chilly, and I caught a cold. Perhaps it was at this time that a more serious illness had a chance to develop.

When I returned to Holland I played a recital with Géza Frid, and ten days later I appeared with the Arnhem Orchestra with Martin Spanjaard conducting for me for the last time. I played Viotti's Concerto No. 22 and Ravel's *Tzigane*. Spanjaard soon retired from his position and shortly afterward commited suicide.

Two works I did not study as a student were Bruch's Concerto in G Minor and Lalo's *Symphonie espagnole*, but I began preparing them both at this time because I was engaged to appear with the orchestra at Liège, where François Rasse was the conductor. Rasse had conducted the Brahms concerto for me at Ostende and now made this new invitation. Unfortunately this engagement in Liège had to be canceled because by now I was very ill.

We went first to a good neighbor who happened to be a doctor, and perhaps this was an error because he did not realize the full extent of my illness. It was only later that another doctor diagnosed pleurisy. These days pleurisy is not so serious an illness as it once was before the discovery of antibiotics. When my father learned of the advanced stage of my illness, he thought it might take me a full ten years to completely recover. I was fortunate in that it only lasted about nine months, but that year, when I was thirty years old, the concert season was lost to this illness.

The Kolisch String Quartet appeared in the Kleine Zaal at the Amsterdam Concertgebouw on 10 February 1934, performing Beethoven's Op. 18, No. 3, Bartók's Third Quartet, and Schubert's quartet, Op. 161. They played the concert from memory as they always did. This tradition had been established at the suggestion of Arnold Schoenberg in 1927 when they were with him in Vienna to celebrate his fifty-third birthday. Before dinner they had played his yet-un-performed First and Third Quartets for the guests. After dinner when the composer requested more music, they were at a loss since they had brought no other scores. However, since they had used the Finale of Beethoven's Quartet Op. 59, No. 3, as an étude at the start of each rehearsal and knew it from memory, they played it by heart to end the birthday party. Schoenberg was excited by this performance and encouraged them to perform from memory in the future, so they began to gradually commit their entire repertoire to memory.[16]

After their Amsterdam concert the Kolisch Quartet visited the Székelys in Nijmegen. They were among the last artists to visit them there, since during his illness Zoltán and Mientje had decided to live on their own.

> Mientje and I decided to have a new home built by the young Dutch architect, Gerrit Rietveld.[17] For several years we had lived only three months of each year in Holland and always in Anna Everts' home on Kwakkenbergweg in Nijmegen, but in 1935 we decided to move to Bloemendaal where Rietveld had found a perfect location for our new home near Santpoort Station.
>
> Bloemendaal is a garden suburb thirteen kilometers west of Haarlem. It was a nice place for Amsterdamers and a lot of them lived there. Near Bloemendaal there was an open-air theater, a miniature lake, botanical gardens, and an aviary. The town spreads out to reach the community of Aerdenhout. It is only ten minutes from the dunes and the sea.
>
> Rietveld had just started his career as an architect and was happy to build our new house, which we symbolically named "The Rhapsody." The house was totally unconventional and built in the functional manner. Everything was electrical, which was not yet the usual thing in Holland, so again this made life easy and gave us a sense of well-being. Although it was a large house, it had an intimate feeling. The main floor was devoted to the living room and studio and was adaptable to chamber music concerts.
>
> While riding on a bus in Budapest, Bartók wrote me on 10 January 1935 concerning a radio concert in Hilversum.[18] A few days later he wrote again to explain the details of how he and Ditta would travel to Holland. They would be our first house guests at The Rhapsody, where he and I would practice at our leisure.[19]

When they arrived, we presented a radio broadcast from Hilversum and played two concerts. The Dutch Section of ISCM had a Bartók evening at the Concertgebouw during which he played his Piano Sonata. Together we played the First Violin Sonata, and the rest was devoted to his songs sung by Bertha Seroen. The other concert was in Rotterdam.

During our days together at The Rhapsody we four must have toasted each other with wine glasses and decided to address each other in the familiar form, since in all the correspondence that came later we addressed each other in that way.

Mientje had prepared a guest book for our new house, and the first to sign it was Bartók when he wrote in Hungarian during this visit to our new home: "Wishing the guest-loving inhabitants of The Rhapsody wine, wheat, peace (and other good things) by its first house-guests, the Bartóks. Santpoort, January 26, 1935."[20]

Chapter Fourteen

The Bartóks in Santpoort

Mientje had a vivid memory of the Bartóks' first visit to The Rhapsody, and she saved several hard-won newspaper stories in her journal. She begins:

> The Bartóks arrived on a Friday, and the next morning began a nice weekend. We were just in the breakfast room, and everything was pleasant with Bartók well rested when suddenly a taxi stopped outside. A young man got out and rang our bell. At once I recognized him as a critic. I wondered what would happen next because Bartók had said he wanted peace and quiet. I thought immediately that if I send this young man away he will be offended, but Bartók said, "I don't want to see anybody!" I replied, "Béla, Zoltán can't tell you, but your music is for me, for the audience, for everyone . . . difficult. This young man has sacrificed his free weekend, paid a lot of money for a taxi from Amsterdam, and if he weren't really interested in helping with the concert, he would not do that." Then Bartók said, "Well, you have a point. Let him come in for ten minutes."

The young critic stayed at The Rhapsody for two hours or so. The article he wrote, entitled "Béla Bartók Speaks: The fable of the faggot," appeared in *Algemeen Handelsblad* on 29 January 1935:

A very creative artist whose work you have known for several years, and admire, but whom you have never met in person suddenly sits very much alive in front of you. This is always a very special sensation. This feeling came over me as I met Béla Bartók in the music room of the violinist, Zoltán Székely, in the beautiful modern villa, Rhapsody, in Santpoort.

The environment was as pleasant as imaginable. The circle was formed by the host and hostess, the composer, his charming young wife who is accompanying her famous husband for the first time abroad, and the writer of this review.

. . . The conversation went in three languages mixed together and in this pleasant atmosphere of a Dutch tea party with Hungarian pastries and the attention of Mrs. Bartók in a nicely lighted music studio, it was not difficult at all.

Between the conversations about other subjects it was possible also to exchange views with the great artist about his work. The conversation was interrupted several times by telephone calls. The material of Bartók's Second Piano Concerto composed in 1932, which he will perform Saturday with the Philharmonic Orchestra of Rotterdam, Eduard Flipse conducting, has not arrived and this upsets the composer somewhat, but soon came the news that the music had arrived in Amsterdam. Less fortunate fared the music for the choir so that this music had to be omitted from the program of the International Society of Contemporary Music.

What remains is very interesting. Bartók's music of genius is still too little known, and it is an important fact that the two concerts this week will fill up the hall. This evening one will hear Bartók and his friend, Zoltán Székely, and the Bartók First Violin Sonata. The Second Sonata was performed here twelve years ago. The program in Rotterdam contains the Piano Concerto and the First Suite, Opus 3, so one will be able to compare a work from Bartók's early period with one of later date. The Hungarian violinist, Zoltán Székely, who after many tours throughout the world settled down in Santpoort, has been since his youth an ardent collaborator with his older compatriot, Bartók, although his violin teacher, Hubay, did not agree with his preference.

The twosome introduced in Amsterdam in April 1923 Bartók's Second Violin Sonata although Székely was not feeling well at that time. In the period in between, Bartók performed little in Holland, and is, therefore, less known here than Ravel or Stravinsky. We hope that the concert this week will change the situation. It is highly important for the Dutch audience to get to know a personality such as this Hungarian who is important not only as a pianist and composer, but also as a collector and arranger of old folk songs.

We talked at length with the musician about this subject, and foregoing his proverbial reserve, he gave us his very interesting explanation.

Publication of Hungarian Folk Songs

It is well known that Béla Bartók, along with Zoltán Kodály, has for many years gathered and transcribed folk songs and peasant dances of his homeland and of other countries. We knew that this very substantial material has been recorded and that these musicians have used many folk songs in their compositions, but we did not know what happened to the bulk of the collection. Bartók has explained that to us. He told us that the material he gathered has been kept several years in manuscript form until at last the Hungarian Academy of Science has initiated a complete publication.

This is being done under the supervision of Bartók and Kodály, and will contain several volumes. About twelve thousand Hungarian songs have been classified, arranged scientifically, organized, and noted down. Talking about this work that comprises an important part of his life work, Bartók became more and more animated. He explained that collectors especially wanted to examine the social function of the folk song which in its origin was an obligatory part of all kinds of festive and sacramental ceremonies.

For this work, one needs to be not only a good musician but also a philosopher, a sociologist, and a choreographer. It is of course impossible to combine all those functions within one person, but one does, as Bartók mentions, what one can. "As far as the musical side is concerned, we can guarantee the genuineness of our work completely. We naturally give the melodies only in the original form, without artistic additions or accompaniments and with the nearly overwhelming amount of material arranged in a clear way, not according to the text, but according to the characteristic peculiarities of the melodies and groups of melodies. This is so that everyone who knows the system can look at the melodic groups as though they were in an etymological dictionary."

Continuing this subject that was so dear to him and near to his heart, the musician informed us of many interesting details about the folk songs. He showed us some smaller publications, brochures with music illustrations, which he has edited before the copious edition was started. Six or seven hundred songs and instrumental melodies from Hungary and other countries have already been edited, explored, and compared.

He pointed out the remarkable similarity of the music of the Hungarians with that of the Russian tribes. He told interesting things about the instruments on which they were played. He also spoke with great appreciation of similar work done in other countries and for which, for instance, in the Rumanian world of art, ample funding is made available. In Bucharest, the musicologist Constantine Brailoiu works in this domain on a large scale and the gramophone company records many folk songs which have a high instructional and documentary value.

With all this interesting news, we nearly missed asking about Bartók's composing. As we asked him, he told us that he not long ago finished a new string quartet, and it will be premiered in Washington. Bartók plays regularly for the radio in Budapest, especially as an interpreter of 18th-century music, for instance Scarlatti. He has arranged these works for piano very modestly, only by writing double octaves which on the harpsichord are produced by registration. He also has great interest in performing pre-classical music on the piano.

Next week Bartók will give a piano recital for the radio and the Saturday concert will also be broadcast. He is astonished about our small country having so many different radio stations. "Don't they know the fable of the faggot?" asked Bartók, and then he told us this instructive fable that follows here as a clever lesson.

A father calls his sons together and gives them a bunch of branches and orders them to break them. One after the other tries it, but without success. Then the father takes the bunch apart and gives every son a branch which now is broken without effort.

The moral of that, it is hoped, will penetrate to the Dutch radio world. Lessons given by a man such as Béla Bartók are really worth consideration.[1]

"The next day, Sunday, a man from *De Telegraaf* came," Mientje recalled.

> He knocked on the door and the windows and waved at Zoltán, and I worried what would happen now, as I said, "Béla, there is another one."
>
> "I won't see anyone," was his response. "But these two newspapers are such competitors that this one will, of course, write down not very pleasant things about your music, and we are so happy that they are interested, at least." Then he said, "I don't want to see him," but by then the door flew open from the big music room, the man stood there with a notebook and pencil and said, "Maestro, how are you?"
>
> Bartók looked at him and said, "Very well, come in," and we all laughed a bit crazily at the odd circumstance.

The critic from *De Telegraaf* wrote an article entitled "With Béla Bartók in Santpoort." It was published the next day in Amsterdam:

> The great Hungarian composer and pianist, who is in our country, has worked in folklore, and is a master of contemporary music. We found Bartók totally at ease, deeply sunken in an easy chair, in the ultramodern house where his friend Zoltán Székely, already many years in our country, lives.
>
> It would be hard to imagine more interesting or more beautiful surroundings as backdrop to the highly interesting personality of Bartók. In the great space where he is seated, his small delicate frame is remarkable in the sea of light that comes through the large front windows from the garden. His silver-white hair seems even whiter and his dark eyes ever brighter. His whole personality has something heroic, something that is hard to define but that impresses you and makes you think this is a personality of importance, a person one meets very rarely. A master.
>
> Shy, discreet, even introverted is his attitude in the first minutes that follow; Bartók does not like to be treated as a celebrity, to be honored as the center of attention. Only after Székely joins in the conversation as his host and has the attention for awhile does one observe that Bartók, after all, is not so unreachable as his reputation suggests.
>
> Slowly, but surely, he unwinds. He tells us how he is pleased to be in Holland again. He inquires about friends

which he made before. "What was the name again," he asked, "of the man who absolutely wanted to have my *Allegro Africaine*?" "Very likely it was a jazz fan who hoped to find real negro rhythms," answers his host, who has also forgotten his name. And if he understood our astonishment about these words, Bartók knew immediately the good man meant his piece, *Allegro barbaro*.

As the ice was broken, the pressure was off, and musical expressions were used. The word "rhythm" came up and Bartók has great interest in things concerning rhythm. He tells us that in Hungary, Rumania,and Bulgaria, for example, one can hear dance tunes and folk songs whose rhythm is a constant source of study, rhythms which inspire the composer and practically force him to use them. All of the current Hungarian music is more or less under the influence of this folk music which is the life of the people.

"You will find this with the young people," he says, then his personality becomes very lively. His eyes are shining and his whole personality has something untamable about it. He takes an envelope which lies at hand before him, improvises a staff on it, and writes notes. "Look here," he says, "for normal, ordinary professional musicians who are not accustomed to this, this brings great difficulties, but these difficulties are there to be conquered."

These strange, rhythmic melodies constitute one of the reasons, according to the opinion of the Master, that the young generation of composers in Hungary makes more music and experiments less than that in countries such as Austria and Czechoslovakia. "There was a time," he says, "that the direction seemed to be absolutely the atonality of the Austrians. Theoretically, it is considered possible, but the consequence is doubtful. I myself never worked this way, and very likely you won't find anybody who does it this way in Hungary. Our folklore sources are still prolific. One speaks sometimes about very complicated jazz rhythms, but can you imagine them compared in the near future with this?" he asked, pointing to his scribbles.

As the Master likes to talk about his native country, we continue in this direction, and we inquire about Hungarian concert life and speak of all the empty halls in Hungary. It seems that there is an overflow of performances and many empty halls, and the public is also making it difficult for young composers. Bartók thinks that in a way this is logical and even necessary. Composers have always had difficulties convincing their contemporaries, and the difficulties they encounter have always born fruit.

Then we come back to Holland. Our people have a special place in the Hungarian hearts. We talk about artistic life here and the new Dutch music. "We know little about this," says the Master. "I heard names from my compatriot, [Pál] Kadosa, whose Piano Concerto was performed in 1933 at the Music Festival of the International Society of Contemporary Music in Amsterdam. But what is in a name? Your young people also certainly have difficulties as everywhere else and, of course, they like to send their manuscripts across the borders."

After a moment of silence, something of his reticence comes back, and in the end he asks what sense it makes to talk so much about music. "One should listen to music and in fact I'm only here to make music and not to talk. I am playing Tuesday for the International Society of Contemporary Music in the chamber music hall of the Concertgebouw, and it gives me pleasure to work together again with my friend, Székely. Twelve years ago, we played my Second Violin Sonata in that same hall and now we will play my First Sonata. Coincidentally on that concert all those years ago, Zoltán was ill, and now we perform for the first time after another extended illness.

"I am going to rehearse this afternoon with Mrs. Bertha Soroen who will sing a series of folk songs arranged by me, and on Tuesday I am going to Rotterdam where I will play my Second Piano Concerto with the Philharmonic Orchestra of Rotterdam with Eduard Flipse, the conductor who was the person who engaged me for this. It is due to the initiative of Eduard Flipse that I am here."

Hereafter we felt the conversation ended. We heard no more about music or concerts. Totally absorbed in his own thoughts, the Master sat down at the grand piano and began to practice. As I left the house, I saw his silver-white hair, like the snow outside, about the lightly silhouetted forehead. Dutch music lovers may expect a few very important musical happenings if the signs don't lie.[2]

"During this visit there was an exceptional concert with the Rotterdam Philharmonic," Mientje recalled:

Since the conductor Eduard Flipse could not entirely carry out his planned program, Béla and Zoltán played the First Violin Sonata in the concert. We went by car from our house to Rotterdam for the rehearsal, and Béla was so excited to go to the dunes since he was a true nature lover and wanted to see them. Even though he had a rehearsal he wanted to stop, then stepped out of the car and just started a little walk around. He was so impressed by the dunes and the sea that he seemed to forget all about his rehearsal and I had to remind him that we must be on our way to Rotterdam.

When we arrived at the rehearsal the orchestra was playing his First Suite, Op. 3, and sounded so poor and weak that I saw his face stiffen. It was not the Amsterdam Concertgebouw nor The Hague; it was just Rotterdam and the music was much too difficult. Suddenly Béla was at the point of leaving the rehearsal. "It is impossible," he said. Then since Zoltán couldn't speak so bluntly, I said, "Béla, the Concertgebouw doesn't even try it. The Hague doesn't even look at you, and now this small orchestra. . . . Flipse has worked hard to get this orchestra to play your difficult work and just now you can't wish more. He is very smart and I am sure it will be better if you tell him what you want." He looked at me as if I had said something terrible, but he walked right up to Flipse and started talking to him.

We were there for many hours, and in the end it all went quite well. I spoke out this way because I was young and because I felt sorry for the conductor and I knew the circumstances. To take that from me, Bartók was unselfish and kind. He did stand there for hours trying to explain what to do and in this episode he was great. On that concert he played the Second Piano Concerto . . . and the First Sonata with Zoltán.

If I remember well, after the concert he said, "I have the feeling that I deserve something," so we went down to the bar. Probably we ate there because there was no other place to eat, and there was a Rumanian gypsy playing the violin. He enjoyed that so much. He got so excited that he went to the man and talked to him about music. He asked him about the rhythm and the *glissandi* that he made since he liked that so much. I still remember his joy when he ran to that man.

From Santpoort Bartók went to Switzerland. Ditta stayed a day longer at The Rhapsody before returning to Budapest. On 4 February Bartók wrote from Basel:

> I arrived here without any problems, only in the early morning a wild Teutonic herd besieged the train, loaded with knapsacks and skis (being Sunday), took all available space, spoiled the air for a half hour, then got off.—Was Ditta able to leave on Sunday morning? I thought of her all day, how she traveled, were there any problems.

Bartók was concerned about his wife and her journey home to Hungary since this was her first time abroad. In Basel the orchestra's conductor Paul Sacher was away on vacation, so there were guest conductors and only brief rehearsal times. Now he had an invitation that concerned him.

> The Berlin Philharmonic invited me on a very short notice either to conduct or as soloist. Naturally I have no intention to respond to such hurried notices. . . .[3]

Sometime after this visit, Bartók's request to be relieved of his piano-teaching duties at the Franz Liszt Academy was approved. By an almost unanimous vote on 16 May 1935, Bartók was elected to membership in the Hungarian Academy of Sciences as a corresponding member, along with a number of eminent medical scientists. His letter expressing gratitude for his election is now exhibited in the Manuscript Archive's display room of the Academy of Sciences.[4]

This was the first official honor he received in his own country although he had been made a Chevalier of the French Legion of Honor five years earlier. From 1935 until his departure for the United States, Bartók spent his working life dealing with the collection of folk music that had accumulated there, devoting himself almost exclusively to his ethnomusicological research.

Four days after his election to the Academy of Sciences, Bartók wrote the Székelys the good news:

> A few days ago the Hungarian Academy of Sciences elected me a "correspondent" (this is the first level of membership), but Kodály was not elected which was rather clumsy if they wanted something of this sort: the reason seems to be that it would be too much for them to admit two musicians at the same time. Why they chose me first I don't know, probably because I am the older one.

So one is exposed to such events; however, we both escaped the Kisfaludy[5] circle. . . .[6]

Recovering from his long illness with pleurisy, Székely began again to play recitals in Holland in the fall of 1935.

I appeared with Géza Frid in Veendam, Leeuwarden, and Haarlem in recitals which featured the Sonata in D Minor of Brahms and other works which we had played frequently over the previous decade.

My parents arrived from Hungary on 4 December 1935 for their first visit to our new home. By coincidence they had been on the same train as Bartók from Budapest to Vienna, had visited with him and shared a turkey leg, and had even brought a letter from him which they delivered to me by hand.[7] He was on a tour which would take him to London where after some years' absence he performed his piano concerto at Queen's Hall. After a month's visit, my parents returned to Hungary on 2 January, and we awaited Bartók who planned to visit us the following week.

Having played the previous night in London, Bartók wrote a postcard to his mother on 8 January while flying—for the only time in his life—aboard a KLM Fokker XXII to reach Holland in time for his concert in Utrecht.[8] He found the experience wonderful although he had been a little frightened by his first takeoff, and admired the vista of an endless field of clouds and glorious sunshine.[9]

"Bartók had an engagement in Utrecht," Mientje recalled:

Zoltán and I went with Géza Frid to hear the concert. Zoltán even turned the pages. Afterward we all went to supper in Amsterdam with Mrs. Révész, then Béla came to The Rhapsody for a few days.

At The Rhapsody he stayed in our guest room. He often came downstairs to the studio and always brought with him the new things to show. Once he and Zoltán rehearsed together and I was busy in the kitchen or somewhere when he said, "You must come in." He began to play a certain passage with a difficult rhythm, then he turned to me and said, "Can you hear that?" With anybody else one might say "Yes, I hear it," but I couldn't lie to Bartók and said, "I don't hear anything. It is impossible. I am an amateur. I love music, but you can't judge this from me." His reply was, "No, if you can't hear it, the others can't hear it either, so I have to write it again."

He must have played that passage a dozen times, and every time he asked, "Did you hear it?" Since I couldn't say "Yes" to Bartók when I didn't hear it, each time I said "No," and he continued to play. Finally, after a dozen repetitions, I did hear it! Such a man, for I was so unimportant and just a music lover, but that was so typical of Bartók to believe that if I couldn't hear this detail, then others would not hear it as well.

I remember one morning when they were rehearsing, a man came to the door selling chickens. In Holland tradesmen often come door-to-door selling dressed fowl ready to use. Our little maid who answered came to me saying, "Madame, Madame, I can get chickens, so shall I take two?" Knowing that Bartók loved chicken, I said "Yes" and didn't even look at them. Later I said to Béla, "We will have something you like for dinner."

That evening when we came to dinner Zoltán tried to cut the chicken, and he could not separate it. He simply could not! I felt so embarrassed and tried to explain to our guest, "Our maid is so young. But surely one can fry a chicken and can't ruin it." Then I realized that they were not meant for frying but were boiling chickens that have to cook for hours!

"There is nothing wrong with the chickens," Bartók said. "Give me a hammer." Laughing all the while, he took the hammer and hammered the chickens and we ate them for dinner. Perhaps he wanted to save me embarrassment. I'll never forget Béla with the hammer at our dinner table.

The next morning that young girl, the maid, came running to me saying that our guest was gone, which made us uneasy, of course. Then a neighbor came and said, "That remarkable guest of yours left a long time ago. He had with him a botanical box." Hearing this, we understood. He came home later with all kinds of little specimens, flowers and plants. While he couldn't plant them for himself, he was a great nature lover, and even at our place, he gathered plants and flowers.

Bartók was very thrifty because he had known hard times. Even at that time he very often traveled in third class even as frail as he was. When he was packing to leave with

Zoltán for Liverpool, he left ten guilders for the little maid, who was not accustomed to getting tips, and this was like giving twenty-five dollars at that time. "Madame, he has made a mistake. If anything he should have given me a guilder, or even nothing," she said. She ran after him down the street where he was having a stroll to say that it was far too much, but when he saw that the little girl had run after him, he assured her that it was not a mistake. He was generous and wanted to make that gesture.

For some years Mientje had arranged the details of Székely's professional engagements, but in 1935 he engaged someone new to assist her in the management of his concerts. This was Antonia Kossar (née Maier). She had been the secretary to Dr. Géza de Koos in Amsterdam and now had established her own firm, Concertdirectie A. Kossar, located at Albrect Dürerstraat 16. Mrs. Kossar married the violinist, Nicholas Roth. A pupil of Hubay, Roth had formed the Budapest Trio in 1927 with his brother, cellist George Roth, and pianist Endre Petri. He came to Holland in 1935 and founded the Musica Antiqua Quartet to perform early music. Later Roth worked at Hilversum as director of chamber music AVRO.

At Székely's suggestion, from 1936 Antonia Kossar also worked for Bartók, eventually arranging some twenty-four engagements for him over the years.[10] During this time letters went back and forth between them all. On 26 July 1935 Bartók wrote to Székely mentioning that since the previous July he had been trying to arrange a brief tour for them in Britain. He had written to Mrs. Kossar that she should try to get something at the BBC. He did not want to ask the BBC directly, but the fact was that he had not played his violin pieces there.[11] Székely felt the same:

> We hoped for an engagement in Scotland while on tour in Britain. Bartók wrote to his friend Eric Chisholm in Glasgow as well as having Mrs. Kossar write to the BBC. While the Glasgow engagement didn't come about, we did go to play in Liverpool, departing together from The Rhapsody after his visit in Santpoort in January.
>
> We played a recital on 16 January 1936 at Rushworth Hall for the Liverpool Music Society with the Sonata, K. 526, of Mozart and the Ravel sonata. On that evening we performed many of Bartók's works including the Second Violin

Sonata and the First Rhapsody, as well as my transcription of
the *Rumanian Folk Dances*.

At the end of spring, after a busy season of concerts, Székely received from Bartók, who was in Vienna, a proposal for their concert
arrangements for Switzerland, where they would give a radio broadcast from Berne. In this letter of 18 May 1936, Bartók was perturbed
with Antonia Kossar, and made a pun on her name, the word *kosár* in
Hungarian meaning "basket."

> I am very glad we can play together in Berne. But I am
> angry at that basket. She organized this matter, too, entirely
> contrary to my instructions. . . .
> Here life continues to be difficult, a lot of trouble. (I even
> had a note from His Majesty's tax office!)[12]

A month later Bartók wrote again to say when he would arrive in
Berne and that he would take a room in a simple hotel, probably the
"de la Gare," asking that Székely bring the piano parts for the Debussy and Ravel sonatas since his own copies were in a thickly bound
edition. He concluded by saying, "It would be nice if Mien could also
come: if you came by car would it be possible?"[13]

In Switzerland, Székely and Bartók rehearsed, and performed the
radio broadcast on 19 June which included Debussy's Sonata for
Violin and Piano, the work that had launched their artistic alliance in
Budapest in 1921.

Székely had always hoped to convince Bartók to write a violin
concerto. He tried to persuade Kodály to do the same, but unfortunately never succeeded. With Bartók he persisted. On 10 August 1936
he proposed again to Bartók that he compose a violin concerto for
him. In Bartók's letter of 17 October 1936 in answer to Székely's question as to whether he would write the violin concerto, Bartók at least
promised to think about it:

> The other thing is certainly feasible. You do know, however,
> that I can only work on such things during the summer thus
> you couldn't expect the manuscript before the end of Sep-
> tember 1937. But, I must warn you! this might be bad busi-
> ness, think it over carefully. If I accept the whole thing—with
> the three year exclusive rights—then I would give you the
> manuscript with the idea that <u>that</u> is what you actually pur-

chased. At any rate, you have time to think it over, we might meet at the end of January and finalize the matter.[14]

Bartók's cautious remark "then I would give you the manuscript with the idea that that is what you actually purchased" establishes his intentions at the outset of their complex negotiations that began in 1936 and continued for many years, causing considerable confusion and misunderstanding. To Székely it seemed clear that their agreement would not constitute the acceptance of a commission or of a long-term business proposition. Rather, Bartók would write the new Violin Concerto out of friendship—the honorarium offered, and accepted, would simply serve the purpose of compensation for the lack of performance fees that would have been paid to Bartók by other artists during the time of Székely's exclusive performance rights.

Bartók began the actual writing of the Violin Concerto one year later. As usual he had very little time to spend on it and so had difficulty completing it; however, he promised Székely that it would be finished in 1938, and it was indeed finished on the very last day of that year, 31 December 1938.

In his letter of 17 October 1936, Bartók also mentioned that he was writing a commissioned work for Paul Sacher following an invitation he had received after parting from Székely in Switzerland. That, of course, was the *Music for Strings, Percussion, and Celesta*, which he finished in Budapest in 1936. The commission was to celebrate the tenth anniversary of the Basel Chamber Orchestra. Bartók writes, "I accepted it for it is better than nothing and I had been planning something like it for quite a while."

After playing with Bartók in Switzerland in 1936, Székely returned to Holland, but only for a few days. Together the Székelys went again to London in late June, where he played a BBC radio broadcast with the Montreal singer Sarah Fischer, a Canadian member of the newly formed British National Opera. Their program contained many contrasting works: Székely began with Viotti's Concerto No. 22; Fischer sang songs of Debussy; and then Székely performed the Prelude and Fugue from Reger's Solo Sonata in G Minor and the *Suite espagnole* by Nin. After Fischer's group of songs by Brahms, Healy-Hutchinson, and Arthur Benjamin, Székely finished the broadcast with some shorter works.

Upon his return to Bloemendaal, Székely became very busy copying the manuscript of his String Quartet, one of the compositions he had decided to enter in the Coolidge Competition in the United States. Székely's String Quartet is in seven short movements and explores many modern devices, including polyrhythm. Unfortunately, this mature work, the last of Székely's compositions, did not succeed in the Coolidge Competition. It was never performed in public and remains unpublished, as does his big Duo for Violin and Cello, which he composed in Nijmegen, a work that Bartók found very interesting.

Carl Flesch had lived in Amsterdam from 1903 to 1908 and during those five years had enjoyed a very successful career. His debut as soloist with Mengelberg and the Amsterdam Concertgebouw Orchestra had taken place shorty after his arrival in the country. Having succeeded the Hubay disciple Bram Eldering as professor at the Amsterdam Conservatory, Flesch often appeared in recitals with pianist Julius Röntgen before he moved to Berlin in 1908.

The Székelys had visited Flesch in 1927 at his home in Baden-Baden. In 1930 they saw him again in Florence, where he was performing Brahms' Violin Concerto. When Flesch visited Holland in early autumn of 1935, he invited Székely for an evening of quartet playing.

> I played quartets with Flesch at the home of his former pupil, Jan Tadema, an amateur violinist who was then a Haarlem publisher. For more than thirty years Flesch had played quartets in the Tadema home during his frequent visits to Holland. They were close friends. I remember that Flesch insisted I play first violin and he play second violin. Perhaps he just wanted to observe what I would do in that situation.
>
> Later that week he visited us at The Rhapsody. "I have a very good memory of my first, but not the last, visit to Sant-poort," he wrote in our guest book after his visit on 2 October 1936.

In his work at the Academy of Sciences, Bartók had come into contact with a Turkish musicologist, Adnan Saygun, and was now interested in searching for resemblances between the peasant music of Turkey and of Hungary. In October Bartók went to Turkey. Bartók's brief search there for materials took him to the ancient Anatolian city of Adana, where with the assistance of Saygun he was successful in collecting new examples of folk song from the peasants.

Bartók sent the Székelys two postcards during his journey to Turkey. From Ankara, dated 15 November 1936, he wrote briefly about the conductor Ernst Praetorius and the Ankara orchestra. He ended the postcard humorously saying, "The weather is lovely and sunny but unfortunately my health has broken down probably because I ate some Circassian hen and ladies' belly buttons."[15]

Ten days later, on 25 November, he wrote again, this time from Adana in South Anatolia:

> Yesterday I visited some nomads, real ones living in a tent complete with camel herds, etc. I was collecting from 7 P.M. until midnight by the light of campfire and my own kerosene lamp, squatting on the ground, kneeling, or cross-legged since they have no such useless things as chair, table, or bed.[16]

At The Rhapsody, the Christmas holiday was spent with friends. Pál Hermann, now the cellist of the Gertler Quartet in Brussels, came from Belgium to be with the Székelys in Santpoort. When he arrived, Székely was completing his preparations for a performance in the northern city of Groningen where he would play Mendelssohn's Violin Concerto. Kor Kruiler, the conductor of the Groningen Orchestra, was planning a celebration concert which Princess Juliana would attend.

A winter's calm descended on The Rhapsody during the first week of 1937. After Hermann's departure, Székely and Frid had begun rehearsing *Capriccio*, a new work by Henk Badings which had been dedicated to Székely, when the good news came from Bartók that he would soon visit Amsterdam.[17]

During this visit he would hear the Amsterdam concert in which his Second Rhapsody appeared, as well as the premiere of *Capriccio* by Badings, give a lecture in Amsterdam on 29 January and stay for a brief time in the home of Dr. Révész, then come to The Rhapsody for a few days so that he and Székely could rehearse together for their own pending engagements.

Ten days later Bartók wrote again to discuss the matter of programs for their London engagement:

> Your special delivery letter [express] came night before yesterday; my answer is not exactly express; it was rather difficult to nail this program together (as you will see below) because of all the English titles. Also I had a lecture yesterday and will have another tomorrow. I have so much to do it is unbelievable. . . .

Bartók was concerned that the programs for both a recital for the London Contemporary Music Centre and a broadcast for the BBC would reach their destinations on time. He wrote humorously about his "flea" pieces, a large group of flea-sized piano pieces that he proposed to play in public for the first time, explaining that with the help of his American students, the translation of the titles from Hungarian to English had been made for twenty-seven pieces from Mikrokosmos. He described the proposed program as rather long-winded but went on to say,

> But at least all these flea pieces are "all in manuscript," "novelty" "very first performance," "nowhere else performed yet," "world premiere," and what you like. Surely this will satisfy the music centre!

Bartók had decided the invitation to broadcast from Paris must not be accepted, that the idea must be given up. He wished to settle the program for their Hilversum broadcast and suggested the Second or First Rhapsody, Mozart's Sonata in A Major, K. 526, or the Debussy sonata, and the Tivador Országh transcription for violin and piano of pieces from his piano work, *For Children*.[18]

When Székely and Frid played at the Concertgebouw on 26 January, Bartók was in the audience to hear his Second Rhapsody and came on stage after the performance to be acknowledged by the audience. In the second half came the premiere of *Capriccio* by Badings. The performance of Bartók's Second Rhapsody and the premiere of *Capriccio* created an exciting evening during which Székely played with phenomenal assurance. As for Badings' new work, Theo van der Bijl wrote in *De Tijd*: "The *Capriccio* is easy to follow, quick and playful music, and here again a thankful and enthusiastic public applauded for the three—soloist, accompanist, and composer."[19]

After Antonia Kossar's continued negotiations achieved improved terms for the proposed French radio broadcast, Bartók relented and the broadcast from Paris was accepted for 31 January 1937. Mientje recalled the unusual circumstances in the studio:

> It was a great event then, the Paris radio. The announcer came out and said, "Now I introduce you to *Béla* Székely and *Zoltán* Bartók." Bartók ran to me and said, "That they don't know my music, I don't care, but that they don't even know my name, that hurts me." So I said to him, "Well, the French

are a bit careless sometimes," but although he was not vain, that was too much. Then they asked, "What country are you from? Oh now I know, you must be Czechs!" But it was a good performance of the Second Sonata despite this unfortunate confusion.

Two days later in Brussels, an entire day was devoted to Bartók's music. There was an afternoon concert of his works for choir and orchestra. That evening both Bartók and Székely appeared as soloists with Franz André conducting the Concert Orchestra of the Institut National Belge de Radio. Bartók played his Second Piano Concerto and Székely performed the Second Rhapsody. Both *Village Scenes* and *The Miraculous Mandarin Suite* were performed in this concert as well. Later Bartók wrote a letter to his Swiss friend, Mrs. Müller-Widmann, and said a few very nice words about this concert, expressing his delight with Székely's performance of the Second Rhapsody.[20]

Antonia Kossar had suggested to the BBC that Bartók and Székely would be in England to fulfill engagements in Manchester in early February. Consequently they were engaged for a broadcast on 4 February in London.[21] The late-night broadcast began with the Sonata in B Minor by Bach, followed by Bartók's playing four of his own short piano pieces. The musicians concluded the broadcast with a performance of Bartók's Second Violin Sonata.

On 8 February 1937 they gave an all-Bartók recital for the London Contemporary Music Centre at Cowdray Hall. As promised by Bartók, the novelty of the concert was a set of twenty-seven small piano pieces under the title *Mikrokosmos*. These were drawn from Bartók's pedagogical masterpiece, 153 progressive pieces for the piano composed between 1926 and 1939.

"The performances could be accepted as models for the interpretation of the First Sonata and Second Rhapsody for Violin and Piano," wrote Marion Scott in the *Musical Times*.

> When this Sonata was first played in London I seem to recollect its asperities of sound bewitched the audience into being so many mental porcupines with their quills out. The Sonata still seems a long, biting work, but when set in the proper perspective—as now by Székely and Bartók—it gains upon the intelligence of an audience because the composer has concentrated an unfaltering intellect upon unwinding the thread of his ideas. . . . The Rhapsody is less stern: salt and

sugar mixed. But for its pungent intellectualisms it might also be a virtuoso piece. Székely played it very well with an appropriate touch of gypsy fiddling. The great event of the evening, however, was the first performance in any country of pieces from *Mikrokosmos* . . . played by Bartók with the firm—often fierce—touch he seems to like.[22]

After this concert at Cowdray Hall in London, Bartók and Székely traveled to Holland to broadcast another all-Bartók recital from the Hilversum studios. The Second Rhapsody, three piano pieces, and Székely's transcription of the *Rumanian Folk Dances* made up the program. Following these concerts and broadcasts in Brussels, Paris, London, and Hilversum, Bartók wrote to Paul Sacher in Basel to speak of Székely and encourage a performance of the Second Rhapsody there. He mentioned the Brussels performance, saying he could not have wished it to be more beautiful.[23]

Four young Hungarians had formed a quartet in Budapest in 1935. They called themselves the New Hungarian String Quartet so that their identity would not to be confused with the Waldbauer-Kerpely Quartet, sometimes called the Hungarian String Quartet on their many tours in Europe. On 12 March 1937 the New Hungarian String Quartet appeared in Amsterdam at the Muzieklyceum. The Székelys invited them to a dinner party at The Rhapsody the next evening—their first meeting with the quartet. Székely and Vilmos Palotai, the cellist of the quartet, had been students together at the Franz Liszt Academy. When they were children their mothers were acquainted and frequently spoke to each other at the academy. Székely had not known what had become of Palotai until he heard of the formation of the New Hungarian String Quartet in Budapest. Like Pál Hermann, Palotai had been a pupil of Adolf Schiffer at the academy, then had gone to Berlin to study with Hugo Becker.

At the end of the evening, after sightreading Székely's new String Quartet so that he might hear it performed for the first time, the members of the quartet—Sándor Végh, László Halmos, Dénes Koromzay, and Vilmos Palotai—signed the The Rhapsody's guest book. This meeting of Zoltán Székely and the New Hungarian String Quartet had momentous implications for the future.

1938–1945

Zoltán Székely with baby Frans at The Rhapsody in 1938. PHOTOGRAPHY
IGMINIA SZÉKELY. THE SZÉKELY COLLECTION.

Chapter Fifteen

The New Hungarian String Quartet

"The New Hungarian String Quartet had already existed for more than two years when we had dinner with the Székelys at The Rhapsody following our Amsterdam concert in March of 1937," recalls Dénes Koromzay, the founding violist of the ensemble:[1]

> When we began in 1935 we were very young graduates of the Academy of Music in Budapest. We graduated at the age of seventeen and were playing in orchestras. One of my closest friends—we had entered the school together and graduated together and went to the same *Concours* [public competitions]—was Sándor Végh.
>
> We had always had the idea that someday we should make a quartet together, but basically the motivating force for forming the quartet was Vilmos Palotai, the original cellist, who was seven or eight years older than us. He had come back to Budapest from studying with Hugo Becker in Berlin and, in his wisdom and experience, had became the moving force.
>
> I can tell you very briefly the story of the birth of the quartet. We simply started to play quartets. We first sat down to rehearse in 1935 and to get ourselves what might eventually become a career. Since we were playing in orchestras to survive, we had to rehearse quartets in the mornings at seven because it left the day free to look after our jobs.

We had grandiose plans! After having rehearsed for a time we would have liked to play Beethoven's Opus 131 or any of the great Schubert quartets, but nobody would listen because at that time those works were played by the Kolisch, Budapest, Busch, Léner, or the other great quartets—you name them—so in order to be heard we had to play pieces which nobody else played.

In the first place, we learned new quartets which at that time our Hungarian friends, young composers from the Kodály school, wrote. We learned them out of friendship and because of admiration, too, but any piece which gave us a possibility of playing, we learned. Those names still hound me—Jerzy Fitelberg, Vladimir Fogel, Alan Bush, and André Jolivet. We learned them in the hope that they would give us the possibility of performing.

Sándor Végh was first violin and Péter Szervánszky, a colleague of ours and a very fine violinist, was the original second violin in a long succession of second violins. Everything would have worked out except for personality clashes between Végh and Szervánsky which somehow are apt to develop between the members of any quartet. Szervánsky soon left and László Halmos became the new second violinist. We knew that in order to establish ourselves, we especially needed to go abroad, outside of Hungary. With Halmos as second violin we finally got out of the country and started to make a name for ourselves.

Bartók's Fifth Quartet was our vehicle. We believed that once we had learned it, it would help us, and it did. During those early performances of the Fifth Quartet, Sándor Végh, László Halmos, Vilmos Palotai, and I were the members of the quartet. We called ourselves the New Hungarian Quartet because there was a resident quartet in Hungary which was called the Waldbauer-Kerpely Quartet for the first twenty-five years of its existence, but when on tour in Europe, was sometimes called the Hungarian String Quartet.

This was a highly meritorious group, probably the only one who cared for contemporary music. They played the Debussy quartet for the first time in Budapest, sometime during the First World War. They were very close friends of Bartók and Kodály, and Bartók's First and Second Quartets are dedicated to them, and they gave the first performances of the Third and Fourth, as well.

Imre Waldbauer happened to be my teacher, my string

quartet coach at the academy, and after my graduation in the spring of 1931 he very kindly accepted me as a friend and invited me to his home quite often. I spent many evenings there, the main motive being that he loved to play bridge and I was a regular bridge player.

One evening I went to Waldbauer's home with Pál Kadosa to play bridge. When I entered his living room I saw that there on the piano lay a new Bartók manuscript. At that time the rumors were going around that Bartók was writing or finishing his Fifth Quartet. "What is this?" I asked. Waldbauer replied, "Béla just sent over his Fifth Quartet. We have to learn it." So I said to him, "Could you loan me the score for just a very short time?" He agreed. "There is no hurry for us, so you can have it for two days."

After finishing our bridge game, I went home, and next morning at seven o'clock, I appeared at our rehearsal with the treasure in my hand. It was just exactly what we were looking for—a vehicle which would carry us. Immediately phone calls went out to our friends, Sándor Veress and Pál Kadosa, young composers at that time but since then established very well, and the excitement of seeing a new Bartók work was such that they came practically in pajamas in ten minutes, and tore apart the score. One took three movements and the other took two, and they went home and copied it.

Later we put the score together again and dutifully took it back to Waldbauer saying nothing. We copied out our individual parts from the newly copied score and started to learn the piece. It was furiously difficult, and being a very young quartet we didn't have any experience yet. Nevertheless we worked very hard, and after three or four weeks we called Bartók and asked whether he would like to hear it.

Bartók certainly had no vanity whatsoever, but there is no composer who doesn't like to listen to his own music, especially when he has never heard it—not even Bartók. The Fifth Quartet was commissioned by the Elizabeth Sprague Coolidge Foundation in Washington, D.C., and the world premiere was to be given by the Kolisch Quartet, who happened to be in America, so they got a copy of the score.[2] At that time they had already played it [8 April 1935], but Bartók had never heard it. So we played it for him and he decided that he would coach it. He worked with us every day for ten days, after which he said "You can play the first performance in Budapest."

How did he think I got a hold of it? Well, after all, it was just a little trick we all laughed about. The point was that we were all obviously a little afraid of what Waldbauer would say and he said something, but I think he was basically glad. They were extremely busy people. He was teaching and playing, they didn't have much time and they knew the piece was difficult, and they graciously consented.

We gave the first performance in Budapest. Certainly both in Vienna and Budapest we had the first performances.[3]

The New Hungarian String Quartet presented the first Austrian performance of Bartók's Fifth Quartet in Vienna for a concert for the Hagebund Society organized by the Austrian Section of the ISCM on 18 February 1936. The concert began with two works they had played earlier at the Prague International Festival with considerable success, new string quartets by Sándor Veress and Alan Bush. Next was a performance of Sándor Jemnitz' Sonata for Solo Cello with Vilmos Palotai as soloist.

The Fifth Quartet by Bartók was of course a work that aroused the greatest expectations, and the New Hungarian Quartet with their accomplished performance of the new masterpiece was well received by Vienna's most illustrious musical audience. Austrian composer Ernst Krenek saw Bartók's quartet as an unusual achievement even for the Hungarian master. When reviewing the concert in Budapest's *Pester Lloyd* on 25 February 1936, he wrote, "His tonal fantasies, which can produce an orchestral fortissimo from a quartet, serve a strict and sovereign musical concept."[4]

Two weeks later at the Franz Liszt Academy, the New Hungarian String Quartet presented the first Hungarian performance of Bartók's Fifth Quartet as well as Beethoven's Op. 95, and Mozart's Piano Quartet, K. 478, with Annie Fischer as pianist. Sándor Jemnitz called Bartók's new work "one of the most perfect products of Hungarian music ever."[5] Noting that all the Bartók faithfuls were at this concert, Pál Spitzer remarked, "In the center of the evening stood Bartók's Fifth Quartet which . . . we are finally able to hear in its home country."[6]

Kálmán Kovács wrote, "Bartók was called to the podium and when he appeared—this moment happened after more than eight years of hiatus—there was a storm of enthusiasm that broke out like a tornado."[7] Koromzay recalls that this performance was memorable for Bartók's having joined the New Hungarian Quartet on stage to receive the applause of the audience:

Bartók had become so fed up with the animosity and disregard, the near-persecution that he was subjected to by officialdom—obviously the last segment who knew what a genius he was—that he said "No," and he wouldn't set his foot on a stage in Hungary. That lasted for years.

I think it was in 1932, when I was playing in the Budapest Concert Orchestra, that the Budapest premiere was set for his Second Piano Concerto with Otto Klemperer conducting. First it was planned that the orchestra would move up to Vienna and play the work, and obviously many people in Budapest were upset about that and asked how come our greatest composer and his important new work won't be played in Budapest. They pressured the organization to make at least a Budapest performance, too, and for that concert the young pianist Louis Kentner had to learn the piece because Bartók would not appear.

Finally in March 1936, when we played the Fifth Quartet in Budapest, Bartók came to hear it. There was a tremendous ovation because the piece is really so overwhelming. Finally Bartók came out with us to take a bow. That was the first time in years that he relented, but after that he began to appear regularly again.

What was the official problem with Bartók? Was it the academy in Budapest? Originally Bartók was a piano teacher. He was appointed to the academy at the age of twenty-two and was the youngest professor ever appointed. At the time when I graduated in 1931 he was already very deep into his folklore research and had stopped teaching piano.

Since Bartók was a professor and Hubay was the director of the academy, they "knew each other" obviously, but Hubay didn't understand him. In the aesthetics class or music history class, I remember one of the very well-known professors talking about Bartók and saying that he was certainly one of the great talents, but unfortunately he had gone mad and this type of music he composes will necessarily disappear. This happened in the same school where Bartók was a colleague—he taught hundreds of youngsters—so you can imagine that when this came back to Bartók he didn't like it.

It was awfully hard for our quartet to finance tours and introductory concerts in the capitals of the world, so it was only with contemporary music that we could make ourselves heard. The 1935 ISCM Festival had been held in Prague, and there we played the First Quartet of Sándor Veress and a 1929 quartet called *Dialectic* by the English composer, Alan Bush. With those works we made a little splash.

In Hungary, Dohnányi joined us on several occasions in performances of his Piano Quintet, Op.1. During those early years, the composer László Lajtha was one of our mentors.[8] He did many very positive things for us, including coaching us in Bartók's Second Quartet. Lajtha had strong connections in France and he helped us with our negotiations there, since at that time we didn't know French well. He had composed several works for quartet including a set of études. We played the pizzicato study from that work. In 1936 another Hungarian composer, Pál Kadosa, a very close friend of Palotai, showed his interest in the New Hungarian Quartet.[9] He composed a work for us, Concerto for String Quartet, which unfortunately we never played.

Then we sold the idea of Bartók's Fifth Quartet being in our possession to the organizer and president of the upcoming ISCM Festival which in 1936 was in Barcelona, very shortly before the Spanish Civil War broke out. He asked that this piece be placed on the program, with Bartók's permission. That resulted in our being invited for the unbelievable fee of their paying our return second-class train expenses from Budapest to Barcelona and our room and board for two weeks. It was unprecedented in our experience.

As I said and as we expected—and we were rewarded even more than we expected—we can thank the beginning of our career and the success we had in the early years to Bartók's Fifth Quartet. The Barcelona Festival was an important event and people interested in contemporary music came from all over the world, and the international press was there.

Those festivals were very meritorious and very interesting, but they were also sometimes somewhat of a bore, since so much music was crammed into those two weeks, three or four concerts daily of choral and chamber music and orchestral works. Most of those works were rather dull and with so much compression it was made worse. Everybody who was there was a firm believer in contemporary music, but you could see discouragement on their faces. Their faith was waning, and perhaps a little Mozart wouldn't have been bad!

I remember seeing Ernest Ansermet who was conducting many works at the festival. I asked him whether he would come to the chamber music concert because the new quartet was a great work. He said he would love to, but he was too tired and "tomorrow morning I cannot."

Bartók's Fifth Quartet was placed at the end of an endless program of chamber music, and people were getting tired since it was the end of the festival.[10] Finally we played, and it is really one of my great memories because from all of those people who, as I said, were shaken in their faith for contemporary music, suddenly came this unbelievable outburst! You never heard such an outburst!

We probably played it well enough, but it was not us but the work that restored their faith. Ernest Ansermet, who had said he could not come, seemingly decided to listen to one movement. He came up, trampling over people and hugging us, with a red face. Restored!

Hearing Bartók's work showed that one really can write great masterpieces in the contemporary idiom. Because that event was very well covered by the international press, it gave us a great boost. Engagements in other countries easily came our way.

Bartók didn't come to Barcelona. By 1936, he was world famous although he never earned much money, but his name was certainly established with those of Schoenberg and Stravinsky as the great composers of the century, at least the first part of the century.

"Bartók's Fifth Quartet was best received of all the works on the program, not only by the critics, but by the audience who loved it immediately," wrote the critic of *Nepszava*.[11] "The success of the chamber concert, actually of the whole festival, was Bartók's enormous Fifth Quartet," wrote Emil Haraszti in *Magyar Dal*, "and with breath held, the audience followed Bartók's thoughts, and after the finale applauded enormously."[12] On 5 May 1936, the Hungarian paper *Magyarság* quoted Amsterdam's *De Telegraaf*: "Bartók's Fifth Quartet was a musical revelation as performed by the wonderful New Hungarian Quartet . . . even Bartók has seldom written a work so rich, wonderful, and original."[13]

The Spanish press was ecstatic about the performances of the New Hungarian String Quartet. The critic of Madrid's *Humanitat* praised their Beethoven playing as ranking among the greatest achievements of chamber music. In Barcelona, the critic for *Rambla* had never heard a quartet with such beauty of tone, wonderful style, and perfect ensemble, in works by both the classical and modern masters.

The New Hungarian Quartet had by now appeared at the Prague International Festival, in Vienna and Budapest, and on tour in Basel,

Geneva, Strasbourg, and London, playing quartets by Sándor Veress and Pál Kadosa and Bartók's Fifth Quartet. They were the only Hungarian participants in the 1936 Barcelona Festival, and the international press promoted their cause on the basis of the great success achieved with the Bartók performance. The Fifth Quartet was perhaps the most outstanding work at the festival.

When the quartet returned to Hungary, they visited the composer Tibor Serly, a pupil of Kodály and a close friend of Palotai. Serly was home for a vacation in Budapest from the United States, where he was a member of the Philadelphia Orchestra.[14] On his way to Budapest in 1937, Serly had stopped in Italy to visit his friend, Ezra Pound, as he had in previous years. The American poet had been living there since 1907 as foreign editor of the journal, *Poetry*. During September the quartet had seen Ezra Pound at the Venice Biennale, where they performed Bartók's Fifth Quartet during a new music festival specializing in contemporary music. Backstage after the concert, the poet had exchanged a few words "in limping German" with Vilmos Palotai whose rich-toned cello playing he found very beautiful, then later had joined the quartet for a midnight meal.[15]

During Serly's visit with the quartet, he told them that a concert of his works was being organized in Budapest which would include his String Quartet. At Palotai's suggestion, the quartet learned Serly's new work and performed it in the concert. Later Palotai asked Serly his opinion of the possibility of the quartet's performing in America. While Serly thought the prospects for this were limited at that time, he reminded him of his contact with Ezra Pound, who organized a series of chamber music concerts in Rapallo. He thought Pound might invite them to play there.

Serly had met Pound some years earlier after writing him a letter criticizing his article, "Antheil and the Treatise on Harmony." In August of 1933, Serly and Géza Frid went to Rapallo as Pound's guests and gave a private performance of Serly's new Viola Concerto at the Villa Andrea. Serly became a frequent performer at Rapallo's Inverno Musicale. His String Quartet was performed there by the Gertler String Quartet in a concert of modern Hungarian music given on 13 January 1935. On 3 March, Serly took part in a concert at Rapallo's Town Hall which featured his Concerto for Viola performed with a piano reduction. Following these concerts, Pound wrote the article, "Tibor Serly, composer," for the *New English Weekly*, acclaiming the compositions of the young Hungarian composer.

No one in the New Hungarian Quartet really knew the significance of Ezra Pound, not being familiar in 1937 with contemporary American literature. However, twenty-four-year-old Koromzay, who wrote to Pound at Serly's suggestion, was soon to learn of it.

Within weeks I had a collection of bizarre letters written by the poet to the quartet. Some were written in four or five languages, including Latin, and I remember that one letter consisted of only two sentences, the first of which filled the front of a page; the second filled the back. I had read a great deal and had friends who were writers, among them one who later became one of the great novelists in Hungary. Recognizing the source of the Rapallo letters, my friend exclaimed, "Do you know these letters are from the man who changed the world of poetry?"

We accepted Pound's invitation to play at Rapallo for "five hundred lire and a night's lodging," and departed for Italy on a trip which took us first to Switzerland to fulfill a radio engagement. When we arrived in Rapallo, Ezra Pound was waiting for us. He invited us to his home which was the attic of an old house with a beautiful view of the Gulf of Tigullian.

The first thing I saw when I entered his attic home was a tremendous, stuffed shark hanging on the wall. When I remarked on it, he replied simply, "I got it from *Ernest*."

At that moment I had no idea who "Ernest" was, but later when he and I took a stroll during which we spoke in German, I mentioned I had read some works by the American writers of "The Lost Generation"—in a Hungarian translation—and that I admired a certain short story by Willa Cather included in the anthology. "Second rate," he retorted. "How can you say that?" I asked, initiating a confrontation with this literary giant during which I soon learned, among other things, that his stuffed shark was a gift from Ernest Hemingway! In retrospect, I smile at the memory of myself as a naïve young man in Rapallo.

Led by Sándor Végh, the New Hungarian String Quartet performed in Paris the following season for Triton, the contemporary chamber music series at the École Normale de Musique. On 8 February 1937 the quartet gave the first performance in Paris of three new works, Jerzy Fitelberg's Quartet No. 3, Mihail Jora's Quartet, Op. 9, and Bartók's Fifth Quartet.

The next week Ezra Pound wrote an article, "The New Hungarian Quartet," in *Il Mare* in which he announced that the quartet was to perform when they stopped in Rapallo on their way from Lyons to Naples. Pound felt this second appearance at Rapallo's Town Hall would unquestionably be an important event for his chamber music series. Two programs were given, one on 4 March, "Mozart-Boccherini, and Composers of Today," and another on 5 March, comprising Bartók's Second and Fifth Quartets on either side of Haydn's Quartet, Op. 20, No. 3.

On 13 March Pound again wrote about the New Hungarian Quartet in *Il Mare*, praising them as the ensemble whose mastery exceeded any quartet he had ever heard. He mentioned that, despite the shamefully small audience that had attended the concerts, the quartet had agreed to return the following season.

Chapter Sixteen

Paris and North Africa

In Budapest during March of 1937, Palotai and Koromzay discussed the significance of the recent meeting with Székely in Holland and came to the conclusion that it would improve the New Hungarian String Quartet tremendously if Székely would join them as first violinist. After further serious discussion, Végh agreed to play second violin, replacing László Halmos, should Székely accept their invitation. While they realized that Halmos' contribution to the recent international success of the quartet was considerable and that releasing him from his position would present him with a difficult professional situation, they decided that the prospect of having Székely as first violinist warranted the change.

Palotai wrote to Székely inviting him to take the leadership of the New Hungarian String Quartet, assuring him that should he decide to do so, Végh would play second violin. Székely's response was positive; however, he would only accept the invitation with a certain condition—the quartet must reside in Holland. Already a prominent soloist in Europe, Székely was not prepared to leave Holland, where he had established an important relationship with the professional musical community during fifteen years of living abroad.

Recalling Székely's condition for joining the New Hungarian Quartet in 1937, Koromzay speaks of the decision to move to Holland:

We were all unmarried and free and moving to Holland wasn't too bad an idea since in the late 1930s the political winds were not exactly blowing our way in Hungary. In fact, the quartet was very badly located if we wanted to play concerts because Germany was completely out of the question with a total Nazi regime, and Nazism was spreading in Hungary too. And so it was western Europe to which we were tending, and Holland was a very convenient location.

Later Bartók certainly *had* to leave Hungary. We didn't have to leave. Bartók was one of the most direct and outspoken men in the world, and he made such strong anti-Nazi statements that he would have been the first to be picked up by the Gestapo when they came, or even by the Hungarian Nazis when they eventually came to power. So he had to leave, and it was a heartbreak for him because he was more Hungarian than anybody could be, with his whole life's work there.

We went to Holland for the quartet, foolishly hoping that there wouldn't be war, or, on the precedent of the First World War believing that Holland might remain neutral. But Holland was invaded, and a Nazi regime was installed, and that produced five horrid years when one couldn't work, couldn't travel, couldn't do anything.

In 1938, after a year in Holland, Sándor Végh decided he wanted to go back to Budapest and do something else. He wasn't satisfied with the second violin position even if the quartet was very successful. History proved his decision right because he made a tremendous career, formed his own quartet, and was probably much happier than if he had stayed.[1]

Having spoken to Pál Hermann, who had left the Gertler Quartet in Brussels, moved to Paris, and was again playing solo recitals, Bartók became concerned about possible restrictions that might be imposed on Székely's solo career by his impending commitment to the New Hungarian String Quartet. He wrote Székely in April to express his concern. Székely recalled:

When I was considering joining the quartet, Bartók wrote and asked me, as he did later from time to time, if I would have time to play the new Violin Concerto during the period of my exclusive performance rights. Because he was beginning to think seriously about the composition of the concerto, in a letter from Budapest on 10 April 1937 he wrote,

"And something else comes to mind: if you join the New Hungarian Quartet, how will you be able to play solos? (that is, regarding the time element). After all, quartet playing implies a lot of restrictions. Also how would it be, would you move to Budapest or would the others move to Holland?"

Ditta wrote a lovely postscript to this letter saying that she had spoken to my parents at Pál Hermann's concert in Budapest.[2]

I wrote Bartók to assure him that once I had the concerto I would set aside time every season to have performances of it during the period of my sole performance rights. He wrote again on 1 May 1937: "If that is the case there is really nothing in the way. Only you didn't mention how you will be able to fit together quartet and solo playing. (I think that was the problem with Pál Hermann); for it would not be good if during the period of your exclusive rights you would have to forego some good opportunities to perform it all because of the quartet."

The text of the draft agreement that follows in Bartók's letter has considerable historical significance. It establishes the genre of the work as a violin concerto, although initially Bartók had wanted to write a work in variation form. In addition, it indicates that the composer had already conceived the work's duration in minutes. The duplication and use of the score and orchestral parts is discussed. Székely's exclusive performance rights are defined in the sixth point ("Székely shall, at the acceptance of the manuscript, pay 500 Dutch florins for the rights described"), and this is of special importance to the negotiations that ensued until 10 December 1940. The text reads as follows:

Agreement between Béla Bartók and Zoltán Székely

1. Béla Bartók will write a Violin Concerto in 1937 of about twenty-one to twenty-five minutes' duration.
2. The sole performance rights of this work will belong to Zoltán Székely until August 31, 1941; this can be extended until August 31, 1944 at Zoltán Székely's wish, of which he must notify Béla Bartók by December 31, 1940.
3. Béla Bartók will have to place a copy of the work's score at Zoltán Székely's disposal by the end of 1937.
4. Zoltán Székely may have the orchestra material produced from this copy once or in duplicate, and will be able to

use this material during the time of the sole performing rights, but he has no right to ask the orchestras or their managers for any compensation for the use of that material. He may not loan this material to anyone else.

5. This orchestra material will stay in Zoltán Székely's possession even after the expiration of the exclusivity period and he himself may use it for public performances; however, he or the concert's management is obliged to pay the usual hire [rental] fees to the publisher.

6. Zoltán Székely shall, at the acceptance of the manuscript mentioned in point three, pay 500 Dutch florins for the rights described in the preceding paragraphs.

7. In case Béla Bartók should be for whatever reason unable to complete this work mentioned above, no indemnification shall be sought from him.

Bartók concluded his letter which contained this draft agreement by saying, "I believe this will be satisfactory. Write it down in two copies, sign them both and I will return one to you with my signature. . . ."[3]

Székely complied by returning the signed copies of the agreement. On 10 June 1937 Bartók wrote again and enclosed one signed copy with his signature and the message: "I am enclosing my signed copy of the agreement—we shall see what the future brings!"[4]

In the summer of 1937 Székely's three new colleagues came to Holland. They settled at Pension Duinlust, a boarding house in Bloemendaal near Santpoort Station. At once the group began rehearsing. Every afternoon the three young Hungarians joined their new first violinist at The Rhapsody to work on string quartets by Haydn, Schubert, Beethoven, and Bartók—repertoire that they had performed on their recent European concert tour.

In 1990 Székely recalled these early rehearsals during which his colleagues shared with him certain memories from having played Bartók's Fifth Quartet in Budapest during coaching sessions with the composer:

Dénes Koromzay told me that Bartók had once stood on a table in order to use the full length of the tape pendulum of the highly accurate balance metronome. "I can still see him standing on top of the table," Dénes said, "when making final decisions about the tempo of the Scherzo (Alla bulgarese) where the beat—for the full bar—is very slow, and ac-

cordingly the length of the pendulum very great. A short
man, he could only let it swing freely if he stood on a table."

Bartók had given up the ordinary metronome because he
didn't trust it anymore, and instead he used the balance
metronome, a device that should be absolutely accurate. Its
pendulum looks like a measuring tape with a complete set of
consecutive numbers on it. That is why in Bartók's later
markings you have all those in-between numbers that do
not correspond to the unique numbers on an ordinary
metronome.

At an earlier period in 1931, Bartók had written to Max
Rostal to say that some of his metronome markings in the
First and Fourth Quartets were not good, probably because
his ordinary metronome was working imperfectly.[5]

Even at that one need not take these markings absolutely
literally. I have seen one of the studies made by László Somfai in 1977 about the piano piece, *Evening in Transylvania*.
Bartók recorded it twice. Somfai made an exact analysis that
also included the rubatos, and the tempos are sometimes radically different between the two performances of the same
piece.

I know by experience that when we played the First
Rhapsody together, I took a more comfortable tempo than
that which Szigeti took on their recording made at the
Library of Congress, a recording which is a little bit on the
nervous side.

Now there is a certain tempo, about 100 to 108 to the
eighth-note, which establishes the character of the *Verbunkos*
or "Recruiting Dance." The *Verbunkos* appears in the First
Rhapsody and in the Violin Concerto and is, of course, in the
same tempo in both. With the marking 100 to 108 to the
eighth-note, you have a certain liberty since two numbers'
difference is quite something in certain cases. Bartók, himself, did not strictly adhere to all those numbers. As well, the
duration in real time found at the end of his scores may not
be his invention. I saw that device in a piece by Joan Manén,
the Spanish composer, who was a very great violin virtuoso.
Manén applied the same idea in one of his last works, where
he noted the exact timing of an actual performance.

When the New Hungarian Quartet began rehearsals in Holland,
Székely's colleagues had considerable interest in continuing to play
Haydn's Quartet, Op. 20, No. 3, which they had performed at Ra-

pallo. This unusual Haydn quartet was the first work they rehearsed with Székely leading the ensemble. They also began work on Beethoven's Op. 95, Schubert's Quartet in A Minor, and, of course, Bartók's Fifth Quartet. The ensemble already had another important engagement for the forthcoming festival of the International Society for Contemporary Music in Paris, so there was a definite and immediate goal from the outset of the rehearsals. They began learning the Quartet No. 2 by Honegger, Milhaud's Quartet No. 9, and the Quartet No. 2 by Sándor Veress, the three works scheduled for the Paris concerts.

The quartet went to Paris in June of 1937 for the ISCM Festival held in conjunction with the Paris International Exposition. In two different chamber music concerts they played first the Honegger work, then later those by Sándor Veress and Darius Milhaud. They soon met the young English composer Elizabeth Maconchy who was at the festival to hear her Second Quartet. Her tense and concentrated instrumental style so appealed to them that they asked her to consider writing her next quartet for them. Maconchy agreed. She immediately began composing her Third Quartet for the New Hungarian String Quartet, who performed the premiere of the new work in London the following season.

Following the performances at the festival, a private concert was arranged for a friend of Ezra Pound and Igor Stravinsky, the Princess Edmond de Polignac, an aristocrat who regularly had chamber music recitals in her palatial home on Avenue Henri Martin. She requested a performance of Schubert's Quartet in D Minor ("Death and the Maiden"), a work not yet in their repertoire; however, she agreed that Schubert's Quartet in A Minor would be an excellent choice for her *soirée,* and it was this work they played, among others.

Imre Kun, the Budapest manager of the New Hungarian Quartet, had encouraged them to make a suitable agreement with the Parisian concert agency, the Bureau de Concerts Marcel de Valmalète, located in the Maison Gaveau at 45–47 rue la Boëtie. Having made this fortunate alliance in 1937, the quartet remained with Valmalète's agency for thirty-five years. At the beginning their concert arrangements were made by the impresario Théo Ysaÿe, a relative of the great violinist, then associated with Valmalète. He managed the quartet's business until Jean Duport, the general secretary of the firm, assumed supervision of their affairs.

Later that summer the quartet had its first trip to North Africa, touring Algeria, French Morocco, and Tunisia, three countries which were then French protectorates. This tour was arranged in Paris by Étienne Morette, a French language teacher who helped organize the musical life in North Africa to serve the cultural needs of the French citizens living there.

They arrived in North Africa at the port of Tangiers near Gibraltar and were met at the pier that morning by a prominent French gentleman, the director of a Tangiers bank, who represented the organization sponsoring the first concert of their tour. He promptly arranged for his Arab chauffeur to drive them around Tangiers for a morning of sightseeing. At noon when they had finished this diversion, the chauffeur invited them to visit his home, a typical shuttered dwelling with an inner courtyard. There they met his wife and children. As they were leaving to return to their hotel, he asked if they wouldn't like to see his *other* home. To the amazement of these young Europeans, he explained that in his other home lived his *second* wife and children. Evidently his two wives did not get along, so he had arranged separate domiciles for his two large families.

Later that day, a French colonel who was a member of the local concert organization invited Koromzay and Végh for a shopping trip in Tangiers' Casbah. At a small shop in the midst of an interminable row of stalls where leatherware, silver, and gold were sold, the colonel prompted the two young musicians to bargain for a small purchase. At the shopkeeper's demand of 800 francs, they laughingly countered, "Forty!" The good-natured shopkeeper joined in their merriment and suggested a price somewhat lower than his original request. They finally reached a stalemate at 200 francs, excused themselves, and moved away along the crowded corridor of shops. Within two blocks the shopkeeper caught up with them with his new proposal—forty francs. Sold!

The North African press greatly admired the New Hungarian String Quartet during this tour. In *l'Echo d'Alger* the reviewer wrote, "I cannot imagine playing more beautiful than the luminous performance they gave."[6] The critic of the *Courrier du Maroc* reported, "These artists bring a wholesome innocence and considerable dash to their playing with its magnificent balance, rich plentitude of tone, and absolute purity of of rhythm."[7]

Bartók wrote Székely once more, this time from Kals in East Tyrol on 15 July 1937. In this letter Bartók answered certain questions Székely had previously asked him regarding the sole performance rights to the Violin Concerto.

I must again return to the Violin Concerto. Please do not take it badly but to be sure I wrote to Universal-Edition concerning the matter without mentioning your name.[8] They agree to everything, but ask for these two following things: (1) that they receive a copy of the work upon completion in order to register the copyright (although I don't understand why a work in manuscript has to be copyrighted, but perhaps for the possible American performance royalties) [;] (2) that "the certain violinist concerned" should report to them all performances of the work (let us say within a month, but perhaps within a half a year if you like that better), so that they can control the incoming royalty especially from America. I don't believe that this presents a problem, thus I ask you that you assume this added obligation in a supplemental declaration. Otherwise everything is fine.

I would like it if you would write me about all of this to Budapest so that I could receive your declaration on my return on the 20th or shortly thereafter. . . . Write me about Paris also. How did it go? And in general how do you function together? Are there many arguments??![9]

Székely made his first recordings in London for Decca as a result of a previous test recording supervised by Fred Gaisberg. These early solo recordings included his transcription of Bartók's *Rumanian Folk Dances* as well as Joan Manén's Chanson—Adagietto, Op. A8, No. 1, and Nicolò Porpora's Sonata in G Major. Géza Frid was the pianist. They recorded the *Rumanian Folk Dances* in a shortened version due to the time limitations of the 78 rpm recording process, omitting the fifth dance, *Poargă românească*.[10]

Antonia Kossar, who arranged these early contracts with Decca, was later able to arrange several other recordings in Holland during the war. Made for educational purposes and marketed only in Holland, these Dutch recordings included Paganini's Caprice No. 24 and the first movement of Beethoven's Violin Concerto. Glazounov's Violin Concerto was recorded with Willem van Otterloo and the Residentie Orchestra of The Hague and was issued by the Dutch section of Decca. The Brahms Violin Concerto was recorded but never released.

While the quartet was still rehearsing in August, Jaap and Loes de Graaff came to visit the Székelys. As house guests at The Rhapsody, they heard the New Hungarian Quartet with great pleasure. They also heard Székely perform the Mendelssohn concerto at the Kurhaus in The Hague with Ignaz Neumark conducting the Residentie Orchestra.

This appearance with Neumark came sixteen years after Székely's Dutch debut, with the same orchestra and conductor with whom he had played the matinee performance during his first visit to Holland.

After this concert in The Hague, the quartet went to Budapest to spend the rest of the summer of 1937. There they rehearsed the late quartets of Beethoven, drawing on the theory of the German scholar Hugo Riemann to solve certain performance problems. In addition, Székely visited Bartók and saw for the first time the unfinished violin part of the new concerto. In 1939 Székely was to involve himself indelibly in the genesis of Bartók's masterpiece when the composer agreed to his proposal to write an alternate ending to the concerto. Székely recalls:

> We had a lot of quartet repertoire to learn, and that is why I hired a nice apartment in Budapest near the Danube so we could rehearse there, as well as in the home of Palotai's mother. While we were working on the Scherzo of Beethoven's Op. 131, a problem arose regarding a passage in which we had difficulty deciding the accentuation. In this movement, as in some faster movements, one bar among several represents the heavy beat and there is no clear indication which bar this is. For instance, when three fast bars represent one unit of meter, Beethoven has sometimes marked *tre battute*, to explain the accentuation, but when this is not marked, such groups are open to many different interpretations since the meaning of a certain bar in syncopation may be a question.
>
> We began discussing Hugo Riemann's theories of form and rhythm in search for a solution. Riemann developed a theory of musical phrasing during the late nineteenth century in which the cadence is always the point of repose and serves as his criterion for understanding the phrasing. In 1937 I didn't yet know the Riemann Theory, but somehow Vilmos Palotai knew it because it had come to his attention when he was studying in Berlin. I remember telephoning Bartók to ask him his opinion, but he also didn't know Riemann's ideas on this problem.
>
> During that stay in Budapest Mientje and I visited both my parents and the Bartóks. I remember very well that during our visit with the Bartóks, he and Ditta played through a new work for us at their home, the Sonata for Two Pianos and Percussion, but of course without the percussion. On that occa-

sion he showed me the first two pages of the violin part of the Violin Concerto beautifully written out, but the piano reduction was nothing yet, just a few notes. I played and he accompanied me at the piano from his sketch, so that much was ready at that time. The conception was ready and fixed as it would be, as it came later, and that seems a very remarkable thing, since the work was only really finished a year later.

At the beginning Bartók suggested that this work be in variation form, but I wanted it to be a big work in the traditional concerto form. Those who have studied this concerto must have noticed with amazement the very unusual thing that the work has two different endings. This is how and why it happened. While studying the newly received copy of the manuscript in 1939 I felt more and more that the end, which was a big *fortissimo* orchestral apotheosis, did not fit the conception of a violin concerto. It seemed to me more like the conclusion of a symphony.

I was so much convinced of the correctness of my feelings that I wrote a letter to Bartók explaining to him that in my opinion a concerto for violin and orchestra is not a challenge—it is more a cooperation, and the violin and the orchestra have to complement each other.

You can imagine my astonishment when fairly soon I got his answer, saying that he went to a concert where Szigeti played two great violin concertos in one evening, the Beethoven and the Brahms, and that after listening to these works he appreciated the validity of my opinion and had accordingly rewritten the end of his concerto. There were very interesting orchestral effects in the original ending which he didn't want to sacrifice. He retained much of this material which he transformed into a version that favored the solo violin. Now everyone plays it in the version he corrected although in the publication the original ending is appended to the score *ad libitum*. One has to study and compare the two endings to see the masterful ease and perfection with which he accomplished this task.

The quartet continued their rehearsals in Holland during the fall of 1937, learning new repertoire to present at their Dutch concerts. In December Pál Hermann came from Paris to visit the Székelys. After the New Year's celebration, the quartet left on tour to France and Italy with Budapest as the final destination.

Ezra Pound announced in *Il Mare* on 21 January 1938 that the

Tigullian Musical Season in Rapallo would again have the participation of the New Hungarian String Quartet. He wrote that while he didn't know the details of the quartet's reorganization, had he been free during the past ten years to tour the centers of Germany and Hungary instead of living in Rapallo, he would have known the high quality of the new first violinist, Zoltán Székely, by direct experience and not only through his fame. Their program for Rapallo would include a quartet by Mozart, Stravinsky's Concertino, Honegger's Quartet No. 2, and the Second Quartet by Sándor Veress.

During the Second World War Ezra Pound broadcast fascist propaganda to the United States from Rome, an act that led to his arrest in 1945, his confinement in Pisa, and his indictment for treason. Judged mentally unfit to answer the indictment, he was committed to St. Elizabeth's Hospital in Washington, D.C., where he remained until 1958, when he was finally released. Charges against him were dropped, and he was allowed to return to Italy. His death in 1972 in Venice marked the passing of a poet, editor, and critic considered by many to be one of the most influential literary figures in modern literature. His remains rest in the Venetian cemetery on the burial island of San Michele, a few steps from the graves of Igor and Vera Stravinsky and Sergei Diaghilev.

The quartet returned to North Africa during March of 1938. Székely recalls going from one seaport to another by an old-fashioned train:

> We toured along the North African coast by train, one day playing, one day traveling, always using the same train with its steam engine and wooden cars. We went down the whole coast of Algeria and Morocco in this way. We played in such places as Fez, Rabat, and Casablanca and finished the tour in Marrakech, where we stayed in Churchill's favorite hotel. Once during this tour we left the train and went by bus through the desert to play a concert in a desert village.

While the quartet was on tour in North Africa, Hitler's *Anschluss* in Vienna signaled an end to Bartók's professional work as a composer in eastern Europe because the owners and editors of Universal-Edition lost control of their publishing house. The performing rights organization that collected Bartók's royalties, the Gesellschaft der Autoren, Komponisten, und Musikverleger, or AKM, was quickly and entirely placed under the control of the Nazis.

Then fifty-seven years old, Bartók began his efforts to find a new publisher, meeting with Ralph Hawkes, the director of Boosey and Hawkes in London, who had flown to Budapest to discuss with Bartók and Kodály the possibility of publishing their works in England. Later in June, when the Bartóks were in London to perform the Sonata for Two Pianos and Percussion at an ISCM concert, the composer reached a final agreement with Boosey and Hawkes, who then acquired the publication rights for all his music.[11]

After the second tour to North Africa, there was a change in the New Hungarian Quartet when Sándor Végh decided to quit and return to Hungary. Székely recalls that the search for a new second violinist began immediately:

> I agreed with Vilmos Palotai that he should approach his old friend, Ödön Pártos, to join the quartet as second violinist. His acceptance of the quartet position would give us the opportunity to have another Hungarian violinist with training similiar to our own. Pártos had been a pupil of Hubay and had studied composition with Kodály. After his training at the academy he had spent five years in Berlin, returning to Budapest in 1933. Pártos did accept our invitation and we tried for awhile to see how things would go.

In the early fall, Koromzay and Palotai returned to Holland from Budapest with Pártos and his wife. In Amsterdam the Székelys and Eva (Susie) Tormay, Koromzay's fiancée, met the returning party at the station to welcome the new quartet member and his wife.

They rehearsed Beethoven's Op. 59, No. 1, with the new violinist during the first weeks of the new 1938–39 concert season. During these rehearsals Pártos may have regretted his decision to join them. He soon disappeared without saying goodbye, leaving a note to tell them that he had gone to take up a position in the Tel Aviv Philharmonic in Israel.[12]

Very soon after the abrupt departure of Pártos, they found an excellent new colleague in Holland, the violinist Alexandre Moskowsky. He was a professor at the Muzieklyceum in Amsterdam, had his own quartet, and had lived in Holland as long as Székely had, although they were not acquainted.

> Moskowsky was recommended to us by Géza Frid. Although I didn't know it at the time, Sascha was eager to em-

igrate to the United States, and in fact, he already had the
visa.

He was Russian, born at Kertch in the Crimea in 1901.
He studied with Leopold Auer in St. Petersburg. After he graduated, Alexander Glazounov, the director of the St. Petersburg Conservatory, helped him to go abroad to Holland.

With Alexandre Moskowsky as second violinist, the quartet appeared in Czechoslovakia at Trencianske-Teplice during the fall of
1938. A few miles from Trencín, the spa at Teplice (with its natural
thermal pool, Zelená Zaba) was the site of an annual music festival.
Many critics from Budapest attended the quartet's concerts at the festival and later reported success. A tour of ten concerts in Czechoslovakia was proposed for the following season as a result. While the
prospect of this tour was cause for celebration, the quartet celebrated
another important event in Trencín, as well. Recently in Budapest,
Dénes Koromzay had married his fiancée, Susie Tormay.

When the quartet had returned to Holland to continue their rehearsals, Székely heard again from Bartók. He was in the process of
changing editors, and new complications had arisen with the Violin
Concerto. Universal-Edition did not want him to go to Boosey and
Hawkes, and he could not finish any work until he was free from Universal-Edition since he had to give them any finished compositions.
However, even one note missing from an unfinished work was sufficient reason for him to retain it in his possession. In view of this he
did not want to finish the concerto at that time, and this was probably at least part of the reason why its completion was long delayed.
From Basel on 28 June 1938, Bartók wrote to Székely:

My situation is still in limbo, at best it will clear itself
somewhat within a few weeks. What is involved is that I
should be freed from the claws of the Viennese robbers but
this is not so simple, it requires a highly diplomatic approach.
If I succeed in escaping the clutch of the Universal-Edition
highwaymen, I will go with another publisher (English). In
that case I can finish the violin concerto by September, but
then the new publisher will have something to say about our
business. If I don't escape them what will happen is what I
told you on the phone. However, there is one hitch in any
case. You told me at that time on the phone that for one year
you will have time to play the work several times but how

much time you will have afterwards is very questionable. (This was my first thought last year when I heard the news about you joining the quartet.) Now then it would be no good for anyone to have such a long term agreement in effect with only a few performances. How do you see it?

I don't write about the deplorable situation in Hungary, I imagine you know the most important aspects. It would be best to emigrate before it is too late; but how and where? Would I achieve anything by it? Too bad I couldn't answer your letter right away, I would have wanted to begin with "Hooray for Székelys!! this is really happy news, we greet the little Székely in advance on the occasion of his entry into the world." Are you sufficiently happy about it?[13]

The congratulatory ending to this letter is a response to the news Székely had written previously to the Bartóks. Mientje was expecting a child. Now he wrote to tell Bartók that he was having exciting weeks with the quartet, that there might be a tour in Czechoslovakia where ten concerts had been proposed as a result of the successful performances at the festival in Trencín, and that the new second violinist, Alexandre Moskowsky, had turned out well. Again he begged him to finish the Violin Concerto and assured him that he would make time and reserve a period for its performance every year. By then the first performances were scheduled for Amsterdam and The Hague with the Amsterdam Concertgebouw Orchestra under the direction of Willem Mengelberg.

The Székely's only child, a son, was born on 19 September 1938 in a Haarlem hospital near Bloemendaal. His parents gave him an old family name—Franciscus Jacobus. He was called Frans. Later he would be known as Frans Székely-Everts, and finally in America, simply as Frank S. Everts. Mientje was well and happy, Frans was strong and healthy, a good boy who didn't cry. Before leaving The Rhapsody after her stay of one month, Mientje's mother, Anna Everts, wrote about her new grandson in the guest book:

Our dear little Frans was born on September 19. Outside there were heavy thunder clouds in the European skies, but in The Rhapsody there was a new little star in the sky and this made everything bright. Everything is so good here. Frans does what he must to become strong. His father is having success in England and Ireland and dreaming and thinking of mother and son.

Plate 57. The New Hungarian String Quartet with Béla Bartók in Budapest in 1935. (Left to right: Sandor Végh, László Halmos, Dénes Koromzay, Vilmos Palotai, and Béla Bartók.) PHOTOGRAPHY JÓSZEF PÉCSI. THE KOROMZAY COLLECTION.

Plate 58. The New Hungarian String Quartet with Ezra Pound in Rapallo in 1937. (Left to right: Dénes Koromzay, Sándor Végh, Ezra Pound, Zoltán Székely, and Vilmos Palotai.) THE KOROMZAY COLLECTION.

Plate 59. The New Hungarian String Quartet in Budapest in 1937. (Left to right: Zoltán Székely, Sándor Végh, Dénes Koromzay, and Vilmos Palotai.) THE KOROMZAY COLLECTION.

Plate 60. The New Hungarian String Quartet at The Rhapsody in 1938. (Left to right: Dénes Koromzay, Alexandre Moskowsky, Zoltán Székely, and Vilmos Palotai.) PHOTOGRAPHY IGMINIA SZÉKELY. THE SZÉKELY COLLECTION.

Plate 61. Bartók's home at 29 Csalán Street in Budapest where he composed the Violin Concerto during 1937–38. PHOTOGRAPHY ADÁM FRIEDRICH.

A very important letter came from Budapest the week of their son's birth. In his letter of 14 September 1938 Bartók wrote extensively about the new Violin Concerto:

> I wanted to write you for a long time, but all my work, etc. Unfortunately, concerning the Universal-Edition case, there are still only "negotiations." I can still only write you as last time that if I don't want to jeopardize the appearance of the concerto for fifty years plus my lifetime then I cannot finish the work now, only three years later. Those Germans are wild beasts and if that man [Ralph Hawkes] is unsuccessful in settling with them they might not let me go just out of spite. In case of an unsuccessful settlement, that is, if we have to wait three years, our agreement naturally is not binding on you; if you want to, you can sign another one with me or you can drop the whole thing. True, after waiting for three years we could hardly talk about six years exclusive rights but, in order that you don't lose on the deal, I would offer that the fee be reduced by one-third. By the way, what the new publisher who is negotiating with Universal-Edition now also doesn't like is the long six year term of exclusivity. I submit the idea that in case I will be able to become free of the U.E., go to the new publisher by the end of December, and therefore finish the concerto and "deliver it" to you, would you consider reducing the length of exclusivity to three years, of course in return for reducing the fee by one-third? It is entirely up to you for, if you don't want to do that, I will naturally respect our original agreement.
>
> Neither while I am alive nor after my death do I want any German publisher to have any of my work even if it means that no work of mine will ever be published again. This is for now what is fixed and final.
>
> I was diligent: the score for the first and second movements is ready, the third movement in sketches (with the exception of the coda that was planned to be short also, by the way) is also ready, five pages of it are already orchestrated. I think the third movement turned out very well, actually a free variation of the first (thus I got the best of you, I wrote variations after all). . . .

Here Bartók refers jokingly to their previous debate over the matter of the form of the new work. While creating the Violin Concerto as Székely had requested, Bartók simultaneously fulfilled his desire to write in a variation form: the third movement, Allegro molto, is a free variation on the opening movement, Allegro non troppo, making a large-scale variation of the entire work. He continues to write candidly of the concerto in a way that was unusual for him when speaking of his own work:

> it is brilliant, effective, with some new things in it; before the coda there is an (orchestra-accompanied) cadenza, about eight minutes. The main theme is in 3/4 time:

> (violin entirely alone). The second section after a few bars of tutti (this already with imitational accompaniment).

Writing the score really takes time, on average <u>at least</u> three to four hours per page! The first and second movements total 51 pages, the third will be around 35 to 40.

However, while I was diligent, you were not! I would need your counter suggestions concerning articulation, etc., after all that is why I gave you the piano reduction so that you could mark in your recommendations (slurs, bowings, etc.) (In the cadenza of the first movement I already eliminated the discomfort in the passage in fifths, in the second movement I also adjusted the penultimate pizzicato variation). Thus, you should now send me the piano score in a hurry with your notes, so that I can enter the slur markings in the score; because that is all that is missing. If you won't do that, I don't know what to do, shall I ask the advice of Zathureczky or Waldbauer? Since I wrote you this concerto it should really be in accordance with your suggestions that I should finalize the violin solo part.

Another question: should I send the copy of the score even during such uncertain times? (of course, only in November, by bringing it with me) and if yes, how many copies do you want besides the obligatory one? (I figure the cost will be around 27 pengős per copy): we have discussed this already, but I have forgotten what you said.

To resume the whole thing: I will finish the work by November–December (except perhaps the coda in the third
movement), in November I can give you the score of the first
and second movements, in December, of the third. But in
case I can't escape the Universal-Edition, we must postpone
the whole thing for three years.[14]

On 30 September, the day that the quartet departed for England,
Székely wrote to Bartók explaining that due to the events of these
weeks he had no time to mark the violin part of the concerto. He felt
that to do a superficial job of the important task of annotating the
violin part would have made no sense; therefore, he asked that the
score be copied without his markings, Bartók indicating only the
slurs he thought appropriate.

At thirty-five, Székely was more deeply commited to thoroughness in such matters than ever before. Never imagining in 1938 how
little time was left to their collaboration, he suggested to his older
colleague that later on they should make a violin part together, with
the final, exact markings. Unfortunately this was not to happen.

Chapter Seventeen

Bartók's New Masterpiece

By 1938 the New Hungarian String Quartet had the assistance of three distinguished concert managements: Bureau de Concert Marcel de Valmalète in France; Concertdirectie Dr. Géza de Koos in Holland; and, in England, Ibbs and Tillet. In October the quartet traveled to London to play several important concerts. When they arrived they invited Miss Emmie Bass, the young secretary at Ibbs and Tillet, to a deluxe three-and-a-half shilling lunch at the Mount Royal Hotel. During lunch they discussed their plans with her since she was to arrange the details of their London concerts. Their meeting with Miss Bass seems a fateful one. She was eventually to have a great influence on the career of the quartet when later she became Mrs. Emmie Tillet. She reigned as managing director at Ibbs and Tillet until the age of eighty and was devoted to the career of the quartet for thirty-five years.

For the London Contemporary Music Centre at Cowdray Hall there was a concert on 4 October of four modern works: Quartet No. 2 by Sándor Veress, Arthur Honegger's Quartet No. 3, Henk Badings' Second Quartet, and the world premiere of Elizabeth Maconchy's new Quartet No. 3, written for the Hungarians. "In sum, there is a fair credit balance from these four new works, all of which had the inestimable advantage of being played by a quartet of quite exceptional brilliance who had, moreover, full understanding of the modern id-

ioms involved," wrote the critic of the *Times*.[1] The reviewer of the
Daily Telegraph commented:

> Three of these compositions—quartets by Henk Badings,
> Elizabeth Maconchy, and Sándor Veress—were dedicated to
> the valiant executants. The performance of their compatriot
> Veress' exacting score, in particular, was impressive in its en-
> ergy and evident thoroughness.
>
> Veress is a pupil of Bartók and Kodály, and his work sug-
> gests that an atmosphere of almost inhuman intellectuality
> is breathed in academic Budapest. It is a strenuous exercise
> in a craggy region high above the vegetated zone. Of the
> evening's music it was the most "contemporary" in the con-
> temporary sense. The Dutchman, Badings, is also a climber,
> uncompromising and dogged. In Holland, too, it seems,
> youth feels that a grim face must be put to the world.
>
> After Badings' rigidity, Miss Maconchy's new one-move-
> ment work, Quartet No. 3, came with an effect of ease and al-
> most charm, though there was nothing slack in this heroic
> elegy. The impression was left that the work might be the
> slow movement of a vast composition, the rest of which
> might be expected to employ other resources of the four
> strings here unexploited.
>
> The elder generation was represented by Arthur Honeg-
> ger's new Quartet No. 3, no doubt the most consummate
> piece of writing of the evening, yet somewhat disappoint-
> ingly elusive, for all the grace and spirit of the style.[2]

On 7 October the New Hungarian String Quartet appeared again
in London at the BBC Broadcasting House in the first of the 1938
season of BBC concerts of contemporary music with Maconchy's
Quartet No. 3 and Honegger's new work. Luigi Dallapiccola's Divertimento for soprano and ensemble with Hélène Ludolph, soprano,
and an ensemble including Koromzay and Palotai, concluded the
program.

The following evening at Wigmore Hall, the New Hungarian
String Quartet appeared in the second series of popular concerts of
chamber music arranged by André Mangeot. These concerts, given in
the hour before dinner on the first Monday of each month, seemed
to have met a real demand, and there was a large audience on this occasion. The program comprised Kodály's Quartet, Op. 10, No. 2, and
Schubert's Op. 161.

The critic of the *London Sunday Times* wrote, "Their inside view of it [Kodály's Quartet No. 2] governed the show of spirit without frenzy, delicacy without threadiness, of which they have the knack."[3] The *Times* found the performances first-rate throughout, combining great vigor with tunefulness, sensitive phrasing, and a fine balance between the four instruments. The Kodály quartet he thought admirably performed: " The slow movement consists of a long cantilena for the first violin which was finely played by Zoltán Székely."[4]

After the London concerts, the ensemble went north to perform in Ireland and Wales. In Belfast the quartet played a more traditional program for the British Music Society of Northern Ireland in Smyth Hall: Mozart's Quartet, K. 387, Beethoven's Op. 59, No. 1, and Smetana's Quartet, Op. 116 ("From My Life"). In Ireland, audiences and critics alike received the performance warmly. Mr. Rathcol wrote in the *Belfast Telegraph*:

> The New Hungarian Quartet . . . gave us what was, all in all, the most fascinating presentation of chamber music locally since the palmy days of the Brodsky Quartet.
> . . . this was Mozart of an aristocratic aloofness with less immediate appeal than by the direct method, but in the end striking deeper, I fancy, for all who had ears to hear.
> . . . I for one shall never forget the exceeding beauty of tone and shape and balance of this performance. . . .
> Technically these players are, with their scale of values, exceedingly accomplished; and it was a valuable lesson for the young people present, who may be disposed to put their trust in drawing the long bow, to note how much was achieved with how little bow-length in those heavenly *pianissimi,* a hardly perceptible half-inch or so. Spiritually it was, above all in the Mozart, playing which was a gift from the gods: and, as such, a gift only for the true in heart.[5]

The same program drew similiar praise in Cardiff where the New Hungarian Quartet was heard as a perfect ensemble with all the technical and interpretive qualities that are usually associated with the artistry of great quartets. The reviewer, who could not recall the equal of the quartet with its fiery temperament, wrote, "All the qualities which go to the successful performance of the string quartet were present—beautiful phrasing, delicacy and vigour, rhythm, and interpretative insight."[6]

Back in London, the quartet played an all-Schubert concert on 31 October for the Schubert Society at the Royal Institute of British Architects. The program included two quartets, the A Minor and the G Major. The Quartet in G Major, Op. 161, which was to become one of the most successful works in the group's repertoire, was written during a ten-day period in the final year of Schubert's life. This last quartet is one of the least played of Schubert's quartets, yet the composer thought so highly of this work that he selected the first movement to be performed by Böhm, Holz, Weiss, and Linke at the only private concert of his life, eight months before his death.

The critic of the *Daily Telegraph and Morning Post* found the group's ensemble and balance impeccable, the variety of tone amazing, and the rhythm a model of flexibility. He wrote of the performance of the two Schubert quartets, "Works so dissimilar demand very different kinds of handling, and the best tribute to the virtuosity, alike technical and interpretative, of the New Hungarian Quartet is that something very like perfection was achieved in both."[7]

After their concert for the Schubert Society, the New Hungarian String Quartet made its earliest recording, in 1938 for His Master's Voice at their London studios on Abbey Road. They recorded two sides of a 78 rpm record with Tchaikovsky's *Andante Cantabile* and the Nocturne from Borodin's String Quartet in D Major. This appeared on the market, but the war interrupted any further recording by the quartet; however, in 1946 they continued with EMI in London recording Haydn, Mozart, Beethoven, and Bartók.

For some years Mientje had been improving her Hungarian, and Bartók often reacted to her enthusiasm for his native language with spontaneous interest. Minetje recalled that, "After a visit to Scotland in February of 1932, Bartók sent me a message written in Hungarian that was obviously intended to help me learn the Hungarian use of the double negative."

It included such words as *never*, *nowhere*, and *nobody* woven into a clever postscript. He wrote that he never played with such a bad violinist, that no one had said anything interesting to him, he would never forget how good it was in Nijmegen, there he never had any rest, was not left in peace except that very day he wrote when he had nothing to do whatever.[8]

On 24 October 1938 Bartók wrote Mientje a polyglot letter congratulating the Székelys on the birth of their son, Frans.

Dear Mien!

It is a shame that we didn't immediately respond after having received the news[9] and that we did not shout forth in a letter: long live the little Francis Jacob,[10] to everyone's joy and the happiness of his parents, hurrah![11] So now we are making up for it several times over and in a polyglot way.— Do not be annoyed by our delay.

Meantime, so much trouble has broken out all over the world, such unrest, such fright—-and now this shocking recoil on the part of the Western countries. One ought to get away from here, from the neighborhood of that pestilential country, far, far away, but where: to Greenland, Cape Colony, the Tierra del Fuego, the Fiji Islands, or somewhere even the Almighty has not heard of!

I got your letter. What Zoltán wrote in it is all right; he just forgot to answer one thing. But now it's all the same; soon—if nothing intervenes—we shall be going to Holland, and I shall meet him; then we will talk it over.

I am afraid you will not quite understand my very genuine Hungarian expressions but I can't help it: in writing to you my mind pours out the most colorful words—And then I didn't want to use that cursed language of our neighbors, whom I hate more than ever.[12]

Our best wishes to you, to your little darling and to your husband.

So long,[13]

Béla

As she often did, Ditta Bartók added a postscript: "From my innermost heart I wish all three of you much joy and happiness. Ditta."[14]

Somewhat earlier Bartók had agreed with Antonia Kossar's arrangements for a broadcast and recital planned for November. In addition to some works that Bartók and Székely would play together, there would be piano solos and works for two pianos, since Ditta was coming with him. On 13 November they broadcast at AVRO, in Hilversum. Together Székely and Bartók played the Mozart Sonata, K. 448, Bartók played solos from *Mikrokosmos*, then he and Ditta played Debussy's *En blanc et noir*. The following day Bartók signed the Székely's guest book for what was to be his last visit to The Rhapsody, although of course they could not know that then. He wrote, "Once more! Béla Bartók. 1938. November 14."

The recital was in the Kleine Zaal of the Amsterdam Concertgebouw on 15 November. This was the last time Székely and Bartók performed together in public. The program included Mozart's Sonata in A Major, K. 526, the First Rhapsody, and Székely's transcription of the *Rumanian Folk Dances*. After the intermission Béla and Ditta Bartók played Debussy's *En blanc et noir* and Bartók's new Sonata for Two Pianos and Percussion with Charles Smit and Theo van Dijk, two percussionists from the Amsterdam Concertgebouw Orchestra, assisting them.

Arntzenius wrote in *De Telegraaf*, "Székely's warm and noble tone color was riveting. The evening left nothing to be desired."[15] Sensing that the two artists made an ideal combination, the critic of the *Nieuwe Rotterdamsche Courante* wrote of their outstanding interpretation of the music, "It was a great privilege to hear the Master play his own work with such a partner as Székely in the First Rhapsody and the *Rumanian Folk Dances*."[16]

Although Székely already had a copy of the manuscript for the first movement of the Violin Concerto, there was no time for them to discuss it in detail. In fact, the violinist had to rush to catch the night train for Switzerland and didn't hear the second half of the concert.

Several important performances of the new Sonata for Two Pianos and Percussion had taken place before this in Basel, Luxembourg, and London. The premiere had been on 16 January 1938 in Basel with the Bartóks as pianists and Fritz Schiesser and Philipp Rühlig as the percussionists. This performance marked Ditta Bartók's first public appearance in a foreign country. In May, the Bartóks played the sonata in Luxembourg. In June they performed it for an ISCM festival in London.

Jaap and Loes de Graaff had moved from London to France in 1937 and now lived on their country estate at Mont de Marsan in the Landes region, about 80 kilometers south of Bordeaux. During 1938 the quartet visited their estate, Beaussiet, and there saw not only "Oom Jaap and Tante Loes" as they were fondly called, but also Pál Hermann and his wife, Ada Weevers, who was Jaap de Graaff's niece. One of Ada Hermann's brothers worked as de Graaff's estate foreman, overseeing the operation of his diversified business interests. At Mont de Marsan this primarily involved producing resin products from the forest and wine from the vineyards. De Graaff's main business affairs had to do with supplying foodstuffs, especially Australian fowl, to the Lyons chain in London.

Mientje approached Oom Jaap to request his assistance in helping Koromzay acquire a fine viola suitable for his performances with
the New Hungarian String Quartet. Koromzay recalls the circumstances of the acquisition:

> At the old Français shop in Paris I found a Venetian viola,
> an instrument by Domenico Busan of the Gofriller School.
> Palotai encouraged me to take it since its unusually large di-
> mensions endowed it with an organ-like tone suitable to en-
> semble playing. Oom Jaap purchased it for my use in the
> quartet and I played this extremely large, eighteen-and-one
> half-inch viola for many years.[17] Unfortunately, I did so to
> my physical detriment as I realized later, when the effects of
> the physical strain became apparent in my playing.
>
> I played this viola for the de Graaffs for the first time dur-
> ing our visit in 1938 when Pál Hermann was at Mont de
> Marsan and joined the quartet in some music-making.

While deeply involved in the final preparation of his new Violin
Concerto, Bartók wrote a letter to Székely on 6 December 1938 which
is a document of instructions regarding how the orchestral parts were
to be copied—what was to be improved and changed—from the copy
of the manuscript score which he had sent three days previously:

> With great difficulty I have finished 60 pages; for the time
> being I sent you three copies on the 3rd, the other two copies
> will follow later. A few folios are not folded at the right place,
> these can be corrected at home. One page turned out too
> big, it must be folded in, unfortunately that one can't be
> corrected.
>
> There are remarks here and there, only in Hungarian;
> would you please translate these into English or French and
> write them into the copies, so that the copyist can write them
> that way as well into the parts.
>
> Call the attention of the copyist to the following:
> 1) at changes of meter he should not write ‖ double lines
> (and in general he should always follow the original).
> 2) the parts of indeterminate-pitch percussion should be
> written on one line, not on five, and he should not scribble in
> clefs, for example 𝄢 for bass drum or 𝄞 for snaredrum!

3) flauto II muta fl. picc. (one part)
   Ob. II muta cor. ing. (one part)
   Clar. II muta clar. basso (one part)
   Fag. I muta contrafag. (one part)
5) after long rests the cues should <u>not</u> be taken from the Violin solo if possible (in general they should be taken from related or neighboring instruments).
6) "tacet" must only be written in exceptional cases (only if it can't cause any confusion about entrances; thus <u>tacet al fine</u> is possible; but at the beginning or middle of movements "tacet" is not suitable.

———————— • ————————

I marked the duration of various sections under the lines so:

Of course, I have already found some typographical errors:
Movement I:
Measure 68 in the viola.

Measure 106 in flute 1. The last quarter note tr. is missing.

Measure 108 in trumpet 1 and 2. two tenuto signs are missing.
Measure 109 in Fl. picc. "muta in fl. 2" is missing.
There will be plenty more errors.

I beg of you to correct the mistakes very carefully and make a list of errors found and of questionable places. And finally, please write the agreed-upon changes on an "agreement addenda" (in two copies) and send them to me so I can sign them.

Yesterday I reached page 71, perhaps there will be another 19 (that is, a total of 90); I would very much like to finish it by Christmas, but I don't know whether it is possible. Perhaps—when 20 pages are ready—I'll have them done and send them, in order not to draw it out so long.

And finally, I strongly recommend that the duplicating of the parts should be done by <u>Lichtpaus</u> [photocopied], and in nice, orderly, flawless fashion. Because, in that case, there might be a possibility that, when the time comes, the publisher will buy from you the photocopied materials. Of course, this is only a suggestion without any guarantee.

Best wishes to all of you from both of us!

Béla[18]

"After Béla's letter in October when he said 'One ought to get away from here—far away,' I began to worry seriously about his situation," Mientje recalled during an interview in 1973.

I wrote to him about my personal concerns because I was much afraid for his safety. Since he was so open-minded and couldn't stand fascism, I was sure that he would get in trouble. Because I was so much younger and we loved him so much I wrote him a letter and told him, "Béla, you can't stay there, you must go. You have to leave Europe somehow." Much later I felt somewhat responsible that he was so unhappy in America, but I knew in 1938 that he was in danger and because he was naïve in a way and couldn't imagine the consequences of his frankness he might have been killed in Europe, so you never know. Of course, he had been to America earlier and while he didn't mention going to America at the time of our letters, he wrote already that one should leave Hungary.

His health was not good and that was a serious worry. Even when he was young he was often ill. At the beginning of our friendship he had some internal disorder and Zoltán's doctor father went to see him. Yes, he was very often ill.

Most of the time there was good clean air on the dunes by the sea and he felt good at our home in Holland, but one day in 1937 when he was our guest he didn't come down in the morning and when Zoltán went up to his room, he was in bed with a high fever.

Immediately we called the doctor because he was so ill. The doctor looked at his throat and he tried every possible thing, but found no reason for this illness, only a high fever. In America, they would have sent him to the hospital to take tests, but they didn't do that in Holland. He was so terribly thin and miserably ill. Of course, at that time they didn't consider leukemia, the illness he finally died of a few years later.

He didn't want to go to the hospital so I assured him he

could stay as long as possible in our home. During that week of illness he was so grateful if one brought him something to drink or had an easy conversation. His illness suddenly stopped.

Another letter to Mientje, written in English on 10 January 1939 in Budapest, arrived from Bartók.

Dear Mien,

your kind and loving letter gave us a kind of emotion not yet experienced: is the situation as bad as you see it?! Of course, since March we are sure there will be a change to worse or to worst which will perhaps make it impossible to work here and even to live here. But in the country you mention, would it be possible to do that work which is so very important for me (I mean the scientific work)? I don't think so. If I can only "vegetate" there, then it would be of no use to change "domicile." I think it extremely difficult to decide something in that way and really I am at a loss what to do. In any case, still we must wait for some more decisive sign of change. Sure, I feel rather uncomfortable to live so very near to the clutches of the nazis or even in the clutches; but to live elsewhere would—it seems at least for the moment—not make things easier.

Bartók continued with further instructions about the Violin Concerto:

Yesterday I posted the following:
(1) 2 copies of pages 1–60 of the violin-concerto; you have to do nothing with these, only keep them at home.
(2) two copies of pages 61–80 of the same work; one of these you have to send immediately to the copyist who is writing the orchestra-parts.

Enclosed in this letter you see a "list of the errors" detected until now, you have to give it also to the copyist except for the last part of it marked with red [encircled], this you have to send to Zoltán.

———— • ————

In two days I will send you the following copies:
(1) Two other copies of pages 61–80; keep them at home.

(2) Three copies of pages 81–96; one of them you must give to the copyist and another you have to send immediately to Zoltán.

(3) One copy of the piano-arrangement of the concerto; this also you must send immediately to Zoltán.

Please will you kindly "acknowledge receipt" of all this material.

——————— • ———————

We will be in Paris from 25 Febr. until 3. March, it is very, very important for both of us: Zoltán and myself to have a meeting there and to be able to go through the work. He must arrange it, as—in any case he is going through Paris just at the same time.

Yours very sincerely,

Béla[19]

Székely sent a postcard to Bartók to confirm the plans to rehearse the Violin Concerto in France. Bartók responded on 8 February 1939 with a postcard telling the name of the hotel in Paris where he and Ditta would stay:

I was happy to read your postcard with the news that you will be in Paris between the 4th and 7th of March. We [the Bartóks] shall stay at the Hotel Vouillemont on the rue Boissy d'Angelas (Madeleine area). Too bad you entered the modifications on the original contract; had you made separate supplementary and post-contracts in 2 copies I would have sent it back signed a long time ago. Now this way I have to look for my original copy, enter the changes etc., in brief, I don't have the time. I will take it to Paris and give it to you. I have discovered a few more unfortunate mistakes (who knows how many are hiding still!) the list of which is on the enclosed page, give it to the copyist immediately.

Warmest greetings until we meet,

Béla.

By the time you are in Paris, you must know your part perfectly![20]

When the opportunity came for them to meet in Paris, Székely and Bartók talked extensively about the Violin Concerto, played and rehearsed it thoroughly. There was just over one month before the first performance.

> We rehearsed every day for four days at the home of Pál Hermann, who was by then living and working in Paris. As we went through the concerto very thoroughly, I made a number of suggestions, probably the most significant one concerning the end of the exposition in the first movement. It was about the orchestral episode between the end of the violin solo and the new entrance in the development section. I felt that those six bars of tutti were not sufficient, and that the section should be somewhat longer. Of course, the moment I made this suggestion he protested, since he had the feeling that it was all right, although for me that modulation was too sudden.
>
> We argued for awhile, then played it through. He thought silently for a few minutes. Again, as so often, he took me by surprise when he said, "All right, I agree, but I have no time to make corrections before I get back to Budapest and it would be too late to write it into the orchestral score and parts, so go ahead and make the change yourself." This I did. When I played it in Amsterdam for the first time, this passage was as I wrote it. The few bars of extension as well as some other modifications which I proposed are incorporated in the final version.[21]
>
> As we worked together, he played at the piano and I played the violin part and we talked over what should be done and how it should be played. I must say that generally he was very pleased and we had not much trouble with it. During these working sessions Bartók made pencil corrections to the copy I used, a reduction for violin and piano. Later these corrections were made in the orchestral score from which Mengelberg conducted the first performance, but that copy of the score disappeared into Mengelberg's possessions.
>
> Bartók intended that some of the percussion instruments be placed in definite positions on the stage. He asked me to convey this information to Mengelberg, which I did. At the rehearsals and the first performance, the harp, the xylophone, and the celesta were very near to me, insuring a certain intimacy of ensemble during passages in the slow movement, for instance, *Un poco più tranquillo* at measure 23.
>
> Perhaps in this matter Bartók was under the influence of

his *Music for Strings, Percussion, and Celesta* which was composed just before the Violin Concerto. In the printed score of that work, he gave explicit instructions for the stringed instruments to be divided into two separate groups and showed a plan for the relative positions on the stage of all the instruments. Perhaps he meant to do likewise in the case of the certain instruments employed in the Violin Concerto, but no such information was printed in the score.

There are a few errors in the printed orchestral score, perhaps not so important, but some that are important. There are a few wrong notes, for instance. There are certain instructions which did get into print, and others that did not, instructions that I wrote in pencil as we talked them over in the rehearsals in Paris.[22]

Regarding the orchestration, Bartók once said, "When I orchestrate, I write it down right away, as though composing, rather than later as instrumentation." In my opinion the concerto is over-orchestrated in some places, although when I played it once at the Banff Centre in Canada with Walter Susskind conducting, he was very enthusiastic about the orchestration. For Bartók the orchestral color is important and the orchestration was a pleasure for him.

Bartók dedicated the Violin Concerto to me with the words "To my dear friend Zoltán Székely" on top of the first page. With these words and the dedication of this splendid work, I felt richly rewarded for my devotion in advancing the music of this great genius.

After Paris we went our separate ways. We never suspected that this was to be the last time we would see each other.

Bartók wrote Mientje from Basel two days later on 9 March 1939:

Dear Mien,

We had very good and long rehearsals together—Zoltán and myself—in Paris, he plays the solo-part of the concerto splendidly indeed. I am sending you enclosed a few bars (alternative), you have to give it immediately to the copyist.—We are in a hurry, are leaving Basel for Budapest in a few minutes. I hope the performance of the concerto will be excellent, what a pity that I can't be present.

Yours, with the kindest regards,

Béla[23]

After his meeting with Bartók in Paris, Székely continued his quartet tour, traveling to Switzerland for two concerts in Vevey and a third concert in Basel.

> I had to travel with great haste after the Basel concert to get back to Amsterdam for the three rehearsals and the performance of the new concerto.
>
> Mengelberg had programmed Beethoven's *Egmont* Overture and the Tchaikovsky Fifth Symphony along with the Bartók Violin Concerto and since these two orchestral works were well known to the Concertgebouw Orchestra, an unusual amount of time was spent rehearsing the new work.[24] In fact, one of the orchestra rehearsals was moved away from the Concertgebouw, which was already in use.
>
> I remember that at my first hearing there were some mistakes in the harp part in the first movement which I had to correct. I gave suggestions to Mengelberg, and, really surprisingly, he accepted them all and tried to do them right away. Even the percussion was placed in the orchestra as Bartók had wished when possible.

Chapter Eighteen

Occupied Holland

Zoltán Székely played the world premiere of Bartók's Violin Concerto with the Amsterdam Concertgebouw under the direction of Willem Mengleberg on 23 March 1939. Two days later they repeated the performance in The Hague. During the period that followed there were performances in Amsterdam, Rotterdam, Arnhem, and in the provinces, and eventually in Brussels before Queen Elisabeth of Belgium.

The Dutch press praised the new work and the performers. Arntzenius wrote in *De Telegraaf*: "Szekely played like a true master. . . . Here we have a great artist, a great soloist who was one with the music."[1] In *Algemeen Handelsblad*, Herman Rutters wrote:

> For a world premiere of a work which Bartók only finished three months ago, the audience's applause was well deserved by Székely, the soloist, the orchestra and Mengelberg. Székely solved the very difficult problems perfectly well. . . . The Concerto is a great work and Székely's interpretation deserves all praise.[2]

"The new Concerto is a great victory," wrote Lou van Strien, the critic of *Nieuwe Rotterdamsche Courant*.

> Bartók has reached new heights and has managed to solve all the problems, has fused all aspects together to form

a new work. But we must hear the work often. With so masterful an interpretation as Székely has played and Mengelberg has conducted, we hope the foundation is laid for the work to be played many times.

Székely played with a crystal-clear and noble tone, and performed with convincing involvement. As an artist, he has reached a well-deserved place among the select few. The coolness that used to exist in his earlier years is gone. Warm, clear, and virtuosic playing is now evident in a special way that is only given to a great artist. This was a great success for everyone.[3]

The second performance in The Hague, which was attended by Princess Juliana, was very well received by the audience. As Székely was applauded, a beautiful bouquet was handed to him tied with ribbons of the national Hungarian colors. This he handed politely to Mengelberg who then asked the orchestra to stand and receive their part of the celebration. The reviewer of the *Nieuwe Rotterdamsche Courante* wrote on 26 March 1939:

The new Concerto is a work that one can love. Bartók is a giant and in this work he uses everything that has arrived in the past and everything is in perfect balance. Székely, Mengelberg, and the orchestra certainly deserved our admiration and our gratitude although all of this is most deserved by the creator, Béla Bartók.[4]

"Székely and Mengelberg solved all their problems with self-evident and perfect knowledge," wrote A. de Wal in *Het Vaderland*, then continued:

Székely's beautiful tone, his freedom, and yet his discipline, his perfect sense of style, his enthusiasm, and lively virtuosity lifted the work very, very high. The orchestra's part was also very well done. Princess Juliana and the public were very enthusiastic.[5]

AVRO recorded the premiere live. For the purposes of broadcast repetitions, the sound engineers from Hilversum made acetate discs of the performance. Székely eventually acquired this recording from AVRO after relayed broadcasts in Europe were completed. Fortunately he and his wife had the foresight to protect the delicate acetate discs over the years. Sometime later, before the Belgian conductor Franz André led an Amsterdam performance, Székely gave him the opportunity to listen to the original discs, and during his study the delicate records were damaged somewhat.

Stored in one of Mientje's hatboxes, the acetate records survived a world war, traveled around the world with the Székelys, and came with them eventually to North America. When the National Recording Branch of the Hungarian Archive Department produced a complete edition of Bartók's works in the 1970s, Székely's permission was asked to include the recording of the world premiere, as a supplement. The original 1939 discs were used as the matrix in spite of their slight damage. The newly remastered LP recording was surprisingly successful from a technical standpoint, and the historical legacy was a welcome addition to the complete edition. In 1989 it was reissued as a compact disc recording.[6] And where are the precious contents of the hatbox today? They were entrusted to the Bartók Archívum in Budapest.

Bartók was not to hear a performance of the Violin Concerto until 1943 in Carnegie Hall. Unfortunately, he was never to hear a performance by Székely for whom he had composed the work. He and Ditta were performing in Budapest the night of the premiere in Amsterdam and evidently did not hear the European radio broadcasts that followed. However, Aladár Tóth and his wife, the pianist Annie Fischer, heard the broadcast in Sweden and wrote to Székely to express their pleasure.

> Aladár Tóth wrote me a lovely letter from Stockholm to say that he and Annie thought the broadcast of the premiere was beautiful, so we enjoyed knowing that Bartók would hear about it from Tóth. I had the sole performing rights for the work for that short period of time and never thought that Bartók would not hear it.
>
> Immediately after the premiere, the New Hungarian Quartet went on tour again, this time in Portugal. When we returned to Holland there was a letter from Bartók. On 3 April 1939 I answered to tell him about the premiere, to send him the press reviews, and to discuss another important matter, the final arrangements to settle my debt with him regarding our agreement. I proposed transferring 1760 pengős, an amount equal to the 500 Dutch guilders we had agreed upon, to a bank of his choice in Budapest.

I told him that at the premiere Mengelberg had seated the percussion instruments as he had wished, fulfilling his plan for a seating arrangement that he hoped would insure the intimacy of the ensemble playing, particularly in the second movement. I also wrote that Mengelberg planned to have a special score copied for himself since he no longer saw very well.

I assured him that Mengelberg was really taken by the concerto and that we had agreed to play it again the next season in Amsterdam and Rotterdam by which time I hoped the performances would go perfectly.[7]

Following the success of the Violin Concerto, the New Hungarian Quartet asked Bartók to write a string quartet especially for them. With Székely as spokesman, this negotiation was conducted entirely by correspondence. To their great joy, Bartók consented. This became his sixth and last quartet.

During the summer Bartók went to Switzerland where he was Paul Sacher's guest at a chalet at Saanen in the massif of Gruyère. There he worked on the new quartet. In a letter dated 18 August 1939 to his son, Béla, Jr., he wrote that he had another commission to fulfill and that it was a string quartet for Székely, for the New Hungarian Quartet.[8] This is the first mention of the commission in the extant literature.

The circumstances that surrounded the commissioning of the Sixth Quartet, the various exchanges of letters between composer and performers, and the final dedication and first performance cannot now be described with certainty by anyone other than Székely.

Although Bartók worked on the new quartet at Saanen, he did not finish the Sixth Quartet in Switzerland. He took it back to Budapest in the fall and continued to work on it there. The Sixth Quartet is the final work he completed in Hungary before going to America. He wrote in September to say that the new quartet was almost finished and asked whether we needed it soon. I answered on 3 October 1939 to tell him that we were very happy that it was so close to completion and asked him to finish it as soon as possible. At that time I mentioned that there was a worry, though, concerning the length of our exclusive rights to the piece. If the war were to last four to five years, by the time it finished our rights would have also expired. Thus I asked him to examine this problem, both with the Violin Concerto and the Sixth Quartet, hoping that surely he would find a solution favorable to both of us.[9]

Later he wrote me a nice letter asking whether we would object to his taking it in his portfolio to America so he could have some new work with him—even though it had been intended for us.

Once there he gave it to the Kolisch Quartet, which was a first-rate ensemble that also played much of his music. Well, I can understand it. He couldn't keep it back. The Kolisch Quartet was there in New York and he was well acquainted with them, so they did the first performance. That is what happened. In the end it doesn't make too much difference, dedicated to the one or to the other, and the Kolisch was a very good quartet. On 20 January 1941 they gave the first performance in New York of this work, written for our quartet but eventually dedicated to them.

The last day of August 1939 was the last day of peace in Europe. At noon Adolf Hitler ordered his armed forces to attack Poland the next day. Before dawn on 1 September a million-and-a-half German troops carried out his command, crossing the Polish borders and converging on Warsaw. Both England and France took immediate action with a declaration of war on Germany two days later. That night the British liner Athenia was torpedoed by a German submarine west of the Hebrides. The Second World War had begun.

During the beginning of the war in Europe, the New Hungarian Quartet still traveled, but in darkened trains and only in the neutral countries: Spain, Portugal, and Switzerland. Escape from Portugal to America was a possibility for some, especially those traveling alone. For Székely this was not an option, as he would not have attempted this difficult course of action with Mientje and Frans.

While the war had ruined all our plans, we hoped to sustain the new season in Holland. We began the 1939–40 season in October with a concert in Hilversum, then ten days later we played in the Kleine Zaal of the Amsterdam Concertgebouw, performing Henk Badings' Second Quartet along with Mozart and Kodály. After a performance in Zwolle for their chamber music series we returned to Amsterdam on 25 October to play Bartók's Second Quartet, Mozart, and Schubert. In November we played in Middelburg, Laren-Blaricum, Rotterdam, and again at the Concertgebouw, where we performed Darius Milhaud's Ninth Quartet, Brahms, and Beethoven. During those eight concerts we presented the works of Kodály, Bartók, Badings, and Milhaud combined with the classical repertoire of Mozart, Haydn, Beethoven, Schubert, and Brahms.

Since it was then still possible to travel to Switzerland, the quartet left Holland at the beginning of December and played again in Vevey. The director of Nestlé Chocolates, Emile Rossier, was a very influential music lover in Vevey and the guiding force of La Société des Arts et Lettres. The Société became a very important organization for the New Hungarian Quartet, and the four performances in Vevey during 1939 established the quartet as a favorite ensemble of the Société. After the war the quartet next appeared there in 1946, no longer called the *New* Hungarian String Quartet. Their artistic metamorphosis complete, they began their second decade with a new name—the Hungarian String Quartet. Their 1946 concert in Vevey marked the beginning of almost yearly visits, during which they presented more than thirty-five concerts for La Société des Arts et Lettres, spanning the lifetime of the quartet.

The Rumanian pianist Clara Haskil lived in Vevey. Later in the 1950s Charlie Chaplin and his wife, Oona, the daughter of playwright Eugene O'Neill, lived near Vevey in the village of Corsier. The Queen of Spain and the Count and Countess Chevreau d'Antraigues resided in the area occasionally. Film stars and writers—George and Benita Sanders, Noel Coward, and Truman Capote—found their way there as well.

After the concerts in Vevey the quartet returned to Holland to play in Nijmegen and Naarde-Bussum before departing for neutral Portugal where they gave two concerts in Lisbon—an all-Beethoven concert and one comprising quartets by Haydn, Sibelius, and Smetana. On 10 March 1940 Székely appeared with the Amsterdam Concertgebouw Orchestra in the fifth performance of the Bartók Violin Concerto. This was the first time since the premiere that the work was heard again in Amsterdam. Willem Mengelberg again conducted, and in addition to the concerto, the orchestra performed Berlioz' *Roman Carnival* Overture and Beethoven's Symphony No. 3.

Herman Rutters wrote in *Algemeen Handelsblad* how fine it was to hear the work again after the premiere the previous year:

The Concerto never crosses the border of being playable, but Bartók knows what can be trusted to Zoltán Székely, to whom the work is dedicated. It is no small thing and Székely again proved that he deserved this trust. He played with great artistry, totally intelligently, yet with virtuosity, spirit, and a noble, warm, expressive tone. The orchestra was supportive and Mengelberg did a fine job.[10]

A month later the Amsterdam Concertgebouw Orchestra traveled to Brussels to perform before Queen Elisabeth of Belgium in the concert hall of the Palais des Beaux-Arts at 23 rue Ravenstein. The concert opened with Weber's *Oberon* Overture and concluded with Brahms' First Symphony. Mengelberg mentioned to the press that the concert hall had "nearly too good an acoustic since one hears everything that happens on the podium and if one would drop a pin, even that would be heard."

Always interested in the violin and its music and hopeful for the new work's future, the Belgian Queen Elisabeth enthusiastically enjoyed the new concerto, as did the audience who had applauded after every movement, as one critic thought, "perhaps more for the virtuosity of Székely than for the new work although this unknown work wasn't so difficult to understand as one might think." Székely was asked back to the stage many times in recognition of his masterly performance.[11]

This journey to Brussels was Székely's last trip from Holland for five years. Upon his return home the next day, the quartet rehearsed for two concerts, one arranged for 9 April in Enschede where Henk Badings' Second Quartet, Beethoven, and Smetana would be played and another appearance the following night in Haarlem at the Stadsschouwburg. An hour before dawn on 9 April German envoys in Copenhagen and Oslo presented the Danish and Norwegian governments with a German ultimatum demanding that they instantly accept without resistance the protection of the Reich, and then landed troops in Denmark and Norway, startling the world with the suddenness of the invasion.

Denmark made no resistance and fell within the hour; however, Norway defied the ultimatum. The quick response of the German government was an air attack. Great Britain entered the conflict on 10 April, when five British destroyers engaged the German navy in Narvik harbor. As the Battle of Norway continued through April,

Hitler made plans to invade Belgium and Holland in early May. The key to the German plan was the seizure by airborne troops of the bridges just south of Rotterdam over the Nieuwe Maas River and those farther southeast over the two estuaries at Dordrect and Moerdijk.

The day before the German invasion, Dénes and Susie Koromzay traveled together by train to the Dutch border. Koromzay recalls:

> My wife's parents, the Tormays, had persuaded Susie to come home to Budapest for the birth of our first child. Susie and I went together by train to the Dutch border and on our way we saw the lines of fortification, the preparations for war that existed on the Dutch side. She left on 9 May and the next morning at four o'clock the invasion of Holland occurred. I was out of touch with her as she traveled alone in the eighth month of her pregnancy during the first day of the attack on Holland.
>
> Somehow I received a telegram that she had arrived safely in Hungary. I didn't see her or my first-born child until late November since there was no possibility of her return to Holland until then.[12]

On 10 May, the first day of attack, Holland resisted. Near Roermond, German troops crossed the Dutch frontier twelve kilometers north of the Belgian border. Parachute troops landed at strategic points near Rotterdam, The Hague, and Amsterdam where Schiphol Airport, the country's largest, was heavily bombed at dawn, while fifty German planes were seen that morning over Nijmegen. The strategic bridges were seized on the morning of 10 May and two days later German troops crossed them, arriving on the south banks of the Nieuwe Maas River near Rotterdam.

The royal family fled on two British destroyers, taking refuge in England, where Queen Wilhelmina was persuaded to remain, declaring London the seat of the Dutch government. At dusk on 14 May, General Winkelmann, the commander-in-chief of the Dutch forces, ordered his troops to lay down their arms and at eleven o'clock the next morning, he signed the official capitulations in the village of Rijsoord, after Rotterdan had become an inferno. Within five days the invasion of Holland was over and the German Occupation had begun.[13]

Although he had no idea at that time that it would be so, in March of 1939 in Paris Székely saw both his friends—Pál Hermann and Béla Bartók—for the last time. It was not until the war ended that he knew of their tragic fates. Bartók died in New York of leukemia on 26 September 1945. Pál Hermann had disappeared in Toulouse, abducted by the Gestapo.

Sometime during the war Pál and Ada Hermann left Paris and went to the relative safety of Jaap de Graaff's country estate at Mont de Marsan. Shortly after, Ada was drowned in a tragic swimming accident in the ocean. Their daughter was given into the care of the Weevers family. Pál was left disconsolate. Due to his restless nature, he felt unsettled at Mont de Marsan. He suddenly decided to make a trip to Toulouse where he had friends. There was a curfew in effect in Toulouse, but not taking this fact seriously, he went out into the streets after dark. He was never seen again.

Somehow his family later removed his cello, although the rooms where he had stayed in Toulouse had been sealed after his abduction by the Nazis. This terrible loss of my friend was only made known to me after the war when Ada Hermann's family, the Weevers, informed us.

During the summer of 1940 Székely still had several solo engagements in occupied Holland. On 11 July he performed Dvořák's Violin Concerto with the Concertgebouw Orchestra in The Hague at the last of the Mengelberg concerts of the summer season. One week later at the Kurhaus he played the Brahms Violin Concerto with Willem van Otterloo conducting the Residentie Orchestra in The Hague.

In the autumn of 1940 Ferdinand Helmann succeeded Louis Zimmermann as First Concertmaster of the Amsterdam Concertgebouw Orchestra, when the venerable leader retired. At the invitation of Willem Mengelberg, Székely joined the Concertgebouw Orchestra that season as second First Concertmaster.

Because everything had become very difficult to manage in Holland, I rented rooms in Amsterdam near the Concertgebouw to overcome the problems of transportation from The Rhapsody, to be able to get to rehearsals and concerts with some ease.

I had certain privileges because of my previous association with the Concertgebouw and was able to keep one of my violins, the Sacconi, in the soloist's room while my Stradivarius and Tononi violins remained safe in Bloemendaal. I was lucky that during the war years nothing happened to the Strad. The Germans could have taken it away, but I seldom mentioned what violin I was playing.

I remember that one day after lunch I decided that I would take a nap. The next day when I arrived at rehearsal, Mengelberg looked at me, wagged his finger, and asked, "Where were you yesterday afternoon? We recorded *Ein Heldenleben*. Fortunately Mr. Helmann plays the solo very well." Because I had heard nothing of this recording engagement, I had slept through a recording of this monumental work, which Richard Strauss had dedicated to Mengelberg. It was fortunate that Mr. Helmann did know the famous solo passage since it was not in my repertoire.

After the Bartóks left for America, the preparation for the publication of the collection of folk songs was left to Kodály, who remained in Hungary during the war working at the Academy of Sciences. In addition to this musicological task, Kodály accepted several commissions for new compositions. During November of 1940 the Amsterdam Concertgebouw Orchestra played the first performance of Kodály's new work, *Peacock Variations*, which had been commissioned for the fiftieth anniversary of the orchestra. Along with the *Hary János Suite*, Kodály's *Peacock Variations* was recorded and now fifty years later has reappeared on compact disc, as has Mengelberg's recording of *Ein Heldenleben*.

Mientje's mother, Anna Everts, visited The Rhapsody during the autumn of 1940 and wrote this message in the guest book:

The big war troubles have come over our country and everything is dark, but out of this dark sky, there is a little ray of sun. It is incredible! Zoltán is Concertmaster of the Amsterdam Concertgebouw Orchestra. I came here to hear about that. I stayed five weeks. . . . Mien and Zoltán are traveling up and down to Amsterdam where Zoltán has some rooms. Frans is a very intelligent child, very sweet as well, and has character. Mien surrounds things with her warm heart and Zoltán has a serene quietness that makes an impression on everything. Even if the future is not sure, Mien has the trust of God, so she doesn't hesitate and she doesn't fear.

The New Hungarian Quartet still had engagements in Holland during this time and on 13 October appeared in The Hague for the chamber music society with Paul Frenkel, pianist, who joined them in the Piano Quartet, Op. 60, by Brahms. A few days later Székely appeared as soloist in Brahms' Violin Concerto for a St. Cecilia's Day concert with the Amsterdam Concertgebouw Orchestra.

In quick succession all three concertmasters of the orchestra appeared as soloists. First there was Ferdinand Helmann who played the Beethoven Violin Concerto, then Székely with his outstanding Brahms performance, and finally the retired concertmaster, Louis Zimmerman, appeared.

While the critics knew Székely as the leader of the New Hungarian String Quartet, they knew him even better as a soloist who had appeared often with the orchestra, and most recently as the champion of the new Bartók Violin Concerto. No doubt they expected that he would give a superior performance of the Brahms concerto, but that his performance would be so surprisingly fine delighted them.

"The most piquant part of the evening was Zoltán Székely's noble, intense performance, of which the finale was sublime," wrote one critic. Another commented, "For years well known in our musical world and now bound even more to Holland by his concertmastership in the Amsterdam Concertgebouw, Székely played Brahms with his inborn, strong musicality, his genuine violinistic talent, and the sureness of his mastery."[14]

After the birth of their son, the Székelys had certain changes made to The Rhapsody. Gerrit Rietveld designed and built a new bedroom for Frans on the second floor. During the first year of the Occupation, still further changes were made when they had a favorite, trustworthy carpenter build new wall panels in the attic with the hope of preserving certain valuable possessions in relative secrecy. Trusted carpenters were kept very busy in those times, as their entire neighborhood in Bloemendaal attempted to increase the security of their properties.

With great ingenuity, Székely created a link with the outside world when he installed a clandestine radio at The Rhapsody.

> With the help of friends, I buried our radio, a Philips, in the garden, having first tuned it to the frequency that would transmit the BBC broadcasts from London.
>
> Having hidden the radio in this way, we bored a hole in the floor beneath the sofa in my studio and arranged a con-

nection for earphones in the leg of my desk. In this way I could lie there on the sofa and listen whenever it was safe to do so. Of course, once the radio was buried there could be no changing of stations, but fortunately the BBC broadcasts were transmitted during the entire Occupation.

In Hungary Bartók had experienced a great personal loss with the death of his mother in late December of 1939. During the months that followed, he prepared himself for the pending, very important second tour to the United States, where he hoped to find sufficient professional support to enable him to stay abroad throughout the war. He sailed from Naples on the SS *Rex*, arriving in New York on 11 April 1940. Two days later he performed with Szigeti in the Coolidge Festival in Washington, D.C. He remained in the United States for five weeks, returning to Hungary on 18 May.

After Bartók's departure from America, Jenő Antal, a violinist of the disbanded Roth Quartet who now lived in Pennsylvania, spoke on Bartók's behalf to both Carl Engel, the president of Schirmer publishers, and Douglas Moore, head of the Music Faculty at Columbia University, in an effort to assist Bartók in finding a scholarly position so that he might emigrate. As a result, Bartók was awarded a one-year grant from Columbia University's Ditson Fund.[15]

The next weeks were anxious ones for the Bartóks, who hurriedly made new travel plans, having received their visas to enter the United States. They played a farewell concert in Budapest on 8 October during which Ditta made her first appearance there as soloist in Mozart's Piano Concerto, K. 413, and together they performed Mozart's Concerto for Two Pianos, K. 365. After this concert they traveled by train through Italy and Switzerland, then by bus to Spain and Portugal where they sailed from Lisbon on the SS *Excalibur*. They arrived in New York City at midnight on 29 October 1940, but their possessions had gone astray and did not appear for weeks.

Very soon after their arrival they performed in two concerts at Town Hall. The first was a recital for the New Friends of Music where they played the Sonata for Two Pianos and Percussion; the second was a recital of Debussy, Bach, Brahms, and Bartók's *Mikrokosmos*. On 25 November Bartók was awarded an honorary Doctor of Music degree by Columbia University. After a brief transcontinental tour of seven cities, they returned to New York, where Bartók began his work at Columbia University in March.

Earlier in April of 1939 while Bartók was still in Hungary, Boosey and Hawkes had proposed the publication of a violin and piano reduction of the Violin Concerto with a note appended to the inside page of the cover restricting the performance of the work with orchestra until October 1942. The availability of this publication in the autumn of 1939 would serve violinists as an aid to studying the new masterpiece while Székely still held the sole performance rights. The publisher had done something similar in the case of Ernest Bloch's Violin Concerto for which Szigeti held the performance rights.[16]

Because a small balance of Bartók's funds remained in a Dutch bank, various unsuccessful plans were now conceived to get these funds to him. The most elaborate plan involved sending a check to Székely's cousin, Frigyes Mártonyi, in Lima, Peru, so that the funds could then be transferred to Joseph Szigeti who was on tour in South America. Unfortunately the check never reached its destination. In such troubled times none of these plans could be relied upon, and by now everyone involved began to realize this.

One week before receiving his honorary degree from Columbia, Bartók drafted what was to be his final letter to Székely who, with his family and the members of the New Hungarian String Quartet, was trapped in occupied Holland with little hope of communications with the outside world.

With his letter dated 10 December 1940 Bartók gave notice that he was reducing the period of time reserving the sole performance rights of the Violin Concerto and that the work would be at the disposal of all performers from 1 September 1941 onward.[17] Bartók advised Székely of this decision in a German-language letter despite his feelings toward the Germans. Obviously, in his increasing anxiety at the time, he wanted to make certain that this letter would reach Székely, regardless of German censorship of the mail. The rather official language of the letter points in this same direction. This decision shortened Székely's reservation by thirteen months and precluded the possibility of an optional extension to 31 August 1944.

Székely, of course, held little expectation of long-term performance rights to the concerto and therefore could only feel relieved that Bartók finally was able to work out a way to receive compensation in his time of need. Yet this response was drowned out in the confusion of those troubled war years, with lost or censored correspondence, failed appointments, change of publisher, then the ultimate catastrophe, the separation of the two friends. Thus in the interest of historical accuracy, Székely later retraced the story of the violin concerto's financial arrangements by discussing, in particular, some otherwise mysterious sentences contained in the extant letters dating from 1936 to 1941.

First of all, I submit that the Violin Concerto was not the result of a commission or a business proposition. Bartók wrote it out of friendship, and the honorarium offered, and accepted, simply served the purpose of compensation for the lack of performance fees that would have been paid by other artists. Bartók still decided to write a contract, thinking that a more thorough description of the agreement would be useful to his publisher.

It is interesting to read that part of his letter to me, dated 17 October 1936, where he answers positively to my often-stated wish that he should write a violin concerto. He writes, "The other thing is certainly feasible. You do know, however, that I can only work on such things during the summer thus you couldn't expect the mansucript before the end of September of 1937. But, I warn you! this might be bad business, think about it. If I accept the whole thing—with the three year exclusive rights—then I would give you the manuscript with the idea that <u>that</u> is what you actually purchased. At any rate, you have time to think it over, we might meet at the end of January and finalize the matter."[18]

Unfortunately, the promised manuscript never reached me, because when the time came for me to receive it, World War Two broke out and the whole thing was forgotten. But, after all, many things happened differently from the way they were planned during the war, and many valuable documents were lost or burned. Among others it is regrettable that the final text of the agreement between us has disappeared. (There is a small hope that, along with a few other letters, this one will be found someday.)

I do have, however, Bartók's letter, dated 1 May 1937, that contains the text of our agreement. I quote the sixth point from it: "Székely Zoltán shall, at the acceptance of the manuscript mentioned in point three, pay 500 Dutch florins for the rights described in the preceding paragraphs."[19]

The world premiere of the Violin Concerto took place on 23 March 1939. In my letter of 3 April 1939, I report the event to Bartók and I also write: "There is another important thing. I would like to settle my debt to you now, since I have received a larger amount in Budapest. Thus you would receive from me 1760 pengős plus 80 for the scores. Also, I would like another five of them, because they are going fast. I hope you will accept my payment, even though it is not completely according to our agreement [i.e., Dutch florins]. Please let me know soon. (To which Budapest bank should I transfer the money?)"

If we compare the two quoted letters, we find the same amount of money. Five hundred Dutch florins equalled 1760 pengős at the time. Bartók preferred foreign currency, as in the agreement. Not needing so many pengős, he only took a portion of the offered amount. Soon after, Bartók needed money and would have accepted pengős as well.

In the meantime, however, war broke out, and I was forced to write him on 3 October 1939: "The war ruined all our plans. I cannot fulfill your request concerning the folk songs [foreign currency]. It would be too risky to send such valuable material by post. The possibility that someone could give it to you in person no longer exists because of the present conditions. But were you not planning to come here?"

Bartók was forced by his desperation and his difficult financial position in New York to find a way for some compensation. He decided to shorten the time of exclusive performance rights, held by me, to allow a U.S. performance of the work in the near future. Bartók's decision did not change my position, since the war had destroyed all further opportunities for me to perform the concerto. Thus it was comforting for me to know that Bartók was compensated both artistically and financially.[20]

When his final letter eventually reached Székely in the winter of 1941, already opened by the censors, Bartók had little hope of contacting his friend and no hope of sustaining a correspondence. He had heard nothing from Székely immediately before leaving Budapest and wrote, "I was expecting a sign of life from you, but unfortunately was therefore of the opinion that postal communication has become impossible."[21] Indeed Bartók and Székely were not able to communicate further, and it was only after the war was over in Europe that the Székelys learned of Bartók's death in New York.

The Violin Concerto was performed for the first time in the United States on 21 and 23 January 1943, at Severance Hall in Cleveland. Tossy Spivakovsky was the soloist, with the Cleveland Sym-

phony Orchestra conducted by Artur Rodzinski. The next performances took place in New York City on 14, 15, and 17 October 1943
at Carnegie Hall. Again Spivakovsky was the soloist. The New York
Philharmonic was conducted by Artur Rodzinski. After these performances, the concerto was quickly taken up by Yehudi Menuhin and
Max Rostal.

Bartók's new Sixth Quartet was performed in New York City at
Town Hall by the Kolisch String Quartet on 20 January 1941, seven
weeks after Bartók's final letter to Székely, which offered no account
of the destiny of this new work commissioned by Székely and the
New Hungarian String Quartet. The program on which it appeared
also included works by Mozart and Schubert.

The Kolisch Quartet with its original members gave a final concert in Chicago while on tour in America in 1939, then disbanded.[22]
The Kolisch Quartet was briefly reorganized a few months later with
Jascha Veissi, violist, and Stefan Auber, cellist, joining the original
violinists, Rudolph Kolisch and Felix Kuhner. It was in this formation
that the Kolisch Quartet presented the first performance of Bartók's
Sixth Quartet in New York.

More than three years later, Rudolph Kolisch again led a performance of Bartók's Sixth Quartet. This performance took place in the
Hall of the New York Times Building for the American League of
Composers on 19 March 1944. On that occasion Kolisch was joined
by Lorna Freedman, violin, Bernard Milofsky, viola, and János Scholz,
cello.

Concert life continued on a limited basis in Holland during the
Occupation. Antonio Votto, an Italian conductor who had often directed operatic performances in Holland, came to conduct the summer concerts of the Residentie Orchestra in Scheveningen, a suburb
of The Hague. Since Carl Schuricht had temporarily left Scheveningen, Votto, a pupil of Toscanini, took his place. Székely performed
Viotti's Concerto No. 22 with Antonio Votto on 16 July 1941 during
this summer series. He had played the work with the Concertgebouw
Orchestra the previous winter, replacing Georg Kulenkampff, who
had canceled his engagement.

About the summer performance in Scheveningen, a critic in The
Hague wrote, "It gives him the opportunity to show his masterful
violin playing, his noble tone, his warm vibrato, his temperament,
and his sophisticated musicality. . . . "[23]

Two days before the Viotti performance, the artistic director of the Amsterdam Concertgebouw, Rudolf Mengelberg (cousin of the conductor) invited Dénes Koromzay to join the Concertgebouw Orchestra as first violist. Koromzay accepted this engagement and began his career with the orchestra on 1 September when the new season was launched.

While the New Hungarian String Quartet still continued to perform in Holland during the 1941–42 season, they were unable to leave the country for engagements elsewhere. A shared Beethoven cycle was arranged in Amsterdam at the Concertgebouw with a number of concerts planned throughout the season by three quartets resident in Holland: the New Hungarian String Quartet, the Sweelinck Quartet, and the New Holland Quartet.

In addition to its Beethoven offering, the New Hungarian Quartet appeared in Arnhem, Rotterdam, Zwolle, Deventer, and Hattum. Székely and Koromzay carried out their duties in the orchestra, and appeared in Amsterdam, Rotterdam, and Haarlem during November as the soloists in performances of Mozart's Symphonie Concertante, K. 364, for violin, viola, and orchestra. The German conductor Eugen Jochum, music director of the Hamburg State Opera, appeared as guest conductor of the Concertgebouw Orchestra for these performances in November.

The artistic life in Holland was drastically affected by the Nazi Occupation during the period that followed. Willem Mengelberg became entangled with the Nazis and held a post in Hitler's German Culture Cabinet. In 1945, he was accused as a collaborator and lived in artistic exile in Zuort, Switzerland, until his death in 1951, a week before his eightieth birthday.

By 1941 it gradually became impossible for musicians in Holland to appear in public concerts without political connections to the German regime. When Mengelberg decided to take the Amsterdam Concertgebouw Orchestra by overnight train to perform in Vienna, Székely refused to travel and ended his tenure as concertmaster of the orchestra. By now, the New Hungarian Quartet no longer appeared in public. Deeply concerned that the concert world would simply forget the quartet during the long silence of the Occupation, they rose to the challenge of their enforced withdrawal from the concert platform: they began to perfect their playing of the Beethoven cycle, the seventeen masterworks the performance and recordings of which were eventually to become one of their marks of greatest distinction.

In a visit to The Rhapsody in December of 1941, Mientje's mother wrote for the last time in the guest book:

Always the war and darkness around us. There have been a lot of things over our heads. The spook of the evacuation. To let go everything that is dear to us. Frans is a boy of four years. Zoltán is no longer in Amsterdam. Everything lies still. I feel the dark clouds, but we are in the hands of God and that is what we believe.

Now the New Hungarian Quartet determined to learn the Beethoven cycle. Nine of the Beethoven quartets were already in their repertoire. The remaining works would be restudied and rehearsed thoroughly throughout the difficult period ahead.

When Dénes Koromzay joined the Amsterdam Concertgebouw Orchestra, he and his family moved from Bloemendaal into Amsterdam where he could more easily get to his orchestra rehearsals. He traveled back to nearby Bloemendaal to rehearse with the quartet since his colleagues had remained there, Alexander and Flossie Moskowsky in their Bloemendaal home and the Székelys at The Rhapsody. Also living in Bloemendaal was another family with the Hungarian surname Székely, but not related to the violinist. This Mrs. Székely—Lon Loelofs—was a celebrated Dutch novelist whose highly successful novels had been translated into eighteen languages. She befriended Vilmos Palotai and sheltered him in her home throughout the war.

Székely speaks of living conditions that became more and more difficult during the passing years of the Nazi Occupation:

There was a problem of heating the room where we rehearsed and of course food was scarce. We had the good fortune that our home, The Rhapsody, had central heating. We even had some oil hidden in a barrel in the garden. We sometimes used this oil as barter since we had lived on our money until there was no more. Often I went to the countryside on my bicycle and bartered with the farmers for some kind of food. Somehow I once got a whole cheese, a big round cheese. Once when Mientje found an egg, she boiled it, divided it, and the quartet had this meagre treat after a strenuous rehearsal. That time was a bad dream.

Suddenly there was talk of evacuation from Bloemendaal.

It was said that we were living too close to the harbor at Ijmuiden where the German U-boats were kept. Finally the orders came. German soldiers would occupy The Rhapsody and we would be evacuated to nearby Aerdenhout, a quiet suburban area of large homes where many wealthy Amsterdamers lived.

We were to share a home with a man and his elderly mother. Mr. Harmens, who owned this house, was to be moved to an upstairs room, we were to live downstairs in improvised quarters, and our maid, Maria, would come with us and share quarters with Harmens' servants. What is more, a part of the house would be made available to German officers as a kind of club. Immediately the Germans decided to move Harmens' elderly mother elsewhere, but after intense negotiations she was allowed to stay as well.

I could not take my radio since it was buried in the garden at The Rhapsody, but we found another radio that had belonged to Mientje's mother. This became our second clandestine radio. Somehow I was able to install it and by giving certain false information I managed to create an electrical outlet so that when the Germans closed off all the electricity and we lighted candles for the evening, I could still switch on the power in the room where we lived and hear the news from London.

With a probability of one in a million, I turned on the radio one evening late in 1944 and heard the Bartók Violin Concerto, which was a staggering surprise! We had heard little news of the musical world outside Holland during the Occupation. Of course we knew the Bartóks were in America, but we had no idea of the fate of the Violin Concerto of which I had originally been given the sole performing rights. It was Menuhin who was playing on the radio broadcast with the BBC Symphony from London. How Menuhin got to London from America in those troubled times I did not know.

Frank Székely-Everts remembers well his family's evacuation to Aerdenhout:

My sixth birthday party was canceled because the Germans took over our home on 19 September 1944. Our family piled the movable furniture on a large cart which was pulled by two horses since there was no gasoline left to fuel a vehicle of any sort. We left our own car at The Rhapsody. I had

spent hours playing in our Opel which was by then stored
on blocks. When we started for Aerdenhout, I rode on the
cart with our possessions; my mother and father and Maria,
our maid, rode on their bicycles.

At Mr. Harmens' house in Aerdenhout we stored our furniture in the garage, leaving enough space for someone to be
hidden behind it. While I was not supposed to know this, at
six years of age I found it remarkable and often went there to
crawl through the furniture hoping to greet anyone that
might be in hiding. Behind the Harmens' house was a
wooded area. I remember frequently seeing people fleeing
through those woods and even once saw someone being
chased by German soldiers.[24]

In Aerdenhout there was an enterprising man who was very interested in music and soon discovered that the Hungarian Quartet
was still hard at work. John de Jong Schouwenburg became one of
the quartet's closest friends and somewhat later the president of the
Amsterdam Concertgebouw. Koromzay speaks of Schouwenburg's
innovative idea to present the quartet in private concerts during the
last year of the Occupation:

> Schouwenburg approached us with the idea of giving
> some private concerts in Aerdenhout during our "forced re-
> tirement." He said, "Since we have to hunt for food on the
> weekdays, let's celebrate the weekend with the New Hungar-
> ian Quartet!"
>
> We had learned the entire Beethoven cycle without being
> able to play it in public. Now Schouwenburg organized a pri-
> vate gathering where we played Saturday afternoon and out
> of this grew such an unbelievable enthusiasm for string quar-
> tet listening that every Saturday and every Sunday we played
> in those homes where there was a little bit more food and a
> little bit more warmth than was usual that winter. We played
> in at least fifteen palatial homes whose owners had by then
> traded away most of their possessions for food.
>
> At first there had been a small charge for admission to
> these private concerts, but since the money was almost
> worthless by then, the organizers decided that each listener
> should bring something, whatever he could. These things
> were left on a table by the door and once when someone
> brought a half pound of beans, the quartet wives counted
> them out and divided them into four parcels, one for each

family. Another time someone brought a half bar of soap. We hadn't seen soap in a year. This was also divided. But despite the harsh times we experienced that winter, these concert events had a spiritual quality as well. At last we were able to do our job again, regardless of the realities of war.

The curfew allowed no one on the streets after ten o'clock at night and the Gestapo could have arrested all of us since such gatherings were forbidden. However, Aerdenhout was a provincial place, and the Germans knew by then that they had lost the war. Those private concerts in Aerdenhout basically saved our sanity because conditions had gradually deteriorated during the last winter until there was nothing— no electricity, the trains weren't running, there was no gas, the distribution systems failed, no rationing. Nothing worked anymore. Total chaos and insecurity.

After that terrible winter, spring came at last. Frequently during the night we heard the Allied planes flying over Holland, then suddenly one day we saw the planes come over in the early morning, flying low and dropping something which was not bombs! Food!

Frank Székely-Everts recalls going home to The Rhapsody at the end of the war.

When the war in Europe ended on 8 May 1945 we immediately made plans to leave Aerdenhout and go home to Bloemendaal. When my family was able to return to The Rhapsody, we found it in poor condition because the German soldiers had been living in it. I remember that my mother had the ruined carpets removed and burned, but because there was no carpet left for sale in Holland, she could not replace them, so she had straw spread on the floors and then covered the straw with cheap fabric. Of course, we were very glad to be home again. The war was over!

1946–1972

The 1968 signature photograph of the Hungarian String Quartet. (Left to right: Gabriel Magyar, Zoltán Székely, Dénes Koromzay, Michael Kuttner). COURTESY OF PATHÉ-MARCONI.

Chapter Nineteen

The Beethoven Cycle

For eight months after the end of the war, the Hungarian Quartet could not travel outside Holland. Their concert manager, Géza de Koos, had temporarily fled to Hungary, and by the fall of 1945 they were still without his assistance. In his absence, a certain Dutch entrepreneur approached them with the proposition of managing their business affairs. He guaranteed a large number of concerts in Holland at unheard-of fees, some of which were never paid; however, during the eight-month period when they could not cross the borders, the quartet played an astounding number of concerts—more than eighty—in both major centers and small villages.

They traveled as they could, sometimes by car—the agent in Bloemendaal had a Chevrolet—other times in an old army bus. Once they lost a wheel near Utrecht when they were on their way to play a concert in Arnhem. There was no way to fix it quickly and no way to communicate with Arnhem since the telephone system was not yet fully operational. When they finally arrived in Arnhem, the hall was dark and the public had gone away.

During the 1945–46 season, the quartet devoted twenty-four concerts to performances of the Beethoven cycle. They also played concerts at Rotterdam, Arnhem, Bilthoven, Nijmegen, Heerlen, Maastricht, Venlo, Harderwijk, Eindhoven, Winschoten, Veendam, and Zwolle, among many other places—and broadcast from Hilversum.

The format of their concerts continued to include two quartets from the works of Mozart, Haydn, Beethoven, or Schubert, and a third quartet that represented a departure from that traditional repertoire: Debussy's String Quartet, Op. 10; César Franck's String Quartet in D Major; Bartók's Second, Third, and Fifth Quartets; or Tchaikovsky's String Quartet No.1, Op. 11.

Two concerts in Haarlem launched the quartet's first post-war season in the fall of 1945, the first on 5 September at the Stadsschouwburg, the second on 26 September at the Gemeentelijke Concertzaal. Unknown to the group, Béla Bartók died at the West Side Hospital in New York City shortly before noon on the day of their second concert.

In one of Bartók's last letters, written on 1 July 1945 to Jenő Zádor in Hollywood, the sixty-four-year-old composer said in closing that he would like to return to Hungary for good.[1] This, of course, was not to happen because of his serious illness. At the hour of his death, his wife, Ditta, and his younger son, Péter, were by his side. The news of Bartók's death did not immediately reach the Hungarian Quartet. They learned of it only later, when their compatriot, Mátyás Seiber, informed them during their first post-war visit to London.

With the continuing, generous financial assistance of the American Society of Composers, Authors, and Publishers (ASCAP), Bartók had received the best possible medical attention during his final illness. Dr. Israel Rappaport, who in 1917 had treated Endre Ady, the great Hungarian poet, became Bartók's principal physician from May 1943 until his death. Granted permission by officials in Washington, D.C., Dr. Rappaport administered penicillin. Bartók was one of the first civilians to whom the new drug was administered, it then being reserved for military use. In the spring of 1944, Bartók's first symptoms of leukemia had been observed by Dr. Rappaport. It was this disease that finally took his life, but not before he composed his four final masterpieces.[2]

The Beethoven cycle, which the quartet had prepared during the war years and played for the private concerts arranged by John de Jong Schouwenburg, was now presented to the public for the first time in Haarlem, then in Blaricum-Laren, Amsterdam, and Utrecht.

Székely arranged the order of the works for each concert by combining quartets from Beethoven's three style periods.

I avoided chronological programs hoping to give greater variety to the public. While we sometimes played the cycle in five concerts, we preferred to play it in six.[3]

At a later period, this six-concert format included two performances of the String Quartet, Op. 130: the first with the Grosse Fuge, Op. 133, as the finale in the way Beethoven originally intended; the second with the alternative Allegro, Op. 130. In our early public performances of the Beethoven cycle in Holland, we used the six-concert format with the exception of the performances in Utrecht where we played all seventeen quartets in five evenings.

At the end of January 1946 Székely took time from the busy schedule of the quartet to appear as soloist at the Amsterdam Concertgebouw in a performance of Viotti's Concerto No. 22 and the Mendelssohn concerto with the Twentsch Kamer Orkest conducted by Claas de Rook. A few days later the quartet left Holland for the first time in five years.

We were afraid that people might have forgotten the Hungarian Quartet during the war, but that was not the case. In February we went to Belgium, France, and England to play concerts that would again establish the quartet in Western Europe. We had such success at our first concert at the Palais des Beaux-Arts in Brussels that the manager of the Beaux-Arts later arranged quite a few concerts for us, since suddenly the quartet was, so to speak, *en vogue* in Belgium.

In France, Valmalète organized a concert at the Salle Gaveau in Paris and another at Mulhouse. In England, Ibbs and Tillet arranged for us to appear in Cambridge and Birmingham. In London we began to broadcast frequently on the BBC and to record again for His Master's Voice. Before returning to Holland, we performed the Beethoven cycle in Paris at the Salle Gaveau, our first performance of the Beethoven cycle outside Holland.

When the quartet was at work in Broadcasting House in London during the spring of 1946, Steuart Wilson, later director of music at the BBC from 1947 until 1950, visited them to explain the British Broadcasting Corporation's plans for establishing the Third Programme. Inaugurated in September of 1946, this new service changed domestic broadcasting in England and its concept was quickly copied by other broadcasting organizations in Europe.

Specifically designed for intelligent lay people, the Third Programme was intended to serve listeners of cultivated taste and interest. Its aim was to broadcast the masterpieces of arts, letters, and music that lend themselves to transmission in sound, without regard to length or difficulty. An absence of fixed points in the schedule facilitated the then-revolutionary plan of devoting the greater part of an evening to a single musical work; and the program policy offered great scope to contemporary music.[4]

New program ideas soon emerged on other radio frequencies. The series called "Music in Miniature" offered an outstandingly successful program that presented chamber music to British audiences not yet fully devoted to that repertoire. The quartet appeared frequently in brief recitals on "Music in Miniature" while the Third Programme soon presented them three or four times each season in performances of both the Beethoven and Bartók cycles.

It was for the Third Programme that the quartet first presented a complete Bartók cycle in 1947. William Glock, who was to become the BBC's controller of music in 1959, wrote about these early broadcasts in *Time and Tide* on 1 February 1947:

> Of course I realize how difficult it is to choose the right performers, or in some cases, even to find anyone adequate at all for works of great importance . . . but I mustn't overstress this point . . . we have certainly had some good playing. On Monday, for example, the Hungarian String Quartet gave the best performance of Bartók I have ever heard.
> It was his Sixth Quartet, and after hearing it played with such imagination and such reverence I wondered how any of us had come to think of Hindemith as a figure of almost equal stature. No, he is a respectable master, but Bartók is a genius. I imagine that Joachim must have played late Beethoven in very much the same spirit as the Hungarian Quartet played the wonderful last movement of this Bartók No. 6. Whatever you do, don't miss No. 1 in the Third Programme next Wednesday.[5]

At the invitation of Walter Legge, the quartet returned to the Abbey Road studios of His Master's Voice to continue the recording career that they had begun tentatively before the war in 1938 when

HMV released a single 78 rpm recording of Tchaikovsky's *Andante Cantabile* and the Nocturne from Borodin's Quartet in D Major. Legge, who was married to the German soprano Elizabeth Schwarzkopf, was director of the classical division at the London branch of the EMI recording company and was a dominant figure in the recording industry. A sophisticated star-maker, he was not only in control of the artistic life of EMI, but was the creator of the London Philharmonia Orchestra and the chief protagonist of Herbert von Karajan who first conducted that orchestra in 1947 and became its chief conductor in 1950.

From 1946 until 1949, the Hungarian String Quartet recorded five important works for HMV on 78 rpm records.[6] The first was Mozart's Quartet No. 15 in D Minor, K. 421, and during these recording sessions an artistic disagreement arose between Legge and Székely.

> Our first Mozart recording was produced by Walter Legge, and it seems he had certain ideas about the Menuetto. He came into the studio and began to tell me how that movement should be played. Of course, he went over such things in the studio with many famous musicians, but for my part I didn't know if he, himself, even was a musician.
>
> In string quartet playing there are unique difficulties, even more so than when you play alone. No one plays exactly the same way twice in the studio, but the differences are often so slight that it doesn't matter as long as the different "takes" fit together successfully and the final recording sounds lively. But when one listens to a recording, and listens too often, it may eventually be said, "every time they do everything the same way." But this is wrong! It is only the natural impression from listening often to the same recording. Recorded playing should be even more perfect than concert playing, since in concert performances the audience listens only to a general impression. When they listen to a record, then a general impression is simply not enough.

Next came Haydn's Quartet in D Major, Op. 64, No. 5 ("Lark"), a work that would eventually be released in three different recordings by the Hungarian String Quartet. A showcase for the first violinist, the recorded finale of the "Lark" was performed remarkably by Székely with his almost unbelievably controlled *spiccato*. In London throughout the 1950s, this recording continued to capture the attention of London musicians and music lovers. A later, equally successful version was made in Paris by Pathé-Marconi and issued on the RCA Victor label in the United States. It was the first recording of the Hungarian Quartet to be marketed abroad by EMI.

In a 1981 interview, Koromzay discussed the quartet's first recording of Bartók's Fifth Quartet in 1946:

> The recording repertoire was always the company's choice and luckily Walter Legge was interested in Bartók's Fifth Quartet. And besides that, at that time our name was associated with the work, and not many other quartets played it. Later in 1949 we recorded the Sixth Quartet of Bartók and began recording Beethoven's Op. 127, as well.
>
> This was still the time of 78 rpm recordings and there were only three "takes" for each side, and between those three, one choice was made. This was a highly critical manuever and quite different from the later, more flexible recording techniques that involved editing tapes.
>
> There came some grave difficulties with Beethoven's Op. 127. We were very difficult and temperamental people and I remember some stormy sessions when the quartet, but particularly Vilmos Palotai, was not satisfied with the sound production. While Legge liked our playing, he soon had enough of the Hungarian Quartet's temperament and so our sessions stopped in London. Our recordings did not resume until we went to Pathé-Marconi in Paris.[7]

Pathé-Marconi, the Paris-based subsidiary of EMI, became the exclusive recording company for the Hungarian String Quartet from 1953 to 1957 after its departure from the London studios. While before the war His Master's Voice (later called British Gramophone Co.) had dominated the industry, by the mid-1950s London-based EMI, the Electric and Musical Industries, Ltd., produced one out of every five records sold worldwide. A general realignment of the subsidiary companies of EMI produced a complex relationship between these various recording companies. British and American Columbia severed their ties. As the North American market grew larger, American Columbia established autonomy in order to override dictates from Britain. To overcome these changes, EMI later established the Angel and Seraphim labels and bought Capitol Records which became its exclusive distributor in North America. American RCA Victor was no longer allowed the European use of the trademark, "His Master's Voice."[8]

After recording Bartók's Fifth Quartet in London in 1946, the quartet returned to Switzerland to perform for Vevey's Société des Arts et Lettres for the first time since 1939. On 15 November at the Théâtre de Vevey, the quartet gave its first public performance of Bartók's Sixth Quartet. While the Sixth Quartet had been published in the United States by Boosey and Hawkes in 1941, the Hungarian Quartet had not seen the score until after the war when Mátyás Seiber had shown them his printed copy during a visit in London.

Five important performances of the Beethoven cycle followed the concerts in Vevey. The quartet played these integral performances in the Amsterdam Concertgebouw, the Palais des Beaux-Arts in Brussels, the Temple St. Jean at Mulhouse, the Conservatoire de Musique in Geneva, and the Teatro alla Scala in Milan, where an audience of 2500 attended the performances during the 1948 festival, Concerti di Primavera.

The first Edinburgh International Festival of Music and Drama took place in the summer of 1947. The great pianist Artur Schnabel performed as soloist on five different occasions at the festival and was frequently joined by Joseph Szigeti, William Primrose, and Pierre Fournier for chamber music concerts. The first Edinburgh Festival, a significant event in Europe's post-war artistic life, appeared to Schnabel to be an incredibly early demonstration of an unbroken faith in unifying human values and virtues. He later wrote, "It leads to the desire for the continuation, for the development of the Festival into a cherished institution, an uninterrupted stimulation of spiritual efforts."[9]

The second Edinburgh Festival opened with a Service of Praise in the Cathedral Church of St. Giles on Sunday, 22 August 1948. Ahead were three weeks resplendent with performances of Mozart's *Don Giovanni* and *Così fan tutte*, Euripides' *Medea* starring John Gielgud, Tyrone Guthrie's production of Lindsay's morality play, *Satire of the Three Estates*, performances by the Amsterdam Concertgebouw Orchestra conducted by both Eduard Van Beinum and Charles Munch, the Augusteo Orchestra of the Santa Cecilia Academy of Rome conducted by Wilhelm Furtwängler, Bernardino Molinari, and Vittorio Gui. Four outstanding British orchestras appeared: the Liverpool Philharmonic conducted by Sir Malcolm Sargent, the BBC Scottish Orchestra conducted by Ian Whyte, the Hallé Orchestra conducted by

John Barbirolli, and the BBC Symphony conducted by Adrian Boult. Canada's Boyd Neel Orchestra performed in a series of ten morning concerts.

The chamber music concerts featured two performances by the Hungarian String Quartet at Freemasons' Hall and three concerts at Usher Hall where Yehudi Menuhin and Louis Kentner performed Beethoven's ten sonatas for violin and piano. The first Hungarian String Quartet concert presented Mozart's String Quartet, K. 387, Schubert's Quartet in D Minor ("Death and the Maiden"), and Bartók's Fifth Quartet. The other concert was an all-Beethoven program with three quartets, Op. 74, Op. 132, and Op. 18, No. 6.

The 1948 festival created the largest broadcasting operation of the year for the staff of the BBC in Scotland. The suspended microphones in Freemasons' Hall brought the Hungarian String Quartet to its largest radio audience to date when untold numbers of listeners scattered across the world heard the opening phrase of the Mozart, K. 387. These festival appearances established the Hungarian Quartet as a favorite ensemble of the Edinburgh Festivals. They were to return on many occasions during the next decades.

Plate 62. The Hungarian String Quartet and their families at Schiphol Airport in Amsterdam before departing for South America in 1949. COURTESY OF KLM, ROYAL DUTCH AIRLINES, AMSTERDAM.

Plate 63. The Hungarian String Quartet on stage at Salle Gaveau in Paris in 1955. PHOTOGRAPHY STUDIO LIPNITZKI. COURTESY OF PATHÉ-MARCONI.

Plate 64. Grand Prix du Disque Diplome from the Académie Charles Cros in 1955. THE SZÉKELY COLLECTION.

Plate 65. The Hungarian String Quartet with Marc Chagall (center) at Vence near the French Riviera in 1958. THE KOROMZAY COLLECTION.

Plate 66. Clara Haskil and members of the Hungarian String Quartet at Vevey, 1958. PHOTOGRAPHY IGMINIA SZÉKELY. THE SZÉKELY COLLECTION.

Plate 67. Zoltán Székely and Aaron Copland at the 1960 Aspen Festival. PHOTOGRAPHY IGMINIA SZÉKELY. THE SZÉKELY COLLECTION.

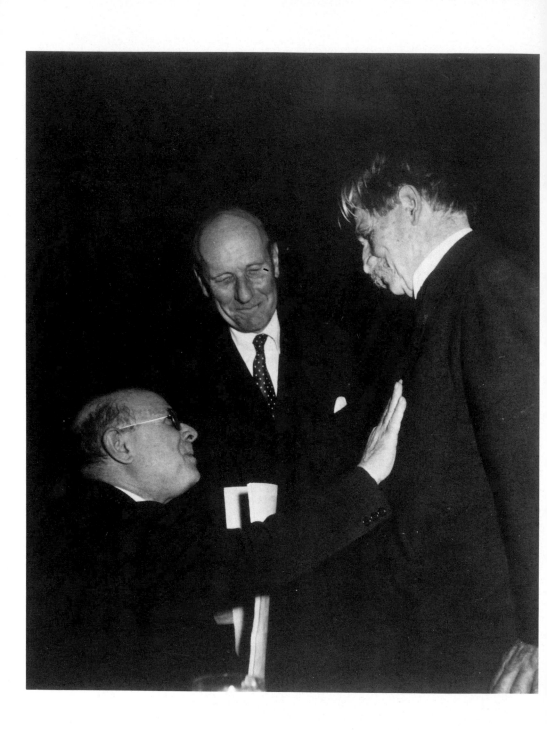

Plate 68. Pablo Casals, Emile Rossier, and Albert Schweitzer in Geneva in 1951. COURTESY OF MARTA CASALS ISTOMIN.

Plate 69. Zoltán Székely, Pablo Casals, and Julius Katchen at the 1962 Prades Festival. PHOTOGRAPHY PUPIER GARANGER. COURTESY OF MARTA CASALS ISTOMIN.

Plate 70. Strijkkwartet. A sculpture of the Hungarian String Quartet by Ubbo Scheffer acquired by the Committee of the Concertgebouw, Amsterdam, where it now stands. PHOTOGRAPHY WIM BECH. COURTESY OF HET CONCERT-GEBOUW NV.

Plate 71. Recording Cecil Effinger's Quartet No. 5 at the University of Colorado in Boulder in 1967. COURTESY OF DR. OAKLEIGH THORNE.

Plate 72. The Hungarian String Quartet with Zoltán Kodály in Budapest in 1967. THE SZÉKELY COLLECTION.

Plate 73. The Hungarian String Quartet at the Franz Liszt Academy in Budapest in 1969. PHOTOGRAPHY LÁSZLÓ TKLÁDI. THE SZÉKELY COLLECTION.

Plate 74. Ditta Bartók and Zoltán Székely in Budapest in 1969. THE SZÉKELY COLLECTION.

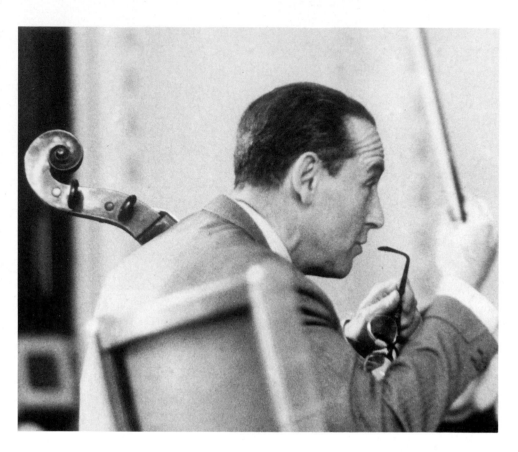

Plate 75. Gabriel Magyar teaching a master class at the University of Alberta in Edmonton in 1971. PHOTOGRAPHY LAWRENCE V. FISHER.

Plate 76. The Hungarian String Quartet and Thomas Rolston, violist, recording a Brahms quintet at the Salle Wagram in Paris in 1971. PHOTOGRAPHY JULIE MAGYAR. THE ROLSTON COLLECTION.

Plate 77. Listening to a "take" at Salle Wagram in Paris in 1971. (Left to right: back row, Thomas Rolston, Gabriel Magyar, and Michael Kuttner; front row, Producer Eric McLeod, Zoltán Székely, and Dénes Koromzay. PHOTOGRAPHY JULIE MAGYAR. THE ROLSTON COLLECTION.

Plate 78. The Hungarian Quartet relaxing in Paris in 1971. PHOTOGRAPHY
SABINE WEISS. COURTESY OF PATHÉ-MARCONI.

Plate 79. Zoltán and Mientje Székely backstage in The Hague in 1971. PHO-
TOGRAPHY DE MAAR. THE SZÉKELY COLLECTION.

Plate 80. The last concert of the Hungarian String Quartet at Colby College in 1972. COURTESY OF THE OFFICE OF COMMUNICATIONS, COLBY COLLEGE.

Chapter Twenty

New York Debut

The French-Canadian Bernard La Berge was one of North America's most important concert managers of chamber music ensembles. He had his office near Carnegie Hall at 119 West 57th Street in New York City, a few blocks from the apartment where the Bartóks had lived until the composer's death in 1945. In the summer of 1948 La Berge visited Paris and negotiated an American tour of thirty concerts for the Hungarian String Quartet with Jean Duport, the quartet's personal representative at the Valmalète agency. This tour included a debut recital at Town Hall in New York City for the New Friends of Music, a prestigious appearance at the Library of Congress in Washington, D.C., for the Gertrude Clarke Whittall Foundation in a concert in memory of Antonio Stradivari, and twenty-eight additional appearances from coast to coast before the many chamber music societies that form a network of sponsors for string quartet concerts in the United States.

The quartet arrived in the United States to begin their first American tour in late October of 1948. They played their first concert in Utica, New York; a day later in New York City, they played a private performance at the Harvard Club on 44th Street, arranged by La Berge so the musicians could have a preliminary appearance in the city before their Town Hall debut. He assured them that the single most important critical review following the Town Hall concert would be the one written by Olin Downes for the *New York Times*.

The New Friends of Music organization opened its thirteenth musical season on 2 November 1948, a season devoted to the music of Bach, Brahms, and Arnold Schoenberg with generous amounts of Mozart, the first of a two-year plan devised to present Mozart's chamber music works.

Robert Hague, critic of the *New York Star*, heralded the debut of the Hungarian String Quartet, not Olin Downes as hoped by La Berge. For Downes' approbation, the La Berge management would have to wait impatiently until another season.

The quartet impressed Robert Hague as a well-balanced ensemble, and he found their playing of Mozart's Quartet, K. 387 expressive, lucid, and persuasive. In a performance of the Quintet in F Minor by Brahms with Rudolf Firkusny, the distinguished young Czech pianist, "The music, with its flow of gentle lyricism punctuated by outspoken drama, was for the most part tellingly revealed."[1] The central portion of the program was given over to a well-received performance by Joseph and Lillian Fuchs of Mozart's Duo for Violin and Viola, K. 424.

The Hungarian Quartet appeared twice more in New York City in concerts at Washington Irving High School and Columbia University, then departed on a tour which took them to Newark, Montclair, Boston, Buffalo, Montreal, Kansas City, Austin, Dallas, San Antonio, Los Angeles, Pasadena, Oakland, Seattle, Portland, Yakima, Rexburg, Provo, Cedar City, Durham, Bridgewater, and finally to Washington, D.C., and the Library of Congress.

Their concert at the Library of Congress observing the anniversary of Stradivari's death took place in the Coolidge Auditorium. They played Mozart's Quartet, K. 458, Kodály's Quartet No. 2, Op.10, and Schubert's Quartet in D Minor ("Death and the Maiden"). The concert was broadcast in its entirety by WQQW-FM.

The twenty-three-year-old Coolidge Auditorium was Elizabeth Sprague Coolidge's gift to the Library of Congress. She had begun her remarkable patronage of chamber music with the South Mountain Chamber Music Festival near Pittsfield, Massachusetts, in 1918. In 1925 the Elizabeth Sprague Coolidge Foundation was created at the Library of Congress, the income from this trust to benefit the Music Division of the Library.[2] In the same year she presented the library with the Coolidge Auditorium, a 512-seat chamber-music hall, and the Coolidge String Quartet, a resident ensemble led by William

Kroll, which performed frequently from Founder's Day in October of 1936 until 1947, when it was succeeded by a quartet led by Kroll under his own name.

At Mrs. Coolidge's suggestion, and under the direction of Harold Spivacke, the foundation helped fund the residencies of several distinguished quartets at American universities. When asked why the Kolisch Quartet did not seek Mrs. Coolidge's intervention before disbanding in America in 1939, Eugene Lehner, the quartet's violist, explained that it was simply due to their naïveté. When she presented the by-then homeless Pro Arte Quartet to the University of Wisconsin at Madison, the members of the disbanded Kolisch Quartet realized that she might have assisted them as well, but by then each had made new professional commitments.[3]

After the Hungarian Quartet's successful performance on 18 December 1948 in Washington, D.C., Harold Spivacke,[4] chief of the music division of the Library of Congress, took an interest in further establishing their American career. As director of the Elizabeth Sprague Coolidge Foundation, Spivacke proposed a university residency for the Hungarian Quartet to be jointly funded by the University of Southern California in Los Angeles and the Coolidge Foundation whose activities he greatly influenced.

When the Hungarian Quartet returned to Europe at Christmas, the La Berge agency began work on the Hungarian Quartet's publicity for the next season, without the benefit of the hoped-for review by Olin Downes, but with the knowledge that the USC residency might become a reality in 1950. La Berge had offered the quartet a second American tour of forty-nine concerts, and they had accepted. These early negotiations indicate the number of chamber music societies at work in the United States at that time and the extent of La Berge's managerial control.

Back home in Holland, the members of the quartet began to consider seriously whether to emigrate to the United States. As he looks back, Székely says, "We began to feel that it might be better to live in America if the quartet was going to have a career there and finally took the opportunity, because at that time life was not yet normal in Europe in the aftermath of the war."

> Unfortunately in the United States our career would coincide with that of the Budapest Quartet who were already perfectly established. The Budapest Quartet originated in

Hungary, of course. The original members—Emil Hauser, Imre Poganyi, István Ipolyi, and Harry Son—had all played in the Budapest Opera Orchestra. Gradually it became a quartet of Russians when Joseph Roisman replaced Hauser, then Alexander Schneider became second violin, and his brother, Mischa Schneider, became the cellist. The violist Ipolyi stayed longest, but eventually Boris Kroyt succeeded him. From 1938 until 1962 the Budapest Quartet gave the Library of Congress concerts for the Whittall Foundation, about twenty each year, for which they used the Stradivarius instruments collected there.

It happened that the Quartetto Italiano came to America about the same time as our quartet and had an enormous success. In the final analysis, we were not in the same situation in America as in Europe where there was no competition whatsoever at that time.

When in 1949 the final decision was made in favor of going to the United States to live and work, each quartet member began to prepare his documents for emigration. At the same time there were European engagements to be played, and a first tour to South America was being planned by Ernesto de Quesada, the president of the Spanish concert management, Sociedad Musical Daniel.

After many concerts that spring in Holland and France, the quartet was engaged to perform the Beethoven cycle in Copenhagen by Wilhelm Hansen who was both an important music publisher and a concert manager in Denmark. They undertook an extended tour in France for Jeunesses Musicales de France. On this tour they were accompanied alternately by either Marc Meunier-Thouret or Jacques Feschotte, two musicologists who lectured for the JMF organization. In addition to the Hungarian String Quartet, André Navarra, cellist, André de Ribaupierre, violinist, Pierre Jamet, flutist, the Quintette Jamet de Paris, and the Quatuor Grégoire de Strasbourg were also touring for JMF during the season.

At the conclusion of the JMF tour, the quartet presented the Beethoven cycle in Bordeaux before returning to London for an extensive series of broadcasts. Once having finished the BBC engagement, which lasted more than a month, they waited impatiently in London for their visas to enter Portugal. They had been engaged for several important concerts in Lisbon where they would present their first public Bartók cycle in two concerts for the Portuguese Section of the International Society of Contemporary Music. On 8 May 1949 with only one day left before the quartet's scheduled departure, the Portuguese Embassy finally contacted them to say that the visas were in order.

In Portugal, as in Spain, the concerts began very late at night and were usually not finished until after midnight. A great Portuguese music lover, Doña Elena Pedroso, frequently received the artists and her guests after concerts, but never before three o'clock in the morning. Near dawn following their final concert in Lisbon, Doña Elena told the quartet that she was glad to hear that they had received the visas in time and soon let them know that this had happened because of her personal intervention. "I have friends in high places," she remarked. "You will please do me the favor of going with your calling cards tomorrow to the prime minister to pay your respects," she said, revealing that it was Prime Minister António de Oliveira Salazar, who had approved the visas at her urgent request.

The next day the quartet did leave their calling cards at the prime minister's office, then went for lunch. When they returned to their hotel to pack for the night journey to Spain, they were pleasantly surprised to find that Prime Minister Salazar had sent each of them his own calling card in return.

They departed from the Lisbon station at a very late hour. When their train approached the Spanish border, a government official approached them and asked for their Portuguese exit visas, something they neither had nor even knew about. They were promptly put off the train with the grim prospect of returning to Lisbon while their Spanish hosts awaited them in Madrid.

They protested this treatment, but the official paid no attention to their entreaties until Alexandre Moskowsky reached into his coat pocket and produced Salazar's official calling card, which fortunately he had kept at hand. With a sudden change of mood and gracious gestures of hospitality, the official politely escorted the Hungarian Quartet back into the train. They sighed with relief as the train jolted into motion to continue the night journey to Madrid, thankful for the magical effect produced by the prime minister's calling card.

Ernesto de Quesada, president of the Sociedad Musical Daniel, a concert agency founded in 1908 in Madrid, arranged a concert tour of three months' duration in Brazil, Argentina, Colombia, and Mexico, ending in Mexico City in late October. Frank Székely-Everts remembers the quartet's departure. His favorite photograph (Plate 62) is one taken of family and friends at Schiphol Airport shortly before the Hungarian Quartet left Amsterdam for Rio de Janeiro on their first South American tour in August of 1949.

> Everyone had come from Bloemendaal to see them off. We gathered at the boarding steps of the aircraft for an extended Hungarian Quartet family photo: Flossy and Sascha Moskowsky with their daughter balanced on his knee; my father and mother with Dénes Koromozay; standing on the steps in front of them am I with my two friends, Val and Dennis Koromzay (we three wear short pants since it is late summer). Their mother, Susie Koromzay, is beside them; nearby is the Jan Smits family with Vili Palotai and his friend, Lon Loelofs, the Dutch author.[5]

The first South American tour began with a Beethoven cycle in Rio de Janeiro where for a week the quartet appeared before the Sociedad de los Amigos de la Música. After Rio de Janeiro, they moved on from one success to another, appearing in Sao Paulo, Bogotá, Buenos Aires, Medellín, then Mexico City.

The intimate Sala Chopin was the setting for the Beethoven cycle in Mexico City. Many Mexican musicians, especially the string players, came to hear the Beethoven cycle hoping to learn from the example of these great European masters. After the second of six concerts, the critic of *Excelsior Mexico* wrote on 27 October 1949, "It is a marvelous thing to observe the manner in which Zoltán Székely harmoniously blends his incredible sonority with the ensemble: the velvety tone of Alexandre Moskowsky, the profound, emphatic accents of Dénes Koromzay's viola, the sweetness of Vilmos Palotai's phrasing. Very rarely have we the occasion to witness such a festival of the spirit."[6]

During the performances of the Beethoven cycle in Mexico City the long-awaited papers arrived confirming the quartet's residency at the University of Southern California. On the appointed day they went to the Office of Immigration and stood before an official with all their documents except the one paper attesting to their being bonafide teachers, a document which they had not known was required.

They were told immediately that this document was crucial, since their entrance into the United States depended not only on their contract with the University of Southern California, but also on evidence of their previous teaching careers.

In the confusion of the moment, they began speaking in Hungarian, conveying to each other their mutual distress that their papers were incomplete. Suddenly the official spoke to them in Hungarian, much to their surprise, asking them to continue their personal discussions elsewhere. He had been attached to the American Embassy in Budapest, was fluent in Hungarian, and did not want to inadvertently overhear their conversation which they had imagined to be a private one until that moment.

Nothing would suffice except that on their return to Europe from Mexico City the documents missing from their portfolios must be obtained. Both Koromzay and Palotai called upon the administration of an institution in France (where they had given master classes in conjunction with concert appearances) to attest to their teaching expertise. Amsterdam's Muzieklyceum wrote on behalf of Moskowsy, and Willem Andriessen, director of the Amsterdam Conservatory, provided the required documents for Székely, who had served on the faculty for a number of years.

With their portfolios complete, they returned to North America. Officials from the Dutch Consulate in Buffalo, New York, met them on the Canadian border at Niagara Falls, Ontario. They looked after their needs, assisted their official entrance into the United States, and finally drove them across the border into New York State. At this official beginning of their residence in the United States, Moskowsky was forty-eight years old; Palotai was forty-five; Székely was forty-four; and Koromzay was the youngest member of the ensemble at thirty-six.

The quartet began its second American tour on 31 October 1949 in Gainesville, Florida, played in Durham, North Carolina, on 3 November, then arrived in Washington, D.C., to appear for the second time in the Coolidge Auditorium at the Library of Congress under the auspices of the Gertrude Clarke Whittall Foundation, performing a concert that included Haydn's Quartet, Op. 76, No. 5, Bartók's Fifth Quartet, and Beethoven's Op. 127.

It was not quite a year since the quartet had made its debut at the Library of Congress. Now they brought Bartók's Fifth Quartet to the platform, and about this performance Elena de Sayn, critic of the *Washington Post* wrote: "The lyric cantilenas, interspersed between the often wild and the fantastic, had imagination and an ingratiating hue, as played, while the tone never lost its mellow quality in the most dramatic and passionate moments."[7]

After nine more concerts which took them again to the Midwest, the quartet returned to Town Hall in New York City to give their second annual concert for the New Friends of Music on 27 November 1949. Brahms' Quartet, Op. 51, No. 1, was followed by a performance of Mozart's Clarinet Quintet, K. 581, with clarinetist Reginald Kell. The concert ended with the Brahms Sextet, Op 18, in a collaboration with violist Milton Katims and Benar Heifetz, the former cellist of the Kolisch Quartet.

Ten days later the quartet appeared again at Town Hall in a recital devoted to string quartets. The critic of the *New York Times,* who found their ensemble remarkable for its sensitivity and cohesion in Bartók's Fourth Quartet, wrote, "The ensemble solved all problems with stunning ease, and the listener was conscious not of problems, but of Bartók's wide-ranging, imaginative musical mind."[8] Jerome Bohm in the *New York Herald Tribune* wrote of the unforgettable experience of the performance: "Such music making is all too rare and is only to be found when such self-effacing, accomplished players unite for the sole purpose of serving the composers whose music they have chosen to interpret."[9]

On this rising tide of positive critical opinion in the New York press, the quartet returned to Europe for a month to be with their families after an absence of five months. They appeared in Amsterdam, then went to Switzerland for concerts in Glarus, Basel, Zurich, and Bern before returning to America for the remaining seventeen concerts of their second tour.

The subscribers of the Los Angeles Music Guild had voted for a return engagement of the Hungarian Quartet. During their second American tour, the quartet returned to southern California to give two concerts for the Music Guild's series. They presented works by Mozart, Schubert, and Dvořák, the Brahms Clarinet Quintet, Op. 115, again with clarinetist Reginald Kell—and Bartók's Fourth Quartet.

A capacity audience arrived at the Wilshire Ebell Theater in Los Angeles in late November of 1949 with high expectations, remembering the remarkable performance of Bartók's Fifth Quartet heard during the quartet's first American tour in 1948. That the players made their performances so clear and exciting to an unprepared public was a good indication of their ability to bring new repertoire successfully to West Coast audiences.

The Los Angeles critics Albert Goldberg and Mildred Norton wrote admiringly about two different aspects of the quartet's great abilities. Goldberg, the critic of the *Los Angeles Times*, who found the new music difficult, praised the Hungarian Quartet ("players as sensational as the music of Bartók's Fourth Quartet") for making it accessible to the public. He wrote, "It would be hard to imagine a performance more devoted, more skillful in the face of abstruse and appalling difficulties, or more imbued with the rarefied spirit of the music."[10] The critic of the *Los Angeles Daily News*, Mildred Norton, wrote of their ability to reveal the standard repertoire with new insight: "A group so consistently fine as the Hungarian String Quartet can still startle the listener with a performance so fresh and compelling, so alive, sensitive, and illuminated, that music of familiar and beloved countenance is suddenly beheld with new and exciting awareness."[11]

In Pasadena, they appeared in the Coleman Chamber Concert series during a season dedicated to Alice Coleman Batchelder, founder and musical director of the series for forty-three years. They closed their first concert there with a performance of Schubert's "Death and the Maiden" Quartet as they had at the Wilshire Ebell Theater in Los Angeles earlier that week. Raymond Kendall, director of the School of Music at USC, reviewed their Schubert performance in Pasadena. He wrote of Schubert's music that it "sometimes becomes almost an act of eternal beauty in itself," and said of the slow movement of the Quartet in D Minor, "of such stuff are these Schubert variations."[12] Kendall expressed his view that the Hungarian Quartet's stylistic unity, both in technique and interpretation, produced artistic results not experienced since the original Pro Arte Quartet had come to the United States.

When the time came to leave Europe, the Székelys sold their treasured home in Bloemendaal. The Rhapsody was bought by their neighbor, a local wine merchant, and Mientje sailed from Rotterdam with Frans on the Nieuw Amsterdam, arriving in New York City on 22 July 1950. The Székelys were soon reunited in California, where they lived in their first home in America, a bungalow in Sherman Oaks, a suburb of Los Angeles.

The musicians soon discovered many expatriate colleagues and friends in California. A large, varied, and distinguished group of European musicians, including celebrities such as Heifetz, Piatigorsky, Primrose, and Schoenberg, had established itself there in the early 1950s. Cellist Stephen Deák was living in California, as were Jenő Kerpely, Lajos Shuk, and Gabor Rejtő. Mario Castelnuovo-Tedesco,

Miklós Rózsa, and Jenő Zador were composing for the film industry in Hollywood. Laurent Halleux and Germain Prévost of the Belgian Pro Arte Quartet were living in southern California, Felix Khuner of the Kolisch Quartet and Ferenc Molnár of the Roth Quartet were settled in the Bay Area near San Francisco, and the Griller Quartet was in residence at the University of California in Berkeley.

It had taken great courage to leave behind the troubled world of Europe. While Bartók escaped the immediate danger of remaining in Hungary in 1939, he found no panacea in North America, but rather the disillusionment of an indifferent New York, the slow death by leukemia—the loss of homeland, social roots, hard-won recognition. While the creation of his final four masterpieces allowed him to retain his artistic identity, he continued to yearn for Hungary until the end of his life. For the Hungarian Quartet the situation was different. Not only had they survived the Occupation in Holland, but their artistry had developed during those years of hardship. After 1945, they had reestablished their European career, garnering new artistic recognition by performing and broadcasting both the Beethoven and Bartók cycles. For the quartet, the question in 1950 was whether a world career could be developed while living and working in California where the lifestyle differed so radically from what they had known in Europe. Two important challenges lay ahead: to gain continued acceptance from the public during their annual American tours arranged by La Berge and to assimilate the quartet into the academic life of the University of Southern California.

In February 1950 they immediately began to make their imprint on the musical life of their new academic home. The University of Southern California, a private institution founded in 1880, had begun a music program in 1883. A century later the School of Music had some six hundred students and a staff of sixty full-time teachers and fifty-five part-time instructors.

During the early 1950s, the Hungarian cellist, Stephen Deák, was head of the stringed instrument department at USC.[13] In 1950 Deák assumed responsibility for a new lecture-demonstration series at the university which featured performances of the Hungarian Quartet during the first spring of its residency. The series, a new venture in the teaching of chamber music literature at USC, was offered by the School of Music in cooperation with University College. A course in the history and literature of the string quartet was presented in a series of fifteen lectures and demonstrations featuring the Hungarian

Quartet. The series began on 14 February and lasted through 23 May 1950. Joining Stephen Deák for individual lectures were several members of the faculty: Pauline Alderman, Ingolf Dahl, Timothy Fetler, Raymond Kendall, and Halsey Stevens.

The Hungarian Quartet played at nine of the fifteen lectures that took place on Tuesday afternoons in Hancock Auditorium on the USC campus. The musical demonstrations for the remaining lectures featured either student quartets or recordings. This was the first opportunity for the Hungarian Quartet to introduce itself to an academic community eager to hear the four men speak about music and play their repertoire.[14] In addition to this series, the quartet played two concerts at Hancock Auditorium under the joint sponsorship of the School of Music and the Elizabeth Sprague Coolidge Foundation of the Library of Congress.

The following year, this lecture series was led by Halsey Stevens[15] and evolved into a seminar on the Bartók Quartets during which the quartet performed the six masterpieces and Stevens lectured. Later, Stevens and the ensemble presented this Bartók seminar at Mills College in Oakland, establishing the Hungarian Quartet in the Bay Area. Székely and Stevens developed a significant rapport during these seminars that led the Hungarian violinist to support the scholar's literary work in progress, *The Life and Music of Béla Bartók*.

The La Berge agency had arranged a third American tour of twenty-three concerts for the fall of 1951. By now many chamber music societies in the United States expected annual concerts by the Hungarian String Quartet. Return engagements became traditional in St. Louis, Kansas City, Dallas, Pittsburgh, and Cleveland, among many other cities, and Harold Spivacke continued to arrange engagements at the Library of Congress as well.

The annual programs of chamber music presented by the Elizabeth Sprague Coolidge Foundation opened in late October of 1951 with the presentation of a new work, the String Quartet No. 4 by the American composer William Schuman. The work had been commissioned by the foundation, and the Hungarian String Quartet presented the premiere.

In a special report in the *New York Times* on 29 October 1951, Downes wrote:

> We listened to a group of four string players, profoundly versed in their art, who sat down as informally as if they were

alone together in their shirtsleeves, finding incomparable happiness and solace for all the ills that a troubled world might bring in making music together.

It was playing by a most finished, sensitive and balanced ensemble, yet playing that was farthest from the precision hitting, smooth shellacked, crack quartet which could be imagined. These men lived in the music and the music lived in them. There was no need to carefully remember a re-hearsed effect, a special pause, or balance, "accelerando" or "ritardando." With an enviable background of experience and of living tradition, these men played instinctively to-gether, and in a way, sentimental as it may sound to say, which went straight from heart to heart.

They revealed completely the spirit of the composers they discoursed. The Beethoven quartet was as simple and direct in expression as it was lofty, tender, nobly sung and not without the due proportion of Beethoven's rugged power.

The supreme triumph of the afternoon was the music of Schubert, played with every nuance, fluctuation, feeling, fancy that this delicious and naive composition contains. Played also, at the proper moments, with wild romantic fantasy.

For Schubert is not only a dreaming lyricist. He can be astonishingly modern, as when, after shuddering tremolo chords, the upper strings persistently repeat a phrase which becomes sharply dissonant over changing harmonies; as when, in the slow movement with its lovely singing theme, a grand and sombre landscape seems suddenly to unfold it-self to the eye.

The scherzo, of course, is one of the most beautiful move-ments in chamber music, and when, in the finale, Schubert prattles happily along, with the laughter of a child, and rem-iniscence of the Rossini whose music he loved in his youth, the listener laughs too—or does so when he hears the music played as adorably as it was today. In the hands of poorer in-terpreters one wishes the movement would end quickly and the composer have done with his repetitions.

Whereas it would have been a delight, this afternoon, if that captivating, radiant music could have gone on minutes longer, one is tempted to conclude that this is the only way to play Schubert!

Had the Hungarian Quartet rested on these laurels they could have rested content. They did more: they gave a performance of William Schuman's new score, which is ultra-modern, and which presents more difficulties of technique and intonation than Beethoven and Schubert together. . . . There is reason to believe that Mr. Schuman, who was present and called repeatedly before the audience to acknowledge their cordial reception of his score, felt the same way.

As for the composition itself, let us say, for the present, that it is the score of a highly progressive composer who is well acquainted with the modern literature of music, knowing his Bartók, Hindemith, Schoenberg, and Berg as well; able to adopt their idioms at will to his own esthetic needs. Whether this composite also reveals the essential William Schuman is something that a closer acquaintance with the music will reveal. At the close of this performance Mrs. Coolidge, who sat in the front row just before the stage, herself joined in the applause for Mr. Schuman.[16]

Chapter Twenty-one

Southern California

Bernard La Berge died in 1950. The Hungarian Quartet was informed that Henry and Ann Colbert had bought the La Berge agency and would continue its operations in New York. At that time the Colberts, who had emigrated from Germany during the war, were employed by the New York organization, New Friends of Music.

In a 1992 interview Dénes Koromzay spoke of the early years of the Colbert–La Berge Concert Management:

> The Colberts established their new office in an apartment on West 57th Street. It was a place where their artists were welcome friends. Agnes Eisenberger, the wife of violist Paul Doktor and granddaughter of the Polish pianist Severin Eisenberger, was engaged by the Colberts and soon became assistant manager of the agency.
>
> In the best New York tradition, the Colberts "thought big" and had expansive plans. They brought Elizabeth Schwarzkopf into their fold. She was with them for a number of years, as were Georg Solti and others. Through good years and bad, we stood with the Colberts who soon seemed to have cornered the quartet market.
>
> Their agency began to offer "packaged seasons" to the sponsors, entire seasons that promised specific performances by quartets under the Colbert management. Because only the

Budapest Quartet was not with them, this method of marketing chamber music was very successful for the Colberts,
until there was a rupture with the Amadeus Quartet, who demanded more certain guarantees.[1]

The Hungarian Quartet appeared in New York for the third consecutive season for the New Friends of Music on 5 November 1950.
The program was organized by the pianist Hortense Monath, who
with bassist Philip Sklar joined the ensemble for a performance of
Schubert's Piano Quintet ("The Trout"). Aaron Copland's *Two Pieces*
(1928) appeared on the program, which also included Schubert's
masterpiece, the String Quartet in G Major, Op. 161. The inclusion of
Copland's music was part of the November celebration in New York
of the American master's fiftieth birthday.

In January 1951 at the Wilshire Ebell Theater in Los Angeles, the
quartet began their first Beethoven cycle in the United States. The
five-concert format was used, with the series ending with the Grosse
Fuge, Op. 133, as the final movement of String Quartet, Op. 130, as
Beethoven had originally intended. Unlike their typical European
performances of the Beethoven cycle, which absorbed five or six consecutive evenings, the five concerts in Los Angeles were played inter-
mittently over a long period, beginning on 3 January and ending on
11 April.

After the opening Beethoven concert in Los Angeles, the quartet
traveled immediately to Mexico City to present a subscription series
of six concerts in the Sala Molière of the Instituto Francés de América
Latina. They played works by Haydn, Mozart, Beethoven, and Schubert, and both Bartók's and Kodály's second quartets.

The ensemble ended its touring season three months later
in Seattle with a concert on 20 April in Meany Hall on the University
of Washington campus. Pat Dunbar, critic of the *Seattle Times*,
wrote:

> One by one, the cares and worries of the Atomic Age were
> gently smoothed away by the Hungarian Quartet last night at
> Meany Hall. The mere fact that there was a public perfor-
> mance of chamber music by a string quartet, and that it was
> attended by a crowd of over 750 people, was reassuring evi-
> dence of the continuity and imperishableness of the great
> musical forms.[2]

In the fall of 1951 the quartet began a tour of South America which had been arranged by Ernesto de Quesada. In Barranquilla on the coast of Colombia, they arrived at the theater to rehearse, but when the stage curtains were opened, thousands of bats flew into the air, disturbed by the intrusion. The quartet fled.

Finally it was decided that the quartet would sit on the apron of the stage in front of the curtains, the bats held at bay on the darkened stage. At the concert the four musicians huddled in an odd configuration, enduring the incredible heat and humidity, air conditioning not being a normal convenience at that time in South America. Throughout the first half of the concert, Palotai watched Koromzay's every move with unusual attentiveness. At the intermission when asked the cause of such vigilance, the cellist reported that a large, green praying mantis had been lurking near Koromzay's feet during the entire Beethoven quartet. During the second half of the concert, everyone kept a sharp lookout.

In Rio de Janeiro, the quartet returned to the Teatro Municipal where they had performed the Beethoven cycle in 1949. Their concert on 10 November 1951 included a performance of the Piano Quintet in F Minor, Op. 34, by Brahms. The pianist was Wilhelm Backhaus, with whom they had performed the quintet earlier in Vevey. When Quesada realized that the great German pianist would be available for another performance while touring in South America, he arranged it for Rio de Janeiro to the mutual satisfaction of the musicians and the delight of the Brazilian audience.

After their reunion with Wilhelm Backhaus, the quartet met Heitor Villa-Lobos, a composer who had visited the United States for the first time in 1944 to conduct his works in Los Angeles, Boston, and New York. In 1947, after having established the Brazilian Academy of Music, Villa-Lobos went again to the United States, then eventually to Europe. After 1950 he traveled widely but always kept his home in Rio de Janeiro; it was there he entertained the Hungarian Quartet.

Villa-Lobos was considered one of the most original composers of his time. In his compositions, which exceed two thousand in number, he was able to relate successfully certain elements of Brazilian folk song to his own eclectic style of composition. This compositional technique interested Székely, who asked to study the scores of his string quartets:

Learning of my interest in these works, Villa-Lobos sent copies of all the scores to Los Angeles. We studied the Quartet No. 6 which is subtitled *Quarteto Brasileiros* and played it often. We recorded it in Paris at the same time as Kodály's Second Quartet. Unfortunately, this release on European Columbia never came out in America. Eventually Villa-Lobos composed fifteen string quartets, but his Quartet No. 6 was the most often played.

Later in New York I met Villa-Lobos again. In his hotel room he served coffee made from Brazilian coffee beans, which he always carried with him on his travels. When I expressed some interest in the possibility of his composing a work for string quartet and orchestra for us, he immediately took manuscript paper and spontaneously began to write down motifs. This was his natural method.

After performing in South America, the quartet immediately began another tour in the United States with twenty-three concerts that took them from Dallas to New York, where they appeared at Town Hall and at the Frick Gallery. They then returned to Texas, where the tour concluded with a concert at the San Pedro Playhouse in San Antonio.

They appeared at the San Francisco Museum of Art on 17 April 1951 in their first concert under the auspices of Mills College in Oakland. Alfred Frankenstein, the esteemed critic of the *San Francisco Chronicle*, wrote about their performance of Bartók's colossal, virtuosic work, the Fourth Quartet: "The Hungarian Quartet left its audience as limp as it was excited, but order was restored with a rich, symphonic performance of Schubert's 'Death and the Maiden.'"[3] This concert was the first of twenty-four concerts the quartet gave in the Bay Area during the following two summers.

For more than a decade the Budapest Quartet had presented a series of summer chamber music concerts at Mills College. When they chose not to return in 1951, the Hungarian Quartet was engaged to replace them for the series' twenty-third summer season at Mills College. The concerts were linked to a concurrent series at the San Francisco Museum of Art, so that the quartet had to travel from Los Angeles to the Bay Area each of six weeks in order to play two concerts. They would perform in Oakland and, two days later, in San Francisco, then return to the USC campus in Los Angeles to carry out their duties there.

Quartets by Mozart, Beethoven, Schubert, and Brahms provided the staple fare of their concerts on the Mills College campus, as well as Brahms' Quintet in F Minor, Op. 34, with pianist Egon Petri. A twentieth-century quartet appeared on each concert as well—works by Darius Milhaud, William Schuman, Walter Piston, David Diamond, Paul Hindemith, and Aaron Copland. Each concert in San Francisco contained works by Beethoven and Haydn and one of the Bartók quartets, resulting in a chronological Bartók cycle over the six-week period.

During the winter season that followed, the quartet undertook its fourth annual American tour for the Colbert–La Berge agency. In February they gave their traditional New York appearance at Town Hall for the New Friends of Music with a performance of two Beethoven works and Walter Piston's Quartet No. 1. About Piston and his music, the critic of the *New York Herald Tribune* wrote, "He is a composer (and it is a work) in which the musical elements—personal and abstract—are beautifully poised and integrated."[4] Having found success with the Piston work, the quartet continued to play it throughout the tour with many well-received performances.

They returned to the stage of the Wilshire Ebell Theater in Los Angeles on 21 March in a unique concert for the Music Guild which opened with the little-played Quartet No. 2 by Juan Arriaga, an early nineteenth-century Spanish composer. The critic of the *Mirror* in Los Angeles wrote about Piston's work that followed, "It would be difficult to imagine Walter Piston's succinct Quartet No. 1 (1933) played with more compelling rhythm or more stunning virtuosity than the Hungarians brought to it last night."[5] After the intermission Mitchel Lurie (clarinet), Joseph Eger (horn), Don Christlieb (bassoon), and Milton Kestenbaum (double bass) joined the quartet for a performance of Schubert's Octet in F Major, Op. 166.

To his surprise, Székely discovered that his old friend, Mario Castelnuovo-Tedesco, was living in the Los Angeles area. When they met again for the first time in decades, he learned that Castelnuovo-Tedesco had just completed a new chamber music work, a piano quintet, and this soon brought them together on the stage in Pasadena.

Jascha Heifetz had played two important works by Castelnuovo-Tedesco in New York during the 1930s. With the New York Philharmonic conducted by Arturo Toscanini, Heifetz performed *The Prophets* for violin and orchestra in 1933, then two years later, the

Violin Concerto No. 3. This brought Castelnuovo-Tedesco immediate success in the United States.

With the help of Heifetz and Toscanini, the Florentine composer emigrated to the United States in 1939 when the political events in Europe forced him to flee Italy. He spent one year in New York, then settled in Beverly Hills. In Hollywood he created the musical scores for *Gaslight*, *Ten Little Indians*, and *The Day of the Fox*, among many others. He appeared frequently as a piano soloist and taught composition, mainly to aspiring composers of film scores.

Mario Castelnuovo-Tedesco appeared as pianist with the Hungarian Quartet at the Pasadena Playhouse on 20 March 1952 in the world premiere of his new Second Piano Quintet. This performance for the Coleman series was a long-awaited artistic collaboration between Castelnuovo-Tedesco and Székely, for whom the gifted composer had written and dedicated his *Variazioni sinfoniche for Violin and Orchestra* in 1930. Castelnuovo-Tedesco had contemplated the composition of the Second Piano Quintet for many years and had finally completed it under the encouragement of Harlow Mills, who wished to have the first performance in the Coleman concerts in Pasadena. Subtitled "Memories of a Tuscan Countryside," its four movements bear descriptive titles: The Hills, The Cypresses, Procession in the Month of May, and The Harvest. The composer returned to Italy after this premiere to take part in the staging of his novel puppet show with voices and instruments, *Aucassin et Nicolette*.

The quartet returned to the Bay Area the next year to celebrate the twenty-fourth summer season of chamber music at Mills College. Darius Milhaud, who for many years had been composer-in-residence at Mills College, was present at the world premiere of his Piano Quintet No. 1, performed by the Hungarian Quartet and Egon Petri on June 29 during the Mills College Centennial. The quartet's six concerts on the Oakland campus during June and July followed a plan that offered, in addition to the celebration of Milhaud's new quintet, two traditional masterworks and one Bartók quartet at each performance.

Each concert of the concurrent series in San Francisco featured a work of Mozart and on various occasions the quartets of Smetana, Ravel, and Brahms. Two assisting artists appeared with the Hungarian Quartet: Gabor Rejtő, cellist, in a performance of the Schubert Quintet, Op. 163, and Agnes Albert, pianist, in the Franck Quintet in F Minor. Twentieth-century quartets by Walter Piston, Aaron Copland,

Heitor Villa-Lobos, Zoltán Kodály, Paul Hindemith, and Darius Milhaud figured prominently in this series.[6]

After two successful years, the Hungarian Quartet's appointment at the University of Southern California came to an end. During a difficult financial period, the institution was unable to continue funding its share of the project conceived by Harold Spivacke, director of the Coolidge Foundation.

Discussing this juncture in the quartet's career, Székly stresses the crucial point that their residency at USC was not a teaching appointment:

> Raymond Kendall had the desire to engage us further but could only do so if we would agree to continue in a teaching capacity. At that time a teaching commitment was not in our plans. We believed in our success all over the world as a performing quartet and decided to discontinue our engagement at USC.
>
> Kendall himself eventually left his position at USC and became associated with a new institute funded by the Chandler Foundation. Many years later, Kendall approached me with the idea of my teaching chamber music in Los Angeles, but I decided in favor of accepting a position in Canada as artist-in-residence at the Banff Centre in Alberta.
>
> Shortly after that, Kendall left his post and began a new career in San Diego.

After the Bay Area concerts in the summer of 1952, violist Dénes Koromzay withdrew from public performances for a period of one year, after twenty intensive years of stage appearances. During his absence from the Hungarian Quartet, Laurent Halleux joined the ensemble as violist.

Laurent Halleux was born at Hodimont-Verviers, France, on 24 January 1897. A violin pupil of César Thomson, he was a member of the celebrated Belgian Pro Arte String Quartet and alternated as leader with Alphonse Onnou during the early years of the ensemble. Later he was second violinist. After 1940 he was in residence at the University of Wisconsin, then took up the viola and played in the MGM studio orchestra in Los Angeles.

After the war, a number of independent recording companies were established in the United States. These included Concert Hall Society in 1947, Westminster in 1949, and somewhat later, Vox,

Urania, Allegro, and Composer Recordings, Inc. Concert Hall Society, which operated as a subscription record club, invited the quartet to make its first recordings in the United States.

In the fall of 1952, with Laurent Halleux as violist, the Hungarian Quartet recorded Schubert's Quartet in D Minor ("Death and the Maiden") in a private studio in Los Angeles for Concert Hall Society. A few weeks later they recorded three additional works for them in a New York studio: Dvořák's Quartet No. 12 in F, Op. 96 ("American"), Glazounov's *Five Novelettes,* Op. 15, and Tchaikovsky's Quartet No. 1 in D Major, Op. 11. These three works were recorded in two sessions on a single day. The amazing quality of these recorded performances is very much akin to the so-called "live performance" recordings of a later era. With the availability of these Concert Hall Society recordings, the quartet's large following in North America had access to the ensemble's recordings for the first time. Their earlier recordings made in London had not been marketed in the United States.

The Hungarian Quartet's European season began in Vevey with two concerts in October, the fourteenth and fifteenth concerts in Vevey since their first appearance there in 1939. After these performances in Switzerland, the quartet was introduced to post-war audiences in Germany, appearing first in Hannover. During the following two decades they appeared frequently in Hamburg, Bremen, Frankfurt, and Munich, and in the Ruhr Valley at Mülheim. Because of its isolation by the Iron Curtain, Berlin was visited less frequently. The quartet's devotion to the classical repertoire, and in particular to the quartets of Beethoven, brought serious attention from the West German audiences. They played often in such towns as Detmold, Oberhausen, Neuss, Lüneburg, Lübeck, Osnabrück, Hanau, Wiesbaden, Marburg, Essen, Duisburg, Gelsenkirchen, Krefeld, and Wuppertal, among many others.

Dénes Koromzay rejoined the Hungarian Quartet during the summer of 1953 for concerts at the Ravinia Festival near Chicago. Immediately after the Ravinia concerts, the quartet embarked for Paris where they soon began their most ambitious and successful recording enterprise to date. For Pathé-Marconi, the Paris-based branch of EMI, they recorded the Beethoven cycle for the first time. In 1955, the Académie Charles Cros recognized the superior artistic achievement of this recording effort by awarding the recording with its prestigious Grand Prix du Disque.

During a period of financial prosperity, the directors of Pathé-

Marconi had asked the Valmalète agency to recommend a string quartet to record the Beethoven cycle. The Hungarian Quartet, with its vast experience in public performances of the Beethoven cycle, was Valmalète's obvious choice. In April of 1953 Pathé-Marconi offered the quartet an exclusive recording contract that would be in effect for four years—from 1 June 1953 to 31 May 1957. Their recordings would be marketed under the European Columbia label.

Pathé-Marconi's invitation came by telegram. In their excitement, the quartet misread the amount of the proposed fee, but still found the offer acceptable—even "minus a zero."

The prestigious company, Les Industries Musicales et Électriques Pathé-Marconi, had no permanent studios in Paris in 1953. The quartet's first recording sessions took place near the Plaza Athenée Hotel in a converted, three-story apartment house called Studio Magellan, on a side street off the Champs-Elysées near the Place de l'Étoile.

The seventeen quartets of the Beethoven cycle were recorded in two sessions over a four-month period. The first session began on 7 September 1953 with Quartet No. 12 (Op. 127) and ended on 17 October with Quartet No. 16, the last quartet, Op. 135. The players returned to Studio Magellan on 9 November to record the remaining five quartets of Op. 18, concluding the project on 8 December 1953, Zoltán Székely's forty-ninth birthday.[7]

From the outset of the first recording session, there was constant interruption from the sound of a jazz recording taking place one floor above. The quartet often had to stop the sessions, their work ruined by the outside sound. When at last the recording of the finale of Op. 127 was completed and heard in its entirety, the producer, Peter de Jongh, was so elated with the results that he ran around the studio shouting, "This is unbelievable. Unbelievable!"

Peter de Jongh assumed his first administrative role at Pathé-Marconi before the Beethoven project was completed. Norbert Gamsohn took over as producer, with Paul Vavasseur as the balance engineer. When de Jongh eventually became an executive at Pathé-Marconi and altogether abandoned his role as a producer in the company, a young Hungarian named Tomaso Gallia became Pathé-Marconi's chief producer. The son of an Italian father and a Hungarian mother, Gallia was the grandson of István Thomán, the piano teacher of Bartók and Dohnányi at the Franz Liszt Academy. For many years Gallia continued to have an outstanding career as a producer for Pathé-Marconi. He found György Cziffra playing in Budapest cafes and engaged him to record for Pathé-Marconi in Paris. When Cziffra, who is best known for his brilliant interpretations of the music of Liszt, achieved eminence as a recording artist in France, Tomaso Gallia became his private secretary.

After the historic Pathé-Marconi recording of the Beethoven cycle, all EMI's subsequent recordings of the Hungarian Quartet were made with the assistance of Eric McLeod, a Scottish-French producer who led the sessions but said very little. McLeod was amiable and civilized, critical but not aggressive; however, he was responsible for the bulk of the recorded legacy of the Hungarian String Quartet, including their second recording of the Beethoven cycle in 1965.

During these initial recording sessions in 1953, the quartet devoted twenty-four days in October, November, and December to four public performances of the complete Beethoven cycle. The first two were scheduled concurrently in Switzerland in October. The quartet moved easily between Geneva and Vevey, appearing alternately at the Théâtre de Vevey and the Théâtre de la Cour St. Pierre. In Vevey, where Laurent Halleux had been expected to appear as violist in the ensemble, the organizers made note in the house programs that Dénes Koromzay had returned to the Hungarian Quartet: *"Pour sa tournée en Europe, le Quatuor Hongrois a pu s'assurer à nouveau le concours de son ancien altiste Monsieur Dénes Koromzay."* After the Swiss concerts, the quartet played the Beethoven cycle twice more during the fall: in Paris at the Salle Gaveau and in Milan for the Società del Quartetto di Milano.

After four public performances and two extended recording sessions of the Beethoven cycle, the quartet returned to the United States after Christmas for the sixth consecutive season of touring for the Colbert agency.

At the end of this American tour, the distinguished cellist Eva Heinitz was invited to appear with the quartet in Seattle in March of 1954. After an extensive career as both cellist and viola da gambist, Heinitz settled in Seattle, where she was professor of cello at the University of Washington. A week before the Seattle performance, she met the quartet after their concert in Yakima, Washington, the center of the apple-growing industry in America, to rehearse the Schubert Quintet, Op. 163. The ensemble had performed the quintet in the past with assisting artists including Henri Honegger, Stephen Deák, and Gabor Rejtő; the occasion to perform the work with Heinitz was a welcome one that brought special pleasure to Vilmos

Palotai, since he and Heinitz had been friends in Berlin where they were both studying with Hugo Becker. At Palotai's invitation, Heinitz took the leading part.

Making their sixth appearance in Seattle's Meany Hall, the quartet performed Haydn's "Lark" and Piston's Quartet No. 4, but the magnificent performance of the Schubert quintet with Heinitz and Palotai playing the cello parts was the climax of the concert. The critic of the *Seattle Post-Intelligencer* called the evening "probably the most rewarding concert of the chamber music season, the engaging performance by the Italian Quartet last fall notwithstanding."[8]

The quartet spent most of the 1954–55 season abroad playing concerts and recording again for Pathé-Marconi in Paris. In mid-September Copenhagen was the venue for a Beethoven cycle, followed by other concerts in Denmark (Herning, Silkeborg, Assens, Faabord, and Svenborg). They traveled to Germany for a concert in Berlin, then returned to Scandinavia for appearances in Stockholm and Gothenburg, Sweden. October was devoted to the English audiences in Birmingham, Bradford, Exeter, Newcastle-on-Tyne, and in the Royal Festival Hall in London. Appearances in Vienna and Paris concluded the fall tour.

Recording sessions began in Paris on 22 November and lasted until three days before Christmas. The quartet returned to the Pathé-Marconi studios for another month in late May. These two periods of recording produced five recordings in the new long-playing format which were released on the European Columbia label and marketed in Europe. Two Schubert works, Quartet Op. 29, No. 1, and Quartet in D Minor ("Death and the Maiden"), were paired as one monophonic, long-playing release. Schubert's Quartet in G Major, Op. 161, was produced as a single release. Quartet No. 6 by Heitor Villa-Lobos and Quartet No. 2, Op. 10, by Zoltán Kodály were recorded at the Schola Cantorum in Paris and paired on one record. Two Haydn works, Op. 76, No. 2 ("Quinten") and Op. 64, No. 5 ("Lark"), were recorded and paired on another release. Quartet No. 2 by Alexander Borodin was released as a single record.

Pathé-Marconi produced an album later in 1956 that contained selected movements drawn from the quartet's entire catalogue of recordings in which Vilmos Palotai had appeared as cellist. This album, "Le Quatour Hongrois: Morceaux Choisis de Quatuors à cordes," contained movements from quartets by Borodin, Schubert, Haydn, Mozart, Beethoven, Tchaikovsky, and Dvořák.[9]

The first issue of the new Columbia recording of the Beethoven cycle was released in midwinter of 1955. The European press was quick to confirm the artistic success of the new recordings, and the sale of the quartet's new Beethoven cycle was instantly successful, as Pathé-Marconi had hoped.

During December, Jacques Feschotte, the musicologist who often accompanied the quartet on its tours for Jeunesses Musicales de France, wrote from Brest to tell Székely about his recent visit in Paris on 17 November with the ailing Arthur Honegger who was by then bedridden.[10] The great musician had greeted Feschotte with his usual kindness. When Feschotte told him that he was planning to leave on a JMF tour with the young artists of the Hungarian String Quartet, Honegger expressed his regret that he had not been able to listen the previous day to his "dear friends who had so admirably interpreted his works" and asked that this be told to them. In this remark Honegger referred to having missed the quartet's concert at the Salle Gaveau in Paris which celebrated the tenth anniversary of Béla Bartók's death. "And tell them also," Honegger said, showing Feschotte his copy of the new recordings of the Beethoven cycle, "that I have the four of them with me for my greatest joy." Feschotte concluded his message to the quartet by saying that on 27 December he was brokenhearted by the news of Honegger's death in Paris.

The quartet returned to Holland in January of 1955 for concerts in Arnhem, The Hague, Bloemendaal, Rotterdam, and Amsterdam. Belgium and France welcomed them in February; Italy did so in March; they spent April in Switzerland; Spain was their host in May. In early June they returned to the recording studios in Paris for several weeks. Then, as part of the 1955 Holland Festival, they finished the season with nine concerts in The Hague, Scheveningen, and Amsterdam devoted to Haydn, Bartók, and Beethoven.

In the Hague Joseph van Voorthuysen, critic of the *Haager Courant*, expressed his belief that the quartet played together as though their musicality shared only one temperament. "It is as though the impossible becomes possible and the maturity of these resoundingly fine musicians demands our biggest respect."[11]

Chapter Twenty-two

Aspen

After two years of intensive touring abroad with one extended period of fourteen months spent in Europe, the quartet returned to the United States. Their recording of the Beethoven cycle had aroused great interest in America. The Colbert–La Berge Concert Management released publicity materials that praised the new recordings and informed the sponsoring chamber music societies of critical opinion expressed by J. F. Kilpatrick of the *Dallas Times Herald* and Harold Schonberg of the *New York Times*, a brilliant critic who had begun his writing career for Vox Productions. In assessing one volume of the recorded cycle, Schonberg wrote, "The Hungarian Quartet offers first-class readings in the three-disk set which is distinguished by interpretations of beautiful tone and fine ensemble." Kilpatrick wrote, "The music is played breathtakingly, as close to mechanical and artistic perfection as it would be good for mortal ears to hear."[1]

After this long absence from the United States, the quartet needed to reestablish itself in the chamber music life of the Americas. The Colberts began to rally the sponsors in thirty cities, reawakening their interest in the Hungarian Quartet, and plans were negotiated with Ernesto de Quesada for another South American tour.

A serious problem confronted the quartet in the spring of 1956. Vilmos Palotai's physician informed him that his health was increasingly threatened by diabetes. A radical change in his lifestyle was demanded, but how to attain this change remained a question. At the height of its popularity, the quartet performed from one hundred to one hundred fifty concerts in each eight-month season. Touring of this magnitude was a stressful business.

From the beginning, Palotai had been a powerful guiding force in the quartet. After considering his doctor's verdict, he approached his colleagues with a proposal designed to dramatically curtail the quartet's concert activities in consideration of his endangered health.

Because his proposal could not be accepted by his colleagues, Vilmos Palotai decided to retire from the quartet he had helped to create twenty-one years earlier. In the spring of 1956 he returned to Switzerland to live. With violinist Arpád Gérecz and his friend of long standing, pianist Georges Solchany, he established the Hungarian Trio, a new ensemble with which he continued to perform at a more relaxed pace.

Replacing the cellist of the quartet had not been something foreseen by the colleagues, but the process had to begin immediately in view of the enormous commitments for the forthcoming season. Gabor Rejtő seemed a logical candidate. This distinguished Hungarian cellist had come to the United States after the war and had been the cello professor at the Eastman School of Music in Rochester, New York, from 1949 to 1954. When Stephen Deák became professor emeritus at USC in 1954, it was Gabor Rejtő who succeeded him. At the time of Rejtő's appointment at USC, many of his devoted cello students followed him from New York to southern California. Rejtő declined the invitation to join the quartet because of his extensive teaching schedule and the demanding concert activities of the Alma Trio, an ensemble he had formed with violinist Roman Totenberg and Adolph Baller, pianist.

At the suggestion of the Colberts, the quartet considered an experienced Austrian cellist living in New York, but this negotiation did not come to fulfillment. The quartet had briefly met the Hungarian cellist, George Bekefi, while on tour in South America. An outstanding virtuoso and a much-admired friend of János Starker, Bekefi was then living in Rio de Janeiro. Koromzay contacted Bekefi when he learned that the cellist had the recommendation of George Mendelssohn, president of Vox Productions. Bekefi, who was now living in the United States, was most enthusiastic about Koromzay's enquiry; however, he had recently signed an orchestra contract, so he was unable to consider joining the quartet. Only a few years hence,

George Bekefi died of cancer shortly after he and violinist Victor Aitay had helped János Starker prepare his book, *An Organized Method of String Playing*, for publication in 1961.

Gabor Rejtő brought another fine Hungarian cellist to the attention of the quartet—Gabriel Magyar. A contemporary of Dénes Koromzay, Magyar was born in Budapest on 5 December 1914. His mother was a pianist. His brother, the violinist Tamás Magyar, was a pupil of Hubay at the Franz Liszt Academy in 1934. Magyar's father, a professor of humanities and classical languages, was a fervent music enthusiast.

Gabriel Magyar began to study the violin as a child, but soon changed to the cello. At the Franz Liszt Academy he was a cello pupil of Anton Friss. He studied chamber music with Leó Weiner and composition with Zoltán Kodály. Magyar graduated with the Master's diploma in 1936. During the earliest period of his career he performed Kodály's Solo Sonata, acclaimed by the composer as the best performance of the work, and gave the first Budapest performance of the Milhaud Cello Concerto, then a new work premiered in Paris in 1935.

Magyar's career was interrupted by the war, but resumed immediately after the Armistice. Successful concerts in Europe were followed by engagements in South America and the United States. In Venezuela, as a soloist and as cellist of the Trio of the National Radio of Caracas, he gave weekly recitals.

When he was invited to join the Hungarian String Quartet in 1956, Magyar was professsor of cello and chamber music at the University of Oklahoma in Norman, where he lived with his Hungarian-born wife, Julie Dora, who had been raised in St. Louis.

Székely made a special trip to Oklahoma to meet Magyar:

> In Norman, Magyar first played for me Schubert's "Arpeggione" Sonata, as I recall. And, of course, we played together and discussed music and quartet playing. He seemed eager to join us, and because I found him an excellent cellist and certainly a highly promising candidate for our quartet, we invited him.
>
> In the beginning his task was great because at that time we had many engagements. We were immediately to present a series of concerts in the San Francisco Museum of Art, and later in July, a major Brahms Festival in Santa Barbara. After the Brahms Festival, we had a brief summer residency at the

University of Oregon in Eugene where we gave three concerts and six lectures.

In a 1992 letter, Gabriel Magyar spoke of his acceptance of the Hungarian Quartet's invitation in 1956 to become cellist of the ensemble:

> When I was approached by the Hungarian String Quartet to join them, I was very happy and after I began my new career in the quartet I was not disappointed. To the contrary, my new role brought even more to my life than I had expected.
>
> I had heard them before and found their playing of the highest caliber, both musically and technically. In 1954, my wife and I drove to Stillwater, Oklahoma, to hear them. After the concert I spoke to the members briefly, little realizing that in the not-too-distant future I would be an enthusiastic partner in their artistry.
>
> I always viewed chamber music as the highest form of music and string quartet music was on the top of my list. It is no small wonder then that I was looking forward tremendously and eagerly to joining them. Nevertheless, I knew that it would not be an easy task to step into the place of Vilmos Palotai, who was a widely reputed and appreciated artist and one of the founders of the quartet.
>
> In early June of 1956 we arrived in Los Angeles, at that time the quartet's home base. We began our rehearsals immediately, rotating the locations where we rehearsed; Zoltán's home was frequented more often than the others, however.
>
> Without my dear wife's fullhearted support in the difficult task of administering the various problems and managing the planning needed to accommodate our itinerant lifestyle of the next sixteen years with the quartet, I could not have succeeded. [2]

The new cellist's formidable task was rehearsing the large repertoire scheduled for an imminent series of six concerts in the Bay Area at the end of the month. It was accomplished with aplomb. The quartet quickly absorbed Magyar's playing into their well-ordered style, even though there had not been a change in personnel for eighteen years. By 5 June 1956, the evening of the first concert in San Francisco, the eighteen works—quartets by Mozart, Haydn, Schubert, Beethoven, Brahms, Debussy, Kodály, Bartók, Maconchy, Copland, Piston, and Milhaud—were ready.

Having settled themselves on the platform, they launched into what had become over the years one of their most succesful works. The first ascending arpeggio of Haydn's "Lark" quartet offered the large San Francisco audience their first encounter with Gabriel Magyar, the new cellist of the Hungarian Quartet. He recalls:

> During my early weeks in the quartet I found their tireless search for interpretation and technical perfection admirable. Zoltán's patience was outstanding. I also found what I had already suspected—that his way of music making was very similar to the principles I had established during my previous musical activities. This facilitated the difficult task of my blending into a previously established, highly successful ensemble. Let others judge to what degree I was successful.
>
> The quartet's approach, first of all, was to the music, its general forms, phrasing, character, mood; then to deciding what technical solutions—fingerings, vibrato, proportioning bow strokes and so on—would best serve those elements previously mentioned. At length we discussed where the leading ideas lie on the instruments and how to balance the dynamics accordingly. Of course, in this process, we had to solve various ensemble problems as well.
>
> Since all four of us had our own ideas about all these elements, it was not an easy task to arrive at a unified conclusion. But I must compliment my colleagues. They were always ready and open to discuss propositions. That does not mean that the process was very peaceful! But, somehow, the miracle always happened and, by the time the actual performance took place, the public and critics alike generally agreed that the Hungarian Quartet had an unusual unity in style and purpose. To an outsider, our discussions over the years would perhaps have seemed to be "a tempest in a teapot," so to speak.[3]

In the many concerts that followed that summer, it was soon apparent that it was within Magyar's powers to adapt his musicality and his remarkably understated virtuosity to the requirements of the quartet repertoire. His unique left-hand technique perfectly suited the demands of unison and octave passages that so often threaten

the intonation of a quartet, his lustrous sonority balanced and complemented the austere beauty of Székely's tone, and he could deliver
the cello's prominent solo passages with distinction and assurance.
After the quartet presented a program of Brahms, Piston, and Debussy
on 19 June at the San Francisco Museum of Art, Clifford Gessler, the
perceptive critic of the *San Francisco Tribune*, conveyed his delight to
his readers, having savored Magyar's "mellow solo tone" in the magnificent Adagio of Piston's Quartet No. 1, a slow movement written
in the American composer's finest style.[4]

Gabriel Magyar's playing revealed unique attributes unlike those
that characterized the magnificent cello playing of Vilmos Palotai
during the twenty-one year period that had preceded. This one would
expect in the case of two splendid, if quite different, cellists, two
artists who portrayed different aspects of the same role. Change had
come to the quartet, and Magyar's playing soon became a much-val-
ued, integral aspect of their performances after 1956.

Regarding Székely's power of concentration, Magyar has this to
say:

> Let me illustrate how intensely Zoltán can concentrate on a
> subject he is interested in. Once we were recording one of
> the Brahms sextets at Salle Wagram on a day that happened
> to be Zoltán's birthday. We secretly agreed that when Zoltán
> gave the cue to start, instead of Brahms, we would play
> "Happy Birthday to you." He stopped playing, looked at the
> score and said, "You know, this could be interpreted in sev-
> eral ways." He heard not a note of our little prank. When we
> burst out laughing, he looked up innocently and asked,
> "What is so funny about this?"[5]

The Hungarian Quartet came to the 1956 Santa Barbara Music
Festival with vast festival experience—Edinburgh, Seville, Menton,
Ravinia, Tanglewood. However, that year the Santa Barbara Festival
was devoted to the chamber music of Johannes Brahms and was
therefore highly specialized. Fortunately, the quartet had already performed the three string quartets of Brahms with Magyar during the
previous weeks in the Bay Area. But there were many other works to
prepare.

The Brahms Festival was launched at the Lobero Theater in Santa
Barbara with two consecutive concerts during which the complete
trios were played by Eudice Shapiro, violinist; Nikolai Graudan, cel-

list; Joanna Graudan, pianist; clarinetist Mitchell Lurie; and Wendell Hoss, French horn. The Hungarian Quartet and guest artists Lee Pattison, pianist; Laurent Halleux, violist; and Gabor Rejtő, cellist, presented the four remaining concerts with the piano quartets and the piano quintet, the string quartets, quintets, and sextets. The final work of the festival was a performance of the Clarinet Quintet, Op. 115. Magyar played the Brahms repertoire complete with the exception of one performance on 29 June, at which time Pattison, Székely, Halleux, and Rejtő took the responsibility of the First Piano Quartet.

When their brief residency at the University of Oregon concluded in August, little time remained to rehearse for their ninth American tour which began in Indianapolis in early fall. In New York they presented a joint recital with John Wummer, flutist, and pianist Arthur Balsam at Carnegie Recital Hall. In Washington, D.C., the quartet performed at the Library of Congress as it had in previous seasons. After twenty-one concerts they arrived in Miami for the final performance of the tour, and then left immediately for Europe.

Dr. Rudolf Goette, their concert manager in Hamburg, had arranged fourteen appearances in Germany in March, with concerts from Bremen to Bayreuth. Their Italian manager, Ada Finzi, organized an Italian tour for April with concerts in Vicenza, Florence, Trieste, Milan, Bolzano, Bologna, and Pesaro. Upon their return to the United States in the spring, the quartet appeared again at Wheeler Auditorium on the University of California campus in Berkeley, then went to Eugene, Oregon, for a second summer residency at the University of Oregon.

After playing in the quartet for a year, Gabriel Magyar had appeared in a broad spectrum of the ensemble's repertoire but had not yet taken part in a Beethoven cycle. This was soon to happen on the quartet's most elaborate Central and South American tour ever: Mexico, Guatemala, Costa Rica, Colombia, Ecuador, Peru, Chile, Argentina, Uruguay, Brazil, and Venezuela. In the Caribbean they performed in Aruba, Curaçao, and Jamaica, finally ending the tour on 25 October in Havana, Cuba. They performed the Beethoven cycle frequently during these three months.

Almost without pause, a tour of the United States began on 29 October in Providence, Rhode Island, and from there the quartet traversed its concert territory playing thirty-three engagements before departing for Europe again in January. During their travels, they appeared in Jordan Hall in Boston for the Mason Music Foundation with a program of Bartók and Beethoven. The critic of the *Christian Science Monitor* concluded his review: "But the final and perhaps the greatest accolade that one may bestow on these great interpreters of great music is that they understand and convey the mingling of personal emotion with formal structure which is the crowning achievement both of Bartók and Beethoven."[6]

They began their European season at the Amsterdam Concertgebouw. In Switzerland they then celebrated Arts et Lettres' three-hundredth concert in the Théâtre de Vevey with Haydn, Brahms, and Debussy. In Vienna at the Mozartsaal, there was a *Kammermusikabend*. In Germany there were broadcast concerts from Baden-Baden.

With the worldwide success of the recordings of the Beethoven cycle, Pathé-Marconi decided there should be more recording sessions. The quartet returned to Paris to record the quartets of Ravel and Debussy at the Schola Cantorum, then at Salle Wagram the Op. 51 quartets of Brahms, Schubert's Quartet in A Minor, Op. 29, and Dvořák's Quartet, Op. 96. Another important recording project launched at this time produced a legacy of piano quintet recordings with pianist Georges Solchany. Four works were recorded: the piano quintets of Dvořák, Franck, Schumann, and Brahms.

Before the end of the recording sessions, Székely fell ill for ten days and was unable to complete the project. Fortunately he recovered and was able to continue the tour, but the quartet had fallen behind in their recording schedule and would have to return to the studio during their holiday period.

After their acclaimed performances at the 1958 Holland Festival in July, they spent ten days performing in Switzerland at the Engadin Festival, a celebration of music near St. Moritz organized by the brother of Walter Shulthess, their Swiss manager and the husband of Stefi Geyer. In early August they returned to the Menton Festival on the French Riviera.

The Russian cellist Michail Cherniavsky attended the concerts in Menton and renewed his friendship with his countryman, Alexandre Moskowsky. The Cherniavsky brothers—violinist Leo, cellist Michail, and pianist Jan—were all born in Odessa. In 1900 they formed the Cherniavsky Trio, toured Russia and Europe with great success, and after an American debut in 1917, eventually settled in Toronto, Canada. In 1958, however, Michail Cherniavsky was living in Vence, an inland town near Menton. After hearing the quartet, he invited them to visit Vence and join him for lunch at his home, which they did. Cherniavsky also invited his friend, the painter Marc Chagall. Vence was a favorite town of artists, the place where Chagall lived during the last twenty years of his life, busy in his studio engaged in what he preferred to call the "chemistry" of his painting.

After the Menton Festival, the quartet appeared in August at the Salzburg Festival in a concert at the Mozarteum: Beethoven's Op. 59, No. 3, Bartók's Sixth Quartet, and Ravel's Quartet in F Major. From this period onward, they appeared regularly at both the Salzburg and the Edinburgh festivals, which fortunately occurred at different times during the summer, allowing both major European festivals to feature the concerts of the Hungarian Quartet.

During the summer of 1958, the quartet had engagements for one or more appearances in festivals at Besançon, Divonne, Constance, Engadin, Menton, Montreux, Amsterdam, and The Hague. Before the ten-month season concluded, they had added seven new recordings to their catalogue and had performed in France, Holland, Belgium, Germany, Italy, Switzerland, and England, playing some 125 concerts including radio and television performances.

The European press was ecstatic. The Colbert agency in New York received the Hungarian Quartet's amazing accolades. From Paris: "If it is possible to surpass perfection, this happened with the interpretation of the last quartets of Beethoven." From Salzburg: "Bartók's Sixth Quartet became a shattering personal confession." From Montreux: "They gave us the impression of having penetrated, felt, meditated everything." And from Amsterdam: "We don't know any other ensemble in our time which could confront us as purely with the musical values of the score, and this places the Hungarian Quartet on a lonely height among the very few."[7]

Clara Haskil, who lived in Vevey, appeared twice with the quartet in Switzerland at the beginning of the 1958–59 season. On 30 September Haskil joined Székely, Koromzay, and Magyar for a performance of Mozart's Piano Quartet, K. 478, and a few days later, she played Brahms' Quintet, Op. 34, with the ensemble.

After the Brahms performance, Emile Rossier, the director of Nestlé Chocolates, gave a reception in his home in Vevey. When the quartet settled down for a hearty post-concert meal, a gentleman approached their table and asked if he might join them. He was Charles Spenser Chaplin, the internationally recognized creator of the inimitable tramp character in films. Rossier had introduced Charlie Chaplin to Clara Haskil. While their conversation had been limited by language difficulties, their friendship was instant, and Chaplin had come to admire Haskil's playing beyond all others. At the table he spoke with the members of the quartet about their concert and Haskil's Brahms performance, and then invited them to a luncheon at his home in the nearby village of Corsier, assuring them that Clara Haskil would be there as well.

Somewhat later, when Chaplin was asked to explain how he and Haskil continued to communicate considering the language barrier, Chaplin simply replied, "I was always a mime." After 1960, the musical life of Vevey was impoverished by her loss. While on tour, Clara Haskil slipped off the step of a train in Brussels, was taken to a hospital, and died there on 7 December 1960.[8]

For more than twenty years, Alexandre Moskowsky, who was fluent in five languages, had dealt with the internal business affairs of the quartet, constantly communicating with a half-dozen concert managers on several continents and bringing order to the quartet's business affairs with Pathé-Marconi. Having been prepared to emigrate to the United States in 1938 before he joined the Hungarian Quartet, Moskowsky was now living happily in America with his Belgian wife, Martine, and had established an enviable career as second violinist of the Hungarian Quartet.

During yet another season of more than a hundred concerts in Europe and the United States, however, Alexandre Moskowsky decided in March of 1959 to retire from the quartet after twenty-one years of concertizing. From that time on, Dénes Koromzay took over the responsibility for the internal management of the group.

The Moskowskys returned to Europe and lived in Paris, where Alexandre played several recitals with his Russian friend, the pianist Bukov, but was unable to secure a new career in France. After a year in Paris, they moved to Israel. There Moskowsky met the Polish violinist Henryk Szeryng who later recommended him for a teaching position in Manchester. Moskowsky remained in England, teaching in Manchester until his death in the late 1960s. Martine Moskowsky moved to Switzerland, where she taught school until her own retirement.

Having returned to Los Angeles after an absence of over a year, the Hungarian Quartet families found themselves momentarily occupied with domestic life. New houses were rented, old homes reopened. The Cleveland Chamber Music Society wrote to Székely asking his advice on the use of their small endowment intended for the commissioning of new chamber music works. The remaining, ongoing business affairs of the quartet were dealt with by Koromzay: the management of the Vancouver International Festival asked for program suggestions for the forthcoming three concerts in August, and the new press books prepared by the Colberts were sanctioned and copies sent to South Africa where plans were pending for a tour.

Dénes Koromzay and Agnes Eisenberger, the executive assistant of the Colbert–La Berge Concert Management, began what was to be a voluminous correspondence regarding the details of the quartet's future engagements in the United States. Interest among the old sponsors was lagging following the quartet's sustained absence during their European tours, so that it was necessary to reestablish the group's image and find new venues for the 1959–60 season.

However, the most urgent matter was finding the best possible violinist to replace Alexandre Moskowsky at the end of summer. It was Gabriel Magyar who brought Michael Kuttner's name to the attention of the quartet. Magyar had known Kuttner at the academy in Budapest. Their fathers had been friends before World War One.

Michael Kuttner seemed a logical choice. He had come to the United States with his own Pro Ideale Quartet, which had been coached by Leó Weiner in Budapest. By 1959 Kuttner was living in New York City and playing as a member of the New York City Center Opera Orchestra. A highly accomplished chamber music player, he was the finest of second violinists. He was approached by the quartet and accepted the position, becoming the fifth and final second violinist, following Szervánsky, Halmos, Végh, and Moskowsky—the second violinists from 1935 to 1959.

Kuttner was fourteen years younger than Székely. He was born in Budapest on 9 February 1918, and studied in the Hubay master class at the Franz Liszt Academy, from which he graduated in 1935 with the coveted Reményi Prize. He devoted his last year at the academy to studying chamber music with Leó Weiner. In the United States, Kuttner's Pro Ideale Quartet became known as the Westminster Quartet when they joined the staff of the Westminster Choir College in Princeton, New Jersey. Kuttner also played with such famous ensembles as the Roth, Jacques Gordon, and Léner quartets. His violin, which he prized highly, was called the "Santa Theresa," made by Petrus Guarnerius in 1704.

In a 1992 letter, Hungarian violinist Kató Havas[9] reminisced about "Misi" Kuttner, the friend of her childhood.

After fifty years' absence, the first place I was taken during a short visit to Hungary was the Academy of Music in Budapest. Once inside the concert hall, I was overwhelmed with memories. It was as if I had never left. The most vivid among them was Kuttner with his sweet smile and curly hair.

There we were again, he the "golden" boy of Ede Zathureczky and I the "golden" child of Imre Waldbauer. The two professors did not always see eye to eye. There was a certain amount of rivalry between them. But this did not affect the friendship between Misi and me.

When I started at the academy at the age of nine in 1929, I think he must have been in his early teens, finishing his studies and on the way to a promising and brilliant career. The age difference did not stop us from becoming friends at Waldbauer's prestigious chamber music sessions, which took the form of master classes and were held for a period of four hours twice a week. Each quartet had to have a prepared work, but sometimes the quartets had to mix and sight-read. I was the only child in these classes. I will never forget Misi's kindness on these daunting occasions. Far from being condescending, he often chose me to play second violin for him and even saw to it that there was a sufficient pile of music on my chair so that I could be at an equal height with the other players. Sometimes he even insisted that I take the first violin part. In return, I had an enormous admiration and respect for him. His tone was sweet and silky and I tried hard, but I am afraid unsuccessfully, to emulate him.

The baroque splendor of the concert hall, with its magnificent organ and tiny balcony over the podium where all the then-famous players had appeared, evoked further memories. During my childhood Waldbauer was adamant that I should hear all the great artists who came to play in Budapest and saw to it that I could always get a free standing ticket in the organ gallery. As I was too small to see over, I have distinct memories of having to stand on a rung so that I could lean over the top. It was often Misi who hung on to my shirt tail as I climbed on the rail during these performances to see the players.

We lost touch during the war years, and the next time I saw him was many years later at László Varga's house in San Francisco. I knew something was up as soon as I arrived because of an unnatural stillness and sure enough, no sooner did I enter the living room when I was scared to death by a

tremendous "Boo!" with Misi jumping out at me from behind the door.

Dear Misi. I am sure he had enriched the lives of all the
people who knew him. As for his role in the Hungarian Quartet, how many quartets are fortunate enough to have a brilliant first violinist play second violin?[10]

When Michael Kuttner joined the Hungarian String Quartet in
1959, the ensemble was made up of four Hungarians for the first time
since 1937. The Colberts were impressed with Kuttner's personality
when they met him in New York. The scant engagements for the
coming season suddenly doubled, and after the Aspen Festival, the
number would double again. In its new formation with Michael Kuttner as second violinist, the Hungarian Quartet moved toward its
period of greatest maturity and unqualified success on the world
music scene.

At the Vancouver International Festival in 1959, Alexandre
Moskowky was quickly approaching the end of his long tenure as
second violinist (after the festival, he played only three more concerts with the quartet, in Bellingham and Seattle). The Colbert agency
had decided that neither Moskowsky's imminent retirement nor
Kuttner's new appointment would be announced to the public until
the 1959–60 season was finished. Chamber music societies would
officially hear the news of the change in personnel during late
summer.

Harry Somers, an outstanding Canadian composer, had been
commissioned to write a string quartet for the 1959 Vancouver International Festival. Years before the opportunity came to compose
this work, Somers had found the quartet's early recording of Bartók's
Fifth Quartet a source of great stimulation and excitement. His new
work, String Quartet No. 3, dedicated to the Hungarian String Quartet, had its world premiere on 12 August 1959. In the decades that followed, the Third Quartet by Harry Somers took its place as a Canadian masterpiece of the midcentury.

In the elegant ballroom of the Hotel Vancouver, the third concert
by the quartet began with Mozart's Quintet in D Major, with Canadian violist Smythe Humphries as assisting artist. Before the intermission came the premiere of Somer's new work, which was well
received by the festival audience. Beethoven's last quartet, Op. 135,
ended the concert.

Earlier in October of 1959, Henry Colbert had proposed that the quartet accept an engagement the following summer at the Aspen Music Festival in Colorado. The Juilliard Quartet, who regularly joined the Aspen staff, was to be on leave, and Norman Singer, the executive director of the Aspen Festival, had asked for the Hungarian Quartet. This proposition placed the quartet in a dilemma since they were already committed to a number of summer festivals in Europe. They realized that the Aspen Festival was of great importance to the musical scene in America, but in addition to the conflict with Europe, accepting the Aspen proposal would again interlock their engagements. They would finish a tour in South Africa on 15 June, rush to the Edinburgh Festival, then cross the Atlantic for the Aspen Festival with hardly a day to spare.

Darius Milhaud asked that his Third Quartet be performed at Aspen in the summer of 1960. Jennie Tourel had indicated her willingness to participate in a performance, having studied the score of this work, in which a mezzo-soprano voice is included in the second of its two movements. She had further suggested that Ottorino Respighi's *Il Tramonto* (1917) for mezzo-soprano and quartet be considered for the same program.

During the spring of 1960, the Hungarian Quartet decided to join the staff at Aspen. At the Colbert agency, Agnes Eisenberger studied the repertoire the Juilliard Quartet had played at Aspen in 1959 in order to avoid duplicating what had recently been presented. In consultation with the Hungarian Quartet, she drew up a list of works by Haydn, Mozart, Beethoven, Schubert, Brahms, Schumann, Ravel, Debussy, Bartók, and Copland—thirty works in all—so that the Aspen programs could be proposed to Norman Singer.

During the course of nine weeks in Aspen, the quartet appeared in fourteen joint recitals with their colleagues Leonard Shure, Hans Hotter, Zara Nelsova, Roman Totenberg, Szymon Goldberg, Nikolai and Joanna Graudan, Adele Addison, Rosina Lhévinne, Eudice Shapiro, and, of course, the ubiquitous piano accompanist, Brooks Smith. With pianist Eugene Istomin, they presented the Quintet in F Minor by Brahms. Milhaud's Quartet No. 1, No. 7, and the two-movement work, Quartet No. 3, performed with Jennie Tourel, were also played. Aaron Copland joined the Hungarian Quartet and clarinetist Earl Bates on 24 August to perform as pianist in a performance of his Sextet for String Quartet, Clarinet, and Piano, a work arranged by the composer in 1933 from his own *Short Symphony*.

To benefit the scholarship fund of the Aspen Music School, the quartet gave two additional full recitals. At the first of two lecture recitals, Koromzay spoke on the Beethoven quartets. Székely gave a special lecture on the music of Bartók, assisted by the tenor Leslie Chabay and violinist Eudice Shapiro, who performed the Second Rhapsody with Brooks Smith. Székely's lecture-recital concluded with Bartók's Third Quartet performed by the Hungarian Quartet.

The quartet's productive activities at the 1960 Aspen Festival—concert appearances, lecture-recitals, and chamber music coachings—emerged as an artistic entity that prompted Norman Singer to ask that they return the following summer. They departed Aspen to begin their thirteenth American tour, knowing that their Colorado summer had been successful; however, at that time they did not know that they would return to Colorado many times in the future in a series of residencies at the University of Colorado in nearby Boulder.

During a day off in Pasadena, where the quartet's next tour was to begin, the Koromzays went to the ocean and there met pianist Rosina Lhévinne on the beach. She invited the players to a reception for her musician friends, including many Aspen colleagues, who planned to celebrate the beginning of the new season with her.

At the peak of Lhévinne's party, the room fell silent when three new guests arrived. "Look! It's Heifetz," someone whispered, as Jascha Heifetz and his wife entered the room with Brooks Smith following close behind them. The momentary silence was broken when another of the guests called out in a loud voice, "Look! It's Brooksie!" Genial laughter erupted, the spirited party resumed, and rather soon Székely and Heifetz were chatting amiably.

After their West Coast series, the quartet performed throughout Texas, Oklahoma, and Arkansas, appearing in many cities where they had not been heard previously. From Little Rock, they continued the tour in more familiar territory and on 14 December, after thirty-six concerts, played in Utica, New York, the scene of their first appearance in the United States in 1948.

The quartet arrived in Europe in January. At the Amsterdam Concertgebouw, Michael Kuttner had his first opportunity to take part in a Beethoven cycle. There was a celebration of the Hungarian Quartet's Silver Jubilee on the last of the six concerts of the cycle, their twenty-second performance in twenty-eight days. The jubilant audience in the sold-out hall rose to its feet and demanded eight curtain calls for "our Hungarians."

The season continued with concerts in Germany, France, Spain, England, and Austria. In late May the festivals began again, with performances in Menton, Engadine, Salzburg, Edinburgh, and Montreux. The Hungarian String Quartet in its ultimate formation—Székely, Kuttner, Koromzay, and Magyar—had crossed the threshold of world fame and would soon appear regularly on six continents as one of the astounding chamber music ensembles of the century.

Chapter Twenty-three

Australia

Pathé-Marconi had in its catalogue the Bartók cycle of string quartets recorded in London by the Végh Quartet. Although the Hungarian Quartet eagerly wished to record the Bartók cycle in Paris, because of market considerations the company did not want to repeat the cycle. When the Hungarian's exclusive recording contract with Pathé-Marconi expired on 31 May 1957, George Mendelssohn, president of Vox Productions, became interested in having the quartet record the Bartók cycle for his own company, but was not then in a position to negotiate such a contract.

Mendelssohn had some influence with Deutsche Grammophon Gesellschaft in Hamburg. Elsa Braun Schiller, a former piano student at the Franz Liszt Academy, was the director of DGG; in Mendelssohn's opinion, Schiller, a powerful figure in the recording industry, could change the fortune of the quartet's recording career as she had for the promising Hungarian conductor, Ferenc Fricsay. He had achieved enormous success through his association with DGG.

Mendelssohn prompted negotiations between DGG and the Hungarian Quartet, hoping that a plan he envisioned for Vox Productions could be realized if they would record the Bartók cycle in Germany. He wanted the quartet to record several works by Haydn for Vox Productions, using the DGG facilities in Hannover when the Bartók cycle was completed. With the possibility of Frau Professor

Schiller's agreement to this plan, he was willing to cede the publishing rights of these new recordings for Germany alone to DGG.

Koromzay began another negotiation at this point. He wrote to Peter de Jongh at Pathé-Marconi to discuss certain aspects of the quartet's expired exclusive contract in which EMI held the rights to their entire recorded repertoire with no limit in time. In his communications with de Jongh, he sought an agreement which would state a reasonable time limit to EMI's rights on their old recordings, without which they could not enter into serious negotiations or long-range projects with any other recording company. Koromzay proposed that de Jongh ask EMI for a release on the records that had been recorded more than five years previously. Because most of their EMI recordings were not on the market in North America, the quartet faced the situation that, for practical purposes, their recordings were not to be found in many places where they regularly performed.

The prospect of recording Haydn's "Lark" in Vienna for Vox Productions intensified the urgency of Koromzay's request since that work was already in the Pathé-Marconi catalogue from 1955. However, no agreement was forthcoming from Pathé-Marconi during May 1957.

When DGG announced an allotment of only eighteen days in late summer to record the Bartók cycle in Hanover, Mendelssohn abandoned his plan of using their recording facilities and began to explore other possibilities. Finally two days in June were set aside for the quartet to record for Vox in a studio in Vienna. Josef Duron would be in charge of production.

With considerable dispatch, the quartet recorded Haydn's Op. 77, No. 2, and the "Lark" in early summer, although they were not able to agree to a publication of the "Lark" until the release was granted by EMI. Since this release was not immediately forthcoming, Koromzay suggested to Vox that they record Haydn's Op. 76, No. 5, at some later date in order to produce two Haydn works for one long-playing release. Fortunately the EMI release for the "Lark" was eventually granted and the quartet's first Haydn recordings for Vox were issued in 1962. One record contained the "Lark" and Op. 77, No. 2. Another offered Op. 76, Nos. 2 and 5. These early Haydn recordings for Vox Productions later appeared in slightly different formats on the Vox budget label, Turnabout.

The recording of two Mozart quartets, the "Hunt" and the "Dissonance," was scheduled for 13–15 September in Paris with George

Kárdár as producer for Vox Productions. Kárdár, a self-assured Hungarian producer, was tremendously perceptive during recording sessions. He scrutinized every detail. At the September recording session, Kárdár was so pleased with the first "take" of the finale of the "Dissonance," he decided that either it be kept—there was something about it that he hated to disturb—or that they start working toward an even better result. Three hours later, they had attained that result.

The recording sessions for Deutsche Grammophon took place in two sessions of nine days each. From 21 to 30 June and from 26 August to 3 September, the DGG engineers recorded the quartet's performance of Bartók's six quartets. O. E. Wohlert was artistic supervisor. The recording engineer was Walter Sommer.

Recalling the recording sessions for the Bartók cycle during the summer of 1961, Székely described some thirty years later what took place:

> We recorded the Bartók cycle in the Beethoven Saal in Hannover. We had a method in mind, but the producer was not entirely agreeable to it. We intended to record certain passages, then to decide ourselves whether or not to proceed or to do them again, much as we had done in our sessions for Pathé.
>
> In the First Quartet, at the end of the second movement when the cello is prominent, then the violin repeats the phrase, I wanted to do this passage again since I didn't feel that it was good enough. "No, that was good," the producer said. "We can't repeat it."
>
> I understood from his point of view that one cannot go on forever, since the job would never be finished. After that, as I recall, we played and he made the decisions. If for him it was good enough, we had to accept his judgment. We just waited to see what would come of that. Fortunately for everyone, in this case it was very successful.

Shortly after the sessions began, there was an unexpected personnel change when several members of Von Karajan's recording crew in Berlin fell ill and the Hannover crew was sent to replace them on short notice. However, the work progressed without further technical incident. The final result was a long-awaited recording of the Bartók cycle which soon came to represent the standard by which future recordings of these great works were measured.

In a letter to Agnes Eisenberger at the Colbert agency, Koromzay outlined the essential activities of the quartet's European season that followed the Bartók recordings in Germany:

> One hundred and fifty people came for a late supper after the concert at the Montreux Festival, and the reception lasted until dawn. The next two days were spent in Paris playing the Bartók Cycle, then German, Dutch, and English tours. We are now going around the whole of France, but with an unexpected break of five days we spent some time at one of our favorite places, Ouchy, on Lake Geneva near Lausanne. In December we go to Budapest to play for the first time since 1938!
>
> When the season is finished we will have had altogether some 130 to 140 concerts for the full year.[1]

The quartet had undertaken a tour for Jeunesses Musicales de France which lasted for twenty days and accounted for their "going around the whole of France"—Lille, Marseille, Toulouse, Bordeaux, Poitiers, Rennes, Nancy, Dijon, Grenoble, Nantes, Tours, Rouen, and Clermont-Ferrand. After the JMF tour, they traveled to Italy in early December for a performance of the Beethoven cycle in Perugia, then appeared in Vicenza, Milan, Venice, and Brescia.

The Hungarian Quartet returned to Hungary after an absence of twenty-three years, arriving in Budapest on 15 December 1961. Hungary was still enduring a period of political change that followed the 1956 revolution. Under the management of Nemzetközi Koncertiroda, the quartet broadcast on Hungarian radio, then performed a recital at the Franz Liszt Academy on 19 December comprised of Haydn's "Lark," Bartók's Fifth Quartet, and Op. 131, Beethoven's late quartet whose seven movements (played without pause) are linked in one enormous, unified masterpiece.

Of the original members of the New Hungarian String Quartet, only Dénes Koromzay remained in 1961 to relive the memory of the first Budapest performance of the Bartók work twenty-five years earlier in the same concert hall on 3 March 1936. Led by their new first violinist, Zoltán Székely, they had returned only once, two years later in 1938, to play for the last time before the German Occupation of Holland which had brought their European concert tours to a halt.

In its ultimate formation—Székely, Kuttner, Koromzay, and Magyar—the Hungarian Quartet returned to Hungary in 1961 to perform before new audiences, many of whom knew the ensemble only by its recordings and illustrious international reputation. These performances sparked a renewal of interest in the Hungarian Quartet and won them a new following for their subsequent visits to their homeland.

During his visits to Hungary in the 1960s, Székely befriended many of the new Bartók scholars of post-war Hungary.

> I met the theorist Ernő Lendvai in Budapest. His work was then considered controversial by many. Nevertheless, he began to publish his writings, and soon not only his books were available, but many articles began to appear in journals such as *Muzsika*. When we first spoke together, Lendvai seemed quite discouraged by the slow acceptance of his new theories about Bartók's composition.
>
> Of course, many Bartók scholars of the new generation were at work in Hungary during this period. I remember attending a public lecture given by János Kárpáti at which József Ujfalussy was present. The work of László Somfai soon gained attention as well.
>
> During one visit, Kodály invited me to join him at the Academy of Sciences where we listened together to a recent recording of the symphony he had completed in 1961. On another occasion, we played Schumann's Piano Quintet with Annie Fisher and visited with her husband, Aladár Tóth, shortly before his death in 1968.
>
> Michael Kuttner always welcomed an opportunity to conduct. On one of the quartet's visits to Budapest, he conducted the National Radio Orchestra, Szimfonikus Zenekara, when I appeared in a broadcast performance of both Bartók rhapsodies.
>
> On the final visit of the quartet to Budapest, the quartet played at the academy for a full house, with members of the audience even seated on the platform. After that concert I visited for the last time with Ditta Bartók, who had been living in Budapest since her return from America after Bartók's death in 1945.

The idea of joining the staff of an American university was not new to the Hungarian Quartet, but after their residency of two years at the University of Southern California in Los Angeles, they had only accepted brief engagements at Mills College and the University of Oregon. In 1958, there had been serious discussions with the administration of Wake Forest College in Winston-Salem, North Carolina, about a possible residency there. However, after serious exploration and study, they abandoned this plan, and the Colbert agency began looking elsewhere for an academic home for the quartet, one that would provide an appropriate base of operations for the ensemble's North American career.

On 19 October 1961, the provost of the University of Colorado wrote to inform the Hungarian Quartet of their appointment as lecturers and quartet-in-residence for the spring semester of the year 1961–62, thus concluding a lengthy process of negotiation between the university and the Colbert agency. Koromzay and Dean Warner Imig immediately launched a correspondence about the repertoire for concerts and the topics for lectures.

After their Budapest concerts in December of 1961, the quartet returned to the United States. They appeared first in Dayton, Ohio, then fulfilled a dozen engagements, including a performance at the Library of Congress in which they presented the String Quartet (1928) by John Alden Carpenter. On 25 February 1962, they performed the final concert of the tour in Omaha, then flew to Boulder, arriving after midnight in a blinding snowstorm. The next morning at the School of Music they delivered their first lecture for a course in the literature of the string quartet.

Within a few days the Hungarian Quartet played their first concert on the Boulder campus since the summer of 1960: Haydn's Op. 77, No. 2, Bartók's Fifth Quartet, and Beethoven's Op. 59, No. 2. The impression of their performance was so powerful and their presence at the University of Colorado was so welcome that at the reception that followed, the president of the university asked whether the quartet would consider coming permanently to Boulder.

During their first residency in Boulder, they played the repertoire that had become their hallmark: classical works by Haydn, Mozart, Beethoven, and Schubert, and twentieth-century masterpieces by Bartók, Webern, Piston, and Hindemith. Their lecture recitals on the quartets of Beethoven and Bartók illuminated their teaching and enriched the academic offering of the School of Music to the satisfaction of Dean Imig, who had considerable interest in the presentation of music as a living art form. The Hungarian Quartet had begun a long, periodic association with the University of Colorado that would extend over three decades, with Dénes Koromzay and the members of the Takács String Quartet carrying their traditions forward into the 1990s.

"M. Duport informed me about the conversation he had with you concerning our planned visit to Australia in 1962," Koromzay wrote to Regina Ridge, the manager of Australia's Musica Viva Society. On behalf of the Hungarian Quartet, he expressed his pleasure that after such a long negotiation, this plan had become a reality. "We are very much looking forward to our first visit to your country and hope to make it a successful one." [2]

The first tour to Australia and New Zealand opened a new territory for the Hungarian Quartet with the promise of performing forty concerts there. Regina Ridge was eager to have the quartet play at Musica Viva's Easter Festival in Mittagong and began trying to arrange this. At the major centers, she planned a shared Beethoven cycle in Sydney, Melbourne, and Adelaide with the participation of the Hungarian Quartet, the Smetana Quartet from Czechoslovakia, and the Tel-Aviv Quartet from Israel. For the New Zealand Federation of Chamber Music Societies, the Hungarian Quartet was asked to play seventeen concerts in eleven cities, among them Wellington, Auckland, and Christchurch.

The proposed repertoire for the Hungarian Quartet's recitals included Anton Webern's Five Movements for String Quartet, Op. 5 (the only work of the second Viennese school which appeared regularly on their concerts), Milhaud's Quartet No. 7, and Bartók's Fifth Quartet in addition to works by Mozart, Haydn, Brahms, Schubert, Debussy, and the Beethoven quartets. They also soon learned that "God Save the Queen" should be added to the list because the national anthem was still traditionally played at the beginning of public concerts in Commonwealth countries.

With considerable geographical miscalculation, an inexperienced manager in New Zealand wrote dutifully to Boulder, Colorado, explaining that the quartet's visas had been sent to Paris, suggesting they pick them up there! After finding a more efficient solution, the quartet departed for Australia, visas in hand, on 16 April 1962, after they had appeared in a concert at Stanford University in Palo Alto and Székely had attended the wedding of his son, Frank Székely-Everts, to Anne Iverson in Los Angeles. Upon their arrival in Sydney on Easter Sunday, they were immediately taken on a three-hour journey by car to Mittagong. After a night's rest they greeted their first

Australian audience, one that included a very large proportion of string players, amateur and professional.

Their Mittagong Easter Festival concert was a rousing success. On hand to chronicle the event, the critic of the *Sydney Morning Herald* was lavish with praise for the quartet and its illustrious leader:

> It would be disingenuous to pretend that the quartet's excellence is a surprise. The recordings made by it have long made it one of the best known international quartets to many music lovers in this country.
>
> These players were expected to be marvellous; and they were.
>
> A surprising number of the quartets which have visited Australia in the last two years have lacked leaders to match some of their other instrumentalists.
>
> Zoltán Székely, in contrast, is a real leader, whose authority is evident as soon as he sits himself at his desk with a kind of resplendent gravity. It needed only the first few bars of Haydn's "Lark" quartet, with the first violin floating transparently over the others strings, to confirm that his stylistic and technical authority was equal to his powers of leadership.
>
> The "Lark" is very much a "first violin" quartet; but in the fugato of the Finale, when every instrument is momentarily on equal terms, the whole ensemble blazed with dazzling precision and clarity.[3]

Four days later a record crowd of 1600 attended the first Beethoven recital in Sydney, the attendance far exceeding Musica Viva's total number of subscribers. "Chamber music played as near to perfection as one can hope to hear was offered by the Hungarian Quartet," wrote the critic of the *Sun* on 27 April 1962, following the opening concert of the shared Beethoven cycle in Sydney's Town Hall. The reviewer concluded that if the standard set by the Hungarian Quartet could be maintained by the two other quartets from Israel and Czechoslovakia, "Chamber music lovers can look forward to the finest Beethoven interpretations available today."[4]

Almost forty concerts later in the small town of Invercargill in New Zealand, the audience that filled the Scottish Hall to capacity, rapt in attention, heart-moving in applause, was an encouraging sight to the organizers of the New Zealand Federation of Chamber Music Societies, since there had been many past occasions on which fine artists had appeared there before more empty seats than people.

The performance of the Hungarian Quartet, characteristically intense, incisive, and virile, "made a profound effect, all the more remarkable because of the absence of all external dramatics," wrote the critic of the *Southland Daily News*. In the presence of artists whose work had been admired for years, but only through recordings, the music lovers were prepared for a shade of disappointment, but there was none. "Each work played was not a repetition but an intensely realized re-creation, with a constant vigilance for any fresh implication which the music may yield."[5]

In 1963, the quartet truly found its stride as a globe-trotting, international chamber music ensemble when they undertook a round-the-world tour which included Egypt, India, Japan, and the city-state of Singapore. Return visits to Japan and Australasia were immediately proposed for 1964. Now a pattern arose in which the University of Colorado brought the quartet back to Boulder after their journeys abroad, eager to share their artistic growth and heightened professionalism.

The players returned to Hungary in March of 1963. Ferenc Bónis reviewed the recital, finding it an even more convincing performance than that of the previous year. Speaking of their great understanding of the secrets of the musical flow, their first-rate instrumental knowledge, rhythm, color, and poetic force, Bónis wrote, "One of the most characteristic things about the Quartet was the artistic knowledge, the consciousness with which they first searched, then expressed all the functions of every note of the work, every harmony, every dynamic marking."[6]

A few weeks later they appeared once more in London's Wigmore Hall, where Ibbs and Tillett had arranged a Beethoven cycle. In these six concerts, the Hungarian Quartet seems to have had a still greater success than on previous occasions in London. Colin Mason, critic of the *London Times*, praised them as unsurpassed interpreters of the Beethoven quartets. Speaking of their supreme control of form, he wrote, "No other quartet team consistently combines such refinement of detail with such largeness of phrase and virility of style, or such homogeneity of tone and ensemble with such individuality of character in the parts."[7]

After the final concert of the Beethoven cycle in Wigmore Hall, Szigeti came backstage to greet Székely:

Szigeti was in London to deal with the publication of his work, *A Violinist's Notebook*. At the end of the conversation about our Beethoven performance, he asked me, "How do you do it?" He was seemingly surprised that I was still playing so many concerts (at my age—sixty!), since by then he had stopped, having reached the age of seventy-one.

I saw him once more at his home near Lake Geneva, when Mientje and I were traveling through Switzerland by automobile. He was past eighty. His violin case was still open, resting on the piano, but I don't think he played at all. Although his daughter visited him there, it looked as though he was otherwise very much alone. Like many elderly people, Szigeti couldn't solve that problem.

Thirteen years earlier in 1950, Pablo Casals, the musical world's great voluntary exile, had reappeared in public after three years of silent protest against Franco's rule in Spain. A celebration in honor of the two-hundredth anniversary of the death of Bach brought musicians and music lovers from around the world to the village of Prades at the foot of Mount Canigou in the French Pyrénées-Orientales. They came to take part with the great Spanish cellist in what was the first of a series of major world festivals. "Very few have the experience of knowing a day—much less a period of weeks—when a considerable number of colleagues and admirers travel thousands of miles to pay them tribute," wrote H. L. Kirk. "For Casals the summer of 1950 was simply the first of more than twenty years during which he was the focus of at least one important international musical event a year."[8]

In September of 1951, having finally breached his silence, Casals traveled to Zurich to conduct his two works, *Los Tres Reyes Magos* from the oratorio *El Pessebre* and *Sardana,* with an ensemble of 120 cellists from all parts of the western world. During that visit he met with his friends Emile Rossier, the music patron from Vevey, and Albert Schweitzer, whom he had not seen for seventeen years. He returned to Prades intent on his unflagging efforts to help bring about world peace and was prepared to play the cello and conduct again in public, but only to that end.

By the summer of 1963, Casals' international activities had increased to include regular appearances at festivals in San Juan and Marlboro, but he returned annually to Prades, lived in his little house at the nearby spa, Molitg-les-Bains, and gave his presence to the later

Prades festivals, which had essentially developed into chamber music festivals. When the Hungarian Quartet arrived for their first appearance at the 1963 Prades Festival, a concert in the Church of St. Pierre, they stayed for one week in the village hotel. Zoltán and Mientje Székely had arrived at Prades by car, avoiding the trip from Perpignan to Vernet-les-Bains on the narrow-gauge railway. Since they had their car, they soon left the local hotel and moved to a spa hotel in Molitg-les-Bains, in order for Székely to rehearse Beethoven's piano trio, Variations, Op. 121a ("Ich bin der Schneider Kakadu"), with Casals and the American pianist, Julius Katchen, who had come from Paris to take part in the festival.

Although Székely had heard Casals play in Amsterdam many years earlier, he only really met him at the Prades Festival during the summer of 1963. Casals was very cordial when he and his young wife Marta received the Székelys at their home, but there was no real opportunity during those busy days for the two men to discourse on any subject, only time to rehearse together Beethoven's Variations, Op. 121a, and a trio by Haydn which they planned to play with Katchen during the festival.

In their concert at the Church of St. Pierre, Székely performed Brahms' Sonata in D Minor, Op. 108, with Katchen, a pianist he had not known previously. During their rehearsals together in Prades, Katchen proposed that they consider recording the three sonatas of Brahms later, but this did not come about.

After 1964, a photograph of Ubbo Scheffer's sculpture, "Strijkkwartet," appeared as a logo on the concert programs and brochures of the Hungarian String Quartet. Chamber music lovers who might never have visited the Amsterdam Concertgebouw nor seen Scheffer's work of art now became familiar with it by seeing its image reproduced in Boulder, New York, London, and beyond.

"Strijkkwartet" won for Ubbo Scheffer the Cultural Prix of Gelderland. The sculpture had been inspired by a Beethoven concert of the Hungarian String Quartet at the Amsterdam Concertgebouw. The enormous work portrays in stone the image of the quartet as it existed before 1956. In creating his work, Scheffer transposed the relative positions of the two violinists, Alexandre Moskowsky appearing on the extreme left and Zoltán Székely at the apex. Vilmos Palotai appears next to Székely while Dénes Koromzay sits at the extreme right, his countenance turned away from the viewer. Scheffer's lively creation has a characteristic expression of power in the heads and hands. The players seem profoundly unified with their instruments and with each other.

In a letter fifty-three years after his early discovery of Zoltán Székely, Ubbo Scheffer reminisced about the creation of his sculpture, "Strijkkwartet."

My first acquaintance with Zoltán was by radio. When I was fourteen years old, I heard the Violin Concerto by Bartók, the first performance in 1939 by the Concertgebouw Orchestra with Mengelberg conducting. As we listened, my father switched off the lights. I was surprised to hear so many dimensions in space. Perhaps this early experience influenced the later composition of my sculpture.

The first sketches I made during a Beethoven cycle by the Hungarian Quartet in the Concertgebouw in Amsterdam. I still have a drawing of Palotai behind his cello. As I reflect on my stone sculpture dedicated to the Hungarian String Quartet, I remember I worked on it almost two years—eleven hours a day.

I was fascinated by the fact that sound-structures in the compositions for string quartet are so physically present on the stage in shape and movement. The right arm describes half a circle in space while playing. I decided that even this movement should be the general architectonic base for the first composition in which a second one could be placed, namely the realistic details, which form a composition of their own.

Therefore, in the first one the surface of the stone was carved in a rough way. In the second one, the faces, hands and instruments are worked out in a smooth way. (Chairs and desks are not essential for making music.) The whole composition is like a fan, the sculpture carved lifesize in a very hard French limestone.

In the expression of the performers I tried to typify the different characters which are inherent in the players of each instrument. The first time when Zoltán and his wife were confronted in my studio with the almost finished work, tears came to Mientje's eyes as she whispered, "They really play."[9]

At the direction of John de Jong Schouwenburg, "Strijkkwartet" was later acquired by the Amsterdam Concertgebouw. It is on permanent exhibition near the entrance to the Kleine Zaal at the Amsterdam Concertgebouw—a tribute to the Hungarian String Quartet, chamber music, and the great Dutch sculptor, Ubbo Scheffer. (An early photograph of "Strijkkwartet" taken in Scheffer's studio appears here as Plate 70.)

Peter Ré, a former pupil of Paul Hindemith at Yale University and a professor of music at Colby College in Waterville, Maine, had founded the Colby Summer School of Music in 1963 with the Juilliard String Quartet as the first faculty-in-residence. Even though the program was very successful under their guidance, the Juilliard Quartet decided to return to Aspen the following summer, but not before granting an interview in the *New York Times* which brought Colby College's new summer school to the attention of the public.

While teaching at Stanford University as a visiting professor in the spring of 1964, Ré learned of the Juilliard Quartet's decision. He immediately approached the Hungarian Quartet, who accepted his invitation to become the faculty-in-residence during July and August of 1964. So successful was this new association that the Hungarian Quartet returned for nine consecutive summers, establishing the Colby Summer School of Music as one of the outstanding chamber music courses in North America.

Unexpected good news arrived on 14 September 1965 from Peter de Jongh, Directeur des Services Artistiques at Pathé-Marconi in Paris. EMI proposed a new recording of the Beethoven cycle. The quartet accepted the invitation and a contract was sent immediately.

Twelve years after the first recording of the Beethoven cycle, studio techniques had improved, significant changes had occurred in the personnel of the quartet, and vast performance experience in the interim had brought a new maturity to the ensemble as was proved by the outstanding recordings created at Salle Wagram in Paris with Eric McLeod as producer for Pathé-Marconi.

The new Beethoven cycle was issued in North America on Angel Records' new label, Seraphim. This label was initially reserved for issuing inexpensive reprints, but in this case the recording was completely new. Seldom had the record lover been offered more quality at less cost: the price was $27.50 for the eleven discs presented in three boxes grouped by style period. *High Fidelity Magazine* was quick to review the new release noting the absence of the "cavernous" reverberation of the previous recording of the Beethoven cycle. The interpretations were seen as far more impressive, "lithe, graceful, and passionate by turn as the players produced engaging colors and textures, along with some not inappropriate grit and asperity."[10]

The new recording of the Beethoven cycle brought the Hungarian Quartet the Grand Prix de Discophile and, for the second time, the Grand Prix du Disque of the Académie Charles Cros. This distinction was all the more remarkable for these circumstances: the same ensemble, the same recording company, and the same magnificent works doubly rewarded within a twelve-year period. In sum, the Hungarian Quartet's new recording of the Beethoven cycle was heralded as a release of major significance.

Meanwhile, Emmie Tillet, the venerable managing director of Ibbs and Tillet in London, conceived a daring plan. She would present the Hungarian Quartet once again in the Beethoven cycle at the apogée of their fame, but not at the Wigmore Hall as she had frequently done in the past. She decided that the Royal Festival Hall on the south bank of the Thames would be the new venue; with this decision an historic event was in the making.

This was the first Beethoven cycle ever attempted in the Royal Festival Hall. It was expected that with popular prices some two thousand people might turn up. Instead, the three-thousand-seat hall was almost sold out six consecutive times, producing a cumulative ticket-holding audience of 13,250 listeners in two weeks for the Hungarian String Quartet's Beethoven performances.

At the conclusion of his lengthy review in the *Guardian* on 8 February 1966, Neville Cardus momentarily put aside his role as critic to make a singular, illuminating confession:

> Whenever the cello melody of the slow movement of Op. 135 is given the melting tone and warm flow and curve that it received in this performance, I am lost to critical awareness. The cradling of the consoling song, then the falling decorations, cadences of the gentlest benediction, take possession of one's head and better-self (for the time being). In such an abnormally uplifted state I personally can only bow the head and thank God and Beethoven that I was given ears to catch this music's unearthly overtones at all. . . . Beethoven was the greatest mind and spirit ever to give himself to, and express himself in music. This concert brought home the fact beautifully, convincingly, and memorably.[11]

Listeners and critics alike had found that Beethoven's music simply took hold of them. In this case the Hungarian Quartet, authentic musicians, aristocrats to their fingertips, were an ensemble of artists whose ability to sustain the concentration of the audience was not frequently encountered. In the *London Times* on 8 February, Colin Mason wrote of their performance of Op. 127: "The serene, withdrawn spiritual quality of their playing . . . made it easy to understand why so many musicians have been fascinated by the idea that music aspires at its most sublime to a state of physical nonexistence."[12]

Chapter Twenty-four

Alberta

The eighteenth American tour for Colbert Artists Management began with a concert in New York City. The quartet opened the new season with fresh confidence, the fruit of their maturity, and an attempt to give even greater credibility to their concert life through performances governed by reason and control. As the public clamored for programs devoted to Beethoven and Bartók, the era of presenting new repertoire began to fade in favor of authoritative, definitive performances of the masterworks that had become their sovereign domain.

A few works identified with the mainstream twentieth-century composers were still sought out by the public in every country. In England they played Walton, Tippett, Britten; in America Piston, Copland, Diamond. The Five Movements for String Quartet, Op. 5, by Anton Webern appeared on their programs, revealed as music of an infinitely moving quality. Music by Milhaud, Villa-Lobos, and Hindemith appeared on many programs, for now it was important to them that they not become merely a repertory ensemble. However, it was the perfection of the Beethoven-Bartók repertoire and the remarkable performances of Haydn, Mozart, and Schubert that had, in fact, brought world recognition and the attendant 150 appearances every season.

In late October, the quartet performed in New York City, went the following day to Cambridge, Massachusetts, for a concert, then returned to New York City for recitals at Columbia University, Queens College, and Hunter College. At Hunter College they appeared in "Mostly Mozart," a concert series arranged by Norman Singer, administrator of the Hunter College Concert Bureau, that also included performances by the Quartetto Italiano and the Juilliard and Fine Arts quartets. After New York, the Hungarians began a fifteen-concert tour with a journey south to Florida and Alabama. They returned to Urbana, then ended their tour in Minneapolis on 8 December, Székely's sixty-third birthday.

After the holiday season, the quartet began its concerts again in January in western Canada with a performance for the Chamber Music Society in Edmonton, Alberta. This organization had been formed in 1952 with a small membership of amateurs who met to play chamber music recreationally. Ten years later it was reorganized on a subscription basis to sponsor concerts by musicians from Canada and abroad. Its eight hundred members filled the University of Alberta's Convocation Hall on 4 January 1967 to hear the Hungarian Quartet play Haydn, Bartók, and Schubert, an event that initiated a significant, ongoing association between the members of the quartet and the Province of Alberta.

The Department of Music of the University of Alberta was host to the ensemble for two days following their performance. During that time they coached student chamber music ensembles. The outstanding Canadian violinist Thomas Rolston, who was then acting chairman of the Department of Music, began to reveal his plans to forge an artistic relationship between the Hungarian Quartet and the University of Alberta. Very soon these plans were extended to include the Banff Centre for Continuing Education located nearby in Banff National Park in the Canadian Rockies.

After his return to Boulder, Koromzay wrote to Rolston on 13 February 1967:

> Many thanks for the kind reception and hospitality you gave us during our recent short stay in Edmonton. We have enjoyed it more than I can tell you and all four of us were very much impressed by the dedication and highly successful work you and your colleagues are doing there for the sake of our common goal—music.

Koromzay expressed the interest of the quartet in Rolston's proposal that they return to the University of Alberta for a more extended stay in the spring of 1968, and concluded:

> I quite realize that the project is ambitious and on closer examination might prove too difficult to achieve . . . but we simply don't want to forgo the chance that perhaps the plan is realistic after all.[1]

As noted earlier, on behalf of Colbert Artists Management, Agnes Eisenberger had launched a major effort to find an academic residency for the Hungarian Quartet in North America. Ironically, as the quartet's activities abroad became more demanding, the agency became less able to produce adequate engagements in North America. Now in its thirty-third year, the quartet was performing on five continents, realizing its earlier concertizing aspirations. Yet the players began to look ahead to their future plans, having decided to reduce to a considerable extent their worldwide concertizing activities from the start of the academic year 1968–69 and to accept instead—if offered—a full residency at an academic institution. The quartet needed a permanent base in North America from which it could more selectively arrange its concerts on the North American continent and thereby decrease the demands of touring abroad.

Specific institutions in Pennsylvania, Vermont, North Carolina, Florida, Maryland, New York, Ohio, Massachusetts, and Tennessee were approached by Eisenberger, but when this led to no fruitful results, the agency wrote individual letters to the 281 colleges and universities who were then members of the National Association of Schools of Music hoping to arouse interest further afield. In this communication, Ann Colbert stated that the Hungarian Quartet would be available from the fall of 1968 and would be prepared to perform, teach their instruments and chamber music literature, and coach string ensembles; Michael Kuttner would be available to teach conducting as well.

Thomas Rolston cabled the good news to Koromzay on 21 April 1967 that the Board of Governors of the University of Alberta had guaranteed the fee for a one-month residency in March of 1968. The terms were accepted and plans were made for the quartet's second visit to Edmonton after the conclusion of an extended European tour the following year.

When this news arrived, the quartet was in the final stage of preparing Cecil Effinger's String Quartet No. 5, recently composed for them. A pupil of Bernard Wagenaar and Nadia Boulanger, Effinger was born in Colorado, studied the violin and the oboe there, and graduated from Colorado College in 1935 as a mathematician. The following year he began his long tenure as a music professor at the University of Colorado in Boulder; after his retirement in 1981, he assumed the position of composer-in-residence. Effinger was an inventor of some reputation. Before the age of computerized music notation in 1954, he created a practical music typewriter, the "Music-writer." In 1969 he designed a "tempo watch" (a metronome to be worn on the wrist), and somewhat later a special typewriter for engineering drawings.

This man of unusual talents was the prolific composer of five symphonies, two operas, and four string quartets. He was eager to present the Hungarian Quartet with a new work in 1967 and had discussed its composition in great detail with Székely, whose opinion as a composer he valued, frequently rewriting passages based on his advice. After its premiere, the new work was recorded during May 1967 by Owl Records, a Boulder-based studio of which Dr. Oakleigh Thorne was president. On this recording Effinger's new quartet was paired with Quincy Porter's String Quartet No. 7, the seventh of nine quartets composed by the well-known American composer and Yale professor before his death the previous year.

The recording sessions took place in Music Hall, the School of Music's concert venue on the Boulder campus. A test pressing was available in June and sent to Maine, where the Hungarian Quartet made its final approval for the release of the new recording in the fall.

In the spring of 1967 the Colby College administration contacted all quartet players who had sent inquiring letters over the recent previous seasons. After five years of operation, the Colby endeavor would require increased enrollment to justify its continuation. When both Joseph Gingold and William Primrose encouraged their students at Indiana University to consider studying with the Hungarian Quartet in Maine, the enrollment did increase and the program continued.

On 30 May the quartet colleagues were packing, on the point of leaving their homes for more than a year. They went first to Maine for the Colby season, then appeared in New York with a performance at Lincoln Center on 3 August in a Mozart festival before departing for Europe, not to return until March of 1968. For the Mid-Summer

Serenade series at Philharmonic Hall (now Avery Fisher Hall), they performed two Mozart quartets, K. 499 and K. 465, with artistic assurance and effortless grace, a difficult achievement in the large hall with its then-uncertain acoustics. With clarinetist David Glazer, they offered the Quintet in A Major, K. 581, before the intermission, and according to critic Robert Sherman, "all five musicians wrought a minor miracle of sensitive beauty."[2]

From the forests of the Vosges in France, Koromzay wrote to Agnes Eisenberger on 21 September to speak of the recent pleasant stay in their lakeside cottage near Waterville, Maine, during their annual engagement at Colby College. He summarized their current touring activity—concerts in Engadin, Santander, Menton, Ascona, Besançon, Stockholm, and Bonn, where the critics had lavished praise on their Beethoven performances. Tours were being negotiated for Australia, South America, and South Africa. The quartet had managed respites along the way, stopping briefly in Pontresina, the caves of Altamira, the Italian lakes, Innsbruck, Stockholm, and Copenhagen. "All this will end next week and the treadmill of six concerts a week starts and continues without interruption until Christmas, but so far everyone is well and we have been playing in our best form. However," Koromzay concluded, "there must come a time when we decide whether or not we go on concertizing for another year and this will come pretty soon."[3]

Their European plans for the months ahead were interesting and challenging, and promised the busiest season they had encountered, a year with concerts all over Europe interspersed with recording sessions. A few new recordings had been proposed. Capitol Records, the American subsidiary of EMI, was interested in marketing an album—all Brahms—to follow up the success of the second recording of the Beethoven cycle. Peter de Jongh had personally driven from Paris to Lyon where the quartet was appearing to offer them Pathé-Marconi's proposition of recording all Brahms chamber music works larger than the piano trios. This huge project would comprise the four works with piano—three piano quartets, Opp. 25, 26, and 60, and the Piano Quintet, Op. 34, with pianist Georges Solchany; the Clarinet Quintet, Op. 115, with David Glazer; the two string quintets, Opp. 88 and 111, and two string sextets, Opp. 18 and 36, with cellist László Varga and Thomas Rolston as violist. The quartet accepted de Jongh's proposal, eager to add these Brahms masterworks to their catalogue of recorded works.

With Georges Solchany they had recorded four piano quintets in Paris and now appeared with him at Salle Gaveau in a performance of the quintets by Brahms and Dvořák. The *International Herald Tribune* ranked Solchany among the world's great chamber music pianists and praised the quartet: "One hears a good many string groups and most of them seem competent enough until he hears the Hungarian Quartet again and realizes that the others are still on the beginner's slope . . . what a marriage of ideas and sound!"[4]

The Hungarian Quartet arrived in Canada on 11 March and were taken to a small residential hotel in Edmonton where they would live for a month. Mientje Székely and Julie Magyar were traveling with the quartet. The day after their arrival, the quartet and their Canadian collegues gathered in the Székely suite to confirm the schedule of activities planned by Rolston and Koromzay. Armed only with a teapot and two china cups, Mientje was completely at ease in her temporary home. As she set out to serve each person, having repeatedly washed the two china cups, she chatted amiably about her recent second trip to Japan with the group. She remarked to the Thomas Rolston, "I've traveled with my husband for forty years. See this little teapot? I always take some personal item along on our trips to give a touch of home to each and every hotel room."

The University of Alberta chamber music students—five young string quartets—had prepared themselves during a two-month period of frantic activity. Earlier in the season, the Netherlands String Quartet had appeared in Edmonton and had coached these ensembles. A major musical event followed in December, a Bach festival during which the violin and cello works and the Brandenburg Concertos had been performed. Before the arrival of the Hungarian Quartet, all five student quartets had presented a full recital so that each ensemble had at least one complete program for the Hungarian Quartet to hear during an intensive schedule of private coachings of more than fifteen works.

Of course there were pleasant intervals amid the grueling work, since the twenty string players had become fast friends in the artistic environment created by Rolston and his colleagues. When two quartets met in the late hours, changing stations on Convocation Hall's stage, they chatted and compared notes on the progress of their concert preparations.

The Hungarian Quartet's four Wednesday concerts on the University of Alberta campus were devoted to Bartók quartets and selected masterpieces of Haydn and Beethoven. Capacity audiences filled the university's Convocation Hall for these performances. On consecutive Mondays, there were lecture recitals designed for the music students during which Koromzay dealt with the Beethoven works and Székely discussed the compositional details of the Bartók quartets. Kuttner gave a public lecture on the Beethoven quartets. Magyar spoke on the topic of the dance movements in the quartet literature with special attention to the works of Beethoven and Bartók. Székely ended the series on 3 April with an informal lecture giving his personal reminiscences of Bartók. His remarks began:

> It always gives me great satisfaction to discuss Bartók's art from any aspect, and especially—it goes without saying—his string quartets or violin works, which I love and on which I have spent so many years of study. This, of course, would be a subject requiring a highly technical, analytical or aesthetical treatment, which I do not intend to offer this evening. Instead, I would like to pay tribute to my illustrious compatriot and dear friend by relating a few things—in a very informal way—about him as a person, his life, his art and about some of my own recollections experienced during my longstanding personal relationship with this great man.
>
> The twenty-three years since Bartók's death are not much in the course of history, yet it is a sufficiently long period for the appraisal, the true judgment of a man's genius. Bartók's art has withstood the ruthless test of time victoriously, so much so that today the whole world recognizes him as one of the great, if not the greatest composer of his period—a composer who, in company with Schoenberg and Stravinsky, decisively influenced the development of our music. But that is not all! Bartók was also a splendid pianist and a scholar of the first rank. Furthermore, Hungary admires him as a great son of the country, who, together with Zoltán Kodály, created a genuine Hungarian art-music and raised its music culture to a level of international significance.[5]

As the month's program unfolded, the crowds grew ever larger as local chamber music lovers arrived at the various events, scores in hand, to learn from the Hungarian Quartet. At every available hour, private consultations ensued during which the quartet discussed with

their Canadian colleagues the many possible ways of intensifying
the musical life in Alberta and thereby assuring the continuance of
chamber music activity in western Canada.

The unasked question was whether the Hungarian Quartet would
consider a permanent home in Alberta. However, as a significant result of these hours together, that question eventually gave way to
the emerging idea of forming an entirely new string quartet in
Canada. The Board of Governors of the University of Alberta approved the plan later in the spring. The University of Alberta String
Quartet came into existence the next fall with Thomas Rolston
and Lawrence Fisher, violinists, Michael Bowie, violist, and Claude
Kenneson, cellist, as the founding members. And in the summer of
1972, the Academy of Chamber Music at the Banff Centre was inaugurated, with the members of the Hungarian String Quartet as the
first faculty.

The Hungarian Quartet returned to Boulder in April for a month
of teaching and concerts on the University of Colorado campus. During that month they left Boulder momentarily to make an unusual
appearance at the Mississippi Arts Festival, where they shared the bill
with actor Hal Holbrook. They played Dvořák to nine thousand people gathered in the Jackson Coliseum, and were afterward entertained
by the governor and his special guests, Joan Crawford, Bobby Gentry,
and the Lennon Sisters.

Later in May, Koromzay again wrote to Rolston in Canada:

> I am sure that I don't have to tell you that all of us en-
> joyed our stay in Edmonton in every respect. The warmth of
> the reception, the responsiveness of the students, and the
> genuine friendship which was offered to us by you and so
> many others made it a very satisfying experience. . . .
> We are genuinely interested in keeping our collaboration
> with the University of Alberta in whatever form this will be
> feasible.[6]

Everyone in the quartet had gone his own way for a vacation.
Following their break, they reconvened for the new season, which
was entirely booked until August of 1969. Still searching for an academic appointment, the quartet pressed the possibility of a permanent residency in Boulder beginning in the academic year 1969–70
and continued to pursue their interest in a similar appointment at
Southwestern University in Memphis, Tennessee. However, it soon

became apparent that the universities' funding difficulties would bring these negotiations to a halt.

The twenty-first American season began on 15 October, and the Hungarian Quartet insisted on maintaining a schedule that would have exhausted a quartet of more youthful players. From Buffalo, the tour took them as far south as Miami, west to Tucson, and eventually to Vancouver, Canada. In an unguarded moment in Grand Central Station in New York, Koromzay's briefcase containing all his quartet parts was stolen, never to be recovered. He continued the tour with unmarked viola parts, reconstructing his annotations as he traveled, but playing from memory as he always had, even though music rested on his stand.

After Vancouver the quartet went again to Europe in January. They began the New Year with a German tour, after which they returned to Paris where the recording sessions of the piano quartets of Brahms with pianist Georges Solchany began at once in Salle Wagram. Performances in Holland, Switzerland, and Austria led them again to Hungary where they played a concert in Budapest on 12 April.

András Pernye, critic of *Magyar Nemzet*, saw them much the same as Olin Downes had nearly twenty years earlier in 1950—as "a group of string players, profoundly versed in their art, who sat down as informally as if they were alone together in their shirtsleeves, finding incomparable happiness and solace for all the ills that a troubled world might bring in making music together."[7] They seemed, no doubt, not older but wiser; it was as though the listener were party to a secret intimacy being shared among them as they played.

Spartan Haydn, irresistible Debussy, then Beethoven's Op. 132 played with understanding and endless seriousness, made up the program. Pernye wrote, "It was miraculous how Zoltán Székely, with unheard-of power, could conquer and fulfill the virtuoso demands of his voice lines, but perhaps it is because his violin playing is without any artificiality and therefore is lasting and worthy."[8]

Only the Smetana Quartet had made three Australian tours for Musica Viva by 1969, but now the Hungarian Quartet also returned for the third time to Australia through the tenacious efforts of the indefatigable manager, Regina Ridge. In a memo dated 1 May 1969, Ridge wrote, "Dear Faithful Ones, Welcome to Musica Viva (and Australia) for your third tour, this time 'coast to coast.' No early morning flights had been booked in deference to Székely's preference for peaceful mornings. . . . Hotel accounts for room and breakfast are to be sent directly to Musica Viva, the per diem allowance is set at five dollars per day."⁹ These were balmy years "down under."

In addition to Beethoven, Schubert, Haydn, Mozart, and Brahms, two contemporary works were to complete the programs: Bartók's Quartet No. 3 and the Quartet, No. 3, Op. 22, by Hindemith. The quartet began their concerts in Perth on 10 May and the following day broadcast for ABC from the Octagon Theatre at the University of Western Australia. From Perth, their concerts took them first to Adelaide where John Horner, critic of the *Advertiser*, wrote, "The various sections of Beethoven's Op. 131 sounded very like improvisations . . . so often have the players played together in intuitive ensemble, like a flock of birds wheeling in perfect formation and effortless beauty." [10] They traveled on to Melbourne, Hobart, Launceston, Springwood in the Blue Mountains, and finally to Sydney, where Romola Costantino declared in the *Sydney Morning Herald*, "Listening to the Hungarian String Quartet the conviction grows that one is hearing not just one of the world's best quartets—one is hearing one of the great quartets of all time." [11]

A day later the banner in the *Australian* in Canberra was, "A performance to make even Beethoven happy," and the critic wrote of the performance of Op. 127, "They glorified the music and invested it with an intellectual conviction that left no room for doubts. . . ."[12] And so it continued with critics and audiences alike in Melbourne, Orange, Newcastle, Toowoomba, Armidale, and Tamworth.

At the conclusion of their Australian tour, the quartet flew to New Zealand for an additional fifteen concerts arranged by Joan Kerr, the manager of the Chamber Music Federation of New Zealand. From Auckland, they made their way to Tauranga, Rotorua, Hamilton, and finally New Plymouth where, to their surprise, pre-concert publicity had suggested that the quartet was to disband and retire. Székely disclaimed this with a statement in the *Daily News*. He made it clear that there were engagements for two full years ahead and, "No, we have no plans to retire yet."[13]

With confident decorum, Székely had put the rumor aside. However, managment was shocked that there had been talk about retirement outside of the confidential circle, where it had already been presumed that Michael Kuttner, in particular, was considering a new career. In December of 1969, Székely would turn sixty-six, an age considered normal for retirement in America. But Székely was at the peak of his artistic powers. His violin playing was at a supreme level of accomplishment, his health was excellent, and his disciplined performances were still admired by audiences around the world. Because there had been no significant progress toward the goal of an academic position for the quartet, the younger members had begun to consider an alternative plan of finding individual university appointments while they were at the height of their reputations as chamber musicians and still young enough to offer at least one sustained decade of service in academic positions.

On 3 July, Owen Jensen, the critic of Wellington's *Evening Post*, wrote about the quartet's eloquence and concluded, "There is nothing mystical about all this, it is simply that the Hungarian Quartet play with the most polished professionalism,"[14] a quality much admired in Australia and New Zealand. From Wellington they flew on 10 July to play in Fiji, on their way back to the United States for their seventh summer residency at Colby College.

The players spent the month of September teaching in Boulder. October was set aside for their third tour to Japan, their first two visits having been in 1963 and 1967. Masumoto Yabuta, the representative for Tokyo's Naoyasu Kajimoto Concert Management, had negotiated their third Japanese tour in Paris with Jean Duport of the Valmàlete Bureau earlier in April. There were nine concerts beginning with a Bartók cycle at the Nissei Theatre in Tokyo and several radio and television appearances. Mr. Kajimoto had requested "popular" programs, an evening's fare of Schubert, Beethoven, Mozart, and Brahms to be played at the Tokyo Bunka Kaikan, in the outlying districts, and at Osaka and Kyoto. After their concert in Kyoto they enjoyed a few days in the ancient city and observed Gagaku, a performance of Japanese music and dance in the court tradition.

On their return flight from Japan, they stopped for a concert in Honolulu. To his delight, Székely was able to visit with Robert Mann of the Juilliard Quartet, who was there on vacation. They discussed the unfinished composition which Mann, violinist and composer, was engrossed in creating during his Hawaiian vacation.

They reached the mainland on 5 November 1969. A brief tour for the Colbert agency took them from Tempe, Arizona, to Miami. After the nine concerts they returned to Boulder at the end of November, ready to vacation for two months, an unusual luxury for the world travelers. But the playing began again in late January of 1970 with a one-month stay in Memphis, Tennessee, then another tour of fifteen concerts on the East Coast which lasted until Easter. In April the quartet arrived once more in Boulder for a six-week residency during which they played their final Beethoven cycle in Colorado and appeared on 21 April in Denver at the University of Colorado Denver Center Auditorium. Thomas MacCluskey, critic of the *Rocky Mountain News*, had the unusual opportunity to hear the quartet perform Debussy's Quartet, Op. 10 on three occasions in less than two weeks, each of which had been a new revelation, but he nevertheless found the Denver performance was "an exceptionally penetrating experience . . . the crowning event."[15]

In December of 1969, the administration of the University of Colorado had told the quartet that they did not have the means for a continuing commitment. On 24 April 1970, after an association of more than eight years, the Hungarian Quartet's official ties with the University of Colorado came to an end. In his farewell message, Associate Dean John Carnes wrote, "The University of Colorado has been enormously enriched by the Hungarian Quartet. Not only have we had the opportunity to hear great music superbly performed, but your contributions to the musical taste and sensitivities of faculty, students, and citizens through your lecture-recitals, workshops, and participation in the Humanities courses have been of great significance . . . you have opened to me and to many others a perspective on world culture which we would not otherwise have had."[16]

On 1 May 1970 the quartet departed from Kennedy International Airport in New York City aboard a Lufthansa flight bound for Buenos Aires where they would play a Beethoven cycle in the Teatro Coliseo to begin what would be their final tour of South America. Another performance of the cycle followed immediately in the new Teatro Guara in Sao Paulo. There were also recitals in Montevideo and Rio de Janeiro.

They returned to New York City on 4 June, but only long enough to change planes. They traversed the Atlantic that day aboard a South African Airways flight bound for Johannesburg. Hans Adler, a concert manager in Johannesburg, had arranged the Hungarian Quartet's fourth trip to South Africa for a rigorous tour of twenty concerts in five weeks. Their friend, Regina Ridge (the manager of Australia's Musica Viva), arrived from Zurich to meet them in Johannesburg on her way home from a European vacation. She went with them to Durban to hear their superb recital there, then the next day to stroll on the beach with her four friends before saying farewell and leaving on the

Johannesburg-Perth flight for her homeward journey. It was the last time they saw her. News came a few years later that the remarkable Miss Ridge had been killed in an automobile accident in Prague. It was the tragic loss of a true friend.

Concerts in East London, Port Elizabeth, Bloemfontein, and Windhoek brought them back to Johannesburg midway in the tour, and from there they went to Rhodesia where they visited Victoria Falls and appeared in Bulawayo, Salisbury, and Livingstone. All three recitals in the great copperbelt of Zambia were well attended, but after the recital in Ndola, Michael Kuttner fell ill, evidently striken with food poisoning, and had to be hospitalized. The others left Ndola the next morning as scheduled; Kuttner, who recovered remarkably fast, met them later in Cape Town to continue the concerts.

To ease the situation of Kuttner's indisposition, Székely, Koromzay, and Magyar formed a trio for the remaining Zambian concert in Lusaka and improvised a program: a Mozart duo for violin and viola, a Beethoven string trio, and a performance of Kodály's Solo Sonata, a demanding work not accessible to every cellist, but one that was securely in Magyar's repertoire.

Kuttner rejoined the quartet for a Beethoven cycle given in eight performances in and around Cape Town, part of which was broadcast by the South African Broadcasting Corporation. On 12 July they flew to London, where Kuttner, not yet quite well, decided to return to New York. Valmàlete arranged for a substitute violinist to join the quartet for one concert in Lyon.

After ten weeks touring South America and South Africa, the quartet reached Maine on 14 July. Close to the seacoast and the mountains, Waterville was an idyllic setting for the weary globe-trotters to have a six-week respite from their travels, carrying out the teaching for which they cared most—coaching string quartets. But their summer at Colby College passed all too quickly in 1970. On 21 August they left Maine for seven months in Europe, not to return to North America until the following March.

Chapter Twenty-five

"Exit without Tears"

The Hungarian Quartet, undisputed masters of the Beethoven string quartet repertoire, played the Beethoven cycle repeatedly for seven months abroad during 1970–71. After performances in Germany and Holland, they arrived in Scotland on 10 November for a Beethoven cycle in Glasgow. One week later they played it again, this time on the South Bank at London's Queen Elizabeth Hall, moving into the larger Royal Festival Hall for the final concert on 30 November.

During a Christmas holiday in Holland, Székely performed for the last time with Géza Frid.

> I played a farewell concert with Géza Frid during one of my last times in Amsterdam. It was a radio broadcast from Hilversum. For that occasion we chose the Sonata in D Minor by Brahms as the main work. Although we had seen each other in recent years when the quartet appeared in Holland, we had not played together for more than thirty years at the time we gave our final broadcast on 20 December 1970.

> At that time Frid was still living in Amsterdam in his same apartment. Four years earlier he had been visited there by our teacher, Zoltán Kodály, and Sarolta, his new wife. This occurred during Kodály's last visit abroad.

> In 1974 Frid celebrated his jubilee concert at the Amsterdam Concertgebouw. Later that year, he fell on the stairs at

home and seriously injured himself. For several years thereafter he lived in a nursing home in Amsterdam. Again he suffered a serious accident and died a few days later from his injuries.

The Mozartsaal in Vienna was the venue for a Beethoven cycle in early January of 1971. Then the quartet returned to Vevey to play Beethoven, Bartók, and Schubert before going on to Lausanne and Geneva. With plans for a transcontinental Bartók tour, they returned to the United States in late February to appear at Colby College for the Student Music Associates. In New York City they presented a Bartók cycle at Hunter College, then began an American tour which took them finally to San Francisco. And then it was back to western Canada.

They arrived in Edmonton directly from San Francisco to spend Easter in snowy Alberta. String quartets by Haydn, Schubert, and Bartók were the fare for the members of the Edmonton Chamber Music Society on the last day of March. The following evening the players joined the enthusiastic Edmonton audience to hear the University of Alberta String Quartet in an all-Bartók concert, while Easter Day was spent with Canadian friends grown accustomed to the yearly visits of the Hungarian Quartet.

Returning to Boulder after an absence of almost a year, the quartet looked forward to a long vacation and the prospect of a reprieve from the concert platform until early July when they would return to Colby College for their eighth consecutive summer. While it was an aspiration that fully formed string quartets would come to Colby for chamber music coachings, the program had prospered by admitting individual players. During the opening days of the course each summer, the quartet assigned these players to newly formed ensembles.

The summer of 1971 witnessed the return of many outstanding individual players, and at last, several pre-formed quartets, thirty-two musicians in all. The Lindsay Quartet, who later took their place at the forefront of English ensembles, came from London to study; another emerging ensemble, the Tokyo Quartet, visited Colby that summer with their teacher Rafael Hillyer in order to play for Székely.

A young Hungarian ensemble, who had auditioned for Koromzay in Budapest, came to Waterville for the 1971 summer course, were coached by the members of the quartet, then returned to Europe to win recognition at the international competitions in Rome and Budapest. Its members were graduates of the Franz Liszt Academy eager to pursue a chamber music career together. Violinists András Kiss and Pál Andrássy, violist Tivador Popa, and cellist Tibor Párkányi called themselves the New Budapest Quartet.

The autumn that followed was a time of change, of endings and of new beginnings. After leaving Maine, the Hungarian Quartet departed for Europe where on 2 September they would embark on a Mediterranean concert cruise. Because he disliked sea voyages, Székely remained in Paris and flew to Tunis to meet the others there when the passengers on the Renaissance went ashore for a concert at Sidi Bou Saîd. The fourth Mediterranean music cruise of the Renaissance had begun at Le Havre with a Grand Ball. Once underway, there were concerts aboard ship and concerts on land at the ports-of-call visited during two weeks: Santiago de Compostela, Málaga, Tunis, Malta, Delphi, Dubrovnik, and Venice. Disembarking in Italy, the passengers left the ship with memories of many fine concerts by Jacqueline Dupré and Daniel Barenboim, Byron Janis, Yehudi Menuhin, Elizabeth Schwarzkopf, and the Hungarian String Quartet.

Until the end of the cruise, the quartet had been concerned with the uncertainty about plans for recording the string quintets of Brahms in Paris. Thomas Rolston, who was living in London for a year, received a telegram from Koromzay telling him that the recording sessions would be reinstated as of 17 September. Within days the five musicians were together in Paris, settled at the Atlantic Hotel on rue de Londres, and ready to begin the Brahms recordings at Salle Wagram with producer Eric McLeod.

During September Pathé-Marconi confirmed that the first two weeks of December were set aside for the final recording session. The great Hungarian cellist László Varga would join Thomas Rolston and the Hungarian Quartet at Salle Wagram to record the remaining string sextets and complete the projected cycle of Brahms recordings.

With the completion of the Brahms quintets in October, the Hungarian Quartet went directly to Milan where George Mendelssohn had engaged Tomaso Gallia to produce their new Mozart recordings for Vox Productions. For their final recording enterprise, the quartet recorded four Mozart quartets, these new recordings to be combined with their previous Vox recordings of the "Dissonance" and the "Hunt" to create an album of the six celebrated Mozart works dedicated to Haydn. In 1991 this recording was reissued by Vox on compact disc.

Directing the editing of the quartet's new recordings was always Székely's privilege. He loved to do this and did it meticulously. He was a perfectionist.

If the recorded playing is not good enough, you cannot make the performance itself better with any new system. Perhaps the engineer can take away some unwanted noise, but the actual performance remains. When the long-playing process was new, Pathé-Marconi transferred our old recording of the "Lark" to the new format. This was a great improvement over the older 78 rpm system. Later we made yet other recordings of the "Lark" and twice recorded Schubert's G Major Quartet, although never in stereo. These are among my personal favorites.

Occasionally, for instance in our recording of the Brahms Piano quintet with Georges Solchany, everything is not as it should be in the studio and later you can hear these differences. In the Brahms quintet, the strings become hazy and have a muted sound in comparison with the piano. This was the result of Solchany's being placed somewhere in the middle of the large studio at Salle Wagram while we were on a podium in one corner. That arrangement was not successful.

Solchany was a very good pianist and played well on these recordings, but he sometimes had strange ideas about balance. One of these ideas was that, in principle, on the piano everything should be evenly loud, so that accompanying parts should be evenly balanced with the treble. On the other hand, our working principle—we learned it from Leó Weiner—was that the soprano must be a little bit clearer, more dominating.

When it came to the editing of the Mozart quartets, I made so many propositions that finally Tomaso Gallia said he couldn't do them, unless he deducted the cost of his labor from our fee. Eventually he did pay less in order to carry out my ideas, a few of which were difficult editing propositions for him, that is true.

The idea was that I give him the very best choices from all the tapes, and these choices were not simply "all in my head" but existed as markings on the score. As I look again at those marked scores, I see one decision that involves only a measure. That doesn't mean that in another "take" that particular measure was bad. I made a choice. It is only that one tries to get the very best example, as perfect as possible. Often I worked at a reduced tape speed with its consequent lower pitch to hear the result more accurately.

Whether the playing was sufficiently precise was the question. In certain instances a producer may not easily recognize imprecise playing when it occurs in a less critical moment in the music. Of course, the engineers were familiar with my ideas, but they didn't know the works as well as we knew them, and that makes all the difference.

Vox sent all the Mozart quartet tapes to me in Switzerland, and I worked very hard on the editing. I was even stricter than usual, proposing that they make certain things louder or softer, or in some new dynamic combinations. On my scores I see some of my written annotations, for instance, "There is a noise at the end of the last note." Whether they fixed that last note or did not, I cannot remember now. In the case of repetitions, I made various choices to make them different so there would be more life. I write here, "It is ugly, but you cannot retake it." In that case, there was no alternative.

It is hard sometimes to make these decisions because it may be that the substitution is a little bit different in sonority from the example at hand, but it is remarkable that we played relatively the same. Of course it was not difficult sometimes, but in the Mozart, there we had a different situation. The simpler the texture, the more difficult is the problem. In Mozart everything is very clear.

After the Mozart recording sessions in Milan, the quartet performed in Holland, France, Belgium, and England. A concert in Rotterdam began their final Dutch tour. It was followed by a radio broadcast from Hilversum, then appearances in Arnhem, The Hague, Deventer, and Amsterdam. The program for their final appearance in the Kleine Zaal of the Amsterdam Concertgebouw was Mozart's Quartet K. 387, Bartók's Second Quartet, and Beethoven's Op. 59, No. 3. As they packed to leave the Hotel Trianon the next day on their way to France and Belgium, Julie Magyar wrote to London to confirm the quartet's acceptance of the Rolstons' invitation to celebrate the final season in late November at their temporary home in South Kensington.

Ibbs and Tillett had announced nine appearances of the quartet in England during November: Oxford, Lancaster, Portsmouth, Monmouth, Bolton, Uttoxeter, Durham, Manchester, and, on Sunday evening 14 November, at London's Queen Elizabeth Hall on the

South Bank. The program for the final concert in London was chosen from repertoire that the London public had come to recognize as signature works of the Hungarian String Quartet for more than thirty years: Haydn's "Lark," the Fifth Quartet of Bartók, and Schubert's Quartet in G Major, Op. 161.

After the concert the quartet made their way to Collingham Gardens where they were greeted by the Rolstons and many friends from the past, among them Dame Eva Turner, Kató Havas, and the Rolstons' daughter, Shauna, who was living abroad for the first time, studying French, and practicing the cello for a forthcoming, brief performance in Dorset for which she received her first notice in The Strad at age five.

Honored in London by their faithful friends and colleagues, the quartet set out for Paris and the final recording sessions at Salle Wagram.

> When we completed the recordings of the Brahms sextets for Pathé in Paris, we said goodbye to our two colleagues who had taken part, Thomas Rolston and László Varga. Later in Los Angeles, I edited these works for Pathé, but unfortunately they were never released, because EMI felt the public would not buy new recordings of our quartet if we were no longer appearing in public concerts.

The quartet returned to the United States in mid-January, then criss-crossed the continent for six weeks playing the final concerts of the twenty-fourth and last American tour in Pennsylvania, North Carolina, Florida, Texas, Oklahoma, a Canadian performance in Vancouver, then Oregon, Nebraska, Indiana, Illinois, and finally Charlottesville, Virginia.

In early May they parted for one month, each family returning home for a brief vacation, the Koromzays to Boulder, the Magyars to St. Louis, and the Székelys and Kuttners to California. The promise of an active summer season lay ahead with both their first Canadian engagement at the Banff Centre's Academy of Chamber Music in June and, during July and August, their last engagement at Colby College where they had spent the previous eight summers teaching.

Three outstanding chamber music students from the United States who had previously studied with the Hungarian Quartet at Colby—violinist Richard Young, violist Louise Schulman, and cellist Cheryll Melott—enrolled in the Banff Centre's fledgling Academy of

Chamber Music in 1972. The enrollment that first year reached the total of twenty-eight string players. Of these, fifteen were young Canadians.

The quartet arrived in the Canadian Rockies on 4 June, coming from different directions, some flying, some driving. Once settled in Rundle Hall on the Banff campus, they began to teach after forming the enrolled students into quartets which would appear in public later in the month representing the master classes. The Hungarian Quartet appeared in two concerts: the first on 11 June included works by Mozart, Schubert, and Debussy; the second on 18 June presented quartets by Haydn, Kodály, and Beethoven. Two lecture recitals were devoted to the quartets of Bartók. Young children from Edmonton's Society for Talent Education visited the campus on 17 June in the company of their parents and teachers. That weekend the members of the quartet taught the youngsters and later played especially for them.

An enthusiastic hiker, Susie Koromzay joined pianist Anton Kuerti and his wife to climb nearby Mount Rundle during her stay at Banff, leaving the campus early one morning intending to return in time for dinner. When the hiking party didn't return on schedule, Koromzay went fishing on the Bow River to calm his anxiety. By nightfall when the hikers were thought to be lost on the mountain, it was too late for the park's helicopter service to initiate a search, but early the next morning the three were located, lost and exhausted, but otherwise well. Campus humor soon spread the word that Mount Rundle was to be renamed Mount Koromzay in honor of the valiant Susie who had spent the chill night unprepared on the mountain side, covered only by her jacket.

The quartet departed from Banff on 1 July to drive across the continent. In Ontario they performed a concert on 8 July in Stratford under the auspices of the Stratford Shakespearean Festival Foundation, then continued on to Waterville, Maine, to begin their ninth summer at Colby College. Surrounded by their outstanding students, many of whom had helped build the chamber music program to its climactic achievement in 1972, the quartet had its most successful summer in Maine.

The evening of 15 August marked an occasion at Colby College that was historic, exhilarating, and at the same time wistfully nostalgic. This was the final appearance of the Hungarian Quartet at

Colby, during their last summer as faculty-in-residence for Colby's Summer School of Music. They played two Beethoven quartets: Op. 59, No. 1, and Op. 131. Robert Strider, president of Colby College, took the opportunity at the end of their performance to offer the profound gratitude of the institution:

> They have contributed to an era in the history of Colby notable for cultural richness. We will miss their perceptive teaching and their extraordinarily sensitive performances of the finest quartets in musical literature. With our thanks may we wish them all well in the years that lie ahead.[1]

The quartet remained another week in Maine to finish their teaching, then on Monday, 21 August 1972, traveled to nearby Hanover, New Hampshire, claimed their reservations at the Hanover Inn, and prepared themselves for their last concert which they performed the following evening at the Hopkins Center at Dartmouth College. The contract for this concert had been signed by Colbert Artists Management on March 3. The program for 14 June chosen by the organizers at Dartmouth was Beethoven's Quartet, Op. 18, No. 4, Kodály's Quartet No. 2, and Schubert's Op. 161.

Dénes Koromzay had written to Agnes Eisenberger at the Colbert Artists Management to tell the news that Michael Kuttner had accepted an invitation to join the staff of Indiana University in Bloomington where he would play in the Berkshire Quartet and pursue his conducting career. "So any rebirth of the Hungarian Quartet, however improbable it was, is not anymore possible. Our swansong will be in Dartmouth—a melancholy occasion."[2]

However, despite the profound personal feelings that this last concert may have aroused in the individual artists of the Hungarian Quartet, the concert itself was indeed an "Exit without tears," as Richard Buell, critic of the *Boston Phoenix,* called it in his historic article on 29 August 1972:

> In the twentieth century (the century of the displaced person, as it has been called), it has been an achievement simply to have survived. But to have survived largely on one's own terms, keeping alive in exile a tradition-based culture of the highest order: this merits our attention and our praise. The Hungarian String Quartet has surely inspired long

thoughts of this kind on other occasions, for they have carried the brilliance of between-the-wars Hungary with them throughout the world for some thirty-seven years.

What is news to the follower of musical happenings is that the "have carried" above must be changed to the simple past tense. The quartet has now disbanded. They gave their last concert at Hopkins Center, Dartmouth College, on the evening of August 22. They retire to teach and play separately.

There was something engagingly unheavy about the entire occasion: not a bit of the *Götterdämmerung* about this quartet. The members straggled into Hanover separately without having planned a rehearsal. Mr. Koromzay, the violist, was content to chat with us until just ten minutes before the concert. "I think I ought to do just a little warming up," he said as we were leaving.

Not that it couldn't have been an intimidating occasion. It was just that they bear the weight of history—the close association with Bartók and Kodály, for instance—with such ease and modesty. . . .

The experience of Székely, Kuttner, Koromzay and Magyar could exemplify rather dolefully the upheavals of European history; it could, that is, if they chose to dwell upon it. One suspects, however, that the resilience of spirit that their playing communicates is not only musical but personal. At least I don't think I'm reading anything that wasn't there into my evaluation of their concert on the 22nd. It just didn't sound like a final concert. The various excellences of the playing which differentiate them from other top-rank quartets were just as much on their own terms as the decision to disband at that particular time and at that level of achievement. There were many things I heard that they could usefully teach some of the more insistently virtuosic young ensembles now on the rise. And it is pleasant to consider that as free individuals (and teachers) they will now be in a position to do just that. I hope that some academic amanuensis will be taking down onto tape and music paper or whatever the perishable expertise, gathered first hand, that these players carry within their heads about some of the most impressive and difficult music of our times. In any case, we and posterity will have their numerous records, and there were a few hundred of us present last Tuesday night who will have a very superior concert to remember. . . .

. . . The encore was the *lento assai* from Beethoven's last (Op. 135) quartet. Stillness.

Afterwards, Mr. Székely, beaming and grandfatherly, said to us, "Yes, I won't have to catch so many planes. But it's only the end of playing in the quartet, not of making music. One can never do that."[3]

Plate 93. Zoltán Székely and Claude Kenneson at Banff in 1992. PHOTOGRA-
PHY MONTE GREENSHIELDS. COURTESY OF THE BANFF CENTRE ARCHIVES.

Plate 92. Zoltán Székely at home in Lloyd Hall in 1991. PHOTOGRAPHY DOREEN
LINDSAY, COURTESY OF THE LINDSAY COLLECTION.

Plate 91. The St. Lawrence String Quartet. First prize winner, Fourth Banff International String Quartet Competition in 1992. (Left to right: Marina Hoover, Barry Shiffman, Lesley Robertson, and Geoff Nuttall.) PHOTOGRAPHY MONTE GREENSHIELDS, COURTESY OF THE BANFF CENTRE ARCHIVES.

Plate 90. Zoltán Székely and Gwen Hoebig working on the Bartók Violin Concerto at the Banff Centre in 1992. PHOTOGRAPHY MONTE GREENSHIELDS. COURTESY OF THE BANFF CENTRE ARCHIVES.

Plate 89. Zoltán Székely and Thomas Rolston in 1991. PHOTOGRAPHY MONTE GREENSHIELDS. COURTESY OF THE BANFF CENTRE ARCHIVES.

Plate 87. The Takács String Quartet and violist Dénes Koromzay performing a Mozart quintet in Boulder. THE KOROMZAY COLLECTION.

Plate 88. The Audubon String Quartet studying Bartók's Fifth Quartet with
Zoltán Székely at the Banff Centre in 1991. (Left to right: Doris Lederer,
Thomas Shaw, David Ehrlich, David Salness, and Zoltán Székely.) PHOTOG-
RAPHY MONTE GREENSHIELDS. COURTESY OF THE BANFF CENTRE ARCHIVES.

Plate 86. Zoltán Székely and the Takács String Quartet at Banff in 1981. (Left to right: Gábor Takács-Nagy, Károly Schranz, Zoltán Székely, Gábor Ormai, and András Fejér.) COURTESY OF THE BANFF CENTRE ARCHIVES.

Plate 85. The Eder String Quartet at Banff in 1983. (Left to right: Pál Eder, Erika Tóth, György Eder, and Zoltán Tóth.) COURTESY OF THE BANFF CENTRE ARCHIVES.

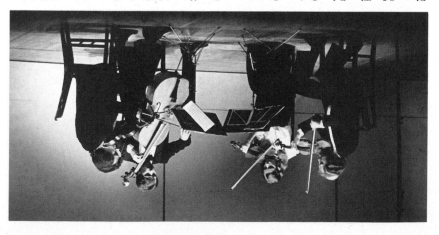

Plate 83. Zoltán Székely, Tibor Serly, and William Primrose at the Banff Centre. PHOTOGRAPHY JOHN MAHLER. COURTESY OF THE BANFF CENTRE ARCHIVES.

Plate 84. The 1981 Béla Bartók Centenary Celebration panel discussion: "The Influence of Folk Music on the Compositions of Béla Bartók." (Left to right: László Somfai, Béla Bartók, Jr., David Leighton, Zoltán Székely, and János Kárpáti.) COURTESY OF THE BANFF CENTRE ARCHIVES.

Plate 82. Zoltán Székely and Isobel Moore in 1991. PHOTOGRAPHY MONTE
GREENSHIELDS, COURTESY OF THE BANFF CENTRE ARCHIVES.

Plate 81. Lorand Fenyves, Zoltán Székely, and Gabriel Magyar at the Banff
Centre in 1978. COURTESY OF THE BANFF CENTRE ARCHIVES.

1973–1993

The Banff Centre. COURTESY OF THE BANFF CENTRE ARCHIVES.

Chapter Twenty-six

The Banff Years

"The inspiration for bringing Zoltán Székely to Banff was Tom Rolston's—and what a brilliant stroke it was!" David Leighton has observed, recalling the events of the early 1970s.

> I particularly remember the Hungarian String Quartet's performance of the first "Razumovsky" quartet of Beethoven in the Margaret Greenham Theatre at Banff. This was one of their last appearances together; they had announced their intention to dissolve the quartet following the summer.
>
> I had been asked to introduce them at a reception following the concert, and I remember facing the daunting job of correctly pronouncing Székely, Magyar, Koromzay, and Kuttner. As a young violin student I had encountered Székely's transcription for violin and piano of Bartók's *Rumanian Folk Dances*, never thinking I would ever meet, let alone become a friend of, the man with the formidable name.[1]

As Leighton has also said:

> Many of the world's greatest musicians are Hungarian and many of them have been to Banff. . . . the leader—the one they all look up to—is Zoltan Székely. He is the Don of the "Hungarian Connection" at Banff.[2]

The Banff Centre's School of Fine Arts became Székely's artistic haven in the summer of 1973, thirty-seven years after it was founded as an institution for continuing education. In the early 1930s, Ned Corbett and Donald Cameron, two visionary Albertans undaunted by the onset of the Great Depression in western Canada, began to plan new fine arts programs for the Department of Extension of the University of Alberta in Edmonton. With the promise of one thousand dollars from a Carnegie grant to finance the undertaking, Corbett established a summer drama course in the village of Banff, situated in Banff National Park in the Rocky Mountains west of the city of Calgary. In the spring of 1933, this newspaper advertisement appeared throughout the province: "School of the Drama, Banff, August 7 to 25. Registration fee $1.00, no tuition fees."

Corbett added art and music courses during the next three years. In the summer of 1936 Donald Cameron combined these fine arts courses to create Banff's School of Fine Arts. A decade later he negotiated a perpetual lease with the National Parks of Canada for a parcel of land on Tunnel Mountain known as the St. Julien site. With this land acquisition and the creation of a new building fund, Cameron had begun the long process of transforming the School of Fine Arts into an institution of national prominence.

The School of Fine Arts offered a course designed for young string players for the first time in 1951. This new venture had an auspicious beginning. Three Canadian violinists destined for international careers—Betty-Jean Hagen, Andrew Dawes, and Kenneth Perkins—enrolled in the string program to study with violinist Clayton Hare.

Vancouver-born violinist Thomas Rolston joined the faculty of the School of Fine Arts in 1965 and with great enthusiasm began the task of building a world-class music program at the Banff Centre. Under his experienced artistic direction, the various choices for study were clearly set forth: chamber music was taught during May and June, and the Canadian Chamber Orchestra brought Canadian orchestral players during July and August for coaching in orchestral playing from such respected conductors as Klaus Tennstedt, Walter Susskind, and Georg Tintner. Those who sought the environment of the instrumental master class to study the solo repertoire found themselves in an ideal circumstance—small classes, distinguished pedagogues, and privileged access to performance during the annual Banff Festival of the Arts.

The next twenty years of vigorous growth saw the campus begin to match physically what it had become artistically and intellectually, a center for the arts nurtured within a constellation of activities devoted to continuing education.[3]

After the final concert by the Hungarian String Quartet at Dartmouth College, Zoltán Székely was no longer heard in the concert halls of the world recreating Beethoven's Op. 131 or Bartók's Fifth Quartet or the miraculous lyricism of Schubert's late quartets. His absence from the world stage as a quartet player impoverished the chamber music community in 1972. Those faithful music lovers who so admired the Hungarian String Quartet and its remarkable leader, whose supremacy in the performance of the Beethoven and Bartók repertoire was undeniable, turned to their record collections to recall the fabled performances.

But Székely had meant what he said to Richard Buell at Dartmouth: "It's only the end of playing in the quartet, not of making music. One can never do that." He and Mientje returned to California in September where they could live quietly while he worked undisturbed in the sanctuary of their little house on North Electric Avenue in Alhambra, very near the home of their son, Frank, a successful Los Angeles businessman.

Székely's first task was a challenging one. Pathé-Marconi had sent the unedited tape recordings of the Brahms quintets and sextets to Alhambra. He immediately began editing them for the sound engineers in Paris, his job made easier by his reprieve from concert playing. Unfortunately these performances were never released to the public, although it is still possible that they may appear someday as archival recordings on compact disc.

As for his violin playing, in 1972 Székely was able to return to his repertoire of the pre-quartet years. He restudied Ravel's Violin Sonata and the sonatas of Brahms and Mozart that had graced his early programs, Beethoven's "Kreutzer" Sonata, and, of course, Bartók's sonatas and rhapsodies.

Perhaps there were only a few other concert violinists in America in 1972 turning seventy, living happily in the present, and still fully capable of sensing imaginatively what his performing career might still encompass. All great artists have, of course, an atmosphere in which they seem most at their ease and at their best: for Székely this ambience was in Alhambra. There he began to prepare the Bartók Violin Concerto for future performances.

His interpretation of the concerto was intact. He had retained the critical, interpretive details unaltered in his mind. His virtuosity had been encouraged and sheltered within the quartet repertoire beyond the bounds of what today seems possible for an aspiring violinist who moves steadily through a traditional solo career on an unswerving path, endlessly repeating performances of only a few popular concertos.

With the vigilance of the fine composer that he had always been, he restudied the structure of the concerto to find what this extraordinary music might now demand of him as a performer. Perhaps the only difficult question was where he should perform it, but that problem would be solved in time.

At age thirty-six when he gave the world premiere of Bartók's Violin Concerto, there was an impression of deceptive ease of execution with nothing wasted on pyrotechnics. The old acetate recording of the first performance yields evidence of this. In 1939 there had been a startling concentration, an unusual aplomb, a spirit daring and committed. However, a significant metamorphosis now began to occur day by day as he conceived a yet-more-profound interpretation of this work, one that would confirm the veracity of András Pernye's opinion that "His violin playing is without any artificiality, therefore lasting and worthy."[4]

Within a few miles of the Székely home in Alhambra, Raymond Kendall was directing the Institute for Special Musical Studies at the University of Southern California, a unique institution flourishing with the support of an endowment from the Chandler Foundation. The presence on the faculty of Gregor Piatigorsky and Jascha Heifetz drew the young virtuosi to the institute in a way unparalleled since Carl Flesch, Leopold Auer, and Emanuel Feuermann had attracted many of the world's most promising students to the Curtis Institute of Music in Philadelphia in the 1920s. Kendall approached Székely with the idea of his teaching chamber music at the institute, but he declined the offer, not wanting at that time to commit himself to an extensive teaching engagement in Los Angeles.

Székely's greatest concern during this period was centered on Mientje's uncertain health. Their marriage had prospered for almost a half century founded on their daily devotion to the interests and needs of one another. Mientje's unflagging ability to keep pace with Székely's artistic lifestyle and to revel in their world travels was a source of amazement to their family and close friends, and her remarkable fidelity to his career brought new strength to them both.

Now inevitable changes in her health suggested themselves—periods of depression and forgetfulness, the possible onset of Alzheimer's disease.

After a year in Alhambra, the Székelys returned to Alberta in the summer of 1973. For a twelve-week period Székely was deeply involved with his teaching and personally happy in the new relationship with his fellow Hungarian, the brilliant pedagogue Lorand Fenyves who now headed the new program. To their great satisfaction Gabriel Magyar joined them to form the faculty for the second season of the Banff Centre's Academy of Chamber Music.

The three Hungarian artists were joined by pianist Ada Bronstein, a Russian-Canadian artist resident in Winnipeg, for a mixed recital on 17 June. Magyar and Bronstein played two works for cello and piano: Sonata in A Major by Luigi Boccherini and Beethoven's Sonata, Op. 102, No. 1. Székely and Fenyves, both Hubay pupils although from quite different periods, played together for the first time. For that occasion they performed a suite of duets from Bartók's *44 Duos for Two Violins*.[5] Fenyves and Magyar ended the evening with a performance of Kodály's masterpiece, the Duo for Violin and Cello.

With pianist Howard Karp, they performed again in the Margaret Greenham Theatre ten days later. This program began with the Trio in E-flat Major by Haydn. Magyar and Karp performed the Sonata, Op. 102, No. 2, by Beethoven, then Fenyves and Maygar played Székely's duo, *Polyphon et Homophon,* Op. 2. After the intermission Lorand Fenyves gave a distinguished performance of the Sonata for Solo Violin by Bartók, a work which he had performed frequently from the time of its first appearance. The violinists ended the program with a repeat performance of the suite drawn from *44 Duos for Two Violins* which had enchanted the audience at the previous concert.

Among those studying in the Academy of Chamber Music in 1973 were young artists soon to take their places in North America's leading string quartets. Some had been at Colby, some were returning for the second season at Banff, all were dedicated and eager to learn. The roster of students included violinists Eva Székely, Eleanor Fruchtman, Magdolna Aldolrolyi-Nagy, Dan Foster, Heilwig von Koenigsloew, and Paul Meyer; violists Mary Wayne Bush, Audrey Pedersen, and Marna Street; cellists Cheryll Melott, Suzanne MacIntosh, and Perry Karp.

In newly formed ensembles, the young artists played concerts of Beethoven and Schubert that set the international standard of the new academy. However, during succeeding years only pre-formed quartets were admitted to the academy. This innovation was designed to improve the quality of study by taking advantage of the previous, communal ensemble experience of the participants. Piano chamber music had its own domain in a program conceived by Isobel Moore and eventually directed by the extraordinary Menahem Pressler, pianist of the Beaux-Arts Trio.

During the Banff Festival of the Arts that concluded the 1973 summer season, a natural consequence of Székely's presence was a pair of concerts, "Tribute to Bartók," in which he was joined by his colleagues in two evenings of chamber music. Pianist Isobel Moore joined Székely on these occasions in performances of the two rhapsodies by Bartók and as a result became the pianist of his choice for the remainder of his public career.

During August, in a concert with Stravinsky's suite from the ballet *Pulcinella* and Murray Adaskin's Diversion for Orchestra, Székely performed Bartók's rhapsodies with the Canadian Chamber Orchestra, conducted by Clifford Evens, and provided the festival with one of its most memorable events. The sound of the Michelangelo Strad filling the Eric Harvie Theatre for the first time drew the attention of Jamie Portman, critic of the *Calgary Herald*, who wrote: "equally hypnotic was the assurance with which Székely probed beneath the surface of the music—offering more than just a superficial contrasting of moods, maintaining a rhythmic tautness which compelled the listener's attention, and offering performances which stressed the epic rather than the merely dramatic nature of the music."[6]

"As I recall, it was Mientje's idea that Zoltán and I play together," Isobel Moore said in a 1992 interview, retracing the events that forged her artistic partnership with Székely two decades earlier.

> While Mientje felt instinctively that we should play together, she was somewhat concerned with the new idea of Zoltán's performing recitals with a woman, although he occasionally had played the big chamber music works with Clara Haskil and Annie Fisher.
>
> She once said to me that she felt Zoltán didn't really like playing with most pianists—that he had only two in his career that he played with often, and only one of them—Béla Bartók—brought him great artistic satisfaction.
>
> Mientje's very genuine aspiration that we play together set things in motion. She built up the flame. In a way that was

what she had done in the case of Bartók. So we started to rehearse and the rehearsing was successful.[7]

After the summer concerts in Banff, Székely returned to Maine in
November of 1973 to appear twice as soloist with orchestra: first in
Bartók's Second Rhapsody and Viotti's Concerto No. 22 with Peter Ré
conducting the Bangor Symphony Orchestra, and then in Bartók's
Violin Concerto with Maine's Portland Symphony Orchestra con-
ducted by Paul Vermel.

Later that fall an invitation came from abroad. When the
Székelys returned to Alhambra from Maine, the Hungarian government asked Székely to come to Budapest to record the rhapsodies
with piano for Hungaroton's projected Béla Bartók Complete Edition. Székely telephoned from Los Angeles to tell Hungaroton that
he wished to record the rhapsodies with a pianist living in Canada.
This was Isobel Moore. "Either I record it in Edmonton, or maybe I
can never do it," he explained. The government agreed. As Moore
recounted:

> I was pleased, of course, when, late in 1973, Zoltán chose
> me as his pianist for this very important recording. I felt com-
> pletely comfortable during our rehearsals. His way of working
> is unstressful. He has endless patience. He is always chal-
> lenged by the problems of the music. I had never rehearsed
> like that before. I was amazed when I would hear his ap-
> proach to things. It was so thoughtful, so perfectly designed,
> yet so free.
>
> My earlier recording experiences had been for radio
> broadcasts and had always occurred during the daytime.
> Recording the two rhapsodies for Hungaroton was quite a
> different adventure. We did it in the dead of night—certainly
> not my style!
>
> Zoltán was absolutely matter-of-fact about all this. The
> Canadian Broadcasting Corporation's recording studio in Ed-
> monton, with its uninspiring design and poor acoustics, was
> more than grim after midnight, but Duncan MacKerchar, a
> gifted and sensitive producer, was in the control booth, my
> husband was turning pages, and Mientje sat in a chair in the
> studio, listening to every note and encouraging us during the
> breaks. By then she had lived with the rhapsodies for forty-
> five years, since the evening in Budapest when Bartók made
> the dedication.

In that situation Zoltán wanted to immediately create the right atmosphere, not being interested in arriving at the final conclusion bar by bar. And he had a methodical plan in mind, as always. First we played right through the whole work to create a model for the editing which Zoltán would do later, and then we recorded in large segments, entire sections, then phrases, then certain problematic passages.

It finally went well after several sessions, and that was that! The next phase of his work began when he and Mientje moved into a small apartment near the University of Alberta, the home of an ever-faithful young violinist, David Zweifel, who vacated it for their comfort. There Zoltán set to work listening to the tapes and making his decisions regarding the editing. When he had finished this task some weeks later, he brought me in to listen to the final results.[8]

In the Béla Bartók Complete Edition, Isobel Moore was the only non-Hungarian among the recording artists. The company's expectation was that the new recording of the two rhapsodies would attain interpretive and historical significance. Clearly Hungaroton was proud to be able to immortalize among its last records such a remarkable moment: "such a harmony of authentic origin and perfect present-day mentality. . . . Bartók's violinist remembers with an awe-inspiring accuracy the style, spirit, and detail of their joint performances."[9]

During the Székelys' extended visit to Edmonton in March of 1974, two important musical events took place in quick succession. Székely and Moore appeared in a recital for the Edmonton Chamber Music Society in Convocation Hall at the University of Alberta on 12 March 1974 performing music by Porpora, Ravel, Bartók, and Brahms. Two weeks later with Pierre Hétu conducting, Székely performed Bartók's two rhapsodies with the Edmonton Symphony Orchestra as part of the 1974 CBC Alberta Festival.

A few days later Hungaroton announced that it would reissue the live recording of the world premiere of Bartók's Violin Concerto as a supplemental recording to the Béla Bartók Complete Edition. The new recording was remastered from the old acetate records Mientje had carried around the world in her hat box.

After an intense month of performing, recording, and editing tapes in Edmonton, Székely's thoughts turned once more to California, where he was scheduled to perform with the San Francisco State University Symphony Orchestra, conducted by László Varga. In a program including orchestral music by Wallingford Riegger and Brahms, Székely appeared as soloist in Bartók's Violin Concerto at McKenna Auditorium; the concert marked the inauguration of the Frank Houser Scholarship.[10] Two days later it was repeated on the campus of the University of California in Berkeley. After hearing the performances, Marilyn Tucker, critic of the *San Francisco Chronicle* wrote, "Székely, with his exquisite, singing performance and superb, effortless artistry, has lost none of his fabled ability as a violinist."[11]

The presence of William Primrose and Cecil Aronowitz added luster to the faculty during Székely's third year teaching in the Academy of Chamber Music. Gerald Stanick taught the viola master class.

Tibor Serly visited Banff later in the summer to discuss Bartók's Viola Concerto in a series of public forums. Thirty years after he had reconstructed Bartók's unfinished Viola Concerto, Serly resolved to write a measure-by-measure exposition of his labors that had extended over a period of two years. He had already begun his essay, "A Belated Account of the Reconstruction of a 20th-Century Masterpiece."[12] He was determined finally to refute claims that the posthumous work was the creation of its reconstructor, in fact to "put the matter to rest."

Serly felt that with the passing of time the Viola Concerto had steadly gained more and more acceptance as a genuine Bartók work deserving of respect and exposure. William Primrose, who had played the world premiere in 1949 and twice recorded the work, still found it "a sensitive and inspired work and a real contribution to the literature of the viola," as he had told Halsey Stevens in May of 1950.[13]

It was, in fact, Halsey Steven's opinion that had launched the controversy and continued to fuel it: "No matter how skillful the reconstruction, it must be admitted that no one but the composer himself could have decided exactly how it was to be done; and for that reason there will always be reluctance to accept the Viola Concerto as an authentic work of Bartók."[14]

Clearly in sympathy with the statement of Halsey Stevens, Székely discussed the subtlety of Bartók's creative processes, referring to the Violin Concerto. "It is clear that the richness of Bartók's *invention* is evident in every measure of the Violin Concerto, for instance. In my opinion, no one but Bartók could have decided how such creation would occur. There is no formula for such creative invention, no model."

Perhaps this matter that plagued Serly could never be satisfactorily put to rest. Those who had an opposing viewpoint continued to hold their ground. However, Serly's visit to Banff was important since it afforded an opportunity for musicians to hear him discuss these matters in person with both Primrose and Székely during the first of several historic forums at the Banff Centre devoted to Bartók's music.

Serly's composition Rondo Fantasy in Stringometrics (1971) for violin and harp provided another interesting topic for discussion during his visit to the Banff Centre. This work is a virtual catalogue of pizzicato effects. Having demonstrated the fourteen different types of pizzicato used in his work, he said, "Imagine what could be done to enhance the performance, of say, the pizzicato movement in Tchaikovsky's Fourth Symphony if orchestral players were truly versed in the subtlety of pizzicato performance."[15]

Tsuyoshi Tsutsumi, who had succeeded Peggy Sampson and Florence Hooten as the Banff Centre's principal cello teacher, suggested to Thomas Rolston that he invite János Starker to teach at Banff. Both Tsutsumi and László Funtek, head of the Theatre Division at the Banff Centre, knew Starker well. Tsutsumi had studied with him at Indiana University. Funtek, who had served with the Red Cross at the end of the Second World War, had personally assisted his emigration to the United States, where he assumed the position of principal cellist of the Dallas Symphony Orchestra, of which Antal Doráti was then conductor.

Starker's acceptance of Rolston's invitation launched a pedagogical renaissance in the cello master classes and a stream of inimitable Starker performances at the subsequent festivals. Székely, Starker, and Moore joined forces in August of 1974 to perform Schubert's Trio, Op. 99, the first time these two Hungarian masters and Isobel Moore had appeared together.

Two days later Székely and Isobel Moore played a recital that included Ravel's Sonata for Violin and Piano. Although Székely had championed the sonata since 1926, he had not found an artistic colleague more receptive to the work than Moore, with the possible exception of Bartók. After almost two decades, she still has a vivid memory of their first performance of the sonata.

> I hadn't played the Ravel sonata before, and, thank goodness, I didn't really know then the magnitude of Zoltán's association with that work, because I would have been overwhelmed.

I must say, at that time I was surprised that we were actually doing it. It was only sometime later that Mientje showed me the photograph of Zoltán and Ravel and told me of the early first performances of the sonata throughout Europe.

Actually playing with him on the stage was even more of a revelation. Everyone seems always to look at him as one of the great musical scholars, and that he is, because in rehearsal his mind rules his heart. But not on the stage. It is the most extraordinary thing, and I think he is aware of it. I'll never forget the end of the first movement of the Ravel sonata. There was a soaring, *bel canto* melody—the most moving thing I've ever accompanied. I've never heard anyone else play it that way. His performance of this work is in the truest spirit of impressionism.

Zoltán derived tremendous pleasure from practicing the works we were to play. Of course he wanted the performances to be good, but regarding the rehearsals, he used to say to me, "We are doing *this* for ourselves, because we want it to be nice."

Sometimes after a concert I wasn't happy with certain things that had happened during my performance, but as time passed and we played together often, we never commented about each other's playing. He was affectionate, but never effusive, but then it is his habit to keep many of his thoughts to himself.

However, the spirit of communication came over him on stage! And we "kept our promises" to each other. He knew that during our work together certain things had to be carefully established—an understanding of structure and form—and within that discipline came freedom. One thing he couldn't stand in chamber music playing was a musician who didn't keep his "musical promises."[16]

In the five years that followed, Székely became strongly identified with the Banff Centre's Festival of the Arts and brought to that celebration performances of Mozart, Beethoven, Schubert—and the contemporary masters—that represented the culmination of his career as a recitalist. In 1975, following the example of the Banff Centre, the Province of Alberta granted Székely special status as Alberta's violinist-in-residence and sent him throughout the province to serve as a world model for the developing musicians of the area.

"Each time Zoltán and Gabriel Magyar returned to Banff, they were accompanied by their wives, Mien Székely and Julie Magyar, who became members of a wonderful, happy, and stimulating music community in Banff," David Leighton remarked during a 1992 interview.

Tom Rolston first proposed the idea of having Zoltán and Mien move permanently to Banff, since Zoltán's main circle of friends was now located in Alberta and his principal teaching responsibilities were those at the Banff Centre.

As president of the Centre, I was very interested in the idea. Not only would Zoltán's presence provide a musical focal point, it would also fit well with our plans for expanding the School of Fine Arts to a year-round program for advanced students and young professionals. We converted several rooms in Lloyd Hall into a comfortable apartment for the Székelys, and in 1976 they moved permanently to Banff.

This began an irregular but continuing series of visits from all sorts of people—Hungarian Television, music teachers, string quartets, old musical colleagues—all coming to see and talk shop with Zoltán. Tibor Serly, William Primrose, his old colleague Dénes Koromzay, Béla Bartók, Jr., and many others came. Early in their stay, Zoltán and Mien decided to become Canadian citizens, which they did in 1976.

The arrangement worked well for several years. Mien was delighted, both with Banff and with the new focus of Zoltán's career. Their son, Frank, came with his family—his wife, Anne, and their sons, Eric and Alec—for an extended visit each Christmas, something the older couple anticipated eagerly. But Mien's health continued to fail, and gradually she became largely confined to their apartment; this was very difficult for Zoltán, but his attachment to Mien was rock-solid and truly touching.[17]

Meanwhile, the other members of the Hungarian String Quartet prospered in their new roles. Gabriel Magyar had become a respected professor at the University of Illinois at Champaign-Urbana, where he taught cello and chamber music. He continued his chamber music coaching at the Banff Centre during the summers. Dénes Koromzay had indeed created another New Hungarian String Quartet, a two-generation ensemble led by Andor Tóth with Richard Young, an outstanding violinist among the former students of the Hungarian Quartet, as second violin, and the young virtuoso Andor Tóth, Jr., as cellist. In residence at Oberlin College in Ohio, Koromzay's New Hungarian String Quartet toured widely in North America and Europe, and recorded the major quartet repertoire for Vox Productions.

To Michael Kuttner's great satisfaction, he continued to pursue a varied career on the staff of Indiana University where he played in the Berkshire String Quartet and conducted the student symphony orchestras. In early September of 1975 when Kuttner failed to appear at an important rehearsal, one of his closest friends went to his home to inquire about him. He discovered that the violinist had died in his sleep during the night. Hundreds of friends and colleagues mourned his passing as the news of his death from a heart attack at age fifty-seven reached them around the world.

Székely became ever-more-closely associated with the University of Alberta String Quartet and in June of 1976 joined them as a lecturer on an American tour. After they presented the Bartók cycle and a series of six lectures at the University of Missouri in Columbia, he returned to Banff in July to appear in a performance of Bartók's Violin Concerto in the Eric Harvie Theatre. In addition to the Bartók work, the program included Beethoven's Symphony No. 2. Walter Susskind conducted the Canadian Chamber Orchestra.

Within a few months Székely played the work again. In the autumn he traveled to Urbana to perform the Bartók concerto at the Krannert Center for the Performing Arts with the Champaign-Urbana Symphony, conducted by Paul Vermel, and to give a master class in violin and ensemble performance at the School of Music of the University of Illinois.

Before hearing the first student quartet at the ensemble class, Székely suddenly pointed to his score, then spoke to the assembled audience: "Even after thirty-five years, you see something you missed. What Beethoven writes is a mysterious thing." He sat alert, unblinking, his chin cupped in his hands as he listened. After a half-dozen repetitions of a passage he had chosen to hear, he began to work. "That's quite good, but I'm not fully convinced yet," he remarked, directing the young players to use their intensity more effectively, where and when it was most needed. At the end of the coaching, he explained the basis for his criticisms by saying simply, "These are my interpretations based on tradition."[18]

As artistic director of the Banff Centre's winter program, Isobel Moore has long observed Székely's pedagogical approach:

Zoltán's principles of playing and teaching have not changed in all these years. For him music making has to be serious, to have content, or he won't do it.

I have to tell young musicians who want to play for Zoltán that he is not interested in their simply playing a work through for him and then asking his opinion of their playing. I think some of the young people are too impatient for his thorough approach. If I see that quality of impatience in them, I don't encourage them to go to him. It won't make either Zoltán or the student happy!

His approach is certainly in the great Hungarian tradition. Whether or not that tradition is completely applicable to the way music should be played today, the thoroughness of the approach is absolutely important. The Hungarian musicians trained in Budapest in the early part of the twentieth century were all touched by this tradition. Generations of that whole musical family were taught the absolute importance of the thorough investigation of the score, and evidently this occurred most frequently in the teaching of Leó Weiner.

I think that this kind of investigation still has to be tied to talent and the art of communication, and, of course, not everyone of that training had that to the same degree, but they all seem to have had certain definite qualities that come from such a disciplined study.

And the extraordinary ones—for instance, Bartók, the pianist? In his case the intellect and the emotion were tied together in the artistic expression. What freedom this could allow him!

As a representative of this great Hungarian tradition, Zoltán, it seems, has not based his musical life entirely on giving concerts, but on something more profound. Certainly he has no fear on stage. He is unusually poised before an audience because he knows that he has looked into everything thoroughly and has done his duty to the composer in his own way during the rehearsals. And while he wants the public to like each concert, his concern is with the music. He has the right motives at heart.

Playing Schubert's Rondo brillant with him was a revelation. All of his great strengths found a focus in this work. In the slow introduction he always performed the most beautiful *bel canto* playing on the violin that can be imagined, then in the faster sections, his incredibly original rhythmic sense was supreme. He seemed always to be playing exactly in time, yet it was not "in time," as we generally think of that.

Zoltán never forces his tone. In fact, he plays completely naturally because he has a remarkable bow control that allows him to sustain his musical ideas. When we played Beethoven's "Ghost" Trio with Tsuyoshi Tsutsumi, I remember that Zoltán planned so few changes of bow in the slow movement that his solutions even challenged Tsuyoshi's great virtuosity.

For Zoltán, any sound that emerges accidentally is wrong. And he hears that more than anything. This gift is quite extraordinary. My own ears became even more conscious of unnecessary, misplaced accents when we worked together.

Zoltán works diligently to bring the accentuation under control. Unfortunately, many of the young musicians who play for him now have a style of playing that allows false accentuation, perhaps because the current trend is so much more physically aggressive than it once was. One has to have a tremendous control not to err in that direction.[19]

In 1977 another invitation came from abroad. Székely was wanted in Budapest. Would he come to Hungary to appear in recitals with Annie Fisher? He no longer considered world travel feasible, and such a journey was now out of the question for Mientje. While his reply was negative, he candidly suggested that only a Budapest performance of Bartók's Violin Concerto would draw him back to Europe. This set a new plan into motion.

In 1977 Székely gave his last concert in Budapest, and that was his final visit to Hungary.

I had not much recent contact with my relatives in Hungary. Only one nephew and his family still lived in Dunavarsányi, near Budapest. Piroska's younger son had been killed in the 1956 revolution. And the musicians I had known best were no more. So that was my last visit to Budapest—the last goodbye. One critic remarked that perhaps it was the eighth wonder of the world that I still played that concerto at my age.

Chapter Twenty-seven

Farewell to Budapest

It was for the autumn festival—Budapest Weeks of the Arts—that Székely performed Bartók's Violin Concerto at the Erkel Színház concert
hall with the Hungarian State Concert Orchestra (Magyar Allami
Hangversenyzenekar), conducted by János Ferencsik.

About the violinist and the performance Lajos Fodor wrote in
Esti Hirlap, "Székely is someone who revealed to us with clarity the
origin of the Violin Concerto with seventy-four-year-old hands, but
with bow strokes led by a fresh, bright mind and spirit . . . his contribution helped make last night's concert truly a celebration of art."[1]

In a letter fifteen years later László Somfai,[2] head of the Bartók
Archívum in Budapest, spoke of Székely's Budapest concert on 26
September 1977:

> I was waiting for the Violin Concerto performance with
> certain nervous expectations.
>
> On the one hand, I knew and admired the historic
> recording of the 1939 world premiere under Mengelberg. It is
> one of the major sources for the study of the style of the Hun-
> garian violin school as Bartók liked it and has helped the
> post-war generations to understand the exact meaning of a
> great many details in Bartók's notation. (As a matter of fact,
> Zoltán Székely left the old discs, which were used for the 1971
> production of the Hungaroton LPX 11753 long-playing edi-
> tion, with me.)

On the other hand, I had a fear that after such a long break from solo playing, while playing so masterfully as the leader of the Hungarian Quartet, he still had the physical power, volume, and attitude to stand up for this often-played Bartók concerto, "his" concerto.

Great men always surprise you. I discovered another side of his instrumental brilliance: he played with perfect soloistic technique, but fortunately without the fashionable heavy tone and vibrato; with a refreshing variety of bow techniques and timbre, with an inspiring differentiation between the crucial notes and the ornamental passages. Those of us who believed that the post-war development of string playing was not at all good for Bartók interpretation (which can easily be demonstrated by the study of subsequent recordings of the Violin Concerto and even the six quartets as presented by star performers), we just felt triumphant. Too bad that the orchestral contribution, in my opinion, was not adequate.

Without saying a word to Zoltán Székely, I soon wrote a letter to [Antal] Doráti and asked his advice of how one could create the proper setting (orchestra, conductor, gramophone company) for making a new studio recording of this magnificent "revival" of the authentic performance. Doráti answered with sympathetic words, but he could not change the fact that the world's big companies already had the Bartók concerto in their catalogues and to replace it, only a young star had a chance.

I was grateful to Zoltán *bácsi* ["Uncle Zoltán," a term of endearment] that with my wife and a young colleague we could speak with him "at the white table" after the concert, and that he was willing to discuss his recollections of Bartók and technical details of the Bartók interpretation in the Hungarian Television studio with me. It is not an overstatement that for the connoisseur this concert in Budapest was a special experience, in my life certainly one of the few historic moments when one could get near to a masterwork in its fully authentic presence.[3]

Almost four years after this historic Budapest performance, the Banff Centre commemorated the centenary of Béla Bartók's birth by including many of Bartók's works in programs of the summer-long 1981 Banff Festival of the Arts. In addition, the Banff School of Fine Arts invited a number of distinguished guests from Budapest to take part in a series of special events—the composer's elder son, Béla Bartók, Jr.,[4] János Kárpáti,[5] László Somfai, and the Sebö Ensemble, a group of musicians who played the peasant instruments and music which had had so much influence on Bartók's compositions. With a crew from Hungarian Radio and Television, the visitors arrived in the Rockies in July, their presence at the Banff Centre made possible, in part, by the assistance of the Hungarian government.

The celebration began and ended with performances of the Bartók Viola Concerto: violist Donald McInnes appeared on 17 July as soloist with the Canadian Chamber Orchestra, and on 15 August, János Starker performed the work in the version for cello and orchestra.

A chamber music concert on 18 July featured the Sonata for Solo Violin (1944), performed by Lorand Fenyves, and *Contrasts* with Fenyves, clarinetist Ronald de Kant, and Ada Bronstein, pianist. Zoltán Székely and Isobel Moore performed the Second Violin Sonata after the intermission. Béla Bartók, Jr., ended the evening with his lecture, "A Personal Perspective of Béla Bartók (1881–1945)."

During this remarkable evening of music and words, Thomas Rolston appeared on stage (much to Székely's surprise) to announce that the Franz Liszt Academy in Budapest had bestowed its highest honor on Zoltán Székely. He was made Honorary Professor of the academy, a gesture extended to only a few world-renowned musicians during the academy's long history beginning in 1875. In receiving this distinction, Professor Székely took his place of honor with Eugène d'Albert, Pablo Casals, Vincent d'Indy, Pietro Mascagni, Jean Sibelius, Richard Strauss, and Arturo Toscanini. After the announcement, Béla Bartók, Jr., presented a special diploma to Székely on behalf of the Franz Liszt Academy before delivering his own lecture.

Hearing Zoltán rehearse with Isobel Moore brought great pleasure to Mientje during the years of her declining health when she was seldom seen in the audience of the concert hall. In preparation for their performance of Bartók's Second Sonata during the Bartók Centenary, they rehearsed exclusively in the Székely apartment, where Mientje rested comfortably in the privacy of her sitting room within earshot of the music she loved best, music that must always have brought to mind her first encounter with the great composer in 1923.

After the Second Sonata was performed in 1981, there would be no further rehearsals with Isobel Moore. Zoltán no longer appeared in public. Several brief periods of debilitating illness came his way, and his increasing deafness become a liability to his concertizing, although not to his teaching.

Twelve years after their last public performance together, Isobel Moore concluded an interview by speaking of that performance with Székely:

> Our performance of the Second Sonata during the Bartók Centenary went well. The work is very difficult, but I had nothing but pleasure with it. Sometime after that performance, a certain moment came in our artistic lives—as it does for everyone—when we no longer played together in public. We didn't discuss this matter then, and perhaps we never will. It was not necessary. Our understanding of each other is deep and constant.
>
> . . . I have a plan for the future. Lorand Fenyves has asked me to perform Bartók's First Sonata with him. I hope this will happen, of course. I love working with Lorand. Although he and Zoltán are very different players, the seriousness of their approach is similar and extraordinary. When I have the work learned, I hope to play it for Zoltán, as a final musical communication, a natural continuation of our partnership.[6] Perhaps in the solitude of his studio in Lloyd Hall, he will play it with me.
>
> I can sum it up without any question at all. Zoltán is a spiritual being when he plays. Music is like a religion to him, and he is a complete believer.
>
> He was the biggest musical influence I ever had. I studied in many places and was exposed to a lot of musicians, but I never met anybody that I admired more.[7]

"The Influence of Folk Music on the Compositions of Béla Bartók" was the title of a panel discussion during the Banff Centre's Béla Bartók Centenary Celebration.[8] Four days after the Székely-Moore performance of Bartók's Second Sonata, David Leighton was moderator for the panel discussion which took place in the Max Bell Auditorium.

The evening began with a performance of Bartók's Second Quartet by the Pacifica String Quartet. Quartet-in-residence for the 1981 summer season at the Banff Centre, the Pacifica Quartet—Marjorie Kransberg and Kiki Collins, violinists, violist Francie Martin, and Dane Richards, cellist—was at that time studying with both Székely and Fenyves.

As moderator, David Leighton welcomed the panelists: "We have here this evening, gathered at the front of this room, probably the four leading experts on Béla Bartók in the world. It is a very distinguished group and we are delighted to have you here." The panel was composed of László Somfai, Béla Bartók, Jr., Zoltán Székely, and János Kárpáti. The dialogue generated during the next hour, especially that between Somfai and Kárpáti, was remarkably unselfconscious and outgoing, to the intellectual delight of the audience.

Leighton's plan for the round-table discussion addressed the relationship between Bartók's scientific research in folklore and his own creative work, including the folkloric influence on the Second Quartet, the circumstances surrounding the work's composition, the problems of its interpretation, and finally a discussion of various related aspects of Bartók's other quartets.

During the course of the evening, in eager pursuit of their exciting subject, the panelists spoke spontaneously without reference to notes. While there was no intention to arrive at definitive conclusions, their discussions on various aspects of Bartók's use of folk music revealed the exceptional creative processes of the master composer.

László Somfai began the discussion by describing a fundamental aspect of Bartók's compositional approach—the idea that the composer's creativity functioned at several levels, alternating between drawing energy either from the expression of his own lyrical self ("ego style") or from "the folk" and their undisputed outpouring, the folk song.

> I would like to point out that in this quartet the folk-music influence is a borderline case. If we think back to the First String Quartet with its three movements, there is a very tragic first movement much more influenced by the romantic style than by folk music, a fine, Beethoven-like sonata form. And we have the wild, big final movement in which, apart from some rhythmic influences of say, Rumanian folk music, there are two islands, two isolated pieces of quasi-quotation of Hungarian folk music. In that work, in fact, folk music does not play a very important role.
>
> In the Second String Quartet (Mr. Kárpáti will agree with me) the folk-music influence is mainly concentrated in the second and third movements. The first movement is in the lyrical "ego style" of Bartók where very few thematic areas have structural or scalar influences of the folk music. Basi-

cally this is a very tragic, appassionato"ego" piece, except the closing theme with its pentatonic formula which certainly has a Hungarian flavor, specifically in the recapitulation. But what is the dramaturgy of the folk music in this piece that makes it so fascinating?

Somfai discussed at some length the art of dramatic composition and theatrical representation, the "dramaturgy" of folk music in Bartók's works. During the course of his remarks, he described the progression from a "puritanical, simple melody" to the eventual transfiguration in which a motif returned "costumed," exuding a Hungarian flavor, a progression from the "ego style" to the big, optimistic Bartókian dramaturgy where the energy is taken not from within the composer, but from without—from the folk element.

Eventually Somfai considered the role of events in the composer's life, upon which he did not want to place undue importance; he said, however,"there is no question about it, the biographical aspect is awfully important in the mood of the composer." He illustrated his point by referring to Bartók's ballet, *The Wooden Prince*, concluding that "This is a beautiful story, and I think there is no question about it that Bartók is the Prince." Somfai continued:

> Bartók deserves our gratitude and excites our interest as a great innovator. Perhaps any lingering doubt about this, our inability to frame any definite opinion of his more difficult works, comes from the fact that they are experimental and thus contain elements that do not fuse harmoniously in our perception. Yet we must remind ourselves that the fault of perception may be ours, for while his experiments were often filled with struggle and he sometimes found himself at an impasse before breaking free in his expression of musical ideas, he eventually did so.

Leighton asked Béla Bartók, Jr., if he had any recollection of the circumstances surrounding the composition of the Second Quartet. Bartók's elder son had witnessed his father's artistic struggle from within his family circle. It was an unexpected pleasure for the audience to hear him speak of his parents and of Zoltán Kodály in a conversational tone after having listened to his more formal lecture a few days earlier in the Margaret Greenham Theatre. His brief remarks made it clear that his father did not compose the movements in the order in which they appear in the completed work. It was the second movement that was written last and had presented Bartók such difficulty.

> In 1917 my father wrote a letter to my mother who was ill and in hospital. "I work very strongly on the Second Quartet," he wrote, "but I have many problems. The first and third movements are ready, finished, but I cannot finish the second movement. Very difficult for me."
>
> After one month, my mother came home, and Zoltán Kodály came to [visit] us. My father talked to him and Kodály made good suggestions to my father, and he accepted them, and after one month it [the second movement] was finished.
>
> Kodály helped . . . and it was often so, and the literature indicates this.

János Kárpáti, author of *Bartók String Quartets* (a critical analysis), spoke next, approaching the difficult question of abstraction:

> I quite agree with Mr. Somfai that in this string quartet the folk music influence is not so important [in quantity] . . . but in the further string quartets from the third to the last string quartet, we know that the folk-music influence is absorbed in the texture of the music, in the musical language of Bartók. So we cannot find one bar, or one phrase, in which there is not some element, some very abstract, structural element [drawn from folk music]. But nevertheless, I think the significance of the folk music in this quartet is very important.

Kárpáti had deduced that the Second Quartet revealed two important elements of folk-music influence, one arising from Bartók's early preoccupation with the folklore of the Carpathian Basin and reflecting an ethnic unity, and another emerging from Bartók's 1913 trip to Nigeria, where he collected important Arab folk-music sources. When describing one compositional aspect of the Second Quartet, Kárpáti referred to the "allegro barbaro" effect. Bartók's first complete assimilation of folk elements in an original work is evident in his piano piece *Allegro barbaro* (1911). The unbridled fury of this work (expressed, in part, by the percussive use of the piano) is often associated with a specific compositional technique used by Bartók to create fast passages in later works.

I think the "allegro barbaro" of the second movement is an Arab "allegro barbaro," and in the interpretation of this string quartet you can hear quite clearly this influence. In this re-mark I refer to both the structure of the scale and the bar-baric ostinato rhythm which is an imitation of Arab peasant music. But I would stress the fact that the whole movement is not an imitation, but serious, straightforward European music influenced by Arab folk music.

To illustrate his point, Kárpáti played a recorded excerpt from Bartók's *44 Duos for Two Violins*. In the *Arabian Dance* for two vio-lins, a brief work from a later period, one can hear approximately the same elements of musical texture as one hears in the Allegro molto capriccioso of the Second Quartet, because in the *Arabian Dance*, "Bartók didn't hide his intentions."

At Kárpáti's request, the Pacifica Quartet again performed the opening of the Allegro molto capriccioso, and then played a variation of the opening theme as it appears later. After listening to the char-acter of the variation, Somfai commented:

For Hungarians this music has a clearly Hungarian charac-ter, similar to the "divertimento" style of the last movement of the *Music for Strings, Percussion, and Celesta*. My point is that when a folk-music element becomes the model for Bar-tók's own theme, the development of it (the dramaturgy of how to make music of it) practically always involves other national features which were equally well known to Bartók; so it is quite natural that after a while, the Arab theme has a little Hungarian coloration to it.

Kárpárti agreed and remarked, "I think Bartók creates a quite per-sonal music, so it is not a pure imitation of Arab music, but a per-sonal, individual work."

There are works in which one can follow Bartók's composi-tional technique in which two, three, or four different kinds of folk music are absorbed in the same piece. In the third movement of the Fifth String Quartet, the so-called Bulgarian scherzo, there are Hungarian structures, Bulgarian structures, and some elements of Slovak folk music—it has a wide range of different folk-music elements that are absorbed into that movement in a quite organic unity.

Somfai responded:

> It is important to bear in mind that in Bartók's own compositions there is more than one case where a clearly Hungarian melody could be really vulgar, but by putting this idiom into, say, a Bulgarian rhythm, Bartók gives it a fine, distinguished character.
>
> There is the well-known example from the Concerto for Orchestra, the fourth movement with its beautiful melody. My Hungarian compatriots recognize that this is a real quotation from a Hungarian operetta. It has a very patriotic text. In quoting it, Bartók refines it by reshaping it rhythmically. In *Contrasts*, the melody in the trio, which is again in a kind of Bulgarian rhythm, has a Hungarian flavor. By combining the two elements—Hungarian flavor and Bulgarian rhythm—Bartók gives it new character.

Kárpáti introduced the subject of formal structure and spoke of the arch supported by two pillars each resting on the outer slow movements (often called arch form). He continued, "In the third movement [of the Second Quartet] there are some very fine and very small elements of Hungarian folk music, but they are hidden in the texture itself, so it is not quite clear how to reveal it."

The Pacifica Quartet played the motif that introduces the last movement of the Second Quartet to illustrate the descending melodic line, and Kárpáti commented:

> We Hungarian musicians feel that the basic character of this last movement is one of mourning. It is very sad—a mourning atmosphere prevails throughout the whole movement. The theme of the movement is like a Hungarian peasant lament, a melody which belongs to the grieving ritual of the peasant life in which the closest member of the family has to lament the death of his father or mother—a dirge.
>
> Naturally it is something much higher than a real dirge, since in the real dirge it is the recitative style that is dominating. The descending line of this melody is very similar to one sort of Hungarian lament.

Kárpáti illustrated the point by playing a recorded fragment of a genuine Hungarian peasant lament, and added, "I don't want to say it is an imitation of this, but behind these feelings of mourning, behind this weeping, we can sense the feeling which is in this piece."

Addressing the Pacifica Quartet, Somfai introduced a question of interpretation, asking if perhaps they had initially played the passage "a bit more beautifully than necessary. Even folk-music-influenced elements became absolutely alien to the original folk style the moment they become part of his composition . . . therefore their performance is in the manneristic, often romantic Bartókian style. You don't have to imitate anything of the peasant performance." He continued by asking Székely, "In this lamenting last movement, would it not be wise to play non-vibrato, or quasi non-vibrato?"

Székely spoke at last:

> In this particular case, not much vibrato is needed. The problem is that the ensemble just didn't build up the vibrato in the proper way. Now, that phrase is very dramatic. You could achieve the intended effect a little better if you were to use a slight, minimal rubato. That makes it more dramatic. We could discuss for a long time the ways to achieve that effect. As for the vibrato speed, I cannot prescribe the solution precisely, but you cannot just play it "straight."
>
> And besides, in this motif with its descending melodic line, one should start a little bit louder in order to achieve a slight decrescendo—just the opposite of what the ensemble has done. The "dropping" quality achieved by an agogic accent on the first note followed by the decrescendo makes the motif more dramatic, but, of course, performing it in this way is not so simple.
>
> At any rate, I wouldn't play it with so much vibrato. I would also play it more quietly and slowly.

Eager to draw Székely into a further discussion of vibrato, Somfai asked directly, "In the Fourth Quartet Bartók already wrote *senza vibrato*, but not in the earlier string quartet scores. Should one play with less vibrato, for instance in this passage, and in others where there is no specific indication?"

Székely responded, "The proportions of the vibrato—fast or slow—are not the same all the time, of course. When less intensity is needed, but the passage is not marked *senza vibrato*, simply start with less vibrato. That is an answer."

Speaking of the formal aspects of the third movement, Somfai remarked about this reflective Lento, "Bartók was very conservative in using the term *Lied* form, the German expression, as he learned it in the class of Koessler." Székely interjected, "It is hard to talk about form here, because I am not of the same opinion as Bartók himself." To this Kárpáti added, "Sometimes Bartók didn't realize, even himself, the real form. He thought always in a classical sense, but instinctively he made something quite different."

Somfai quickly took the opportunity to say, "He was very conscious [of formal elements] when making the music, so he did not have to concern himself unduly about development and relationship and being economic because that was the way he worked." Kárpáti pointed out, "Another example for this is the Fourth String Quartet . . . Bartók himself wrote the analysis in the pocket score. There is a theme in this quartet (the second theme) and Bartók wrote in his analysis that this is a transitional theme, something secondary . . . but it is a very important theme." Somfai countered suddenly, "But who said that transitional themes are not important? In many Haydn and Beethoven sonatas, that is the most exciting part of the sonata form!"

Admiring the accelerating tempo of the discussion, Leighton said jokingly to the audience, "You can see that this was not rehearsed! I have to tell you that before we came in, Professor Székely asked me what could he possibly contribute to the discussion this evening, and I think he has demonstrated already just how much he can contribute! Perhaps we can talk now about the evolution of the later quartets and the influence of folk music in those works."

Somfai launched into a discussion of the positive-negative relationship of Bartók's use of the folk-music elements:

> What is the dramaturgical role of folk music in his string quartets? Is it good or bad, positive or negative? In *The Wooden Prince,* the folk element, whether in the *verbunkos* style or folk-song style, quite clearly represents the negative world.
>
> Even in the Second Quartet, the most barbaric [elements] set against the freedom of the lyric sections come from the folk music. It is probably safe to say that in the development of Bartók's concept, the [abstracted] folk music [element] in certain pieces was used to express negative aspects in the dramaturgy of the form. But this changed considerably from the Third String Quartet on.

Kárpáti again spoke of the abstraction of the folk elements: "I think that in the case of the Third Quartet, the folk-music elements are so incorporated into the musical language, it is impossible to detach them in some concrete form. These elements are quite in the musical texture itself."

Somfai continued:

> Wouldn't you say that this "Boy dance" in the *seconda parte* is quite a direct quotation? This is a very unusual structure, a one-movement piece marked *prima parte; seconda parte; ricapitulazione de prima parte*, and *coda*. As you have correctly described it, it starts with lyrical, "ego" material, with lots of romantic elements. This is a very alien and very pessimistic world. Then comes this much more open, dancing *seconda parte*. So in the dramaturgy of the piece, to put it simply, the folk music represents the positive world. From the Third Quartet on, if I'm not wrong, the folk music is always the sunny or the optimistic, and usually appears as the ending movement.

"You are right," Kárpáti agreed. "and beginning from this Third Quartet, it is always the last movement which we can say is always optimistic."

> There are very small elements of folk music, only a three-note [motif], very typical of Hungarian folk music. There is a small, original form of the pentatonic scale, the basic element of pentatonicism, and this three-note [motif] becomes the structural element of the whole *prima parte*; so in this case, I think that the folkloristic element is not quite clear. I agree with Mr. Somfai that in the *seconda parte*, this is quite a real folk dance, but I couldn't say whether it is Hungarian or Rumanian . . . Eastern European, perhaps, but it is not quite clear. In this context, I would like to quote Bartók himself from an interview given to Denijs Dille in 1937: "The melodic world of my string quartets doesn't essentially differ from that of folk songs. It is just that their setting is more strict."

This was a very important declaration, I think.

Somfai returned to the question of form:

How about speaking of the bridge [arch] form of the Fourth and Fifth Quartet? That is a very dangerous topic indeed, because people are very much impressed by the symmetry of this form, where the first and last, and second and fourth movements use the same thematic material, and in the middle there is a kind of bridge, which can be slow or fast. In fact it is too easy to make too much of this symmetry.

Because this is a very sophisticated audience, I would like to tell you what interests me about this question. I think the bridge form, or the palindromic form—starting and ending with the same material—was one of Bartók's great discoveries and one of his great toys. Not to say more.

As you probably know, he used this symmetrical, palindromic form in a one-movement formation as well in multi-movement, cyclic form. One of the loveliest, the earliest crystal-clear uses of it is in the *Three Rondos on Folk Tunes*. Now, it was a great challenge to him to make this form work, but after a while he tried to get away from it, and there are many kinds of ways to get away from the symmetrical form; for example, having the same material in the first and last movement but doing something completely different in the middle part as in the variation movement of the Violin Concerto.

Now why do I make such a big fuss over this symmetry? Because this symmetry was very soon combined with the symmetry of the first movement, for example presenting the themes in reverse order as in the Fifth Quartet, first movement, or not just in reverse order, but presenting them in inversion in the recapitulation.

Now to put it very simply, how many good melodies, good themes, can you figure out that are equally good and musical if they are in an inversion? How many musical sequences can you find that are natural, beautiful, and straightforward, which can be played in retrograde? One might succeed occasionally in using retrograde, but even Bartók got tired of it, because his music was limited by it.

If you look at the thematic material of the Fifth Quartet, first movement, the intervals which could be used in this piece are very, very limited. . . . I don't know if I am alone with this opinion, but that is why I told you that I think the palindromic form was one of Bartók's greatest discoveries, but a dangerous toy.

Kárpáti spoke of symmetry and asymmetry:

In Bartók's life-work there are some compositions in which he was wavering between the symmetrical forms and the asymmetrical forms, the three- or five-movement, or the two- or four-movement form. . . . After the Fifth String Quartet, which is in five movements, he chose the four-movement form for his last quartet.

Both musicologists continued to discuss Bartók's use of palindromic formal structures, illustrating their remarks with examples drawn from the literature. "We musicologists are working on *this*," Somfai declared, directing attention to details of the form he had illustrated on the blackboard. "We should care much about *this*," he concluded, pointing to the schemata of the unifed whole. "Bartók is not static at all. He is very dynamic."

Leighton eventually brought the discussion to a close by asking for questions from the audience, who responded eagerly. That Bartók's compositional processes remain elusive is certain, since he ultimately worked within the realm of art, not science. But to the panelists it was a certainty that those processes are in some ways observable. They continued to share their observations of the phenomenon throughout the enthusiastic exchange that filled the remaining time.

Perhaps the pinnacle of the Banff celebration of Bartók's Centenary was reached with this discussion, "The Influence of Folk Music on the Compositions of Béla Bartók." The dialogue between Somfai and Kárpáti, Székely's interjections on interpretation, and the telling remarks by Béla Bartók, Jr., brought the audience nearer to understanding Bartók's unique qualities. His power of imagination, with its immense audacity and fertility, his superb mastery of the architectural forms, and his uncanny ability to abstract folklore—these are the qualities that give his masterpieces universality.

Chapter Twenty-eight

The Academy of String Quartets

During the 1980s Zoltán Székely dedicated himself to teaching chamber music. In ten consecutive sessions of the Banff Centre's Academy of String Quartets, many outstanding ensembles came from all over the world to study with him during the intensive spring terms. With his colleagues Fenyves, Magyar, and Koromzay (who returned to Banff in 1979 after some years' absence), he formed the nucleus of a distinguished faculty.

Two outstanding Hungarian ensembles—the Eder Quartet and the Takács Quartet—came to study with Székely in the early 1980s. The ensembles shared a bountiful common background. Both were founded while the members were students of the Franz Liszt Academy in Budapest.[1] Both studied with András Mihály; the Takács Quartet was coached by Sándor Devich after 1977. In quick succession the two quartets received international acclaim by winning important string quartet competitions in Europe.[2]

In 1981 the Takács Quartet came to Banff to study the Bartók string quartets with Székely, although they had already recorded the cycle for Hungaroton. When they returned to Budapest, they appeared on Hungarian Television in a documentary telecast in which they were coached by Dénes Koromzay. Before parting with the Takács Quartet, Koromzay, who was again on the staff of the University of Colorado, suggested that during their forthcoming tour in the United States he would arrange a gala concert for them in Boulder.

Their first appearance there proved so successful that the University of Colorado invited them to return for six weeks in 1983. The following year they made a third visit and began preparing the Beethoven cycle under Koromzay's direction. After several shorter residencies on the Boulder campus, they were invited to join the staff of the University of Colorado as quartet-in-residence, which they did. The Takács Quartet continued to live and work in Colorado while still actively pursuing their international concert and recording career.

During their rehearsals of the classical literature, puzzling over the phrasing or the rhythm, a member of the Takács Quartet may joke, "Well, we haven't had a letter from Beethoven," meaning there are many interpretations. But they do have an unusual link to Bartók. They feel they know what he wanted, that they understand Bartók's intentions. After their intensive study in Banff with Székely and their ongoing professional association with their mentor, Koromzay, the Takács Quartet indeed has "a letter from Bartók."

The first Banff International String Quartet Competition was one of many events planned to mark the fiftieth anniversary in 1983 of the Banff Centre's School of Fine Arts. The jury was a distinguished one: violinists Andrew Dawes (Canada) of the Orford Quartet and Emanuel Hurwitz (U.K.) of the Aeolian Quartet, violists Raphael Hillyer (U.S.) and Piero Farulli (Italy), past members of the Juilliard Quartet and Quartetto Italiano respectively, and cellists Mischa Schneider (U.S.) formerly of the Budapest Quartet and Ede Banda (Hungary) of the Tatrai Quartet.

The triumvirate of artistic directors for the competition— Fenyves, Rolston, and Székely—had the daunting task of examining all serious applications from around the world and finally selecting ten competing quartets. Kenneth Murphy, executive director of the competition, has commented about the Banff Centre's "Competition with a difference."

> We like to think of the week's event as mainly a festival of string quartet playing. In order to emphasize this festival atmosphere, and to play down the competitive aspect of the event, we have ignored some of the traditions of music competitions. Indeed, although there is a jury sitting quietly at the back of the hall for each session, there is nothing else to suggest that a competition is in progress until the end of the fourth day, when the first eliminations are announced.

We do not, for example, eliminate some of the competitors after their first performance. No quartets are eliminated until every group has performed about ninety minutes of music from their chosen repertoire of complete works from the classical and romantic periods, a twentieth-century composition, and the imposed piece.

However, although we have done everything possible to make the Banff competition a fair one, it remains a difficult one. The competition is intended for ensembles of international caliber who hope to make the study and performance of the vast literature of the string quartet the main focus of their professional careers. This is a grueling event for the contestants—a test of their stamina as well as of their musicianship.

The success of a competition is not in the degree of fame achieved by the winners, but in the degree to which all the competitors benefit from the experience of having taken part. The Banff competition has been designed to ensure that, although there will be winners, there will be no losers.[3]

The five winners of the 1983 competition were (in order): the Colorado Quartet (U.S.), the Hagen Quartet (Austria), the Lydian Quartet (U.S.), which was judged to have given the best performance of the imposed piece, *Movement for String Quartet* by Harry Somers; the Mendelssohn Quartet (U.S.), and the Eder Quartet (Hungary).

Nine years after the competition, violinist Julie Rosenfeld reflected on the Colorado Quartet's having won the first competition—the greatest endurance test her quartet had ever faced. "One of the most rewarding things for us after we won in 1983 was actually sitting down with the jury and talking to them about what they liked and didn't like in our playing . . . then the chance to come back to Banff and study with people like Zoltán Székely and Lorand Fenyves."[4]

Although the first competition was conceived as a one-time event, in April of 1986 a second competition was held at Banff. Once more a distinguished international jury was assembled.[5] Ten quartets competed. After a festive week of recitals, four winners emerged (in order): the Franciscan Quartet (U.S.), the Carmina Quartet (Switzerland), the Lark Quartet (U.S.), and the Cavani Quartet (U.S.). The Quatuor Parisii (France) was judged to have given the best performance of the imposed piece, *Three Archetypes* by John Hawkins.

With the international reputation of the competition well-established, a third competition took place in 1989. After listening to the unidentified tapes of twenty-nine prospective contestants, all three of the preliminary jurors—Zdenek Konicek, Eugene Lehner, and Gerald Stanick—attested to the unusually high level of accomplishment of the ten quartets they chose for the competition. As before, the jury was made up of luminaries from the international quartet community.[6] The four winners of the third Banff International String Quartet Competition were (in order): the Quatuor Manfred (France), the Cassatt Quartet (U.S.), which was judged to have given the best performance of the imposed piece, Allan Bell's *Arche II*, the Keller Quartet (Hungary), and the Brindisi Quartet (U.K.).

During the 1980s the Banff Centre had begun to provide advanced training and development for professional artists already embarked on promising careers. Formal courses were being replaced by short-term and long-term residencies. Winners of the Banff International String Quartet Competition were encouraged to return to the Banff Centre where they could further enhance their careers under the guidance of Zoltán Székely and Lorand Fenyves, while being provided with facilities, space, technical support, and opportunities for collaboration and experimentation.

For Zoltán Székely, the new decade dedicated to teaching chamber music became a time of prize winning after the Franz Liszt Academy conferred an honorary professorship on him during the Bartók Centenary in 1981. The Béla Bartók Award in 1982 and the Zoltán Kodály Award in 1983 came to Székely, the violinist; later for Székely, the composer, the Bartók-Pásztory Prize in 1987.

To mark the occasion of his eightieth birthday on 8 December 1983, Székely was awarded the Order of the Flag of Honor, a state award which recognizes substantial contributions made by Hungarians living abroad. Gyula Budal, Hungary's ambassador to Canada, came to Banff to bestow the decoration. The scroll, with its citation signed by both Pál Lasonczi, president of the council, and Inre Katona, secretary, stated: "The President's Council of the Hungarian People's Republic wishes to honor Zoltán Székely, violinist, for his outstanding artistic endeavors and his activities in strengthening international relations in the musical art. We present him with the Order of the Flag of the Hungarian People's Republic."

In 1987 Mientje began living at Banff's Mineral Springs Hospital, and no day passed without Székely's going to the hospital to spend several hours with her during the early evening. After more than sixty-five years together there continued to be daily communication between them, even though Mientje did not always recognize him. On those occasions they spent their time together in silent communion in her room.

In September of 1990 Mientje lapsed into a coma. After one week, she passed away without having regained consciousness. She was ninety-two.

A memorial service was held in Banff within a few days. Surrounded by his family and friends, Székely sat pensively as the Hungarian Quartet's recording of the lento assai from Beethoven's last quartet sounded his farewell. Far from Holland where she had been born in 1898, Mientje Székely was buried in Banff's tranquil, rustic cemetery. The release from her long illness may have been a blessing, but nothing has blunted the edge of Zoltán Székely's sorrow at the loss.

Shortly after Mientje's death, Székely found it possible, during a period of changing political climate in Hungary, to divest himself of property he had possessed since the death of his parents. To Piroska's surviving son, Székely gave the family home in rural Dunavarsányi where his nephews had grown up.

Having read Mientje's obituary in Holland, three of Székely's former students with whom he had lost touch now sent their condolences and restored the friendships that had been nurtured between pupil and teacher a half-century earlier. These violinists he had known as young girls were now women in their seventies; all had pursued careers in Holland and were now enjoying their retirements. Drawn together once more by their efforts to reach Székely whom they had not seen for decades, they soon met in Amsterdam for a reunion lunch, together again as they had been in their youth in the 1930s.

String quartets as diverse as the Audubon Quartet from Virginia and the Atlantic Quartet from Canada's Maritime Provinces arrived throughout the winter to study, and Székely rallied from his period of mourning to meet the demands of his teaching.

The Atlantic Quartet came to study Bartók's First Quartet, and Haydn and Mendelssohn quartets as well. Székely's teaching regimen became even more austere and demanding. During the carefully planned coaching sessions there was no indulgence, no recourse to poetic imagery, only the facts of the music itself were considered through the study of its formal structures.

The Audubon Quartet, resident ensemble of the Virginia Poly-
technic Institute and State University in Blacksburg, Virginia, is at
home in the major concerts hall of the world. In Lincoln Center, the
Kennedy Center, the Academy of Santa Cecilia in Rome, and London's Wigmore Hall, they are hailed by critics for their technical virtuosity and luminous sound, for their interpretations of the classical
masterworks and their outstanding presentation of new quartets such
as David Baker's *Through a Vale of Tears*, Ezra Laderman's Quartet No.
6, or *American Dreams* by Peter Schickele.

Prepared to restudy Bartók's Fifth Quartet during a brief winter
residency at the Banff Centre, the Audubon Quartet called upon Székely the evening before starting their work together. After the genial
social amenities were concluded, he requested, to their surprise, that
first thing the next day they play a Mozart quartet. By this means he
would acquaint himself with their artistic capabilities and, once assured of their musicianship and ensemble skills, launch the most appropriate work on Bartók's Fifth Quartet. When the Audubon Quartet departed a week later, their view of Bartók's masterpiece was
subtly enhanced by his solutions to its performance problems. As a
parting gesture of gratitude, they gave Székely a gift which he soon
learned to enjoy, a portable compact disc player upon which he could
listen to the reissue of the Hungarian Quartet's 1953 Beethoven cycle.

Somewhat later, their performance of the Fifth Quartet in Los
Angeles aroused the interest of Herbert Glass, critic of the *Los Angeles
Times*, who wrote: "Bartók's Fifth Quartet was set forth without the
rhythmic ferocity and craggy articulation many ensembles—notably,
these days the Emerson Quartet and the Alban Berg Quartet—bring
to the composer's scores, but instead, the Audubon offered a more
lyrical, less intense approach, rather like what one hears from the
best Hungarian ensembles."[7]

Such critical review of opposing styles in Bartók performances
began early in the 1950s, when the Hungarian Quartet's early appearances in the United States drew comparisons with those of the
Juilliard Quartet. Robert Mann, leader of the Juilliard Quartet, wrote
candidly of the phenomenon in *The Strad* magazine:

There were two very different ways of interpreting Bartók in
the earlier days. One, typified by the Juilliard style, was
thrusting and exciting, very powerful emotionally, and dramatic. The other was the Hungarian Quartet's version, and

these were people who knew Bartók intimately. Their style was much smoother and not so driving, and if there's a difference between *our* approach then and now . . . I'd say that we have tried to endorse some of the qualities of both worlds.[8]

Many outstanding chamber music artists periodically join the faculty of the Academy of Chamber Music to serve the changing needs of the international participants who arrive each spring. Bonnie Hampton,[9] the distinguished American cellist who teaches in the academy, discussed her impressions of Székely's teaching in a 1992 interview.

I had just finished my own teaching when one of the young French-Canadian quartets invited me to join them for their coaching with Zoltán Székely. They would be working on the variation movement from Beethoven's Op. 18, No. 5.

When we arrived at Székely's studio, it was obvious that he was prepared to work with them on this particular Beethoven movement. He began by discussing Beethoven's displacement of the bar-lines by a half-bar in these variations. It was an interesting concept that would help the quartet avoid a false metric phrasing and remain receptive to the larger concept of the movement with its natural phrase shapes.

After discussing that matter for a while, he asked them to play, but soon stopped them. He began working in minute detail over every rhythmic stress, every chordal balance, every nuance of the musical ideas that concerned shaping of the phrases. He brought their attention to bear on exactly what they were hearing at any given moment. I was fascinated to observe this fine musical mind at work.

I soon had to leave for a final rehearsal of a Mendelssohn sonata with Ruth Laredo, since we were performing it that evening. When we reached the end of the first movement and paused to consider what we had done, I suddenly questioned myself in view of what I had just observed in Székely's teaching. The experience had brought to my mind many things which are easily overlooked, and I realized my own awareness had been raised.

Later I asked the young quartet what had happened after I had departed for my own rehearsal. They explained that finally they had played the movement through after two hours of hard work. They felt that Székely's coaching had given them a new concept. A broader vision had emerged from the careful scrutiny of the minute details.

It seems to me that as musicians we are either "detail people" or "overview people." Whether our performances are mosaics and the challenge is to reach the whole or whether we begin with a sense of the whole and must go back searching for the details—there is surely a strong argument for working in either direction. But I think my observation of Székely's teaching was the clearest example I had seen of how such detailed work can have fruition in achieving clarity of the whole.

I know from studying with Casals that he insisted on considering every note, every musical relationship. Yet, as we know, his playing (and certainly in his later years, his conducting) ultimately had the greatest clarity of vision.

I remember a rehearsal of Schumann's Fourth Symphony at the Casals Festival in Puerto Rico during which the musicians of that exceptional orchestra—concertmasters, chamber music artists, and many seasoned orchestral players, some of whom had been in Toscanini's orchestra as young men—submitted themselves to Casals' influence and were amazed by his way of working. He began with meticulous scrutiny of the first few lines of the music. The work went very slowly for almost an hour, but everyone worked with the best will, even the very seasoned orchestral veterans who had a vast experience with the work. Finally Casals released the orchestra from these demands and played the first movement from beginning to end. When the last chord sounded, the players leapt to their feet and applauded him. It was a revelation! It was as though one had heard the work for the first time. The orchestra's remarkable reaction to the experience was one of spontaneous joy.

Both Casals and Székely remained devoted to raising one's awareness in this way, knowing that the brain-ear conception is heightened and the music is finally heard "as though for the first time." With these great men, the pedagogical approach is not a planned maneuver in the sense of "I will do it this way and cause that to happen," but rather the living of a certain attitude toward music-making. They have an insight into musical thinking that is sublime.[10]

In 1992 winter weather ended abruptly in March. The snow melted during unusually balmy days. The early arrival of spring was welcome, the greening of the campus of the Banff Centre a heartening sight. As the winter term drew to a close with a flurry of concert activity and teaching, Székely was at work preparing himself for the arrival of Gwen Hoebig,[11] the distinguished Canadian violinist, now concertmaster of the Winnipeg Symphony Orchestra. She was coming for coaching on the Bartók Violin Concerto before her forthcoming performances in Winnipeg. His table covered with scores, annotated violin parts, photocopies of manuscripts, the Stradivarius open in its case, Székely reminded himself that he should review for her the many details in this complicated work.

> Gwen should be told Bartók's idea for the placement of the harp, the celesta. It can improve the possibility for good ensemble playing, especially in the variation movement where there are certain critical passages between the solo violin and these instruments.
> If the French horn goes too slowly here, what must one do? This passage is difficult. It requires concentration. It is hard to accommodate any problems in the orchestra. Will they respond easily, quickly? That depends, in part, on the conductor. Mengelberg was not always at home in new music, but he understood how to make this tutti sound. Whose marking is this? Susskind's? Susskind was amazed by the orchestration, so full of nuance, color, but I find this passage with the xylophone was not such a good idea of Bartók's. The intonation is difficult.

The return to the Banff Centre was a homecoming for Gwen Hoebig. She had studied there for ten summers during which she often appeared as a recitalist and as soloist with the Banff Centre's resident ensemble, the Canadian Chamber Orchestra.

"I first came to the Banff Centre in 1968 to study with David Martin when I was a child," Gwen Hoebig said in a recent interview.

> Then it was still only a summer school and the campus was not yet developed with its present facilities—the music wing, the recording studios, the theater complex. My brother, Desmond, who is a cellist, and I went down to the town every day where our group met to work at the elementary school on Squirrel Street.
> I returned in subsequent summers to study with Lorand Fenyves and David Zafer. After a decade I was told by Thomas

Rolston that during the summer of 1979 I might study the Bartók Violin Concerto with Zoltán Székely.

I vividly remember the feeling of entering his apartment in Lloyd Hall. Once across that threshold, the pace of life slowed, although the study was very intense. As we began to work, no detail slipped by him unnoticed, and in the sanctuary of his studio, the different manuscripts and editions were always consulted for tempo markings, articulations, and fingerings he had used for many of his own performances.

From the first entrance of the violin, we went over every detail carefully. At that time I had no idea of the style or phrasing of this concerto, but soon all the inflections of the music derived from the Hungarian language were brought to my attention. I was challenged with many solutions of fingerings and bowings until he was satisfied that everything had been considered. But unfortunately during the next few years no opportunity arose for me to perform the work.

Coming back to Banff in 1992 to prepare the Bartók concerto with Székely for performance was a dream come true. To me he seems unchanged, still as firm in his musical convictions as ever, yet completely flexible in his approach to my playing. He has so much insight into this work and shares it generously. I realized that much I had learned during my earlier study with him had lasted intact with me—a testimory to his precision as a teacher. I hope that these final details will remain with me as strongly.[12]

When it was known that Gwen Hoebig would perform the Bartók Violin Concerto in an impromptu session in Roubakine Hall, accompanied at the piano by her husband, David Moroz, a crowd gathered. Many of the young international students knew Zoltán Székely only as the dedicatee of Bartók's great masterpiece. His rare presence in Roubakine Hall caused an excited response. A half-hour later with the closing measures of the concerto, thunderous applause broke out. Gwen Hoebig put down her violin and walked to Székely's side.

"That was fine, Gwen," he whispered, his eyes twinkling with approval. These few words, sufficient approbation from the source of such knowledge, were a very genuine compliment given with an affectionate handshake.

In his early nineties, Székely continues to plan each day's activities as he has always done. He scrutinizes the daily newspapers to keep abreast of world events, studies the musical works that constantly demand his attention, and reads again the monuments of the violin literature to bring himself ever closer to the wisdom of such men as Leopold Mozart and Carl Flesch. Despite his increasing deafness, he systematically practices the violin, although he no longer appears in public nor demonstrates passages during coaching sessions.

When the opportunity arises, he eagerly indulges his avid, lifelong interest in tennis—now through the medium of television. He watches the important matches with absolute concentration, mesmerized by the strategies of the new players, momentarily oblivious to Beethoven or Bartók, or the sound of ringing doorbells and telephones.

He enjoys brief shopping forays in the village of Banff. Once he arrives on the corner of Wolf and Bear streets, having been driven down the winding road on Tunnel Mountain in his ancient blue Dodge, he consults his terse shopping list. A few items to be found in the grocery, the hardware store, and the pharmacy usually complete his list. The sight of the great violinist slowly making his way along the village streets arouses the palpable joy of recognition in many who have witnessed his peregrinations during the last two decades. If now he murmurs, "Langsam, langsam" ("Slow, slow"), somewhat discouraged by his shortened stride and slow progress, it is only because he prefers to get his shopping finished quickly, then return home to Lloyd Hall.

Letters from colleagues, friends, and relatives arrive almost daily, as well as greetings from the more than one hundred young string quartets to whom he has become a source of information and inspiration. Indeed, as the mentor of the Academy of String Quartets, Zoltán Székely is an integral part of the great legacy of the Banff Centre, the history of which David Leighton has expressed so eloquently:

> The history of the Centre is, above all, the story of individuals, men and women with a common purpose: to create on a mountainside overlooking the Bow Valley in the Rocky Mountains a school to foster the flowering and maturing of the arts and management in Canada and around the world. These individuals comprise a brilliant parade of artists, builders, and dreamers who shared a vision and made it come true.[13]

Rarely does a world-class string quartet emerge in Canada, although the Hart House String Quartet, Canada's most famous chamber ensemble of the first half of the twentieth century, established an enviable artistic reputation from its first appearance in 1923. Among the post-war Canadian quartets, the Orford Quartet attained similar recognition on the international scene.

Only one Canadian quartet, Edmonton's Debut Quartet, has been accepted into any of the first three Banff International String Quartet Competitions. In 1992 the St. Lawrence String Quartet was accepted for the fourth competition.

The St. Lawrence Quartet was formed in 1989 by four of Canada's most gifted young string players—violinists Geoff Nuttall and Barry Shiffman, violist Lesley Robertson, and cellist Marina Hoover. These four instrumentalists of uncommon ability trained variously at the University of Toronto, the Curtis Institute, Juilliard, and Yale University. While fulfilling a two-year residency at Hartt School of Music under the guidance of the Emerson Quartet, the young Canadians lived in New York, rehearsed, concertized, and in the summer of 1991 entered the Melbourne International Competition and Canada's Glory of Mozart Competition, winning second prize in both events.

Recently named teaching assistants to the members of the Juilliard Quartet, the St. Lawrence Quartet lives and works in New York City. There they presented a highly successful debut recital on 17 November 1992, performing Mozart's String Quartet, K. 465 ("Dissonance"), Alban Berg's String Quartet, Op. 3, and Beethoven's Op. 131."The evening's tour de force was, appropriately, Alban Berg's Quartet (Op. 3), a thunderous announcement of musical individuality," wrote Alex Ross in the *New York Times*. "In the future, this quartet should make its presence felt."[14] The St. Lawrence Quartet did make its presence felt one week later by repeating this program at the Kennedy Center in Washington, D.C. Mark Carrington wrote in the *Washington Post*, "Like partners in a high-wire act, the St. Lawrence has complete faith in its skills and vision . . . by listening intently, we for a minute can share that thrill."[15]

In a 1992 interview, Marina Hoover spoke of their work with Székely at the Banff Centre.

> We returned to Banff in the summer of 1991 to prepare for the Melbourne Competition. As members of the academy we coached with both Thomas Brandis from Berlin and Zoltán Székely.
>
> Geoff and I had worked with Mr. Székely three years ear-

lier on Beethoven's Op. 135 and he was glad to see us return with the St. Lawrence Quartet. He seemed interested in our quartet and worked hard with us on both Beethoven's Op. 131 and the Third Quartet of Bartók, the first major contemporary quartet we had learned and a work that was by then sufficiently developed for us to present it to him in a serious way.

His coachings are difficult. You have to have a lot of patience to work in such detail as he explains, for instance, the articulations that the Hungarian Quartet adopted over a long period. We tried to absorb these musical details into our own style.[16]

Like the previous three competitions, the Fourth Banff International String Quartet Competition captured the interest of young professional quartets around the world. Marjan Mozetich's work, *Lament in the Trampled Garden*, a poetic and dramatically lyrical piece that made great demands upon the performers' interpretational skill, was commissioned by the Canadian Broadcasting Corporation as the imposed work for 1992. The preliminary jury—Lorand Fenyves, Jaroslav Karlovsky, and Martha Strongin Katz—selected ten outstanding ensembles, among them the St. Lawrence Quartet.

In mid-April the members of the jury began to arrive. From the United States came violinist Earl Carlyss, twenty-year veteran of the Juilliard Quartet, and Julie Rosenfeld, leader of the Colorado Quartet, who had won the competition in 1983. They were joined by cellist Philip de Groote (U.K.) of the Chilingirian Quartet, violinists Andrew Dawes of the Orford Quartet (chairman of the jury), and Sándor Devich (Hungary) of the Bartók String Quartet, now head of the chamber music department at the Franz Liszt Academy, and two violists, Jaroslav Karlovsky of both the Prague and the Czech String Quartets and Milan Skampa of the Smetana String Quartet.

For three days, the quartets appeared in the Margaret Greenham Theatre in performances of their chosen repertoire of classical, romantic, and contemporary works. On the fourth day Marjan Mozetich joined the jury to hear consecutive performances of his *Lament in the Trampled Garden* before a capacity audience of chamber music connoisseurs. The second playing was by the St. Lawrence Quartet. With this performance—later acknowledged by the jury as the outstanding performance of the new work—they established themselves at the forefront of the competitors.

After the semifinals, four quartets appeared in the Eric Harvie Theatre for the final round. This change of venue from the intimacy of the Margaret Greenham Theatre to the larger hall brought a new reality to the competition. An audience of eight hundred filled the hall to hear the Mandelring Quartet (Germany) play the Brahms' Quartet, Op. 51, No. 1; the Ying Quartet (U.S.) play Schubert's masterpiece, Op. 161; the Amati Quartet (Switzerland) perform Op. 51, No. 2, by Brahms; and the St. Lawrence Quartet play Beethoven's Op. 131.

Andrew Dawes announced the winners: fourth prize to the Amati Quartet, third to the Manderling Quartet, second to the Ying Quartet—and with this news came the realization that the St. Lawrence Quartet had won the first prize. Applause erupted from the audience as the Canadians appeared on stage to accept the honor, then a few minutes later, to perform Mozetich's *Lament in the Trampled Garden* in a live radio broadcast to the nation produced by the Canadian Broadcasting Corporation. A few hours later while flying to New York City, the St. Lawrence Quartet gave telephone press interviews via satellite from their Air Canada jet.

Székely, who had retired to his apartment after having heard the St. Lawrence Quartet perform Beethoven's Op. 131, did not know the outcome of the competition until the following day, when on Sunday morning he was pleased to hear of the triumph of the young Canadians.

With the departure of the jury, the competitors, and the chamber music audience, quiet returned to the Banff Centre. During the days that followed, Székely returned to his study of David Blum's book, *The Art of Quartet Playing*.[17]

I read with interest the book of the Guarneri Quartet. They have intelligent solutions to many problems. I am particularly interested because the Hungarian Quartet faced these same problems and solved many of them in a similar way. It is good that they think about these things. Many quartets do not.

They speak of the dynamic markings in Beethoven. It is true, for instance, that not every composer uses the *pianissimo* with the intent that Beethoven does, and as the Guarneri Quartet remarks, Beethoven sometimes indicates *pianissimo* followed by a crescendo and then *piano*. The question does arise as to whether a *subito piano* is actually intended. And the *sforzando* certainly is not a static effect, but must always be considered within the dynamic range in which it appears.

Some of these specific problems come up because young quartets simply aren't taught to read the music well and to take all these markings into consideration. As a violinist, I was not taught this thoroughly as a boy in Hubay's class, since, of course, the solo repertoire has a somewhat different character and other demands, but the study of all the dynamic markings in the classical quartets is very important. I had to learn this during thirty-five years playing quartets.

These are all things one thinks about if one is studying the music seriously. What one does with this knowledge is perhaps for each person a little different, but the markings must be studied and considered carefully since these matters are especially significant in Beethoven.

And for some of these problems there are no clear answers. The notation only imperfectly conveys the exact meaning. Every quartet that plays the Grosse Fuge has to question Beethoven's notation when he writes twice the same pitch, connects them with the slur mark, but it is not a tie. The Guarneri Quartet mentions the Piano Sonata, Op. 110, in which Beethoven does something similiar and marks each note with a change of finger. This marking must indicate sounding both notes.

The Hungarian Quartet arrived at the solution to make a kind of pulsation with the bow and the vibrato, so the second note of each group is barely articulated, but there is definitely a sense of two notes. Not a tie.

I remember once after a Beethoven cycle in Paris, Klemperer came backstage at the Salle Gaveau, and we spoke of this passage and Beethoven's notation. Klemperer was very interested in the Grosse Fuge and agreed with our solution, the kind of pulsation I referred to. He and I also agreed that sometimes what Beethoven writes is mysterious.

Having revived this distant memory of Otto Klemperer backstage at Salle Gaveau, Zoltán Székely closed his book and sat musing in his favorite chair, surrounded as always by bookcases overflowing with well-worn string quartet scores, his Stradivarius violin, the "Michelangelo," nearby in its open case. But precisely at one o'clock Zoltán Székely will rise from his chair, pull on his cap, and leave his apartment in Lloyd Hall. As he has done every afternoon for almost two decades, the great *primarius* will make his way down the woodland path to lunch, perhaps glancing fleetingly at the mountain panorama as he strolls—and no doubt thinking further about Beethoven's Grosse Fuge.

Béla Bartók Letters

The collection of extant correspondence between Béla Bartók and the Székelys comes from the period 1923 to 1940. Carefully preserved by Mientje Székely for seventy years, most of this correspondence survived the troubled years of World War Two, although some important documents were lost including the final text of the agreement between Bartók and Székely regarding the Violin Concerto. The collection was brought to the United States by the Székelys in 1950 where it now remains with Frank Székely-Everts.

The forty-six items in the collection comprise twenty-eight letters, thirteen postcards, four greetings from guest books, and one undated postscript. Thirty-five of the forty-six items appear in various forms in the text. Their location in the text is indicated in the citation that precedes each item. All of the items can be read in their entirety and in chronological order in Appendix A.

The correspondence originally written in Hungarian or German appears in an English translation by János Csaba and Almut Chateau that preserves Bartók's unique style of personal expression, his idiosyncratic punctuation, and several brief musical examples in his own script. The sons of Béla Bartók—Béla Bartók, Jr., (Budapest) and Péter Bartók (Florida)—have made possible the publication of their father's unpublished letters to the Székelys in this book. The brief musical examples in A-6, A-21, A-38, A-41, A-43, and A-44 are published by permission of Boosey and Hawkes, Inc. Originally published as number 213 in *Béla Bartók Letters* by János Demény, A-39 is republished by permission of Faber and Faber Ltd.

A-1. *To Zoltán Székely, Berg en Dalscheweg 127, Nijmegen, Holland. (Original in Hungarian.) See Chapter Seven, p. 60.*

Budapest, 1923, January 19.

Dear Székely!

I received your letter with thanks. Yesterday a letter from Prunières came in which he writes he isn't in a position to pay you. Indeed nor could he arrange any private engagements for me as he could last year, thus this time the whole concert is canceled.

I enclose a letter to Calvocoressi (music writer and critic, his address: 6 Boulton's Square, London, S.W. 3) in which I recommend you to him.

Around the 25th I will send the piano and violin parts of the sonata as well as the violin part of the Stravinsky.

Many greetings,

Bartók

A-2. *To Zoltán Székely, Berg en Dalscheweg 127, Nijmegen, Holland. (Postcard. Original in German.) See Chapter Seven, p. 60.*

Budapest, 25 February 1923.

Dear Székely!

I am sorry that you cannot come to the concert. It was impossible to postpone the thing, so the concert will take place and the Stravinsky cannot be played, of course. [Ede] Zathureczky will play the Sonata; it will go quite well, I believe.

I ask you to send back the Sonata and the Stravinsky parts <u>as soon as possible</u>.

With greetings and best wishes,

Bartók

A-3. *To Zoltán Székely, c/o Fam. Bloemen, Jacob Obrechtstraat 49, Amsterdam. Redirected to Berg en Dalscheweg 127, Nijmegen, Holland. (Postcard. Original in Hungarian.) See Chapter Seven, p. 65.*

[London] 1923. May 1.

Dear Székely!

The concert in Utrecht will be on May 11. I will arrive there that morning, thus we can have a thorough and <u>calm</u> rehearsal in the afternoon. I hope you have completely recovered and won't get sick before Utrecht.

Many greetings,

Bartók

A-4. To Zoltán Székely, Berg en Dalscheweg 127, Nijmegen, Holland. (Postcard. Original in Hungarian.) See Chapter Seven, p. 65.

7. Sidney Place, London S.W. 7.
1923. May 4.

Dear Székely!

They found more engagements here for me than I expected, therefore I cannot return before the 13th. I sent a telegram and a letter to Suikerman that he should move the concert in Utrecht to the 14th or 15th. I hope he will be able to do it; I asked him to notify you of the new date. I seem to remember that you are free on these days. If the Utrecht concert will take place, I will arrive there on the morning of the concert and plan to stay at the Hotel des Pays-Bas.

Many greetings,

Bartók

A-5. To Zoltán Székely, Berg en Dalscheweg 127, Nijmegen, Holland. (Postcard. Original in Hungarian.) See Chapter Seven, p. 65.

London, 1923. May 8.

Dear Székely,

Suikerman has not responded to date concerning the concert in Utrecht, thus no doubt it will be canceled; I have to make a decision about when I leave here regardless of Utrecht. I depart on the evening of the 14th because even on that afternoon I have some business here which, of course, I would not have accepted if I had received news from Suikerman; but now I cannot wait any longer. I am sorry that the concerts in Holland had this many hurdles. Would you please send the sonata to my address in Budapest. I haven't yet spoken with Taylor or Goosens.

Many greetings,

Bartók

A-6. A greeting from Béla Bartók dated 12 October 1925 written in the Everts' guest book at their home, Berg en Dalscheweg 127, Nijmegen, Holland. The greeting contains a fragment of music entitled Perpetuum mobile *which comprises two motifs from the Dance Suite and one from the Rhapsody. (Original in Hungarian.)*

For remembrance,
Nijmegen, 12 Oct.1925
Béla Bartók.

A-7. To Zoltán Székely, Kwakkenbergweg 275, Nijmegen, Holland. (Postcard. Original in Hungarian.) See Chapter Twelve, p. 132.

Budapest, III. Kavics u. 10.
1930. March 24.

Dear Székely!

Mr. Schamschula (he is the one who should have organized this concert in Prague as well as the one in Brno as he told me himself) has not written to this day, thus the concert in Prague will most likely not materialize. It is actually better for me since I have been ill for three weeks—I have had some skin inflammation and its results bother me (general itching, etc.) so I don't even know if I can go to Berlin on April 3rd where I would have to play with Szigeti.

The Universal-Edition asked me whether we reserve the right to the orchestral performances of the Second Rhapsody next season, for it seems that someone wants to play it somewhere. I'll let you decide this and hope to hear from you about it very soon. Have you any opportunities to play the Rhapsody in a few places? N.B., the First Rhapsody will be free next year.

The problem in Liège is that no one seems to be able to pay the conductor's fee. I do not pay for anything on principle. I have no idea how they managed until now; no one has ever asked me for money for such a purpose before. I suppose Furtwängler and Talich have conducted gratis.

Best wishes to you both,

Bartók

A-8. To Zoltán Székely, Kwakkenbergweg 275, Nijmegen, Holland. (Original in Hungarian.) See Chapter Thirteen, p. 138.

Vienna, 1931. December 17.

Dear Székely!

I haven't had a reply to my postcard yet. . . .

I would very much like to know whether you will be in Nijmegen the last week of February because I might be able to visit you. It seems I will have a few free days (that Ithma is unable to fill).

Are you planning to come to Budapest? Last year you were planning to, but didn't!

I managed to put together a new piano concerto. Disconnecting myself from all economic problems, I worked for a few weeks in enforced peace. Since then I hardly even have time for copying. We are swamped by problems not the least of which is finding a new home (for May). It is as if it were an impossibility to find a five-room villa for rent (for sale there are any number, but we would need three times the money than we have). If we cannot find one I don't know what will happen for I vowed I'd rather be hanged than live in the same house with strangers. (My neighbors bought a radio last year, a piano this year! The latter was positioned so that it manages to pollute all of our rooms. There are days when one hears fifty times the charming melody of [a silly song]). . . .

Until then best wishes for you all,

Béla Bartók

P.S. I forgot to mention that my piano Sonatina was just published transcribed for violin and piano; also I wrote 44 little duos for two violins at the beginning of summer (similar to "For children"); unfortunately their publication keeps on being postponed.

A-9. To Zoltán Székely, Kwakkenbergweg 275, Nijmegen, Holland. (Original in Hungarian.) See Chapter Thirteen, pp. 138–39.

Budapest, III. Kavics u.1931. December 29.

Dear Székely!

Thank you for your two cards. . . .

On the 21st of February (probably in the afternoon) I will play my piano concerto in Paris. And on the eve of February 29th in Glasgow I play in a new musical organization (solo, voice, etc.). Thus I could arrive in Nijmegen on the morning of the 22nd and if I could leave there on the evening of the 27th, by way of the Hook of Holland and London, could be in Glasgow on the evening of the 28th. What type of concert would be possible?

I am happy that you will be home at the end of February and my long overdue visit will be possible. Then we can discuss all the details.

Best wishes to you all and a Happy New Year,

Bartók

A-10. To Zoltán Székely, Kwakkenbergweg 275, Nijmegen, Holland. (Original in Hungarian.)

Frankfurt, 1932. February 1.

Dear Székely!

I received your letter. I play in Paris on the afternoon of February 21st and plan to leave on the 1 A.M. train so by way of Rosendaal I would arrive in Nijmegen around 11 A.M. on the 22nd. You probably know the exact time of arrival of that train. . . .

I could hardly believe it would be possible to play a concert there, during these times!!

I am looking forward to seeing you again and until then, warmest greetings to everyone.

Bartók

A-11. *To Zoltán Székely, Kwakkenbergweg 275, Nijmegen, Holland. (Original in Hungarian.)*

Zurich, 1933. July 18.

Dear Székely!

I spent a few weeks in Switzerland for health reasons. . . .
The situation is more and more depressing. We must now touch our reserves—as long as they last.
It would be so good if you could come to Budapest in the fall!

Many greetings to you both,

Bartók

A-12. *To Zoltán Székely, Kwakkenbergweg 275, Nijmegen, Holland. (Postcard. Original in German.) Chapter Thirteen, p. 142.*

Budapest II. Csalán út. 27.
20 October 1933.

Dear Mien and Zoltán!

Unfortunately it seems that even £10 is too much for the Scots so Glasgow is out. Mr. Chisholm does at least send his thanks for Zoltán's coorperation but unfortunately, etc. etc.—! Now I should like to find out whether the concert in Budapest planned by Zoltán and M. [Mien] will take place or not so that when I am in London I know what to do about the matter I discussed with Zoltán. My address in London is: in care of Mr. Duncan Wilson, 7, Sydney Square, S.W. 7. I shall be in London from November 4 to 8.

Many greetings!

Bartók

A-13. *To Zoltán Székely, Kwakkenbergweg 275, Nijmegen, Holland. (Original in Hungarian.) See Chapter Thirteen, p. 142.*

London, 1933. November 8.

Dear Székely!

I received your letter today [in London], however, as I was in Glasgow last week, now I can no longer speak with the people there. But I add for "consolation" that Mr. Chisholm couldn't do anything anyway for he couldn't get me any performances either in Glasgow or Edinburgh although he wanted to.

Too bad that the concert in Budapest will not take place. . . .

Many greetings to you all and wishing a permanent improvement in your mother-in-law's health!

Béla Bartók

A-14. *To Zoltán Székely, Kwakkenbergweg 275, Nijmegen, Holland. (Original in Hungarian/German.) See Chapter Thirteen, p. 144.*

Budapest, 1935. January 10.

Dear Székelys!

(I am writing with pencil because I am sitting on a bus.) I just received your letter of the 8th. I haven't received any telegrams from Mrs. "Basket!" [Antonia Kossar] Therefore, I am sending the program, by registered mail, also to the <u>radio address you wrote in your letter</u>, as follows:

			Publisher
1.	From 15 Hungarian Peasant Songs No. 6 (Ballade) No. 7–15 (Old Dance Tunes)	} 9' }	Universal Edition
2.	Suite (Op. 14) in 4 movements	10' }	Universal-Ed.
3.	Allegro barbaro	2' }	
4.	Sonatine	4'	Rózsavölgyi
5.	Rumanian Folk Dances	5'	Univ. Ed.
6.	Evening in the village	2' }	Charles Rozsnyai
7.	Bear dance	2' }	
8.	I. Rumanian Dance	<u>5'</u>	Rózsavölgyi
		39'	

In case they only want 30 minutes, then 4 and 5 can be left out, but if they want a longer program then the following can be added:

Kodály 1. Transylvanian Song	2' }	Universal [Edition]
Epitaph	2' }	

I ask you to please call the radio station A.V.R.O. and ask whether they received my letter, sent at the same time as this one; and, if they have not received it, to give them the above program.—We both are very happy that the thing was successful and that Ditta can also travel. Hopefully nothing will happen between now and then.

Next week I will write you in detail about our arrival. I believe that we will be there on the evening of the 27th.

Best wishes and in a hurry,

Bartók

A-15. To Zoltán Székely, Pension Duinlust, Santpoort Station, Holland. (Original in German/Hungarian.) See Chapter Thirteen, p. 144.

Budapest, II. Csalán út, 27.
16 January 1935.

Dear Székelys!

Mrs. Basket's letter (not telegram) arrived a day after your letter; I immediately telegraphed her and also sent her the program. (She wished to receive the program on the <u>previous day</u> which was unfortunately not possible because of the belated arrival of her letter. I hope that has not led to any mishap).

In order to be able to practice at leisure at your house we are planning to leave here at 4 P.M. on Friday, the 25th; we have to change trains in Utrecht at about 10 P.M. on the 26th and shall arrive in Amsterdam at about 11 P.M. How shall we get from there to Haarlem? (You did write to say that we should travel on to Haarlem, didn't you?)

So please write and give me exact details including the address of your house and perhaps also your telephone number (just in case); you will probably meet us with the car at Haarlem station (would it not be better just to go as far as Amsterdam?). Will your house really be all finished and habitable by the 26th?! Please send an answer by return of post!

With many greetings,

Béla Bartók

A-16. To Zoltán Székely, Pension Duinlust, Santpoort Station, Holland. (Postcard. Original in German.)

Budapest, II. Csalán út, 27.
1935. January 22.

Dear Székelys!

So we shall be arriving in Amsterdam around 10 P.M. on January 26 (by the train leaving Budapest at 4:45 P.M. on January 25, of course we shall change in Utrecht), then we shall take the first available train to Haarlem, where we hope you will be waiting for us.—We do not know your address, but I assume that your house is in Santpoort, too.

Until we see each other then, many greetings,

your Bartók

A-17. A greeting from the Bartóks written on the first page of the Székelys'
guest book at their new home, The Rhapsody, Joh. Verhulstweg, 70, Sant-
poort Station, Holland. 1935. January 26. (Original in Hungarian.) See
Chapter Thirteen, p. 145 and Plate 54.

Wishing the guest-loving inhabitants of the "Rhapsody" wine,
wheat, peace (and other good things) by its first house-guests. The
Bartóks.

Santpoort, 1935. January 26.

A-18. To Zoltán Székely, Joh. Verhulstweg, 70, Santpoort Station, Hol-
land. (Postcard: Les Diablerets. Original in Hungarian.) See Chapter Four-
teen, p. 154.

Basel, 1935. February 4.

Dear Mien and Zoltán!

I arrived here without any problems, only in the early morning a
wild Teutonic herd besieged the train, loaded with knapsacks and
skis (being Sunday), took all available space, spoiled the air for a half
hour, then got off.—Was Ditta able to leave on Sunday morning? I
thought of her all day, how she traveled, were there any problems.

The conductor here (Sacher) is on holidays away from Basel; they
have guest conductors. Here, too, the rehearsal times are fairly short,
but there are no other problems so far, therefore I am calmer here
than in Holland. The Berlin Philharmonic invited me on a very short
notice either to conduct or as soloist. Naturally I have no intention to
respond to such hurried notices.

Thank you for everything you did for us and best wishes to you
both,

Béla

A-19. To Zoltán Székely, Joh. Verhulstweg, 70, Santpoort Station, Hol-
land. (Original in Hungarian.) See Chapter Fourteen, p. 154.

Budapest, 1935. May 20.

Dear Zoltán and Mien!

Do not be angry for my not replying immediately. . . .

A few days ago the Hungarian Academy of Sciences elected me a
"correspondent" (this is the first level of membership), but Kodály

was not elected which was rather clumsy if they wanted something of this sort: the reason seems to be that it would be too much for them to admit two musicians at the same time. Why they chose me first I don't know, probably because I am the older one.

So one is exposed to such events; however, we both escaped the Kisfaludy Circle (did we tell you last time about this business?).

This is the most "noteworthy" news, nothing more noteworthy seems to be able to happen.

Best wishes to both of you from both of us,

Béla

A-20. To Zoltán Székely, Joh. Verhulstweg, 70, Santpoort Station, Holland. (Original in Hungarian.) See Chapter Fourteen, p. 157.

Budapest II. Csalán út 27.
1935. July 26.

Dear Mien and Zoltán!

Because of an unpleasant incident we had only two weeks [csak 2 hétig] vacation in the Tátra mountains and had to return home hastily [sebtiben]. Mrs. Kossar's letter was forwarded to me, I answered her from there accepting the two things mentioned in the hope—I wrote to her—that the concert in Hilversum will also happen.

I am very happy that we shall play together, however the 35 guineas in Liverpool are very little for the two of us, hardly worth crossing [átkelni] the sea. I wrote Mrs. Kossar that she [ő] should try to get something for the two of us at the BBC. (I, myself, do not want to ask that.): my violin pieces have not been played there with me [énvelem]. If we could get 25 guineas per person the excursion [kiruc-canás] would be worth it.

Mr. Eric Chisholm also asks whether I will be near them next year (I am surprised that his Active Society still exists). I would recommend to him also a pure violin and piano evening if he could pay us £10 per person. (There we can ask only pounds not guineas, they are Scottish.) Last time I got £15 from them, I went there from London. If we get 10 each, we will still clear £6 if we don't have to hand over the tithe [dézsmát] to Mrs. Kossar (considering the smallness of the fee, she should agree to forfeit her commission, especially since she did not get us this engagement). Also it would only take one and a half to two days once we are already in Liverpool. Glasgow would be best on January 14th (perhaps 15th?) and, for me, Hilversum radio on the 9th, the BBC preferably after the 16th. Write all this to Mrs. Kossar.

In Liverpool it would be best to play all "modern" things (what kind of concert is it? who organizes it?) for example, the Second Violin and Piano Sonata, one or both Rhapsodies, some smaller transcriptions, then Ravel and Debussy. In Glasgow only my things: both Sonatas, either Rhapsody plus transcriptions. I sent a program proposal to Mrs. Kossar for the BBC concert (again only my pieces). . . .

I hope you are well. I already mentioned that our vacation did not turn out as well as we needed it. Otherwise we are well, more or less.

I will write to Chisholm today, assuming your approval; if I am wrong, we can cancel it later. But I would like your answer concerning this as soon as possible. Of course, they may not have the £20!

Best wishes to you both,

Béla

P.S. The words underlined in red are recommended to Mien's attention.

A-21. A greeting from Béla Bartók written in the guest book at The Rhapsody, Joh. Verhulstweg, 70, Santpoort Station, Holland, 1936. January 10–14. The greeting contains a fragment of music from the First Rhapsody. (Original in Hungarian.)

Once again in Santpoort on Jan. 10–14, 1936. Béla Bartók

A-22. To Zoltán Székely, Joh. Verhulstweg, 70, Santpoort Station, Holland. (Original in Hungarian.) See Chapter Fourteen, p. 158.

Vienna, 1936. May 18.

Dear Mien and Zoltán!

I came here for the day. . . .

I am very glad we can play together in Berne. But I am angry at that basket. She organized this matter, too, entirely contrary to my instructions; and then what she did with that trio business! But it may not have been very serious anyway. We will talk about all this.

How are you? Here life continues to be difficult, a lot of trouble.

(I even had a note from His Majesty's tax office!) I wait to hear from you and until then, greetings to you both,

Béla

A-23. To Zoltán Székely, Joh. Verhulstweg, 70, Santpoort Station, Holland. (Original in Hungarian.) See Chapter Fourteen, p. 158.

[Budapest II. Csalán út 27.]
3. VI. 1936.

Dear Zoltán!

I hope you have received my letter from Vienna. . . . I leave here on the afternoon of June 17th and arrive in Berne at 4:50 P.M. on the 18th. I will take a room in a simpler hotel, the "Hirschen," the "Jura," or most probably the "de la Gare." Look for me first in the latter. When will you, or both of you arrive, and where will you stay?

I would ask you to bring the piano parts as well of the Debussy and Ravel Sonatas so I would have to carry less, (i.e., I have them only in a thickly-bound edition.) . . . And really finally, write me a postcard if you can immediately after receiving this letter to let me know if everything is well.

It would be nice if Mien could also come: if you came by car would it be possible?

Warmest greetings to you both,

Béla

P.S. All of good old Mrs. Kossar's other plans came to naught, no Strasburg or anything else. Therefore I will go from Berne to an inexpensive place on the 20th for about ten days (this way my travel expense will be paid for by my fee from Berne).

A-24. To Zoltán Székely, Joh. Verhulstweg, 70, Santpoort Station, Holland. (Original in Hungarian.)

Budapest II, Csalán út 27.
1936. June 12.

Dear Zoltán!

What you sent me has safely arrived. I read with a certain satisfaction that you are not satisfied with Berne either. But then I can't understand why you had to accept it. Mrs. Kossar had begged me in her first letter to accept it in your interest because she was hoping to introduce you there so that she could work for you there in the future. She mentioned some previous cancellations that had caused you to lose credibility there and this would make it all up. She had hoped for a total fee of 500 of which I would get 300 and you 200 because the travel from Budapest cost 200.

At this time I scratched my head and took out a pencil. I figured that I would have 6 pengős net profit. Then I scratched my head some more and had the idea to combine this with my vacation in June. Then came her second letter and the news that the total fee would be only 450. Then I thought to divide it as 275 and 175 considering my possible vacation, otherwise I would have lost on this deal. But I don't understand why she didn't tell you any of this! Why does she get her percentage if she doesn't even take care of the necessary correspondence?!

And now the problem is that because of some illness I had large unexpected expenses that used up the otherwise modest amount set aside for my vacation. Now I don't know what to do; if I come back straight from Berne then I really lose. All in all, this is bad business!! I would not have mentioned to you any of this had you not written that you were also dissatisfied and if you hadn't asked what proportions did Mrs. Kossar offer me. Now you know that of the 450 total fee we divide 275 plus 175. I'm beginning to dislike this Mrs. Kossar!

Warmest greetings until we meet,

Béla

P.S. You will bring the piano parts of the Debussy and the Ravel, won't you!

A-25. To Zoltán Székely, Joh. Verhulstweg, 70, Santpoort Station, Holland. (Original in Hungarian.) See Chapter Fourteen, pp. 158–59, and Chapter Eighteen, p. 221.

[Budapest II. Csalán út 27.]
1936. October 17.

Dear Mien and Zoltán!

Oh dear, oh dear! I should have written you much sooner! But if you only knew what a stressful life I lead, what works tower over my poor head, you would understand my long silence. . . .

The other thing is certainly feasible.[1] You do know, however, that I can only work on such things during the summer thus you couldn't expect the manuscript before the end of September 1937. But, I must warn you! this might be bad business, think it over carefully. If I accept the whole thing—with the three year exclusive rights—then I would give you the manuscript with the idea that <u>that</u> is what you actually purchased. At any rate, you have time to think it over, we might meet at the end of January and finalize the matter.

Mrs. Kossar didn't excel this year, it appears I don't play anywhere else in Holland but Hilversum; England and Ireland appear also uncertain so far (it seems the Irish would want us to play sonatas).

That commission from Basel was for string orchestra and some other instruments.[2] I was asked to do it after I said goodbye to you in Switzerland. I accepted it for it is better than nothing and I had been planning something like it for quite a while. Of course, this one is only reserved until its first performance (at an anniversary concert on January 21st). I would be happy to hear from you soon—perhaps you have more time!!

Our warmest greetings to you both,

the Bartóks

1. Bartók refers to the proposed violin concerto.
2. Music for Strings, Percussion, and Celesta.

A-26. To Zoltán Székely, Joh. Verhulstweg, 70, Santpoort Station, Holland. (Postcard: Ankara Kalesi. Original in Hungarian.) See Chapter Fourteen, p. 161.

Ankara, Légation de Hongrie,
1936. November 15.

Dear Mien and Zoltán!

I am here in the middle of Asia Minor and I must warn you, don't come here for a [concert] tour because, as a foreigner, you would have to give up <u>90%</u> of your fee as taxes. Of course, that is not relevant to me as I—don't get any fee. [Ernst] Praetorius is quite good, the orchestra less so! The weather is lovely and sunny but unfortunately my health has broken down probably because I ate some Circassian hen and ladies' belly buttons.

Warmest greetings,

Béla

A-27. To Zoltán Székely, Joh. Verhulstweg, 70, Santpoort Station, Holland. (Postcard: Adana Göränüsü. Original in Hungarian.) See Chapter Fourteen, p. 161.

Adana (South Anatolia), 1936. November 25.

Dear Mien and Zoltán!

Yesterday I visited some nomads, real ones living in a tent complete with camel herds, etc. I was collecting from 7 P.M. until midnight by the light of campfire and my own kerosene lamp, squatting on the ground, kneeling, or cross-legged since they have no such useless things as chair, table, or bed.

Warmest greetings,

Béla

A-28. To Zoltán Székely, Joh. Verhulstweg, 70, Santpoort Station, Holland. (Original in Hungarian.) See Chapter Fourteen, p. 161.

Budapest, II. Csalán út 29.
1937. January 2.

Dear Zoltán!

. . . Your mail arrived before Christmas.

Concerning my stay there, the story is that the Révész family has asked me to stay with them at least this once. Considering among other things my lecture on the 26th it will be good if I stay with them a couple of days; then I could go to your place for a day or two in view of our rehearsals. Anyway we shall see and discuss it all there. I will probably arrive in Amsterdam on the evening of the 24th, thus can be at your concert on the 25th.

That Paris thing—as I wrote to Mrs. Kossar—cannot be accepted, the fee is so laughably small. We must not devalue ourselves. If the French are so miserly or clumsy that they are unable to pay decent fees, they should be left to themselves and take care of each other's business.

A long time ago I demanded from the Universal-Edition that they change the parts of the Second Rhapsody; I believe that they have done it, but to be sure you should check with them on a postcard.

We send our best to Mien and you, and Happy New Year!

Béla

A-29. To Zoltán Székely, Joh. Verhulstweg, 70, Santpoort Station, Holland. (Original in Hungarian.) See Chapter Fourteen, pp. 161–62.

Budapest, 1937. January 12.

Dear Székelys!

Your special delivery letter [express] came on the night before yesterday; my answer is not exactly express; it was rather difficult to nail this program together (as you will see below) because of all the English titles. Also I had a lecture yesterday and will have another tomorrow. I have so much to do it is unbelievable. Too bad you didn't write sooner about this matter for I also received a letter from Mrs. Hart a few days ago with similar content. Of course I was surprised and sent an angry postcard to the basket, because I thought it was all her fault. In other words: I firmly asked her what all this meant? why she didn't let me know about it, etc.

With the help of my American pupils I luckily or not so luckily succeeded in "translating" this program yesterday and I already sent it to Mrs. Hart; to be sure, I send it to you as well. To wit:

I.   <u>First Sonata</u> for Violin and Piano

II. <u>Seventeen easy piano pieces from "Mikrokosmos"</u>: 15' 20"

      Melody against double stops

      Wandering

      à la Russe

      Five-tone scale

      Like a folksong

      Parallel minor sixths

      Variations

      Merriment

      Clashing sounds

      1. Chromatic Invention

      2. Chromatic Invention

      Sixths and Triads

      Alternating Thirds

      Fourths

      Melody

      Staccato

      Chords together and opposed

            Interval

III. <u>Ten piano pieces from "Mikrokosmos"</u>: 19'
      Syncopes
      Whole-tone scale
      Free variations
      From the Diary of a Fly
      Divided Arpeggios
      March
      Minor Seconds—Major Sevenths
      3. Chromatic Invention
      Unison
      Ostinato
IV. Second Rhapsody for Violin and Piano

——————— • ———————

    A rather long-winded program! But at least these many flea pieces are all in "manuscript," "novelty," "very first performance," "nowhere else performed yet," "world premiere," and what you like. Surely this will satisfy the music center!

    However, <u>let us not bother with</u> those greedy, stingy, niggardly, miserly French. It hurts me because otherwise I like them very much, the French language is music to my ears, I prefer reading in French, etc.—but to make music with them, <u>that</u> is impossible!! At least as long as they are so introverted and don't care for anything but their money bags. And now it is not possible anyway: this excursion would take too much out of me, after all we have to rehearse together and I must also practice—I could not do that at home now, everything was decided in the last minute—In a word, Paris is impossible. We must give up the idea.

    And now, what shall we play in Hilversum? I would suggest:

    1. Second (or First?) Rhapsody for violin and piano.

    2. Mozart A Major? or the Debussy Sonata? (no Ravel!)

    3. The <u>Országh transcriptions</u> (7' 30"). (These are not difficult, you could easily learn them, actually they are <u>my</u> transcriptions.) You should make up the program out of these, after all I don't even know how many minutes they want.

    Warmest greetings, and I conclude my letter in haste.

    Béla

P.S. At the Contemporary, we must play the First Violin Sonata if at the BBC we play the other one. We have time to learn it.

A-30. *To Zoltán Székely, Joh. Verhulstweg, 70, Santpoort Station, Holland. (Postcard: Bern—Bundeshäuse. Original in Hungarian.)*

Basel, 1937. January 23.

Dear Zoltán,

I arrive in Amsterdam on the eve of the 24th, will meet you at your concert on the 25th and then we can discuss when, how much, where we should rehearse. Unfortunately my lecture was postponed until the 29th but somehow we can arrange the time to rehearse. The premiere here went quite well, at any rate they played with great care and endeavor, the conductor is good.

Warmest regards to you both,

Béla

A-31. *To Zoltán Székely, Joh. Verhulstweg, 70, Santpoort Station, Holland. (Postcard. Original in Hungarian.)*

[Basel, 1937] January 28.

[no salutation]

I only wanted to write in a hurry to remind you not to forget the "10 Easy" [Pieces] and Allegro barbaro. . . .

Many greetings,

Béla

A-32. *To Zoltán Székely, Joh. Verhulstweg, 70, Santpoort Station, Holland. (Postcard: Nijmegen, Groote Markt. Original in Hungarian.)*

Budapest, 1937. March 17.
(II. Csalán út 27)

Dear Székelys!

What happened to you???! It has been more than a month since we last saw each other and no news from you. . . . Hope there is nothing the matter? Presently you two are probably moving about in Switzerland (I can't remember exactly when you were planning to be in Lugano). When you come home write us, don't be so lazy. You also didn't do anything concerning the Violin Concerto!!

Warmest regards,

Béla and Ditta

A-33. To Zoltán Székely, Joh. Verhulstweg, 70, Santpoort Station, Holland. (Original in Hungarian.) See Chapter Sixteen, p. 179.

Budapest, 1937. April 10.

Dear Zoltán!

I received your letter. . . .

Concerning the contract plan there are two difficulties. First, the length of sole performance rights: <u>We always talked about *three* years</u> with the option of another three years. The latter seems to me a bit too long—I rather thought of two years—but I could accept the three also. Thus exclusive rights from September 1, 1938 through August 31, 1941 (and, of course, even before September 1, 1938) optional extension, September 1, 1941 until August 31, 1944.

We could also say that the exclusive rights are from January 1, 1938 until August 31, 1941 (i.e., there is no possibility of performance before January 1, the copying cannot be done earlier).

The other difficulty is that you want to use the material even after September 1, 1941 or after September 1, 1944. Although personally I would not object to it; but <u>I don't have the legal right</u> to make such agreement. As long as my work is unpublished I can give the sole manuscript to whomever I please, in this case to you; but as soon as it is published, all rights to produce, lend, etc. the material belong to Universal-Edition. Therefore you could and should have to discuss your request with Universal-Edition. Yet you say I should not mention this to anyone.

Thus now you will have to decide whether I should approach Universal-Edition with this idea or you would rather forego the idea. Of course it is possible that Universal-Edition will not accept it but we shall see that at the time.

Finally I would like a little more freedom concerning the length of the piece: let us say between twenty to twenty-six minutes?

About all this . . . write me right away, for I would like to have it all decided. I must say: you are lazy! You could have easily written it all down at the time in London so we could have taken care of the whole thing without all this correspondence.

And something else comes to mind: if you join the New Hungarian Quartet, how will you be able to play solos? (that is, regarding the time element). After all, quartet playing implies a lot of restrictions. Also how would it be, would you move to Budapest or would the others move to Holland?

Warmest greetings,

Béla

[postscript from Ditta Bartók]

P.S. Dear Mien and Zoltán!

First of all I would like to say that I miss you both; you used to come here more often! Béla has said so many good and lovely things about you, the time that he spent with you, I was sad that I could not be there with you. And the little handkerchief is so lovely and beautiful!! When I want to look pretty I always carry it with me, and you do know, Mien, that I would like to look that way quite often?! Thank you so much, lots of hugs for it.

I saw Zoltán's parents at [Pál Hermann's] concert. We talked about you a lot.

I wonder if Béla has told you how much he loved playing with you, Zoltán? For he often wrote about it, mentioned it to me.

Warmest greetings and hugs,

Ditta

A-34. To Zoltán Székely, Joh. Verhulstweg, 70, Santpoort Station, Holland. (Original in Hungarian.) See Chapter Sixteen, pp. 179–80, and Chapter Eighteen, p. 221.

Budapest, 1937. May 1.

Dear Zoltán!

If that is the case then there is really nothing in the way. Only you didn't mention how you will be able to fit together quartet and solo playing (I think that was the problem with Pál Hermann); for it would not be good if during the period of your exclusive rights you would have to forego some good opportunities to perform it all because of the quartet. Nonetheless, I hereby draft the agreement as follows.

Agreement between Béla Bartók and Zoltán Székely

1. Béla Bartók will write a violin concerto in 1937 of about twenty-one to twenty-five minutes' duration.
2. The sole performance rights of this work will belong to Zoltán Székely until August 31, 1941; this can be extended until August 31,

1944 at Zoltán Székely's wish, of which he must notify Béla Bartók by December 31, 1940.

3. Béla Bartók will have to place a copy of the work's score at Zoltán Székely's disposal by the end of 1937.

4. Zoltán Székely may have the orchestra material produced from this copy once or in duplicate, and will be able to use this material during the time of the sole performing rights, but he has no right to ask the orchestras or their managers for any compensation for the use of that material. He may not loan this material to anyone else.

5. This orchestra material will stay in Zoltán Székely's possession even after the expiration of the exclusivity period and he himself may use it for public performances, however, he or the concert's management is obliged to pay the usual hire fees to the publisher.

6. Zoltán Székely shall, at the acceptance of the manuscript mentioned in point three, pay 500 Dutch florins for the rights described in the preceding paragraphs.

7. In case Béla Bartók should for whatever reason be unable to complete this work mentioned above, no indemnification shall be sought from him.

——————— • ———————

I believe this will be satisfactory. Write it down in two copies, sign them both and I will return one to you with my signature. . . .

Warmest regards to both of you,

Béla

A-35. *To Zoltán Székely, Joh. Verhulstweg, 70, Santpoort Station, Holland. (Original in Hungarian.) See Chapter Sixteen, p. 180.*

Budapest, 1937. June 10.

Dear Mien and Zoltán!

I am only able to answer you now and probably you are not home. . . . I leave here for about a month on June 17.

I am enclosing my signed copy of the agreement—we shall see what the future brings!

All good things and warmest greetings,

Béla

A-36. To Zoltán Székely, Joh. Verhulstweg, 70, Santpoort Station, Holland. (Original in Hungarian.) See Chapter Sixteen, p. 184.

Kals (East Tyrol), 1937. July 15.

Dear Mien and Zoltán!

We have been vacationing here for several weeks; my resting time is over and I plan to return to Budapest next week so that I can start working again on the 21st of July. . . .

I must again return to the violin concerto. Please do not take it badly but to be sure I wrote to Universal-Edition concerning the matter without mentioning your name. They agree to everything, but ask for the two following things: (1) that they receive a copy of the work upon completion in order to register the copyright (although I don't understand why a work in manuscript has to be copyrighted, but perhaps for the possible American performance royalties); (2) that "the certain violinist concerned" should report to them all performances of the work (let us say within a month, but perhaps within a half a year if you like that better), so that they can control the incoming royalty especially from America. I don't believe that this presents a problem, thus I ask you that you assume this added obligation in a supplemental declaration. Otherwise everything is fine.

I would like it if you would write an answer to me about all of this to Budapest so that I could receive your declaration on my return on the 20th or shortly thereafter . . . Write me about Paris also. How did it go? And in general how do you function together? Are there many arguments??!

Warmest regards to you both,

Béla and Ditta

A-37. To Zoltán Székely, Joh. Verhulstweg, 70, Santpoort Station, Holland. (Original in Hungarian.) See Chapter Sixteen, pp. 189–90.

Basel, 1938. June 28.

Dear Mien and Zoltán!

Now I have waited a long time with my reply, but it would not have helped if I had written earlier, I couldn't have written anything positive, in fact, I can't even do that now. N.B. You wrote that [Vilmos] Palotai will call me and that [Ödön] Pártos would like something, but nobody called; yet I know that Palotai had arrived in Budapest several days before I left.

My situation is still in limbo, at best it will clear itself somewhat within a few weeks. What is involved is that I should be freed from the claws of the Viennese robbers but this is not so simple, it requires a highly diplomatic approach. If I succeed in escaping the clutch of the Universal-Edition highwaymen, I will go with another publisher (English). In that case I can finish the violin concerto by September, but then the new publisher will have something to say about our business. If I don't escape them what will happen is what I told you on the phone. However, there is one hitch in any case. You told me at that time on the phone that for one year you will have time to play the work several times but how much time you will have afterward is very questionable. (This was my first thought last year when I heard the news about you joining the quartet). Now then, it would be no good for anyone to have such a long term agreement in effect with only a few performances. How do you see it?

I don't write about the deplorable situation in Hungary, I imagine you know the most important aspects. It would be best to emigrate before it is too late; but how and where? Would I achieve anything by it? Too bad I couldn't answer your letter right away, I would have wanted to begin with "Hooray for the Székelys!! this is really happy news, we greet the little Székely in advance on the occasion of his entry into the world." Are you sufficiently happy about it?

We are going to <u>Braunwald</u> (Switzerland), Hotel Tödiblick, until July 17, then from there home. When I know anything certain, I'll write. You should, too.

Warmest greetings from both of us to all three (!) of you,

Béla

A-38. To Zoltán Székely, Joh. Verhulstweg, 70, Santpoort Station, Holland. (Original in Hungarian.) See Chapter Sixteen, pp. 191–93.

Budapest, 1938. September 14.

Dear Zoltán!

I wanted to write to you for a long time, but all my work, etc. Unfortunately, concerning the Universal-Edition case, there are still only "negotiations." I can still only write to you as last time that if I don't want to jeopardize the appearance of the concerto for fifty years plus my lifetime then I cannot finish the work now, only three years later. Those Germans are wild beasts and if that man is unsuccessful in settling with them they might not let me go just out of spite. In case of an unsuccessful settlement, that is, if we have to wait three years, our agreement naturally is not binding on you; if you want to, you can sign another one with me or you can drop the whole thing. True, after waiting for three years we could hardly talk about six years exclusive rights but, in order that you don't lose on the deal, I would offer that the fee be reduced by one-third. By the way, what the new publisher who is negotiating with Universal-Editions now also doesn't like is the long six-year term of exclusivity. I submit the idea that in case I will be able to become free of the U.E., go to the new publisher by the end of December, and therefore finish the Concerto and "deliver it" to you, would you consider reducing the length of exclusivity to three years, of course in return for reducing the fee by one-third? It is entirely up to you for, if you don't want to do that, I will naturally respect our original agreement.

Neither while I am alive nor after my death do I want any German publisher to have any of my work even if it means that no work of mine will ever be published again. This is for now what is fixed and final.

I was diligent: the score for the first and second movements is ready, the third movement in sketches (with the exception of the coda that was planned to be short also, by the way) is also ready, five pages of it are already orchestrated. I think the third movement turned out very well, actually a free variation of the first (thus I got the best of you, I wrote <u>variations after all</u>), it is brilliant, effective, with some new things in it; before the coda there is an (orchestra-accompanied) cadenza, about eight minutes. The main theme is in 3/4 time:

(violin entirely alone) The second section after a few bars of tutti (this already with imitational accompaniment).

Writing the score really takes time, on average <u>at least</u> three to four hours per page! The first and second movements total 51 pages, the third will be around 35 to 40.

However, while I was diligent, you were not! I would need your counter suggestions concerning articulation, etc., after all that is why I gave you the piano reduction so that you could mark in your recommendations (slurs, bowings, etc.) (In the cadenza of the first movement I already eliminated the discomfort in the passage in fifths, in the second movement I also adjusted the penultimate pizzicato variation). Thus, you should now send me the piano score in a hurry with your notes, so that I can enter the slur markings in the score; because that is all that is missing. If you won't do that, I don't know what to do, shall I ask the advice of Zathureczky or Waldbauer?! Since I wrote you this concerto it should really be in accordance with your suggestions that I should finalize the violin solo part.

Another question: should I send you the copy of the score even during such uncertain times? (of course, only in November, by bringing it with me) and if yes, how many copies do you want besides the obligatory one? (I figure the cost will be around 27 pengős per copy): We have discussed this already, but I have forgotten what you said.

To resume the whole thing: I will finish the work by November–December (except perhaps the coda in the third movement), in November I can give you the score of the first and second movements, in December, of the third one. But in case I can't escape the Universal-Edition, we must postpone the whole thing for three years.

——————— · ———————

Concerning the concert in Amsterdam, I am very happy it turned out this way; it did not even occur to me that you were also asked to play. Mrs. Kossar wrote: (a) some violin-piano works with you, (b) piano solo, (c) two pianos. For (a) I recommend the First Rhapsody plus the Országh transcriptions, that is about 20 minutes. Since (b) is about 25 minutes, we do not need another composer's work. But I am awaiting Mrs. Kossar's reply about this.

Best wishes and good luck to Mien. Let us know about the baby's arrival. Have a nice trip and good work.

Warmest greetings,

Béla

N.B. I am sorry to hear that the concerto will be first performed at the Concertgebouw. I am very angry with them and even if by chance I happened to be around, I would not go to the concert. Actually why didn't it work out with the BBC? Could you inform me of the exact details?

A-39. To Mien Székely, Joh. Verhulstweg, 70, Santpoort Station, Holland. (A polyglot letter.) See Chapter Seventeen, p. 198.

[Budapest] 1938. October 24.

Dear Mien!

It is a shame that we didn't immediately respond after having received the news[1] and that we did not shout forth in a letter: Long live the little Francis Jacob,[2] to everyone's joy and the happiness of his parents, hurrah![3] So now we are making up for it several times over and in a polyglot way.—Do not be annoyed by our delay.

Meantime, so much trouble has broken out all over the world, such unrest, such fright—-and now this shocking recoil on the part of the Western countries. One ought to get away from here, from the neighborhood of that pestilential country, far, far away, but where: to Greenland, Cape Colony, the Tierra del Fuego, the Fiji Islands, or somewhere even the Almighty has not heard of!

I got your letter. What Zoltán wrote in it is all right; he just forgot to answer one thing. But now it's all the same; soon—if nothing intervenes—we shall be going to Holland, and I shall meet him; then we will talk it over.

I am afraid you will not quite understand my very genuine Hungarian expressions but I can't help it: in writing to you my mind pours out the most colorful words—And then I didn't want to use that cursed language of our neighbors, whom I hate more than ever.[4]

Our best wishes to you, to your little darling and to your husband.

So long,[5]

Béla

From my innermost heart I wish all three of you much joy and happiness.

Ditta

1. que nous n'avons pas immédiatement répondu après avoir reçu les nouvelles . . .

2. evviva il Francesco Jacopo, vive le petit François Jacobe . . .
3. živio! să trăiască! Yasasïn küçük oğlunuz!
4. Et puis je n'ai pas voulu faire usage de questa maledetta lingua dei nostri vicini, que j'abhorre plus que jamais.
5. A bientôt

A-40. *A greeting from Béla Bartók written in the Székelys' guest book at The Rhapsody, Joh. Verhulstweg, 70, Santpoort Station, Holland. 1938. November 14. (Original in Hungarian.)*

Once more!

Béla Bartók. 1938. November 14.

A-41. *To Zoltán Székely, Joh. Verhulstweg, 70, Santpoort Station, Holland. (Original in Hungarian.) See Chapter Seventeen, pp. 200–02.*

Budapest, 1938. December 6.

Dear Zoltán!

With great difficulty I have finished 60 pages, for the time being I sent you three copies on the 3rd, the other two copies will follow later. A few folios are not folded at the right place, these can be corrected at home. One page turned out too big, it must be folded in, unfortunately that one can't be corrected.

There are remarks here and there, only in Hungarian; would you please translate these into English or French and write them into the copies, so that the copyist can write them that way as well into the parts.

Call the attention of the copyist to the following:

1) at changes of meter he should not write ‖ double lines (and in general he should always follow the original).

2) the parts of indeterminate-pitch percussion should be written on one line, not on five, and he should not scribble in clefs, for example 𝄢 for bass drum or 𝄞 for snaredrum!

3) flauto II muta fl. picc. (one part)
   Ob. II muta cor. ing. (one part)
   Clar. II muta clar. basso. (one part)
   Fag. I muta contrafag. (one part)

5) after long rests the cues should <u>not</u> be taken from the Violin solo
if possible (in general they should be taken from related or neighboring instruments).

6) "tacet" must only be written in exceptional cases (only if it can't
cause any confusion about entrances; thus <u>tacet al fine</u> is possible;
but at the beginning or middle of movements "tacet" is not suitable).

———————— • ————————

I marked the duration of various sections under the lines so:

Of course, I have already found some typographical errors:
Movement I:
Measure 68 in the viola.

Measure 106 in Flute 1. the last quarter note tr. is missing.

Measure 108 in trumpet 1 and 2. two tenuto signs are missing.
Measure 109 in Fl. picc. "muta in fl. 2" is missing.
There will be plenty more errors.

I beg of you to correct the mistakes very carefully and make a list
of errors found and of questionable places. And finally, please write
the agreed-upon changes on an "agreement addenda" (in two copies)
and send them to me so I can sign them.

Yesterday I reached page 71, perhaps there will be another 19
(that is, a total of 90); I would very much like to finish it by Christmas, but I don't know whether it will be possible. Perhaps—when 20
pages are ready—I'll have them done and send them, in order not to
draw it out so long.

And finally, I strongly recommend that the duplicating of the
parts should be done by <u>Lichtpaus</u> [photocopy], and in nice, orderly,
flawless fashion. Because, in that case, there might be a possibility
that, when the time comes, the publisher will buy from you the photocopied material. Of course, this is only a suggestion without any
guarantee.

Best wishes to all of you from both of us!

Béla

A-42. To Mien Székely, Joh. Verhulstweg, 70, Santpoort Station, Holland.
(Original in English/French.) See Chapter Seventeen, pp. 203–04.

Budapest, II. Csalán út, 29.
10 January 1939.

Dear Mien,

your kind and loving letter gave us a kind of emotion not yet experienced: is the situation as bad as you see it?! Of course, since
March we are sure there will be a change to worse or to worst which
will perhaps make it impossible to work here and even to live here.
But in the country you mention, would it be possible to do that work
which is so very important for me (I mean the scientific work)? I
don't think so. If I can only "vegetate" there, then it would be of no
use to change "domicile." I think it extremely difficult to decide
something in that way and really I am at a loss what to do. In any
case, still we must wait for some more decisive sign of change. Sure,
I feel rather uncomfortable to live so very near to the clutches of the
nazis or even in the clutches; but to live elsewhere would—it seems
at least for the moment—not make things easier.

—————   •   —————

Yesterday I posted the following:
(1) 2 copies of pages 1–60 of the violin-concerto; you have nothing to do with these, only keep them at home.
(2) two copies of pages 61–80 of the same work; one <u>of these</u> you
have to send immediately to the copyist who is writing the orchestra-
parts.
Enclosed in this letter you see a "list of the errors" detected until
now, you have to give it also to the copyist, except the last part of it
marked with red, this you have to send to Zoltán.

—————   •   —————

In two days I will send you the following copies:
(1) Two other copies of pages 61–80; keep them at home.
(2) Three copies of pages 81–96; one of them you must give to the
copyist, and another you have to send immediately to Zoltán.
(3) One copy of the piano-arrangement of the concerto; this also
you must send immediately <u>to Zoltán</u>.
Please, will you kindly acknowledge receipt of all this material.

———— • ————

We will be in Paris from 25 Febr. until 3 March, it is very important for both of us: Zoltán and myself to have a meeting there and to be able to go through the work. He <u>must</u> arrange it, as—in any case he is going through Paris just at the same time.

Yours very sincerely,

Béla

A-43. To Zoltán Székely, Joh. Verhulstweg, 70, Santpoort Station, Holland. (Original in Hungarian.) See Chapter Seventeen, p. 204.

Budapest, 1939. February 8.

Dear Zoltán!

I was happy to read your postcard with the news that you will be in Paris between the 4th and 7th of March. We [the Bartóks] shall stay at the Hotel Vouillemont on the rue Boissy d'Angelas (Madeleine area). Too bad you entered the modifications on the original contract; had you made separate supplementary and post-contracts in <u>2 copies</u> I would have sent it back signed a long time ago. Now this way I have to look for my original copy, enter the changes, etc. in brief, I don't have the time. I will take it to Paris and give it to you. I have discovered a few more unfortunate mistakes (who knows how many are hiding still!) the list of which is on the enclosed page, <u>give it to the copyist immediately</u>.

Warmest greetings until we meet,

Béla

By the time you are in Paris, you must know your part perfectly!

In the solo violin part there is the following change: I movement, page 17 at measure 155.

The fifth in the cadence, D flat–A flat, you objected to, is perfectly playable by throwing the finger across from the E string to the A string! Let us keep it!

A-44. To Mien Székely, Joh. Verhulstweg, 70, Santpoort Station, Holland.
(Original in English.) See Chapter Seventeen, p. 206.

Basel, 9. March 1939.

Dear Mien,

We had very good and long rehearsals together—Zoltán and my-self—in Paris, he plays the solo-part of the concerto splendidly indeed. I am sending you enclosed a few bars (alternative), you have to give it immediately to the copyist.—We are in a hurry, are leaving Basel for Budapest in a few minutes. I hope the performance of the concerto will be excellent, what a pity that I can't be present.

Yours, with the kindest regards,

Béla

[The second page of the letter contains nine corrections to the concerto, dated 8 Febr. [Mar.?] 1939:]

A-45. To Zoltán Székely, Verhulst Straat, 70, Santpoort Station, Holland, Europa. Draft typed on November 18, 1940, contains return address c/o Boosey and Hawkes, 43 West 23, New York City. Handwritten copy dated 10 December 1940 was received in an envelope marked "opened by the authorities." (Original in German.) See Chapter Eighteen, pp. 220 and 222.

110-31, 73 Road, Forest Hills, Long Island, N.Y., U.S.A.
10 December 1940.

Dear Zoltán!

After my five-week stay in the USA in the spring, I went back again to Budapest. I was expecting a sign of life from you, but unfortunately was therefore of the opinion that postal communication has become impossible.

Concerning your last letter of the spring, I discovered with regret that there are no possibilities for your plans in the USA.

Now I have returned here—this time with my wife—and discovered that nothing has arrived from South America for Szigeti, although there would have been sufficient time in the spring for the necessary arrangements. Since I have therefore received only 1/3 of the money for the Violin Concerto, and since I see absolutely no possibility of being able to get the remaining 2/3 of the sum, I am forced to shorten by 1/3 the period of time reserving the performance rights of my Violin Concerto; I am doing this in the knowledge that I have every right to do so. Therefore the work will be at the disposal of all performers from Sept. 1, 1941 onwards.

I hope that you and your family are well; we should be happy to receive news from you.

Warmest greetings to you all,

Béla Bartók

A-46. The original letter to which this undated postscript to Mien Székely was attached is now lost; however, her Hungarian typescript of the exercise it contained has been preserved. Written by Béla Bartók from London after a visit to Glasgow ca. February 1932, the exercise is obviously intended to help her learn the Hungarian use of the double negative and includes such words as never, nowhere, and nobody. See Chapter Seventeen, p. 197.

Kedves Mien! Soha sehol sem játszottam olyan rossz hegedűssel, mint Glasgowban. Sehol semmikor senki semmi érdekeset nem mon-

dott nekem ezen a héten. Soha sem felejtem el, milyen jó volt Nij-
megenben pihenni. Itt soha sincs semmi nyugtom, sose lehetek
békességben, a mai napot kivéve, amikor semmiféle dolgom sem volt.
Mindyájukat sokszor üdvözli sok köszönettel. Bartók

　　(*Dear Mien! Never, nowhere have I played with such a bad violinist as
in Glasgow. Nowhere, not at any time, has anyone said anything interesting to me this week. I shall never forget how good it was to rest in Nijmegen.
Here I never have any rest, never am I left in peace, except today when I had
nothing to do. Many greetings to all of you with thanks. Bartók*)

Performance Practice

ˋ
1. BARTOK QUARTET CYCLE

During the spring of 1976, Zoltán Székely and the members of the University of Alberta String Quartet filmed a working session to discuss in detail numerous passages from the Bartók cycle. Székely's responses to the quartet's questions illuminate various difficult aspects of performance practice in the Bartók quartet cycle.

His remarks refer to a broad range of considerations and are characteristic of his approach to solving the problems of the Bartók cycle. In every instance his remarks reveal his musical erudition as well as his vast and distinguished practical experience.

Here are excerpts from the film's transcript. References are to musical scores published by Boosey and Hawkes.

Regarding accentuation in Quartet No.1, Lento (movement one), Vc. part, before figure 2, two measures, BH No. 24, p. 3:

Quartet: Where the cello has accents marked with the vertical symbol in this *cantabile* passage, should those notes be played tenuto?

Székely: That symbol indicates an agogic accent.[1] It presents a difficult problem every time it comes up. I asked this question of Bartók, and even he, himself, could not explain entirely, completely clearly, what he wanted in such cases. But this is not a dynamic accent, it is an agogic accent. When that symbol appears in this *cantabile* passage, it is an indication that notes marked that way must "come out" at that moment with the imitation.

Regarding the use of two symbols, the horizontal accent $>$ and the vertical accent $\wedge$ as in Quartet No. 4, Prestissimo, con sordino (movement two), Vn. 1 part, after figure 85, three measures, BH No. 77, p. 22:

Quartet: In Bartók's notation what is the difference in these two accents, one that has a horizontal symbol [$>$], the other that has a vertical one [$\wedge$]?

Székely: That horizontal symbol is a sort of *sforzando*, more or less, so it is a dynamic accent. The vertical symbol indicates a purely agogic accent, a musical nuance. You cannot express the vertical symbol as an agogic accentuation by any other means than with that symbol, but it is not an accent in the sense of *sforzando*.

But how can one express it since the difference between the two accents is somewhat ambiguous? I would have discussed that question with Bartók later had the opportunity presented itself, but it did not. I did not see him again after 1939.

Regarding the use of two symbols, the comma [$\mathbf{9}$] as in Quartet No. 4, Allegretto pizzicato (movement four), all voices before figure 90, two measures, BH No. 77, p. 42; the vertical beam [I] as in Quartet No. 4, Allegro molto (movement five), all voices, before figure 373, one measure, BH No. 77, p. 64:

Quartet: What is the specific meaning of the two symbols, the comma [$\mathbf{9}$] and the vertical beam [I] ?

Székely: The diffference between the comma and the vertical beam or straight line[2] is something like the difference between the two accents I have spoken about. That is to say, while the accent symbolized by the comma is an imaginary accent, the vertical beam is an imaginary rest. The comma indicates a definite break in the sound; that is, an additional value in the form of a brief silence is added to the bar.

The exact meaning of the two symbols is again ambiguous as in the case of the symbol used for the slur which can indicate either a phrasing or a bowing. The question is "what is what?"

Even if a composer is as precise as Bartók was, there are ideas which cannot be realized in the traditional notation. Yes! The notation is not exact enough.

Regarding the use of the secondary dotted bar-line [┆] as in Quartet No. 5, Allegro (movement one), all voices at letter A and the continuing passage, BH No. 78, p. 8:

Quartet: Do these secondary dotted bar-lines have to do with the phrasing and the grouping of notes?

Székely: Bartók's use of the secondary dotted bar-line is perhaps a little more indicative of something specific than the other notational devices I've mentioned. Both in this passage and in the Fourth Quartet, the secondary dotted bar-line indicates polyrhythm.[3]

Regarding the use of beams that leap bar-lines as in Quartet No. 5, Allegro (movement one), all voices in numerous passages, BH No. 78, p. 7 (this system of beams appears frequently in Quartets Nos. 3 to 6 as well):

Quartet: In certain passages in the Fifth Quartet where beamed groups cross the bar-lines, how do you perceive Bartók's notation in this case?

Székely: I try to write it down in my violin part as I hear it in my mind, not as Bartók notates it with beams over the bar-line. I notate it as I hear it because this particular notation is sometimes slightly variable and undetermined [imprecise]. Bartók had the idea—as one sees in the Fourth Quartet—to notate everything in 4/4 meter thinking that everybody gets confused otherwise and the music becomes difficult to play, especially in the orchestra works. But you can see from my violin part that the real rhythm has nothing to do with 4/4 meter. Nothing! There is 3/8, 4/8, and 5/8, and for every voice it is a little bit different.

I notate such passages as I hear them, as what I think I hear in the music, because I don't want to play looking at a 4/4 marking if the meter is 5/8, for instance. If you read in 4/4 as he marks it, then you have to remember to eliminate things in your mind, like all these bar-lines, and that is confusing.

What is the function of the bar-line? That is the question. Following the Riemann Theory,[4] the bar-line is nothing else but the indication of the "heavy part" of the motif, so that which is *between* the bar-lines never belongs together. Rather, it is always that which is *over* the bar-lines that belongs together and that is the confusing thing about our traditional notation.

It is a pity that from the beginning when students begin to learn notation, nobody tells them that fact. Everybody says, "Ah, the bar-line! What is *between* belongs together." Almost never! This problem really means that not everything is quite well put down in writing, even in Bartók's notation of folklore. It is sometimes dubious what exists from the "middle of the bar" to the next "middle of the bar."

Following the Riemann Theory, it would very often be the case that phrases end in the middle of the bar. In many Beethoven and Mozart works, the bar-line is in the wrong place. One of the very clear mistakes of this type is in the slow movement of Beethoven's Op. 135. The same thing exists in the slow movement of Op. 59, No. 1. That happens in Bartók's quartets, and in his folklore notation, as well.

Of course, the Riemann Theory doesn't cover every situation, and sometimes there is such a difficult problem that one doesn't know what is what. The basic idea of the Riemann Theory is excellent, in my opinion. It offers the most help of any theory, in this regard, but, of course, in Bartók's quartets one finds much more complicated things and mixtures than Riemann had in mind. When one tries to analyze the music of César Franck with its enchained harmonies[5]—one dips into the other—one doesn't always know where is the beginning and where is the end of the motif. That is also sometimes the case in Bartók's music.

Regarding the articulation in Quartet No. 5, Allegro (movement one), all voices at letter B, BH 78, p. 9:

Quartet: How are the eighth-note upbeats articulated in this leap of the minor tenth?

Székely: Don't make the utmost effort to slur the eighth-note upbeats to the main note in this case. Don't make a maximum effort to play legato, but also don't make "breaks" by making the eighth-note upbeats short. Do it as it is natural. That is to say, don't connect the upbeats to the main note with all your ability, but neither make short notes. Even if you break between the notes, have

accents on every note. Keep accents on the upper notes. That is
again the agogic accent, but you cannot express it with just plain
accents. As I have mentioned, there is not a sufficiently clear indication in the notation because Bartók could not completely explain it either. But there is a feeling that these notes must be
heavy, so that is the musical meaning!

Regarding the articulation in Quartet No. 5, Allegro (movement one),
all voices before figure 30, one measure, BH No. 78, p. 10:

Quartet: What about the accents above the tenuto symbol?

Székely: Express it with heavier notes than just an accent, but in no
way stopped. Don't be afraid that it may not be entirely sustained, as in tenuto. That is not the idea. When I played the Second Rhapsody, Bartók said, "Play it like a peasant!" The gypsies
do not play with lifted bowings, but rather "on the string," and
this was what he had in mind. That was his idea in using this
symbol. The thing is that articulation which is natural is good.

Regarding the articulation in Quartet No. 5, Andante (movement
four), all voices at letter A, BH No. 78, p. 54:

Quartet: What is the best method for solving the ensemble problem
here as we change tempo and articulation simultaneously? Leading the eighth-note upbeats takes away our nervousness, but
makes us physically active since we all "lead."

Székely: Make no big stop, because in the next section you have it entirely legato, so it should go right into the next note.

Quartet: But what does the second violinist do since he is playing
legato until the very moment of the *ricochet* bowing?

Székely: Well, the others playing legato have a hard time, too, but
they manage it somehow!

Quartet: We must change from quarter-note equals metronome 70
(*poco slargando e rubato*) to quarter-note equals 84 (*Più andante*);
that is to say, the quarter-note equaling 84 is quite a bit faster
than what has gone before. But at letter A how can the second violin enter smoothly and at the same time change the tempo
without any specific definition in the connection?

Székely: How can one exactly determine the new tempo? There is no
technique for certain things like that. Besides, it is technically

difficult to play the *saltato* bowing "in a certain tempo." It is also an individual matter. Perhaps one plays a little bit faster, takes a shade of difference in the tempo, when playing alone than when playing with others.

Regarding the articulation in Quartet No. 3, Allegro, Seconda parte, all voices (fugal entrances), before figure 31, one measure and continuing, BH No. 76, p. 20:

Quartet: What about the articulation of the fugue?

Székely: The Hungarian Quartet played the entrances, the first two interjections which are sixteenth-note groups, "on the string." There is a sequence of different articulations: first *leggiero*, then *punta d'arco*, then *ponticello*. So, three different things.

Regarding the *glissandi* in Quartet No. 3, Ricapitulazione della prima parte, all voices at figure 10 to the end of the movement, BH No. 76, p. 37.

Quartet: Do you use the note's full value as notated in these *glissandi?*

Székely: From the period of 1927 on, you have to use the full value of the note in the *glissando*. In that second style period it is meant that way, although before that it was not a clear principle. Here in the Third Quartet it already is a principle that one uses the full value of the note from the point where the *glissando* is marked. It is up to your musical taste if sometimes you feel that a note needs a little longer duration before the *glissando* begins, and in such a case the *glissando* does not start right away. But Bartók marks what he wants.

Regarding the *glissandi* (pizzicati) in Quartet No. 6, Burletta (movement three), all voices, at figure 97 and continuing, BH No. 25, p. 37:

Quartet: How does one sustain the sound in the *pizzicato glissando* so that the terminal pitch will sound?

Székely: Imagine that you are a guitarist. Play practically with the fingernail. If you press your finger very hard, then you could get almost the same results. You must use the same finger—whether the *glissando* goes down or up. You will lose the sound if you change fingers.

Regarding the direction of movement in playing the broken chords in Quartet No. 3, Ricapitulazione della prima parte, Vc. part after figure 13, four measures and continuing, BH No. 76, p. 38:

Quartet: Is the introduction of arrows to show the direction of the broken chord exceptional?

Székely: Bartók uses a system of arrows in the piano works, too. I would say that is just one of his principles. He differentiates between breaking the chords up or down and marks it so, but maybe for the cello he does not always mark it. Some confusion crops up here and there.

Regarding the pizzicato chords in Quartet No. 3, Allegro (Seconda parte), Vc. part, beginning measure 5, BH No. 76, p. 9:

Quartet: Are the three-note chords always played unbroken?

Székely: Yes. Did you play it with one finger, two fingers, three fingers? Play it with three fingers, otherwise it is hard to play the chord so that the soprano note comes out.

Regarding the Scherzo of Quartet No. 4, Prestissimo, con sordino, BH No. 77, p. 18:

Quartet: If only we can we learn "one little secret" that you have regarding the Scherzo of Quartet No. 4—If we could just find one!

Székely: One thing is this: if you have a correct bowing and are not troubled by the "up" and "down" directions, then that is better, but everyone has to find the correct bowing for himself. It should be that one arrives automatically on the heavy beat. That is the easiest way.

What I think is important is that one realizes that, although marked 6/8, it changes into 9/8 every time. However, that fact everyone has to feel for himself.

Quartet: Do you just feel that, or do you mark it?

Székely: I mark it *à la Bartók* with dotted lines. In this case, insofar as it is important, Bartók has an accent on it, and therefore you automatically feel the begining of the bar, for instance, in the seventh bar from the beginning. It is in 9/8 even if he did not change the bar, because otherwise in 6/8 you have a syncopation accent and that doesn't fit with the answer. If you feel that passage in

6/8 as it is notated, then you arrive at different places with the accents, and that confuses the meaning of the music. In time you exactly "feel" the music, but it is better if you have its nature clearly in mind. Otherwise you will probably get confused.

Quartet: Did the Hungarian Quartet ever facilitate the playing of those interchanging violin parts in the fast pizzicato passages at figure 51?

Székely: Yes. In that example we made a "little arrangement." Those are the details which do not change the music at all. It is much wiser to rearrange certain things, and we did so even in Beethoven. With certain rearrangements the music remains exactly as it was, perhaps even better because it is more exactly realized. In this Bartók passage, since the viola and cello continue, we arranged it so that the alternating pizzicato passages remained in only one part, not exchanging with the others, because that is very difficult.

Quartet: Is it possible at figure 185 to redistribute certain notes so as to avoid playing so many perfect fifths?

Székely: The voicing is correct exactly as it is written, but, of course, the listener doesn't hear your voicing. Perhaps he will hear whether the chord is there and in tune. In these cases we occasionally redistributed the notes.

Quartet: Some aspects of the pizzicato playing are extremely difficult. Do you have any advice on that?

Székely: Very few know how to deal with these pizzicato passages simply because they don't think enough about it. One must experiment.

2. CHAMBER MUSIC

These excerpts are from conversations that took place from 1990 to 1992 between Zoltán Székely and Claude Kenneson regarding performance problems in chamber music. During this period topical conversations were frequently recorded for inclusion in the proposed Székely Archive at the Banff Centre.

Székely: Some problems that occur in the music of Bartók's second style period disappeared from his later music, which was simpler.

In the time of the Fourth Quartet, he tried some complicated devices. Halsey Stevens wrote about this in his book. Stevens was so fond of the Fourth Quartet, particularly on account of the first movement. That Allegro is one of Bartók's most abstract compositions.

For the normal listener, Bartók is already difficult, at least in this second style period which is a period of extremities from the Third Quartet on, and including the first movement of the Fourth Quartet.

Kenneson: How do you imagine Bartók conceived the poly-rhythm of the Scherzo (*Alla bulgarese*) of the Fifth Quartet?

Székely: Not everything about the passages in polyrhythm is a complete success. Some aspects are theoretical. The rhythm in itself is very complicated, and when the syncopation is added as a further complication, the ensemble playing becomes difficult. Whether that is just an invention he tried, or whether he really felt that polyrhythm—a very complicated feeling if you want to do it as it is written—I don't know.

Kenneson: Whenever I performed those passages, I was never entirely convinced of the absolute stability of my rhythm in relation to the other players since I always had some misgivings about what they were doing at any given moment. Do you think these things necessarily become clearer with greater experience?

Székely: Slowly one comes to those convictions. Vilmos Palotai asserted that he could feel this polyrhythm, but I am not certain if it is possible. If polyrhymic passages are complex, then one cannot always feel it. When playing, you hear only that there is some impression of confusion in it.

I remember a certain conductor who said he had a talent that allowed him to talk to somebody and then when someone else began to talk at the same time, he could follow it all. Now that is wonderful for a conductor, but I don't know whether it was true or not.

Kenneson: In the Scherzo (*Alla bulgarese*), Bartók clearly marks the rise and fall of the dynamics, but when everyone begins to surge towards loudness, the polyrhythm is somewhat endangered since the strictness tends to go out of the tempo.

Székely: That is fine on paper, but to realize it fully so that it makes the correct effect is very difficult. It is similiar to certain twelve-tone compositions where you have no grip on it since the relations themselves accomplish the effect.

In fact, to a certain degree, polyphony has the same problems. It is almost unbelievable that Bach could improvise a fugue and play it logically and well. Perhaps if one's whole musical life were spent in the style period, it could be possible that some of those earlier musicians were able to accomplish these feats.

Kenneson: In the trio of the Scherzo (*Alla bulgarese*), I could rarely get a clear impression of the complex first violin part since it moved so quickly in its ostinato figures—and perhaps because I was so preoccupied playing the cello part.

Székely: That passage makes a coloristic impression.

Kenneson: Must it be understood what is merely coloristic and what is structural—what is going to bind the parts together?

Székely: Yes, but that is relatively simple. Where it is polyrhythmic, that is hard—if you are honest!

Kenneson: There is a real problem when the music apparently begins to have nothing to do with what you see printed on the page, that is to say, when the notation looks different than the music sounds. I was tempted to find some way to accomplish the playing, but not necessarily with Bartók's notated rhythm. I simply wanted theoretically to be "in the right place at the right time." But actually one can sustain that kind of mental manipulation for only a few measures at a time, because one's perceptions can't hold on to any trickery for long, since it is not essentially the same as the real rhythm. But what of the polytonal passages?

Székely: In Bartók's piano work, Bagatelles, Op. 6, the first Bagatelle is a study in polytonality written about six months before the First Quartet. Theoretically it is and certainly was a bold feat, especially when nobody yet wrote such things. Certain polytonal passages in the music of Milhaud or Stravinsky, for instance, that came years later during their own polytonal experiments, are easier to follow than the polytonality of these Bagatelles.

By the way, do you know the name Enrico Bossi? He was an Italian composer and an organ virtuoso. He composed a piano piece, not of any significance, that was a kind of farce. He played a certain bass together with a soprano that was, strangely enough, a half tone higher than one expected. After a few bars, one absolutely got used to the effect, but when suddenly he gives this up and places both parts in the same tonality, one is momentarily perplexed by what has happened. It is a strange experience to hear this, but because the distance between the parts is great, somehow you combine the parts in your mind. He wrote this for fun, of course. A farce.

Kenneson: Did you feel in your frequent performances of the Fifth Quartet over thirty-five years that its performance problems were eventually solved, or were you concerned when you approached them anew?

Székely: One learns the nature of it. When there is no counterpoint, it is simple, but as it is written, there are certain passages where the imitations cause you to feel that something unusual happens. At any rate, after studying his music for years, knowing his style, system, and technique, one is able to see his intentions much more clearly.

Kenneson: It is the despair of string quartet playing that it doesn't matter how well each person plays his instrument, if together the four cannot realize the music.

Székely: Yes, certain passages are difficult in this respect. At figure 35 in this Scherzo one tries not to feel it, but here there is a combination of nine, that is to say, three plus three plus three and the motif is in 9/8. Perhaps you have to force yourself in such cases, but I don't know whether it is possible to play it in the way it is notated.

Kenneson: If one is playing the cello part, when the others pulse that accompaniment it makes one want to reach out and connect to it somehow, which is not at all the correct solution. Of course, there is some relief when two play the same rhythm because the rhythmic texture is simpler.

Székely: When a passage is instrumentally complicated one must be strict, but, of course, must always play the passage as music.

Kenneson: Do you think Bartók ever thought to take pity on those who would play these passages, or did he just write them in the passion of creativity?

Székely: It is hard to say. There are certain problems in the violin sonatas. In the last movement of the First Sonata, Bartók didn't play as though he were a metronome. Once he said to me,

"When I played this with Márta Linz, she played it right away and well." Linz was a Hubay pupil who learned that violin part and seems to have had an instinct about the rhythm. If one can hear certain cues in the piano part, then every time that cue comes, it dictates the rhythm. He writes 5/8, but within the 5/8 there are variations—longer, then shorter motifs. Of course, he played this passage in musical groups, not in metronomic groups.

Kenneson: That is a different matter, isn't it? Playing musical groupings makes it function, makes it practical.

Székely: In such cases, the violinist must be able to accommodate the pianist, in fact. It seems that Márta Linz could emancipate herself from these rhythmic problems. Whenever that particular high note came in the piano part, it served as a sign. That is the problem in these complicated rhythms that, by nature, if you accent one note, then that accent dictates the distance to the next, if you play it musically. If you don't do that, then it is unnatural and difficult.

Kenneson: Once when writing about string quartet intonation, Robert Mann of the Juilliard Quartet mentioned that the Hungarian Quartet played in an even-tempered intonation.[6] I've read that in your quartet rehearsals during the mid-1960s the size of the interval of the third was still a matter of debate after thirty years. Many quartet players unfamiliar with the discipline of playing in an even-tempered intonation would find that astonishing.

Székely: It is true that in the early period of the Hungarian Quartet's career, we adopted the philosophy that good intonation for our quartet was the outcome of using the even-tempered scale.

Our quartet's vibrato was tempered, as well as its intonation. I tried to avoid excessive vibrato and instead aimed for purity of tone. In principle, we held back the sonorities called for in a dramatic climax until the right moments. In the slow movements I searched for moments of peace without the constant intensity that besets some quartets. That result we achieved with a quality of tone dependent on almost immeasurable factors: hardly perceptible dynamic change, proportioned bowstrokes, nuanced vibrato, the use of tenuto.

We were always concerned with questions of tempo. If one compares our two recordings of the Beethoven cycle made over a long period of time—twelve years—it will be discovered that in the later recording we had abandoned some of the especially fast *tempi*. In the same way a composer ripens as he grows older, we came to new decisions after repeated performances since there is no proof except in public performances. In the second Beethoven cycle recording we tried very hard to make perfect performances that would stand as models, but in principle you cannot compare recorded performances with live ones.

Kenneson: Do you wish to say anything about the inherent difficulties for the first violinist who has a strong background experience as a soloist? In earlier periods it was certainly true that often the first violinist dominated quartet playing in every way, the others becoming merely subservient to a "soloistic" approach.

Székely: Sometimes in quartet playing, the first violinist must make his part fit for the sake of the other voices. Perhaps one could play a passage more beautifully, but the nature of quartet playing doesn't allow too much freedom. It is so subtle. You have to learn that while it is beautiful, it is also somewhat restrictive. It gives the impression of freedom, but it is not free. Of course, it is mainly at the beginning of one's experience that one has to learn that. You simply must forget how freely you play when you are a soloist. You learn this all the time: it is a little bit impersonal, and perhaps not the playing that your heart dictates.

3. STRING QUARTETS

On 2 March 1980 at the Festival of String Quartets, where performances were given by three Alberta string quartets in residence at the Banff Centre, Zoltán Székely talked to the ensembles about several topics related to string quartet playing. The ensembles were the University of Alberta String Quartet, the Aurora String Quartet, and the Relevé String Quartet.

Beethoven's Quartet, Op. 131, has some difficult rhythmic problems that can prove very confusing. Of course, it is possible to interpret this music in different ways, but I have my own way and have written it down.

These problems appear mainly in the Scherzo, where, as in some faster movements, one bar among several represents the heavy beat and there is no clear indication which bar this is. For

instance, when three fast bars represent one unit of meter, Beethoven has sometimes marked *tre battute*, but when this is not
marked, such groupings are open to many different interpretations since the meaning of a certain bar in syncopation may be a
question.

Sometimes the composer doesn't realize exactly what will
happen in performance and leaves these matters to chance, so
to speak, by not marking his own, definite interpretation. According to the Riemann Theory, the harmonic cadence is always
the point of repose and was always the criterion in Riemann's
mind for understanding the phrasing. In the works of both
Brahms and Beethoven there are passages whose phrasing is ambiguous. One can have long discussions in this regard. For instance, in the second movement of Brahms' Violin Concerto it
seems that the bar-line is misplaced by a half-bar. However, one
cannot absolutely say this is the case, for eventually it changes
position. In the slow movements of Quartets Op. 59, No.1, and
Op. 135 of Beethoven there is evidence of a misplaced bar-line. In
Op. 59, No.1, every phrase ends in the middle of the bar.

I learned when I was young that the classicists often notate
music this way. In some Mozart works, exactly the same phrase
returns in a reprise somewhat changed, a half-bar different from
the first appearance, because a shortened bar has appeared in the
meantime. In music a lot of things are possible. We can feel
something at the start of a classical work, then change our sense
of the phrasing later on.

When we come to contemporary music, where we miss our
traditional harmonic basis, we have to take other measurements.
That is a fact. The very latest contemporary music is different
from Bartók's music in this respect. In Bartók's time, before midcentury, one had the feeling that a certain melodic line or a certain phrase had to "go somewhere." The music went from step to
step since we still had in our blood the remnants of the eight-
bar-phrase tradition which is now often nonexistent. Soon we
must have a new theory to answer the questions that come from
the latest developments.

With the music of Bartók we are somewhere in-between the
classicists and that which is new. When you read his music and
study his harmonizations with their chromaticism, you observe
where he scrupulously puts the accidentals, trying to suggest to

you that a certain note indicates a change in the harmony, one which we probably don't hear anymore. As Paul Hindemith has said, "The note is the note" so whether it is written this or that way matters not. But in Bartók's music when we feel that a certain chord has a traditional identity and a particular note is an alteration of that chord, then that note appears to have a definite harmonic function. So Bartók tries to explain his harmonization in notation based on the classical principles, but this doesn't always work. The same problem occurs with the rhythm. Sometimes we cannot determine exactly what is meant even in the folklore examples. Sometimes we hesitate.

Beethoven gave metronome markings to the quartets of the middle period, but there are none in the late quartets. It is not so much the exact number, but that the metronome markings indicate the character of the music. Because the exact metronome markings don't prove to be instrumentally practical in every case, you have to consider Beethoven's intention regarding the character. However, his metronome markings are not far off, except in the Quartet, Op. 18, No. 6. The marking for the first movement is not possible. It would be worthwhile to examine the manuscript and see if there is anything doubtful in the handwriting, for this is far off. He asks 160, and it should be around 120. That is the only metronome marking in the quartets which is that far off. All the others you can consider as giving the indication of the character of the piece. In general, the markings are a little bit faster than we are used to.

I heard a performance of the Op. 59, No. 3, by the very good New York quartet, the New Music Quartet. They played the fugato in the tempo according to Beethoven's extremely fast metronome markings, and it can be played. There are more ensembles now who try to follow the original marks—which is correct to do—and most of the time you will find that we, the Hungarian String Quartet, adopted whatever was the marking.

But in that fugato we dropped one or two numbers slower. If you compare our first recording of the Beethoven cycle with our second, here and there you will notice that we have calmed the *tempi* since some were a little bit on the fast side. Our later recording seems to be played in somewhat more comfortable *tempi*.

I remember once in Paris where we had just finished performing a Beethoven cycle at Salle Gaveau, a certain director of a recording company played a record of Op. 18, No. 4, for us, then asked, "What do you think of that?" And we said, "Very well played. A little bit fast." And he said, "That is you. The Hungarian Quartet!" When the cycle was transmitted on the radio, he had copied it. So we can learn something from listening to even our own recordings.

In Heifetz's recording of the Mendelssohn concerto, he plays the Finale faster than anyone else plays it, and we say, "Very brilliant. Very good," but in fact, it is not what Mendelssohn meant. So this shows that if you play something extremely well, then you can permit yourself to play about with a certain tempo.

Who knows what is in the minds of composers? Mostly they mark *tempi* at the beginning when the work is composed, and seemingly at that period it is so vivid and so fresh that they sometimes mark it a little bit on the fast side while it is still so lively in their imaginations. Later they may accept it a little bit slower.

4. BEETHOVEN CYCLE PERFORMANCE PLANS

From 1945 until 1972, the Hungarian String Quartet presented the complete Beethoven cycle in more than fifty performances in the major music centers of the world. Zoltán Székely always planned the order of these cyclic performances with a preference for mixing quartets from the three style periods in each concert rather than presenting chronological performances.

Here are a few of his characteristic plans for the order of the Beethoven cycle. While the cycle was occasionally presented in a five-concert format, a six-concert format was standard practice. In the later period, Székely planned two performances of Op. 130 during each cycle. It was played once with the traditional Allegro finale; in another concert the work would appear with the Op. 133 (Grosse Fuge) as the final movement, as Beethoven had originally intended it.

Two typical five-concert plans:

Plan for Teatro alla Scala, Milan, 1948

Concert 1. Op. 18, No. 1, Op. 127; Op. 59, No. 1
Concert 2. Op. 18, No. 2; Op. 131; Op. 59, No. 2
Concert 3. Op. 18, No. 3; Op. 132; Op. 59, No. 3

Concert 4. Op. 18, No. 4; Op. 74; Op. 18, No. 5; Op. 95
Concert 5. Op. 18, No. 6; Op. 133; Op. 135; Op. 130

Plan for Mexico City, 1957

Concert 1. Op. 18, No. 4; Op. 59, No. 1; Op. 131
Concert 2. Op. 18, No. 5; Op. 59, No. 2; Op. 18, No. 1; Op. 59, No. 3
Concert 3. Op. 18, No. 3; Op. 127; Op. 135
Concert 4. Op. 18, No. 2; Op. 74; Op. 130 with Fugue
Concert 5. Op. 95; Op. 132; Op. 18, No. 6

Three typical six-concert plans:

Plan for Vevey, Switzerland, 1953

Concert 1. Op. 18, No. 4; Op. 127; Op. 59, No. 3
Concert 2. Op. 18, No. 5; Op. 135; Op. 59, No. 2
Concert 3. Op. 18, No. 3; Op. 133; Op. 59, No. 1
Concert 4. Op. 18, No. 2; Op. 74; Op. 130
Concert 5. Op. 18, No. 1; Op. 95; Op. 132
Concert 6. Op. 18, No. 6; Op. 131

Plan for Zurich, 1954

Concert 1. Op. 18, No. 2; Op. 59, No. 1; Op. 18, No. 3
Concert 2. Op. 18, No. 1; Op. 59, No. 3; Op. 18, No. 6
Concert 3. Op. 18, No. 5; Op. 59, No. 2; Op. 18, No. 4
Concert 4. Op. 130; Op. 133; Op. 74
Concert 5. Op. 95; Op. 135; Op. 127
Concert 6. Op. 132; Op. 131

Plan for London, 1970

Concert 1. Op. 18, No. 1; Op. 127; Op. 59, No. 3
Concert 2. Op. 18, No. 2; Op.130; Op. 95
Concert 3. Op. 18, No. 5; Op. 18, No. 4; Op. 131
Concert 4. Op. 18, No. 3; Op. 74; Op. 132
Concert 5. Op. 130 with Fugue; Op. 59, No. 1
Concert 6. Op. 18, No. 6; Op. 59, No. 2; Op. 135

Members of the Hungarian String Quartet (1935–1972)

Four young musicians—Sándor Végh, Péter Szervánsky, Dénes Koromzay, and Vilmos Palotai—formed a string quartet in Budapest in 1935. They called their ensemble "new" to avoid a conflict of identity with the well-established Waldbauer-Kerpely String Quartet, often called the Hungarian String Quartet on its European tours. In 1945 at the end of World War Two, the New Hungarian String Quartet emerged from five years of artistic exile in Occupied Holland called simply the Hungarian String Quartet, the name it retained until 1972 when it was disbanded. During the 1970s Dénes Koromzay formed yet a third Hungarian String Quartet and once again called it "new."

During the period 1935 to 1938, the New Hungarian String Quartet had several changes of personnel including a succession of second violinists: Szervánsky, László Halmos, Végh (who assumed this role when Zoltán Székely became first violinist in 1937), Ödön Pártos (whose tenure was very brief), and the Russian violinist Alexandre Moskowky. From 1938 to 1956 the first permanent formation of the quartet—Székely, Moskowsky, Koromzay, and Palotai—brought the ensemble to world prominence.

When Palotai retired from the quartet for health reasons in 1956, Gabriel Magyar became the cellist. Moskowsky retired in 1959 at which time Michael Kuttner became the second violinist. From 1959 to 1972 the second permanent formation of the quartet—Székely, Kuttner, Koromzay, and Magyar—established the Hungarian String Quartet as one of the world's leading chamber music ensembles.

ORIGINAL MEMBERS OF THE NEW HUNGARIAN STRING QUARTET

Sándor Végh (b. 1912). Born in Klausenburg on 17 May 1912, Végh was educated in Budapest at the Franz Liszt Academy where he studied violin with Jenő Hubay and chamber music with Leó Weiner. He founded the Hungarian Trio in 1931 and the New Hungarian String Quartet in 1935. First violinist of the quartet from 1935 until 1937, he became second violinist for the 1937–38 season, then returned to Hungary. In 1940 he became professor at the Franz Liszt Academy and founded the Végh String Quartet which soon established an international reputation. In 1946 he moved to Switzerland, led a violin and chamber music master class at the Basel Musikakademie, and was professor at the Freiburg-im-Breisgau Hochschule.

Péter Szervánsky (b. ca. 1910). The original second violinist of the New Hungarian String Quartet, Szervánsky performed with the ensemble during the 1935–36 season. A graduate of the Franz Liszt Academy in 1933, he was a member of Jenő Hubay's master class from 1931 to 1933. He later lived in South America.

Dénes Koromzay (b. 1913). Koromzay was violist of the Hungarian String Quartet throughout its existence. Born in Budapest on 18 May 1913, he lived in Arad, Hungary, for the first twelve years of his life. His father was president of a railroad company. He began piano lessons at the age of five. His first teacher soon recognized his unusual talent and absolute pitch and persuaded him to take up the violin instead.

At twelve, Koromzay entered the Franz Liszt Academy in Budapest where during the next six years he received his musical training. His violin teacher was Jenő Hubay. At seventeen he was awarded his Master's diploma. He studied composition with Albert Siklos, and received his degree in composition and in conducting at the age of eighteen.

That same year he participated in the International Concours for Violin in Vienna where he won a prize. The following year he went to Berlin where he studied in Carl Flesch's master class at the Hochschule für Musik. He began a promising solo career, was heard in many recitals and broadcasts in Budapest, Vienna, and Berlin, and accepted the position of assistant concertmaster in the Budapest Concert Orchestra.

When the New Hungarian String Quartet was formed in 1935, he took up the viola, an instrument for which he always had a special affection and which he very often played in student performances of chamber music. While living in Holland during the war, he accepted the position of principal violist of the Amsterdam Concertgebouw Orchestra offered to him by Willem Mengelberg. During his long and distinguished career he owned several violas, including instruments made by Domenico Busan and Michel Decanet (Venice 1766).

After the Hungarian String Quartet was disbanded in 1972, Koromzay again established a New Hungarian String Quartet. This ensemble with violinists Andor Tóth and Richard Young, and cellist, Andor Tóth, Jr., had a successful international career for eight years and recorded much of the quartet repertoire. Koromzay teaches at the University of Colorado in Boulder. In 1982 he was presented the Bartók Award; in 1983 he received the Kodály Award.

Vilmos Palotai (1904–1972). Palotai was the cellist of the Hungarian String Quartet from its inception in 1935 until 1956. Born in Budapest on 21 May 1904, he studied at the Franz Liszt Academy with Adolf Shiffer, then later in Berlin with Hugo Becker. He also studied conducting with Herman Scherchen. It was during these studies in Strasbourg in 1933 that he conducted a performance of Bartók's Second Piano Concerto with the composer as soloist. His instruments were a Bergonzi-Gofriller and a Vuillaume.

In 1956 after leaving the Hungarian String Quartet due to illness, he went to Switzerland and established the Hungarian Trio with Arpád Gérecz, violin, and Georges Solchany, piano. He died in Switzerland in 1972.

László Halmos (b. ca. 1910). Halmos succeeded Szervánsky as second violinist of the New Hungarian Quartet and appeared with the ensemble during the 1936–37 season. A graduate of the Franz Liszt Academy, he was a pupil of Imre Waldbauer. He toured Europe with the quartet and took part in the early performances of Bartók's Fifth Quartet.

Ödön Pártos (1907–1977). When Végh left the New Hungarian Quartet at the conclusion of the 1937–38 season, Pártos agreed to join the quartet. He rehearsed as second violinist for a brief period in September 1938 but did not appear with the ensemble in concert (see Chapter Sixteen). Born in Budapest on 1 October 1907, he was a graduate of the Franz Liszt Academy where he studied the violin with Jenő Hubay and composition with Zoltán Kodály. After leaving the academy, he spent five years in Berlin, returning to Budapest in 1933. In 1938 Pártos went to Israel where he had a distinguished career as a violist-composer. He was first violist of the Tel Aviv Philharmonic (later the Israel Philharmonic) until 1956. For sixteen years, from 1940 until 1956, he was violist of the Israeli String Quartet. He was appointed Director of the Tel Aviv Academy of Music in 1951. He died in Israel in 1977.

Alexandre Moskowsky (1901–1969). After the brief tenure of Pártos, Moskowsky joined the New Hungarian Quartet and was second violinist of the ensemble from 1938 until 1959. He was born at Kertch in the Crimea in southern Russia on 22 October 1901. His father, a physician, was an excellent amateur singer. Moskowsky's formal musical education started when he was five. At fourteen he had already graduated from the State Conservatory in his provincial town and was appearing in local concerts. He was sent to St. Petersburg to study in Leopold Auer's master class in 1916. When the outbreak of the Revolution interrupted his musical studies, he returned to the Crimea where he studied literature and history.

Later he completed his musical education by obtaining his degree, Master of Music and Virtuosity, at the St. Petersburg Conservatory. Here the director, Alexander Glazunov, singled him out for a particular favor. Glazunov's friends in Germany and Holland wished to help a young and gifted Russian artist, and Glazunov obtained the permit from the authorities to allow Moskowsky to go abroad.

He settled in Holland in 1923 and became the leader of the Moskowsky String Quartet and professor of violin at the Amsterdam Musieklyceum before joining the New Hungarian String Quartet in 1938. His violins were a Guarnerius del Gesù, 1733, the so-called "Pugnani del Gesù," and an instrument by Giovanni Roggeri. Moskowsky was a passionate linguist with complete fluency in six languages.

Zoltán Székely (b.1903). Székely was first violinist of the Hungarian String Quartet for thirty-five years, from 1937 to 1972.

MEMBERS OF THE HUNGARIAN STRING QUARTET AFTER 1952

Laurent Halleux (b.1897). Halleux was violist of the Hungarian String Quartet during the 1952–53 season when Dénes Koromzay was on leave from the ensemble. Halleux was born at Hodimont-Verviers, France, on 24 January 1897 and was a violin pupil of César Thomson. He was a member of the celebrated Belgian Pro-Arte String Quartet and alternated as leader with Alphonse Onnou during the early years of that quartet. Later he was second violinist. After 1940 he was in residence at the University of Wisconsin, then took up the viola and played in the MGM studio orchestra in Los Angeles, and with both the Roth and Hungarian string quartets.

Gabriel Magyar (b. 1914). After Palotai retired from the Hungarian String Quartet in 1956 due to illness, Magyar joined the ensemble and was cellist from 1956 until 1972. Born in Budapest on 5 December 1914, he was introduced to music at an early age. His brother, Tamás Magyar, was a distinguished violinist. His mother was a pianist, and his father, professor of humanities and classical languages, was a fervent music enthusiast. Gabriel Magyar began to play the violin first, but soon took up the cello. He studied at the Franz Liszt Academy with Anton Friss and graduated with the Master's diploma in 1936. He studied chamber music with Leó Weiner and composition with Zoltán Kodály.

Among highlights of his career as a young virtuoso were performances of the Kodály Solo Sonata, acclaimed by the composer, and the first Budapest performance of Darius Milhaud's Cello Concerto. His career was interrupted by the war but resumed immediately after the Armistice. Successful concerts in Europe were followed by engagements in South America and the United States. As solo cellist and member of the Trio of the National Radio of Caracas, Venezuela, he gave weekly recitals. Before joining the Hungarian String Quartet, he was professor of cello and chamber music at the University of Oklahoma.

His instruments were a cello by Giovanni Baptista Gabrielli, 1751, and a Grancino cello. After the disbanding of the Hungarian

String Quartet, Magyar was a professor at the University of Illinois and taught at the Banff Centre in Canada.

Michael Kuttner (1918–1975). After Moskowsky retired from the Hungarian String Quartet in 1959, Kuttner joined the ensemble and was second violinist from 1959 until 1972. He was born in Budapest on 9 February 1918. His father was a friend of Gabriel Magyar's father before World War One. His cousin is the distinguished Hungarian cellist, László Varga.

At the age of seventeen, Kuttner graduated from the Franz Liszt Academy where he had studied in the Hubay master class and won the coveted Reményi Prize. He devoted his last year there to chamber music study under Leó Weiner.

Kuttner organized his own quartet in 1935, and soon this ensemble, the Pro Ideale String Quartet, was invited to join the faculty of the Westminster Choir College in Princeton, New Jersey, where it was known as the Westminster String Quartet. Later Kuttner played with the Roth, Gordon, and Léner quartets. He owned a Petrus Guarnerius violin, 1704, called the "Santa Theresa." After the disbanding of the Hungarian String Quartet, Kuttner taught at Indiana University. He died in Bloomington, Indiana, in 1975.

Compositions and First Performances by Zoltán Székely

COMPOSITIONS BY ZOLTAN SZÉKELY

1. Sonata, Op. 1, Violino Solo
Published by Universal-Edition, No. 8466, Copyright 1926.
Composed during 1919–20. Completed 1920, Budapest.
Dedicated to Mr. and Mrs. J. de Graaff-Bachiene.
Four movements:
    1. Appassionato, ma in tempo molto moderato
    2. Scherzo
    3. Intermezzo
    4. Finale (Molto Allegro con brio)

2. Adagio and Scherzo for Piano
Unpublished.
Composed during 1919–20. Completed July 1920, Budapest.
Two movements:
    1. Adagio
    2. Scherzo (Vivace)

3. Trio for Violin, Viola, and Cello
Unpublished (intended as Opus 2).
Composed during 1918–21. Completed 1921, Budapest.
Four movements:

1. Moderato
2. Vivace ma non troppo
3. Moderato poco adagio
4. Allegretto grazioso. [alternate finale, Allegro vivace]

4. Allegro for Violin and Orchestra (or piano)
Unpublished.
Composed during 1920–23. Orchestrated version with completed
   score; version for violin and piano. Completed 1923, Nijmegen.
One movement:
   1. Allegro

5. Polyphon et Homophon, Op. 2. Duo for Violin and Cello
Published by Universal-Edition, No. 8696, Copyright 1927.
Composed during 1923–25. Completed April 1925, Nijmegen.
Two movements:
   1. Andante espressivo
   2. Con fuoco

6. Duo for Violin and Cello
Unpublished.
Composed during 1922–25. Completed June 1925, Nijmegen.
Three movements:
   1. Allegro moderato (1923–June 1925)
   2. Largo (February 1924)
   3. Presto (January–March 1922)
   4. Variations (not completed)

7. Concerto for Cello and Orchestra
Unpublished.
Composed during 1926–27. Begun 5 July 1926, Pontresina, Switzerland; completed 12 August 1927, Baden-Baden/Nijmegen. One
   movement exists (planned as the third movement) in version for
   cello and piano.

8. String Quartet
Unpublished.
Composed during 1935–37. Completed 1937, Santpoort.
Seven movements:
   1. Moderato ma non troppo
   2. Presto
   3. Molto moderato
   4. Andante sostenuto
   5. Quasi cadenza; Presto grazioso, come una danza
   6. Sostenuto e Appassionato
   7. Finale (molto vivace)

FIRST PERFORMANCES BY ZOLTAN SZÉKELY

Violin and Orchestra:

Béla Bartók (1881–1945)
Second Rhapsody for Violin and Orchestra.
Orchestrated version published by Universal-Edition, 1929; republished by Boosey and Hawkes, 1949.
Composed in 1928. Considerable revision during the decade 1929–39.
Dedicated to Zoltán Székely. (To Zoltán Székely)
World premiere: Budapest, 24 November 1929. Zoltán Székely, violin soloist, the Budapest Philharmonic, Ernst von Dohnányi conducting.

Concerto No. 2 for Violin and Orchestra.
Published by Boosey and Hawkes in 1946. Piano reduction published by Boosey and Hawkes in 1941.
Composed during 1937–38. Completed 31 December 1938.
Dedicated to Zoltán Székely. (To my dear friend Zoltán Székely)
World premiere: Amsterdam, 23 March 1939. Zoltán Székely, violin soloist, the Amsterdam Concertgebouw Orchestra, Willem Mengelberg conducting.

Mario Castelnuovo-Tedesco (1895–1968)
Variazioni sinfoniche for Violin and Orchestra.
Published by Universal-Edition.
Composed in 1930.
Dedicated to Zoltán Székely.
World premiere: Rome, 19 February 1930. Zoltán Székely, violin soloist, Orchestra of the Accademia di Santa Cecilia, Mario Rossi conducting.

Guillaume Landré (b. 1905)
Concerto for Violin and Chamber Orchestra.
Unpublished.
Composed in 1928.
World premiere: Amsterdam, 24 January 1932. Zoltán Székely, violin soloist, the Amsterdam Concertgebouw Orchestra, Pierre Monteux conducting.

Violin Solo:

Willem Pijper (1894–1947)
Sonata for Violin Solo.
Published by Stichting Donemus.

Composed in 1931.
Dedicated to Zoltán Székely.
World premiere: Amsterdam, 22 March 1932. Concert for the Dutch
   section of ISCM in Kleine Zaal, Amsterdam Concertgebouw.

Zoltán Székely (b. 1903)
Sonata Op. 1 for Violino Solo.
Published by Universal-Edition, 1926.
Composed during 1919–20. Completed 1920, Budapest.
Dedicated to Mr. and Mrs. J. de Graaff-Bachiene.
World premiere: Venice, 4 September 1925. Concert for International
   Festival of ISCM in Gran Teatro La Fenice.

Violin and Piano:

Henk Badings (b. 1907)
Capriccio for Violin and Piano.
Published by B. Schott's Söhne, Mainz.
Composed in 1936.
Dedicated to Zoltán Székely.
World premiere: Amsterdam, 26 January 1937. Zoltán Székely, violin,
   and Géza Frid, piano. Concert in Groot Zaal, Amsterdam Con-
   certgebouw.

Béla Bartók
Second Rhapsody for Violin and Piano.
Published by Universal-Edition in 1929. Revised in 1945 and repub-
   lished by Boosey and Hawkes in 1947.
Composed in 1928. Considerable revision during the decade 1929
   to 1939.
Dedicated to Zoltán Székely. (To Zoltán Székely)
World premiere: Amsterdam, 19 November 1928. Zoltán Székely,
   violin, and Géza Frid, piano. Concert in Groot Zaal, Amsterdam
   Concertgebouw.

Lou Lichtveld (?)
Sonata for Violin and Piano.
Unpublished.
Composed in 1924.
World premiere: Nijmegen, May 1925. Zoltán Székely, violin, and
   Eduard Van Beinum, piano. Concert at Canisius College, Nij-
   megen.

Antal Molnár (b.1890)
Suite for Violin and Piano.
Published by Rózsavölgy (Budapest).

Composed in 1934.
Dedicated to Zoltán Székely.
World premiere: Budapest, ca. 1934. Zoltán Székely, violin, and Géza
    Frid, pianist.

Transcriptions for Violin and Piano:

Béla Bartók
Rumanian Folk Dances, transcribed by Zoltán Székely.
Published by Universal-Edition, 1926.
Originally composed for piano solo in 1915 and dedicated to Ion
    Buşiţia.
Transcribed for violin and piano by Zoltán Székely, Nijmegen, 1925.
World premiere: Arnhem, 5 October 1925. Zoltán Székely, violin,
    and Béla Bartók, piano. Concert in Nieuwe Concertzaal of Musis
    Sacrum, Arnhem.

Violin and Cello:

Pál Hermann (1901–ca.1944)
Duo for Violin and Cello.
Unpublished.
Composed during 1929–30.
World premiere: London, 13 March 1930. Zoltán Székely, violin, and
    Pál Hermann, cello. Concert at the Wigmore Hall.

Erwin Schulhoff (1894–1942)
Duo for Violin and Cello.
Unpublished.
World premiere: London, 19 February 1929. Zoltán Székely, violin,
    and Pál Hermann, cello. Concert for the London Contemporary
    Music Centre, the British section of the ISCM, in the Court
    House, Marylebone Lane.

Mátyás Seiber (1905–1960)
Sonata da camera for Violin and Cello.
Published by J. and W. Chester.
World premiere: Frankfurt, 22 May 1928. Zoltán Székely, violin, and
    Pál Hermann, cello. Concert for the Frankfurter Kammer-
    musikgemeinde.

Zoltán Székely
Polyphon et Homophon, Op. 2.
Published by Universal-Edition, No. 8696, Copyright 1927.
Composed during 1923–25. Completed April 1925, Nijmegen
World premiere: Cologne, 2 June 1926. Zoltán Székely, violin, and Pál

Hermann, cello. Concert for Gesellschaft für Neue Musik of Cologne.

Ernst Toch (1887–1964)
Sonata for Violin and Cello, Op. 37.
Unpublished.
World premiere: Amsterdam, 23 March 1932. Zoltán Székely, violin, and Pál Hermann, cello. Concert for the Dutch section of ISCM in the Concertzaal of the Amsterdam Conservatorioum.

Appendix E

Discography

THE SOLO RECORDINGS OF ZOLTAN SZÉKELY, VIOLINIST

Béla Bartók (1881–1945)
Concerto No. 2 for Violin and Orchestra (1937–38)
Zoltán Székely, violin
Amsterdam Concertgebouw Orchestra, Willem Mengelberg con-
ducting
Recorded in Amsterdam in the Groote Zaal of the Amsterdam Con-
certgebouw at the first performance on March 23, 1939
Hungaroton LPX 11573 [LP]; Philips 426 104-2 [CD]

Béla Bartók
Rhapsody No. 1 for Violin and Piano (1928)
Rhapsody No. 2 for Violin and Piano (1928)
Zoltán Székely, violin
Isobel Moore, piano
Recorded at the studios of the Canadian Broadcasting Corporation,
Edmonton, Canada, for Hungaroton in 1974
Hungaroton [LP] SLPX H357; Hungaroton [CD] HCD 31038

Béla Bartók
Rumanian Folk Dances (transcribed for violin and piano by Zoltán
Székely)
Nos. 1, 2, 3, 4, and 6 only
Zoltán Székely, violin

432

Géza Frid, piano
Recorded in London for His Master's Voice at the Abbey Road Studios
ca. 1937
Decca [78] D-K872; TA 3025-1
Pearl Records [CD] (Pavilion Records Ltd.) BVA II

Alexander Glazounov (1865–1936)
Concerto in A Minor, Op. 82, for Violin and Orchestra
Zoltán Székely, violin
Residentie Orchestra of The Hague, Willem Van Otterloo conducting
Recorded in Holland ca. 1942
Van Decca [78] X10110/2

Joan Manén (1883–1971)
Chanson—Adagietto, Op. A8, No. 1, for Violin and Piano
Zoltán Székely, violin
Géza Frid, piano
Recorded in London for His Master's Voice at the Abbey Road Studios
ca. 1937
Decca [78] D-K872 TA 3025-1

Nicolò Antonio Porpora (1686–1768)
Sonata in G Major for Violin and Piano
Zoltán Székely, violin
Géza Frid, piano
Recorded in London for His Master's Voice at the Abbey Road Studios
ca. 1937
Decca [78] D-K863 D-25877. TA 3022-1, 3023-II

THE RECORDINGS OF THE HUNGARIAN STRING QUARTET

Béla Bartók
Quartet No. 5 (1934)
The Hungarian String Quartet (Székely, Moskowsky, Koromzay,
Palotai)
Recorded in London for EMI at the Abbey Road Studio ca. 1946
Decca [78] G.C. (HMV) 3511-4

Béla Bartók
Quartet No. 6 (1939)
The Hungarian String Quartet (Székely, Moskowsky, Koromzay,
Palotai)
Recorded in London for EMI at the Abbey Road Studio ca. 1946
Decca [78] G. BD (HMV) 9389-92; HMV DB 9370-2, 3 TWA

Béla Bartók
6 Streichquartette (Six String Quartets):
First Quartet, Op. 7 (1908)
Second Quartet, Op. 17 (1917)
Third Quartet (1927)
Fourth Quartet (1928)
Fifth Quartet (1934)
Sixth Quartet (1939)
The Hungarian String Quartet (Székely, Kuttner, Koromzay, Magyar)
Recorded in Hannover at the Beethovensaal during two periods, 21 to
    30 June 1961, 26 August to 3 September 1961. Liner notes by
    John S. Weissmann; artistic supervision by O. E. Wohlert; Walter
    Sommer, recording engineer
Deutsche Grammophon Gesellschaft 18650/2 Hi Fi [LP]; 138650/52
    Stereo [LP]

Ludwig van Beethoven (1770–1827)
Quartet in E-flat Major, Op. 127
The Hungarian String Quartet (Székely, Moskowsky, Koromzay,
    Palotai)
Recorded in London at the Abbey Road Studio of EMI ca. 1949.
Decca [78]

Ludwig van Beethoven
Complete String Quartets
The Hungarian String Quartet (Székely, Moskowsky, Koromzay,
    Palotai)
The Early Quartets (Nos. 1–6)
Stereo and Mono CCA 1070/1072
The Middle Quartets (Nos. 7–11)
Stereo and Mono CCA 1073/1075
The Late Quartets (Nos. 12–17)
Stereo and Mono CCA 1076/1079
Mono 30010/30019
European Columbia FCX 240-249; Angel 35106 to 35115 or Album
    3512C (Op. 18); 3513C (Opp. 59, 74, 95); 3514D (Opp. 127, 130,
    131, 132, 133, 135)
Recorded in Paris at the I.M.E. Pathé-Marconi Studio Magellan in two
    sessions, 7 September to 17 October 1953; 9 November to 8
    December 1953. Norbert Gamsohn, producer; Paul Vavasseur,
    balance engineer
Awarded Grand Prix du Disque Diplôme of the Académie Charles
    Cros, 1955

Ludwig van Beethoven (1770–1827)
The Complete Quartets
The Hungarian String Quartet (Székely, Kuttner, Koromzay, Magyar)
Beethoven: The Early Quartets, Nos. 1–6 (Vol. 1)
Stereo CCA 1070/1072; later as HQS 1155, 6, and 7: Seraphim S-6005;
    S-IC6005
Beethoven: The Middle Quartets, Nos. 7–11 (Vol. 2)
Stereo CCA 1073/1075; later as HQS 1159, 60, and 61: Seraphim S-
    6006; S-IC6006
Beethoven: The Late Quartets, Nos. 12–15 and Grosse Fuge (Vol. 3)
Stereo 1076/1079; later as HQS 1178, 79, and 80: Seraphim S-6007; S-
    ID 6007
Recorded in Paris for I.M.E. Pathé-Marconi at Salle Wagram in 1965.
    Eric McLeod, producer
Awarded Grand Prix du Disque Diplôme of the Académie Charles
    Cros and the Grand Prix de Discophile

Alexander Borodin (1834–1887)
Nocturne (Andante, third movement) from String Quartet No. 2 in D
    Major
The New Hungarian String Quartet (Székely, Moskowsky, Koromzay,
    Palotai)
Recorded in London for HMV at the Abbey Road Studio in 1938
G-C3106 [78] (G-HMV; C-Columbia in U.S. and Europe): SEL 1610
    EMI/Col.

Alexander Borodin
String Quartet No. 2 in D Major
The Hungarian String Quartet (Székely, Moskowsky, Koromzay,
    Palotai)
Recorded in Paris for I.M.E. Pathé-Marconi in 1956. Liner notes by
    Jean Cotte
EMI/ European Columbia [LP] 33 CX1581

Johannes Brahms (1833–1897)
String Quartet, Op. 51, No. 1
String Quartet, Op. 51, No. 2
The Hungarian String Quartet (Székely, Moskowsky, Koromzay,
    Magyar)
Recorded in Paris at the Schola Cantorum for I.M.E. Pathé-Marconi in
    1958. Liner notes by Jean-Jacques Normand
European Columbia FCX 782.

Johannes Brahms
String Quartet in B-flat Major, Op. 67

The Hungarian String Quartet (Székely, Kuttner, Koromzay, Magyar)
Recorded in Paris at Salle Wagram for I.M.E. Pathé-Marconi in 1968.
    Liner notes by Georges Bect
EMI: [LP] 2C O65-10.736X

Johannes Brahms
Quintet, Op. 88, for strings
Quintet, Op. 111, for strings
Sextet, Op. 18, for strings
Sextet, Op. 36, for strings
The Hungarian String Quartet (Székely, Kuttner, Koromzay, Magyar)
    with Thomas Rolston, va., and László Varga, vc.
Recorded in Paris at Salle Wagram for I.M.E. Pathé-Marconi. Quintets
    recorded in September 1971; sextets recorded from 15 November
    until 15 December 1971. Not released

Johannes Brahms
Quartet, Op. 25, for piano and strings
Quartet, Op. 26, for piano and strings
Quartet, Op. 60, for piano and strings
Members of the Hungarian String Quartet (Székely, Koromzay, Mag-
    yar) and Georges Solchany, piano
Recorded in Paris at Salle Wagram for I.M.E. Pathé-Marconi in 1968
European Columbia FCX

Johannes Brahms
Quartet, Op. 60, for piano and strings
Members of the Hungarian String Quartet (Székely, Koromzay, Mag-
    yar) and Georges Solchany, piano
Recorded in Stuttgart at Jansen Studio for Vox Productions before
    1968
TV 4037; S4037S

Johannes Brahms
Quintet in F Minor, Op. 34, for piano and strings
The Hungarian String Quartet (Székely, Moskowsky, Koromzay, Mag-
    yar) and Georges Solchany, piano
Recorded in Paris at Salle Wagram for I.M.E. Pathé-Marconi in De-
    cember 1958
EMI: [LP] 2C 065-10.730/3

Johannes Brahms
Quintet, Op. 115, for clarinet and strings
The Hungarian String Quartet (Székely, Kuttner, Koromzay, Magyar)
    and David Glazer, clarinet
Recorded in Paris at Salle Wagram for I.M.E. Pathé-Marconi in De-

cember 1968. Liner notes by Georges Bect
EMI: [LP] 2C 065-10.737X

Claude Debussy (1862–1918)
String Quartet in G Minor, Op. 10
The Hungarian String Quartet (Székely, Moskowsky, Koromzay, Magyar)
Recorded in Paris at the Schola Cantorum for I.M.E. Pathé-Marconi in September 1958. Liner notes by Robert Cushman
European Columbia [LP] SCX 781

Antonin Dvořák (1841–1904)
String Quartet No. 12 in F Major, Op. 96 ("American")
The Hungarian String Quartet (Székely, Moskowsky, Halleux, Palotai)
Recorded in private studio in New York City for Concert Hall Society in September 1952
CHS 1157

Antonin Dvořák
String Quartet No. 12 in F Major, Op. 96 ("American")
The Hungarian String Quartet (Székely, Moskowsky, Koromzay, Magyar)
Recorded in Paris for I.M.E. Pathé-Marconi in 1956. Liner notes by Jean Cotte
European Columbia FCX 783

Antonin Dvořák
Piano Quintet in A Major, Op. 81
The Hungarian String Quartet (Székely, Moskowsky, Koromzay, Magyar) with Georges Solchany, piano
Recorded in Paris for I.M.E. Pathé-Marconi in December 1958
EMI DF 740.009

Cecil Effinger (b. 1914)
String Quartet No. 5 [1963] (Dedicated to the Hungarian String Quartet)
The Hungarian String Quartet (Székely, Kuttner, Koromzay, Magyar)
Recorded at the University of Colorado, Boulder, for Owl Studios, October 1967
Owl 10 [Boulder, Colorado] ORLP-10

César Franck (1822–1890)
Quintet in F Minor (1879) for piano and strings
The Hungarian String Quartet (Székely, Moskowsky, Koromzay, Magyar) with Georges Solchany, piano
Recorded in Paris at Salle Wagram for I.M.E. Pathé-Marconi in

December 1958. Liner notes by Jean-Jacques Normand
EMI: FCX 807

Alexander Glazounov
Five Novelettes, Op. 15
1. Alla Spagnuola. 2. Orientale. 3. Interludium in modo antico. 4.
    Valse 5. All'Hungherese.
The Hungarian String Quartet (Székely, Moskowsky, Halleux, Palotai)
Recorded in private studio in New York City for Concert Hall Society
    in September 1952
Concert Hall Society CHS 1183

Franz Josef Haydn (1732–1809)
String Quartet in D Major, Op. 64, No. 5 ("Lark")
The Hungarian String Quartet (Székely, Moskowsky, Koromzay,
    Palotai)
Recorded in London at the Abbey Road Studio of EMI ca. 1946 [78]
Released in the United States as RCA Victor [LP] DG LRC 9089:
    LM(x)1076

Franz Josef Haydn
String Quartet in D Minor, Op. 76, No. 2 ("Quinten")
The Hungarian String Quartet (Székely, Moskowsky, Koromzay,
    Palotai)
Recorded in Paris for I.M.E. Pathé-Marconi ca. 1956
EMI/European Columbia 33 CX1527

Franz Josef Haydn
String Quartet in D Major, Op. 64, No. 5 ("Lark")
The Hungarian String Quartet (Székely, Moskowsky, Koromzay,
    Palotai)
Recorded in Paris for I.M.E. Pathé-Marconi ca. 1956
EMI/European Columbia 33 CX1527

Franz Josef Haydn
String Quartet in D Major, Op. 64, No. 5 ("Lark")
The Hungarian String Quartet (Székely, Kuttner, Koromzay, Magyar)
Recorded in Vienna, June 1962
Vox PL 12.080; Turnabout 34251/3; Turnabout TV340628 coupled
    with Dekány String Quartet playing Op. 33, Nos. 2 and 3

Franz Josef Haydn
String Quartet in F Major, Op. 77, No. 2
The Hungarian String Quartet (Székely, Kuttner, Koromzay, Magyar)
Recorded in Vienna, June 1962
Vox PL 12.080; Turnabout 34251/3

Franz Josef Haydn
String Quartet in D Minor, Op. 76, No. 2
The Hungarian String Quartet (Székely, Kuttner, Koromzay, Magyar)
Recorded in Vienna, June 1962
Vox PL 12.610; Turnabout 4012; released in 1962. Liner notes by
    Harry Halbreich

Franz Josef Haydn
String Quartet in D Major, Op. 76, No. 5
The Hungarian String Quartet (Székely, Kuttner, Koromzay, Magyar)
Recorded in Vienna, June 1962
Vox PL 12.610; Turnabout 4012; released in 1962. Liner notes by
    Harry Halbreich

Zoltán Kodály (1882–1967)
String Quartet No. 2, Op. 10
The Hungarian String Quartet (Székely, Moskowsky, Koromzay,
    Palotai)
Recorded in Paris at the Schola Cantorum for I.M.E. Pathé-Marconi in
    1955. Liner notes by Marcel Marnat
European Columbia FCX 467

Wolfgang Amadeus Mozart (1756–1791)
Quartet No. 15 in D minor, K. 421
The Hungarian String Quartet (Székely, Moskowsky, Koromzay,
    Palotai)
Recorded in London at the Abbey Road Studio for EMI ca. 1946
RCA Victor Set 1299

Wolfgang Amadeus Mozart
The Six String Quartets Dedicated to Haydn
No. 14 in G Major, K. 387; VS 4127
No. 15 in D Minor, K. 421; VS 4128
No. 16 in E-flat Major, K. 428; VS 4129
No.17 in B-flat Major, K. 458 ("The Hunt") VS 4130: Turn. 34251/3:
    Vox 12130
No. 18 in A Major, K. 464; VS 4131
No. 19 in C Major, K. 465 ("Dissonant")
The Hungarian String Quartet (Székely, Kuttner, Koromzay, Magyar)
Nos. 14, 15, 16, and 18 recorded in Milan for Vox with addition of
    Nos. 17 and 19 (K. 458 and 465) recorded earlier at Studio Jansen
    in Stuttgart for Vox
VS 4132: Turn. 34251/3 Vox 12130; Vox SSVBX 589 [LP]

Quincy Porter (1897–1966)
String Quartet No. 7

The Hungarian String Quartet (Székely, Kuttner, Koromzay, Magyar)
Recorded at the University of Colorado, Boulder, for Owl Studios, October 1967
Owl 10 [Boulder, Colorado] ORLP-10

Maurice Ravel (1875–1937)
String Quartet in F Major
The Hungarian String Quartet (Székely, Moskowsky, Koromzay, Magyar)
Recorded in Paris at the Schola Cantorum for I.M.E. Pathé-Marconi in September 1958. Liner notes by Robert Cushman
European Columbia [LP] SCX 781

Franz Schubert (1797–1828)
Menuet from String Quartet in A Minor, Op. 29, No. 1, D804
The Hungarian String Quartet (Székely, Moskowsky, Koromzay, Palotai)
Recorded in Paris for I.M.E. Pathé-Marconi ca. 1956
EMI: Mono 730 070

Franz Schubert
String Quartet in A Minor, Op. 29, No. 1, D804
The Hungarian String Quartet (Székely, Moskowsky, Koromzay, Magyar)
Recorded in Paris at the Schola Cantorum for I.M.E. Pathé-Marconi in 1958. Liner notes by Jean Cotte
European Columbia FCX 783; Vox [LP] CT-2184; Vox 12520

Franz Schubert
String Quartet in D Minor, Op. Posth., D810 ("Death and the Maiden")
The Hungarian String Quartet (Székely, Moskowsky, Halleux, Palotai)
Recorded in Los Angeles for Concert Hall Society in September 1952
Concert Hall Society CHS 1152

Franz Schubert
String Quartet in D Minor, Op. Posth., D810 ("Death and the Maiden")
The Hungarian String Quartet (Székely, Moskowsky, Koromzay, Palotai)
Recorded in Paris for I.M.E. Pathé-Marconi ca. 1956
EMI: Mono 730 070

Franz Schubert
String Quartet in D Minor, Op. Posth., D810 ("Death and the Maiden")

The Hungarian String Quartet (Székely, Kuttner, Koromzay, Magyar)
Recorded in Paris
Vox 512.520

Franz Schubert
String Quartet in G Major, Op. 161, D887
The Hungarian String Quartet (Székely, Moskowsky, Koromzay, Palotai)
Recorded in Paris for I.M.E. Pathé-Marconi ca. 1956. Liner notes by J. P. Guézec
EMI: FCX 464; European Columbia [LP] 2C 063 11.308; Angel [LP] 45004

Franz Schubert
String Quartet in G Major, Op. 161, D887
The Hungarian String Quartet (Székely, Kuttner, Koromzay, Magyar)
Recorded in Paris at Salle Wagram for I.M.E. Pathé-Marconi
EMI: 2/3036-11308; 2C 061-10.693 [LP]; [Vox CT-2184 [LP]: Vox 12520]

Franz Schubert
String Quintet in C Major, Op. 163, D956
The Hungarian String Quartet (Székely, Kuttner, Koromzay, Magyar) and László Varga, vc.
Recorded in Paris at Salle Wagram for I.M.E. Pathé-Marconi in 1971. Liner notes by Philippe Andriot
EMI: CO69-12093

Franz Schubert
Quintet in A Major ("Trout"), D667 for Piano, Violin, Viola, Cello, and Double Bass
Members of the Hungarian String Quartet (Székely, Koromzay, Magyar), Louis Kentner, piano, and Georg Hörtnagel, double bass
Recorded in Stuttgart at Studio Jansen in 1963. Produced by George Kárdár
Vox 12.690; Turnabout 34140

Robert Schumann (1810–1856)
Piano Quintet in E-flat Major, Op. 44
The Hungarian String Quartet (Székely, Moskowsky, Koromzay, Magyar) and Georges Solchany, piano
Recorded in Paris at Salle Wagram for I.M.E. Pathé-Marconi in December 1958
EMI DF 740.002

Piotr Ilyitch Tchaikovsky (1840–1893)
Andante Cantabile (second movement) from String Quartet No. 1 in
    D Major, Op. 11
The New Hungarian String Quartet (Székely, Moskowsky, Koromzay,
    Palotai)
Recorded in London for HMV at the Abbey Road Studio in 1938
G-C3106 [78] (G-HMV; C-Columbia in U.S. and Europe); SEL 1610
    EMI/Col

Piotr Ilyitch Tchaikovsky
String Quartet No. 1 in D Major, Op. 11
The Hungarian String Quartet (Székely, Moskowsky, Halleux, Palotai)
Recorded in New York City for Concert Hall Society in September
    1952
Concert Hall Society CHS 1183

Heitor Villa-Lobos (1890–1959)
String Quartet No. 6 in E Minor ("Quarteto Brasileiros")
The Hungarian String Quartet (Székely, Moskowsky, Koromzay,
    Palotai)
Recorded in Paris at the Schola Cantorum for I.M.E. Pathé-Marconi in
    1955. Liner notes by Marcel Marnat
European Columbia FCX 467

"Morceaux Choisis de Quatuors à cordes"
The Hungarian String Quartet (Székely, Moskowsky, Koromzay,
    Palotai)
Side A:
(a) Alexander Borodin
     Notturno (Andante, third movement) from Quartet No. 2 in D
     Major
(b) Franz Schubert
     Scherzo (Allegro vivace, third movement) from Quartet in G
     Major, Op. 161
(c) Joseph Haydn
     Serenade (Andante cantabile, second movement) from Quartet in
     F Major, Op. 3, No. 5 [Haydn's authorship not certain]
(d) W. A. Mozart
     Menuet (Allegretto, third movement) from Quartet In D Minor,
     K. 421
(e) Joseph Haydn
     Finale (Vivace, fourth movement) from Quartet in D Major, Op.
     64, No. 5 ("Lark")
Side B:

(a) Franz Schubert
Menuet (Allegretto, third movement) from Quartet in A Minor, Op. 29
(b) Ludwig van Beethoven
Alla Danza Tedesca (fourth movement) from Quartet in B-flat Major, Op. 130
(c) Piotr Ilyitch Tchaikovsky
Andante cantabile (second movement) from Quartet in D Major, Op. 11
(d) Antonin Dvořák
Finale (vivace ma non troppo, fourth movement) from Quartet in F Major, Op. 96 ("American")
Recorded in Paris for I.M.E. Pathé-Marconi in 1955. [This anthology of movements represents the last released recording of the personnel 1938–1956.]
European Columbia FCX 469

Notes

1903–1923

Chapter One

1. Bálint Sárosi, *Gypsy Music* (Cigányzene), trans. by Fred MacNicol (Budapest: Corvina Kiadó, 1978), p. 208.

Chapter Two

1. Halsey Stevens, *The Life and Music of Béla Bartók* (1st ed., rev.; New York: Oxford University Press, 1964), p. 324.
2. Ferenc Bónis, *Béla Bartók: His Life in Pictures and Documents* (Bartók Béla élete: Képekben és dokumentumokban), trans. by Lili Halápy, trans. rev. by Bertha Gaster and Ferenc Bónis (1st ed., rev.; Budapest: Corvina Kiadó, 1981), p. 62.
3. János Demény, ed., *Béla Bartók Letters*, trans. by Péter Balabán and István Farkas, trans. rev. by Elisabeth West and Colin Mason (London: Faber and Faber, 1971), letter 11, p. 27.
4. Bónis, *Béla Bartók*, p. 63.
5. Stevens, *Bartók*, p. 29.
6. Stevens, *Bartók*, p. 339.
7. "Hangversenykrónika" (Concert Chronicles), unsigned review, unidentified newspaper (Budapest), ca. March 1922.
8. Joseph Szigeti, *With Strings Attached* (New York: Alfred A. Knopf, 1947), p. 104.
9. Leó Weiner (1885–1960), Hungarian composer and chamber

music teacher. Weiner was born in Budapest. He studied with Hans Koessler at the Franz Liszt Academy and later in Germany and France. He became a professsor at the Franz Liszt Academy in 1908 and retired in 1949. His compositions, imbued with a Hungarian character, are romantic in style.

10. The Léner String Quartet appeared first in Budapest in 1919. The original members were Jenő Léner (1894–1948), first violin; József Smilovits (b. 1894), second violin; Sándor Roth (1896–1952), violist; and Imre Hartmann (1895–ca.1957), cellist. Antal Molnár's book, A Léner-Vonósnégyes (The Léner String Quartet), gives a full account of the long and varied career of Jenő Léner and the various artists who played in his quartets.

11. George Herzog (1902–1983), Hungarian musicologist. Herzog was born in Budapest. He emigrated to the United States in the 1920s where he studied and later taught anthropology at Columbia University. In 1941 he influenced the decision to appoint Bartók to a research position at Columbia. A distinguished ethnomusicologist, Herzog also taught at Indiana University.

12. Unpublished letter from Leó Weiner to Zoltán Székely, Budapest, ca. 1925.

13. Dénes Koromzay, interview by Thomas Rolston, The Banff Centre, Banff, Alberta, Canada, 5 June 1981.

Chapter Three

1. Jenő Hubay (1858–1937), celebrated Hungarian violinist, pedagogue, and composer. Hubay was born in Budapest. He studied with his father, Karl Huber, and later with Joachim and Vieuxtemps, succeeding the latter as professor at the Brussels Conservatory in 1882. Upon his return to Budapest where he became director of the Franz Liszt Academy from 1919 to 1934, he established himself as one of the most important violin teachers in Europe. He was the leader of the Hubay-Popper String Quartet.

2. Bónis, Béla Bartók, fig. 123, p. 98.

3. Demény, ed., Béla Bartók Letters, letter 66, pp. 99–100.

4. Malcolm Gillies, Bartók Remembered (London: Faber and Faber, 1990), p. 64.

5. Antal Molnár's Bartók analysis is "Bartók kvartettje" (Bartók Quartets), Zeneközlöny 9 (1911), p. 275. His monograph on Kodály is Kodály Zoltán (Budapest: Népszeru Zenefüzetek [Popular Musical Booklets], 1936).

6. Stevens, Bartók, p. 44.

7. Bónis, Béla Bartók, fig. 324, p. 208.

8. Maria Zipernovszky, Hubay Jenő. Hegedütanitási Módszere (Jenő

Hubay: Violin teaching method)(Budapest: Dr. Vajna és Bokor, 1962). The class rolls are confirmed by Zipernovsky's tables, p. 229.

9. Zipernovszky, *Hubay*. See the many testimonial articles in Zipernovsky's book.

10. Zoltán Kodály (1882–1967), celebrated Hungarian composer. Kodály was born at Kecskemet and brought up in a musical family. He wrote a Mass at the age of sixteen, then enrolled at the University of Budapest but also studied composition with Hans Koessler at the Franz Liszt Academy. He was closely associated with Bartók in ethnomusicological research. Kodály was appointed assistant director of the Franz Liszt Academy in 1919. He won worldwide recognition as a composer.

11. László Eősze, *Zoltán Kodály: His Life and Work* (Budapest: Corvina Kiadó, 1962), p. 25.

12. Bónis, *Béla Bartók*, p. 134.

Chapter Four

1. Nándor Zsolt (1887–1936), Hungarian violinist. Zsolt was born in Esztergom. He studied with Hubay. From 1908 he was for some years second concertmaster in the Queen's Hall Orchestra in London. After 1920 he was a violin teacher in Budapest and composed violin and piano works, a piano quintet, a toccata for piano, and a symphony.

2. Béla Bartók, "Kodály's New Trio a Sensation Abroad," *Musical Courier* (19 August 1920).

3. Unsigned review, unidentified newspaper (Budapest), ca. 1920.

4. Béla Szigeti, Hungarian violist and pedagogue. He taught at the Scuola Superiore de Musica in Milan and later at the Musikakademie in Zurich. His booklet, *Das Vibrato*, was highly endorsed by Georges Enesco and Jenő Léner.

5. Unsigned review, unidentified newspaper (Budapest), ca. 1920.

6. Aladár Tóth (1898–1968), Hungarian music critic. Tóth was the principal critic for the Budapest newspaper *Pesti Napló*. From 1946 to 1956, he was director of the Budapest State Opera. Tóth was a fervent admirer of the music of Bartók and Kodály.

7. Révész' book *Erwin Nyiregyházi: Psychologische Analyse eines musikalisch hervorragenden Kindes* was published in Leipzig in 1916. It was later republished in an English translation as *The Psychology of a Musical Prodigy* (New York: Harcourt, Brace, and Co., 1925).

8. Unsigned review, unidentified newspaper (Esztergom), October 1920.

9. Unsigned review, unidentified newspaper (Nagymegyer), Octo-

ber 1920.

10. Pál Karnács, whose father owned a piano store in Budapest, was the only student of the master class who had a phonograph and was the first of Székely's peers to have heard Heifetz and Kreisler recordings for the first time on his own machine.

11. Tóth's remarks appear in an unidentified issue of *Nyugat*, after April 1921. *Nyugat* (West) was a significant literary journal founded in 1908 which played an important role in the development of modern Hungarian literature. As its name suggests, the periodical proclaimed a revival that was based on the literary spirit in western Europe according to Zoltán Kodály in his lecture "Confession" to the Nyugat Circle of Friends, 23 December 1932 (printed in *Nyugat* 36, 1932).

12. Zoltán Székely's composition, Sonate, Op. 1, Violino Solo, was published in 1926 by Universal-Edition, Vienna (as 8466), dedicated to his Dutch patrons, Mr. and Mrs. Jaap de Graaf-Bachiene. The work is cast in four movements: Appassionato, ma in tempo molto moderato; Scherzo; Intermezzo; Finale—Molto allegro con brio.

13. Márta Ziegler Bartók (1893–1955) was the composer's first wife.

14. Béla Bartók, "Lettera di Budapest," *Il Pianoforte* (Turin) 2, no. 9 (September 1921).

15. Review signed Izor Béldi, *Pesti Hirlap* (Budapest), 26 April 1921.

16. Review signed Géza Molnár, *Pester Lloyd* (Budapest), 24 April 1921.

17. Review signed Aladár Tóth, *Nyugat* (Budapest), ca. Spring 1921.

Chapter Five

1. János Kárpáti, liner notes for the compact disc recording *Bartók: The Two Sonatas for Violin and Piano*, Hungaroton, Stereo HCD 11655-2.

2. "Uj magyar hegedümüvész" (New Hungarian violin artist), unsigned interview, unidentified newspaper (Budapest), ca. 1920.

3. "Székely Zoltán: hegedühangversenye" (Zoltán Székely: concert violinist), unsigned review, unidentified newspaper (Budapest), ca. 1920.

4. Unsigned review, unidentified newspaper (Budapest), ca. 1920.

5. "Karácsonyi hangversenyek" (Christmas concert), unsigned review, unidentified newspaper (Budapest), ca. 1920.

6. Unsigned review, *Neues Wiener Journal* (Vienna), 29 December 1921.

7. Unsigned review, unidentified newspaper (Budapest), January 1922.

8. Lorand Fenyves (b.1918), Hungarian violinist. Fenyves studied at the Franz Liszt Academy with Oszkár Studer and Jenő Hubay. He emigrated to Palestine in 1936 and became concertmaster of the new Palestine Symphony Orchestra (later the Israel Philharmonic) and formed the Fenyves String Quartet with his sister, Alice Fenyves, second violin; Ödön Pártos, viola; and László Vinaze, cello. He later founded the Israeli String Quartet, one of the outstanding chamber music ensembles in Israel for twenty years. Fenyves moved to Geneva in 1957 as concertmaster of the Orchestre de la Suisse Romande. In 1966 he joined the Faculty of Music of the University of Toronto and has since had a distinguished career in Canada.

9. Zoltán Kodály, "Oeuvres Nouvelles de Béla Bartók," *Le Revue Musicale* (Paris) 3, no. 7 (March 1922), p. 172.

10. Review signed Aurél Kern, *Magyarság* (Budapest), 19 January 1921.

11. Demény, ed., *Béla Bartók Letters*, letters 114, 115, and 116, pp. 155–57.

12. Malcolm Gillies, *Bartók in Britain: A Guided Tour* (Oxford: Clarendon Press, 1989), pp. 35–37.

13. Denijs Dille, ed., *Documenta Bartókiana*, vol. 3 (Budapest: Akadémiai Kiadó, 1968), letter 64, p. 114.

14. Dille, ed., *Documenta*, vol. 3, letter 66, p. 115; and 67, p. 118.

15. Demény, ed., *Béla Bartók Letters*, letter 119, pp. 160–61.

16. Anton Haefeli gives a comprehensive account of the International Society for Contemporary Music in his book, *Die Internationale Gesellschaft für Neue Musik (IGNM)*.

17. Review signed Keleti, *Pesti Hirlap* (Budapest), 3 February 1922.

18. Unpublished testimonial statement by Dr. Jenő Hubay (1858–1937), director of the Franz Liszt Academy, Budapest, 22 March [1922].

Chapter Six

1. Nijmegen is an old imperial city on the Waal River in Holland. It still has the ruins of the Valkhof, the court once occupied by Charlemagne.

2. An excerpt from Igminia Everts' personal travel diary, 1920.

3. Georg Schnéevoight (1872–1947), Finnish conductor and cellist. Schnéevoight was born in Viborg, Finland. He was a cello pupil of Schröder, Klengel, and Jacobs. He conducted orchestras in Germany, Holland, Russia, and Scandinavia and in Los Angeles between 1927 and 1929. After 1932 Schnéevoight was general director of the National Opera in Riga, Latvia.

4. Adrienne Gombocz, ed., *Béla Bartók Családi Levelei* (Béla Bartók family letters) (Budapest: Zenemükiadó, 1981), letter 433, p. 334.
5. Gombocz, *Családi Levelei*, letter 435, p. 336.
6. Gombocz, *Családi Levelei*, letter 436, p. 336.
7. Unsigned review, *Nijmeegsche Courant* (Nijmegen), 4 November 1922.
8. Unsigned review, *Nieuwe Arnhemsche Courant* (Arnhem), 6 November1922.
9. Friedrich Hermann (1828–1907), German composer. Hermann was born in Leipzig. He studied viola at the Leipzig Conservatory, then became a member of the Leipzig Gewandhaus Orchestra. He was the violist of the celebrated Joachim String Quartet.
10. Unpublished testimonial statement by Willem Mengelberg (1871–1951), Amsterdam, December 1922.

Chapter Seven

1. Henri Prunières (1886–1942), founder of *La Revue Musicale*, organizer of concerts at the Théâtre du Vieux Colombier, and head of the French section of the International Society for Contemporary Music. He had met and assisted Bartók the previous season in Paris.
2. Previously unpublished letter from Béla Bartók to Zoltán Székely, Budapest, 19 January 1923. See Appendix A-1.
3. Igminia Székely states that this letter of introduction contained only the message"Herewith I introduce you to my friend, Zoltán Székely." The brief note was sold at auction at Sotheby's in London during the 1930s.
4. Previously unpublished letter from Béla Bartók to Zoltán Székely, Budapest, 23 February 1923. See Appendix A-2.
5. Unpublished testimonial statement by Eugene Goosens (1893–1962), London, February 1923.
6. Unpublished testimonial statement by Sir Henry Wood (1869–1944), Queen's Hall, London, February 1923.
7. Unsigned review, *Berliner Börsen-Zeitung* (Berlin), 5 April 1923.
8. Gombocz, *Családi Levelei*, letters 439 and 440, pp. 338–39.
9. Igminia Székely, interview by David Leighton, The Banff Centre, summer 1973.
10. Gillies, *Bartók in Britain*, p. 109.
11. Previously unpublished letter from Béla Bartók to Zoltán Székely, London, 1 May 1923. See Appendix A-3.
12. This refers to four additional engagements arranged during Bartók's March visit to England.

13. Suikerman was a minor Dutch concert manager.
14. Previously unpublished letter from Béla Bartók to Zoltán Székely, London, 4 May 1923. See Appendix A-4.
15. Jelly d'Arányi (1895–1966), Hungarian violinist. D'Arányi was born in Budapest. She was the grandniece of Joseph Joachim and a celebrated pupil of Hubay. Bartók's two violin sonatas, Ravel's *Tzigane*, and Vaughan Williams' Violin Concerto are all dedicated to her. In 1937 she proclaimed that Schumann's spirit appeared to her and revealed the secret of his unpublished Violin Concerto.

    The earliest performances of Bartók's Second Sonata for Violin and Piano progressed as follows: first performance, Imre Waldbauer and Bartók, Berlin, 7 February 1923; second performance, Ede Zathureczky and Bartók, Budapest, 27 February 1923; third and fourth performances, Zoltán Székely and Bartók, Amsterdam and Rotterdam, 28 and 29 April 1923; fifth performance, Jelly d'Arányi and Bartók, London, 7 May 1923.
16. This refers to a recital at Normanhurst Court, a girls' school in Battle, Sussex.
17. Previously unpublished letter from Béla Bartók to Zoltán Székely, London, 8 May 1923. See Appendix A-5.
18. Unsigned review, *Het Handelsblad* (Amsterdam), 28 April 1923.
19. Unsigned review, *Nieuwe Rotterdamsche Courant* (Rotterdam), 29 April 1923.
20. Unsigned review, *Dagblad van Rotterdam* (Rotterdam), 30 April 1923.
21. János Kárpati, liner notes for the long-playing recording *Bartók: The Two Sonatas for Violin and Piano*, Hugaroton production HCD 11644-2.
22. Bónis, *Bartók*, p. 21.
23. Review signed Theo van der Bul, *De Tijd* (The Hague), 5 May 1923.

Chapter Eight

1. Ditta Pásztory Bartók (1903–1982), second wife of the composer. She studied piano with Bartók for an extended period, then was his partner in two-piano recitals from 1938. It was for her that Bartók wrote his last composition, the Concerto No. 3 for Piano and Orchestra, immediately before his death in 1945. In 1946 she returned to Budapest where she lived in seclusion; however, during the 1960s she began to perform again and in this period recorded the Third Concerto which was written for her.
2. Unpublished testimonial statement by Eugène Ysaÿe (1858–

1931), Le Zoute, Belgium, 12 September 1923.

3. Review signed Jeanne Landré, *Nijmeegsche Courant* (Nijmegen), 12 October 1923.

4. Alfredo d'Ambrosio (1871–1914), Italian composer and violinist. D'Ambrosio was born in Naples and studied composition there with Enrico Bossi. He was a violin pupil of both Pablo de Sarasate and August Wilhelmj. He settled in Nice, where he taught and was the leader of a string quartet. He served as concertmaster of the Monte Carlo Orchestra as well.

5. Review signed A. M. C., *ABC Madrid* (Madrid), 11 December 1923.

6. Poldowsky was the pen name of Henri Wieniawsky's daughter, Irene Regine Wieniawsky, better known in London circles as Lady Dean Paul.

7. Unsigned review, *El Sol* (Madrid), 12 December 1923.

8. H. L. Kirk, *Pablo Casals* (New York: Holt, Rinehart, and Winston, 1974), p. 339.

9. Review signed Señor Walter, *La Vanguardia* (Barcelona), 20 December 1923.

10. Unsigned review, *Diario del Comercio* (Barcelona), 19 December 1923.

11. Unsigned review, *La Publicitat* (Barcelona), 20 December 1923.

12. These concerts began with music of Veracini and Bach, then the Violin Concerto, Op. 45, of Christian Sinding. Paul Schramm appeared as soloist performing Schumann's *Papillons* and a polonaise by Chopin or alternately the *Handel Variations* by Brahms. After the intermission the group of genre pieces included Hubay's *Elegia and Lepke,* and d'Ambrosio's *Serenate.* The concerts concluded alternately with Vieuxtemps' *Ballade et Polonaise* or Scharwenka's *Alla Polacca.*

13. Unsigned review, *Vlissingen Courante* (Vlissingen), 31 January 1924.

14. Review signed L. C., *De Nieuwe Courant* (Amsterdam), 27 January 1924.

1924–1937

Chapter Nine

1. Unsigned review, *The Daily Telegraph* (London), 11 April 1924.

2. Duo pianists Bartlett and Robertson commissioned a concerto for two pianos and orchestra from Bartók in 1944. This projected work was never written.

3. Unsigned review, *The Morning Post* (London), 11 April 1924.

4. Unsigned review, *South Wales News*, 12 April 1924.
5. Unsigned review, *The Daily Express* (London), 11 April 1924.
6. Unsigned review, *The Daily Telegraph* (London), 11 April 1924.
7. Unsigned review, *The Daily Telegraph* (London), 28 April 1924.
8. Unsigned review, *The Daily Mail* (London), 26 April 1924.
9. Unsigned review, *The Daily Graphic* (London), 26 April 1924.
10. Unsigned review, *The Daily Telegraph* (London), 5 May 1924.
11. Sándor Kőszegi continued to play both violin and viola in the New York Philharmonic until his death on 15 December 1937 at age fifty-seven.
12. Unsigned review, *De Telegraaf* (Amsterdam), 7 March 1925.
13. Unsigned review, *De Avond Post* (The Hague), 12 March 1925.
14. Review signed Marc Pincherle, *Le Monde Musical* (Paris), April 1925.
15. Although Walter Frey's name appears on the printed program of this concert, it was Felix Petyrek who performed Ravel's *Tzigane* with Székely. Petyrek had taught piano at the Mozarteum in Salzburg, then for the Orchestral School of the Berlin Hochschule für Musik. In 1925 he was living in Italy. Petyrek had several compositions performed at the ISCM festivals.
16. Max Butting's *Cinque Piccoli Pezzi* for string quartet was performed by Il Quartetto Veneziano. Ladislav Vycpálek's *Two Songs from Probuzení* were sung by Signora Fleischerowa accompanied by Vaclav Stepán. The Zika String Quartet (whose violinist, Richard Zika, was the leader of the Prague String Quartet from 1920 until 1932) performed Leos Janácek's String Quartet No. 1, a work based on an episode from Tolstoy's story "The Kreutzer Sonata."
17. Unsigned review, *Musical Courier* (New York), 1 October 1925.
18. Unsigned review, *Neue Wiesbadener Zeitung* (Wiesbaden), 16 September 1925.
19. Unsigned review, *Leipziger Neueste Nachrichten* (Leipzig), 15 September 1925.
20. Unsigned review, *Prager Presse* (Prague), 16 September 1925.
21. Review signed Prof. Hans Hermann, *Signale* (Berlin), 30 September 1925.
22. The Viennese Quartet performed Erich Korngold's String Quartet, Op. 16. Gaspar Cassadó and Alfredo Casella played Arthur Honegger's Sonata for Cello and Piano. The woodwind players, including Louis Fleury and Paul Hagemann, flutists; Louis Gaudard, oboist; Henri Delacroix, clarinetist; and Georges Hermans, bassoonist joined forces to present Jacques Ibert's *Two Pieces* and Vittorio Rieti's Sonata for Piano and Winds with Rieti playing the piano part. The flutist Louis Fleury and Mme. Fleury-

Monchablon played Albert Roussel's *Four Pieces for Flute and Piano*.

23. Zoltán Székely, interview by Aladár Tóth, *Pesti Napló* (Budapest), 11 November 1925.

24. János Demény, ed., *Bartók Béla Levelei* (Béla Bartók Letters), vol. 3 (Budapest: Zenemükiadó, 1955), letter 104, p. 177.

25. Unsigned review, unidentified newspaper (Arnhem), 5 October 1925.

26. Unsigned review, *Het Daagblad van Arnhem* (Arnhem), 5 October 1925.

27. Unsigned review, *Utrechtisch Nieuwsblad* (Utrecht), 7 October 1925.

28. Székely's cadenza for Brahms' Violin Concerto was composed in 1921 and first performed in Budapest on 25 November 1921. Székely composed cadenzas for many concertos including those by Mozart, Viotti, and Glazounov.

29. Review signed Jeanne Landré, *Nijmeedsche Courant* (Nijmegen), 30 October 1925.

30. Review signed W. H., *De Gelderlander* (Nijmegen), 31 October 1925.

31. Géza Frid (1904–1971), Hungarian pianist and composer. Frid was born on 25 January 1904 in Máramarossziget. In 1912 he moved to Budapest where he studied composition with Kodály and piano with Bartók. He graduated from the Franz Liszt Academy in 1924. In 1926 he undertook a concert tour in Italy. The premiere performances of Frid's First String Quartet occurred in 1927 in Budapest and London. From 1927 to 1929 he concertized throughout Europe with Zoltán Székely, then settled in Amsterdam where Székely engaged him as his accompanist.

    Frid lived the rest of his life in Holland, and in addition to his performances, he continued to compose. From 1948 until 1974 he appeared frequently as a pianist, touring in Indonesia, the Soviet Union, Israel, and North and South America. In 1974 he presented his jubilee concert at the Amsterdam Concertgebouw.

32. Review signed Aladár Tóth, *Pesti Napló* (Budapest), 10 November 1925.

33. Review signed Péntek, *Szegedi Napló* (Szeged), 20 November 1925.

34. Václav Talich (1883–1961), Czechoslovakian conductor. Talich conducted the Prague Philharmonic Orchestra from 1919 to 1935. He gave a celebrated performance of Bartók's Dance Suite in Budapest which convinced the composer of his ability to orchestrate.

35. Review signed Sándor Jemnitz, *Népszava* (Budapest), 25 Novem-

ber 1925.

36. Review signed Aladár Tóth, *Pesti Napló* (Budapest), 26 November 1925.

Chapter Ten

1. Unsigned review, *Il Cittadino* (Genoa), 3 December 1925.
2. Review signed Adam, *l'Ora* (Palermo), 7–8 December 1925.
3. Unsigned review, *Gazzetta di Venezia* (Venice), 11 December 1925.
4. Unsigned review, *Donaueschingen Tageblatt* (Donaueschingen),15 December 1925.
5. Unsigned review, *Birmingham Gazette*, 9 February 1926.
6. Bálint Sárosi, *Dohnányi Ernő* (Budapest: Zenemükiadó,1971). See Bartók's letter to Dohnányi, p. 119.
7. The Dohnányi cycle in Berlin was divided into three concerts. The first evening was devoted to composer and conductor with the Suite in F-sharp Minor, Op. 19; the Violin Concerto, Op. 27; and *Ruralia Hungarica*, Op. 32B in its first Berlin performance. Two days later the next concert included Beethoven's *Coriolanus* Overture and the "Emperor" Concerto as well as Dohnányi's *Festival Overture* and *Variations on a Nursery Song*, Op. 25; and the final concert presented Dohnányi playing his Passacaglia on a Beethoven Theme, a group of his own shorter pieces, and the Liszt Piano Sonata in B Minor.
8. Review signed Dr. L. Schmidt, *Berliner Tageblatt* (Berlin), 31 March 1926.
9. Georg Kulenkampff (1898–1948), German violinist. Kulenkampff was born in Bremen. He studied in Berlin with Ernst Wendel and Willy Hess. In 1919 he embarked on a solo career, then in 1923 became professor at the Berlin Hochschule. Later he formed a trio with pianist Edwin Fischer and cellist Enrico Mainardi. He fled Germany in 1943, settled in Switzerland, and taught at the Lucerne Conservatory until his death.
10. Review signed Theo van de Bijl, *De Tijd* (Amsterdam), 26 March 1926.
11. Review signed L. M. G. Arntzenius, *De Telegraaf* (Amsterdam), 26 March 1926.
12. Review signed L. M. G. Arntzenius, *De Telegraaf* (Amsterdam), 1 April 1926.
13. Dante Alderighi (1898–1968), Italian pianist and composer. Alderighi was born in Taranto. He went to Rome as a youth to study with Giovanni Sgambati and Malipiero. After appearing in many piano recitals, Alderighi began to write music criticism and to

compose. In 1936, he became a piano professor at the Accademia di Santa Cecilia in Rome.

14. Unsigned review, *Il Giorno* (Naples), 15 December 1926.
15. Unsigned review, *La Tribuna* (Rome), 15 December 1926.
16. Unsigned review, *Il Messaggero* (Rome), 14 December 1926.
17. Unsigned review, *Il Popolo di Roma* (Rome), 14 December 1926.
18. Unsigned review, *Il Messaggero* (Rome), 17 December 1926.
19. Unsigned review (probably dictated by Benito Mussolini), *Il Piccolo* (Rome), 21 December 1926.

Chapter Eleven

1. Unsigned review, *Prager Tagblatt* (Prague), 14 October 1927.
2. Review signed Paul Sanden, *Het Volk* (Amsterdam), 29 November 1927.
3. Review signed L. M. G. Arntzenius, *De Telegraaf* (Amsterdam), 29 November 1927.
4. Gombocz, ed., *Családi Levelei*, letter 622, pp. 453–54.
5. Demény, ed., *Béla Bartók Letters*, letter 140, p. 190.
6. "A Sonata Recital by Joseph Szigeti and Béla Bartók," recorded at the Library of Congress, Washington, D.C., on April 13, 1940, issued as SRV-304/5 by Vanguard Recording Society, Inc.
7. Gillies, *Bartók in Britain*, p. 74.
8. Gombocz, ed., *Családi Levelei*, letter 655, p. 473.
9. Unsigned review, *Morning Post* (London), 8 March 1929.
10. Unsigned review, *The Daily Telegraph* (London), 8 March 1929.

Chapter Twelve

1. Archie Orenstein, *A Ravel Reader* (New York: NYU Columbia University Press, 1990), p. 300.
2. Unpublished letter from Universal-Edition to Mientje Székely, Vienna, 9 April 1929.
3. Gombocz, *Családi Levelei*, letter 663, p. 477.
4. Unsigned review (probably dictated by Benito Mussolini), *Il Lavaro Fascista* (Rome), 17 April 1929.
5. Review signed Claude Berniers, *Le Phare* (Littoral), 8 September 1929.
6. Review signed Géza Molnár, *Pester Lloyd* (Budapest), 26 November 1929.
7. Review signed Aladár Tóth, *Pesti Napló* (Budapest), 26 November 1929.
8. Review signed Emil Haraszti, *Budapest Hirlap* (Budapest), 26 November 1929.
9. A statement by Béla Bartók, *Budapest Hirlap* (Budapest), 27 No-

vember 1929.

10. The two books by Emil Haraszti are *Bartók Béla* (Budapest: Kortársaink,1930) and *Béla Bartók: His Life and Works* (Paris: Lyrebird Press, 1938).

11. Review signed Palma Ottlik, *Pesti Hirlap* (Budapest), 27 November 1929.

12. Unsigned review, *Pester Lloyd* (Budapest), 27 November 1929.

13. Henri Marteau (1875–1934), French violinist. Marteau was born at Reims. He studied in Paris with Léonard and Garcin. In 1900 he was appointed professor at the Geneva Conservatory; in 1908 he succeeded Joachim at the Königliche Hochschule für Musik in Berlin. In 1920 he became a naturalized Swedish citizen. Later between periods of teaching in Prague, Leipzig, and Dresden, he continued his concert appearances.

14. Review signed Aladár Tóth, *Pesti Napló* (Budapest), 28 November 1929.

15. Previously unpublished letter from Béla Bartók to Zoltán Székely, Budapest, 24 March 1930. See Appendix A-7.

Chapter Thirteen

1. Stevens, *Bartók*, p. 312, note 27.

2. Gillies, *Bartók in Britain*, p. 74.

3. János Kárpáti, *Bartók's String Quartets* (Bartók vonósnégyesei), trans. by Fred MacNicol (Budapest: Corvina Press, 1975), p. 209.

4. Review signed Aladár Tóth, *Pesti Napló* (Budapest), 22 March 1929. Tóth praised "the demanding cello solo which Jenő Kerpely interpreted with the noble ardor of a really poetic spirit."

5. Kárpáti, *Bartók's String Quartets*, p. 210.

6. Gerald Moore, *Am I Too Loud?* (London: Hamish Hamilton Ltd., 1962), p. 67.

7. Unsigned review, *De Avond Post* (The Hague), 4 August 1931.

8. Previously unpublished letter from Béla Bartók to Zoltán Székely, Vienna, 17 December 1931. See Appendix A-8.

9. Previously unpublished letter from Béla Bartók to Zoltán Székely, Budapest, 29 December 1931. See Appendix A-9.

10. Gombocz, ed., *Családi Levelei*, letter 750, p. 524.

11. Unsigned review, unidentified newspaper (Amsterdam), 25 January 1932.

12. Unsigned review, *De Maasbode* (Amsterdam), 25 January 1932.

13. Previously unpublished letter from Béla Bartók to the Székelys, Budapest, 20 October 1933. See Appendix A-12.

14. Previously unpublished letter from Béla Bartók to Zoltán Székely, London, 8 November 1933. See Appendix A-13.

15. The state of Hyderabad was dissolved in 1956, and its territory was divided among Andra Pradesh, Mysore, and Bombay.
16. David Harp,"Recalling the Kolisch String Quartet," *Chamber Music* 5, no. 1 (Spring 1988), p. 41.
17. Gerrit Rietveld (1884–1964), Dutch architect. Rietveld was born in Utrecht. Until its demise in 1931, Rietveld belonged to an artistic movement of architects founded in 1917 by Theo van Doesburg in Leiden called de Stijl group.
18. Previously unpublished letter from Béla Bartók to Zoltán Székely, Budapest, 10 January 1935 See Appendix A-14.
19. Previously unpublished letter from Béla Bartók to the Székelys, Budapest, 16 January 1935. See Appendix A-15.
20. Previously unpublished greeting from Béla Bartók to the Székelys, Budapest, 16 January 1935. See Appendix A-17.

Chapter Fourteen

1. "Béla Bartók Speaks," unsigned interview, *Het Algemeen Handelsblad* (Amsterdam), 29 January 1935.
2. "With Béla Bartók at Santpoort," unsigned interview, *De Telegraaf* (Amsterdam), 28 January 1935.
3. Previously unpublished letter from Béla Bartók to the Székelys, Basel, 4 February 1935. See Appendix A-18.
4. Gillies, *Bartók Remembered*, p. 158.
5. Demény, ed., *Béla Bartók Letters*, letter 187, p. 245. On 29 December 1935, the Kisfaludy Society awarded Bartók the Greguss Medal in consideration of what was incorrectly called the *first* performance in 1929 of his Orchestral Suite, No. 1, Op. 3, a work first performed earlier in 1909. Angered by the circumstances that influenced this decision, Bartók wrote the society declaring, "I do not wish to accept the Greguss Medal neither now, nor in the future, nor during my lifetime, nor after my death."
6. Previously unpublished letter from Béla Bartók to the Székelys, Budapest, 20 May 1935. See Appendix A-19.
7. Gombocz, ed., *Családi Levelei*, letter 786, p. 545.
8. Gillies, *Bartók in Britain*, p. 90.
9. Gombocz, ed., *Családi Levelei*, letter 792, p. 549.
10. János Demény, "Letters between Bartók and the Dutch Concert Manager Kossar" (Korrespondenz zwischen Bartók und der holländischen Konzertdiretion Kossar), *Documenta Bartokiana* 6 (1981), pp. 153–233. This article concerns concert engagements arranged by Antonia Kossar for Bartók as reflected in 104 letters.
11. Previously unpublished letter from Béla Bartók to the Székelys, Budapest, 26 July 1935. See Appendix A-20.

12. Previously unpublished letter from Béla Bartók to the Székelys, Vienna, 18 May 1936. See Appendix A-22.
13. Previously unpublished letter from Béla Bartók to Zoltán Székely, Budapest, 3 June 1936. See Appendix A-23.
14. Previously unpublished letter from Béla Bartók to the Székelys, Budapest, 17 October 1936. See Appendix A-25.
15. Previously unpublished postcard from Béla Bartók to the Székelys, Ankara (Turkey), 15 November 1936. The ladies' belly buttons to which Bartók refers is a Turkish confection. See Appendix A-26.
16. Previously unpublished postcard from Béla Bartók to the Székelys, Adana, South Anatolia (Turkey), 25 November 1936. See Appendix A-27.
17. Previously unpublished letter from Béla Bartók to Zoltán Székely, Budapest, 2 January 1937. See Appendix A-28.
18. Previously unpublished letter from Béla Bartók to the Székelys, Budapest, 12 January 1937. See Appendix A-29.
19. Review signed Theo van der Bijl, *De Tijd* (Amsterdam), 27 January 1937.
20. Stevens, *Bartók*, p. 83.
21. Gillies, *Bartók in Britain*, p. 92.
22. Review signed Marion M. Scott, *Musical Times* (London), March 1937.
23. Demény, ed., *Bartók Béla Levelei* (Béla Bartók Letters), vol. 3, p. 422.

1938–1945

Chapter Fifteen

1. Koromzay, interview by Thomas Rolston, The Banff Centre, 5 June 1981.
2. According to Jonathan Kuhner, son of the late Felix Kuhner of the Kolisch Quartet, Bartók sent a detailed letter, in German, to the Kolisch Quartet which they received before the premiere. The letter contained instructions for performing certain passages in the new work.
3. Kárpáti, *Bartók's String Quartets*, p. 226. Mrs. Coolidge possessed the sole right of performance for nine months. Six months after the premiere in Washington, D.C., by the Kolisch Quartet, she called upon the Belgian Pro Arte Quartet to perform the work, sending them the parts in November of 1935 and entrusting them with a few performances, one of which was in Marseille on

13 December 1935.

4. Review signed Ernst Krenek, *Pester Lloyd* (Budapest), 25 February 1936.

5. Review signed Sándor Jemnitz, *Nepszava* (Budapest), 4 March 1936.

6. Review signed Pál Spitzer, *Pester Lloyd* (Budapest), 4 March 1936.

7. Review signed Kálmán Kovács, *Pesti Napló* (Budapest), 4 March 1936.

8. László Lajtha (1891–1963), Hungarian composer. Lajtha was born in Budapest. He studied at the Franz Liszt Academy, then in 1913 became an associate of the Ethnographical Department of the Hungarian National Museum. In 1919 he became professor of composition and also of musical ethnology at the Budapest Conservatory. Although he frequently lived in Paris, Budapest remained the center of his activities, and in 1952 he became professor of musical folklore at the Franz Liszt Academy.

9. Pál Kadosa (1903–1983), Hungarian composer. Kadosa was born at Leva. He studied at the Franz Liszt Academy with Kodály, then taught in Budapest from 1927 to 1943. In 1928 he helped organize a modern musical society eventually incorporated in the International Society for Contemporary Music. In 1945 he became professor of piano at the Franz Liszt Academy and vice-president of the Hungarian Arts Council.

10. The Barcelona Festival program on 21 April 1936 included Walter Piston's Sonata for Flute and Piano; Egon Wellesz' *Five Sonnets*, Op. 52, for soprano and string quartet, based on the works of Elizabeth Barrett Browning; Benjamin Britten's Suite for Violin and Piano, Op. 6; André Souris' *Quelques Airs de Clarisse de Jurenville* for mezzo soprano and string quartet; and Manuel Blancafort's three pieces for piano, *Les Ombres Perennes*. Béla Bartók's String Quartet No. 5 concluded the program.

11. Unsigned review, *Nepszava* (Budapest), 3 May 1936.

12. Review signed Emil Haraszti, *Magyar Dal* (Budapest), 1 September 1936.

13. An excerpt from an unsigned review in *De Telegraaf* (Amsterdam) quoted in *Magyarság* (Budapest), 5 May 1936.

14. Tibor Serly (1900–1978), Hungarian composer and violinist. Serly was born in Losonc but taken to the United States as a child. At age twenty-two he returned to Hungary and studied composition in Budapest with Kodály and Bartók and violin with Hubay. Serly completed the final seventeen measures of Bartók's Third Piano Concerto and reconstructed the unfinished Viola Concerto from the extant sketches after the composer's death in 1945.

15. R. Murray Schafer, ed., *Ezra Pound and Music: The Complete Criti- cism* (New York: New Directions Books, 1977), p. 401.

Chapter Sixteen

1. The Végh String Quartet was founded in Budapest in 1940. Its members were Sándor Végh and Sándor Zóldy, violins; Georges Janzer, viola; and Pál Szabó, cello.
2. Previously unpublished letter from Béla Bartók to Zoltán Székely, Budapest, 10 April 1937. See Appendix A-33.
3. Previously unpublished letter from Béla Bartók to Zoltán Székely, Budapest, 1 May 1937. See Appendix A-34.
4. Previously unpublished letter from Béla Bartók to the Székelys, Budapest, 10 June 1937. See Appendix A-35.
5. Demény, ed., *Béla Bartók Letters*, letter 162, p. 217. While re- hearsing Bartók's First and Fourth Quartets, violinist Max Rostal had doubts as to the correctness of the metronome markings and wrote Bartók to check them. Bartók's reply is contained in letter 162.
6. Unsigned review, *l'Echo d'Alger* (Algiers), ca. July 1937.
7. Unsigned review, *Courrier Du Maroc* (Casablanca), ca. July 1937.
8. This probably refers to the matter discussed in the letter of 10 April 1937, i.e., "As long as my work is unpublished I can give the sole manuscript to whomever I please, in this case to you. As soon as it is published, however, all rights to produce, lend, etc.! the materials belong to Universal-Edition. Therefore you would have to discuss your request with Universal-Edition. . . . "
9. Previously unpublished letter from Béla Bartók to the Székelys, Kals (East Tyrol), 15 July 1937. See Appendix A-36.
10. The 1936 recording of Székely's transcription of Bartók's *Ruman- ian Folk Dances* was reissued in 1989 in the anthology, *The Recorded Violin: The History of the Violin on Record*, compiled from the collection of Raymond Glaspole of Oxford by Pearl Records (Pavilion Recordings Ltd., Sussex, England).
11. Stevens, *Bartók*, p. 85.
12. Ödön Pártos (1907–1977), Hungarian violist and composer. Pár- tos was born in Budapest. He studied at the Franz Liszt Academy with Hubay and Kodály. After 1938, Pártos had a distinguished career as a violist-composer in Israel. He was first violist of the Tel Aviv Philharmonic (later the Israel Philharmonic) until 1956 For sixteen years, from 1940 to 1956, he was violist of the Israeli String Quartet led by Lorand Fenyves. In 1951 he became direc- tor of the Tel Aviv Academy of Music. In 1971 he returned to the Netherlands to experiment on the possiblity of thirty-one-tone

scales proposed by the seventeenth-century Dutch physicist and mathematician, Christiaan Huggens.

13. Previously unpublished letter from Béla Bartók to the Székelys, Basel, 28 June 1938. See Appendix A-37.
14. Previously unpublished letter from Béla Bartók to Zoltán Székely, Budapest, 14 September 1938. See Appendix A-38.

Chapter Seventeen

1. Unsigned review, *The Times* (London), 7 October 1938.
2. Review signed R. C., *The Daily Telegraph* (London), 5 October 1938.
3. Unsigned review, *The London Sunday Times* (London), 9 October 1938.
4. Unsigned review, *The Times* (London), 10 October 1938.
5. Review signed Rathcol, *The Belfast Telegraph*, 15 October 1938.
6. Unsigned review, *Western Mail South Wales News* (Cardiff), 26 October 1938.
7. Unsigned review, *The Daily Telegraph and Morning Post* (London), 2 November 1938.
8. The original text of the exercise is now lost; however, Mientje Everts' Hungarian typescript has been preserved. See Appendix A-46.
9. que nous n'avons pas immédiatement répondu après avoir reçu les nouvelles. . . .
10. evviva il Francesco Jacopo, vive le petit François Jacobe. . . .
11. živio! să trăiască! Yasasïn Yasasinküçük oğlunuz!
12. Et puis je n'ai pas voulu faire usage de questa maledetta lingua dei nostri vicini, que j'abhorre plus que jamais.
13. A bientôt.
14. A polyglot letter from Béla Bartók to Mien Székely, Budapest, 24 October 1938 previously published by János Demény, ed., *Béla Bartók Letters* (London: Faber and Faber, 1971), letter 213, pp. 273–274. See Appendix A-39.
15. Review signed L. M. G. Arntzenius, *De Telegraaf* (Amsterdam), 16 November 1938.
16. Unsigned review, *Nieuwe Rotterdamsche Courante* (Rotterdam), 16 November 1938.
17. In the 1970s, this Busan viola was reduced in size to slightly over forty-three centimeters (seventeen inches). While still very large, it is successfully played by Michael Tree, violist of the Guarneri String Quartet.
18. Previously unpublished letter from Béla Bartók to Zoltán Székely, Budapest, 6 December 1938. Bartók's list had no number 4. See

Appendix A-41.

19. Previously unpublished letter from Béla Bartók to Mientje Székely, Budapest, 10 January 1939. See Appendix A-42.

20. Previously unpublished letter from Béla Bartók to Zoltán Székely, Budapest, 8, February 1939. See Appendix A-43.

21. Changes were made in Bartók's Violin Concerto during the rehearsals in Paris, 25 February to 3 March 1939. Székely's modification to the final version of movement one (approved by Bartók) amounts to the repetition of a few measures.

    This is the technical scheme of Székely's modification to movement one: (1) Bartók's original measure 105 marked *piano* is repeated as new measure 106 marked *subito mezzo piano*. This adds one measure. (2) Bartók's original measure 106 marked *mezzo forte* is repeated as new measure 107 marked *crescendo*. This adds another measure. (3) Bartók's original measures 109 and 110 are augmented from two to four measures by extending the trill into an entire measure; the original quarter-note upbeat in the horns is augmented into half-notes arriving at the section marked *quasi a tempo*. This solution (which added only six measures to movement one) refined the proportions of this section as intended. Later in Amsterdam, this modification was entered into the orchestra score from which Mengelberg conducted the first performance, and even later incorporated into the printed score.

22. In movement two, measure 15 should be marked *ritenuto* and measure 16 *a tempo molto legato*. Three measures later, the end of measure 19 should also be marked *ritenuto* and measure 20 *tranquillo*. These details were agreed upon by Székely and Bartók and notated in pencil by Bartók in Székely's copy of the piano reduction. They were probably forgotten later by Bartók since they do not appear in the printed score. In addition, some wrong notes were corrected. Certainly there were violinistic changes made that were intended to produce a more satisfactory sonority without altering the musical sense of these passages. For instance, some double-stopping replaced simple arpeggios to give a richer texture; Székely also made enharmonic notational corrections that are sometimes the most logical solution for the violinist.

23. Previously unpublished letter from Béla Bartók to Mientje Székely, Basel, 9 March 1939. See Appendix A-44.

24. Walter Susskind conducted a performance of Bartók's Violin Concerto at the Banff Festival of the Arts in 1976. Székely was soloist with the Canadian Chamber Orchestra on that occasion. Susskind had attended Mengelberg's three rehearsals for the premiere of the work in March 1939.

Chapter Eighteen

1. Review signed L. M. G. Arntzenius, *De Telegraaf* (Amsterdam), 24 March 1939.
2. Review signed Herman Rutters, *Algemeen Handelsblad* (Amsterdam), 24 March 1939.
3. Review signed Lou van Strien, *Nieuwe Rotterdamsche Courant*, 24 March 1939.
4. Unsigned review, *Nieuwe Rotterdamsche Courant*, 26 March 1939.
5. Review signed A. de Wal, *Het Vaderland* (The Hague), 26 March 1939.
6. A 1989 release on compact disc of the first performance of Bartók's Violin Concerto, Philips 426 104-2.
7. Previously unpublished letter from Zoltán Székely to Béla Bartók, Santpoort, 3 April 1939.
8. Demény, ed., *Béla Bartók Letters*, letter 219, p. 278.
9. Previously unpublished letter from Zoltán Székely to Béla Bartók, [Santpoort] 3 October 1939.
10. Review signed Herman Rutters, *Algemeen Handelsblad* (Amsterdam), 11 March 1940.
11. Unsigned review, unidentified newspaper (Amsterdam), 7 April 1940.
12. Dénes Koromzay, a week-long series of interviews by Claude Kenneson, The Banff Centre, February 1992.
13. For a more complete account of the Dutch Occupation see William L. Shirer's book, *The Rise and Fall of the Third Reich* (1960. New York: Simon and Schuster, 1990).
14. Two fragments from unidentified newspapers (Amsterdam), 19 October 1940.
15. Gillies, *Bartók Remembered*, account by Jenő Antal, pp.171–72.
16. Dille, ed., *Documenta*, vol. 3, letter 159, p. 239.
17. Previously unpublished letter from Béla Bartók to Zoltán Székely, New York, 10 December 1940. See Appendix A-45.
18. Previously unpublished letter from Béla Bartók to the Székelys, Budapest, 17 October 1936. See Appendix A-25.
19. Previously unpublished letter from Béla Bartók to Zoltán Székely, Budapest, 1 May 1937. See Appendix A-34.
20. Drawn from a statement by Zoltán Székely in the Bartók Archívum, Budapest, dated 27 December 1967.
21. Previously unpublished letter from Béla Bartók to Zoltán Székely, New York, 10 December 1940. See Appendix A-45.
22. When war broke out in Europe, the members of the Kolisch Quartet decided to remain in the United States. Cellist Benar Heifetz joined the Philadelphia Symphony Orchestra as solo cellist, and

violist Eugene Lehner joined the Boston Symphony Orchestra.
23. Unsigned review, unidentified newspaper (The Hague), 17 July 1941.
24. Frank Székely-Everts, interview by Claude Kenneson, Banff, Alberta, Canada, 22 September 1990.

1946–1972

Chapter Nineteen

1. Demény, ed., *Béla Bartók Letters*, letter 285, p. 346.
2. Gillies, *Bartók Remembered*, pp.194–96.
3. See Appendix B, Performance Practice, section 4.
4. Oscar Thompson and Bruce Bohle, eds., *The International Cyclopedia of Music and Musicians*, tenth ed. (New York: Dodd, Mead, and Company, 1975), "British Broadcasting Corporation (BBC)," p. 291.
5. "Notes on the Third Programme," editorial signed William Glock, *Time and Tide* (London), 1 February 1947.
6. See Appendix E, Discography.
7. Dénes Koromzay interview, Banff, summer 1981.
8. Thompson, ed., *The International Cyclopedia*, "Recorded Music IV," p. 1792.
9. "Impressions of the Edinburgh Festival," article signed Artur Schnabel, souvenir program of the Edinburgh International Festival of Music and Drama, 1948, pp. 14–15.

Chapter Twenty

1. Review signed Robert Hague, *New York Star* (New York), 3 November 1948.
2. H. Wiley Hitchcock and Stanley Sadie, eds., *The New Grove Dictionary of American Music*, vol. 1 (London: Macmillan Press, 1980). See Coolidge, Elizabeth (Penn) Sprague, p. 491.
3. David Harp,"Recalling the Kolisch String Quartet," *Chamber Music* 5 (Spring 1988), p. 19.
4. Harold Spivacke (1904–1977), American music librarian and administrator. Spivacke was born in New York City and educated at New York University and the University of Berlin, where he received the Doctor of Philosophy degree in 1933. He returned to New York to become research assistant to Olin Downes at *The New York Times* and joined the staff of the Library of Congress the following year. He was chief of the Music Division from 1935 until his retirement in 1972.

5. Frank Székely-Everts, interview by Claude Kenneson, Banff, 22 September 1990.
6. Review signed Junius, *Excelsior Mexico* (Mexico City), 27 October 1949.
7. Review signed Elena de Sayn, *The Washington Post*, (Washington, D.C.), 5 November 1949.
8. Review signed H. T., *The New York Times*, 9 December 1949.
9. Review signed Jerome Bohm, *The New York Herald Tribune*, 9 December 1949.
10. Review signed Albert Goldberg, *Los Angeles Times*, 25 November 1948.
11. Review signed Mildred Norton, *Los Angeles Daily News*, 6 April 1950.
12. Review signed Raymond Kendall, *Los Angeles Mirror*, 28 November 1948.
13. Stephen Deák (1897–1975), Hungarian cellist and author. Deák was a pupil of David Popper from 1911 to 1913 at the Franz Liszt Academy and made his debut as a concert soloist in Budapest in 1919. He joined the faculty of the Curtis Institute of Music in Philadelphia in 1927, and later taught at the Peabody Conservatory in Baltimore and the University of Southern California, where he was head of the stringed instruments department. Deák is the author of several pedagogical works and the biography of David Popper.
14. During the course of the lecture-demonstration series the quartet performed the following works: Haydn's Quartet Op. 20, No. 4; Mozart's Quartets K. 458 and K. 590; Beethoven's Quartets, Op. 18, No.1; Op. 59, No. 1; Op. 131; and Op. 132; Schubert's Quartet in D Minor ("Death and the Maiden"); Schumann's Quartet, Op. 41, No. 1; the quartets of Franck and Debussy; Walter Piston's Quartet No. 4; and Bartók's Quartets Nos. 1 and 6.
15. Halsey Stevens (1908–1989), American musicologist and composer. Stevens was born in Scott, New York, and educated at Syracuse University and in California where he studied composition with Ernest Bloch. In 1950 he was Associate Professor at USC. An outstanding composer and a musicologist whose writings had been published in the leading journals, Stevens became a distinguished Bartók scholar. In 1953 he published the first English-language biography of Bartók, *The Life and Music of Béla Bartók*.
16. Review signed Olin Downes, *The New York Times*, 29 October 1950.

Chapter Twenty-one

1. Dénes Koromzay, a week-long series of interviews by Claude Kenneson, The Banff Centre, February 1992.
2. Review signed Pat Dunbar, *The Seattle Times*, 21 April 1951.
3. Review signed Alfred Frankenstein, *San Francisco Chronicle*, 19 April 1951.
4. Review signed P. G.-H., *The New York Herald Tribune*, 4 February 1952.
5. Unsigned review, *The Mirror* (Los Angeles), 20 March 1952.
6. Twentieth-century quartets that were played during the twenty-four concerts of the summers of 1951 and 1952 were: the six quartets by Béla Bartók (played twice); Quartets No. 7 and No. 9 by Darius Milhaud; Quartet No. 4 by William Schuman; Quartets No. 1 and No. 4 by Walter Piston; Quartet No. 3 by David Diamond; Quartet No. 5 by Paul Hindemith (played twice); *Two Pieces* (1928) by Aaron Copland; Quartet No. 3 by Elizabeth Maconchy; Quartet No. 2, Op. 10, by Zoltán Kodály; and the quartets by Ravel and Debussy. The quartets by Maconchy and Villa-Lobos were given their first performances in San Francisco on these occasions.
7. The seventeen quartets of the Beethoven cycle were recorded in two sessions over a four-month period. The first session began on 7 September 1953 with Quartet No. 12, Op. 127; continued with Quartets No. 8, Op. 59, No. 2 ("Razumovsky"); No. 10, Op. 74 ("Harp"); No. 13, Op. 130; Grosse Fuge, Op. 133; No. 7, Op. 59, No. 1 ("Razumovsky"); No. 11, Op. 95 ("Serioso"); No. 9, Op. 59, No. 3 ("Razumovsky"); No. 14, Op. 131; No. 15, Op. 132; and No. 3, Op.18, No. 3; and ended on 17 October with No. 16, the last quartet, Op. 135. The second session began on 9 November, and the remaining five quartets of Op. 18 were recorded in the following order: Nos. 5, 6, 2, and 1, concluding with No. 4 on 8 December 1953.
8. Review signed J. V., *Seattle Post-Intelligencer*, 13 March 1954.
9. Appendix E, Discography.
10. Unpublished letter from Jacques Feschotte to Zoltán Székely, Brest (France), December 1955.
11. Review signed J. van Voorthuysen, *Haager Courant* (The Hague), 24 June 1955.

Chapter Twenty-two

1. Excerpts from Colbert–La Berge Concert Management's announcement of the Hungarian Quartet's transcontinental tour, February–April 1956.

2. Unpublished letter from Gabriel Magyar to Claude Kenneson, Urbana, Illinois, 19 March 1992.
3. Unpublished letter from Gabriel Magyar, Urbana, 19 March 1992.
4. Review signed Clifford Gessler, *San Francisco Tribune*, 20 June 1956.
5. Unpublished letter from Gabriel Magyar, Urbana, 19 March 1992.
6. Review signed J. W., *The Christian Science Monitor* (Boston), 8 November 1957.
7. These excerpts are drawn from the following sources: *Aux Écouts* (Paris), 28 March 1958; *Salzburger Volksblatt* (Salzburg),16 August 1958; *Feuilles d'Avis* (Montreux), 4 October 1958; *De Telegraaf* (Amsterdam), 15 July 1958.
8. Charles Chaplin, *Charles Chaplin* (New York: Penguin Books, 1964), pp. 472–73.
9. Kató Havas (b. 1920), Hungarian violinist and teacher. Havas was born in Kolozsvár, Transylvania, on 5 November 1920. From the age of nine, she studied at the Franz Liszt Academy with Imre Waldbauer. Her debut in America was at Carnegie Hall at the age of seventeen, and was acclaimed by the critics. Soon after, she withdrew from professional life with the start of a family. During this period she evolved her revolutionary method of teaching (*The New Approach to Violin Playing*), emerging later as a distinguished pedagogue. In 1992 Havas was awarded the American String Teachers Association's International Award recognizing her "unparalleled achievements" as a teacher.
10. Unpublished letter from Kató Havas to Claude Kenneson, Oxford, 30 January 1992.

Chapter Twenty-three

1. Unpublished letter from Dénes Koromzay to Agnes Eisenberger, Paris, 12 November 1961.
2. Unpublished letter from Dénes Koromzay to Regina Ridge, Los Angeles, 20 September, 1960.
3. Unsigned review, *Sydney Morning Herald*, 23 April 1962.
4. Unsigned review, *The Sun* (Sydney), 27 April 1962.
5. Unsigned review, *The Southland Daily News* (Invercargill, New Zealand), 31 May 1962.
6. Review signed Ferenc Bónis, *Muzsika* (Budapest), 8 March 1963.
7. Review signed Colin Mason, *The London Times*, 23 March 1963.
8. H. L. Kirk, *Pablo Casals* (New York: Holt, Rinehardt, and Winston, 1974), p. 461.

9. Unpublished letter from Ubbo Scheffer to Claude Kenneson, Arnhem, 20 April 1992.
10. "Beethoven: Quartets for Strings," *High Fidelity Magazine*, May 1967, p. 73.
11. Review signed Neville Cardus, *The Guardian* (Manchester), 8 February 1966.
12. Review signed Colin Mason, *The London Times*, 8 February 1966.

Chapter Twenty-four

1. Unpublished letter from Dénes Koromzay to Thomas Rolston, Boulder, 13 February 1967.
2. Review signed Robert Sherman, unidentified newspaper (New York), 4 August 1967.
3. Unpublished letter from Dénes Koromzay to Agnes Eisenberger, Vosges Mountains (France), 21 September 1967.
4. Review signed Priscilla Witter, *International Herald Tribune* (Paris), 27–28 January 1968.
5. From a lecture by Zoltán Székely, Convocation Hall, University of Alberta, Edmonton, 3 April 1968.
6. Unpublished letter from Dénes Koromzay to Thomas Rolston, Boulder, 21 May 1968.
7. Review signed Olin Downes, *The New York Times*, 29 October 1950.
8. Review signed András Pernye, *Magyar Nemzet* (Budapest) 12 April 1969.
9. Memo to the Hungarian Quartet from Regina Ridge, Sydney, 1 May 1969.
10. Review signed John Horner, *The Advertiser* (Adelaide), 15 May 1969.
11. Review signed Romola Costantino, *The Sydney Morning Herald*, 21 May 1969.
12. Review signed Wolfgang Wagner, *The Australian*, Canberra, 2 June 1969.
13. "String Quartet has no plan of retirement," unsigned article, *The Daily News*, New Plymouth (New Zealand), 21 June 1969.
14. Review signed Owen Jensen, *The Evening Post* (Wellington), 3 July 1969.
15. Review signed Thomas MacCluskey, *Rocky Mountain News* (Denver), 22 April 1970.
16. Unpublished letter from John R. Carnes, associate dean, College of Arts and Sciences, University of Colorado, to Zoltán Székely, Boulder, 24 April 1970.

Chapter Twenty-five

1. Homage by Robert Strider, president of Colby College, Given Auditorium, Colby College, Waterville, Maine, 15 August 1972.
2. Unpublished letter from Dénes Koromzay to Agnes Eisenberger, Boulder, 18 May 1972.
3. Richard Buell, "Exit without Tears," *Boston Phoenix*, 29 August 1972.

1973–1993

Chapter Twenty-six

1. David Leighton in conversation with Claude Kenneson, The Banff Centre, 27 April 1992.
2. Leighton, David, *Artists, Builders and Dreamers: 50 Years at the Banff School*. Research and photograph selection by Peggy Leighton. Toronto: McClelland and Stewart Limited, 1982.
3. Concurrent with the growth of this artistic plan came the physical expansion of the existing campus. In 1968 the Eric Harvie Theatre opened, replacing the Banff Avenue Auditorium as the principal performance venue. With the addition of the Margaret Greenham Theatre, rehearsal rooms, and teaching studios, the new Theatre Complex was complete. Other buildings came steadily during the next two prosperous decades: Lloyd Hall, a large residence and fine arts resource library combined; Glyde Hall housing the Walter Phillips Gallery; the Max Bell Building with its lecture hall that was often purloined as a concert venue at the peak of the musical season; the Sally Borden Building, a much needed recreation center with magnificent athletic facilities; the studios of the Leighton Artist Colony; the Roubakine Auditorium; and in 1989 the Jeanne and Peter Lougheed Building with its recording studios and facilities for technical services.
4. Review signed András Pernye, *Magyar Nemzet* (Budapest), 12 April 1969.
5. The suite of duets from Bartók's *44 Duos for Two Violins* included No. 21, New Year's Song; No. 23, Song of the Bride; No. 28, Sadness; No. 33, Song of the Harvest; No. 37, Prelude and Canon; No. 39, Serbian Dance; No. 42, Arabian Dance; No. 43, Pizzicato; and No. 44, Transylvanian Dance.
6. Review signed Jamie Portman, *The Calgary Herald*, 13 August 1973.
7. Isobel Moore, interview by Claude Kenneson, Banff, April 1992.
8. Isobel Moore interview, Banff, April 1992.

9. Liner notes from *Béla Bartók Complete Edition*, Hungaroton SLPX 11357.
10. The Frank Houser Scholarship inaugurated at the concert on 7 May 1974 was to benefit music students studying orchestral instruments at San Francisco State University, where the late Professor Houser, former concertmaster of the San Francisco Symphony Orchestra, had taught for many years.
11. Review signed Marilyn Tucker, *San Francisco Chronicle*, 9 May 1974.
12. Tibor Serly, "A Belated Account of the Reconstruction of a 20th-Century Masterpiece," *The College Music Symposium* 15 (Spring 1975), pp. 7–25.
13. Stevens, *Béla Bartók*, p. 253.
14. Stevens, *Béla Bartók*, p. 228.
15. Tibor Serly in conversation with Claude Kenneson, The Banff Centre, August 1975.
16. Isobel Moore interview, Banff, April 1992.
17. David Leighton in conversation, Banff, 27 April 1992.
18. Zoltán Székely, unsigned interview, *Champaign-Urbana News Gazette*, 19 November 1976.
19. Isobel Moore interview, Banff, April 1992.

Chapter Twenty-seven

1. Review signed Lajos Fodor, *Esti Hirlap* (Budapest), 27 September 1977.
2. László Somfai, Hungarian musicologist, head of the Bartók Archives, the Institute for Musicology of the Hungarian Academy of Sciences, and professor of musicology at the Franz Liszt Academy. A specialist in eighteenth-century music history, Somfai has published extensive writings including two books: *Haydn: His Life and Work in Contemporary Pictures* and with Dénes Bartha, *Haydn as an Opera Conductor*. He has also written *Anton Webern* and *Eighteen Bartók Studies* (Budapest, 1981), and the important article on Béla Bartók in the *New Grove Dictionary of Music and Musicians*.
3. Unpublished letter from László Somfai to Claude Kenneson, Budapest, 23 April 1992.
4. Béla Bartók, Jr. (b. 1910). An engineer in Hungary, Béla Bartók, Jr., has contributed several biographical documents to the Bartók literature since 1955, including *Apám életének krónikája* (Chronicle of my father's life). (Budapest: Zenemükiadó,1981).
5. János Kárpáti, Hungarian musicologist, is head librarian and lecturer in musicology at the Franz Liszt Academy. He is author of

several important works on Bartók including *Bartók's String Quartets* (Budapest, 1967, rev. 1976 as *Bartók's Chamber Music*) and two other books, *Arnold Schoenberg* and *Asian Music*.

6. Isobel Moore and Lorand Fenyves did perform Bartók's First Sonata during the 1992 Banff Festival of the Arts. Before the performance they rehearsed the work several times for Székely in his apartment, eliciting the expected response—intelligent and probing questions regarding the details of their playing. Later during a visit with Fenyves, Székely remarked, "Never before have I heard Isobel sing musical examples as she did in yesterday's rehearsal! She has a fine voice."

7. Isobel Moore interview, Banff, April 1992.

8. The account of the panel discussion that follows was drawn from The Banff Centre's archival videotape 2432-34.

Chapter Twenty-eight

1. The Eder Quartet—Pál Eder and Erika Tóth, violins; Zoltán Tóth, viola; and György Eder, cello—began in 1972. The Takács Quartet—Gábor Takács-Nagy and Károly Schranz, violins; Gábor Ormai, viola; and András Fejér, cello—was founded in 1975.

2. The Eder Quartet won first prize at the Evian International String Quartet Competition in 1976. The Takács Quartet won both first prize and the special Critics' Prize at Evian the following year. The Eder Quartet was honored at the ARD (German Radio Network) Competition in Munich in 1977, then came to the United States to study with Raphael Hillyer at Yale University's summer school at Norfolk, Connecticut. The Takács Quartet won the International String Quartet Competition at Budapest in 1978; after appearing at Interforum in Keszthely, they were invited to Bordeaux, where they were awarded the festival gold medal. In the spring of 1979 they attended a master course given by the Amadeus Quartet, and then won first prize at Portsmouth in Britain.

3. Kenneth Murphy, interview by Claude Kenneson, Banff, April 1992. Statements reflect those in various official publications of the Banff Internatonal String Quartet Competition.

4. "Quartet competition is a tough test," interview with Julie Rosenfeld by Eric Dawson, *Calgary Herald*, 25 April 1992.

5. Violinists Thomas Brandis (Germany), Felix Galimir (U.S.), and Sidney Griller (U.K.), all founding members of the quartets bearing their names, Andrew Dawes (Canada) of the Orford Quartet, Bretislav Novotny (Czechoslovakia) of the Prague Quartet, and Jaap Schröder (Holland) of the Netherlands, Esterhazy, and

Smithson Quartets.

6. Violinists Andrew Dawes (Canada) of the Orford Quartet and Koichiro Harada (Japan) of the Tokyo Quartet, violists Scott Nickrenz (U.S.) founding violist of both the Lenox and the Vermeer quartets, Gerald Stanick (Canada) of the Fine Arts Quartet, Serge Collot (France) of the Quatuor Parrenin, and Artur Paciorkiewicz (Poland) of the Varsovia Quartet, and cellist Martin Lovett (U.K.) of the Amadeus Quartet.

7. Review signed Herbert Glass, *Los Angeles Times*, 15 January 1991.

8. Andrew Kenner, "Juilliard String Quartet," *The Strad*, 92 (November 1981), p. 505.

9. Bonnie Hampton (b. 1935), American cellist. Hampton was born in Oakland, California. She began her cello studies with Margaret Rowell and was later a pupil of Colin Hampton of the Griller Quartet. She studied with Pablo Casals in Europe and Puerto Rico. An outstanding chamber music artist, she has appeared as cellist of the Hampton-Schwartz Duo, the Naumburg Award-winning Francesco Trio, and the Sequoia String Quartet, and as guest artist with the Griller, Budapest, Lenox, Guarneri, and Juilliard string quartets. She is director of the Chamber Music Center, San Francisco Conservatory.

10. Bonnie Hampton, interview by Claude Kenneson, Banff, May 1992.

11. Gwen Hoebig, Canadian violinist. Hoebig was born in Vancouver and began studying the violin with her father at age five. At The Banff Centre she studied with Lorand Fenyves, David Zafer, and Zoltán Székely over a period of ten years. She studied with John Loban and Steven Staryk in Canada, with Ivan Galamian and Sally Thomas in New York, and graduated from the Juilliard School. She became an experienced competition violinist, winning the Canadian Music Competition, the CBC Talent Festival, and the S. C. Eckhardt-Gramaté competitions in Canada. Later she appeared in international competitions in Glasgow, Montreal, and Munich. She is the concertmaster of the Winnipeg Symphony Orchestra.

12. Gwen Hoebig, interview by Claude Kenneson, Banff, March 1992.

13. Leighton, *Artists*, p. 155.

14. Review signed Alex Ross, *The New York Times*, 25 November 1992.

15. Review signed Mark Carrington, *The Washington Post*, 4 December 1992.

16. Marine Hoover, interview by Claude Kenneson, Edmonton, May 1992.

17. David Blum, *The Art of Quartet Playing* (New York: Alfred A. Knopf, 1986).

Appendix B

1. Hugo Riemann coined the German term *Agogik* in 1884 when referring to an accent created by duration rather than by loudness or metrical position.
2. The vertical beam or straight line is a nontraditional symbol in music notation introduced by Bartók.
3. Polyrhythm is the simultaneous use of two or more rhythms that are not readily perceived as deriving from one another or as simple manifestations of the same meter; sometimes called cross-rhythm.
4. The German scholar Hugo Riemann developed a theory of musical phrasing during the late nineteenth century in which the harmonic cadence was always the point of repose and served as his criterion for understanding the phrasing.
5. Enchained harmonies refers to Franck's use of chromaticism which at times undermines the procedures of traditional harmonic progression to such a degree that his music is not easily described as belonging to a single key.
6. Even-tempered intonation is based on adherence to the even-tempered scale with twelve fixed and equidistant semitones—as found on the piano.

Selected Bibliography

Books:

Bartók, Béla, Jr. *Apám életének krónikája* (Chronicle of my Father's Life). Budapest: Zenemükiadó,1981.

Blum, David. *The Art of Quartet Playing*. New York: Alfred A. Knopf, 1986.

Bónis, Ferenc. *Bartók Béla élete: Képekben és dokumentumokban* (Béla Bartók: His life in pictures and documents). Translated by Lili Halápy, translation revised by Bertha Gaster and Ferenc Bónis. Budapest: Corvina Kiadó, 1981.

Chaplin, Charles. *Charles Chaplin*. New York: Penguin Books, 1964.

Deák, Stephen. *David Popper*. Neptune City, New Jersey: Paganiniana Publications, 1980.

Demény, János, ed. *Bartók Béla Levelei* (Béla Bartók Letters), vol. 3. Budapest: Zenemükiadó Vállalat, 1955.

———. *Béla Bartók Letters*. Translated by Péter Balabán and István Farkas, translation revised by Elisabeth West and Colin Mason. London: Faber and Faber, 1971.

Dille, Denijs, ed. *Documenta Bartókiana*, vol. 3. Mainz: Schott's Söhne, 1968.

Eősze, László. *Zoltán Kodály: His Life and Work*. Budapest: Corvina Press, 1962.

Everts, Igminia. *Travel Diary, 1920*. (Unpublished).

Gillies, Malcolm. *Bartók in Britain: A Guided Tour*. Oxford: Clarendon Press, 1989.

————. *Bartók Remembered*. London: Faber and Faber, 1990.

Gombocz, Adrienne, ed. *Bartók Béla Családi Levelei* (Béla Bartók family letters). Budapest: Zenemükiadó, 1981.

Hitchcock, H. Wiley, and Stanley Sadie, eds. *The New Grove Dictionary of American Music*, vol. 1. London: Macmillan Press, Ltd., 1980.

Haraszti, Emil. *Bartók Béla*. Budapest: Kortársaink,1930.

————. *Béla Bartók: His Life and Works*. Paris: Lyrebird Press, 1938.

Haefeli, Anton. *Die Internationale Gesellschaft für Neue Musik (IGNM)*. Zurich: Atlantis Musikbuch-Verlag, 1982.

Kárpáti, János. *Bartók vonósnégyesei* (Bartók's String Quartets). Translated by Fred MacNicol. Budapest: Corvina Press, 1975.

Kirk, H. L. *Pablo Casals*. New York: Holt, Rinehart, and Winston, 1974.

Leighton, David. *Artists, Builders and Dreamers: 50 Years at the Banff School*. Research and photograph selection by Peggy Leighton. Toronto: McClelland and Stewart Limited, 1982.

Molnár, Antal. *Kodály Zoltán*. Budapest: Népszeru Zenefüzetek (Popular Musical Booklets), 1936.

————. *A Léner-Vonósnégyes* (The Léner String Quartet). Budapest: Zenemükiadó,1968.

Moore, Gerald. *Am I Too Loud?* London: Hamish Hamilton Ltd., 1962.

Orenstein, Archie. *A Ravel Reader*. New York: NYU Columbia University Press, 1990.

Révész, Géza. *Erwin Nyiregyházi: Psychologische Analyse eines musikalisch hervorragenden Kindes* (Erwin Nyiregyházi: the psychology of a musical prodigy). Leipzig, 1916.

Sárosi, Bálint. *Dohnányi Ernő*. Budapest: Zenemükiadó, 1971.

————. Cigányzene (Gypsy Music). Translated by Fred MacNicol. Budapest: Corvina Press, 1978.

Schafer, R. Murray, ed. *Ezra Pound and Music: The Complete Criticism*. New York: New Directions Books, 1977.

Shirer, William L. *The Rise and Fall of the Third Reich*. 1960. New York: Simon and Schuster, 1990.

Stevens, Halsey. *The Life and Music of Béla Bartók*. New York: Oxford University Press, 1953.

Szigeti, Joseph. *With Strings Attached*. New York: Alfred A. Knopf, 1947.

Thompson, Oscar, and Bruce Bohle, eds. *The International Cyclopedia of Music and Musicians*. New York: Dodd, Mead, and Company, 1975.

Zipernovszky, Maria. *Hubay Jenő: Hegedütanitási Módszere* (Jenő Hubay: Violin teaching method). Budapest: Dr. Vajna és Bokor, 1962.

Articles:

Bartók, Béla. "Kodály's new trio a sensation abroad." *Musical Courier* (August 1920).

———. "Lettera di Budapest" (Letter from Budapest). *Il Pianoforte* 2, 9 (September 1921).

Demény, János, ed. "Korrespondenz zwischen Bartók und der holländischen Konzertdirektion Kossar" (Letters between Bartók and the Dutch concert manager Kossar). *Documenta Bartókiana* 6 (1981), pp. 153–229.

Glock, William. "Notes on the Third Programme." *Time and Tide* (February 1947).

Harp, David. "Recalling the Kolisch String Quartet." *Chamber Music* 5, 1 (Spring 1988), pp. 19, 41.

Kárpáti, János. Liner notes for compact disc recording *Bartók: The Two Sonatas for Violin and Piano*, Hungaroton, Stereo HCD 11655-2.

———. Liner notes for the long-playing recording *Bartók: The Two Sonatas for Violin and Piano*, Hungaroton production HCD 11644-2.)

Kenner, Andrew. "Juilliard String Quartet." *The Strad* 92 (November 1981), p. 505.

Kodály, Zoltán. "Oeuvres nouvelles de Béla Bartók" (New works of Béla Bartók). *La Revue Musicale* 3, 7 (March 1922), p. 172.

Molnár, Antal. "Bartók kvartettje" (Bartók quartet). *Zeneközlöny* 9 (1911), p. 275.

Schnabel, Artur. Impressions of the Edinburgh Festival. "*Souvenir program of the Edinburgh International Festival of Music and Drama*, (1948)," pp. 14–15.

Serly, Tibor. "A belated account of the reconstruction of a 20th-century masterpiece." *The College Music Symposium* 15 (Spring 1975), pp. 7–25.

Newspapers consulted:

ALGERIA Algiers: *l'Echo Alger*. AUSTRALIA Adelaide: *The Advertiser*. Canberra: *The Australian*. Sydney: *Sydney Morning Herald, Sun*. AUSTRIA Salzburg: *Salzburger Volksblatt*. Vienna: *Neues Wiener Journal*. BELGIUM Littoral: *Le Phare*. CANADA Calgary: *Calgary Herald*. CZECHOSLOVAKIA Prague: *Prager Presse, Prager Tagblatt*. FRANCE Paris: *Aux Écouts, Le Monde Musical*. GERMANY Donaueschingen: *Donaueschingen Tageblatt*. Berlin: *Berliner Börsen-Zeitung, Berliner Tageblatt, Signale*. Leipzig: *Leipziger Neueste Nachrichten*. Wiesbaden: *Neue Wiesbadener Zeitung*. HOLLAND Amsterdam: *Algemeen Handelsblad, Het Volk, De Maasbode, De Nieuwe Courant, De Telegraaf, De Tijd*. Arnhem: *Daagblad van Arn-*

*hem, Nieuwe Arnhemsche Couran*t. The Hague: *Avondpost, Haager Courant, Het Vaderland.* Nijmegen: *De Gelderlander, Nijmeegsche Courant.* Rotterdam: *Dagblad van Rotterdam, Nieuwe Rotterdamsche Courant.* Utrecht: *Utrechtisch Nieuwsblad.* Vlissingen: *Vlissingen Courant.* HUNGARY Budapest: *Budapest Hirlap, Esti Hirlap, Magyar Dal, Magyar Nemzet, Magyarság, Népsava, Pester Lloyd, Pesti Hirlap, Pesti Napló.* Szeged: *Szegedi Napló.* ITALY Genoa: *Il Cittadino.* Naples: *La Tribuna.* Rome: *Il Lavaro Fascista, Il Messaggero, Il Piccolo, Il Popolo di Roma.* Venice: *Gazzetta di Venezia.* Palermo (Sicily): *l'Ora.* MEXICO Mexico City: *Excelsior Mexico.* MOROCCO Casablanca: *Courrier du Maroc.* NEW ZEALAND Invercargill: *The Southland Daily News.* New Plymouth: *Daily News.* Wellington: *Evening Post.*SPAIN Barcelona: *Diario del Comercio, La Publicitat, La Vanguardia.* Madrid: *ABC Madrid, El Sol.* SWITZERLAND Montreux: *Feuilles d'Avis.* UNITED KINGDOM Birmingham: *Birmingham Gazette.* Cardiff: *Western Mail, South Wales News.* Belfast: *Belfast Telegraph.* London: *Daily Express, Daily Graphic, Daily Mail, Daily Telegraph, London Sunday Times, Morning Pos*t, *The Times.* Manchester: *Guardian.* UNITED STATES Boston: *Boston Phoenix, Christian Science Monitor.* Champaign-Urbana: *Champaign-Urbana News Gazette.* Denver: *Rocky Mountain News.* Los Angeles: *Los Angeles Daily News, Los Angeles Mirror, Los Angeles Times.* New York City: *New York Herald Tribune, New York Star, The New York Times.* Seattle: *Seattle Post-Intelligencer, Seattle Times.* San Francisco: *San Francisco Chronicle, San Francisco Tribune.* Washington, D.C.: *Washington Post.*

Index

Abrányi, Emil, *conductor*, 38
Adler, Hans, *concert manager (South Africa)*, 306
Albert, Agnes, *pianist*, 257
d'Albert, Eugène, *pianist*, 93, 338
Alderighi, Dante, *pianist*, 55, 102–03
Alexander, Arthur, *pianist*, 98
Amadeus String Quartet, 253
d'Ambrosio, Alfredo, *composer*, 54–55, 71, 73, 75, 80–81, 96–97, 123
Andriessen, Willem, *pianist*, 245
André, Franz, *conductor*, 163, 210
Ansermet, Ernest, *conductor*, 172–73
Antal, Jenő, *violinist*, 219
Antonicelli, Giuseppe, *conductor*, 122
d'Aranyi, Jelly, *violinist*, 10, 35, 37, 42–43, 45, 65, 73
Arriaga, Juan, *composer*, 256
Aspen Festival (1960), 277–78
Atlantic String Quartet, 354
Auber, Stefan, *cellist*, 223
Audubon String Quartet, 354–55
Auer, Leopold, *violinist*, 9, 189, 324
Augustin, Hans, *concert manager (Holland)*, 51
Aulin, Tor, *composer*, 38, 80, 111

Backhaus, Wilhelm, *pianist*, 254
Badings, Henk, *composer*, 161–62, 194–95, 212–14
Balbian-Verster, Rie de, *painter*, 63
Balsam, Arthur, *pianist*, 270
Banff Centre, The, 1, 206, 258, 296, 330–31
Banff Academy of Chamber Music, 302, 313–14, 325–26, 356–57
Banff Academy of String Quartets, 350, 360
Banff International String Quartet Competition, 351–53, 362–63
Banff School of Fine Arts, 322–23, 337
Bárány, Irma, *violinist*, 21
Bartlett (Robertson), Ethel, *pianist*, 79
Bartók, Béla, *composer-pianist*, 8–9, 27, 69–70, 132, 197–98, 237, 301, 328, 369–417
 as composer: 19–20, 25–26, 43–44, 67–68, 106–07, 112–13, 133–34, 139, 144–57, 158–59, 168–76, 178–81, 184–86, 189–93, 200–07, 210–12, 339–49, 358–59
 as performer: 32–37, 55, 59–60, 62–67, 89–94, 118–19,

[Bartók, Béla, *as performer*]
162–64, 198–99, 204–06
WORKS:
Allegro barbaro, 25, 33, 89–90,
151, 342
Arabian Dance. See 44 Duos for
Two Violins
14 Bagatelles, Op. 6, 52
Concerto for Orchestra, 344
Concerto No. 1 for Piano, 107
Concerto No. 2 for Piano, 138,
147, 152–53, 163, 171
Concerto for Viola, 329–30, 338
Concerto for Violin (1907–08),
52
Concerto for Violin (1937–38),
57, 66, 72, 114, 158–59,
178–81, 183–86, 189–93,
199–211, 213–14, 220–23,
226, 291, 323, 327–29,
333–37, 348, 358–59
Contrasts, 338, 344
Dance Suite for Orchestra, 70,
91
Duke Bluebeard's Castle, Op. 11,
43
44 Duos for Two Violins, 138–39,
325, 343
Evening in Transylvania, 181
For Children, 138, 162
*8 Hungarian Folksongs (Nyolc
magyar népdal)* for voice and
piano, 43, 145, 152
*8 Improvisations on Hungarian
Peasant Songs (Rögtönzések
magyar paraszdalokra)*, Op. 20,
for piano, 41–42
Mikrokosmos, 162–64, 198, 219
Miraculous Mandarin, The, Op.
19, 33, 135, 163
*Music for Strings, Percussion, and
Celesta*, 159, 206, 343
Out of Doors, 118, 134, 164
2 Portraits, Op. 5, 52
Quartet cycle (performances of
the), 234, 242, 249, 263, 280,
282, 301, 305, 309, 333, 350,
403–10
Quartet No. 1, Op. 7, 19, 59,
168, 340, 354
Quartet No. 2, Op. 17, 19, 23,
25, 168, 212, 232, 253, 312,

339–44, 346
Quartet No. 3 (1927), 133–34,
168, 232, 278, 304, 346–47,
362
Quartet No. 4 (1928), 25, 114,
134, 168, 246–47, 255,
345–46, 348, 411
Quartet No. 5 (1934), 168–78,
182, 223, 232, 236–38, 245–
46, 276, 285–86, 313, 323,
343, 348–49, 355–56, 411–13
Quartet No. 6 (1939), 20,
211–12, 234, 237, 272
Quintet for Piano and Strings
(1904), 9, 19–20
Rhapsody, Op. 1, 9, 91, 134
Rhapsody No. 1 for Violin, 55,
113–15, 118, 127–28, 134,
158, 162, 199, 323
Rhapsody No. 2 for Violin, 55,
113, 116, 118, 127–28, 134,
140–41, 161–64, 278, 323
Rondos on Folk Tunes, 348
*Rumanian Folk Dances from
Hungary (Magyarországi román
népti táncok)* transcribed by
Székely, 89–90, 94, 100, 111,
118, 122, 124, 130, 141, 158,
164, 184, 199, 321
Sonata for Piano (1926), 106,
118, 145
Sonata for Two Pianos and
Percussion, 185, 188, 199,
219
Sonata for Violin and Piano
(1903), 8–9, 23
Sonata No. 1 for Violin and
Piano, 37, 42–43, 55, 92, 145,
147, 152–53, 163, 323
Sonata No. 2 for Violin and
Piano, 44, 51, 55, 59–60, 63,
66–67, 123, 147, 152, 157,
163, 323
Sonata for Solo Violin, 325, 338
Sonatina (for piano), 137
Suite No. 1, Op. 3, 147, 153
Swing Song, 96
Valse (Ma Mie que danse). See *2
Portraits*, Op. 5
5 Village Scenes, 134, 163
Wooden Prince, The, 23, 43, 341,
346

Bartók Jr., Béla, *elder son of the
    composer*, 338, 340–42, 349
Bartók, Ditta Pásztory, *second wife
    of the composer*, 70, 112–13,
    144–47, 153–54
Bartók, Péter, *younger son of the
    composer*, 232
Bartók, Márta Ziegler, *first wife of
    the composer*, 33, 51, 64, 70, 342
Bates, Earl, *clarinetist*, 277
Bax, Arnold, *composer*, 61, 80–81
Becker, Hugo, *cellist*, 62, 164, 167,
    262
Beecham, Sir Thomas, *conductor*,
    61, 135
Beimel, György, *violinist*, 21, 29
Beinum, Eduard van, *conductor*, 86,
    109, 237
Bekefi, János, *cellist*, 265–66
Berg, Alban, *composer*, 106–07, 361
Berg (Haraszti), Lily, *composer*, 128
Bériot, Charles de, *violinist*, 31
Berlioz, Hector, *composer*, 91
Bernard, Robert, *composer*, 118
Beethoven quartet cycle, 224,
    227–28, 231–34, 237, 242, 244,
    248, 253, 259–64, 270–71, 278,
    283, 292–94, 299, 306–08, 355,
    364, 417–19
Bliss, Arthur, *composer*, 43
Bloch, Ernest, *composer*, 40–41, 89,
    97, 102, 136, 220
Bloch, Joseph, *violinist*, 8, 11, 21
Blum, David, *author*, 363
Bónis, Ferenc, *musicologist*, 19, 67,
    288
Boosey and Hawkes, *music
    publisher*, 116, 188–89, 220, 237
Borodin, Alexander, *composer*, 197,
    235, 262
Borotra, Jean, *tennis player*, 111
Bossi, Enrico, *composer*, 31, 39,
    412–13
Boulanger, Lili, *composer*, 54, 100
Boulanger, Nadia, *composition
    teacher*, 54, 298
Boult, Sir Adrian, *conductor*, 61, 73,
    238
Brailoiu, Constantine, *musicologist*,
    149
Breuer, Marianna, *violinist*, 21
Braun, Endre, *violinist*, 21

Bronstein, Ada, *pianist*, 325, 338
Bruch, Max, *composer*, 17, 31, 143
Budal, Gyula, *Hungarian diplomat*,
    353
Budapest String Quartet, 168,
    241–42, 253, 255
Buell, Richard, *critic*, 315–16, 323
Burkard, Heinrich, *conductor*, 96
Busan, Domenico, *viola maker*, 200
Bush, Alan, *composer*, 168, 170, 172
Bușiția, Ion, *Rumanian art master*,
    89–90

Calvocoressi, Michel, *critic*, 60, 121
Cameron, Donald, *administrator*,
    322
Capet, Lucien, *violinist*, 117
Carnes, John, *administrator*, 306
Carpenter, John Alden, *composer*,
    285
Casals, Pablo, 73, 112, 289–90, 338,
    357
Casals (Istomin), Marta, *cellist*, 290
Cassadó, Gaspar, *cellist*, 86, 130
Cassela, Alfredo, *composer*, 102–03,
    131, 133
Castelnuovo-Tedesco, Mario,
    composer, 130, 256–57
    WORKS:
    Aucassin et Nicolette, 257
    Capitan Fracassa, 110, 117
    Concerto No. 3 for Violin, 257
    "The Prophets" for Violin and
        Orchestra (1933), 256
    Second Piano Quintet, 257
    Ritmi, 95, 103
    Variazioni sinfoniche for Violin
        and Orchestra, 131, 257
Cather, Willa, *author*, 175
Cebrain (Hubay), Countess Rosa,
    39, 41
Chabay, Leslie, *tenor*, 278
Chagall, Marc, *painter*, 272
Chaliapin, Feodor, *bass*, 81, 134–35
Chaminade, Cecile, *composer*, 96,
    103
Chaplin, Charles Spencer
    ("Charlie"), *actor*, 213, 272–73
Cherniavsky, Michail, *cellist*,
    271–72
Chisholm, Eric, *friend of Bartók*,
    142, 157

Churchill, Winston, 103, 187
Clarke, Rebecca, *composer*, 98
Colbert, Ann and Henry, *concert
  managers (U.S.)*, 252, 265, 274,
  276–77
Colbert–La Berge Concert
  Management, *concert managers
  (U.S.)*, 252, 256, 264, 274,
  276–77, 283, 285, 295, 297
Colby College summer school, 292,
  309–10, 314–15, 325
Coolidge, Elizabeth Sprague, *music
  patron*, 240–41, 251
Coolidge Auditorium, 240, 243
Coolidge Competition, 14, 41, 88,
  160
Coolidge Foundation, 169, 240,
  249, 258
Coolidge String Quartet, 240–41
Copland, Aaron, *composer*, 107,
  137, 253, 256–57, 268, 277, 295
Corbett, Ned, *administrator*, 322
Cornelis, Evert, *conductor*, 56
Crawford, Grace, *soprano*, 43
Cui, César, *composer*, 31
Curzon, Sir Clifford, *pianist*, 120

Dancla, Charles, *violinist*, 11
Deák, Stephen, *cellist*, 247–48, 261,
  265
Debussy, Claude, *composer*, 20, 41,
  45, 56
  WORKS:
  En Blanc et Noir, 198–99, 219
  Préludes (for piano), 34, 41, 86
  String Quartet, Op. 10, 168, 232,
    268–69, 271, 277, 286, 303,
    314
  Sonata for Cello and Piano, 139
  Sonata for Violin and Piano,
    33–35, 55, 139, 158, 162
Dent, Edward J., *music scholar*, 42
Deutsch, Max, *pianist*, 55, 85
Diamond, David, *composer*, 256,
  295
Dickenson-Auner, Mary, *violinist*,
  37, 43,
Dienzl, Oszkár, *pianist*, 35
Dille, Denijs, *musicologist*, 347
Dodd, William, *bow maker*, 105
Dohnanyi, Ernő, *composer-pianist*,
  20, 26, 29–31, 44, 70, 74, 93,

97–99, 117, 127
  WORKS:
  Concerto for Violin, Op. 28, 18,
    97–99
  Festival Overture, 70
  Piano Quintet, Op. 1, 172
  Ruralia Hungarica, 98
Doráti, Antal, *conductor*, 330, 337
Dósa, Lidi, *peasant folk singer*, 41–42
Downes, Olin, *music critic*, 240–41,
  249–51, 303
Drdla, Franz, *composer*, 31
Duport, Jean, *concert manager
  (France)*, 182, 239, 286, 305
Duron, Josef, *record producer
  (Vienna)*, 281
Dutch String Quartet, 125
Dvořák, Antonin, *composer*, 18,
  54–56, 62, 72–73, 79, 96, 99,
  117, 127, 130, 216, 259, 262,
  271, 300, 302

Edinburgh Festival (1947–48),
  237–38
Eder String Quartet, 350
Edmonton Chamber Music Society,
  296, 309, 328
Effinger, Carl, *composer*, 298
Eisenberger (Doktor), Agnes, *concert
  manager (U.S.)*, 252, 274, 277,
  283, 297, 299, 315
Elisabeth, Queen of Belgium, 208,
  214
Ember, Ferran, *pianist*, 55, 73
Engel, Carl, *musicologist*, 219
Ensor, James, *painter*, 126
Evans, Edwin, *music scholar*, 61
Evens, Clifford, *conductor*, 326
Everts Family, 48, 51, 53, 84
Everts, Anna de Balbian-Verster,
  *mother of Igminia (Mientje)
  Székely-Everts*, 49, 89, 100–01,
  135, 139, 190, 217, 224
Everts, Guus, *cousin of Igminia
  (Mientje) Székely-Everts*, 109–10
Everts, Igminia. See Igminia
  (Mientje) Székely-Everts
Everts, Jacobus, *father of Igminia
  (Mientje) Székely-Everts*, 49, 100
Everts, Jeanne, *sister of Igminia
  (Mientje) Székely-Everts*, 100–01

Fachiri, Adila d'Arányi, *violinist*, 42, 45, 61, 73
Fehér, Ilona, *violinist*, 21
Fehér, Miklós, *violinist*, 21
Fenyves, Lorand, *violinist*, 40, 115, 324, 338–39, 350–53, 358, 362
Ferencsik, János, *conductor*, 336
Feschotte, Jacques, *musicologist*, 242, 263
Feuermann, Emanuel, *cellist*, 35, 111, 324
Finzi, Ada, *concert manager (Italy)*, 270
Firkusny, Rudolf, *pianist*, 240
Fischer (Tóth), Annie, *pianist*, 170, 210, 284, 326, 335
Fischer, Sarah, *soprano*, 159
Fisher, Edwin, *pianist*, 85
Fitelberg, Gregor, *conductor*, 136
Fitelberg, Jerzy, *composer*, 136, 168, 176
Fitzner, Rudolf, *violinist*, 9–10
Fitzner String Quartet, 9
Flesch, Carl, *violinist*, 49, 130, 160, 324, 360
Flipse, Eduard, *conductor*, 141, 147–53
Fogel, Vladimir, *composer*, 168
Fournier, Pierre, *cellist*, 237
Franck, César, *composer*, 71, 127, 232, 271, 406
Franco, Francisco, 289
Franz Ferdinand, *Archduke of Austro-Hungarian Empire*, 7
Frenkel, Paul, *pianist*, 218
Freedman, Lorna, *violinist*, 223
Frid, Géza, *pianist*, 91–92, 95–96, 103, 108–11, 117–18, 120–26, 130–31, 136–37, 139, 141, 143, 155, 161, 174, 184, 188, 308–09
Friss, Antal, *cellist*, 266
Fuchs, Joseph and Lillian, *violin-viola duo*, 240
Furtwängler, Wilhelm, *conductor*, 107, 237

Gade, Niels, *composer*, 62
Gaisberg, Fred, *EMI recording engineer*, 125–26, 184
Gallia, Tomaso, *recording engineer*, 260–61, 310–11
Gamsohn, Norbert, *Pathé-Marconi*

record producer, 260
Gérecz, Árpád, *violinist*, 265
Gershwin, George, 137
Gertler, André, *violinist*, 10,
Gertler String Quartet, 161, 174, 178
Gervey, Erzsi, *soprano*, 34
Geyer (Shultess), Stefi, *violinist*, 52, 92, 271
Gingold, Joseph, *violinist*, 84, 298
Glazer, David, *clarinetist*, 299
Glazounov, Alexander, *composer*, 189
WORKS:
Concerto for Violin and Orchestra (1904), 32, 56, 108–10, 117, 122, 184
Five Novelettes, Op. 15, 259
Glock, William, *BBC music controller*, 234
Godwin, Paul, *violist*, 104
Goette, Rudolf, *concert manager (Germany)*, 270
Goldmark, Karl, *composer*, 54
Gool, Marcel van, *pianist*, 49, 55, 68, 72, 75
Goudoever, Henri van, *conductor*, 141
Goosens, Eugene, *conductor*, 60–61, 65
Granados, Enrique, *composer*, 73
Graaff, Jaap de, *art patron*, 82, 104–05, 118–20, 125–26, 184, 199–200, 216
Graaff-Bachienne, Loes de, *wife of the art patron*, 82, 118–20, 184
Grintken, Tilla van der, *friend of Mientje Everts*, 100
Gruber, Emma Sándor. See Kodály, Emma Gruber
Gruenberg, Louis, *composer*, 137
Guadagnini, Giovanni, *violin maker*, 28
Guarneri String Quartet, 363–64
Guarnerius, Petrus, *violin maker*, 142, 274
Gustav, King of Sweden, 101, 112

Hajós, László, *violinist*, 21
Halleux, Laurent, *violinist-violist*, 248, 258–59, 270
Halmos, László, *violinist*, 164, 168,

[Halmos, László]
    177, 274
Halvorsen, Johan, *composer*, 125,
    131
Hampton, Bonnie, *cellist*, 356–57
Hansen, Wilhelm, *concert manager
    (Denmark)*, 242
Haraszti, Emil, *music critic*, 128–29,
    173
Harmens family, 226–27
Haskil, Clara, *pianist*, 213, 272–73,
    326
Havas, Kató, *violinist*, 274–75, 313
Hawkes, Ralph, *music publisher*, 188
Heifetz, Benar, *cellist*, 246
Heifetz, Jascha, 112, 247, 256–57,
    278, 324, 418
Heinitz, Eva, *cellist*, 261–62
Helmann, Ferdinand, *violinist*, 105,
    217–18
Hemingway, Ernest, 175
Henrik, Wilhelmus, *pianist*, 40
Hermann, Emilia, *violinist*, 22
Hermann, Friedrich, *violist-
    composer*, 39, 57, 125, 131
Hermann, Pál, *cellist-composer*, 14,
    23–26, 29, 31, 39, 44, 61, 85–86,
    97–98, 106, 111, 118–20, 125,
    128, 131, 136, 139–41, 161, 164,
    178–79, 186, 199–200, 205,
    215–16
Hermann, Ada Weevers, *wife of Pál
    Hermann*, 199, 216
Herrmann, Emil, *instrument dealer*,
    28, 130
Herrnfeld, Anna, *violinist*, 21
Hertzka, Emil, *director of Universal-
    Edition*, 89
Herzfeld, Victor von, *violinist-
    composer*, 44, 62
Herzog, George, *pianist*, 14
Hétu, Pierre, *conductor*, 328
Hindemith, Paul, *composer*, 43, 88,
    96, 106–07, 234, 256, 258, 285,
    292, 295, 417
    WORKS:
    Hin und Zurück, 106
    Quartet No. 3, Op. 22, 304
    Sonata for Cello Solo (1923), 98
    Sonata for Violin Solo, Op. 31,
        No. 1, 136
Hitler, Adolf, 103, 212, 224

Hoebig, Gwen, *violinist*, 358–59,
Holt, Henry, *impresario*, 81
Holt, Márta, *daughter of Bella
    Poganyi*, 84
Honegger, Arthur, *composer*, 43, 87,
    100, 107, 263
    WORKS:
    Quartet No. 2 (1934), 182, 187
    Quartet No. 3 (1936), 194–95
    Le Roi David, 100
Honegger, Henri, *cellist*, 261
Hoover, Marina, *cellist*, 361–62
Hubay, Jenő, *violinist-composer*,
    9–12, 17–19, 21–23, 27–29, 35,
    37–41, 45, 48, 55–56, 102–03,
    147, 160, 171, 188, 266, 274,
    325, 364, 414
    WORKS:
    Ballade and Humoreske, Op. 104,
        22
    Concerto all'antica (Concerto No.
        4), 23, 31, 35, 37–38
    Csárdas scène, 92, 97, 126, 131
    Elegia and Lepke, 45
    Variations on a Hungarian Theme,
        56, 81
    Waltzer Paraphrase, Op. 105, 22
Hubay-Popper String Quartet, 11,
    22, 40, 62
Huber, Karl, *violinist*, 11
Humphries, Smythe, *violist*, 276
Hungarian String Quartet, 164,
    167–78, 180–89, 193–97,
    210–14, 217–18, 224–25,
    227–28, 231–317
Hydari, Sir Akbar, 142–43

Ibbs and Tillett, *concert managers
    (UK)*, 119, 194, 233, 288, 312
Imig, Warner, *administrator*, 285
Inghelbrecht, Désiré, *composer*, 80
International Society for
    Contemporary Music, 42–44,
    86–89, 100, 106–07, 117–18,
    140–41, 145, 147, 152, 170–73,
    182, 188, 199, 243
Istomin, Eugene, *pianist*, 277
Iverson (Székely-Everts), Anne. See
    Székely-Everts, Anne (Iverson)

Jäger, Johann, *conductor*, 71
Jámbor, Agi, *pianist*, 7, 111

Jámbor, Madame, *piano teacher*, 7
Jemnitz, Sándor, *composer*, 92, 170
Joachim, Joseph, *violinist-composer*,
    35, 38, 45, 62, 234
Jochum, Eugen, *conductor*, 224
Jolivet, André, *composer*, 168
Jongen, Joseph, *composer*, 123, 126
Jongh, Peter de, *Pathé-Marconi
    record producer*, 260, 281, 292,
    299
Jora, Mihail, *composer*, 176
Juliana, *Princess of the Netherlands*,
    161, 209
Juilliard String Quartet, 277, 292,
    296, 305, 355, 414
Juon, Paul, *composer*, 51, 55–56

Kadosa, Pál, *composer*, 152, 169,
    172, 174
Kálmán, Lilla, *violinist*, 21, 29
Karajan, Herbert von, *conductor*,
    235, 282
Kárdár, George, *Vox record producer*,
    282
Károlyi, Count Mihály, 26
Karp, Howard, *pianist*, 325
Kárpáti, János, *musicologist*, 37, 67,
    284, 338, 340, 342–44, 347–49
Katchen, Julius, *pianist*, 290
Katims, Milton, *violist*, 246
Kedrish, Ödön, 4
Kedroff Vocal Quartet, 81, 97
Keleti, Lily, *pianist*, 14
Kell, Reginald, *clarinetist*, 246
Kendall, Raymond, *administrator*,
    247, 258, 324
Kentner, Louis, *pianist*, 136, 171,
    238
Kerékjártó, György, *violinist*, 30
Kernács, Pál, *violinist*, 21, 31
Kerpely, Jenő, *cellist*. 19–20, 34,
    134, 246. See also Waldbauer-
    Kerpely String Quartet
Kerper, Willem, *pianist*, 55
Kerr, Joan, *concert manager (New
    Zealand)*, 304
Khuner, Felix, *violinist*, 223, 246
Kirk, H. L., *author*, 289
Klemperer, Otto, *conductor*, 171,
    364
Kochanski, Paul, *violinist*, 36
Kodály, Zoltán, *composer*, 3, 14,

17–21, 32–33, 42–44, 73, 84, 86,
    88–89, 91, 111, 119–20, 122,
    129, 168, 174, 188, 195, 266,
    301, 308, 341–42, 353
WORKS:
    Duo for Violin and Cello, Op. 7,
        25–26, 39, 44, 98, 119–20,
        125, 141, 307, 325
    Hary János Suite (1927), 122, 217
    *Il pleure dans mon coeur comme il
        pleut sur la ville*, 118
    Méditation, 118
    Peacock Variations (1938–39),
        217
    Psalmus Hungaricus, Op. 13, 70,
        100, 104
    Serenade for Two Violins and
        Viola, Op. 12, 29, 43
    String Quartet No. 1, Op. 2, 19,
        26
    String Quartet No. 2, Op. 10,
        25–26, 195–96, 212–13, 240,
        253, 262, 268, 314–15
    Sonata for Cello and Piano, Op.
        4, 20
    Sonata for Cello Solo, Op. 8, 26,
        44, 266, 307
    Symphony (1961), 284
    Székely keserves, 118
    Zongoramuszika, Op. 11, 19, 36,
        118
Kodály, Emma Gruber, *first wife of
    the composer*, 24, 104
Kodály, Sarolta Péczely, *second wife
    of the composer*, 308
Koessler, Hans, *composition teacher*,
    8, 346
Kolisch, Rudolf, *violinist*, 107, 223
Kolisch (Vienna) String Quartet,
    106, 133–34, 143–44, 168–69,
    212, 223, 241
Koncz, János, *violinist*, 17, 92
Koos, Géza de, *concert manager
    (Holland)*, 50–51, 157, 194, 231
Kornstein (Kenton), Egon, *violist*,
    20
Koromzay, Dénes, *violist*, 15–16,
    164, 167–178, 180–81, 183,
    188–89, 195, 200, 215, 224–25,
    227–28, 236, 244–45, 252–53,
    259, 266, 273, 279–86, 290,
    296–97, 302, 307, 309–10,

[Koromzay, Dénes]
  313–16, 321, 332, 350–51
Koromzay, Dennis and Val, *sons of*
  the violist, 244
Koromzay, Susie (Eva) Tormay, *wife*
  of the violist, 189, 215, 244, 314
Kósa, György, *pianist*, 44
Kossar, Antonia, *concert manager*
  (Holland), 126, 157–58, 162–63,
  184, 198
Kőszegi, Sándor, *violinist*, 7–8, 10,
  12, 83
Kovács, Sándor, *piano teacher*, 19
Krauss, Ernst, *concert manager*
  (Holland), 74
Kreisler, Fritz, 73, 81, 97, 103, 123,
  131
Kreutzer, Rodolphe (the violin
  études of), 10, 12
Kruiler, Kor, *conductor*, 161
Kuerti, Anton, *pianist*, 314
Kuhner, Felix, *violinist*, 223
Kulenkampff, Georg, *violinist*, 99,
  223
Kun, Béla, *founder of the Hungarian*
  Communist Party, 26
Kun, Imre, *concert manager*
  (Hungary), 182
Kuttner, Michael, *violinist*, 274–76,
  279, 283–84, 297, 301, 307, 313,
  315, 321, 333

La Berge, Bernard, *concert manager*
  (U.S.), 239–41, 248–49, 252
Lajtha, László, *composer*, 172
Lalo, Edouard, *composer*, 17, 143
Landré, Guillaume, *composer*,
  140–41
Landré, Willem, *composer*, 140–41
Lasonczi, Pál, *president of Hungarian*
  Peoples' Council, 353
Lavasseur, Paul, *Pathé-Marconi*
  balance engineer, 260
Lazar, Filip, *composer*, 126
Léderer, István, *Budapest store*
  owner, 18
Legge, Walter, *EMI record producer*,
  234–26
Lehner, Eugene, *violist*, 241, 353
Leighton, David S. R., *administrator*,
  62, 321, 332, 339–41, 349, 360

Lendvai, Ernő, *music theorist*, 284
Léner String Quartet, 14, 168, 274
Les Six, 43
Lichtveld, Lou, *composer*, 86
Lier, Bertus van, *composer*, 141
Linz, Márta, *violinist*, 414
Liszt, Franz, *composer*, 18, 37
Lléhvinne, Rosina, *pianist*, 278
Loelofs-Székely, Lon, *author*, 225,
  244

Maconchy, Elizabeth, *composer*,
  182, 194–95, 268
MacKerchar, Duncan, *radio*
  producer, 327
McCormack, John, *tenor*, 81–83
McLeod, Eric, *Pathé-Marconi record*
  producer, 261, 292, 310
Magyar, Gabriel, *cellist*, 266–70,
  274, 279, 283, 301, 307, 313,
  316, 321, 325, 332, 350
Magyar, Julie Dora, *wife of the*
  cellist, 267, 300, 312
Magyar, Támas, *violinist*, 266
Mahler, Gustav, *composer*, 56
Malipiero, Gian Francesco,
  composer, 73, 84, 102
Manén, Joan, *composer*, 22, 73, 96,
  123, 131, 181, 184
Mangeot, André, *concert manager*
  (UK), 195
Mann, Robert, *violinist*, 305,
  355–56, 414
Martinu, Bohuslav, *composer*, 141
Marteau, Henri, *violinist*, 129
Mártonyi, Károly, *husband of*
  Piroska (Székely) Mártonyi, 101
Mártonyi, Friges, *cousin of Zoltán*
  Székely, 102, 220
Maucotel et Deschamp, *instrument*
  dealers, 105
Mayer, Dorothy Moulton, *music*
  patron, 42, 60
Meller, Erich, *pianist*, 38
Mendelssohn, George, *president of*
  Vox Productions, 265, 280–81,
  310
Mengelberg, Rudolf, *artistic director*
  of Amsterdam Concertgebouw, 224
Mengelberg, Willem, *conductor*,
  56–58, 99, 190, 206–09, 211,

216–17, 224, 291, 336
Menuhin, Yehudi, 223, 226, 238, 310
Meunier-Thouret, Marc, *musicoloist*, 242
"Michelangelo" *(popular name of Székely's 1718 Stradivarius violin)*, 2, 28, 82, 105, 126, 131, 326, 364
Milhaud, Darius, *composer*, 43, 73, 80, 256–58, 268, 295, 412
WORKS:
Cello Concerto No. 1, 266
L'Enlèvement d'Europa, 106
Piano Quintet No. 1, 257
Le Printemps, 75
String Quartet No. 1, 277
String Quartet No. 3, 277
String Quartet No. 7, 277, 286
String Quartet No. 9, 182, 213
Sonata for Violin and Piano (1917), 130, 137
Milofsky, Bernard, *violist*, 223
Möller, Max, *instrument dealer*, 141–42
Molnár, Antal, *musicologist*, 19–20,
Monath, Hortense, *pianist*, 253
Monteux, Pierre, *conductor*, 91, 140
Moore, Douglas, *administrator*, 219
Moore, Gerald, *pianist*, 135
Moore, Isobel, *pianist*. See Rolston, Isobel Moore
Morette, Etienne, *concert manager (France)*, 183
Moroz, David, *pianist*, 359
Moskowsky, Alexandre, *violinist*, 188–89, 225, 243–45, 271, 273
Moskowsky, Flossie, *first wife of the violinist*, 225, 244
Moskowsky, Martine, *second wife of the violinist*, 273
Muck, Karl, *conductor*, 48–49, 56, 61
Müller-Widmann, Annie (Mrs. Oscar), *friend of Bartók*, 163
Murphy, Kenneth, *administrator*, 351–52
Musica Viva, *concert management (Australia)*, 286–87, 303–04
Mussolini, Benito, 103, 123–25, 131

Nagy, Izabella, *soprano*, 34
Naoyasu Kajimoto, *concert management (Japan)*, 305
Nemzetközi Koncertiroda, *concert management (Hungary)*, 283
Netherlands String Quartet, 104, 300
Neumark, Ignaz, *conductor*, 51, 184–85
New Holland String Quartet, 224
New Music String Quartet, 417
Newton, Ivor, *pianist*, 55, 97, 134–35
Nin, Joaquín, *composer*, 136, 159
Nürnberger, *family of German bow makers*, 105
Nyiregyházi, Erwin, *pianist*, 30–31

Offenbach, Jacques, *composer*, 6
Offers, Maartje, *contralto*, 125
Onnou, Alphonse, *violinist*, 258
Ormandy, Eugene, *violinist*, 14
Országh, Tivador, *composer*, 162
Ouchard, Emile, *bow maker*, 105
Otterloo, Willem van, *conductor*, 184, 216

Pacifica String Quartet, 339, 343–45
Paganini, Niccolò, *violinist-composer*, 37, 110, 123–24, 184
Palotai, Vilmos, *cellist*, 164, 167, 170, 174, 177, 185, 188, 195, 200, 225, 236, 244, 254, 262, 264–65, 267, 291, 411
Pártos, István, *violinist*, 45, 48–49, 68
Pártos, Ödön, *violinist*, 188
Pecatte, Dominique, *bow maker*, 105
Péczely, Sarolta. See Kodály, Sarolta (Péczely)
Pedroso, Doña Elena, *music patron*, 243
Pernye, András, *music critic*, 303, 324
Peto, Mrs. Imré, *soprano*, 40
Petri, Egon, *pianist*, 256–57
Petyrek, Felix, *pianist*, 55, 86–87
Piatigorsky, Gregor, *cellist*, 247, 324
Picasso, Pablo, *painter*, 88
Pierné, Gabriel, *conductor*, 85

Pijper, Willem, *composer*, 140–41, 143
Pique, François, *violin maker*, 28
Piston, Walter, *composer*, 256–57, 268–69, 285, 295
Pizetti, Ildebrando, *composer*, 110, 117
Poganyi, Bella, *cousin of Zoltán Székely*, 84
Poldowsky, (Lady Dean Paul), *composer*, 73
Polignac (Singer), Princesse Edmond de, 182
Popper, Dávid, *cellist*, 19, 23. See also Hubay-Popper String Quartet
Porpora, Nicola, *composer*, 184, 328
Porter, Quincy, *composer*, 298
Poulenc, Francis, *composer*, 43, 137
Pound, Ezra, *poet*, 174–76, 182, 186–87
Powell, Lionel, *concert manager (UK)*, 81, 83, 97, 134
Praetorius, Ernst, *conductor*, 117, 161
Primrose, William, *violist*, 237, 247, 298, 329, 332
Pro Arte String Quartet (Belgium), 134, 241, 247, 258
Probst-Jones, William, *pianist*, 143
Pro Ideale String Quartet, 274
Prunières, Henri, *musicologist*, 43, 59

Quartetto Italiano, 242–43, 262, 296
Queseda, Ernesto de, *concert manager (Spain)*, 242–43, 254

Rácz, Laczi, *gypsy violinist*, 3–4
Rappaport, Israel, *Bartók's New York physician*, 232
Rasse, François, *conductor*, 126, 143
Ravel, Maurice, *composer*, 20, 43, 73, 87, 103, 121–22, 148
  WORKS:
  Pièce en forma de Habanera (1907), 73, 75
  Quartet in F (1903), 271–72, 277
  Sonata for Violin and Cello (1920–22), 86, 117, 119–20, 131, 139, 330
  Sonata for Violin and Piano (1923–27), 109–11, 121, 126, 129, 157, 323, 328, 330
  Trio for Violin, Cello, and Piano (1914), 34, 136
  Tzigane for Violin and Orchestra (1924), 56, 86–87, 91–92, 96–98, 100, 102, 108, 117, 121–22, 125, 131, 136–37, 139, 143
Raalte, Albert van, *conductor*, 132, 137
Ré, Peter, *composer*, 292, 327
Reger, Max, *composer*, 17, 159
Reiner, Fritz, *conductor*, 61, 70, 83
Reinitz, Béla, *composer-critic*, 26
Rejtő, Gabor, *cellist*, 257, 261, 266, 270
Révész, Géza, *psychologist*, 30–31, 42, 155, 161
Ridge, Regina, *concert manager (Australia)*, 286, 303, 306–07
Riemann, Hugo, *music theorist*, 185, 405–06, 416
Rieti, Vittorio, *composer*, 87, 103
Rietveld, Gerrit, *architect*, 144, 218
Rimsky-Korsakov, Nikolay, *composer*, 74
Robertson, Rae, *pianist*, 55, 79–80
Rodzinski, Artur, *conductor*, 223
Roger-Ducasse, Jean, *composer*, 75
Rolston, Isobel Moore, *pianist*, 55, 114–15, 313, 326–28, 330–31, 333–35, 338–39
Rolston, Shauna, *cellist*, 313
Rolston, Thomas, *violinist*, 296–97, 299–301, 302, 310, 312–13, 321–22, 330, 332, 338
Rook, Claas de, *conductor*, 233
Rossi, Mario, *conductor*, 130
Rossini, Giacchino, *composer*, 6, 250
Rossier, Emile, *music patron*, 213, 272, 289
Rostal, Max, *violinist*, 181, 223
Roth, Nicholas, *violinist*, 157
Roth String Quartet, 111, 219, 274
Rubenstein, Erna, *violinist*, 45, 68, 74, 92

Sacconi, Simone, *violin maker*, 105, 130–31

Sacher, Paul, *conductor*, 53, 154, 164, 211
St. Lawrence String Quartet, 361–63
Saint-Saëns, Camille, *composer*, 97, 117, 125
Salazar, Antonio de Oliveira, 243
Salter, Norbert, *concert manager (Germany)*, 108
Sándor, László, *violinist*, 21, 40
Santa Barbara Festival (1956), 269–70
Sarasate, Pablo de, *violinist-composer*, 97, 102
Saygun, Adnan, *musicologist*, 160
Scharwenka, Philipp, *composer*, 38, 45, 72, 81, 95
Scheffer, Ubbo, *sculptor*, 290–92
Schiffer, Adolf, *cellist*, 23, 31, 164
Schiller, Elsa Braun, *director of DGG*, 280–81
Schnabel, Artur, *pianist*, 111, 237
Schneeberger, Hans-Heinz, *violinist*, 53
Schnéevoight, George, *conductor*, 50
Schoenberg, Arnold, *composer*, 44, 73, 84, 86, 88, 106, 143–44, 173, 232, 240, 247, 301
WORKS:
Drei Klavierstücke, Op. 11, 34
Quartet No. 1, Op. 7, 144
Quartet No. 3, Op. 30, 144
Transfigured Night (Sextet for Strings, Op. 4), 20
Scholz, János, *cellist*, 223
Schouwenberg, John de Jong, *director of Amsterdam Concertgebouw*, 227, 232, 291
Schramm, Paul, *pianist*, 55, 74–75
Schulhoff, Erwin, *composer*, 107, 118
Schuman, William, *composer*, 249–51, 256
Schuricht, Carl, *conductor*, 136, 223
Schwarzkoph, Elizabeth, *soprano*, 235, 252, 310
Schweitzer, Albert, *organist*, 289
Scotney, Evelyn, *soprano*, 81, 97, 137
Scott, Cyril, *composer*, 38, 44–45, 73, 80

Seiber, Mátyás, *composer*, 111, 118, 232, 237
Serly, Tibor, *composer*, 174–75, 329–30, 332
Shapiro, Eudice, *violinist*, 269, 278
Shulthess, Walter, *concert manager (Switzerland)*, 271
Sibelius, Jean, *composer*, 23, 37, 50, 57, 213, 338
Siklós, Albert, *composer*, 44
Sinding, Christian, *composer*, 12, 31, 54, 73
Singer, Norman, *administrator*, 277, 296
Sinigaglia, Leone, *composer*, 31, 80, 96, 130
WORKS:
Concerto for Violin, Op. 20, 130, 132
Danza piemontese, Op. 31, 132
Overture to *La Baruffe Chiozote*, Op. 32, 132
Rapsodia piemontese, 54–56, 75, 95–97, 123, 130, 136–37
Smetana, Bedrich, *composer*, 196, 213–14
Smith, Brooks, *pianist*, 278
Smits, Jan, *father-in-law of Vilmos Palotai*, 244
Sociedad Musical Daniel, *concert managers (Spain)*, 242
Soeren, Bertha, *soprano*, 145, 152
Solchany, Georges, *pianist*, 265, 271, 299–300, 303, 310
Solti, Sir George, *conductor*, 16, 252
Somers, Harry, *composer*, 276, 352
Somfai, László, *musicologist*, 115, 181, 336–42, 344–49
Sommer, Walter, *DGG recording engineer*, 282
Spanjaard, Martin, *conductor*, 55, 71, 91, 108, 126, 143
Spivacke, Harold, *librarian*, 241, 258
Spivakovsky, Tossy, *violinist*, 222–23
Spohr, Louis, *violinist-composer*, 29
Stanford, Sir Charles, *composer*, 53
Starker, János, *cellist*, 16, 265–66, 330, 338
Steuermann, Eduard, *pianist*, 37, 43
Stevens, Halsey, *musicologist*, 8, 249, 329, 411

Strauss, Richard, *composer*, 57, 107, 217, 338
Strausz family, 5, 102
Stravinsky, Igor, *composer*, 43, 73, 84, 86, 88, 107, 148, 173, 182, 187, 301, 412
  WORKS:
  Concertino for String Quartet, 187
  Piano Rag Music (1920), 34
  Pulcinella (Suite), 326
  Quatre Chants Russe, 34
  Suite from *l'Histoire du Soldat* (1919), 60
Stravinsky, Vera, *wife of the composer*, 187
Strider, Robert, *president of Colby College*, 315
Suikerman, *concert manager (Holland)*, 65
Suk, Josef, *composer*, 72, 102
Susskind, Walter, *conductor*, 206, 322, 333
Sweelinck String Quartet, 224
Székely-Everts, Franciscus Jacobus (known as Frans, later Frank), *son of Zoltán and Igminia Székely*, 190, 197–98, 212, 224, 226–27, 243–44, 247, 286, 323, 332
Székely-Everts, Alec and Eric, *sons of Frank and Anne Székely-Everts*, 332
Székely-Everts, Anne Iverson, *wife of Frank Székely-Everts*, 286, 332
Székely-Everts, Igminia (Mientje) *wife of Zoltán Székely*, 1, 47–51, 62–64, 85, 87, 89, 100–01, 104, 109–12, 119–25, 135–36, 139, 143–46, 150–53, 155–59, 162, 185, 190, 197–98, 200, 202–03, 206, 210, 212, 225, 247, 289–91, 300, 323–24, 326–28, 331–32, 335, 353–54
Székely, Erzsébet Strausz, *mother of Zoltán Székely*, 2, 4, 7, 28, 51, 84, 155, 185
Székely, László, *father of Zoltán Székely*, 2–7, 45, 47–48, 83–84, 117, 143, 155, 185
Székely, Piroska (Mártonyi), *sister of Zoltán Székely*, 2, 4, 7, 31, 84, 101, 111, 335, 354

Székelyhidy, Ferenc, *tenor*, 104
Szenkár, Jenő, *conductor*, 135
Szerémi, Gusztáv, *violist*, 30, 39
Szervánsky, Péter, *violinist*, 168, 274
Szigeti, Joseph, *violinist*, 10–11, 22, 45, 91, 113–15, 122–23, 127–28, 181, 186, 219–20, 237, 288–89
Szigety, Béla, *violist*, 29
Szikla, Adolf, *pianist*, 34
Szymanovsky, Karol, *composer*, 36, 43, 110, 136

Tabbernal, Bernard, *pianist*, 55, 85, 99
Tadema, Jan, *pupil of Carl Flesch*, 160
Takács String Quartet, 286, 350–51
Talich, Václav, *conductor*, 93
Tango, Egisto, *conductor*, 23
Tarnay, Alajos, *piano teacher*, 12
Telmányi, Emil, *violinist*, 18–19, 45, 92
Temesváry, János, *violinist*, 19
Tchaikovsky, Piotr, *composer*, 40, 99, 197, 207, 232, 235, 259, 262, 330
Thibaud, Jacques, *violinist*, 49, 70–71, 73
Thoman, István, *piano teacher*, 30, 260
Thomson, César, *violinist*, 258
Thorne, Oakleigh, *record producer*, 298
Tilden, Bill, *tennis player*, 111
Tillet, Emmie Bass, *concert manager (UK)*, 194, 293
Toch, Ernst, *composer*, 106–07, 111, 141
Tononi, Carlo, *violin maker*, 141–42
Toscanini, Arturo, *conductor*, 57, 223, 256–57, 338, 357
Tóth, Aladár, *music critic*, 30–31, 34, 88, 91, 93–94, 128–30, 210, 284
Tóth, János, *violin maker*, 28–29, 93
Tourel, Jennie, *soprano*, 277
Tsutsumi, Tsuyoshi, *cellist*, 330, 335

Ujfalussy, Jozsef, *musicologist*, 284
Universal-Edition, *music publisher (Austria)*, 37, 89–90, 116, 119, 122, 184, 187, 189, 193

University of Alberta, 296–97, 300–02
University of Alberta Board of Governors, 297, 362
University of Alberta String Quartet, 302, 309, 333, 403–10
University of Southern California, 241, 244, 248–49, 255, 258

Valmalète, Marcel de, *concert manager (France)*, 182, 194, 233, 239, 260, 305
Varèse, Edgar, *composer*, 83, 139
Varga, László, *cellist*, 275, 299, 310, 313, 328
Varvara, Traselli, *concert manager (Sicily)*, 95
Vaughan Williams, Ralph, *composer*, 61
Vavasseur, Paul, *balance engineer EMI*, 260
Vecsey, Ferenc, *violinist*, 10, 23, 30, 38, 45, 91–92
Végh, Sándor, *violinist*, 15, 164, 168, 175, 177–78, 183, 188, 274
Végh String Quartet, 280
Veissi, Jascha, *violist*, 233
Venetian School of violin making, 142
Verhuyck-Coulon, Gaston, *concert manager (Belgium)*, 134
Veress, Sándor, *composer*, 169–71, 174, 182, 187, 194–95
Vermel, Paul, *conductor*, 327, 333
Vieuxtemps, Henri, *violinist-composer*, 13, 51, 96, 126
Vigneron, Joseph, *bow maker*, 105
Villa-Lobos, Heitor, *composer*, 254–55, 258, 262, 295
Viotti, Giovanni Battista, *composer*, 12, 56, 137, 143, 159, 233
Volkman, Robert, *composer*, 40
Votto, Antonio, *conductor*, 223
Vries, Willem de, *organist*, 53

Waldbauer, Imre, *violinist*, 10, 19–20, 27, 29, 34–35, 44, 59, 112, 168–70, 192, 275
Waldbauer-Kerpely String Quartet, 19–20, 29, 59, 133–34, 164, 168
Webern, Anton, *composer*, 43, 285–86, 295

Weiner, Leó, *composer*, 7, 12, 13–15, 26, 88, 266, 274, 311, 334
WORKS:
Quartet No. 1, Op. 3 (1908), 14
Quartet No. 2, Op. 13 (1922), 14
Sonata No. 1 for Violin and Piano, Op. 9, 14
Sonata No. 2 for Violin and Piano, Op. 11, 14
String Trio (1909), 14
Violin Fantasy (uncompleted), 15
Weiss, Maria, *pianist*, 13
Wieniawsky, Henri, *violinist-composer*, 18
Wilhelmina, *Queen of the Netherlands*, 215
Wilson, Duncan and Freda, *friends of Bartók*, 64, 135
Wilson, Steuart, *BBC director of music*, 233
Winkelmann, General, *Dutch commander*, 215
Wohlert, O. E., *DGG record producer*, 282
Wolff, Ernst, *pianist*, 55, 62
Wood, Sir Henry, *conductor*, 60–61, 137
Wummer, John, *flutist*, 270

Yabuta, Masumoto, *concert manager (Japan)*, 305
Ysaÿe, Eugène, *violinist*, 70–71, 73, 75, 81, 105, 126
Ysaÿe, Theo, *concert manager (France)*, 182

Zádor, Jenő, *composer*, 232, 248
Zala, Mor, *Budapest music store owner*, 18
Zathureczky, Ede, *violinist*, 10, 18, 21, 31, 60, 192, 275
Zeitlin, Lev, *violinist*, 9
Zilcher, Herman, *composer*, 45
Zimmerman, Louis, *violinist*, 216, 218
Zipernovsky, Maria, *author*, 40
Zoltán, Siegmund, *uncle of Zoltán Székely*, 5
Zsámboky, Miklós, *cellist*, 40
Zsolt, Nándor, *violinist-conductor*, 29, 31